Lecture Notes in Computer Sci

Edited by G. Goos, J. Hartmanis, and J. van

Springer

Berlin
Heidelberg
New York
Barcelona
Hong Kong
London
Milan
Paris
Tokyo

Maria Carla Calzarossa   Salvatore Tucci (Eds.)

Performance Evaluation of Complex Systems: Techniques and Tools

Performance 2002 Tutorial Lectures

Springer

Series Editors

Gerhard Goos, Karlsruhe University, Germany
Juris Hartmanis, Cornell University, NY, USA
Jan van Leeuwen, Utrecht University, The Netherlands

Volume Editors

Maria Carla Calzarossa
Università di Pavia, Dipartimento di Informatica e Sistemistica
via Ferrata 1, 27100 Pavia, Italy
E-mail: mcc@alice.unipv.it

Salvatore Tucci
Ufficio per l'Informatica, la Telematica e la Statistica
Presidenza del Consiglio dei Ministri
via della Stamperia 8, 00187 Roma, Italy
E-mail: tucci@torvergata.it

Cataloging-in-Publication Data applied for

Die Deutsche Bibliothek - CIP-Einheitsaufnahme

Performance evaluation of complex sytems : techniques and tools ;
performance 2002 tutorial lectures / Maria Carla Calzarossa ; Salvatore
Tucci (ed.). - Berlin ; Heidelberg ; New York ; Hong Kong ; London ; Milan ;
Paris ; Tokyo : Springer, 2002
   (Lecture notes in computer science ; Vol. 2459)
   ISBN 3-540-44252-9

CR Subject Classification (1998): C.4, C.2, D.2.8, D.4, F.1, H.4

ISSN 0302-9743
ISBN 3-540-44252-9 Springer-Verlag Berlin Heidelberg New York

This work is subject to copyright. All rights are reserved, whether the whole or part of the material is
concerned, specifically the rights of translation, reprinting, re-use of illustrations, recitation, broadcasting,
reproduction on microfilms or in any other way, and storage in data banks. Duplication of this publication
or parts thereof is permitted only under the provisions of the German Copyright Law of September 9, 1965,
in its current version, and permission for use must always be obtained from Springer-Verlag. Violations are
liable for prosecution under the German Copyright Law.

Springer-Verlag Berlin Heidelberg New York,
a member of BertelsmannSpringer Science+Business Media GmbH

http://www.springer.de

© Springer-Verlag Berlin Heidelberg 2002
Printed in Germany

Typesetting: Camera-ready by author, data conversion by PTP-Berlin, Stefan Sossna e.K.
Printed on acid-free paper   SPIN: 10871194   06/3142   5 4 3 2 1 0

Preface

The fast evolution and the increased pervasiveness of computers and communication networks have led to the development of a large variety of complex applications and services which have become an integral part of our daily lives. Modern society widely relies on information technologies. Hence, the Quality of Service, that is, the efficiency, availability, reliability, and security of these technologies, is an essential requirement for the proper functioning of modern society.

In this scenario, performance evaluation plays a central role. Performance evaluation has to assess and predict the performance of hardware and software systems, and to identify and prevent their current and future performance bottlenecks.

In the past thirty years, many performance evaluation techniques and tools have been developed and successfully applied in studies dealing with the configuration and capacity planning of existing systems and with the design and development of new systems. Recently, performance evaluation techniques have evolved to cope with the increased complexity of the current systems and their workloads. Many of the classical techniques have been revisited in light of the recent technological advances, and novel techniques, methods, and tools have been developed.

This book is organized around a set of survey papers which provide a comprehensive overview of the theories, techniques, and tools for performance and reliability evaluation of current and new emerging technologies. The papers, by leading international experts in the field of performance evaluation, are based on the tutorials presented at the IFIP WG 7.3 International Symposium on Computer Modeling, Measurement, and Evaluation (*Performance 2002*) held in Rome on September 23–27, 2002.

The papers address the state of the art of the theoretical and methodological advances in the area of performance and reliability evaluation as well as new perspectives in the major application domains. A broad spectrum of topics is covered in this book. Modeling and verification formalisms, solution methods, workload characterization, and benchmarking are addressed from a methodological point of view. Applications of performance and reliability techniques to various domains, such as, hardware and software architectures, wired and wireless networks, Grid environments, Web services, real–time voice and video applications, are also examined.

This book is intended to serve as a reference for students, scientists, and engineers working in the areas of performance and reliability evaluation, hardware and software design, and capacity planning.

Finally, as editors of the book, we would like to thank all authors for their valuable contributions and their effort and cooperation in the preparation of their manuscripts.

July 2002   Maria Carla Calzarossa
                                                        Salvatore Tucci

Table of Contents

G-Networks: Multiple Classes of Positive Customers, Signals, and Product Form Results

Erol Gelenbe

School of Electrical Engineering and Computer Science
University of Central Florida
Orlando, FL 32816
erol@cs.ucf.edu

Abstract. The purpose of this tutorial presentation is to introduce G-Networks, or Gelenbe Networks, which are product form queueing networks which include normal or positive customers, as well as negative customers which destroy other customers, and triggers which displace other customers from one queue to another. We derive the balance equations for these models in the context of multiple customer classes, show the product form results, and exhibit the traffic equations which – in this case, contrary to BCMP and Jackson networks - are non-linear. This leads to interesting issues of existence and uniqueness of the steady-state solution. Gelenbe Network can be used to model large scale computer systems and networks in which signaling functions represented by negative customers and triggers are used to achieve flow and congestion control.

1 Introduction

In this survey and tutorial, we discuss a class of queueing networks, originally inspired by our work on neural networks, in which customers are either "signals" or positive customers.

Positive customers enter a queue and receive service as ordinary queueing network customers; they constitute queue length. A signal may be of a "negative customer", or it may be a "trigger". Signals do not receive service, and disappear after having visited a queue. If the signal is a trigger, then it actually transfers a customer from the queue it arrives to, to some other queue according to a probabilistic rule. On the other hand, a negative customer simply depletes the length of the queue to which it arrives if the queue is non-empty. One can also consider that a negative customer is a special kind of trigger which simply sends a customer to the "outside world" rather than transferring it to another queue. Positive customers which leave a queue to enter another queue can become signals or remain positive customers.

Additional primitive operations for these networks have also been introduced in [12]. The computation of numerical solutions to the non-linear traffic equations of some of these models have been discussed in [6]. Applications to networking problems are reported in [17]. A model of doubly redundant systems using G-networks, where work is scheduled on two different processors and then cancelled

M.C. Calzarossa and S. Tucci (Eds.): Performance 2002, LNCS 2459, pp. 1–16, 2002.
© Springer-Verlag Berlin Heidelberg 2002

at one of the processors if the work is successfully completed at the other, is presented in [7]. The extension of the original model with positive and signals [4] to multiple classes was proposed and obtained in various papers [9,11,15,19].

Some early neural network applications of G-networks are summarized in a survey article [18]. From the neural network approach, the model in [9] was applied to texture generation in colour images in an early paper [10].

The present survey Includes the results presented in [20], where multiple classes of positive and signals are discussed, and we also include multiple classes of triggers. Thus in this paper we discuss G-Networks with **multiple classes of positive customers and one or more classes of signals**.

Three types of service centers with their corresponding service disciplines are examined:

- Type 1 : first-in-first-out (FIFO),
- Type 2 : processor sharing (PS),
- Type 4 : last-in-first-out with preemptive resume priority (LIFO/PR).

With reference to the usual terminology related to the BCMP theorem [2], we exclude from the present discussion the Type 3 service centers with an infinite number of servers **since they will not be covered by our results**. Furthermore, in this paper we deal only with exponentially distributed service times.

In Section 2 we will prove that these multiple class G-Networks, with Type 1, 2 and 4 service centers, have product form.

2   The Model

We consider networks with an arbitrary number n of queues, an arbitrary number of positive customer classes K, and an arbitrary number of signal classes S. External arrival streams to the network are independent Poisson processes for positive customers of some class k and signals of some class c. We denote by $\Lambda_{i,k}$ the external arrival rate of *positive* customers of class k to queue i and by $\lambda_{i,m}$ be the external arrival rate of *signals* of class m to queue i.

Only positive customers are served, and after service they may change class, service center and nature (positive signal), or depart from the system. The movement of customers between queues, classes and nature (positive to signal) is represented by a Markov chain.

At its arrival in a non-empty queue, a signal selects a positive customer as its "target" in the queue in accordance with the service discipline at this station. If the queue is empty, then the signalsimply disappears. Once the target is selected, the signaltries to *trigger the movement of* the selected customer. A negative customer, of some class m, succeeds in *triggering the movement of* the selected positive customer of some class k, at service center i with probability $K_{i,m,k}$. With probability $(1 - K_{i,m,k})$ it does not succeed. A signal disappears as soon as it tries to *trigger the movement of* its targeted customer. Recall that signal is either exogenous, or is obtained by the transformation of a positive customer as it leaves a queue.

A positive customer of class k which leaves queue i (after finishing service) goes to queue j as a positive customer of class l with probability $P^+[i,j][k,l]$, or as a signal of class m with probability $P^-[i,j][k,m]$. It may also depart from the network with probability $d[i,k]$. Obviously we have for all i,k:

$$\sum_{j=1}^{n}\sum_{l=1}^{R} P^+[i,j][k,l] \;+\; \sum_{j=1}^{n}\sum_{m=1}^{S} P^-[i,j][k,m] \;+\; d[i,k] = 1 \qquad (1)$$

We assume that all service centers have exponential service time distributions. In the three types of service centers, each class of positive customers may have a distinct service rate
rik. When the service center is of Type 1 (FIFO) we place the following constraint on the service rate and the *movement triggering* rate due to incoming signals:

$$rik + \sum_{m=1}^{S} K_{i,m,k}\lambda_{i,m} = c_i \qquad (2)$$

Note that this constraint, together with the constraint (3) given below, have the effect of producing a *single positive customer class equivalent* for service centers with FIFO discipline. The following constraints on the *movement triggering* probability are assumed to exist. Note that because services are exponentially distributed, positive customers of a given class are indistinguishable for *movement triggering* because of the Markovian property of service time.

- The following constraint must hold for all stations i of Type 1 and classes of signals m such that $\sum_{j=1}^{n}\sum_{l=1}^{R} P^-[j,i][l,m] > 0$

  for all classes of positive customers a and b, $K_{i,m,a} = K_{i,m,b}$ $\qquad (3)$

  This constraint implies that a signal of some class m arriving from the network does not "distinguish" between the positive customer classes it will try to trigger the movement, and that it will treat them all in the same manner.
- For a Type 2 server, the probability that any one positive customer of the queue is selected by the arriving signalis $1/c$ if c is the total number of customers in the queue.

For Type 1 service centers, one may consider the following conditions which are simpler than (2) and (3):

$$\begin{aligned} r_{ia} &= r_{ib} \\ K_{i,m,a} &= K_{i,m,b} \end{aligned} \qquad (4)$$

for all classes of positive customers a and b, and all classes of signals m. Note however that these new conditions are more restrictive, though they do imply that (2), 3) hold.

2.1   State Representation

We denote the state at time t of the queueing network by a vector $x(t) = (x_1(t), ..., x_n(t))$. Here $x_i(t)$ represents the state of service center i. The vector $x = (x_1..., x_n)$ will denote a particular value of the state and $|x_i|$ will be the total number of customers in queue i for state x.

For Type 1 and Type 4 servers, the instantaneous value of the state x_i of queue i is represented by the vector of elements whose length is the number of customers in the queue and whose jth element $x_{i,j}$ is the class index of the jth customer in the queue. Furthermore, the customers are ordered according to the service order (FIFO or LIFO); it is always the customer at the head of the list which is in service. We denote by $c_{i,1}$ the class number of the customer in service and by $c_{i,\infty}$ the class number of the last customer in the queue.

For a PS (Type 2) service station, the instantaneous value of the state x_i is represented by the vector $(x_{i,k})$ which is the number of customers of class k in queue i.

3   Main Theorem

Let $P(x)$ denote the stationary probability distribution of the state of the network. It is given by the following product form result.

Theorem 1 *Consider a G-network with the restrictions and properties described in the previous sections. If the system of non-linear equations:*

$$q_{i,k} = \frac{\Lambda_{i,k} + \Lambda_{i,k}^+}{r_{i,k} + \sum_{m=1}^{S} K_{i,m,k}[\lambda_{i,m} + \lambda_{i,m}^-]} \tag{5}$$

$$\Lambda_{i,k}^+ = \sum_{j=1}^{n} \sum_{l=1}^{R} P^+[j,i][l,k] r_{j,l} q_{j,l}$$

$$+ \sum_{j=1}^{n} \sum_{l=1}^{R} \sum_{h=1}^{n} \sum_{m=1}^{S} \sum_{s=1}^{R} r_{j,l} q_{j,l} P^-[j,h][l,m] K_{h,m,s} q_{h,s} Q[h,i][s,k]$$

$$+ \sum_{j=1}^{n} \sum_{m=1}^{S} \sum_{s=1}^{R} \lambda_{j,m} K_{j,m,s} q_{j,s} Q[j,i][s,k] \tag{6}$$

$$\lambda_{i,m}^- = \sum_{j=1}^{n} \sum_{l=1}^{R} P^-[j,i][l,m] r_{j,l} q_{j,l} \tag{7}$$

has a solution such that for each pair i,k : $0 < q_{i,k}$ and for each station i : $\sum_{k=1}^{R} q_{i,k} < 1$, then the stationary probability distribution of the network state is:

$$P(x) = G \prod_{i=1}^{n} g_i(x_i) \tag{8}$$

where each $g_i(x_i)$ depends on the type of service center i. The $g_i(x_i)$ in (5) have the following form :

FIFO. *If the service center is of Type 1, then*

$$g_i(x_i) = \prod_{n=1}^{|x_i|} q_{i,v_{i,n}} \tag{9}$$

PS. *If the service center is of Type 2, then*

$$g_i(x_i) = |x_i|! \prod_{k=1}^{R} \frac{(q_{i,k})^{x_{i,k}}}{x_{i,k}!} \tag{10}$$

LIFO/PR. *If the service center is of Type 4, then*

$$g_i(x_i) = \prod_{n=1}^{|x_i|} q_{i,v_{i,n}} \tag{11}$$

and G is the normalization constant.

Notice that $\Lambda_{i,k}^+$ may be written as:

$$\Lambda_{i,k}^+ = \sum_{j=1}^{n} \sum_{l=1}^{R} r_{j,l} q_{j,l} P^+[j,i][l,k]$$

$$+ \sum_{j=1}^{n} \sum_{l=1}^{R} \sum_{m=1}^{S} q_{j,l} Q[j,i][l,k] K_{j,m,l}[\lambda_{j,m} + \lambda_{j,m}^-] \tag{12}$$

The conditions requiring that $q_{i,k} > 0$ and on that their sum over all classes at each center be less than 1 simply insure the existence of the normalizing constant G in (8) and the stability of the network.

4   Proof of the Main Result

The proof follows the same lines as that for a similar result but more restrictive result in [20] which does not cover the case of triggers. The reader who is not interested in the technical details may prefer to skip this section. We begin with some technical Lemmas.

Lemma 1 *The following flow equation is satisfied:*

$$\sum_{i=1}^{n} \sum_{k=1}^{R} \Lambda_{i,k}^+ + \sum_{i=1}^{n} \sum_{m=1}^{S} \lambda_{i,m}^-$$

$$= \sum_{i-1}^{n} \sum_{k=1}^{R} q_{i,k} r_{i,k}(1 - d[i,k])$$

$$+ \sum_{i=1}^{n} \sum_{k=1}^{R} \sum_{j=1}^{n} \sum_{l=1}^{R} \sum_{m=1}^{S} q_{j,l} Q[j,i][l,k] K_{j,m,l}[\lambda_{j,m} + \lambda_{j,m}^-]$$

Proof : Consider (12), then sum it for all the stations and all the classes and exchange the order of summations in the right-hand side of the equation :

$$\sum_{i=1}^{n}\sum_{k=1}^{R}\Lambda_{i,k}^{+} = \sum_{j=1}^{n}\sum_{l=1}^{R}r_{j,l}q_{j,l}\left(\sum_{i=1}^{n}\sum_{k=1}^{R}P^{+}[j,i][l,k]\right)$$
$$+ \sum_{i=1}^{n}\sum_{k=1}^{R}\sum_{j=1}^{n}\sum_{l=1}^{R}\sum_{m=1}^{S}q_{j,l}Q[j,i][l,k]K_{j,m,l}[\lambda_{j,m}+\lambda_{j,m}^{-}]$$

Similarly, using equation (7)

$$\sum_{i=1}^{n}\sum_{m=1}^{S}\lambda_{i,m}^{-} = \sum_{j=1}^{n}\sum_{l=1}^{R}r_{j,l}q_{j,l}\left(\sum_{i=1}^{n}\sum_{m=1}^{S}P^{-}[j,i][l,m]\right)$$

Furthermore:

$$\sum_{i=1}^{n}\sum_{k=1}^{R}\Lambda_{i,k}^{+} + \sum_{i=1}^{n}\sum_{m=1}^{S}\lambda_{i,m}^{-}$$
$$= \sum_{j=1}^{n}\sum_{l=1}^{R}r_{j,l}q_{j,l}\left(\sum_{i=1}^{n}\sum_{k=1}^{R}P^{+}[j,i][l,k] + \sum_{i=1}^{n}\sum_{m=1}^{S}P^{-}[j,i][l,m]\right)$$
$$+ \sum_{i=1}^{n}\sum_{k=1}^{R}\sum_{j=1}^{n}\sum_{l=1}^{R}\sum_{m=1}^{S}q_{j,l}Q[j,i][l,k]K_{j,m,l}[\lambda_{j,m}+\lambda_{j,m}^{-}]$$

According to the definition of the routing matrix P (equation (1)), we have

$$\sum_{i=1}^{n}\sum_{k=1}^{R}\Lambda_{i,k}^{+} + \sum_{i=1}^{n}\sum_{m=1}^{S}\lambda_{i,m}^{-}$$
$$= \sum_{j=1}^{n}\sum_{l=1}^{R}r_{j,l}q_{j,l}(1 - d[j,l])$$
$$+ \sum_{i=1}^{n}\sum_{k=1}^{R}\sum_{j=1}^{n}\sum_{l=1}^{R}\sum_{m=1}^{S}q_{j,l}Q[j,i][l,k]K_{j,m,l}[\lambda_{j,m}+\lambda_{j,m}^{-}]$$

Thus the proof of the Lemma is complete.

□

In order to carry out the algebraic manipulations of the stationary Chapman-Kolmogorov (global balance) equations, we introduce some notation and develop intermediate results:

– The state dependent service rates for customers at service center j will be denoted by $M_{j,l}(x_j)$ where x_j refers to the state of the service center and l is the class of the customer concerned. From the definition of the service rate rjl, we obtain for the three types of stations :

FIFO and LIFO/PR $M_{j,l}(x_j) = r_{j,l}1_{\{c_{j,1}=l\}}$,
PS $M_{j,l}(x_j) = r_{j,l}\frac{x_{j,l}}{|x_j|}$.

- $N_{j,l}(x_j)$ is the *movement triggering* rate of class l positive customers due to external arrivals of all the classes of signals:
  FIFO and LIFO/PR $N_{j,l}(x_j) = 1_{\{c_{j,1}=l\}} \sum_{m=1}^{S} K_{j,m,l}\lambda_{j,m}$
  PS $N_{j,l}(x_j) = \frac{x_{j,l}}{|x_j|} \sum_{m=1}^{S} K_{j,m,l}\lambda_{j,m}$.

- $A_{j,l}(x_j)$ is the condition which establishes that it is possible to reach state x_j by an arrival of a positive customer of class l
  FIFO $A_{j,l}(x_j) = 1_{\{c_{j,\infty}=l\}}$,
  LIFO/PR $A_{j,l}(x_j) = 1_{\{c_{j,1}=l\}}$,
  PS $A_{j,l}(x_j) = 1_{\{|x_{j,l}|>0\}}$.

- $Z_{j,l,m}(x_j)$ is the probability that a signal of class m, arriving from the network, will *trigger the movement of* a positive customer of class l.
  FIFO and LIFO/PR $Z_{j,l,m}(x_j) = 1_{\{c_{j,1}=l\}}K_{j,m,l}$
  PS $Z_{j,l,m}(x_j) = \frac{x_{j,l}}{|x_j|}K_{j,m,l}$.

- $Y_{j,m}(x_j)$ is the probability that a signal of class m which enters a non empty queue, will not *trigger the movement of* a positive customer.
  FIFO and LIFO/PR $Y_{j,m}(x_j) = \sum_{l=1}^{R} 1_{\{c_{j,1}=l\}}(1 - K_{j,m,l})$
  PS $Y_{j,m}(x_j) = \sum_{l=1}^{R}(1 - K_{j,m,l})\frac{x_{j,l}}{|x_j|}$.

Denote by $(x_j + e_{j,l})$ the state of station j obtained by *adding to the $j-th$ queue a positive customer of class l*. Let $(x_i - e_{i,k})$ be the state obtained by removing from the end of the list of customers in queue, a class k customer if it is there; otherwise $(x_i - e_{i,k})$ is not defined.

Lemma 2 *For any Type 1, 2, or 4 service center, the following relations hold:*

$$M_{j,l}(x_j + e_{j,l})\frac{g_j(x_j + e_{j,l})}{g_j(x_j)} = r_{j,l}q_{j,l} \qquad (13)$$

$$N_{j,l}(x_j + e_{j,l})\frac{g_j(x_j + e_{j,l})}{g_j(x_j)} = \sum_{m=1}^{S}(K_{j,m,l}\lambda_{j,m})q_{j,l} \qquad (14)$$

$$Z_{j,l,m}(x_j + e_{j,l})\frac{g_j(x_j + e_{j,l})}{g_j(x_j)} = K_{j,m,l}q_{j,l} \qquad (15)$$

The proof is purely algebraic.

□

Remark : As a consequence, we have from equations (12), (7) and (13):

$$\Lambda_{i,k}^{+} = \sum_{j=1}^{n}\sum_{l=1}^{R} M_{j,l}(x_j + e_{j,l})\frac{g_j(x_j + e_{j,l})}{g_j(x_j)}P^{+}[j, i][l, k]$$

$$+ \sum_{j=1}^{n}\sum_{l=1}^{R}\sum_{m=1}^{S} q_{j,l}Q[j, i][l, k]K_{j,m,l}[\lambda_{j,m} + \lambda_{j,m}^{-}] \qquad (16)$$

and

$$\lambda_{i,m}^{-} = \sum_{j=1}^{n} \sum_{l=1}^{R} M_{j,l}(x_j + e_{j,l}) \frac{g_j(x_j + e_{j,l})}{g_j(x_j)} P^{-}[j,i][l,m] \tag{17}$$

Lemma 3 *Let i be any Type 1, 2, or 4 station, and let $\Delta_i(x_i)$ be:*

$$\Delta_i(x_i) = \sum_{m=1}^{S} \lambda_{i,m}^{-} Y_{i,m}(x_i)$$

$$- \sum_{k=1}^{R} (M_{i,k}(x_i) + N_{i,k}(x_i))$$

$$+ \sum_{k=1}^{R} A_{i,k}(x_i)(\Lambda_{i,k} + \Lambda_{i,k}^{+}) \frac{g_i(x_i - e_{i,k})}{g_i(x_i)}$$

Then for the three types of service centers, $1_{\{|x_i|>0\}} \Delta_i(x_i) = \sum_{m=1}^{S} \lambda_{i,m}^{-} 1_{\{|x_i|>0\}}$.

The proof of Lemma 3 is in a separate subsection at the end of this paper in order to make the text somewhat easier to follow.

□

Let us now turn to the proof of Theorem 1. The global balance equation of the networks which are considered is:

$$P(x) \left[\sum_{j=1}^{n} \sum_{l=1}^{R} (\Lambda_{j,l} + M_{j,l}(x_j) 1_{\{|x_j|>0\}} + N_{j,l}(x_j) 1_{\{|x_j|>0\}}) \right]$$

$$= \sum_{j=1}^{n} \sum_{l=1}^{R} P(x - e_{j,l}) \Lambda_{j,l} A_{j,l}(x_j) 1_{\{|x_j|>0\}}$$

$$+ \sum_{j=1}^{n} \sum_{l=1}^{R} P(x + e_{j,l}) N_{j,l}(x_j + e_{j,l}) D[j,l]$$

$$+ \sum_{j=1}^{n} \sum_{l=1}^{R} P(x + e_{j,l}) M_{j,l}(x_j + e_{j,l}) d[j,l]$$

$$+ \sum_{i=1}^{n} \sum_{j=1}^{n} \sum_{l=1}^{R} \sum_{m=1}^{S} M_{j,l}(x_j + e_{j,l}) P(x + e_{j,l}) P^{-}[j,i][l,m] Y_{i,m}(x_i) 1_{\{|x_i|>0\}}$$

$$+ \sum_{i=1}^{n} \sum_{j=1}^{n} \sum_{l=1}^{R} \sum_{m=1}^{S} M_{j,l}(x_j + e_{j,l}) P(x + e_{j,l}) P^{-}[j,i][l,m] 1_{\{|x_i|=0\}}$$

$$+ \sum_{i=1}^{n} \sum_{j=1}^{n} \sum_{k=1}^{R} \sum_{l=1}^{R} M_{j,l}(x_j + e_{j,l}) P(x - e_{i,k} + e_{j,l}) P^{+}[j,i][l,k] A_{i,k}(x_i) 1_{\{|x_i|>0\}}$$

$$+ \sum_{i=1}^{n} \sum_{j=1}^{n} \sum_{k=1}^{R} \sum_{l=1}^{R} N_{j,l}(x_j + e_{j,l}) P(x - e_{i,k} + e_{j,l}) Q[j,i][l,k] A_{i,k}(x_i) 1_{\{|x_i|>0\}}$$

$$+ \sum_{i=1}^{n} \sum_{j=1}^{n} \sum_{k=1}^{R} \sum_{l=1}^{R} \sum_{m=1}^{S} M_{j,l}(x_j + e_{j,l}) P(x + e_{i,k} + e_{j,l}) P^-[j,i][l,m] Z_{i,k,m}$$

$$(x_i + e_{i,k}) D[i,k]$$

$$+ \sum_{i=1}^{n} \sum_{j=1}^{n} \sum_{k=1}^{R} \sum_{l=1}^{R} \sum_{m=1}^{S} \sum_{h=1}^{n} \sum_{s=1}^{R} (M_{j,l}(x_j + e_{j,l}) P(x + e_{i,k} + e_{j,l} - e_{h,s}) P^-[j,i][l,m]$$

$$Z_{i,k,m}(x_i + e_{i,k}) Q[i,h][k,s] A_{h,s}(x_h) 1_{\{|x_h|>0\}})$$

We divide both sides by $P(x)$, assume that there is a product form solution, and apply Lemma 2:

$$\sum_{j=1}^{n} \sum_{l=1}^{R} (\Lambda_{j,l} + M_{j,l}(x_j) 1_{\{|x_j|>0\}} + N_{j,l}(x_j) 1_{\{|x_j|>0\}})$$

$$= \sum_{j=1}^{n} \sum_{l=1}^{R} \frac{g_j(x_j - e_{j,l})}{g_j(x_j)} \Lambda_{j,l} A_{j,l}(x_j) 1_{\{|x_j|>0\}}$$

$$+ \sum_{j=1}^{n} \sum_{l=1}^{R} \sum_{m=1}^{S} \lambda_{j,m} K_{j,m,l} q_{j,l} D[j,l] \quad + \quad \sum_{j=1}^{n} \sum_{l=1}^{R} r_{j,l} q_{j,l} d[j,l]$$

$$+ \sum_{i=1}^{n} \sum_{j=1}^{n} \sum_{l=1}^{R} \sum_{m=1}^{S} r_{j,l} q_{j,l} P^-[j,i][l,m] Y_{i,m}(x_i) 1_{\{|x_i|>0\}}$$

$$+ \sum_{i=1}^{n} \sum_{j=1}^{n} \sum_{l=1}^{R} \sum_{m=1}^{S} r_{j,l} q_{j,l} P^-[j,i][l,m] 1_{\{|x_i|=0\}}$$

$$+ \sum_{i=1}^{n} \sum_{j=1}^{n} \sum_{k=1}^{R} \sum_{l=1}^{R} r_{j,l} q_{j,l} P^+[j,i][l,k] A_{i,k}(x_i) \frac{g_i(x_i - e_{i,k})}{g_i(x_i)} 1_{\{|x_i|>0\}}$$

$$+ \sum_{i=1}^{n} \sum_{j=1}^{n} \sum_{k=1}^{R} \sum_{l=1}^{R} \sum_{m=1}^{S} \lambda_{j,m} K_{j,m,l} q_{j,l} Q[j,i][l,k] A_{i,k}(x_i) \frac{g_i(x_i - e_{i,k})}{g_i(x_i)} 1_{\{|x_i|>0\}}$$

$$+ \sum_{i=1}^{n} \sum_{j=1}^{n} \sum_{k=1}^{R} \sum_{l=1}^{R} \sum_{m=1}^{S} r_{j,l} q_{j,l} P^-[j,i][l,m] K_{i,m,k} q_{i,k} D[i,k]$$

$$+ \sum_{i=1}^{n} \sum_{j=1}^{n} \sum_{h=1}^{n} \sum_{l=1}^{R} \sum_{k=1}^{R} \sum_{s=1}^{R} \sum_{m=1}^{S} r_{j,l} q_{j,l} P^-[j,i][l,m] K_{i,m,k} q_{i,k} Q[i,h][k,s]$$

$$\frac{g_h(x_h - e_{h,s})}{g_h(x_h)} A_{h,s}(x_h) 1_{\{|x_h|>0\}}$$

We now apply (7) to the fourth, fifth, eigth and ninth terms of the second member of the equation:

$$\sum_{j=1}^{n}\sum_{l=1}^{R}(\Lambda_{j,l} + M_{j,l}(x_j)1_{\{|x_j|>0\}} + N_{j,l}(x_j)1_{\{|x_j|>0\}})$$

$$= \sum_{j=1}^{n}\sum_{l=1}^{R}\frac{g_j(x_j - e_{j,l})}{g_j(x_j)}\Lambda_{j,l}A_{j,l}(x_j)1_{\{|x_j|>0\}}$$

$$+ \sum_{j=1}^{n}\sum_{l=1}^{R}\sum_{m=1}^{S}\lambda_{j,m}K_{j,m,l}q_{j,l}D[j,l] \quad + \quad \sum_{j=1}^{n}\sum_{l=1}^{R}r_{j,l}q_{j,l}d[j,l]$$

$$+ \sum_{i=1}^{n}\sum_{m=1}^{S}\lambda_{i,m}^{-}Y_{i,m}(x_i)1_{\{|x_i|>0\}}$$

$$+ \sum_{i=1}^{n}\sum_{m=1}^{S}\lambda_{i,m}^{-}1_{\{|x_i|=0\}}$$

$$+ \sum_{i=1}^{n}\sum_{j=1}^{n}\sum_{k=1}^{R}\sum_{l=1}^{R}r_{j,l}q_{j,l}P^{+}[j,i][l,k]A_{i,k}(x_i)\frac{g_i(x_i - e_{i,k})}{g_i(x_i)}1_{\{|x_i|>0\}}$$

$$+ \sum_{i=1}^{n}\sum_{j=1}^{n}\sum_{k=1}^{R}\sum_{l=1}^{R}\sum_{m=1}^{S}\lambda_{j,m}K_{j,m,l}q_{j,l}Q[j,i][l,k]A_{i,k}(x_i)\frac{g_i(x_i - e_{i,k})}{g_i(x_i)}1_{\{|x_i|>0\}}$$

$$+ \sum_{i=1}^{n}\sum_{k=1}^{R}\sum_{m=1}^{S}\lambda_{i,m}^{-}K_{i,m,k}q_{i,k}D[i,k]$$

$$+ \sum_{i=1}^{n}\sum_{j=1}^{n}\sum_{l=1}^{R}\sum_{k=1}^{R}\sum_{m=1}^{S}\lambda_{j,m}^{-}K_{j,m,l}q_{j,l}Q[j,i][l,k]\frac{g_i(x_i - e_{i,k})}{g_i(x_i)}A_{i,k}(x_i)1_{\{|x_i|>0\}}$$

We group the first, sixth, seventh and ninth terms of the right side of the equation, and pass the two last terms of the first member to the second:

$$\sum_{j=1}^{n}\sum_{l=1}^{R}(\Lambda_{j,l})$$

$$= -\sum_{i=1}^{n}\sum_{k=1}^{R}(M_{i,k}(x_i) + N_{i,k}(x_i))1_{\{|x_i|>0\}}$$

$$+ \sum_{i=1}^{n}\sum_{k=1}^{R}\frac{g_i(x_i - e_{i,k})}{g_i(x_i)}A_{i,k}(x_i)1_{\{|x_i|>0\}}(\Lambda_{i,k} + \Lambda_{i,k}^{+})$$

$$+ \sum_{i=1}^{n}\sum_{m=1}^{S}\lambda_{i,m}^{-}Y_{i,m}(x_i)1_{\{|x_i|>0\}}$$

$$+ \sum_{j=1}^{n} \sum_{l=1}^{R} \sum_{m=1}^{S} \lambda_{j,m} K_{j,m,l} q_{j,l} D[j,l] \quad + \quad \sum_{j=1}^{n} \sum_{l=1}^{R} r_{j,l} q_{j,l} d[j,l]$$

$$+ \sum_{i=1}^{n} \sum_{m=1}^{S} \lambda_{i,m}^{-} 1_{\{|x_i|=0\}}$$

$$+ \sum_{i=1}^{n} \sum_{k=1}^{R} \sum_{m=1}^{S} \lambda_{i,m}^{-} K_{i,m,k} q_{i,k} D[i,k]$$

We now apply Lemma 3 to the sum of the three first terms of the second equation:

$$\sum_{j=1}^{n} \sum_{l=1}^{R} \Lambda_{j,l}$$

$$= \sum_{i=1}^{n} \sum_{m=1}^{S} \lambda_{i,m}^{-} 1_{\{|x_i|>0\}}$$

$$+ \sum_{j=1}^{n} \sum_{l=1}^{R} \sum_{m=1}^{S} \lambda_{j,m} K_{j,m,l} q_{j,l} D[j,l] \quad + \quad \sum_{j=1}^{n} \sum_{l=1}^{R} r_{j,l} q_{j,l} d[j,l]$$

$$+ \sum_{i=1}^{n} \sum_{m=1}^{S} \lambda_{i,m}^{-} 1_{\{|x_i|=0\}}$$

$$+ \sum_{j=1}^{n} \sum_{k=1}^{R} \sum_{m=1}^{S} \lambda_{j,m}^{-} K_{j,m,k} q_{j,k} D[j,k]$$

Now we group the first and fourth terms, and the second and fifth terms of the right side of the equation.

$$\sum_{j=1}^{n} \sum_{l=1}^{R} \Lambda_{j,l}$$

$$= \sum_{i=1}^{n} \sum_{m=1}^{S} \lambda_{i,m}^{-}$$

$$+ \sum_{j=1}^{n} \sum_{l=1}^{R} \sum_{m=1}^{S} q_{j,l} K_{j,m,l} (\lambda_{j,m} + \lambda_{j,m}^{-}) D[j,l]$$

$$+ \sum_{j=1}^{n} \sum_{l=1}^{R} r_{j,l} q_{j,l} d[j,l]$$

Substituting the value of $D[j,l]$ and the value of $d[j,l]$,

$$\sum_{j=1}^{n} \sum_{l=1}^{R} \Lambda_{j,l}$$

$$= \sum_{i=1}^{n}\sum_{m=1}^{S}\lambda_{i,m}^{-} \;+\; \sum_{j=1}^{n}\sum_{l=1}^{R}\sum_{m=1}^{S}q_{j,l}K_{j,m,l}(\lambda_{j,m}+\lambda_{j,m}^{-}) \;+\; \sum_{j=1}^{n}\sum_{l=1}^{R}q_{j,l}r_{j,l}$$

$$- (\sum_{i=1}^{n}\sum_{j=1}^{n}\sum_{l=1}^{R}\sum_{k=1}^{R}\sum_{m=1}^{S}q_{j,l}K_{j,m,l}Q[j,i][l,k](\lambda_{j,m}+\lambda_{j,m}^{-})$$

$$+ \sum_{i=1}^{n}\sum_{j=1}^{n}\sum_{l=1}^{R}\sum_{k=1}^{R}r_{j,l}q_{j,l}P^{+}[j,i][l,k])$$

$$- \sum_{i=1}^{n}\sum_{j=1}^{n}\sum_{l=1}^{R}\sum_{m=1}^{S}q_{j,l}r_{j,l}P^{-}[j,i][l,m]$$

and substituting for q_{jl} in the second and third terms and grouping them we have:

$$\sum_{j=1}^{n}\sum_{l=1}^{R}\Lambda_{j,l}$$

$$= \sum_{i=1}^{n}\sum_{m=1}^{S}\lambda_{i,m}^{-}$$

$$+ \sum_{j=1}^{n}\sum_{l=1}^{R}\Lambda_{j,l} \;+\; \sum_{j=1}^{n}\sum_{l=1}^{R}\Lambda_{j,l}^{+}$$

$$- \sum_{j=1}^{n}\sum_{l=1}^{R}\Lambda_{j,l}^{+} \;-\; \sum_{i=1}^{n}\sum_{m=1}^{S}\lambda_{i,m}^{-}$$

which yields thefollowing equality which is obviously satisfied,

$$\sum_{j=1}^{n}\sum_{l=1}^{R}\Lambda_{j,l} \;=\; \sum_{j=1}^{n}\sum_{l=1}^{R}\Lambda_{j,l},$$

concluding the proof.

As in the BCMP [2] theorem, we can also compute the steady state distribution of the number of customers of each class in each queue. Let y_i be the vector whose elements are $(y_{i,k})$ the number of customers of class k in station i. Let y be the vector of vectors (y_i). We omit the proof of the following result.

Theorem 2 *If the system of equations (5), (6) and (7) has a solution then, the steady state distribution $\pi(y)$ is given by*

$$\pi(y) = \prod_{i=1}^{n} h_i(y_i) \tag{18}$$

where the marginal probabilities $h_i(y_i)$ have the following form :

$$h_i(y_i) = (1 - \sum_{k=1}^{R} q_{i,k})|y_i|! \prod_{k=1}^{R} [(q_{i,k})^{y_{i,k}}/y_{i,k}!] \tag{19}$$

4.1   Proof of Lemma 3

The proof of Lemma 3 consists in algebraic manipulations of the terms in the balance equations related to each og the the three types of stations.

LIFO/PR. First consider an arbitrary LIFO station and recall the definition of Δ_i :

$$
\begin{aligned}
1_{\{|x_i|>0\}}\Delta_i(x_i) = {}& 1_{\{|x_i|>0\}} \sum_{k=1}^{R} A_{i,k}(x_i)(\Lambda_{i,k} + \Lambda_{i,k}^+)\frac{g_i(x_i - e_{i,k})}{g_i(x_i)} \\
& - 1_{\{|x_i|>0\}} \sum_{k=1}^{R} M_{i,k}(x_i) \quad - \quad 1_{\{|x_i|>0\}} \sum_{k=1}^{R} N_{i,k}(x_i) \\
& + 1_{\{|x_i|>0\}} \sum_{m=1}^{S} \lambda_{i,m}^- Y_{i,m}(x_i)
\end{aligned}
$$

We substitute the values of $Y_{i,m}$, $M_{i,k}$, $N_{i,k}$ and $A_{i,k}$ for a LIFO station :

$$
\begin{aligned}
1_{\{|x_i|>0\}}\Delta_i(x_i) = {}& 1_{\{|x_i|>0\}} \sum_{k=1}^{R} 1_{\{c_{i,1}=k\}} \, (\Lambda_{i,k} + \Lambda_{i,k}^+)/q_{i,k} \\
& - 1_{\{|x_i|>0\}} \sum_{k=1}^{R} 1_{\{c_{i,1}=k\}} \, r_{i,k} \\
& - 1_{\{|x_i|>0\}} \sum_{k=1}^{R} 1_{\{c_{i,1}=k\}} \sum_{m=1}^{S} K_{i,m,k}\lambda_{i,m} \\
& + 1_{\{|x_i|>0\}} \sum_{m=1}^{S} \lambda_{i,m}^- \sum_{k=1}^{R} 1_{\{c_{i,1}=k\}}(1 - K_{i,m,k})
\end{aligned}
$$

We use the value of $q_{i,k}$ from equation (5) and some cancellations of termsto obtain:

$$
\begin{aligned}
1_{\{|x_i|>0\}}\Delta_i(x_i) &= 1_{\{|x_i|>0\}} \sum_{k=1}^{R} 1_{\{c_{i,1}=k\}}(\sum_{m=1}^{S} K_{i,m,k}\lambda_{i,m}^- + \sum_{m=1}^{S} \lambda_{i,m}^-(1 - K_{i,m,k}) \\
&= 1_{\{|x_i|>0\}} \sum_{m=1}^{S} \lambda_{i,m}^- \sum_{k=1}^{R} 1_{\{c_{i,1}=k\}}
\end{aligned}
$$

and as $1_{\{|x_i|>0\}} \sum_{k=1}^{R} 1_{\{c_{i,1}=k\}} = 1_{\{|x_i|>0\}}$, we finally get the result :

$$
1_{\{|x_i|>0\}}\Delta_i(x_i) = 1_{\{|x_i|>0\}} \sum_{m=1}^{S} \lambda_{i,m}^- \tag{20}
$$

FIFO. Consider now an arbitrary FIFO station :

$$1_{\{|x_i|>0\}}\Delta_i(x_i) = 1_{\{|x_i|>0\}}\sum_{k=1}^{R}A_{i,k}(x_i)(\Lambda_{i,k}+\Lambda_{i,k}^{+})\frac{g_i(x_i-e_{i,k})}{g_i(x_i)}$$

$$-1_{\{|x_i|>0\}}\sum_{k=1}^{R}M_{i,k}(x_i) \quad - \quad \sum_{k=1}^{R}1_{\{|x_i|>0\}}N_{i,k}(x_i)$$

$$+1_{\{|x_i|>0\}}\sum_{m=1}^{S}\lambda_{i,m}^{-}Y_{i,m}(x_i)$$

Similarly, we substitute the values of $Y_{i,m}$, $M_{i,k}$, $N_{i,k}$, $A_{i,k}$ and $q_{i,k}$:

$$1_{\{|x_i|>0\}}\Delta_i(x_i) = 1_{\{|x_i|>0\}}\sum_{k=1}^{R}1_{\{c_{i,\infty}=k\}}(r_{i,k}+\sum_{m=1}^{S}K_{i,m,k}\lambda_{i,m}+\sum_{m=1}^{S}K_{i,m,k}\lambda_{i,m}^{-})$$

$$-1_{\{|x_i|>0\}}\sum_{k=1}^{R}1_{\{c_{i,1}=k\}}r_{i,k}-1_{\{|x_i|>0\}}\sum_{k=1}^{R}1_{\{c_{i,1}=k\}}\sum_{m=1}^{S}K_{i,m,k}\lambda_{i,m}$$

$$+1_{\{|x_i|>0\}}\sum_{m=1}^{S}\lambda_{i,m}^{-}\sum_{k=1}^{R}1_{\{c_{i,1}=k\}}(1-K_{i,m,k})$$

We separate the last term into two parts, and regroup terms:

$$1_{\{|x_i|>0\}}\Delta_i(x_i) = 1_{\{|x_i|>0\}}\sum_{k=1}^{R}1_{\{c_{i,\infty}=k\}}\ (r_{i,k}+\sum_{m=1}^{S}K_{i,m,k}\lambda_{i,m}+\sum_{m=1}^{S}K_{i,m,k}\lambda_{i,m}^{-})$$

$$-1_{\{|x_i|>0\}}\sum_{k=1}^{R}1_{\{c_{i,1}=k\}}\ (r_{i,k}+\sum_{m=1}^{S}K_{i,m,k}\lambda_{i,m}+\sum_{m=1}^{S}K_{i,m,k}\lambda_{i,m}^{-})$$

$$+1_{\{|x_i|>0\}}\sum_{m=1}^{S}\lambda_{i,m}^{-}\sum_{k=1}^{R}1_{\{c_{i,1}=k\}}$$

Conditions (2) and (3) imply that the following relation must hold:

$$\sum_{k=1}^{R}1_{\{c_{i,\infty}=k\}}\ (r_{i,k}+\sum_{m=1}^{S}K_{i,m,k}\lambda_{i,m}+\sum_{m=1}^{S}K_{i,m,k}\lambda_{i,m}^{-}) =$$

$$\sum_{k=1}^{R}1_{\{c_{i,1}=k\}}\ (r_{i,k}+\sum_{m=1}^{S}K_{i,m,k}\lambda_{i,m}+\sum_{m=1}^{S}K_{i,m,k}\lambda_{i,m}^{-})$$

Thus, as $1_{\{|x_i|>0\}}\sum_{k=1}^{R}1_{\{c_{i,1}=k\}} = 1_{\{|x_i|>0\}}$, we finally get the expected result :

$$1_{\{|x_i|>0\}}\Delta_i(x_i) = 1_{\{|x_i|>0\}}\sum_{m=1}^{S}\lambda_{i,m}^{-} \tag{21}$$

PS. Consider now an arbitrary PS station :

$$1_{\{|x_i|>0\}}\Delta_i(x_i) = 1_{\{|x_i|>0\}}\sum_{k=1}^{R} A_{i,k}(x_i)(\Lambda_{i,k}+\Lambda_{i,k}^{+})\frac{g_i(x_i-e_{i,k})}{g_i(x_i)}$$

$$- 1_{\{|x_i|>0\}}\sum_{k=1}^{R} M_{i,k}(x_i) \quad - \sum_{k=1}^{R} 1_{\{|x_i|>0\}} N_{i,k}(x_i)$$

$$+ 1_{\{|x_i|>0\}}\sum_{m=1}^{S} \lambda_{i,m}^{-} Y_{i,m}(x_i)$$

As usual, we substitute the values of $Y_{i,m}$, $M_{i,k}$, $N_{i,k}$, $A_{i,k}$:

$$1_{\{|x_i|>0\}}\Delta_i(x_i) = 1_{\{|x_i|>0\}}\sum_{k=1}^{R} 1_{\{|x_{i,k}|>0\}}\frac{(\Lambda_{i,k}+\Lambda_{i,k}^{+})}{q_{i,k}}\frac{x_{i,k}}{|x_i|}$$

$$- 1_{\{|x_i|>0\}}\sum_{k=1}^{R} r_{i,k}\frac{x_{i,k}}{|x_i|}$$

$$- 1_{\{|x_i|>0\}}\sum_{k=1}^{R} \frac{x_{i,k}}{|x_i|}\sum_{m=1}^{S} K_{i,m,k}\lambda_{i,m}$$

$$+ 1_{\{|x_i|>0\}}\sum_{m=1}^{S}\sum_{k=1}^{R} \lambda_{i,m}^{-}\frac{x_{i,k}}{|x_i|}(1-K_{i,m,k})$$

Then, we apply equation (5) to substitute $q_{i,k}$. After some cancelations of terms we obtain :

$$1_{\{|x_i|>0\}}\Delta_i(x_i) = 1_{\{|x_i|>0\}}\sum_{k=1}^{R} \frac{x_{i,k}}{|x_i|}\sum_{m=1}^{S} K_{i,m,k}\lambda_{i,m}^{-}$$

$$+ 1_{\{|x_i|>0\}}\sum_{m=1}^{S}\sum_{k=1}^{R} \lambda_{i,m}^{-}\frac{x_{i,k}}{|x_i|}(1-K_{i,m,k})$$

Finally we have:

$$1_{\{|x_i|>0\}}\Delta_i(x_i) = 1_{\{|x_i|>0\}}\sum_{k=1}^{R} \frac{x_{i,k}}{|x_i|}\sum_{m=1}^{S} \lambda_{i,m}^{-} \qquad (22)$$

Since $1_{\{|x_i|>0\}}\sum_{k=1}^{R}\frac{x_{i,k}}{|x_i|} = 1_{\{|x_i|>0\}}$, once again, we establish the relation we need. This concludes the proof of Lemma 3.

□

References

1. Kemmeny, J.G., Snell, J.L. "Finite Markov Chains", Von Nostrand, Princeton, 1965.

2. Baskett F., Chandy K., Muntz R.R., Palacios F.G. "Open, closed and mixed networks of queues with different classes of customers", *Journal ACM*, Vol. 22, No 2, pp 248–260, April 1975.

3. Gelenbe E. "Random neural networks with negative and positive signals and product form solution", *Neural Computation*, Vol. 1, No. 4, pp 502–510, 1989.

4. Gelenbe E. "Product form queueing networks with negative and positive customers", *Journal of Applied Probability*, Vol. 28, pp 656–663, 1991.

5. Gelenbe E., Glynn P., Sigmann K. "Queues with negative customers", *Journal of Applied Probability*, Vol. 28, pp 245–250, 1991.

6. Fourneau J.M. "Computing the steady-state distribution of networks with positive and negative customers", *Proc. 13-th IMACS World Congress on Computation and Applied Mathematics*, Dublin, 1991.

7. E. Gelenbe, S. Tucci "Performances d'un système informatique dupliqué", *Comptes-Rendus Acad. Sci.*, t 312, Série II, pp. 27–30, 1991.

8. Gelenbe E., Schassberger R. "Stability of G-Networks", *Probability in the Engineering and Informational Sciences*, Vol. 6, pp 271–276, 1992.

9. Fourneau, J.M., Gelenbe, E. "Multiple class G-networks," *Conference of the ORSA Technical Committee on Computer Science, Williamsburg, VA*, Balci, O. (Ed.), Pergamon, 1992.

10. Atalay, V., Gelenbe, E. "Parallel algorithm for colour texture generation using the random neural network model", *International Journal of Pattern Recognition and Artificial Intelligence*, Vol. 6, No. 2 & 3, pp 437–446, 1992.

11. Miyazawa, M. " Insensitivity and product form decomposability of reallocatable GSMP", *Advances in Applied Probability*, Vol. 25, No. 2, pp 415–437, 1993.

12. Henderson, W. " Queueing networks with negative customers and negative queue lengths", *Journal of Applied Probability*, Vol. 30, No. 3, 1993.

13. Gelenbe E. "G-Networks with triggered customer movement", *Journal of Applied Probability*, Vol. 30, No. 3, pp 742–748, 1993.

14. Gelenbe E., "G-Networks with signals and batch removal", *Probability in the Engineering and Informational Sciences*, Vol. 7, pp 335–342, 1993.

15. Chao, X., Pinedo, M. "On generalized networks of queues with positive and negative arrivals", *Probability in the Engineering and Informational Sciences*, Vol. 7, pp 301–334, 1993.

16. Henderson, W., Northcote, B.S., Taylor, P.G. "Geometric equilibrium distributions for queues with interactive batch departures," *Annals of Operations Research*, Vol. 48, No. 1–4, 1994.

17. Henderson, W., Northcote, B.S., Taylor, P.G. "Networks of customer queues and resource queues", *Proc. International Teletraffic Congress 14*, Labetoulle, J. and Roberts, J. (Eds.), pp 853–864, Elsevier, 1994.

18. Gelenbe, E. "G-networks: an unifying model for neural and queueing networks", *Annals of Operations Research*, Vol. 48, No. 1–4, pp 433–461, 1994.

19. Chao, X., Pinedo, M. "Product form queueing networks with batch services, signals, and product form solutions", *Operations Research Letters*, Vol. 17, pp 237–242, 1995.

20. J.M. Fourneau, E. Gelenbe, R. Suros "G-networks with multiple classes of positive and negative customers," *Theoretical Computer Science*, Vol. 155, pp. 141–156, 1996.

21. Gelenbe, E., Labed A. "G-networks with multiple classes of customers and triggers", to appear.

Spectral Expansion Solutions for Markov-Modulated Queues

Isi Mitrani

Computing Science Department, University of Newcastle
isi.mitrani@ncl.ac.uk

1 Introduction

There are many computer, communication and manufacturing systems which give rise to queueing models where the arrival and/or service mechanisms are influenced by some external processes. In such models, a single unbounded queue evolves in an environment which changes state from time to time. The instantaneous arrival and service rates may depend on the state of the environment and also, to a limited extent, on the number of jobs present.

The system state at time t is described by a pair of integer random variables, (I_t, J_t), where I_t represents the state of the environment and J_t is the number of jobs present. The variable I_t takes a finite number of values, numbered $0, 1, \ldots, N$; these are also called the environmental *phases*. The possible values of J_t are $0, 1, \ldots$. Thus, the system is in state (i, j) when the environment is in phase i and there are j jobs waiting and/or being served.

The two-dimensional process $X = \{(I_t, J_t) \; ; \; t \geq 0\}$ is assumed to have the Markov property, i.e. given the current phase and number of jobs, the future behaviour of X is independent of its past history. Such a model is referred to as a *Markov-modulated queue* (see, for example, Prabhu and Zhu [21]). The corresponding state space, $\{0, 1, \ldots, N\} \times \{0, 1, \ldots\}$ is known as a *lattice strip*.

A fully general Markov-modulated queue, with arbitrary state-dependent transitions, is not tractable. However, one can consider a sub-class of models which are sufficiently general to be useful, and yet can be solved efficiently. We shall introduce the following restrictions:

- (i) There is a threshold M, such that the instantaneous transition rates out of state (i, j) do not depend on j when $j \geq M$.
- (ii) the jumps of the random variable J are bounded.

When the jumps of the random variable J are of size 1, i.e. when jobs arrive and depart one at a time, the process is said to be of the *Quasi-Birth-and-Death* type, or QBD (the term *skip-free* is also used, e.g. in Latouche et al. [12]). The state diagram for this common model, showing some transitions out of state (i, j), is illustrated in figure 1.

The requirement that all transition rates cease to depend on the size of the job queue beyond a certain threshold is not too restrictive. Note that we impose no limit on the magnitude of the threshold M, although it must be pointed out that

M.C. Calzarossa and S. Tucci (Eds.): Performance 2002, LNCS 2459, pp. 17–35, 2002.
© Springer-Verlag Berlin Heidelberg 2002

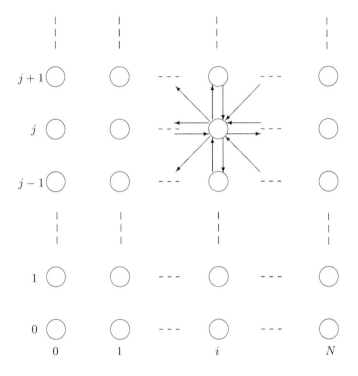

Fig. 1. State diagram of a QBD process

the larger M is, the greater the complexity of the solution. Similarly, although jobs may arrive and/or depart in fixed or variable (but bounded) batches, the larger the batch size, the more complex the solution.

The object of the analysis of a Markov-modulated queue is to determine the joint steady-state distribution of the environmental phase and the number of jobs in the system:

$$p_{i,j} = \lim_{t \to \infty} P(I_t = i,\, J_t = j) \; ; \; i = 0, 1, \ldots, N \; ; \; j = 0, 1, \ldots . \tag{1}$$

That distribution exists for an irreducible Markov process if, and only if, the corresponding set of balance equations has a positive solution that can be normalized.

The marginal distributions of the number of jobs in the system, and of the phase, can be obtained from the joint distribution:

$$p_{\cdot,j} = \sum_{i=0}^{N} p_{i,j} \, . \tag{2}$$

$$p_{i,\cdot} = \sum_{j=0}^{\infty} p_{i,j} \ . \tag{3}$$

Various performance measures can then be computed in terms of these joint and marginal distributions.

There are three ways of solving Markov-modulated queueing models exactly. Perhaps the most widely used one is the *matrix-geometric* method [18]. This approach relies on determining the minimal positive solution, R, of a non-linear matrix equation; the equilibrium distribution is then expressed in terms of powers of R.

The second method uses generating functions to solve the set of balance equations. A number of unknown probabilities which appear in the equations for those generating functions are determined by exploiting the singularities of the coefficient matrix. A comprehensive treatment of that approach, in the context of a discrete-time process with an M/G/1 structure, is presented in Gail et al. [5].

The third (and arguably best) method is the subject of this tutorial. It is called *spectral expansion*, and is based on expressing the equilibrium distribution of the process in terms of the eigenvalues and left eigenvectors of a certain matrix polynomial. The idea of the spectral expansion solution method has been known for some time (e.g., see Neuts [18]), but there are rather few examples of its application in the performance evaluation literature. Some instances where that solution has proved useful are reported in Elwalid et al. [3], and Mitrani and Mitra [17]; a more detailed treatment, including numerical results, is presented in Mitrani and Chakka [16]. More recently, Grassmann [7] has discussed models where the eigenvalues can be isolated and determined very efficiently. Some comparisons between the spectral expansion and the matrix-geometric solutions can be found in [16] and in Haverkort and Ost [8]. The available evidence suggests that, where both methods are applicable, spectral expansion is faster even if the matrix R is computed by the most efficient algorithm.

The presentation in this tutorial is largely based on the material in chapter 6 of [13] and chapter 13 of [14].

Before describing the details of the spectral expansion solution, it would be instructive to show some examples of systems which are modelled as Markov-modulated queues.

2   Examples of Markov-Modulated Queues

We shall start with a few models of the Quasi-Birth-and-Death type, where the queue size increases and decreases in steps of 1.

2.1   A Multiserver Queue with Breakdowns and Repairs

A single, unbounded queue is served by N identical parallel servers. Each server goes through alternating periods of being operative and inoperative, independently of the others and of the number of jobs in the system. The operative and inoperative periods are distributed exponentially with parameters ξ and η, respectively. Thus, the number of operative servers at time t, I_t, is a Markov process on the state space $\{0, 1, \ldots, N\}$. This is the environment in which the queue evolves: it is in phase i when there are i operative servers (see [15,20]).

Jobs arrive according to a Markov-Modulated Poisson Process controlled by I_t. When the phase is i, the instantaneous arrival rate is λ_i. Jobs are taken for service from the front of the queue, one at a time, by available operative servers. The required service times are distributed exponentially with parameter μ. An operative server cannot be idle if there are jobs waiting to be served. A job whose service is interrupted by a server breakdown is returned to the front of the queue. When an operative server becomes available, the service is resumed from the point of interruption, without any switching overheads. The flow of jobs is shown in figure 2.

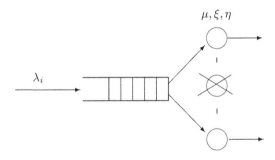

Fig. 2. A multiserver queue with breakdowns and repairs

The process $X = \{(I_t, J_t) \, ; \, t \geq 0\}$ is QBD. The transitions out of state (i, j) are:

(a) to state $(i - 1, j)$ $(i > 0)$, with rate $i\xi$;
(b) to state $(i + 1, j)$ $(i < N)$, with rate $(N - i)\eta$;
(c) to state $(i, j + 1)$ with rate λ_i;
(d) to state $(i, j - 1)$ with rate $\min(i, j)\mu$.

Note that only transition (d) has a rate which depends on j, and that dependency vanishes when $j \geq N$.

Remark. Even if the breakdown and repair processes were more complicated, e.g., if servers could break down and be repaired in batches, or if a server breakdown triggered a job departure, the queueing process would still be QBD. The environmental state transitions can be arbitrary, as long as the queue changes in steps of 1.

In this example, as in all models where the environment state transitions do not depend on the number of jobs present, the marginal distribution of the number of operative servers can be determined without finding the joint distribution first. Moreover, since the servers break down and are repaired independently of each other, that distribution is binomial:

$$p_{i,\cdot} = \binom{N}{i} \left(\frac{\eta}{\xi+\eta}\right)^i \left(\frac{\xi}{\xi+\eta}\right)^{N-i} \quad ; \quad i = 0, 1, \ldots, N \;. \tag{4}$$

Hence, the steady-state average number of operative servers is equal to

$$E(X_t) = \frac{N\eta}{\xi+\eta} \;. \tag{5}$$

The overall average arrival rate is equal to

$$\lambda = \sum_{i=0}^{N} p_{i,\cdot}\lambda_i \;. \tag{6}$$

This gives us an explicit condition for stability. The offered load must be less than the processing capacity:

$$\frac{\lambda}{\mu} < \frac{N\eta}{\xi+\eta} \;. \tag{7}$$

2.2 Manufacturing Blocking

Consider a network of two nodes in tandem, such as the one in figure 3. Jobs arrive into the first node in a Poisson stream with rate λ, and join an unbounded queue. After completing service at node 1 (exponentially distributed with parameter μ), they attempt to go to node 2, where there is a finite buffer with room for a maximum of $N-1$ jobs (including the one in service). If that transfer is impossible because the buffer is full, the job remains at node 1, preventing its server from starting a new service, until the completion of the current service at node 2 (exponentially distributed with parameter ξ). In this last case, server 1 is said to be 'blocked'. Transfers from node 1 to node 2 are instantaneous (see [1,19]).

Fig. 3. Two nodes with a finite intermediate buffer

The above type of blocking is referred to as 'manufacturing blocking'. (An alternative model, which also gives rise to a Markov-modulated queue, is the 'communication blocking'. There node 1 *does not start* a service if the buffer is full.)

In this system, the unbounded queue at node 1 is modulated by a finite-state environment defined by node 2. We say that the environment, I_t, is in state i if there are i jobs at node 2 and server 1 is not blocked ($i = 0, 1, \ldots, N - 1$). An extra state, $I_t = N$, is needed to describe the situation where there are $N - 1$ jobs at node 2 and server 1 is blocked.

The above assumptions imply that the pair $X = \{(I_t, J_t) ; t \geq 0\}$, where J_t is the number of jobs at node 1, is a QBD process. Note that the state $(N, 0)$ does not exist: node 1 may be blocked only if there are jobs present.

The transitions out of state (i, j) are:

(a) to state $(i - 1, j)$ $(0 < i < N)$, with rate ξ;
(b) to state $(N - 1, j - 1)$ $(i = N, \ j > 0)$, with rate ξ;
(c) to state $(i + 1, j - 1)$ $(0 \leq i < N - 1, \ j > 0)$, with rate μ;
(d) to state (N, j) $(i = N - 1, \ j > 0)$, with rate μ;
(e) to state $(i, j + 1)$ with rate λ.

The only dependency on j comes from the fact that transitions (b), (c) and (d) are not available when $j = 0$. In this example, the j-independency threshold is $M = 1$.

Because the environmental process is coupled with the queueing process, the marginal distribution of the former (i.e., the number of jobs at node 2), cannot be determined without finding the joint distribution of I_t and J_t. Nor is the stability condition as simple as in the previous example.

2.3   Phase-Type Distributions

There is a large and useful family of distributions that can be incorporated into queueing models by means of Markovian environments. Those distributions are 'almost' general, in the sense that any distribution function either belongs to this family or can be approximated as closely as desired by functions from it.

Let I_t be a Markov process with state space $\{0, 1, \ldots, N\}$ and generator matrix $\tilde{A}$. States $0, 1, \ldots, N - 1$ are transient, while state N, reachable from any of the other states, is absorbing (the last row of $\tilde{A}$ is 0). At time 0, the process starts in state i with probability α_i ($i = 0, 1, \ldots, N-1; \alpha_1 + \alpha_2 + \ldots + \alpha_{N-1} = 1$). Eventually, after an interval of length T, it is absorbed in state N. The random variable T is said to have a 'phase-type' (PH) distribution with parameters $\tilde{A}$ and α_i (see [18]).

The exponential distribution is obviously phase-type ($N = 1$). So is the Erlang distribution—the convolution of N exponentials (exercise 5 in section 2.3). The corresponding generator matrix is

$$\tilde{A} = \begin{bmatrix} -\mu & \mu & & & \\ & -\mu & \mu & & \\ & & \ddots & \ddots & \\ & & & -\mu & \mu \\ & & & & 0 \end{bmatrix} ,$$

and the initial probabilities are $\alpha_0 = 1$, $\alpha_1 = \ldots = \alpha_{N-1} = 0$.

Another common PH distribution is the 'hyperexponential', where $I_0 = i$ with probability α_i, and absorbtion occurs at the first transition. The generator matrix of the hyperexponential distribution is

$$\tilde{A} = \begin{bmatrix} -\mu_0 & & & & \mu_0 \\ & -\mu_1 & & & \mu_1 \\ & & \ddots & & \vdots \\ & & & -\mu_{N-1} & \mu_{N-1} \\ & & & & 0 \end{bmatrix} .$$

The corresponding probability distribution function, $F(x)$, is a mixture of exponentials:

$$F(x) = 1 - \sum_{i=0}^{N-1} \alpha_i e^{-\mu_i x} .$$

The PH family is very versatile. It contains distributions with both low and high coefficients of variation. It is closed with respect to mixing and convolution: if X_1 and X_2 are two independent PH random variables with N_1 and N_2 (non-absorbing) phases respectively, and c_1 and c_2 are constants, then $c_1 X_1 + c_2 X_2$ has a PH distribution with $N_1 + N_2$ phases.

A model with a single unbounded queue, where either the interarrival intervals, or the service times, or both, have PH distributions, is easily cast in the framework of a queue in Markovian environment. Consider, for instance, the M/PH/1 queue. Its state at time t can be represented as a pair (I_t, J_t), where J_t is the number of jobs present and I_t is the phase of the current service (if $J_t > 0$). When I_t has a transition into the absorbing state, the current service completes and (if the queue is not empty) a new service starts immediately, entering phase i with probability α_i.

The PH/PH/n queue can also be represented as a QBD process. However, the state of the environmental variable, I_t, now has to indicate the phase of the current interarrival interval and the phases of the current services at all busy servers. If the interarrival interval has N_1 phases and the service has N_2 phases, the state space of I_t would be of size $N_1 N_2^n$.

2.4   Checkpointing and Recovery in the Presence of Faults

The last example is not a QBD process. Consider a system where transactions, arriving according to a Poisson process with rate λ, are served in FIFO order by a single server. The service times are i.i.d. random variables distributed exponentially with parameter μ. After N consecutive transactions have been completed, the system performs a checkpoint operation whose duration is an i.i.d. random variable distributed exponentially with parameter β. Once a checkpoint is established, the N completed transactions are deemed to have departed. However, both transaction processing and checkpointing may be interrupted by the occurrence of a fault. The latter arrive according to an independent Poisson process with rate ξ. When a fault occurs, the system instantaneously rolls back to the last established checkpoint; all transactions which arrived since that moment either remain in the queue, if they have not been processed, or return to it, in order to be processed again (it is assumed that repeated service times are resampled independently) (see [11,8]).

This system can be modelled as an unbounded queue of (uncompleted) transactions, which is modulated by an environment consisting of completed transactions and checkpoints. More precisely, the two state variables, $I(t)$ and $J(t)$, are the number of transactions that have completed service since the last checkpoint, and the number of transactions present that have not completed service (including those requiring re-processing), respectively.

The Markov-modulated queueing process $X = \{[I(t), J(t)] ; t \geq 0\}$, has the following transitions out of state (i, j):

(a) to state $(0, j + i)$, with rate ξ;
(b) to state $(0, j)$ $(i = N)$, with rate β;
(c) to state $(i, j + 1)$, with rate λ;
(d) to state $(i + 1, j - 1)$ $(0 \leq i < N, \ j > 0)$, with rate μ;

Because transitions (a), resulting from arrivals of faults, cause the queue size to jump by more than 1, this is not a QBD process.

3   Spectral Expansion Solution

Let us now turn to the problem of determining the steady-state joint distribution of the environmental phase and the number of jobs present, for a Markov-modulated queue. We shall start with the most commonly encountered case, namely the QBD process, where jobs arrive and depart singly. The starting point is of course the set of balance equations which the probabilities $p_{i,j}$, defined in 1, must satisfy. In order to write them in general terms, the following notation for the instantaneous transition rates will be used.

(a) Phase transitions leaving the queue unchanged: from state (i, j) to state (k, j) $(0 \leq i, k \leq N ; i \neq k)$, with rate $a_j(i, k)$;
(b) Transitions incrementing the queue: from state (i, j) to state $(k, j + 1)$ $(0 \leq i, k \leq N)$, with rate $b_j(i, k)$;
(c) Transitions decrementing the queue: from state (i, j) to state $(k, j - 1)$ $(0 \leq i, k \leq N ; j > 0)$, with rate $c_j(i, k)$.

It is convenient to introduce the $(N+1) \times (N+1)$ matrices containing the rates of type (a), (b) and (c): $A_j = [a_j(i,k)]$, $B_j = [b_j(i,k)]$ and $C_j = [c_j(i,k)]$, respectively (the main diagonal of A_j is zero by definition; also, $C_0 = 0$ by definition). According to the assumptions of the Markov-modulated queue, there is a threshold, M ($M \geq 1$), such that those matrices do not depend on j when $j \geq M$. In other words,

$$A_j = A ; \; B_j = B ; \; C_j = C , \; j \geq M . \tag{8}$$

Note that transitions (b) may represent a job arrival coinciding with a change of phase. If arrivals are not accompanied by such changes, then the matrices B_j and B are diagonal. Similarly, a transition of type (c) may represent a job departure coinciding with a change of phase. Again, if such coincidences do not occur, then the matrices C_j and C are diagonal.

By way of illustration, here are the transition rate matrices for some of the examples in the previous subsection.

Multiserver Queue with Breakdowns and Repairs

Since the phase transitions are independent of the queue size, the matrices A_j are all equal:

$$A_j = A = \begin{bmatrix} 0 & N\eta & & & \\ \xi & 0 & (N-1)\eta & & \\ & 2\xi & 0 & \ddots & \\ & & \ddots & \ddots & \eta \\ & & & N\xi & 0 \end{bmatrix} .$$

Similarly, the matrices B_j do not depend on j:

$$B = \begin{bmatrix} \lambda_0 & & & \\ & \lambda_1 & & \\ & & \ddots & \\ & & & \lambda_N \end{bmatrix} .$$

Denoting

$$\mu_{i,j} = \min(i,j)\mu ; \quad i = 0, 1, \ldots, N ; \quad j = 1, 2, \ldots ,$$

the departure rate matrices, C_j, can thus be written as

$$C_j = \begin{bmatrix} 0 & & & \\ & \mu_{1,j} & & \\ & & \ddots & \\ & & & \mu_{N,j} \end{bmatrix} ; \; j = 1, 2, \ldots ,$$

These matrices cease to depend on j when $j \geq N$. Thus, the threshold M is now equal to N, and

$$
C = \begin{bmatrix} 0 & & & \\ & \mu & & \\ & & \ddots & \\ & & & N\mu \end{bmatrix}.
$$

Manufacturing Blocking

Remember that the environment changes phase without changing the queue size either when a service completes at node 2 and node 1 is not blocked, or when node 1 becomes blocked (if node 1 is already blocked, then a completion at node 2 changes both phase and queue size). Hence, when $j > 0$,

$$
A_j = A = \begin{bmatrix} 0 & 0 & & & \\ \xi & 0 & 0 & & \\ & \ddots & \ddots & \ddots & \\ & & \xi & 0 & \mu \\ & & & 0 & 0 \end{bmatrix} \quad ; \; j = 1, 2, \dots \; .
$$

When node 1 is empty $(j = 0)$, it cannot become blocked; the state $(N, 0)$ does not exist and the matrix A_0 has only N rows and columns:

$$
A_0 = \begin{bmatrix} 0 & & & \\ \xi & 0 & & \\ & \ddots & \ddots & \\ & & \xi & 0 \end{bmatrix} \quad ;
$$

Since the arrival rate into node 1 does not depend on either i or j, we have $B_j = B = \lambda I$, where I is the identity matrix of order $N + 1$. The departures from node 1 (which can occur when $i \neq N - 1$) are always accompanied by environmental changes: from state (i, j) the system moves to state $(i + 1, j - 1)$ with rate μ for $i < N - 1$; from state (N, j) to state $(N - 2, j - 1)$ with rate ξ. Hence, the departure rate matrices do not depend on j and are equal to

$$
C_j = C = \begin{bmatrix} 0 & \mu & & & & \\ 0 & 0 & \mu & & & \\ & & \ddots & \ddots & & \\ & & & \ddots & 0 & \mu \\ & & & & 0 & 0 & 0 \\ & & & & \xi & 0 & 0 \end{bmatrix}.
$$

Balance Equations

Using the instantaneous transition rates defined at the beginning of this section, the balance equations of a general QBD process can be written as

$$p_{i,j} \sum_{k=0}^{N} [a_j(i,k) + b_j(i,k) + c_j(i,k)]$$

$$= \sum_{k=0}^{N} [p_{k,j} a_j(k,i) + p_{k,j-1} b_{j-1}(k,i) + p_{k,j+1} c_{j+1}(k,i)] , \qquad (9)$$

where $p_{i,-1} = b_{-1}(k,i) = c_0(i,k) = 0$ by definition. The left-hand side of (9) gives the total average number of transitions out of state (i,j) per unit time (due to changes of phase, arrivals and departures), while the right-hand side expresses the total average number of transitions into state (i,j) (again due to changes of phase, arrivals and departures). These balance equations can be written more compactly by using vectors and matrices. Define the row vectors of probabilities corresponding to states with j jobs in the system:

$$\mathbf{v}_j = (p_{0,j}, p_{1,j}, \ldots, p_{N,j}) ; \ j = 0, 1, \ldots . \qquad (10)$$

Also, let D_j^A, D_j^B and D_j^C be the diagonal matrices whose ith diagonal element is equal to the ith row sum of A_j, B_j and C_j, respectively. Then equations (9), for $j = 0, 1, \ldots$, can be written as:

$$\mathbf{v}_j [D_j^A + D_j^B + D_j^C] = \mathbf{v}_{j-1} B_{j-1} + \mathbf{v}_j A_j + \mathbf{v}_{j+1} C_{j+1} , \qquad (11)$$

where $\mathbf{v}_{-1} = \mathbf{0}$ and $D_0^C = B_{-1} = 0$ by definition.

When j is greater than the threshold M, the coefficients in (11) cease to depend on j:

$$\mathbf{v}_j [D^A + D^B + D^C] = \mathbf{v}_{j-1} B + \mathbf{v}_j A + \mathbf{v}_{j+1} C , \qquad (12)$$

for $j = M + 1, M + 2, \ldots$.

In addition, all probabilities must sum up to 1:

$$\sum_{j=0}^{\infty} \mathbf{v}_j \mathbf{e} = 1 , \qquad (13)$$

where $\mathbf{e}$ is a column vector with $N + 1$ elements, all of which are equal to 1.

The first step of any solution method is to find the general solution of the infinite set of balance equations with constant coefficients, (12). The latter are normally written in the form of a homogeneous vector difference equation of order 2:

$$\mathbf{v}_j Q_0 + \mathbf{v}_{j+1} Q_1 + \mathbf{v}_{j+2} Q_2 = \mathbf{0} ; \ j = M, M + 1, \ldots , \qquad (14)$$

where $Q_0 = B$, $Q_1 = A - D^A - D^B - D^C$ and $Q_2 = C$. There is more than one way of solving such equations.

Associated with equation (14) is the so-called 'characteristic matrix polynomial', $Q(x)$, defined as

$$Q(x) = Q_0 + Q_1 x + Q_2 x^2 . \tag{15}$$

Denote by x_k and $\mathbf{u}_k$ the 'generalized eigenvalues', and corresponding 'generalized left eigenvectors', of $Q(x)$. In other words, these are quantities which satisfy

$$det[Q(x_k)] = 0 ,$$
$$\mathbf{u}_k Q(x_k) = \mathbf{0} ; \ k = 1, 2, \ldots, d , \tag{16}$$

where $det[Q(x)]$ is the determinant of $Q(x)$ and d is its degree. In what follows, the qualification *generalized* will be omitted.

The above eigenvalues do not have to be simple, but it is assumed that if one of them has multiplicity m, then it also has m linearly independent left eigenvectors. This tends to be the case in practice. So, the numbering in (16) is such that each eigenvalue is counted according to its multiplicity.

It is readily seen that if x_k and $\mathbf{u}_k$ are any eigenvalue and corresponding left eigenvector, then the sequence

$$\mathbf{v}_{k,j} = \mathbf{u}_k x_k^{j-M} ; \ j = M, M + 1, \ldots , \tag{17}$$

is a solution of equation (14). Indeed, substituting (17) into (14) we get

$$\mathbf{v}_{k,j} Q_0 + \mathbf{v}_{k,j+1} Q_1 + \mathbf{v}_{k,j+2} Q_2 = x_k^{j-M} \mathbf{u}_k [Q_0 + Q_1 x_k + Q_2 x_k^2] = \mathbf{0} .$$

By combining any multiple eigenvalues with each of their independent eigenvectors, we thus obtain d linearly independent solutions of (14). On the other hand, it is known that there cannot be more than d linearly independent solutions. Therefore, any solution of (14) can be expressed as a linear combination of the d solutions (17):

$$\mathbf{v}_j = \sum_{k=1}^{d} \alpha_k \mathbf{u}_k x_k^{j-M} ; \ j = M, M + 1, \ldots , \tag{18}$$

where α_k $(k = 1, 2, \ldots, d)$, are arbitrary (complex) constants.

However, the only solutions that are of interest in the present context are those which can be normalized to become probability distributions. Hence, it is necessary to select from the set (18), those sequences for which the series $\sum \mathbf{v}_j \mathbf{e}$ converges. This requirement implies that if $|x_k| \geq 1$ for some k, then the corresponding coefficient α_k must be 0.

So, suppose that c of the eigenvalues of $Q(x)$ are strictly inside the unit disk (each counted according to its multiplicity), while the others are on the circumference or outside. Order them so that $|x_k| < 1$ for $k = 1, 2, \ldots, c$. The corresponding independent eigenvectors are $\mathbf{u}_1$, $\mathbf{u}_2$, ..., $\mathbf{u}_c$. Then any normalizable solution of equation (14) can be expressed as

$$\mathbf{v}_j = \sum_{k=1}^{c} \alpha_k \mathbf{u}_k x_k^{j-M} ; \ j = M, M + 1, \ldots , \tag{19}$$

where α_k $(k = 1, 2, \ldots, c)$, are some constants.

Expression (19) is referred to as the 'spectral expansion' of the vectors $\mathbf{v}_j$. The coefficients of that expansion, α_k, are yet to be determined.

Note that if there are non-real eigenvalues in the unit disk, then they appear in complex-conjugate pairs. The corresponding eigenvectors are also complex-conjugate. The same must be true for the appropriate pairs of constants α_k, in order that the right-hand side of (19) be real. To ensure that it is also positive, the real parts of x_k, $\mathbf{u}_k$ and α_k should be positive.

So far, expressions have been obtained for the vectors $\mathbf{v}_M$, $\mathbf{v}_{M+1}$, ...; these contain c unknown constants. Now it is time to consider the balance equations (11), for $j = 0, 1, \ldots, M$. This is a set of $(M + 1)(N + 1)$ linear equations with $M(N+1)$ unknown probabilities (the vectors $\mathbf{v}_j$ for $j = 0, 1, \ldots, M-1$), plus the c constants α_k. However, only $(M+1)(N+1)-1$ of these equations are linearly independent, since the generator matrix of the Markov process is singular. On the other hand, an additional independent equation is provided by (13).

In order that this set of linearly independent equations has a unique solution, the number of unknowns must be equal to the number of equations, i.e. $(M + 1)(N + 1) = M(N + 1) + c$, or $c = N + 1$. This observation implies the following

Proposition 1 *The QBD process has a steady-state distribution if, and only if, the number of eigenvalues of $Q(x)$ strictly inside the unit disk, each counted according to its multiplicity, is equal to the number of states of the Markovian environment, $N+1$. Then, assuming that the eigenvectors of multiple eigenvalues are linearly independent, the spectral expansion solution of (12) has the form*

$$\mathbf{v}_j = \sum_{k=1}^{N+1} \alpha_k \mathbf{u}_k x_k^{j-M} \; ; \; j = M, M + 1, \ldots . \tag{20}$$

In summary, the spectral expansion solution procedure consists of the following steps:

1. Compute the eigenvalues of $Q(x)$, x_k, inside the unit disk, and the corresponding left eigenvectors $\mathbf{u}_k$. If their number is other than $N + 1$, stop; a steady-state distribution does not exist.
2. Solve the finite set of linear equations (11), for $j = 0, 1, \ldots, M$, and (13), with $\mathbf{v}_M$ and $\mathbf{v}_{M+1}$ given by (20), to determine the constants α_k and the vectors $\mathbf{v}_j$ for $j < M$.
3. Use the obtained solution in order to determine various moments, marginal probabilities, percentiles and other system performance measures that may be of interest.

Careful attention should be paid to step 1. The 'brute force' approach which relies on first evaluating the scalar polynomial $det[Q(x)]$, then finding its roots, may be very inefficient for large N. An alternative which is preferable in most cases is to reduce the quadratic eigenvalue-eigenvector problem

$$\mathbf{u}[Q_0 + Q_1 x + Q_2 x^2] = \mathbf{0} , \tag{21}$$

to a linear one of the form $\mathbf{u}Q = x\mathbf{u}$, where Q is a matrix whose dimensions are twice as large as those of Q_0, Q_1 and Q_2. The latter problem is normally solved by applying various transformation techniques. Efficient routines for that purpose are available in most numerical packages.

This linearization can be achieved quite easily if the matrix $C = Q_2$ is non-singular. Indeed, after multiplying (21) on the right by Q_2^{-1}, it becomes

$$\mathbf{u}[H_0 + H_1 x + I x^2] = \mathbf{0} , \tag{22}$$

where $H_0 = Q_0 C^{-1}$, $H_1 = Q_1 C^{-1}$, and I is the identity matrix. By introducing the vector $\mathbf{y} = x\mathbf{u}$, equation (22) can be rewritten in the equivalent linear form

$$[\mathbf{u}, \mathbf{y}] \begin{bmatrix} 0 & -H_0 \\ I & -H_1 \end{bmatrix} = x[\mathbf{u}, \mathbf{y}] . \tag{23}$$

If C is singular but B is not, a similar linearization is achieved by multiplying (21) on the right by B^{-1} and making a change of variable $x \to 1/x$. Then the relevant eigenvalues are those outside the unit disk.

If both B and C are singular, then the desired result is achieved by first making a change of variable, $x \to (\gamma + x)/(\gamma - x)$, where the value of γ is chosen so that the matrix $S = \gamma^2 Q_2 + \gamma Q_1 + Q_0$ is non-singular. In other words, γ can have any value which is not an eigenvalue of $Q(x)$. Having made that change of variable, multiplying the resulting equation by S^{-1} on the right reduces it to the form (22).

The computational demands of step 2 may be high if the threshold M is large. However, if the matrices B_j ($j = 0, 1, \ldots, M-1$) are non-singular (which is often the case in practice), then the vectors $\mathbf{v}_{M-1}, \mathbf{v}_{M-2}, \ldots, \mathbf{v}_0$ can be expressed in terms of $\mathbf{v}_M$ and $\mathbf{v}_{M+1}$, with the aid of equations (11) for $j = M, M-1, \ldots, 1$. One is then left with equations (11) for $j = 0$, plus (13) (a total of $N+1$ independent linear equations), for the $N+1$ unknowns x_k.

Having determined the coefficients in the expansion (19) and the probabilities $p_{i,j}$ for $j < N$, it is easy to compute performance measures. The steady-state probability that the environment is in state i is given by

$$p_{i,\cdot} = \sum_{j=0}^{M-1} p_{i,j} + \sum_{k=1}^{N+1} \alpha_k u_{k,i} \frac{1}{1 - x_k} , \tag{24}$$

where $u_{k,i}$ is the ith element of $\mathbf{u}_k$.

The conditional average number of jobs in the system, L_i, given that the environment is in state i, is obtained from

$$L_i = \frac{1}{p_{i,\cdot}} \left[\sum_{j=1}^{M-1} j p_{i,j} + \sum_{k=1}^{N+1} \alpha_k u_{k,i} \frac{M - (M-1) x_k}{(1 - x_k)^2} \right] . \tag{25}$$

The overall average number of jobs in the system, L, is equal to

$$L = \sum_{i=0}^{N} p_{i,\cdot} L_i . \tag{26}$$

The spectral expansion solution can also be used to provide simple estimates of performance when the system is heavily loaded. The important observation in this connection is that when the system approaches instability, the expansion (19) is dominated by the eigenvalue with the largest modulus inside the unit disk, x_{N+1}. That eigenvalue is always real. It can be shown that when the offered load is high, the average number of jobs in the system is approximately equal to $x_{N+1}/(1 - x_{N+1})$.

3.1 Batch Arrivals and/or Departures

Consider now a Markov-modulated queue which is not a QBD process, i.e. one where the queue size jumps may be bigger than 1. As before, the state of the process at time t is described by the pair (I_t, J_t), where I_t is the state of the environment (the operational mode) and J_t is the number of jobs in the system. The state space is the lattice strip $\{0, 1, \ldots, N\} \times \{0, 1, \ldots\}$. The variable J_t may jump by arbitrary, but bounded amounts in either direction. In other words, the allowable transitions are:

(a) Phase transitions leaving the queue unchanged: from state (i, j) to state (k, j) $(0 \le i, k \le N \; ; \; i \ne k)$, with rate $a_j(i, k)$;
(b) Transitions incrementing the queue by s: from state (i, j) to state $(k, j + s)$ $(0 \le i, k \le N \; ; \; 1 \le s \le r_1 \; ; \; r_1 \ge 1)$, with rate $b_{j,s}(i, k)$;
(c) Transitions decrementing the queue by s: from state (i, j) to state $(k, j - s)$ $(0 \le i, k \le N \; ; \; 1 \le s \le r_2 \; ; \; r_2 \ge 1)$, with rate $c_{j,s}(i, k)$,

provided of course that the source and destination states are valid.

Obviously, if $r_1 = r_2 = 1$ then this is a Quasi-Birth-and-Death process.

Denote by $A_j = [a_j(i, k)]$, $B_{j,s} = [b_{j,s}(i, k)]$ and $C_{j,s} = [c_{j,s}(i, k)]$, the transition rate matrices associated with (a), (b) and (c), respectively. There is a threshold M, such that

$$A_j = A \; ; \; B_{j,s} = B_s \; ; \; C_{j,s} = C_s \; ; \; j \ge M \; . \tag{27}$$

Defining again the diagonal matrices D^A, D^{B_s} and D^{C_s}, whose ith diagonal element is equal to the ith row sum of A, B_s and C_s, respectively, the balance equations for $j > M + r_1$ can be written in a form analogous to (12):

$$\mathbf{v}_j \left[D^A + \sum_{s=1}^{r_1} D^{B_s} + \sum_{s=1}^{r_2} D^{C_s} \right] = \sum_{s=1}^{r_1} \mathbf{v}_{j-s} B_s + \mathbf{v}_j A + \sum_{s=1}^{r_2} \mathbf{v}_{j+s} C_s \; . \tag{28}$$

Similar equations, involving A_j, $B_{j,s}$ and $C_{j,s}$, together with the corresponding diagonal matrices, can be written for $j \le M + r_1$.

As before, (28) can be rewritten as a vector difference equation, this time of order $r = r_1 + r_2$, with constant coefficients:

$$\sum_{\ell=0}^{r} \mathbf{v}_{j+\ell} Q_\ell = \mathbf{0} \; ; \; j \ge M \; . \tag{29}$$

Here, $Q_\ell = B_{r_1-\ell}$ for $\ell = 0, 1, \ldots r_1 - 1$,

$$Q_{r_1} = A - D^A - \sum_{s=1}^{r_1} D^{B_s} - \sum_{s=1}^{r_2} D^{C_s} ,$$

and $Q_\ell = C_{\ell-r_1}$ for $\ell = r_1 + 1, r_1 + 2, \ldots r_1 + r_2$.

The spectral expansion solution of this equation is obtained from the characteristic matrix polynomial

$$Q(x) = \sum_{\ell=0}^{r} Q_\ell x^\ell . \tag{30}$$

The solution is of the form

$$\mathbf{v}_j = \sum_{k=1}^{c} \alpha_k \mathbf{u}_k x_k^{j-M} \ ; \ j = M, M+1, \ldots , \tag{31}$$

where x_k are the eigenvalues of $Q(x)$ in the interior of the unit disk, $\mathbf{u}_k$ are the corresponding left eigenvectors, and α_k are constants $(k = 1, 2, \ldots, c)$. These constants, together with the the probability vectors $\mathbf{v}_j$ for $j < M$, are determined with the aid of the state-dependent balance equations and the normalizing equation.

There are now $(M + r_1)(N + 1)$ so-far-unused balance equations (the ones where $j < M + r_1$), of which $(M + r_1)(N + 1) - 1$ are linearly independent, plus one normalizing equation. The number of unknowns is $M(N+1)+c$ (the vectors $\mathbf{v}_j$ for $j = 0, 1, \ldots, M - 1$), plus the c constants α_k. Hence, there is a unique solution when $c = r_1(N + 1)$.

Proposition 2 *The Markov-modulated queue has a steady-state distribution if, and only if, the number of eigenvalues of $Q(x)$ strictly inside the unit disk, each counted according to its multiplicity, is equal to the number of states of the Markovian environment, $N+1$, multiplied by the largest arrival batch, r_1. Then, assuming that the eigenvectors of multiple eigenvalues are linearly independent, the spectral expansion solution of (28) has the form*

$$\mathbf{v}_j = \sum_{k=1}^{r_1*(N+1)} \alpha_k \mathbf{u}_k x_k^{j-M} \ ; \ j = M, M+1, \ldots . \tag{32}$$

For computational purposes, the polynomial eigenvalue-eigenvector problem of degree r can be transformed into a linear one. For example, suppose that Q_r is non-singular and multiply (29) on the right by Q_r^{-1}. This leads to the problem

$$\mathbf{u} \left[\sum_{\ell=0}^{r-1} H_\ell x^\ell + I x^r \right] = \mathbf{0} , \tag{33}$$

where $H_\ell = Q_\ell Q_r^{-1}$. Introducing the vectors $\mathbf{y}_\ell = x^\ell \mathbf{u}$, $\ell = 1, 2, \ldots, r - 1$, one obtains the equivalent linear form

$$[\mathbf{u}, \mathbf{y}_1, \ldots, \mathbf{y}_{r-1}] \begin{bmatrix} 0 & & & -H_0 \\ I & 0 & & -H_1 \\ & \ddots & \ddots & \vdots \\ & & I & -H_{r-1} \end{bmatrix} = x[\mathbf{u}, \mathbf{y}_1, \ldots, \mathbf{y}_{r-1}].$$

As in the quadratic case, if Q_r is singular then the linear form can be achieved by an appropriate change of variable.

Example: Checkpointing and Recovery

Consider the transaction processing system described in section 2.4. Here $r_1 = N$ and $r_2 = 1$ (the queue size is incremented by 1 when jobs arrive and by $1, 2, \ldots, N$ when faults occur; it is decremented by 1 when a transaction completes service. The threshold M is equal to 0. The matrices A, B_s and C_s are given by:

$$A_j = A = \begin{bmatrix} 0 & & & \\ 0 & 0 & & \\ & \vdots & & \\ \beta & 0 & \ldots & 0 \end{bmatrix} \quad ; \ j = 0, 1, \ldots.$$

The only transition which changes the environment, but not the queue, is the establishment of a checkpoint in state (N, j).

$$B_{j,1} = B_1 = \begin{bmatrix} \lambda & & & \\ \xi & \lambda & & \\ 0 & 0 & \lambda & \\ & & & \ddots & \\ & & & & \lambda \end{bmatrix} \quad ; \ j = 0, 1, \ldots.$$

The queue size increases by 1 when a job arrives, causing a transition from (i, j) to $(i, j + 1)$, and also when a fault occurs in state $(1, j)$; then the new state is $(0, j + 1)$.

$$B_{j,2} = B_2 = \begin{bmatrix} 0 & & & \\ 0 & 0 & & \\ \xi & 0 & 0 & \\ & \vdots & & \\ 0 & 0 & \ldots & 0 \end{bmatrix} \quad ; \ j = 0, 1, \ldots.$$

The queue size increases by 2 when a fault occurs in state $(2, j)$, causing a transition to state $(0, j + 2)$. The other B_s matrices have a similar form, until

$$B_{j,N} = B_N = \begin{bmatrix} 0 & & & \\ 0 & 0 & & \\ & \vdots & & \\ \xi & 0 & \ldots & 0 \end{bmatrix} \quad ; \ j = 0, 1, \ldots.$$

There is only one matrix corresponding to decrementing queue:

$$C_{j,1} = C_1 = \begin{bmatrix} 0 & \mu & & & \\ & 0 & \mu & & \\ & & \ddots & \ddots & \\ & & & 0 & \mu \\ & & & & 0 \end{bmatrix} \; ; \; j = 1, 2, \ldots \; .$$

The matrix polynomial $Q(x)$ is of degree $N + 1$. According to Proposition 2, the condition for stability is that the number of eigenvalues in the interior of the unit disk is $N(N + 1)$.

References

1. J.A. Buzacott and J.G. Shanthikumar, *Stochastic Models of Manufacturing Systems*, Prentice-Hall, 1993.
2. J.N. Daigle and D.M. Lucantoni, Queueing systems having phase-dependent arrival and service rates, in *Numerical Solutions of Markov Chains*, (ed. W.J. Stewart), Marcel Dekker, 1991.
3. A.I. Elwalid, D. Mitra and T.E. Stern, Statistical multiplexing of Markov modulated sources: Theory and computational algorithms, *Int. Teletraffic Congress*, 1991.
4. M. Ettl and I. Mitrani, Applying spectral expansion in evaluating the performance of multiprocessor systems, *CWI Tracts* (ed. O. Boxma and G. Koole), 1994.
5. H.R. Gail, S.L. Hantler and B.A. Taylor, Spectral analysis of M/G/1 type Markov chains, *RC17765, IBM Research Division*, 1992.
6. I. Gohberg, P. Lancaster and L. Rodman, *Matrix Polynomials*, Academic Press, 1982.
7. W.K. Grassmann and S. Drekic, An analytical solution for a tandem queue with blocking, *Queueing Systems*, 36, pp. 221–235, 2000.
8. B.R. Haverkort and A. Ost, Steady-State Analysis of Infinite Stochastic Petri Nets: Comparing the Spectral Expansion and the Matrix-Geometric Method, *Procs., 7th Int. Workshop on Petri Nets and Performance Models*, San Malo, 1997.
9. A. Jennings, *Matrix Computations for Engineers and Scientists*, Wiley, 1977.
10. A.G. Konheim and M. Reiser, A queueing model with finite waiting room and blocking, *JACM*, 23, 2, pp. 328–341, 1976.
11. L. Kumar, M. Misra and I. Mitrani, Analysis of a Transaction System with Checkpointing, Failures and Rollback, *Computer Performance Evaluation* (Eds T. Field, P.G. Harrison and U. Harder), LNCS 2324, Springer, 2002.
12. G. Latouche, P.A. Jacobs and D.P. Gaver, Finite Markov chain models skip-free in one direction, *Naval Res. Log. Quart.*, 31, pp. 571–588, 1984.
13. I. Mitrani, *Probabilistic Modelling*, Cambridge University Press, 1998.
14. I. Mitrani, The Spectral Expansion Solution Method for Markov Processes on Lattice Strips, Chapter 13 in *Advances in Queueing*, (Ed. J.H. Dshalalow), CRC Press, 1995.
15. I. Mitrani and B. Avi-Itzhak, A many-server queue with service interruptions, *Operations Research*, 16, 3, pp.628-638, 1968.

16. I. Mitrani and R. Chakka, Spectral expansion solution for a class of Markov models: Application and comparison with the matrix-geometric method, to appear in *Performance Evaluation*, 1995.

17. I. Mitrani and D. Mitra, A spectral expansion method for random walks on semi-infinite strips, *IMACS Symposium on Iterative Methods in Linear Algebra*, Brussels, 1991.

18. M.F. Neuts, *Matrix Geometric Solutions in Stochastic Models*, John Hopkins Press, 1981.

19. M.F. Neuts, Two queues in series with a finite intermediate waiting room, *J. Appl. Prob.*, 5, pp. 123–142, 1968.

20. M.F. Neuts and D.M. Lucantoni, A Markovian queue with N servers subject to breakdowns and repairs, *Management Science*, 25, pp. 849–861, 1979.

21. N.U. Prabhu and Y. Zhu, Markov-modulated queueing systems, *QUESTA*, 5, pp. 215–246, 1989.

M/G/1-Type Markov Processes: A Tutorial*

Alma Riska and Evgenia Smirni

Department of Computer Science
College of William and Mary
Williamsburg, VA 23187-8795
{riska,esmirni}@cs.wm.edu

Abstract. M/G/1-type processes are commonly encountered when modeling modern complex computer and communication systems. In this tutorial, we present a detailed survey of existing solution methods for M/G/1-type processes, focusing on the matrix-analytic methodology. From first principles and using simple examples, we derive the fundamental matrix-analytic results and lay out recent advances. Finally, we give an overview of an existing, state-of-the-art software tool for the analysis of M/G/1-type processes.

Keywords: M/G/1-type processes; matrix analytic method; Markov chains.

1 Introduction

Matrix analytic techniques, pioneered by Marcel Neuts [25,26], provide a framework that is widely used for the exact analysis of a general and frequently encountered class of queueing models. In these models, the embedded Markov chains are two-dimensional generalizations of elementary GI/M/1 and M/G/1 queues [13], and their intersection, i.e., quasi-birth-death (QBD) processes. GI/M/1 and M/G/1 Markov chains model systems with interarrival and service times characterized, respectively, by *general* distributions rather than simple exponentials and are often used as the modeling tool of choice in modern computer and communication systems [24,30,35,6,18]. As a consequence, considerable effort has been placed into the development of efficient matrix-analytic techniques for their analysis [26,21,8,9,11,15]. Alternatively, GI/M/1 and M/G/1 Markov chains can be analyzed by means of eigenvalues and eigenvectors [7].

The class of models that can be analyzed using M/G/1-type Markov chains includes the important class of BMAP/G/1 queues, where the arrival process is a batch Markovian arrival process (BMAP) [17,26,3]. Special cases of BMAPs include phase-type renewal processes (e.g., Erlang or Hyperexponential processes) and non-renewal processes (e.g., the Markov modulated Poisson process). The importance of BMAPs lies in their ability to be more effective and powerful

---

* This work has been supported by National Science Foundation under grands EIA-9974992, CCR-0098278, and ACI-0090221.

© Springer-Verlag Berlin Heidelberg 2002

traffic models than the simple Poisson process or the batch Poisson process, as they can effectively capture dependence and correlation, salient characteristics of Internet traffic [27,12,33].

In this paper, we focus on the solution techniques for M/G/1-type Markov chains. Neuts [25] defines various classes of infinite-state Markov chains with a repetitive structure, whose state space[1] is partitioned into the boundary states $\mathcal{S}^{(0)} = \{s_1^{(0)}, \ldots, s_m^{(0)}\}$ and the sets of states $\mathcal{S}^{(i)} = \{s_1^{(i)}, \ldots, s_n^{(i)}\}$, for $i \geq 1$, that correspond to the repetitive portion of the chain. For the class of M/G/1-type Markov chains, the infinitesimal generator $\mathbf{Q}_{M/G/1}$ has upper block Hessenberg form:

$$\mathbf{Q}_{M/G/1} = \begin{bmatrix} \widehat{\mathbf{L}} & \widehat{\mathbf{F}}^{(1)} & \widehat{\mathbf{F}}^{(2)} & \widehat{\mathbf{F}}^{(3)} & \widehat{\mathbf{F}}^{(4)} & \cdots \\ \widehat{\mathbf{B}} & \mathbf{L} & \mathbf{F}^{(1)} & \mathbf{F}^{(2)} & \mathbf{F}^{(3)} & \cdots \\ \mathbf{0} & \mathbf{B} & \mathbf{L} & \mathbf{F}^{(1)} & \mathbf{F}^{(2)} & \cdots \\ \mathbf{0} & \mathbf{0} & \mathbf{B} & \mathbf{L} & \mathbf{F}^{(1)} & \cdots \\ \mathbf{0} & \mathbf{0} & \mathbf{0} & \mathbf{B} & \mathbf{L} & \cdots \\ \vdots & \vdots & \vdots & \vdots & \vdots & \ddots \end{bmatrix}. \tag{1}$$

We use the letters "L", "F", and "B" to describe "local", 'forward", and "back-ward" transition rates, respectively, in relation to a set of states $\mathcal{S}^{(i)}$ for $i \geq 1$, and a "$\widehat{}$" for matrices related to $\mathcal{S}^{(0)}$.

For systems of the M/G/1-type, matrix analytic methods have been proposed for the solution of the basic equation $\boldsymbol{\pi} \cdot \mathbf{Q}_{M/G/1} = \mathbf{0}$ [26], where $\boldsymbol{\pi}$ is the (infinite) stationary probability vector of all states in the chain. Key to the matrix-analytic methods is the computation of an auxiliary matrix called $\mathbf{G}$. Traditional solution methodologies for M/G/1-type processes compute the stationary probability vector with a recursive function based on $\mathbf{G}$. Iterative algorithms are used to determine $\mathbf{G}$ [20,16].

Another class of Markov-chains with repetitive structure that commonly occurs in modeling of computer systems is the class of GI/M/1-type processes, whose infinitesimal generator $\mathbf{Q}_{GI/M/1}$ has a lower block Hessenberg form:

---

[1] We use calligraphic letters to indicate sets (e.g., $\mathcal{A}$), lower case boldface Roman or Greek letters to indicate row vectors (e.g., $\mathbf{a}$, $\boldsymbol{\alpha}$), and upper case boldface Roman letters to indicate matrices (e.g., $\mathbf{A}$). We use superscripts in parentheses or subscripts to indicate family of related entities (e.g., $\mathcal{A}^{(1)}$, $\mathbf{A}_1$), and we extend the notation to subvectors or submatrices by allowing sets of indices to be used instead of single indices (e.g., $\mathbf{a}[\mathcal{A}]$, $\mathbf{A}[\mathcal{A}, \mathcal{B}]$). Vector and matrix elements are indicated using square brackets (e.g., $\mathbf{a}[1]$, $\mathbf{A}[1, 2]$). $RowSum(\cdot)$ indicates the diagonal matrix whose entry in position (r, r) is the sum of the entries on the rth row of the argument (which can be a rectangular matrix). $Norm(\cdot)$ indicates a matrix whose rows are normalized. $\mathbf{0}$ and $\mathbf{1}$ indicate a row vector or a matrix of 0's, or a row vector of 1's, of the appropriate dimensions, respectively.

$$\mathbf{Q}_{GI/M/1} = \begin{bmatrix} \mathbf{\hat{L}} & \mathbf{\hat{F}} & \mathbf{0} & \mathbf{0}\ \mathbf{0} \cdots \\ \mathbf{\hat{B}}^{(1)} & \mathbf{L} & \mathbf{F} & \mathbf{0}\ \mathbf{0} \cdots \\ \mathbf{\hat{B}}^{(2)} & \mathbf{B}^{(1)} & \mathbf{L} & \mathbf{F}\ \mathbf{0} \cdots \\ \mathbf{\hat{B}}^{(3)} & \mathbf{B}^{(2)} & \mathbf{B}^{(1)} & \mathbf{L}\ \mathbf{F} \cdots \\ \vdots & \vdots & \vdots & \vdots\ \vdots\ \ddots \end{bmatrix}. \tag{2}$$

The solution of GI/M/1-type processes is significantly simpler than the solution of M/G/1-type processes because of the *matrix geometric* relation [25] that exists among the stationary probabilities of sets $\mathcal{S}^{(i)}$ for $i \geq 1$. This property leads to significant algebraic simplifications resulting in the very elegant matrix-geometric solution technique that was pioneered by Neuts and that was later popularized by Nelson in the early '90s [23,24]. Key to the matrix-geometric solution is a matrix called $\mathbf{R}$ which is used in the computation of the steady-state probability vector and measures of interest.

Quasi-Birth-Death (QBD) processes are the intersection of M/G/1-type and GI/M/1-type processes and their infinitesimal generator has the structure depicted in Eq.(3).

$$\mathbf{Q}_{QDB} = \begin{bmatrix} \mathbf{\hat{L}} & \mathbf{\hat{F}} & \mathbf{0} & \mathbf{0} & \mathbf{0} \cdots \\ \mathbf{\hat{B}} & \mathbf{L} & \mathbf{F} & \mathbf{0} & \mathbf{0} \cdots \\ \mathbf{0} & \mathbf{B} & \mathbf{L} & \mathbf{F} & \mathbf{0} \cdots \\ \mathbf{0} & \mathbf{0} & \mathbf{B} & \mathbf{L} & \mathbf{F} \cdots \\ \vdots & \vdots & \vdots & \vdots & \vdots\ \ddots \end{bmatrix}. \tag{3}$$

Since QBDs are special cases of both M/G/1-type processes and GI/M/1-type processes, either the matrix-analytic method or the matrix-geometric solution can be used for their analysis. The matrix-geometric solution is the preferable one because of its simplicity. Both matrices $\mathbf{G}$ and $\mathbf{R}$ are defined for QBD processes. We direct the interested reader to [16] for recent advances on the analysis of QBD processes.

Key to the solution of Markov chains of the M/G/1, GI/M/1, and QBD types, is the existence of a repetitive structure, as illustrated in Eqs. (1), (2), and (3), that allows for a certain recursive procedure to be applied for the computation of the stationary probability vector $\boldsymbol{\pi}^{(i)}$ corresponding to $\mathcal{S}^{(i)}$ for $i \geq 1$. It is this recursive relation that gives elegance to the solution for the case of $GI/M/1$ (and consequently QBD) Markov chains, but results in unfortunately more complicated mathematics for the case of the M/G/1-type.

The purpose of this tutorial is to shed light into the existing techniques for the analysis of Markov chains of the M/G/1 type that are traditionally considered not easy to solve. Our intention is to derive from first principles (i.e., global balance equations) the repetitive patterns that allow for their solution and illustrate that the mathematics involved are less arduous than initially feared.

Our stated goals and outline of this tutorial are the following:

– Give an overview of the matrix-geometric solution of GI/M/1 and QBD processes and establish from first principles why a geometric solution exists (Section 2).

– Use first principles to establish the most stable recursive relation for the case of M/G/1-type processes and essentially illustrate the absence of any geometric relation among the steady state probabilities of sets $\mathcal{S}^{(i)}$, $i \geq 0$, for such chains (Section 3).
– Present an overview of the current state of the art of efficient solutions for M/G/1-type processes (Section 4).
– State the stability conditions for M/G/1-type processes (Section 5).
– Summarize the features of an existing software tool that can provide M/G/1-type solutions (Section 6).

Our aim is to make these results more accessible to performance modelers. We do this by presenting simplified derivations that are often example driven and by describing an existing tool for the solution of such processes.

2 Matrix Geometric Solutions for GI/M/1-Type and QBD Processes

In this section we give a brief overview[2] of the matrix geometric solution technique for GI/M/1-type and QBD processes. While QBDs fall under both the M/G/1 and the GI/M/1-type cases, they are most commonly associated with GI/M/1 processes because they can be both solved using the very well-known matrix geometric approach [25].

Key to the general solution for the generator of Eqs.(2) and (3) is the assumption that a geometric relation[3] holds among the stationary probability vectors $\boldsymbol{\pi}^{(i)}$ of states in $\mathcal{S}^{(i)}$ for $i \geq 1$:

$$\forall i \geq 1, \; \boldsymbol{\pi}^{(i)} = \boldsymbol{\pi}^{(1)} \cdot \mathbf{R}^{i-1}, \tag{4}$$

where, in the GI/M/1-type case, $\mathbf{R}$ is the solution of the matrix equation

$$\mathbf{F} + \mathbf{R} \cdot \mathbf{L} + \sum_{k=1}^{\infty} \mathbf{R}^{k+1} \cdot \mathbf{B}^{(k)} = \mathbf{0}, \tag{5}$$

and can be computed using iterative numerical algorithms. The above equation is obtained from the balance equations of the repeating portion of the process, i.e., starting from the third column of $\mathbf{Q}_{GI/M/1}$. Using Eq.(4) and substituting in the balance equation that corresponds to the second column of $\mathbf{Q}_{GI/M/1}$, and together with the normalization condition

$$\boldsymbol{\pi}^{(0)} \cdot \mathbf{1}^T + \boldsymbol{\pi}^{(1)} \cdot \sum_{i=1}^{\infty} \mathbf{R}^{i-1} \cdot \mathbf{1}^T = 1 \quad \text{i.e.,} \quad \boldsymbol{\pi}^{(0)} \cdot \mathbf{1}^T + \boldsymbol{\pi}^{(1)} \cdot (\mathbf{I} - \mathbf{R})^{-1} \cdot \mathbf{1}^T = 1,$$

we obtain the following system of linear equations

---

[2] In this section and in the remainder of this tutorial we assume continuous time Markov chains, or CTMCs, but our discussion applies just as well to discrete time Markov chains, or DTMCs.

[3] This is similar to the simplest degenerate case of a QBD process, the straight forward birth-death M/M/1 case.

$$[\boldsymbol{\pi}^{(0)}, \boldsymbol{\pi}^{(1)}] \cdot \begin{bmatrix} \mathbf{e} & (\mathbf{L}^{(0)})^{\diamond} & \widehat{\mathbf{F}}^{(1)} \\ (\mathbf{I} - \mathbf{R})^{-1} \cdot \mathbf{e} & \left(\sum_{k=1}^{\infty} \mathbf{R}^{k-1} \cdot \widehat{\mathbf{B}}^{(k)} \right)^{\diamond} & \mathbf{L} + \sum_{k=1}^{\infty} \mathbf{R}^{k} \cdot \mathbf{B}^{(k)} \end{bmatrix} = [\mathbf{1}, \mathbf{0}],$$

(6)

that yields a unique solution for $\boldsymbol{\pi}^{(0)}$ and $\boldsymbol{\pi}^{(1)}$. The symbol "$\diamond$" indicates that we discard one (any) column of the corresponding matrix, since we added a column representing the normalization condition. For $i \geq 2$, $\boldsymbol{\pi}^{(i)}$ can be obtained numerically from Eq. (4), but many useful performance metrics such as expected system utilization, throughput, or queue length can be expressed explicitly in closed-form using $\boldsymbol{\pi}^{(0)}$, $\boldsymbol{\pi}^{(1)}$, and $\mathbf{R}$ only (e.g., the average queue length is simply given by $\boldsymbol{\pi}^{(1)} \cdot (\mathbf{I} - \mathbf{R})^{-2} \cdot \mathbf{1}^{T}$) [23].

In the case of QBD processes, Eq. (5) simply reduces to the matrix quadratic equation

$$\mathbf{F} + \mathbf{R} \cdot \mathbf{L} + \mathbf{R}^{2} \cdot \mathbf{B} = \mathbf{0},$$

while $\boldsymbol{\pi}^{(0)}$ and $\boldsymbol{\pi}^{(1)}$ are obtained as the solution of the following system of linear equations [24]:

$$[\boldsymbol{\pi}^{(0)}, \boldsymbol{\pi}^{(1)}] \cdot \begin{bmatrix} \mathbf{e} & (\mathbf{L}^{(0)})^{\diamond} & \widehat{\mathbf{F}}^{(1)} \\ (\mathbf{I} - \mathbf{R})^{-1} \cdot \mathbf{e} & (\widehat{\mathbf{B}})^{\diamond} & \mathbf{L} + \mathbf{R} \cdot \mathbf{B} \end{bmatrix} = [\mathbf{1}, \mathbf{0}].$$

Again, the average queue length is given by the same equation as in the GI/M/1 case.

2.1   Why Does a Geometric Relation Hold for QBD Processes?

There is a clear intuitive appeal to the fact that a geometric relation holds for QBD processes. In this section, we first focus on the reasons for the existence of this relationship via a simple example. Our first example is a QBD process that models an $M/Cox_2/1$ queue. The state transition diagram of the CTMC that models this queue is depicted in Figure 1. The state space $\mathcal{S}$ of this CTMC is divided into subsets $\mathcal{S}^{(0)} = \{(0,0)\}$ and $\mathcal{S}^{(i)} = \{(i,1), (i,2)\}$ for $i \geq 1$, implying that the stationary probability vector is also divided in the respective subvectors $\boldsymbol{\pi}^{(0)} = [\pi(0,0)]$ and $\boldsymbol{\pi}^{(i)} = [\pi(i,1), \pi(i,2)]$, for $i \geq 1$. The block-partitioned infinitesimal generator $\mathbf{Q}_{QBD}$ is a infinite block tridiagonal matrix as defined in Eq.(3) and its component matrices are:

$$\widehat{\mathbf{L}} = [-\lambda], \qquad \widehat{\mathbf{F}} = [\lambda \quad 0], \qquad \widehat{\mathbf{B}} = \begin{bmatrix} 0.2\mu \\ \gamma \end{bmatrix},$$

$$\mathbf{B} = \begin{bmatrix} 0.2\mu & 0 \\ \gamma & 0 \end{bmatrix}, \qquad \mathbf{L} = \begin{bmatrix} -(\lambda + \mu) & 0.8\mu \\ 0 & -(\lambda + \gamma) \end{bmatrix}, \qquad \mathbf{F} = \begin{bmatrix} \lambda & 0 \\ 0 & \lambda \end{bmatrix}.$$

(7)

To illustrate the existence of the geometric relationship among the various stationary probability vectors $\boldsymbol{\pi}^{(i)}$, we use the concept of stochastic complementation [22]. A detailed summary of some important results on stochastic complementation is presented in Appendix A. We partition the state space into two subsets; $\mathcal{A} = \cup_{j=0}^{j=i} \mathcal{S}^{(j)}$ and $\overline{\mathcal{A}} = \cup_{j=i+1}^{\infty} \mathcal{S}^{(j)}$, i.e., a set with finite number of

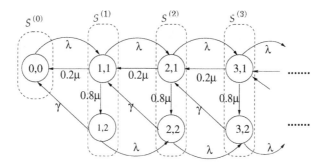

Fig. 1. The CTMC modeling an $M/Cox_2/1$ queue.

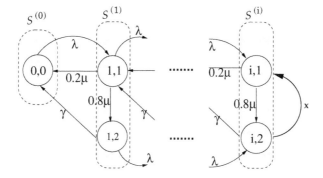

Fig. 2. The CTMC of the stochastic complement of $\mathcal{A} = \cup_{j=0}^{j=i} \mathcal{S}^{(j)}$ of the CTMC modeling an $M/Cox_2/1$ queue.

states and a set with an infinite number of states, respectively. The stochastic complement of the states in $\mathcal{A}$ is a new Markov chain that "skips over" all states in $\overline{\mathcal{A}}$. This Markov chain includes states in $\mathcal{A}$ only but all transitions out of $\mathcal{S}^{(i)}$ (i.e., the boundary set) to $\mathcal{S}^{(i+1)}$ (i.e., the first set in $\overline{\mathcal{A}}$) need to be "folded back" to $\mathcal{A}$ (see Figure 2). This folding introduces a new direct transition with rate x that ensures that the stochastic complement of the states in $\mathcal{A}$ is a stand-alone process. Because of the structure of this particular process, i.e., $\mathcal{A}$ is entered from $\overline{\mathcal{A}}$ *only* through state $(i, 1)$, x is simply equal to λ (see Lemma 1 in Appendix A). Furthermore, because of the repetitive structure of the original chain, this rate does not depend on i (which essentially defines the size of set $\mathcal{A}$).

The steady state probability vector $\overline{\pi} = [\overline{\pi}^{(0)}, \cdots, \overline{\pi}^{(i)}]$ of the stochastic complement of the states in $\mathcal{A}$ relates to the steady state probability $\pi_\mathcal{A}$ of the original process with: $\overline{\pi} = \pi_\mathcal{A}/\pi_\mathcal{A} \cdot \mathbf{1}^T$. This implies that if a relation exists between $\overline{\pi}^{(i-1)}$ and $\overline{\pi}^{(i)}$, then the same relation holds for $\pi^{(i-1)}$ and $\pi^{(i)}$.

The flow balance equations for states $(i, 1)$ and $(i, 2)$ in the stochastic complement of $\mathcal{A}$, are:

$$(0.2\mu + 0.8\mu)\overline{\pi}^{(i)}[1] = \lambda\overline{\pi}^{(i-1)}[1] + \lambda\overline{\pi}^{(i)}[2],$$

$$(\gamma + \lambda)\overline{\pi}^{(i)}[2] = \lambda\overline{\pi}^{(i-1)}[2] + 0.8\mu\overline{\pi}^{(i)}[1],$$

which can further be expressed as:

$$(-\mu\overline{\pi}^{(i)}[1] + \lambda\overline{\pi}^{(i)}[2]) = -\lambda\overline{\pi}^{(i-1)}[1],$$

$$(0.8\mu\overline{\pi}^{(i)}[1] - (\gamma + \lambda)\overline{\pi}^{(i)}[2]) = -\lambda\overline{\pi}^{(i-1)}[2].$$

This last set of equations leads us to the following matrix equation

$$\begin{bmatrix} \overline{\pi}^{(i)}[1], \overline{\pi}^{(i)}[2] \end{bmatrix} \begin{bmatrix} -\mu & 0.8\mu \\ \lambda & -(\gamma + \lambda) \end{bmatrix} = - \begin{bmatrix} \overline{\pi}^{(i-1)}[1], \overline{\pi}^{(i-1)}[2] \end{bmatrix} \begin{bmatrix} \lambda & 0 \\ 0 & \lambda \end{bmatrix},$$

which implies that the relation between $\pi^{(i-1)}$ and $\pi^{(i)}$ can be expressed as

$$\pi^{(i)} = \pi^{(i-1)}\mathbf{R}, \tag{8}$$

where matrix $\mathbf{R}$ is defined as

$$\mathbf{R} = - \begin{bmatrix} \lambda & 0 \\ 0 & \lambda \end{bmatrix} \cdot \begin{bmatrix} -\mu & 0.8\mu \\ \lambda & -(\gamma + \lambda) \end{bmatrix}^{-1} = -\mathbf{F}\left(\mathbf{L} + \mathbf{F}\begin{bmatrix} 1 & 0 \\ 1 & 0 \end{bmatrix}\right)^{-1}. \tag{9}$$

Applying Eq.(8) recursively, one can obtain the result of Eq.(4). Observe that in this particular case an explicit computation of $\mathbf{R}$ is possible (i.e., there is no need to compute $\mathbf{R}$ [28] via an iterative numerical procedure as in the general case). This is a direct effect of the fact that in this example backward transitions from $\mathcal{S}^{(i)}$ to $\mathcal{S}^{(i-1)}$ are directed toward a single state only. In Appendix B, we give details on the cases when matrix $\mathbf{R}$ can be explicitly computed.

2.2   Generalization: Geometric Solution for the GI/M/1 Processes

We generalize the finding in the previous example by considering a GI/M/1-queue with infinitesimal generator $\mathbf{Q}_{GI/M/1}$ similarly to the proof given in [14]. To evaluate the relation between $\pi^{(i-1)}$ and $\pi^{(i)}$ for $i > 1$, we construct the stochastic complement of the states in $\mathcal{A} = \cup_{j=0}^{i}\mathcal{S}^{(j)}$ ($\overline{\mathcal{A}} = \mathcal{S} - \mathcal{A}$). The stochastic complement of states in $\mathcal{A}$ has an infinitesimal generator defined by the following relation

$$\overline{\mathbf{Q}} = \mathbf{Q}[\mathcal{A}, \mathcal{A}] + \mathbf{Q}[\mathcal{A}, \overline{\mathcal{A}}] \cdot (-\mathbf{Q}[\overline{\mathcal{A}}, \overline{\mathcal{A}}])^{-1} \cdot \mathbf{Q}[\overline{\mathcal{A}}, \mathcal{A}],$$

where

$$\mathbf{Q}[\mathcal{A},\mathcal{A}] = \begin{bmatrix} \widehat{\mathbf{L}} & \widehat{\mathbf{F}} & \cdots & 0 & 0 \\ \widehat{\mathbf{B}}^{(1)} & \mathbf{L} & \cdots & 0 & 0 \\ \vdots & \vdots & \vdots & \vdots & \vdots \\ \widehat{\mathbf{B}}^{(i-1)} & \mathbf{B}^{(i-2)} & \cdots & \mathbf{L} & \mathbf{F} \\ \widehat{\mathbf{B}}^{(i)} & \mathbf{B}^{(i-1)} & \cdots & \mathbf{B}^{(1)} & \mathbf{L} \end{bmatrix}, \quad \mathbf{Q}[\mathcal{A},\overline{\mathcal{A}}] = \begin{bmatrix} 0\;0\;0\;0\;\cdots \\ 0\;0\;0\;0\;\cdots \\ \vdots\;\vdots\;\vdots\;\vdots\;\vdots \\ 0\;0\;0\;0\;\cdots \\ \mathbf{F}\;0\;0\;0\;\cdots \end{bmatrix},$$

$$\mathbf{Q}[\overline{\mathcal{A}},\mathcal{A}] = \begin{bmatrix} \widehat{\mathbf{B}}^{(i+1)} & \mathbf{B}^{(i)} & \cdots & \mathbf{B}^{(1)} \\ \widehat{\mathbf{B}}^{(i+2)} & \mathbf{B}^{(i+1)} & \cdots & \mathbf{B}^{(2)} \\ \widehat{\mathbf{B}}^{(i+3)} & \mathbf{B}^{(i+2)} & \cdots & \mathbf{B}^{(3)} \\ \widehat{\mathbf{B}}^{(i+4)} & \mathbf{B}^{(i+3)} & \cdots & \mathbf{B}^{(4)} \\ \vdots & \vdots & \vdots & \vdots \end{bmatrix}, \quad \mathbf{Q}[\overline{\mathcal{A}},\overline{\mathcal{A}}] = \begin{bmatrix} \mathbf{L} & \mathbf{F} & 0 & 0 & \cdots \\ \mathbf{B}^{(1)} & \mathbf{L} & \mathbf{F} & 0 & \cdots \\ \mathbf{B}^{(2)} & \mathbf{B}^{(1)} & \mathbf{L} & \mathbf{F} & \cdots \\ \mathbf{B}^{(3)} & \mathbf{B}^{(2)} & \mathbf{B}^{(1)} & \mathbf{L} & \cdots \\ \vdots & \vdots & \vdots & \vdots & \ddots \end{bmatrix}.$$

$$(10)$$

Observe that $\mathbf{Q}[\overline{\mathcal{A}},\overline{\mathcal{A}}]$ is the same matrix for any $i > 1$. We define its inverse to be as follows

$$(-\mathbf{Q}[\overline{\mathcal{A}},\overline{\mathcal{A}}])^{-1} = \begin{bmatrix} \mathbf{A}_{0,0} & \mathbf{A}_{0,1} & \mathbf{A}_{0,2} & \mathbf{A}_{0,3} & \cdots \\ \mathbf{A}_{1,0} & \mathbf{A}_{1,1} & \mathbf{A}_{1,2} & \mathbf{A}_{1,3} & \cdots \\ \mathbf{A}_{2,0} & \mathbf{A}_{2,1} & \mathbf{A}_{2,2} & \mathbf{A}_{2,3} & \cdots \\ \mathbf{A}_{3,0} & \mathbf{A}_{3,1} & \mathbf{A}_{3,2} & \mathbf{A}_{3,3} & \cdots \\ \vdots & \vdots & \vdots & \vdots & \vdots \end{bmatrix}. \tag{11}$$

From the special structure of $\mathbf{Q}[\mathcal{A},\overline{\mathcal{A}}]$ we conclude that the second term in the summation that defines $\overline{\mathbf{Q}}$ is a matrix with all block entries equal to zero except the very last block row, whose block entries $\mathbf{X}_j$ are of the form:

$$\mathbf{X}_j = \mathbf{F} \cdot \sum_{k=0}^{\infty} \mathbf{A}_{0,k} \widehat{\mathbf{B}}^{(j+1+k)} \quad j = i$$

and

$$\mathbf{X}_j = \mathbf{F} \cdot \sum_{k=0}^{\infty} \mathbf{A}_{0,k} \mathbf{B}^{(j+1+k)}, \quad 0 \le j < i.$$

Note that $\mathbf{X}_0 = \mathbf{F} \cdot \sum_{k=0}^{\infty} \mathbf{A}_{0,k} \mathbf{B}^{(1+k)}$ which means that $\mathbf{X}_0$ does not depend on the value of $i > 1$. The infinitesimal generator $\overline{\mathbf{Q}}$ of the stochastic complement of states in $\mathcal{A}$ is determined as

$$\overline{\mathbf{Q}} = \begin{bmatrix} \widehat{\mathbf{L}} & \widehat{\mathbf{F}} & \cdots & 0 & 0 \\ \widehat{\mathbf{B}}^{(1)} & \mathbf{L} & \cdots & 0 & 0 \\ \vdots & \vdots & \vdots & \vdots & \vdots \\ \widehat{\mathbf{B}}^{(i-1)} & \mathbf{B}^{(i-2)} & \cdots & \mathbf{L} & \mathbf{F} \\ \widehat{\mathbf{B}}^{(i)} + \mathbf{X}_i & \mathbf{B}^{(i-1)} + \mathbf{X}_{i-1} & \cdots & \mathbf{B}^{(1)} + \mathbf{X}_1 & \mathbf{L} + \mathbf{X}_0 \end{bmatrix}. \tag{12}$$

Let $\overline{\pi}$ be the stationary probability vector of the CTMC with infinitesimal generator $\overline{\mathbf{Q}}$ and $\pi_{\mathcal{A}}$ the steady-state probability vector of the CTMC of states in

$\mathcal{A}$ in the original process, i.e., the process with infinitesimal generator $\mathbf{Q}_{GI/M/1}$. There is a linear relation between $\overline{\pi}$ and $\pi_{\mathcal{A}}$ given in the following equation:

$$\overline{\pi} = \frac{\pi_{\mathcal{A}}}{\pi_{\mathcal{A}} \cdot \mathbf{1}^T}. \tag{13}$$

Since $\overline{\pi}\overline{\mathbf{Q}} = \mathbf{0}$, we obtain the following relation

$$\overline{\pi}^{(i)} \cdot (\mathbf{L} + \mathbf{X}_0) = -\overline{\pi}^{(i-1)} \cdot \mathbf{F}$$

implying:

$$\pi^{(i)} \cdot (\mathbf{L} + \mathbf{X}_0) = -\pi^{(i-1)} \cdot \mathbf{F}.$$

The above equation holds for any $i > 1$, because their matrix coefficients do not depend on i. By applying it recursively over all vectors $\pi^{(i)}$ for $i > 1$, we obtain the following geometric relation

$$\pi^{(i)} = \pi^{(1)} \cdot \mathbf{R}^{i-1} \quad \forall \, i \geq 1.$$

Matrix $\mathbf{R}$, the geometric coefficient, has an important probabilistic interpretation: the entry (k, l) of $\mathbf{R}$ is the expected time spent in the state l of $\mathcal{S}^{(i)}$, before the first visit into $\mathcal{S}^{(i-1)}$, expressed in time unit Δ^i, given the starting state is k in $\mathcal{S}^{(i-1)}$. Δ^i is the mean sojourn time in the state k of $\mathcal{S}^{(i-1)}$ for $i \geq 2$ [25, pages 30-35].

3   Why M/G/1 Processes Are More Difficult

For M/G/1-type processes there is no geometric relation among the various probability vectors $\pi^{(i)}$ for $i \geq 1$ as in the case of QBD and GI/M/1-type processes. In this section, we first demonstrate via a simple example why such a geometric relation does not exist and then we generalize and derive Ramaswami's recursive formula, i.e., the classic methodology for the solution of M/G/1 chains.

3.1   Example: A $BMAP_1/Cox_2/1$ Queue

Figure 3 illustrates a Markov chain that models a $BMAP_1/Cox_2/1$ queue. This chain is very similar with the one depicted in Figure 1, the only difference is that the new chain models bulk arrivals of unlimited size. The infinitesimal generator $\mathbf{Q}_{M/G/1}$ of the process is block partitioned according to the partitioning of the state space $\mathcal{S}$ of this CTMC into subsets $\mathcal{S}^{(0)} = \{(0,0)\}$ and $\mathcal{S}^{(i)} = \{(i,1),(i,2)\}$ for $i \geq 1$. The definition of the component matrices of $\mathbf{Q}_{M/G/1}$ is as follows:

$$\widehat{\mathbf{L}} = [-2\lambda], \qquad \widehat{\mathbf{B}} = \begin{bmatrix} 0.2\mu \\ \gamma \end{bmatrix}, \qquad \widehat{\mathbf{F}}^{(i)} = [0.5^{i-1}\lambda \quad 0] \; i \geq 1,$$

$$\mathbf{B} = \begin{bmatrix} 0.2\mu & 0 \\ \gamma & 0 \end{bmatrix}, \mathbf{L} = \begin{bmatrix} -(2\lambda + \mu) & 0.8\mu \\ 0 & -(2\lambda + \gamma) \end{bmatrix}, \mathbf{F}^{(i)} = \begin{bmatrix} 0.5^{i-1}\lambda & 0 \\ 0 & 0.5^{i-1}\lambda \end{bmatrix} i \geq 1.$$

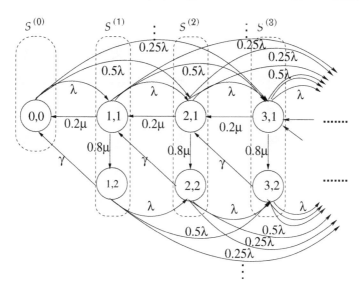

Fig. 3. The CTMC that models a $BMAP_1/Cox_2/1$ queue.

In the following, we derive the relation between $\boldsymbol{\pi}^{(i)}$ for $i \geq 1$ and the rest of vectors in $\boldsymbol{\pi}$ using stochastic complementation, i.e., similarly to the approach described in Section 2. First we partition the state space $\mathcal{S}$ into two partitions $\mathcal{A} = \cup_{j=0}^{j=i} \mathcal{S}^{(j)}$ and $\overline{\mathcal{A}} = \cup_{j=i+1}^{\infty} \mathcal{S}^{(j)}$ and then we construct the stochastic complement of states in $\mathcal{A}$. The Markov chain of the stochastic complement of states in $\mathcal{A}$, (see Figure 4), illustrates how transitions from states $(j, 1)$ and $(j, 2)$ for $j \leq i$ and state $(0, 0)$ to states $(l, 1)$ and $(l, 2)$ for $l > i$ are folded back to state $(i, 1)$, which is the single state to enter $\mathcal{A}$ from states in $\overline{\mathcal{A}}$. These "back-folded" transitions are marked by $x_{k,h}$ for $k \leq i$ and $h = 1, 2$ and represent the "correction" needed to make the stochastic complement of states in $\mathcal{A}$, a stand-alone process. Because of the single entry state in $\mathcal{A}$ the stochastic complement of states in $\mathcal{A}$ for this example can be explicitly derived (see Lemma 1 in Appendix A) and the definition of rates $x_{k,h}$ is as follows:

$$x_{k,h} = 2 \cdot 0.5^{i-k}\lambda = 0.5^{i-k-1}\lambda, \quad i \geq 1, \quad k \leq i, \quad h = 1, 2.$$

The flow balance equations for states $(i, 1)$ and $(i, 2)$ for the stochastic complement of states in $\mathcal{A}$ are:

$$\begin{aligned}
(0.2\mu + 0.8\mu)\overline{\boldsymbol{\pi}}^{(i)}[1] = {} & 2\lambda\overline{\boldsymbol{\pi}}^{(i)}[2] \\
& + 2 \cdot 0.5^{i-1}\lambda\overline{\boldsymbol{\pi}}^{(0)}[1] \\
& + 2 \cdot 0.5^{i-2}\lambda\overline{\boldsymbol{\pi}}^{(1)}[1] + 0.5^{i-2}\lambda\overline{\boldsymbol{\pi}}^{(1)}[2] + \dots \\
& + 2 \cdot 0.5^{i-i}\lambda\overline{\boldsymbol{\pi}}^{(i-1)}[1] + 0.5^{i-i}\lambda\overline{\boldsymbol{\pi}}^{(i-1)}[2]
\end{aligned}$$

and

$$(2\lambda + \gamma)\overline{\boldsymbol{\pi}}^{(i)}[2] = 0.8\mu\overline{\boldsymbol{\pi}}^{(i)}[1] + 0.5^{i-2}\lambda\overline{\boldsymbol{\pi}}^{(1)}[2] + \dots + 0.5^{i-i}\lambda\overline{\boldsymbol{\pi}}^{(i-1)}[2].$$

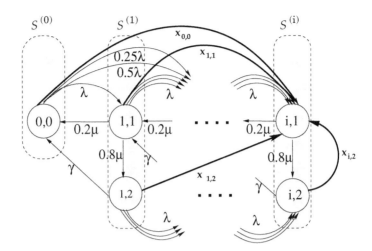

Fig. 4. Stochastic complement of $BMAP_1/Cox_2/1$-type queue at level i.

In the above equalities we group the elements of $\overline{\pi}^{(i)}$ on the left and the rest of the terms on the right in order to express their relation in terms of the block matrices that describe the infinitesimal generator $\overline{\mathbf{Q}}$ of the stochastic complement of states in $\mathcal{A}$. By rearranging the terms, the above equations can be re-written as:

$$-\mu\overline{\pi}^{(i)}[1] + 2\lambda\overline{\pi}^{(i)}[2] = -(2 \cdot 0.5^{i-1}\lambda\overline{\pi}^{(0)}[1]$$
$$+ 2 \cdot 0.5^{i-2}\lambda\overline{\pi}^{(1)}[1] + 0.5^{i-2}\lambda\overline{\pi}^{(1)}[2] + \dots$$
$$+ 2 \cdot 0.5^{i-i}\lambda\overline{\pi}^{(i-1)}[1] + 0.5^{i-i}\lambda\overline{\pi}^{(i-1)}[2])$$

and

$$0.8\mu\overline{\pi}^{(i)}[1] - (2\lambda + \gamma)\overline{\pi}^{(i)}[2] = -(0.5^{i-2}\lambda\overline{\pi}^{(1)}[2] + \dots + 0.5^{i-i}\lambda\overline{\pi}^{(i-1)}[2]).$$

We can now re-write the above equations in the following matrix equation form:

$$[\overline{\pi}^{(i)}[1], \ \overline{\pi}^{(i)}[2]] \cdot \begin{bmatrix} -\mu & 0.8\mu \\ 2\lambda & -(2\lambda + \gamma) \end{bmatrix} = -\left(\overline{\pi}^{(0)}[1] \begin{bmatrix} 2 \cdot 0.5^{i-1}\lambda & 0 \end{bmatrix}\right.$$
$$+ [\overline{\pi}^{(1)}[1], \ \overline{\pi}^{(1)}[2]] \begin{bmatrix} 2 \cdot 0.5^{i-2}\lambda & 0 \\ 0.5^{i-2}\lambda & 0.5^{i-2}\lambda \end{bmatrix} + \dots$$
$$\left. + [\overline{\pi}^{(i-1)}[1], \ \overline{\pi}^{(i-1)}[2]] \begin{bmatrix} 2 \cdot 0.5^{i-i}\lambda & 0 \\ 0.5^{i-i}\lambda & 0.5^{i-i}\lambda \end{bmatrix}\right).$$

By substituting $[\overline{\pi}^{(i)}[1], \ \overline{\pi}^{(i)}[2]]$ with $\overline{\pi}^{(i)}$ and expressing the coefficient matrices in the above equation in terms of the component matrices of the infinitesimal generator $\overline{\mathbf{Q}}$ of the stochastic complement of states in $\mathcal{A}$, we obtain[4]:

---

[4] Recall that $\overline{\pi}$ is the stationary probability vector of the stochastic complement of states in $\mathcal{A}$ and $\pi[\mathcal{A}]$ is the stationary probability vector of states in $\mathcal{A}$ in

$$\overline{\pi}^{(i)} \cdot (\mathbf{L} + \sum_{j=1}^{\infty} \mathbf{F}^{(j)} \mathbf{G}) = -(\overline{\pi}^{(0)} \sum_{j=i}^{\infty} \widehat{\mathbf{F}}^{(j)} \mathbf{G} + \overline{\pi}^{(1)} \sum_{j=i-1}^{\infty} \mathbf{F}^{(j)} \mathbf{G} + \dots + \overline{\pi}^{(i-1)} \sum_{j=1}^{\infty} \mathbf{F}^{(j)} \mathbf{G}),$$

where $\mathbf{G}$ is a matrix with the following structure:

$$\mathbf{G} = \begin{bmatrix} 1 & 0 \\ 1 & 0 \end{bmatrix}.$$

Note that at this point, we have introduced a new matrix, $\mathbf{G}$, that has an important probabilistic interpretation. In this specific example, the matrix $\mathbf{G}$ can be explicitly derived [28]. This is a direct outcome of the fact that all states in set $\mathcal{S}^{(i)}$ for $i \geq 1$ return to the same *single* state in set $\mathcal{S}^{(i-1)}$. Equivalently, the matrix $\mathbf{B}$ of the infinitesimal generator $\mathbf{Q}_{M/G/1}$ has only a single column different from zero.

3.2 Generalization: Derivation of Ramaswami's Recursive Formula

In this section, we investigate the relation between $\boldsymbol{\pi}^{(i)}$ for $i > 1$ and $\boldsymbol{\pi}^{(j)}$ for $0 \leq j < i$ for the general case in the same spirit as [34]. We construct the stochastic complementation of the states in $\mathcal{A} = \cup_{j=0}^{i} \mathcal{S}^{(j)}$ ($\overline{\mathcal{A}} = \mathcal{S} - \mathcal{A}$). We obtain

$$\mathbf{Q}[\mathcal{A}, \mathcal{A}] = \begin{bmatrix} \widehat{\mathbf{L}} & \widehat{\mathbf{F}}^{(1)} & \dots & \widehat{\mathbf{F}}^{(i-1)} & \widehat{\mathbf{F}}^{(i)} \\ \widehat{\mathbf{B}} & \mathbf{L} & \dots & \widehat{\mathbf{F}}^{(i-2)} & \widehat{\mathbf{F}}^{(i-1)} \\ \vdots & \vdots & \vdots & \vdots & \vdots \\ 0 & 0 & \dots & \mathbf{L} & \mathbf{F} \\ 0 & 0 & \dots & \mathbf{B} & \mathbf{L} \end{bmatrix}, \quad \mathbf{Q}[\mathcal{A}, \overline{\mathcal{A}}] = \begin{bmatrix} \widehat{\mathbf{F}}^{(i+1)} & \widehat{\mathbf{F}}^{(i+2)} & \widehat{\mathbf{F}}^{(i+3)} & \dots \\ \mathbf{F}^{(i)} & \mathbf{F}^{(i+1)} & \mathbf{F}^{(i+2)} & \dots \\ \vdots & \vdots & \vdots & \dots \\ \mathbf{F}^{(2)} & \mathbf{F}^{(3)} & \mathbf{F}^{(4)} & \dots \\ \mathbf{F}^{(1)} & \mathbf{F}^{(2)} & \mathbf{F}^{(3)} & \dots \end{bmatrix},$$

$$\mathbf{Q}[\overline{\mathcal{A}}, \mathcal{A}] = \begin{bmatrix} 0 & 0 & \dots & 0 & \mathbf{B} \\ 0 & 0 & \dots & 0 & 0 \\ 0 & 0 & \dots & 0 & 0 \\ 0 & 0 & \dots & 0 & 0 \\ \vdots & \vdots & \vdots & \vdots & \vdots \end{bmatrix}, \quad \mathbf{Q}[\overline{\mathcal{A}}, \overline{\mathcal{A}}] = \begin{bmatrix} \mathbf{L} & \mathbf{F}^{(1)} & \mathbf{F}^{(2)} & \mathbf{F}^{(3)} & \dots \\ \mathbf{B} & \mathbf{L} & \mathbf{F}^{(1)} & \mathbf{F}^{(2)} & \dots \\ 0 & \mathbf{B} & \mathbf{L} & \mathbf{F}^{(1)} & \dots \\ 0 & 0 & \mathbf{B} & \mathbf{L} & \dots \\ \vdots & \vdots & \vdots & \vdots & \ddots \end{bmatrix}.$$

The stochastic complement for states in $\mathcal{A}$ has an infinitesimal generator defined as follows

$$\overline{\mathbf{Q}} = \mathbf{Q}[\mathcal{A}, \mathcal{A}] + \mathbf{Q}[\mathcal{A}, \overline{\mathcal{A}}] \cdot (-\mathbf{Q}[\overline{\mathcal{A}}, \overline{\mathcal{A}}])^{-1} \cdot \mathbf{Q}[\overline{\mathcal{A}}, \mathcal{A}].$$

---

the original M/G/1 process. They relate to each other based on the equation $\overline{\pi} = \pi[\mathcal{A}]/(\pi[\mathcal{A}]\mathbf{1}^T)$, which implies that any relation that holds among subvectors $\overline{\pi}^{(j)}$ for $j \leq i$ would hold for subvectors $\pi^{(j)}$ for $j \leq i$ as well

Observe that $\mathbf{Q}[\overline{\mathcal{A}}, \overline{\mathcal{A}}]$ is the same matrix for any $i \geq 1$. We define its inverse to be as follows

$$(-\mathbf{Q}[\overline{\mathcal{A}}, \overline{\mathcal{A}}])^{-1} = \begin{bmatrix} \mathbf{A}_{0,0} & \mathbf{A}_{0,1} & \mathbf{A}_{0,2} & \mathbf{A}_{0,3} & \cdots \\ \mathbf{A}_{1,0} & \mathbf{A}_{1,1} & \mathbf{A}_{1,2} & \mathbf{A}_{1,3} & \cdots \\ \mathbf{A}_{2,0} & \mathbf{A}_{2,1} & \mathbf{A}_{2,2} & \mathbf{A}_{2,3} & \cdots \\ \mathbf{A}_{3,0} & \mathbf{A}_{3,1} & \mathbf{A}_{3,2} & \mathbf{A}_{3,3} & \cdots \\ \vdots & \vdots & \vdots & \vdots & \vdots \end{bmatrix}. \tag{14}$$

From the special structure of $\mathbf{Q}[\overline{\mathcal{A}}, \mathcal{A}]$ we conclude that the second term of the above summation is a matrix with all block entries equal to zero except the very last block column, whose block entries $\mathbf{X}_j$ are of the form:

$$\mathbf{X}_i = \sum_{k=0}^{\infty} \widehat{\mathbf{F}}^{(i+1+k)} \cdot \mathbf{A}_{k,0} \cdot \mathbf{B}$$

and

$$\mathbf{X}_j = \sum_{k=0}^{\infty} \mathbf{F}^{(j+1+k)} \cdot \mathbf{A}_{k,0} \cdot \mathbf{B}, \quad 0 \leq j < i.$$

The infinitesimal generator $\overline{\mathbf{Q}}$ of the stochastic complement of states in $\mathcal{A}$ is determined as

$$\overline{\mathbf{Q}} = \begin{bmatrix} \widehat{\mathbf{L}} & \widehat{\mathbf{F}}^{(1)} & \cdots & \widehat{\mathbf{F}}^{(i-1)} & \widehat{\mathbf{F}}^{(i)} + \mathbf{X}_i \\ \widehat{\mathbf{B}} & \mathbf{L} & \cdots & \mathbf{F}^{(i-2)} & \mathbf{F}^{(i-1)} + \mathbf{X}_{i-1} \\ \vdots & \vdots & & \vdots & \vdots \\ \mathbf{0} & \mathbf{0} & \cdots & \mathbf{L} & \mathbf{F}^{(1)} + \mathbf{X}_1 \\ \mathbf{0} & \mathbf{0} & \cdots & \mathbf{B} & \mathbf{L} + \mathbf{X}_0 \end{bmatrix}. \tag{15}$$

We define $\overline{\boldsymbol{\pi}}$ to be the steady-state probability vector of the CTMC with infinitesimal generator $\overline{\mathbf{Q}}$ and $\boldsymbol{\pi}_{\mathcal{A}}$ the steady-state probability vector of the CTMC with infinitesimal generator $\mathbf{Q}_{M/G/1}$ corresponding to the states in $\mathcal{A}$. There is a linear relation between $\overline{\boldsymbol{\pi}}$ and $\boldsymbol{\pi}_{\mathcal{A}}$:

$$\overline{\boldsymbol{\pi}} = \frac{\boldsymbol{\pi}_{\mathcal{A}}}{\boldsymbol{\pi}_{\mathcal{A}} \cdot \mathbf{1}^T}. \tag{16}$$

From the relation $\overline{\boldsymbol{\pi}}\,\overline{\mathbf{Q}} = \mathbf{0}$, it follows that

$$\overline{\boldsymbol{\pi}}^{(i)} \cdot (\mathbf{L} + \mathbf{X}_0) = -(\overline{\boldsymbol{\pi}}^{(0)} \cdot (\widehat{\mathbf{F}}^{(i)} + \mathbf{X}_i) + \sum_{j=1}^{i-1} \overline{\boldsymbol{\pi}}^{(j)} \cdot (\mathbf{F}^{(i-j)} + \mathbf{X}_{i-j})) \quad \forall i \geq 1$$

and

$$\boldsymbol{\pi}^{(i)} \cdot (\mathbf{L} + \mathbf{X}_0) = -(\boldsymbol{\pi}^{(0)} \cdot (\widehat{\mathbf{F}}^{(i)} + \mathbf{X}_i) + \sum_{j=1}^{i-1} \boldsymbol{\pi}^{(j)} \cdot (\mathbf{F}^{(i-j)} + \mathbf{X}_{i-j})) \quad \forall i \geq 1. \tag{17}$$

The above equation shows that there in no geometric relation between vectors $\boldsymbol{\pi}^{(i)}$ for $i \geq 1$, however it provides a recursive relation for the computation of the steady-state probability vector for M/G/1 Markov chains. In the following, we further work on simplifying the expression of matrices $\mathbf{X}_j$ for $0 \leq j \leq i$.

From the definition of the stochastic complementation (see Appendix A) we know that an entry $[r, c]$ in $(-\mathbf{Q}[\overline{\mathcal{A}}, \overline{\mathcal{A}}]^{-1} \cdot \mathbf{Q}[\overline{\mathcal{A}}, \mathcal{A}])$ [5] represents the probability that starting from state $r \in \overline{\mathcal{A}}$ the process enters $\mathcal{A}$ through state c. Since $\mathcal{A}$ is entered from $\overline{\mathcal{A}}$ only through states in $\mathcal{S}^{(i)}$ we can use the probabilistic interpretation of matrix $\mathbf{G}$ to figure out the entries in $(-\mathbf{Q}[\overline{\mathcal{A}}, \overline{\mathcal{A}}]^{-1}) \cdot \mathbf{Q}[\overline{\mathcal{A}}, \mathcal{A}]$. An entry $[r, c]$ in $\mathbf{G}^j$ for $j > 0$ represents the probability that starting from state $r \in \mathcal{S}^{(i+j)}$ for $i > 0$ the process enters set $\mathcal{S}^{(i)}$ through state c. It is straightforward now to define

$$(-\mathbf{Q}[\overline{\mathcal{A}}, \overline{\mathcal{A}}]^{-1}) \cdot \mathbf{Q}[\overline{\mathcal{A}}, \mathcal{A}] = \begin{bmatrix} \mathbf{0} \, \mathbf{0} \cdots \mathbf{0} \, \mathbf{G} \\ \mathbf{0} \, \mathbf{0} \cdots \mathbf{0} \, \mathbf{G}^1 \\ \mathbf{0} \, \mathbf{0} \cdots \mathbf{0} \, \mathbf{G}^2 \\ \mathbf{0} \, \mathbf{0} \cdots \mathbf{0} \, \mathbf{G}^3 \\ \vdots \, \vdots \quad \vdots \, \vdots \end{bmatrix}. \tag{18}$$

The above result simplifies the expression of $\mathbf{X}_j$ as follows

$$\mathbf{X}_i = \sum_{k=1}^{\infty} \widehat{\mathbf{F}}^{(i+k)} \cdot \mathbf{G}^k \quad \text{and} \quad \mathbf{X}_j = \sum_{k=1}^{\infty} \mathbf{F}^{(j+k)} \cdot \mathbf{G}^k, \quad 0 \leq j < i. \tag{19}$$

This is in essence Ramaswami's recursive formula. We will return to this in the following section after we elaborate on matrix $\mathbf{G}$, its implications, and its probabilistic interpretation.

4 General Solution Method for M/G/1

For the solution of M/G/1-type processes, several algorithms exist [2,20,26]. These algorithms first compute matrix $\mathbf{G}$ as the solution of the following equation:

$$\mathbf{B} + \mathbf{L}\mathbf{G} + \sum_{i=1}^{\infty} \mathbf{F}^{(i)} \mathbf{G}^{i+1} = \mathbf{0}. \tag{20}$$

The matrix $\mathbf{G}$ has an important probabilistic interpretation: an entry (r, c) in $\mathbf{G}$ expresses the conditional probability of the process first entering $\mathcal{S}^{(i-1)}$ through state c, given that it starts from state r of $\mathcal{S}^{(i)}$ [26, page 81][6]. Figure 5 illustrates the relation of entries in $\mathbf{G}$ for different paths of the process. From the probabilistic interpretation of $\mathbf{G}$ the following structural properties hold [26]

- if the M/G/1 process with infinitesimal generator $\mathbf{Q}_{M/G/1}$ is recurrent then $\mathbf{G}$ is row-stochastic,

---

[5] Only the entries of the last block column of $(-\mathbf{Q}[\overline{\mathcal{A}}, \overline{\mathcal{A}}]^{-1}) \cdot \mathbf{Q}[\overline{\mathcal{A}}, \mathcal{A}]$ are different from zero.

[6] The probabilistic interpretation of $\mathbf{G}$ is the same for both DTMCs and CTMCs.

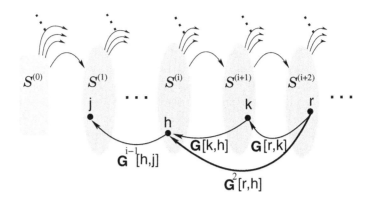

Fig. 5. Probabilistic interpretation of **G**.

- to any zero column in matrix **B** of the infinitesimal generator $\mathbf{Q}_{M/G/1}$, there is a corresponding zero column in matrix **G**.

The **G** matrix is obtained by solving iteratively Eq.(20). However, recent advances show that the computation of **G** is more efficient when displacement structures are used based on the representation of M/G/1-type processes by means of QBD processes [20,2,1,16]. The most efficient algorithm for the computation of **G** is the cyclic reduction algorithm [2].

4.1   Ramaswami's Formula

From Eqs.(17) and (19) and the aid of matrix **G**, we derive Ramaswami's recursive formula [29], which is numerically stable because it entails only additions and multiplications[7]. Ramaswami's formula defines the following recursive relation among stationary probability vectors $\boldsymbol{\pi}^{(i)}$ for $i \geq 0$:

$$\boldsymbol{\pi}^{(i)} = -\left(\boldsymbol{\pi}^{(0)}\widehat{\mathbf{S}}^{(i)} + \sum_{k=1}^{i-1} \boldsymbol{\pi}^{(k)}\mathbf{S}^{(i-k)}\right)\mathbf{S}^{(0)^{-1}} \quad \forall i \geq 1, \tag{21}$$

where, letting $\mathbf{F}^{(0)} \equiv \mathbf{L}$, matrices $\widehat{\mathbf{S}}^{(i)}$ and $\mathbf{S}^{(i)}$ are defined as follows:

$$\widehat{\mathbf{S}}^{(i)} = \sum_{l=i}^{\infty} \widehat{\mathbf{F}}^{(l)}\mathbf{G}^{l-i}, \; i \geq 1, \quad \mathbf{S}^{(i)} = \sum_{l=i}^{\infty} \mathbf{F}^{(l)}\mathbf{G}^{l-i}, \; i \geq 0. \tag{22}$$

Observe that the above auxiliary sums represent the last column in the infinitesimal generator $\overline{\mathbf{Q}}$ defined in Eq.(15). We can express them in terms of matrices $\mathbf{X}_i$ defined in Eq.(19) as follows:

$$\widehat{\mathbf{S}}^{(i)} = \widehat{\mathbf{F}}^{(i)} + \mathbf{X}_i, \; i \geq 1 \quad \mathbf{S}^{(i)} = \mathbf{F}^{(i)} + \mathbf{X}_i, \; i \geq 0.$$

---

[7] Subtractions on these type of formulas present the possibility of numerical instability [26,29].

Given the above definition of $\boldsymbol{\pi}^{(i)}$ for $i \geq 1$ and the normalization condition, a unique vector $\boldsymbol{\pi}^{(0)}$ can be obtained by solving the following system of m linear equations, i.e., the cardinality of set $\mathcal{S}^{(0)}$:

$$\boldsymbol{\pi}^{(0)} \left[\left(\widehat{\mathbf{L}}^{(0)} - \widehat{\mathbf{S}}^{(1)} \mathbf{S}^{(0)^{-1}} \widehat{\mathbf{B}} \right)^{\diamond} \mid \mathbf{1}^T - \sum_{i=1}^{\infty} \widehat{\mathbf{S}}^{(i)} \left(\sum_{j=0}^{\infty} \mathbf{S}^{(j)} \right)^{-1} \mathbf{1}^T \right] = [\mathbf{0} \mid 1], \quad (23)$$

where the symbol "$\diamond$" indicates that we discard one (any) column of the corresponding matrix, since we added a column representing the normalization condition. Once $\boldsymbol{\pi}^{(0)}$ is known, we can then iteratively compute $\boldsymbol{\pi}^{(i)}$ for $i \geq 1$, stopping when the accumulated probability mass is close to one. After this point, measures of interest can be computed. Since the relation between $\boldsymbol{\pi}^{(i)}$ for $i \geq 1$ is not straightforward, computation of measures of interest requires generation of the whole stationary probability vector.

4.2   Special Case: Explicit Computation of G

A special case of M/G/1-type processes occurs when $\mathbf{B}$ is a product of two vectors, i.e., $\mathbf{B} = \boldsymbol{\alpha} \cdot \boldsymbol{\beta}$. Assuming, without loss of generality, that $\boldsymbol{\beta}$ is normalized, then $\mathbf{G} = \mathbf{1}^T \cdot \boldsymbol{\beta}$, i.e., it is derived explicitly [28,30].

For this special case, $\mathbf{G} = \mathbf{G}^n$, for $n \geq 1$. This special structure of matrix $\mathbf{G}$ simplifies the form of matrices $\widehat{\mathbf{S}}^{(i)}$ for $i \geq 1$, and $\mathbf{S}^{(i)}$ for $i \geq 0$ defined in Eq.(22):

$$\begin{aligned} \widehat{\mathbf{S}}^{(i)} &= \widehat{\mathbf{F}}^{(i)} + \left(\sum_{j=i+1}^{\infty} \widehat{\mathbf{F}}^{(j)} \right) \cdot \mathbf{G}, \quad i \geq 1 \\ \mathbf{S}^{(i)} &= \widehat{\mathbf{F}}^{(i)} + \left(\sum_{j=i+1}^{\infty} \mathbf{F}^{(j)} \right) \cdot \mathbf{G}, \quad i \geq 0, \mathbf{F}^{(0)} \equiv \mathbf{L}. \end{aligned} \quad (24)$$

The major gain of this special case is the fact that $\mathbf{G}$ does not need to be either computed or fully stored.

4.3   Fast FFT Ramaswami's Formula

[19] gives an improved version of Ramaswami's formula. Once $\boldsymbol{\pi}^{(0)}$ is known using Eq.(23), the stationary probability vector is computed using matrix-generating functions associated with block triangular Toeplitz matrices[8]. These matrix-generating functions are computed efficiently by using fast Fourier transforms (FFT).

The algorithm of the Fast FFT Ramaswami's formula is based on the fact that in practice it is not possible to store an infinite number of matrices to express the M/G/1-type process. Assuming that only p matrices can be stored then the infinitesimal generator $\mathbf{Q}_{M/G/1}$ has the following structure

---

[8] A Toeplitz matrix has equal elements in each of its diagonals allowing the use of computationally efficient methods.

$$\mathbf{Q}_{M/G/1} = \begin{bmatrix} \widehat{\mathbf{L}} & \widehat{\mathbf{F}}^{(1)} & \widehat{\mathbf{F}}^{(2)} & \widehat{\mathbf{F}}^{(3)} & \widehat{\mathbf{F}}^{(4)} & \cdots & \widehat{\mathbf{F}}^{(p)} & \mathbf{0} & \mathbf{0} & \cdots \\ \widehat{\mathbf{B}} & \mathbf{L} & \mathbf{F}^{(1)} & \mathbf{F}^{(2)} & \mathbf{F}^{(3)} & \cdots & \mathbf{F}^{(p-1)} & \mathbf{F}^{(p)} & \mathbf{0} & \cdots \\ \mathbf{0} & \mathbf{B} & \mathbf{L} & \mathbf{F}^{(1)} & \mathbf{F}^{(2)} & \cdots & \mathbf{F}^{(p-2)} & \mathbf{F}^{(p-1)} & \mathbf{F}^{(p)} & \cdots \\ \mathbf{0} & \mathbf{0} & \mathbf{B} & \mathbf{L} & \mathbf{F}^{(1)} & \cdots & \mathbf{F}^{(p-3)} & \mathbf{F}^{(p-2)} & \mathbf{F}^{(p-1)} & \cdots \\ \vdots & \vdots & \vdots & \vdots & \vdots & \ddots & \vdots & \vdots & \vdots & \ddots \\ \mathbf{0} & \mathbf{0} & \mathbf{0} & \mathbf{0} & \mathbf{0} & \cdots & \mathbf{F}^{(1)} & \mathbf{F}^{(2)} & \mathbf{F}^{(3)} & \cdots \\ \mathbf{0} & \mathbf{0} & \mathbf{0} & \mathbf{0} & \mathbf{0} & \cdots & \mathbf{L} & \mathbf{F}^{(1)} & \mathbf{F}^{(2)} & \cdots \\ \mathbf{0} & \mathbf{0} & \mathbf{0} & \mathbf{0} & \mathbf{0} & \cdots & \mathbf{B} & \mathbf{L} & \mathbf{F}^{(1)} & \cdots \\ \mathbf{0} & \mathbf{0} & \mathbf{0} & \mathbf{0} & \mathbf{0} & \cdots & \mathbf{0} & \mathbf{B} & \mathbf{L} & \cdots \\ \vdots & \vdots & \vdots & \vdots & \vdots & \vdots & \vdots & \vdots & \vdots & \ddots \end{bmatrix}. \tag{25}$$

Because there are only p matrices of type $\widehat{\mathbf{F}}^{(i)}$ and $\mathbf{F}^{(i)}$, there are only p sums of type $\widehat{\mathbf{S}}^{(i)}$ and $\mathbf{S}^{(i)}$ to be computed. Therefore, the computation of $\boldsymbol{\pi}^{(i)}$ for $i > 0$ using Ramaswami's formula, i.e., Eq.(21), depends only on p vectors $\boldsymbol{\pi}^{(j)}$ for $max(0, i - p) \leq j < i$. Define

$$\tilde{\boldsymbol{\pi}}^{(1)} = [\boldsymbol{\pi}^{(1)}, ..., \boldsymbol{\pi}^{(p)}] \quad \text{and} \quad \tilde{\boldsymbol{\pi}}^{(i)} = [\boldsymbol{\pi}^{(p(i-1)+1)}, ..., \boldsymbol{\pi}^{(pi)}] \quad \text{for} \quad i \geq 2. \tag{26}$$

The above definition simplifies the formalization of Ramaswami's formula since $\tilde{\boldsymbol{\pi}}^{(i)}$ depends only on the values of $\tilde{\boldsymbol{\pi}}^{(i-1)}$ for $i > 1$. If we apply Ramaswami's formula for vectors $\boldsymbol{\pi}^{(1)}$ to $\boldsymbol{\pi}^{(p)}$, we obtain the following equations

$$\begin{aligned} \boldsymbol{\pi}^{(1)} &= -\boldsymbol{\pi}^{(0)}\widehat{\mathbf{S}}^{(1)}(\mathbf{S}^{(0)})^{-1} \\ \boldsymbol{\pi}^{(2)} &= -(\boldsymbol{\pi}^{(0)}\widehat{\mathbf{S}}^{(2)} + \boldsymbol{\pi}^{(1)}\mathbf{S}^{(1)})(\mathbf{S}^{(0)})^{-1} \\ \boldsymbol{\pi}^{(3)} &= -(\boldsymbol{\pi}^{(0)}\widehat{\mathbf{S}}^{(3)} + \boldsymbol{\pi}^{(1)}\mathbf{S}^{(2)} + \boldsymbol{\pi}^{(2)}\mathbf{S}^{(1)})(\mathbf{S}^{(0)})^{-1} \\ &\vdots \\ \boldsymbol{\pi}^{(p)} &= -(\boldsymbol{\pi}^{(0)}\widehat{\mathbf{S}}^{(p)} + \boldsymbol{\pi}^{(1)}\mathbf{S}^{(p-1)} + ... + \boldsymbol{\pi}^{(p-1)}\mathbf{S}^{(1)})(\mathbf{S}^{(0)})^{-1} \end{aligned} \tag{27}$$

We rewrite the above equations in the following form:

$$\begin{aligned} \boldsymbol{\pi}^{(1)}\mathbf{S}^{(0)} &= -\boldsymbol{\pi}^{(0)}\widehat{\mathbf{S}}^{(1)} \\ \boldsymbol{\pi}^{(2)}\mathbf{S}^{(0)} + \boldsymbol{\pi}^{(1)}\mathbf{S}^{(1)} &= -\boldsymbol{\pi}^{(0)}\widehat{\mathbf{S}}^{(2)} \\ \boldsymbol{\pi}^{(3)}\mathbf{S}^{(0)} + \boldsymbol{\pi}^{(2)}\mathbf{S}^{(1)} + \boldsymbol{\pi}^{(1)}\mathbf{S}^{(2)} &= -\boldsymbol{\pi}^{(0)}\widehat{\mathbf{S}}^{(3)} \\ &\vdots \\ \boldsymbol{\pi}^{(p)}\mathbf{S}^{(0)} + \boldsymbol{\pi}^{(p-1)}\mathbf{S}^{(1)} + ... + \boldsymbol{\pi}^{(1)}\mathbf{S}^{(p-1)} &= -\boldsymbol{\pi}^{(0)}\widehat{\mathbf{S}}^{(p)} \end{aligned} \tag{28}$$

Define

$$\mathbf{Y} = \begin{bmatrix} \mathbf{S}^{(0)} & \mathbf{S}^{(1)} & \mathbf{S}^{(2)} & \cdots & \mathbf{S}^{(p-1)} \\ \mathbf{0} & \mathbf{S}^{(0)} & \mathbf{S}^{(1)} & \cdots & \mathbf{S}^{(p-2)} \\ \mathbf{0} & \mathbf{0} & \mathbf{S}^{(0)} & \cdots & \mathbf{S}^{(p-3)} \\ \vdots & \vdots & \vdots & \ddots & \vdots \\ \mathbf{0} & \mathbf{0} & \mathbf{0} & \cdots & \mathbf{S}^{(0)} \end{bmatrix} \quad \text{and} \quad \mathbf{b} = \left[\widehat{\mathbf{S}}^{(1)}, \widehat{\mathbf{S}}^{(2)}, \widehat{\mathbf{S}}^{(3)}, \cdots, \widehat{\mathbf{S}}^{(p)}\right]. \tag{29}$$

The set of equations in Eq.(28) can be written in a compact way by using the definitions in Eq.(26) and Eq.(29).

$$\tilde{\pi}^{(1)} = -\pi^{(0)} \cdot \mathbf{b} \cdot \mathbf{Y}^{-1}. \tag{30}$$

We apply Ramswami's formula for all vectors $\pi^{(j)}$, $p(i-1)+1 \le j \le pi$ in $\tilde{\pi}^{(i)}$ for $i > 1$.

$$\begin{aligned}
\pi^{(p(i-1)+1)} &= -\big(\pi^{(p(i-2)+1)}\mathbf{S}^{(p)}+\ldots+\ \pi^{(p(i-1))}\mathbf{S}^{(1)}\big)\ \ (\mathbf{S}^{(0)})^{-1}\\
\pi^{(p(i-1)+2)} &= -\big(\pi^{(p(i-2)+2)}\mathbf{S}^{(p)}+\ldots+\ \pi^{(p(i-1)+1)}\mathbf{S}^{(1)}\big)\ \ (\mathbf{S}^{(0)})^{-1}\\
\pi^{(p(i-1)+3)} &= -\big(\pi^{(p(i-2)+3)}\mathbf{S}^{(p)}+\ldots+\ \pi^{(p(i-1)+2)}\mathbf{S}^{(1)}\big)\ \ (\mathbf{S}^{(0)})^{-1}\\
&\ \vdots\\
\pi^{(p(i-1)+p)} &= -\big(\pi^{(p(i-2)+p)}\mathbf{S}^{(p)}+\ldots+\pi^{(p(i-1)+p-1)}\mathbf{S}^{(1)}\big)\ (\mathbf{S}^{(0)})^{-1}
\end{aligned}$$

These equations can be rewritten in the following form

$$\begin{aligned}
\pi^{(p(i-1)+1)}\mathbf{S}^{(0)} &= -\big(\pi^{(p(i-2)+1)}\mathbf{S}^{(p)}+ \ldots +\pi^{(p(i-1))}\mathbf{S}^{(1)}\big)\\
\pi^{(p(i-1)+2)}\mathbf{S}^{(0)} + \pi^{(p(i-1)+1)}\mathbf{S}^{(1)} &= -\big(\pi^{(p(i-2)+2)}\mathbf{S}^{(p)}+ \ldots +\pi^{(p(i-1))}\mathbf{S}^{(2)}\big)\\
\pi^{(p(i-1)+3)}\mathbf{S}^{(0)} + \ldots + \pi^{(p(i-1)+1)}\mathbf{S}^{(2)} &= -\big(\pi^{(p(i-2)+3)}\mathbf{S}^{(p)}+ \ldots +\pi^{(p(i-1))}\mathbf{S}^{(3)}\big)\\
&\ \vdots\\
\pi^{(p(i-1)+p)}\mathbf{S}^{(0)} + \ldots + \pi^{(p(i-1)+1)}\mathbf{S}^{(p-1)} &= -\pi^{(p(i-1))}\mathbf{S}^{(p)}.
\end{aligned}$$

The above set of equations can be written in a matrix form as

$$\tilde{\pi}^{(i)} = -\tilde{\pi}^{(i-1)} \cdot \mathbf{Z}\mathbf{Y}^{-1} \qquad i \ge 2, \tag{31}$$

where matrix $\mathbf{Y}$ is defined in Eq.(29) and the definition of matrix $\mathbf{Z}$ is given by the following

$$\mathbf{Z} = \begin{bmatrix}
\mathbf{S}^{(p)} & \mathbf{0} & \cdots & \mathbf{0} & \mathbf{0} \\
\mathbf{S}^{(p-1)} & \mathbf{S}^{(p)} & \cdots & \mathbf{0} & \mathbf{0} \\
\vdots & \vdots & \ddots & \vdots & \vdots \\
\mathbf{S}^{(2)} & \mathbf{S}^{(3)} & \cdots & \mathbf{S}^{(p)} & \mathbf{0} \\
\mathbf{S}^{(1)} & \mathbf{S}^{(2)} & \cdots & \mathbf{S}^{(p-1)} & \mathbf{S}^{(p)}
\end{bmatrix}. \tag{32}$$

The Fast Ramaswami's Formula consists of the set of equations defined in Eq.(30) and Eq.(31). The effectiveness of the representation of the Ramaswami's formula in the form of Eq.(30) and Eq.(31) comes from the special structure of matrices $\mathbf{Y}$ and $\mathbf{Z}$. The matrix $\mathbf{Y}$ is an upper block triangular Toeplitz matrix and the matrix $\mathbf{Z}$ is a lower block triangular Toeplitz matrix. Using fast Fourier transforms one can compute efficiently the inverse of a Toeplitz matrix or the multiplication of a vector with a Toeplitz matrix [19]. Although the use of Fourier transforms for matrix operations may result in numerical instabilities, in numerous test cases the above algorithm has not experienced instability [19, 21].

4.4   ETAQA-M/G/1

ETAQA[31] is an aggregation-based technique that computes only $\boldsymbol{\pi}^{(0)}$, $\boldsymbol{\pi}^{(1)}$ and $\sum_{i=2}^{\infty} \boldsymbol{\pi}^{(i)}$ for an M/G/1-type processes by solving a finite system of linear equations. Distinctively from the classic techniques of solving M/G/1-type processes, this method recasts the problem into that of solving a finite linear system in $m + 2n$ unknowns, where m is the number of states in the boundary portion of the process and n is the number of states in each of the repetitive "levels" of the state space, and are able to obtain exact results. The ETAQA methodology uses basic, well-known results for Markov chains. Assuming that the state space $\mathcal{S}$ is partitioned into sets $\mathcal{S}^{(j)}$, $j \geq 0$, instead of evaluating the probability distribution of *all* states in each $\mathcal{S}^{(j)}$, we calculate the *aggregate* probability distribution of n classes of states $\mathcal{T}^{(i)}$, $1 \leq i \leq n$, appropriately defined (see Figure 6).

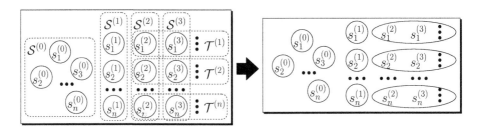

Fig. 6. Aggregation of an infinite $\mathcal{S}$ into a finite number of states.

The following theorem formalizes the basic ETAQA result.

Theorem 1. [ETAQA] *Given an ergodic CTMC with infinitesimal generator* $\mathbf{Q}_{M/G/1}$ *having the structure shown in Eq.(1), with stationary probability vector* $\boldsymbol{\pi} = [\boldsymbol{\pi}^{(0)}, \boldsymbol{\pi}^{(1)}, \boldsymbol{\pi}^{(2)}, ...]$ *the system of linear equations*

$$\mathbf{x} \cdot \mathbf{X} = [1, \mathbf{0}] \tag{33}$$

where $\mathbf{X} \in \mathbb{R}^{(m+2n) \times (m+2n)}$ *is defined as follows*

$$\mathbf{X} = \begin{bmatrix} \mathbf{1}^T & \widehat{\mathbf{L}} & \widehat{\mathbf{F}}^{(1)} - \sum_{i=3}^{\infty} \widehat{\mathbf{S}}^{(i)} \cdot \mathbf{G} & (\sum_{i=2}^{\infty} \widehat{\mathbf{F}}^{(i)} + (\sum_{i=3}^{\infty} \widehat{\mathbf{S}}^{(i)} \cdot \mathbf{G})^{\diamond} \\[2ex] \mathbf{1}^T & \widehat{\mathbf{B}} & \mathbf{L} - \sum_{i=2}^{\infty} \mathbf{S}^{(i)} \cdot \mathbf{G} & (\sum_{i=1}^{\infty} \mathbf{F}^{(i)} + \sum_{i=2}^{\infty} \mathbf{S}^{(i)} \cdot \mathbf{G})^{\diamond} \\[2ex] \mathbf{1}^T & \mathbf{0} & \mathbf{B} - \sum_{i=1}^{\infty} \mathbf{S}^{(i)} \cdot \mathbf{G} & (\sum_{i=1}^{\infty} \mathbf{F}^{(i)} + \mathbf{L} + \sum_{i=1}^{\infty} \mathbf{S}^{(i)} \cdot \mathbf{G})^{\diamond} \end{bmatrix} \tag{34}$$

admits a unique solution $\mathbf{x} = [\boldsymbol{\pi}^{(0)}, \boldsymbol{\pi}^{(1)}, \boldsymbol{\pi}^{(*)}]$, *where* $\boldsymbol{\pi}^{(*)} = \sum_{i=2}^{\infty} \boldsymbol{\pi}^{(i)}$.

ETAQA approach is in the same spirit as the one presented in [5,4] for the exact solution of a very limited class of QBD and M/G/1-type Markov chains, but in distinct contrast to these works, the above theorem does not require any restriction on the form of the chain's repeating pattern, thus can be applied to *any* type of M/G/1 chain.

ETAQA provides a recursive approach to compute metrics of interest once $\boldsymbol{\pi}^{(0)}$, $\boldsymbol{\pi}^{(1)}$, and $\boldsymbol{\pi}^{(*)}$ have been computed. We consider measures that can be expressed as the expected reward rate:

$$r = \sum_{j=0}^{\infty} \sum_{i \in \mathcal{S}^{(j)}} \rho_i^{(j)} \pi_i^{(j)},$$

where $\rho_i^{(j)}$ is the *reward rate* of state $s_i^{(j)}$. For example, to compute the expected queue length in steady state, where $\mathcal{S}^{(j)}$ represents the system states with j customers in the queue, we let $\rho_i^{(j)} = j$. To compute the second moment of the queue length, we let $\rho_i^{(j)} = j^2$.

Since our solution approach obtains $\boldsymbol{\pi}^{(0)}$, $\boldsymbol{\pi}^{(1)}$, and $\sum_{j=2}^{\infty} \boldsymbol{\pi}^{(j)}$, we rewrite r as

$$r = \boldsymbol{\pi}^{(0)} \boldsymbol{\rho}^{(0)T} + \boldsymbol{\pi}^{(1)} \boldsymbol{\rho}^{(1)T} + \sum_{j=2}^{\infty} \boldsymbol{\pi}^{(j)} \boldsymbol{\rho}^{(j)T},$$

where $\boldsymbol{\rho}^{(0)} = [\rho_1^{(0)}, \dots, \rho_m^{(0)}]$ and $\boldsymbol{\rho}^{(j)} = [\rho_1^{(j)}, \dots, \rho_n^{(j)}]$, for $j \geq 1$. Then, we must show how to compute the above summation without explicitly using the values of $\boldsymbol{\pi}^{(j)}$ for $j \geq 2$. We can do so if the reward rate of state $s_i^{(j)}$, for $j \geq 2$ and $i = 1, \dots, n$, is a polynomial of degree k in j with arbitrary coefficients $\mathbf{a}_i^{[0]}, \mathbf{a}_i^{[1]}, \dots, \mathbf{a}_i^{[k]}$:

$$\forall j \geq 2, \ \forall i \in \{1, 2, \dots, n\}, \qquad \rho_i^{(j)} = \mathbf{a}_i^{[0]} + \mathbf{a}_i^{[1]} j + \dots + \mathbf{a}_i^{[k]} j^k. \qquad (35)$$

The definition of $\rho_i^{(j)}$ illustrates that the set of measures of interest that one can compute includes any moment of the probability vector $\boldsymbol{\pi}$ as long as the reward rate of the ith state in each set $\mathcal{S}^{(j)}$ has the same polynomial coefficients for all $j \geq 2$.

We compute $\sum_{j=2}^{\infty} \boldsymbol{\pi}^{(j)} \boldsymbol{\rho}^{(j)T}$ as follows

$$\begin{aligned} \sum_{j=2}^{\infty} \boldsymbol{\pi}^{(j)} \boldsymbol{\rho}^{(j)T} &= \sum_{j=2}^{\infty} \boldsymbol{\pi}^{(j)} \left(\mathbf{a}^{[0]} + \mathbf{a}^{[1]} j + \dots + \mathbf{a}^{[k]} j^k \right)^T \\ &= \mathbf{r}^{[0]} \mathbf{a}^{[0]T} + \mathbf{r}^{[1]} \mathbf{a}^{[1]T} + \dots + \mathbf{r}^{[k]} \mathbf{a}^{[k]T}, \end{aligned} \qquad (36)$$

and the problem is reduced to the computation of $\mathbf{r}^{[l]} = \sum_{j=2}^{\infty} j^l \boldsymbol{\pi}^{(j)}$, for $l = 0, \dots, k$. We show how $\mathbf{r}^{[k]}$, $k > 0$, can be computed recursively, starting from $\mathbf{r}^{[0]}$, which is simply $\boldsymbol{\pi}^{(*)}$.

$$\mathbf{r}^{[k]} \cdot [(\mathbf{B} + \mathbf{L} + \sum_{j=1}^{\infty} \mathbf{F}^{(j)})^{\circ} \mid (\sum_{j=1}^{\infty} j^k \mathbf{F}^{(j)} - \mathbf{B}) \mathbf{1}^T] = [\mathbf{b}^{[k]} \mid c^{[k]}], \qquad (37)$$

where the definitions of $\mathbf{b}^{[k]}$, $c^{[k]}$, $\widehat{\mathbf{F}}_{[k,j,h]}$, and $\mathbf{F}_{[k,j,h]}$ are as follows

$$\mathbf{b}^{[k]} = - \left(\boldsymbol{\pi}^{(0)} \widehat{\mathbf{F}}_{[k,1,1]} + \boldsymbol{\pi}^{(1)} (2^k \mathbf{L} + \mathbf{F}_{[k,1,2]}) + \sum_{l=1}^{k} \binom{k}{l} \mathbf{r}^{[k-l]} (\mathbf{L} + \mathbf{F}_{[l,1,1]}) \right),$$

$$c^{[k]} = -(\boldsymbol{\pi}^{(0)} \sum_{j=2}^{\infty} j^k \widehat{\mathbf{F}}_{[0,j,0]} \mathbf{1}^T + \boldsymbol{\pi}^{(1)} \sum_{j=1}^{\infty} (j+1)^k \mathbf{F}_{[0,j,0]} \mathbf{1}^T + \sum_{l=1}^{k} \binom{k}{l} \mathbf{r}^{[k-l]} \sum_{j=1}^{\infty} j^l \mathbf{F}_{[0,j,0]} \mathbf{1}^T)$$

$$\widehat{\mathbf{F}}_{[k,j,h]} = \sum_{l=j}^{\infty} (l+h)^k \cdot \widehat{\mathbf{F}}^{(l)}, \qquad \mathbf{F}_{[k,j,h]} = \sum_{l=j}^{\infty} (l+h)^k \cdot \mathbf{F}^{(l)}, \qquad j \geq 1.$$

As an example, we consider $\mathbf{r}^{[1]}$, which is used to compute measures such as the first moment of the queue length. In this case,

$$\mathbf{b}^{[1]} = -\boldsymbol{\pi}^{(0)} \sum_{j=1}^{\infty} (j+1) \widehat{\mathbf{F}}^{(j)} - \boldsymbol{\pi}^{(1)} (2\mathbf{L} + \sum_{j=1}^{\infty} (j+2) \mathbf{F}^{(j)}) - \boldsymbol{\pi}^{(*)} (\mathbf{L} + \sum_{j=1}^{\infty} (j+1) \mathbf{F}^{(j)})$$

$$c^{[1]} = -\boldsymbol{\pi}^{(0)} \sum_{j=2}^{\infty} j \widehat{\mathbf{F}}_{[0,j]} \mathbf{1}^T - \boldsymbol{\pi}^{(1)} \sum_{j=1}^{\infty} (j+1) \mathbf{F}_{[0,j]} \mathbf{1}^T - \boldsymbol{\pi}^{(*)} \sum_{j=1}^{\infty} j \mathbf{F}_{[0,j]} \mathbf{1}^T$$

5   Conditions for Stability

We briefly review the conditions that enable us to assert that the CTMC described by the infinitesimal generator $\mathbf{Q}_{M/G/1}$ in Eq.(1) is stable, that is, admits a probability vector satisfying $\boldsymbol{\pi} \mathbf{Q}_{M/G/1} = \mathbf{0}$ and $\boldsymbol{\pi} \mathbf{1}^T = 1$.

First observe that the matrix $\widetilde{\mathbf{Q}} = \mathbf{B} + \mathbf{L} + \sum_{j=1}^{\infty} \mathbf{F}^{(j)}$ is an infinitesimal generator, since it has zero row sums and non-negative off-diagonal entries. The conditions for stability depend on the irreducibility of matrix $\widetilde{\mathbf{Q}}$.

If $\widetilde{\mathbf{Q}}$ is irreducible then there exists a unique positive vector $\widetilde{\boldsymbol{\pi}}$ that satisfies the equations $\widetilde{\boldsymbol{\pi}} \widetilde{\mathbf{Q}} = \mathbf{0}$ and $\widetilde{\boldsymbol{\pi}} \mathbf{1}^T = 1$. In this case, the stability condition for the M/G/1-type process with infinitesimal generator $\mathbf{Q}_{M/G/1}$ [26] is given by the following inequality

$$\widetilde{\boldsymbol{\pi}}(\mathbf{L} + \sum_{j=1}^{\infty} (j+1) \mathbf{F}^{(j)}) \mathbf{1}^T = \widetilde{\boldsymbol{\pi}}(\mathbf{L} + \sum_{j=1}^{\infty} \mathbf{F}^{(j)}) \mathbf{1}^T + \widetilde{\boldsymbol{\pi}} \sum_{j=1}^{\infty} j \mathbf{F}^{(j)} \mathbf{1}^T < 0.$$

Since $\mathbf{B} + \mathbf{L} + \sum_{j=1}^{\infty} \mathbf{F}^{(j)}$ is an infinitesimal generator, then $(\mathbf{B} + \mathbf{L} + \sum_{j=1}^{\infty} \mathbf{F}^{(j)}) \mathbf{1}^T = \mathbf{0}$. By substituting in the condition for stability the term $(\mathbf{L} + \sum_{j=1}^{\infty} \mathbf{F}^{(j)}) \mathbf{1}^T$ with its equal $(-\mathbf{B} \mathbf{1}^T)$, the condition for stability can be re-written as:

$$\widetilde{\boldsymbol{\pi}} \sum_{j=1}^{\infty} j \mathbf{F}^{(j)} \mathbf{1}^T < \widetilde{\boldsymbol{\pi}} \mathbf{B} \mathbf{1}^T. \tag{38}$$

As in the scalar case, the equality in the above relation results in a null-recurrent CTMC.

In the example of the $BMAP_1/Cox_2/1$ queue depicted in Figure 3 the infinitesimal generator $\widetilde{\mathbf{Q}}$ and its stationary probability vector are

$$\widetilde{\mathbf{Q}} = \begin{bmatrix} -0.8\mu & 0.8\mu \\ \gamma & -\gamma \end{bmatrix} \quad \text{and} \quad \widetilde{\boldsymbol{\pi}} = \begin{bmatrix} \dfrac{\gamma}{\gamma + 0.8\mu}, & \dfrac{0.8\mu}{\gamma + 0.8\mu} \end{bmatrix},$$

while

$$\sum_{j=1}^{\infty} j\mathbf{F}^{(j)} = \begin{bmatrix} 4\lambda & 0 \\ 0 & 4\lambda \end{bmatrix}.$$

The stability condition is expressed as

$$\left[\frac{\gamma}{\gamma + 0.8\mu}, \frac{0.8\mu}{\gamma + 0.8\mu}\right] \cdot \begin{bmatrix} 4\lambda & 0 \\ 0 & 4\lambda \end{bmatrix} \cdot \begin{bmatrix} 1 \\ 1 \end{bmatrix} < \left[\frac{\gamma}{\gamma + 0.8\mu}, \frac{0.8\mu}{\gamma + 0.8\mu}\right] \cdot \begin{bmatrix} 0.2\mu & 0 \\ \gamma & 0 \end{bmatrix} \cdot \begin{bmatrix} 1 \\ 1 \end{bmatrix},$$

which can be written in the following compact form

$$4\lambda < \frac{\mu \cdot \gamma}{0.8\mu + \gamma}.$$

If $\widetilde{\mathbf{Q}}$ is reducible, then the stability condition is different. By identifying the absorbing states in $\widetilde{\mathbf{Q}}$, its state space can be rearranged as follows

$$\widetilde{\mathbf{Q}} = \begin{bmatrix} \mathbf{C}_1 & \mathbf{0} & \cdots & \mathbf{0} & \mathbf{0} \\ \mathbf{0} & \mathbf{C}_2 & \cdots & \mathbf{0} & \mathbf{0} \\ \vdots & \vdots & \ddots & \vdots & \mathbf{0} \\ \mathbf{0} & \mathbf{0} & \cdots & \mathbf{C}_k & \mathbf{0} \\ \mathbf{D}_1 & \mathbf{D}_2 & \cdots & \mathbf{D}_k & \mathbf{D}_0 \end{bmatrix}, \tag{39}$$

where the blocks $\mathbf{C}_h$ for $1 \leq h \leq k$ are irreducible and infinitesimal genera-tors. Since the matrices $\mathbf{B}$, $\mathbf{L}$ and $\mathbf{F}^{(i)}$ for $i \geq 1$ have non-negative off-diagonal elements, they can be restructured similarly and have block components $\mathbf{B}_{\mathbf{C}_h}$, $\mathbf{B}_{\mathbf{D}_l}$, $\mathbf{L}_{C_h}$, $\mathbf{L}_{D_l}$, and $\mathbf{F}_{C_h}^{(i)}$, $\mathbf{F}_{D_l}^{(i)}$ for $1 \leq h \leq k$, $0 \leq l \leq k$, and $i \geq 1$.

This implies that each of the sets $\mathcal{S}^{(i)}$ for $i \geq 1$ is partitioned into subsets that communicate only through the boundary portion of the process, i.e., states in $\mathcal{S}^{(0)}$. The stability condition in Eq.(38) should be satisfied by all the irreducible blocks identified in Eq.(39) in order for the M/G/1-type process to be stable as summarized below:

$$\widetilde{\boldsymbol{\pi}}^{(h)} \sum_{j=1}^{\infty} j\mathbf{F}_{C_h}^{(i)} \mathbf{1}^T < \widetilde{\boldsymbol{\pi}}^{(h)} \mathbf{B}_{\mathbf{C}_h} \mathbf{1}^T \qquad \forall 1 \leq h \leq k. \tag{40}$$

6 MAMSolver: A Matrix-Analytic Methods Tool

In this section we briefly describe the MAMSolver [32] software tool[9] for the solution of M/G/1-type, GI/M/1-type, and QBD processes. MAMSolver is a collection of the most efficient solution methodologies for M/G/1-type, GI/M/1-type, and QBD processes. In contrast to existing tools such as MAGIC [36] and MGMTool [10], which provide solutions only for QBD processes, MAMSolver provides implementations for the classical and the most efficient algorithms that solve M/G/1-type, GI/M/1-type, and QBD processes. The solution provided by MAMSolver consists of the stationary probability vector for the processes under

---

[9] Available at `http://www.cs.wm.edu/MAMSolver/`

study, the queue length and queue length distribution, as well as probabilistic indicators for the queueing model such as the caudal characteristic [16].

MAMSolver provides solutions for both DTMCs and CTMCs. The matrix-analytic algorithms are defined in terms of matrices, making matrix manipulations and operations the basic elements of the tool. The input to MAMSolver, in the form of a structured text file, indicates the method to be used for the solution and the finite set of matrices that accurately describe the process to be solved. Several tests are performed within the tool to insure that special cases are treated separately and therefore efficiently.

To address possible numerical problems that may arise during matrix operations, we use well known and heavily tested routines provided by the Lapack and BLAS packages[10]. Methods such as LU-decomposition, GMRES, and BiCGSTAB are used for the solution of systems of linear equations.

The solution of **QBD** processes starts with the computation of the matrix **R** using the logarithmic reduction algorithm [16]. However for completeness we provide also the classical iterative algorithm. There are cases when **G** (and **R**) can be computed explicitly [28]. We check if the conditions for the explicit computation hold in order to simplify and speedup the solution. The available solution methods for QBD processes are matrix-geometric and ETAQA.

The classic matrix geometric solution is implemented to solve **GI/M/1** processes. The algorithm goes first through the classic iterative procedure to compute **R** (to our knowledge, there is no alternative more efficient one). Then, it computes the boundary part of the stationary probability vector. Since there exists a geometric relation between vectors $\boldsymbol{\pi}^{(i)}$ for $i \geq 1$, there is no need to compute the whole stationary probability vector.

M/G/1 processes require the computation of matrix **G**. More effort has been placed on efficient solution of M/G/1 processes. MAMSolver provides the classic iterative algorithm, the cyclic-reduction algorithm, and the explicit one for special cases. The stationary probability vector is computed recursively using either Ramaswami's formula or its fast FFT version. ETAQA is the other available alternative for the solution of M/G/1 processes.

For a set of input and output examples and the source code of MAMSolver, we point the interested reader to the tool's website
http://www.cs.wm.edu/MAMSolver/.

7   Concluding Remarks

In this tutorial, we derived the basic matrix analytic results for the solution of M/G/1-type Markov processes. Via simple examples and from first principles, we illustrated why the solution of QBD and GI/M/1-type processes is simpler than the solution of M/G/1-type processes. We direct the interested reader in the two books of Neuts [25,26] for further reading as well as to the book of Latouche and Ramaswami [16]. Our target was to present enough material for

---

[10] Available from http://www.netlib.org.

a modeler to solve performance models with embedded Markov chains of the M/G/1 form.

References

1. D. A. Bini and B. Meini. Using displacement structure for solving non-skip-free M/G/1 type Markov chains. In A. Alfa and S. Chakravarthy, editors, *Advances in Matrix Analytic Methods for Stochastic Models*, pages 17–37, Notable Publications Inc. NJ, 1998.

2. D. A. Bini, B. Meini, and V. Ramaswami. Analyzing M/G/1 paradigms through QBDs: the role of the block structure in computing the matrix G. In G. Latouche and P. Taylor, editors, *Advances in Matrix-Analytic Methods for Stochastic Models*, pages 73–86, Notable Publications Inc. NJ, 2000.

3. L. Breuer. Parameter estimation for a class of BMAPs. In G. Latouche and P. Taylor, editors, *Advances in Matrix-Analytic Methods for Stochastic Models*, pages 87–97, Notable Publications Inc. NJ, 2000.

4. G. Ciardo, A. Riska, and E. Smirni. An aggregation-based solution method for M/G/1-type processes. In B. Plateau, W. J. Stewart, and M. Silva, editors, *Numerical Solution of Markov Chains*, pages 21–40. Prensas Universitarias de Zaragoza, Zaragoza, Spain, 1999.

5. G. Ciardo and E. Smirni. ETAQA: an efficient technique for the analysis of QBD processes by aggregation. *Performance Evaluation*, vol. 36-37, pages 71–93, 1999.

6. J. N. Daige and D. M. Lucantoni. Queueing systems having phase-dependent arrival and service rates. In J. W. Stewart, editor, *Numerical Solution of Markov Chains*, pages 179–215, Marcel Dekker, New York, 1991.

7. H. R. Gail, S. L. Hantler, and B. A. Taylor. Use of characteristic roots for solving infinite state Markov chains. In W. K. Grassmann, editor, *Computational Probability*, pages 205–255, Kluwer Academic Publishers, Boston, MA, 2000.

8. W. K. Grassmann and D. A. Stanford. Matrix analytic methods. In W. K. Grassmann, editor, *Computational Probability*, pages 153–204, Kluwer Academic Publishers, Boston, MA, 2000.

9. D. Green. Lag correlation of approximating departure process for MAP/PH/1 queues. In G. Latouche and P. Taylor, editors, *Advances in Matrix-Analytic Methods for Stochastic Models*, pages 135–151, Notable Publications Inc. NJ, 2000.

10. B. Haverkort, A. Van Moorsel, and A. Dijkstra. MGMtool: A Performance Analysis Tool Based on Matrix Geometric Methods. In R. Pooley, and J. Hillston, editors, *Modelling Techniques and Tools*, pages 312–316, Edinburgh University Press, 1993.

11. D. Heyman and A. Reeves. Numerical solutions of linear equations arising in Markov chain models. *ORSA Journal on Computing*, vol. 1 pages 52–60, 1989.

12. D. Heyman and D. Lucantoni. Modeling multiple IP traffic streams with rate limits. In Proceedings of the 17th International Teletraffic Congress, Brazil, Dec. 2001.

13. L. Kleinrock. Queueing systems. Volume I: Theory, Wiley, 1975.

14. G. Latouche. A simple proof for the matrix-geometric theorem. *Applied Stochastic Models and Data Analysis*, vol. 8, pages 25–29, 1992.

15. G. Latouche and G. W. Stewart. Numerical methods for M/G/1 type queues. In G. W. Stewart, editor, *Computations with Markov chains*, pages 571–581, Kluwer Academic Publishers, Boston, MA, 1995.

16. G. Latouche and V. Ramaswami. *Introduction to Matrix Geometric Methods in Stochastic Modeling.* ASA-SIAM Series on Statistics and Applied Probability. SIAM, Philadelphia, PA, 1999.

17. D. M. Lucantoni. The BMAP/G/1 queue: A tutorial. In L. Donatiello and R. Nelson, editors, *Models and Techniques for Performance Evaluation of Computer and Communication Systems*, pages 330–358. Springer-Verlag, 1993.

18. D. M. Lucantoni. *An algorithmic analysis of a communication model with retransmission of flawed messages.* Pitman, Boston, 1983.

19. B. Meini. An improved FFT-based version of Ramaswami's formula. *Comm. Statist. Stochastic Models*, vol. 13, pages 223–238, 1997.

20. B. Meini. Solving M/G/1 type Markov chains: Recent advances and applications. *Comm. Statist. Stochastic Models*, vol. 14(1&2), pages 479–496, 1998.

21. B. Meini. *Fast algorithms for the numerical solution of structured Markov chains.* Ph.D. Thesis, Department of Mathematics, University of Pisa, 1998.

22. C. D. Meyer. Stochastic complementation, uncoupling Markov chains, and the theory of nearly reducible systems. *SIAM Review*, vol. 31(2) pages 240–271, June 1989.

23. R. Nelson. Matrix geometric solutions in Markov models: a mathematical tutorial. Research Report RC 16777 (#742931), IBM T.J. Watson Res. Center, Yorktown Heights, NY, Apr. 1991.

24. R. Nelson. *Probability, Stochastic Processes, and Queueing Theory.* Springer-Verlag, 1995.

25. M. F. Neuts. *Matrix-geometric solutions in stochastic models.* Johns Hopkins University Press, Baltimore, MD, 1981.

26. M. F. Neuts. *Structured stochastic matrices of M/G/1 type and their applications.* Marcel Dekker, New York, NY, 1989.

27. B. F. Nielsen. Modeling long-range dependent and heavy-tailed phenomena by matrix analytic methods. In *Advances in Matrix-Analytic Methods for Stochastic Models,* G. Latouche and P. Taylor, editors, Notable Publications, pages 265–278, 2000.

28. V. Ramaswami and G. Latouche. A general class of Markov processes with explicit matrix-geometric solutions. *OR Spektrum*, vol. 8, pages 209–218, Aug. 1986.

29. V. Ramaswami. A stable recursion for the steady state vector in Markov chains of M/G/1 type. *Comm. Statist. Stochastic Models*, vol. 4, pages 183–263, 1988.

30. V. Ramaswami and J. L. Wang. A hybrid analysis/simulation for ATM performance with application to quality-of-service of CBR traffic. *Telecommunication Systems*, vol. 5, pages 25–48, 1996.

31. A. Riska and E. Smirni. An exact aggregation approach for M/G/1-type Markov chains. In the *Proceedings of the ACM International Conference on Measurement and Modeling of Computer Systems (ACM SIGMETRICS '02)*, pages 86–96, Marina Del Rey, CA, 2002.

32. A. Riska and E. Smirni. MAMSolver: a Matrix-analytic methods tools. In T. Field et al. (editors), *TOOLS 2002, LNCS 2324*, pages 205–211, Springer-Verlag, 2002.

33. A. Riska, M. S. Squillante, S.-Z. Yu, Z. Liu, and L. Zhang. Matrix-analytic analysis of a MAP/PH/1 queue fitted to web server data. 4th *Conference on Matrix-Analytic Methods* (to appear), Adelaide, Australia, July 2002.

34. H. Schellhaas. On Ramaswami's algorithm for the computation of the steady state vector in Markov chains of M/G/1 type. *Comm. Statist. Stochastic Models*, vol. 6, pages 541–550, 1990.

35. M. S. Squillante. Matrix-analytic methods: Applications, results and software tools. In G. Latouche and P. Taylor, editors, *Advances in Matrix-Analytic Methods for Stochastic Models*, Notable Publications Inc. NJ, 2000.
36. M. S. Squillante. MAGIC: A computer performance modeling tool based on matrix-geometric techniques. In G. Balbo and G. Serazzi, editors, Computer Performance Evaluation: Modeling Techniques and Tools, North-Holland, Amsterdam, pages 411–425, 1992.

Appendix A: Stochastic Complementation

Here, we briefly outline the concept of stochastic complementation [22]. While [22] introduces the concept of stochastic complementation for DTMCs with finite state spaces we define it instead for the infinite case, a straightforward extension, and state the results in terms of CTMCs.

Partition the state space $\mathcal{S}$ of an ergodic CTMC with infinitesimal generator matrix $\mathbf{Q}$ and stationary probability vector π, satisfying $\pi\mathbf{Q} = \mathbf{0}$, into two disjoint subsets, $\mathcal{A}$ and $\overline{\mathcal{A}}$.

Definition 1. [22] (Stochastic complement) The stochastic complement of $\mathcal{A}$ is

$$\overline{\mathbf{Q}} = \mathbf{Q}[\mathcal{A}, \mathcal{A}] + \mathbf{Q}[\mathcal{A}, \overline{\mathcal{A}}](-\mathbf{Q}[\overline{\mathcal{A}}, \overline{\mathcal{A}}])^{-1}\mathbf{Q}[\overline{\mathcal{A}}, \mathcal{A}], \qquad (41)$$

where $(-\mathbf{Q}[\overline{\mathcal{A}}, \overline{\mathcal{A}}])^{-1}[r, c]$ represents the mean time spent in state $c \in \overline{\mathcal{A}}$, starting from state $r \in \overline{\mathcal{A}}$, before reaching any state in $\mathcal{A}$, and $((-\mathbf{Q}[\overline{\mathcal{A}}, \overline{\mathcal{A}}])^{-1}\mathbf{Q}[\overline{\mathcal{A}}, \mathcal{A}])[r, c']$ represents the probability that, starting from $r \in \overline{\mathcal{A}}$, we enter $\mathcal{A}$ through state c'. □

The stochastic complement $\overline{\mathbf{Q}}$ is the infinitesimal generator of a new CTMC which mimics the original CTMC but "skips over" states in $\overline{\mathcal{A}}$. The following theorem formalizes this concept.

Theorem 2. [22] *The stochastic complement $\overline{\mathbf{Q}}$ of $\mathcal{A}$ is an infinitesimal generator and is irreducible if $\mathbf{Q}$ is. If α is its stationary probability vector satisfying $\alpha\overline{\mathbf{Q}} = \mathbf{0}$, then $\alpha = Norm(\pi[\mathcal{A}])$.* □

This implies that the stationary probability distribution α of the stochastic complement differs from the corresponding portion of the stationary distribution of the original CTMC $\pi[\mathcal{A}]$ only by the constant $\pi[\mathcal{A}]\mathbf{1}^T$, which represents the probability of being in $\mathcal{A}$ in the original CTMC.

There are cases where we can take advantage of the special structure of the CTMC and explicitly generate the stochastic complement of a set of states $\mathcal{A}$. To consider these cases, rewrite the definition of stochastic complement in Eq.(41) as

$$\overline{\mathbf{Q}} = \mathbf{Q}[\mathcal{A}, \mathcal{A}] + RowSum(\mathbf{Q}[\mathcal{A}, \overline{\mathcal{A}}])\mathbf{Z}, \qquad (42)$$

where $\mathbf{Z} = Norm(\mathbf{Q}[\mathcal{A}, \overline{\mathcal{A}}]) \, (-\mathbf{Q}[\overline{\mathcal{A}}, \overline{\mathcal{A}}])^{-1}\mathbf{Q}[\overline{\mathcal{A}}, \mathcal{A}]$. The rth diagonal element of $RowSum(\mathbf{Q}[\mathcal{A}, \overline{\mathcal{A}}])$ represents the rate at which the set $\mathcal{A}$ is left from its rth

state to reach any of the states in $\overline{\mathcal{A}}$, while the rth row of $\mathbf{Z}$, which sums to one, specifies how this rate should be redistributed over the states in $\mathcal{A}$ when the process eventually reenters it.

Lemma 1. (Single entry) If $\mathcal{A}$ can be entered from $\overline{\mathcal{A}}$ only through a single state $c \in \mathcal{A}$, the matrix $\mathbf{Z}$ defined in Eq. (42) is trivially computable: it is a matrix of zeros except for its cth column, which contains all ones.   □

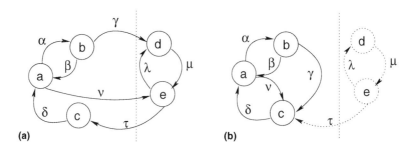

Fig. 7. Stochastic Complementation for a finite Markov chain.

We choose the simple finite Markov chain depicted in Figure 7(a) to explain the concept of stochastic complementation. The state space of this Markov chain is $\mathcal{S} = \{a, b, c, d, e\}$. We construct the stochastic complement of the states in set $\mathcal{A} = \{a, b, c\}$ ($\overline{\mathcal{A}} = \{d, e\}$), as shown in Figure 7(b). The matrices used in Eq.(41) for this example are:

$$
\mathbf{Q}[\mathcal{A}, \mathcal{A}] = \begin{bmatrix} -(\alpha + \nu) & \alpha & 0 \\ \beta & -(\gamma + \beta) & 0 \\ \delta & 0 & -\delta \end{bmatrix}, \qquad \mathbf{Q}[\mathcal{A}, \overline{\mathcal{A}}] = \begin{bmatrix} 0 & \nu \\ \gamma & 0 \\ 0 & 0 \end{bmatrix},
$$

$$
\mathbf{Q}[\overline{\mathcal{A}}, \mathcal{A}] = \begin{bmatrix} 0 & 0 & 0 \\ 0 & 0 & \tau \end{bmatrix}, \qquad \mathbf{Q}[\overline{\mathcal{A}}, \overline{\mathcal{A}}] = \begin{bmatrix} -\mu & \mu \\ \lambda & -(\lambda + \tau) \end{bmatrix}.
$$

Observe that in this case one can apply Lemma 1 to trivially construct the stochastic complement, since $\mathcal{A}$ is entered from states in $\overline{\mathcal{A}}$ only through state c. There are only two transitions from states in $\mathcal{A}$ to states in $\overline{\mathcal{A}}$; the transition with rate γ from state b to state d and the transition with rate ν from state a to state e. These two transitions are folded back into $\mathcal{A}$ through state c, which is the single entry in $\mathcal{A}$. The following derivation shows that because of the special single entry state the two folded transitions have the original rates, γ and ν respectively.

$$
\mathbf{Z} = Norm(\mathbf{Q}[\mathcal{A}, \overline{\mathcal{A}}])(-\mathbf{Q}[\overline{\mathcal{A}}, \overline{\mathcal{A}}])^{-1}\mathbf{Q}[\overline{\mathcal{A}}, \mathcal{A}] = \begin{bmatrix} 0 & 1 \\ 1 & 0 \\ 0 & 0 \end{bmatrix} \cdot \begin{bmatrix} \frac{\lambda + \tau}{\mu\tau} & \frac{1}{\tau} \\ \frac{\lambda}{\mu\tau} & \frac{1}{\tau} \end{bmatrix} \cdot \begin{bmatrix} 0 & 0 & 0 \\ 0 & 0 & \tau \end{bmatrix} = \begin{bmatrix} 0 & 0 & 1 \\ 0 & 0 & 1 \\ 0 & 0 & 0 \end{bmatrix},
$$

which further results in:

$$RowSum(\mathbf{Q}[\mathcal{A}, \overline{\mathcal{A}}]) \cdot \mathbf{Z} = \begin{bmatrix} \nu & 0 & 0 \\ 0 & \gamma & 0 \\ 0 & 0 & 0 \end{bmatrix} \cdot \begin{bmatrix} 0 & 0 & 1 \\ 0 & 0 & 1 \\ 0 & 0 & 0 \end{bmatrix} = \begin{bmatrix} 0 & 0 & \nu \\ 0 & 0 & \gamma \\ 0 & 0 & 0 \end{bmatrix}.$$

Appendix B: Explicit Computation of R

QBD processes are defined as the intersection of M/G/1 and GI/M/1-type processes. Hence, both matrix $\mathbf{G}$ (characteristic for M/G/1) and matrix $\mathbf{R}$ (characteristic for GI/M/1) can be defined for a QBD process as solutions of the following quadratic equations [16]:

$$\mathbf{B} + \mathbf{L}\mathbf{G} + \mathbf{F}\mathbf{G}^2 = 0, \qquad \mathbf{F} + \mathbf{R}\mathbf{L} + \mathbf{R}^2\mathbf{B} = 0.$$

If matrix-geometric is used to solve a QBD process then the relation between $\boldsymbol{\pi}^{(i)}$ and $\boldsymbol{\pi}^{(i-1)}$ for $i > 1$ is expressed in terms of $\mathbf{R}$

$$\boldsymbol{\pi}^{(i)} = \boldsymbol{\pi}^{(i-1)}\mathbf{R},$$

If matrix-analytic is the solution method then the relation between $\boldsymbol{\pi}^{(i)}$ and $\boldsymbol{\pi}^{(i-1)}$ is based on Ramaswami's recursive formula:

$$\boldsymbol{\pi}^{(i)} = -\boldsymbol{\pi}^{(i-1)}\mathbf{S}^{(1)}(\mathbf{S}^{(0)})^{-1},$$

where $\mathbf{S}^{(1)} = \mathbf{F}$ and $\mathbf{S}^{(0)} = (\mathbf{L} + \mathbf{F}\mathbf{G})$, i.e., the only auxiliary sums (see Subsection 4.1) used in the solution of M/G/1 processes that are defined for a QBD process. The above equations allow the derivation of the fundamental relation between $\mathbf{R}$ and $\mathbf{G}$ [16, pages 137-8],

$$\mathbf{R} = -\mathbf{F}(\mathbf{L} + \mathbf{F}\mathbf{G})^{-1}. \tag{43}$$

Obviously, for the case of QBD processes, knowing $\mathbf{G}$ (or $\mathbf{R}$) implies a direct computation of $\mathbf{R}$ (or $\mathbf{G}$). Computing $\mathbf{G}$ is usually easier than computing $\mathbf{R}$: $\mathbf{G}$'s computation is a prerequisite to the computation of $\mathbf{R}$ in the logarithmic reduction algorithm, the most efficient algorithm to compute $\mathbf{R}$ [16]. If $\mathbf{B}$ can be expressed as a product of two vectors

$$\mathbf{B} = \boldsymbol{\alpha} \cdot \boldsymbol{\beta},$$

where, without loss of generality $\boldsymbol{\beta}$ is assumed to be a normalized vector, then $\mathbf{G}$ and $\mathbf{R}$ can be explicitly obtained as

$$\mathbf{G} = \mathbf{1} \cdot \boldsymbol{\beta}, \qquad \mathbf{R} = -\mathbf{F}(\mathbf{L} + \mathbf{F}\mathbf{1} \cdot \boldsymbol{\beta})^{-1}.$$

Representative examples, where the above condition holds, are the queues $M/Cox/1$, $M/Hr/1$, and $M/Er/1$, whose service process is Coxian, Hyperexponential, and Erlang distribution respectively.

An Algorithmic Approach to Stochastic Bounds

J.M. Fourneau and N. Pekergin

PRiSM, Université de Versailles Saint-Quentin en Yvelines,
45 Av. des Etats Unis, 78000 Versailles, France

Abstract. We present a new methodology based on the stochastic ordering, algorithmic derivation of simpler Markov chains and numerical
analysis of these chains. The performance indices defined by reward functions are stochastically bounded by reward functions computed on much
simpler or smaller Markov chains. This leads to an important reduction
on numerical complexity. Stochastic bounds are a promising method to
analyze QoS requirements. Indeed it is sufficient to prove that a bound
of the real performance satisfies the guarantee.

1 Introduction

Since Plateau's seminal work on composition and compact tensor representation
of Markov chains using Stochastic Automata Networks (SAN), we know how to
model Markov systems with interacting components and large state space [29,30,
31]. The main idea of the SAN approach is to decompose the system of interest
into its components and to model each component separately. Once this is done,
interactions and dependencies among components can be added to complete the
model. The stochastic matrix of the chain is obtained after summations and
Kronecker (or tensor) products of local components. The benefit of the SAN approach is twofold. First, each component can be modeled much easier compared
to the global system. Second, the space required to store the description of components is in general much smaller than the explicit list of transitions, even in
a sparse representation. However, using this representation instead of the usual
sparse matrix form increases the time required for numerical analysis of the
chains [6,15,37,33]. Note that we are interested in performance indices R defined
as reward functions on the steady-state distribution (i.e. $R = \sum_i r(i)\pi(i)$) and
we do not try to compute transient measures. Thus the numerical computation
of the analysis is mainly the computation of the steady-state distribution and
then the summation of the elementary rewards $r(i)$ to obtain R. The first step
is in general the most difficult because of the memory space and time requirements (see Steward's book [34] for an overview of usual numerical techniques for
Markov chains). The decomposition and tensor representation has been generalized to other modeling formalisms as well : Stochastic Petri nets [13], Stochastic
Process Algebra [20]. So we now have several well-founded methods to model
complex systems using Markov chains with large state space.

Despite considerable works [7,12,15,37], the numerical analysis of Markov
chains, is still a very difficult problem when the state space is too large or the

M.C. Calzarossa and S. Tucci (Eds.): Performance 2002, LNCS 2459, pp. 64–88, 2002.
© Springer-Verlag Berlin Heidelberg 2002

eigenvalues badly distributed. Fortunately enough, while modeling high speed networks, it is often sufficient to satisfy the requirements for the Quality of Service (QoS) we expect. Exact values of the performance indices are not necessary in this case and bounding some reward functions is often sufficient.

So, we advocate the use of stochastic bounds to prove that the QoS requirements are satisfied. Our approach differs from sample path techniques and coupling theorem applied to models transformation (see [27] for an example on Fair Queueing delays comparison based on sample-paths), as we only consider Markov chains and algorithmic operations on stochastic matrices. Assume that we have to model a problem using a very large Markov chain. We need to compute its steady-state distribution in order to obtain reward functions (for instance, the cell loss rates for a finite capacity buffer). The key idea of the methodology is to design a new chain such that the reward functions will be upper or lower bounds of the exact reward functions. This new chain is an aggregated or simplified model of the former one. These bounds and the simplification criteria are based on some stochastic orderings applied to Markov processes (see Stoyan [35] and other references therein). As we drastically reduced the state space or the complexity of the analysis, we may now use numerical methods to efficiently compute a bound of the rewards.

Several methods have been proposed to bound rewards : resolution of a linear algebra problem and polyhedra properties by Courtois and Semal [8,9], Markov Decision Process by Van Dijk [38] and various stochastic bounds (see [35,22,32] and references therein). Here we present recent results based on stochastic orders and structure-based algorithms combined with usual numerical techniques. Thus the algorithms we present can be easily implemented inside software tools based on Markov chains. Unlike former approaches which are either analytical or not really constructive, this new approach is only based on simple algorithms. These algorithms can always be applied, even if the quality of the bounds may be sometimes not enough accurate.

We survey the results in two steps : first how to obtain a bounding matrix and a bound of the distributions and in a second step how to simplify the numerical computations. We present several algorithms based on stochastic bounds and structural properties of the chains and some examples to show the effectiveness of the approach. In section 2, we define the "st" and "icx" stochastic orderings and we give the fundamental theorem on the stochastic matrices. We also present Vincent's algorithm [1] which is the starting point of all the algorithms for the "st" ordering presented here. Then we present, in section 3, several algorithms for "st" bounds based on structures: upper-Hessenberg, lumpability, stochastic complement [26], Class C Matrices. Section 4 is devoted to the analysis of a real problem: the loss rates of a finite buffer with batch arrivals and modulation, Head of Line service discipline and Pushout buffer management. Such systems have been proposed for ATM networks [18]. The example here is only slightly simplified to focus on the algorithmic aspects. The reduction algorithms we have used on this example has divided the state-space by ten for several analysis. Finally, in section 5, we present some algorithms for "icx" ordering.

2   Strong Stochastic Bounds

For the sake of simplicity, we restrict ourselves to Discrete Time Markov Chains (DTMC) with finite state space $E = \{1, \ldots, n\}$ but continuous-time models can be considered after uniformization. Here we restrict ourselves to "st" stochastic ordering. The definitions and results for "icx" ordering are presented in section 5. In the following, n will denote the size of matrix P and $P_{i,*}$ will refer to row i of P.

First, we give a brief overview on stochastic ordering for Markov chains and we obtain a set of inequalities to imply bounds. Then we present a basic algorithm proposed by Vincent and Abuamsha [1] and we explain some of its properties.

2.1   A Brief Overview

Following [35], we define the strong stochastic ordering by the set of non-decreasing functions or by matrix K_{st}.

$$
K_{st} = \begin{bmatrix}
1 & 0 & 0 & \ldots & 0 \\
1 & 1 & 0 & \ldots & 0 \\
1 & 1 & 1 & \ldots & 0 \\
\vdots & \vdots & \vdots & \ddots & \vdots \\
1 & 1 & 1 & \ldots & 1
\end{bmatrix}
$$

Definition 1 *Let X and Y be random variables taking values on a totally ordered space. Then X is said to be less than Y in the strong stochastic sense, that is, $X <_{st} Y$ if and only if $E[f(X)] \leq E[f(Y)]$ for all non decreasing functions f whenever the expectations exist.*

If X and Y take values on the finite state space $\{1, 2, \ldots, n\}$ with p and q as probability distribution vectors, then X is said to be less than Y in the strong stochastic sense, that is, $X <_{st} Y$ if and only if $\sum_{j=k}^{n} p_j \leq \sum_{j=k}^{n} q_j$ for $k = 1, 2, \ldots, n$, or briefly: $pK_{st} <_{st} qK_{st}$.

Important performance indices such as average population, loss rates or tail probabilities are non decreasing functions. Therefore, bounds on the distribution imply bounds on these performance indices as well. It is important to know that st-bounds are valid pour the transient distributions as well. We do not use this property as we are mainly interested in performance measures on the the steady-state. To the best of our knowledge, such a work has still to be done to link st-bounds and numerical analysis for the computation of transient distributions.

It is known for a long time that monotonicity [21] and comparability of the one step transition probability matrices of time-homogeneous MCs yield sufficient conditions for their stochastic comparison. This is the fundamental result we use in our algorithms. First let us define the st-comparability of the matrix and the st-monotonicity.

Definition 2 *Let P and Q be two stochastic matrices. $P <_{st} Q$ if and only if $PK_{st} \leq QK_{st}$. This can be also characterized as $P_{i,*} <_{st} Q_{i,*}$ for all i.*

Definition 3 *Let P be a stochastic matrix, P is st-monotone if and only if for all u and v, if $u <_{st} v$ then $uP <_{st} vP$.*

Hopefully, st-monotone matrices are completely characterized (this is not the case for other orderings, see [4]).

Definition 4 *Let P be a stochastic matrix. P is $<_{st}$-monotone if and only if $K_{st}^{-1} P K_{st} \geq 0$ component-wise.*

Thus we get:

Property 1 *Let P be a stochastic matrix, P is st-monotone if and only if for all i, $j > i$, we have $P_{i,*} <_{st} P_{j,*}$*

Theorem 1 *Let $X(t)$ and $Y(t)$ be two DTMC and P and Q be their respective stochastic matrices. Then $X(t) <_{st} Y(t), t > 0$, if*

- $X(0) <_{st} Y(0)$,
- *st-monotonicity of at least one of the matrices holds,*
- *st-comparability of the matrices holds, that is, $P_{i,*} <_{st} Q_{i,*}$ $\forall i$.*

Thus, assuming that P is not monotone, we obtain a set of inequalities on elements of Q :

$$\begin{cases} \sum_{k=j}^{n} P_{i,k} \leq \sum_{k=j}^{n} Q_{i,k} & \forall\, i,j \\ \sum_{k=j}^{n} Q_{i,k} \leq \sum_{k=j}^{n} Q_{i+1,k} & \forall\, i,j \end{cases} \tag{1}$$

2.2   Algorithms

It is possible to derive a set of equalities, instead of inequalities. These equalities provides, once they have been ordered (in increasing order for i and in decreasing order for j in system 2), a constructive way to design a stochastic matrix which yields a stochastic bound.

$$\begin{cases} \sum_{k=j}^{n} Q_{1,k} = \sum_{k=j}^{n} P_{1,k} \\ \sum_{k=j}^{n} Q_{i+1,k} = max(\sum_{k=j}^{n} Q_{i,k}, \sum_{k=j}^{n} P_{i+1,k}) & \forall\, i,j \end{cases} \tag{2}$$

The following algorithm [1] constructs an st-monotone upper bounding DTMC Q for a given DTMC P. For the sake of simplicity, we use a full matrix representation for P and Q. Stochastic matrices associated to real performance evaluation problems are usually sparse. And the sparse matrix version of all the algorithms we present here is straightforward. Note that due to the ordering of the indices, the summations $\sum_{j=l}^{n} q_{i-1,j}$ and $\sum_{j=l+1}^{n} q_{i,j}$ are already computed when we need them. And they can be stored to avoid computations. However, we let them appear as summations to show the relations with inequalities 1.

Algorithm 1   Construction of the optimal st-monotone upper bounding DTMC Q:

$q_{1,n} = p_{1,n}$;
for $i = 2, 3, \ldots, n$ do $q_{i,n} = \max(q_{i-1,n}, p_{i,n})$; od
for $l = n - 1, n - 2, \ldots, 1$, do $q_{1,l} = p_{1,l}$;
    for $i = 2, 3, \ldots, n$, do $q_{i,l} = \max(\sum_{j=l}^{n} q_{i-1,j}, \sum_{j=l}^{n} p_{i,l}) - \sum_{j=l+1}^{n} q_{i,j}$; od
od

Definition 5 *We denote by $v(P)$ the matrix obtained after application of Algorithm 1 to a stochastic matrix P.*

First let us illustrate Algorithm 1 on a small matrix. We consider a 5×5 matrix for $P1$ and we compute matrix Q, and both steady-state distributions.

$$P1 = \begin{bmatrix} 0.5 & 0.2 & 0.1 & 0.2 & 0.0 \\ 0.1 & 0.7 & 0.1 & 0.0 & 0.1 \\ 0.2 & 0.1 & 0.5 & 0.2 & 0.0 \\ 0.1 & 0.0 & 0.1 & 0.7 & 0.1 \\ 0.0 & 0.2 & 0.2 & 0.1 & 0.5 \end{bmatrix} \quad Q = v(P1) = \begin{bmatrix} 0.5 & 0.2 & 0.1 & 0.2 & 0.0 \\ 0.1 & 0.6 & 0.1 & 0.1 & 0.1 \\ 0.1 & 0.2 & 0.5 & 0.1 & 0.1 \\ 0.1 & 0.0 & 0.1 & 0.7 & 0.1 \\ 0.0 & 0.1 & 0.1 & 0.3 & 0.5 \end{bmatrix}$$

Their   steady-state   distributions   are   respectively π_{P1} $=$ $(0.180, 0.252, 0.184, 0.278, 0.106)$ and $\pi_Q = (0.143, 0.190, 0.167, 0.357, 0.143)$. Their expectations are respectively 1.87 and 2.16 (we assume that the first state has index 0 to compute the reward $f(i) = i$ associated to the expectation). Remember that the strong stochastic ordering implies that the expectation of f on distribution π_{P1} is smaller than the expectation of f on distribution π_Q for all non decreasing functions f.

It may happen that matrix $v(P)$ computed by Algorithm 1 is not irreducible, even if P is irreducible. Indeed due to the subtraction operation in inner loops, some elements of $v(P)$ may be zero even if the elements with the same indices in P are positive. We have derived a new algorithm which try to keep almost all transitions of P in matrix $v(P)$ and we have proved a necessary and sufficient condition on P to obtain an irreducible matrix (the proof of the theorem is omitted for the sake of readability):

Theorem 2 *Let P be an irreducible finite stochastic matrix. Matrix Q computed from P by Algorithm 2 is irreducible if and only if every row of the lower triangle of matrix P contains at least one positive element.*

Even if matrix $v(P)$ is reducible, it has one essential class of states and the last state belongs to that class. So it is still possible to compute the steady-state distribution for this class. We do not prove the theorem but we present an example of a matrix $P2$ such that $v(P2)$ is reducible (i.e. states 0, 1 and 2 are transient in matrix $v(P2)$).

$$P2 = \begin{bmatrix} 0.5 & 0.2 & 0.1 & 0.2 & 0.0 \\ 0.1 & 0.7 & 0.1 & 0.0 & 0.1 \\ 0.2 & 0.1 & 0.5 & 0.2 & 0.0 \\ 0.0 & 0.0 & 0.0 & 0.7 & 0.3 \\ 0.0 & 0.2 & 0.2 & 0.1 & 0.5 \end{bmatrix} \quad Q = v(P2) = \begin{bmatrix} 0.5 & 0.2 & 0.1 & 0.2 & 0.0 \\ 0.1 & 0.6 & 0.1 & 0.1 & 0.1 \\ 0.1 & 0.2 & 0.5 & 0.1 & 0.1 \\ 0.0 & 0.0 & 0.0 & 0.7 & 0.3 \\ 0.0 & 0.0 & 0.0 & 0.5 & 0.5 \end{bmatrix}$$

In the following, ϵ is an arbitrary positive value. And we assume that a summation with a lower index larger than the upper index is 0.

Algorithm 2 Construction of an st-monotone upper bounding DTMC without transition deletion:

$q_{1,n} = p_{1,n}$;
for $i = 2, 3, \ldots, n$ do $q_{i,n} = \max(q_{i-1,n}, p_{i,n})$; od
for $l = n - 1, n - 2, \ldots, 1$, do $q_{1,l} = p_{1,l}$;
    for $i = 2, 3, \ldots, n$, do
        $q_{i,l} = \max(\sum_{j=l}^{n} q_{i-1,j}, \sum_{j=l}^{n} p_{i,l}) - \sum_{j=l+1}^{n} q_{i,j}$;
        if $(q_{i,l} = 0)$ and $(p_{i,l} > 0)$ and $(\sum_{j=l+1}^{n} q_{i,j} < 1)$ then
            $q_{i,l} = \epsilon \times (1 - \sum_{j=l+1}^{n} q_{i,j})$
    od
od

2.3 Properties

Algorithm 1 has several interesting properties which can be proved using a max-plus formulation [10] which appears clearly in equation 2.

Theorem 3 *Algorithm 1 provides the smallest st-monotone upper bound for a matrix P: i.e. if we consider U another st-monotone upper bounding DTMC for P then $Q <_{st} U$ [1].*

However bounds on the probability distributions may still be improved. The former theorem only states that Algorithm 1 provides the smallest matrix. We have developed new techniques to improve the accuracy of the bounds on the steady-state π which are based on some transformations on P [10].

We have studied a linear transformation for stochastic matrices $\alpha(P, \delta) = (1 - \delta)I + \delta P$, for $\delta \in (0, 1)$. This transformation has no effect on the steady-state distribution but it has a large influence on the effect of Algorithm 1. We have proved in [10] that if the given stochastic matrix is not row diagonally dominant, then the steady-state probability distribution of the optimal st-monotone upper bounding matrix corresponding to the row diagonally dominant transformed matrix is better in the strong stochastic sense than the one corresponding to the original matrix. And we have established that the transformation $P/2 + I/2$ provides the best bound for the family of linear transformation we have considered. More precisely:

Theorem 4 *Let P be a DTMC of order n, and two different values $\delta_1, \delta_2 \in (0, 1)$ such that $\delta1 < \delta2$, Then $\pi_{v(\alpha(P, \delta 1))} <_{st} \pi_{v(\alpha(P, \delta 2))} <_{st} \pi_{v(P)}$.*

One may ask if there is an optimal value of δ. When the matrix is row diagonal dominant (RDD), its diagonal serves as a barrier for the perturbation moving from the upper-triangular part to the strictly lower-triangular part in forming $v(P)$.

Definition 6 *A stochastic matrix is said to be row diagonally dominant (RDD) if all of its diagonal elements are greater than or equal to 0.5.*

Corollary 1 *Let P be a DTMC of order n that is RDD. Then $v(P)$ and $v(\alpha(P))$ have the same steady-state probability distribution.*

Corollary 1 implies that one cannot improve the steady-state probability bounds by choosing a smaller δ value to transform an already RDD DTMC. And $\delta = 1/2$ is sufficient to transform an arbitrary stochastic matrix into a RDD one. This first approach was then generalized to transformations based on a set of polynomials which gives better (i.e. more accurate) bounds [5]. Let us first introduce these transformations and their basic properties.

Definition 7 *Let $\mathcal{D}$ be the set of polynomials $\Phi()$ such that $\Phi(1) = 1$, Φ different of Identity, and all the coefficients of Φ are non negative.*

Proposition 1 *Let $\Phi()$ be an arbitrary polynomial in $\mathcal{D}$, then $\Phi(P)$ has the same steady-state distribution than P*

Theorem 5 *Let Φ be an arbitrary polynomial in $\mathcal{D}$, Algorithm 1 applied on $\Phi(P)$ provides a more accurate bound than the steady-state distribution of Q i.e.:*

$$\pi_P <_{st} \pi_{v(\Phi(P))} <_{st} \pi_{v(P)}$$

For a stochastic interpretation of this result and a proof based on linear algebra see [5]. Corollary 1 basically states that the optimal transformation if we restrict ourselves to degree 1 polynomials is $\phi(X) = X/2 + 1/2$. Such a result is still unknown for arbitrary degree polynomials, even if it is clear that the larger the degree of Φ, the more accurate the bound $v(\Phi(P))$. This is illustrated in the example below. Let us consider stochastic matrix $P3$ and we study the polynomials $\phi(X) = X/2 + 1/2$ and $\psi(X) = X^2/2 + 1/2$.

$$P3 = \begin{bmatrix} 0.1 & 0.2 & 0.4 & 0.3 \\ 0.2 & 0.3 & 0.2 & 0.3 \\ 0.1 & 0.5 & 0.4 & 0 \\ 0.2 & 0.1 & 0.3 & 0.4 \end{bmatrix}$$

First, let us compute $\phi(P3)$ and $\psi(P3)$.

$$\phi(P3) = \begin{bmatrix} 0.55 & 0.1 & 0.2 & 0.15 \\ 0.1 & 0.65 & 0.1 & 0.15 \\ 0.05 & 0.25 & 0.7 & 0 \\ 0.1 & 0.05 & 0.15 & 0.7 \end{bmatrix} \quad \psi(P3) = \begin{bmatrix} 0.575 & 0.155 & 0.165 & 0.105 \\ 0.08 & 0.63 & 0.155 & 0.135 \\ 0.075 & 0.185 & 0.65 & 0.09 \\ 0.075 & 0.13 & 0.17 & 0.625 \end{bmatrix}$$

Then, we apply operators v to obtain the bounds on matrices :

$$v(\phi(P3)) = \begin{bmatrix} 0.55 & 0.1 & 0.2 & 0.15 \\ 0.1 & 0.55 & 0.2 & 0.15 \\ 0.05 & 0.25 & 0.55 & 0.15 \\ 0.05 & 0.1 & 0.15 & 0.7 \end{bmatrix} \quad v(\psi(P3)) = \begin{bmatrix} 0.575 & 0.155 & 0.165 & 0.105 \\ 0.08 & 0.63 & 0.155 & 0.135 \\ 0.075 & 0.185 & 0.605 & 0.135 \\ 0.075 & 0.13 & 0.17 & 0.625 \end{bmatrix}$$

And,

$$v(P3) = \begin{bmatrix} 0.1 & 0.2 & 0.4 & 0.3 \\ 0.1 & 0.2 & 0.4 & 0.3 \\ 0.1 & 0.2 & 0.4 & 0.3 \\ 0.1 & 0.2 & 0.3 & 0.4 \end{bmatrix}$$

Finally, we compute the steady-state distributions for all matrices:

$$\begin{cases} \pi_{v(P3)} = (0.1, 0.2, 0, 3667, 0.3333) \\ \pi_{v(\phi(P3))} = (0.1259, 0.2587, 0, 2821, 0.3333) \\ \pi_{v(\psi(P3))} = (0.1530, 0.2997, 0, 2916, 0.2557) \\ \pi_{P3} = (0.1530, 0.3025, 0, 3167, 0.2278) \end{cases}$$

Clearly, bounds obtained by polynomial ψ are more accurate than the other bounds.

2.4   Time and Space Complexity

It must be clear at this point that Algorithm 1 builds a matrix Q which is, in general, as difficult as P to analyze. This first algorithm is only presented here to show that inequalities 1 have algorithmic implications. Concerning complexity of Algorithm 1 on sparse matrix, we do not have positive results. Indeed, it may be possible that matrix Q has many more positive elements than matrix P and it may be even completely filled. For instance:

$$P4 = \begin{bmatrix} 0.5 & 0.2 & 0.1 & 0.1 & 0.1 \\ 1.0 & 0.0 & 0.0 & 0.0 & 0.0 \\ 1.0 & 0.0 & 0.0 & 0.0 & 0.0 \\ 1.0 & 0.0 & 0.0 & 0.0 & 0.0 \\ 1.0 & 0.0 & 0.0 & 0.0 & 0.0 \end{bmatrix} \quad Q = v(P4) = \begin{bmatrix} 0.5 & 0.2 & 0.1 & 0.1 & 0.1 \\ 0.5 & 0.2 & 0.1 & 0.1 & 0.1 \\ 0.5 & 0.2 & 0.1 & 0.1 & 0.1 \\ 0.5 & 0.2 & 0.1 & 0.1 & 0.1 \\ 0.5 & 0.2 & 0.1 & 0.1 & 0.1 \end{bmatrix}$$

More generally, it is easy to build a matrix P with $3n$ positive elements resulting in a completely filled matrix $v(P)$. Of course the algorithms we survey in the next section provide matrices with structural or numerical properties. Most of them do not suffer the same complexity problem.

3   Structure Based Bounding Algorithms for "st" Comparison

We can also use the two sets of constraints of system 1 and add some structural properties to simplify the resolution of the bounding matrix. For instance, Algorithm 3 provides an upper bounding matrix which is upper-Hessenberg (i.e.

the low triangle except the main sub-diagonal is zero). Therefore the resolution by direct elimination is quite simple. In the following we illustrate this principle with several structures associated to simple resolution methods and present algorithms to build structure based st-monotone bounding stochastic matrices. Most of these algorithms do not assume any particular property or structure for the initial stochastic matrix.

3.1   Upper-Hessenberg Structure

Definition 8 *A matrix H is said to be upper-Hessenberg if and only if $H_{i,j} = 0$ for $i > j + 1$.*

The paradigm for upper-Hessenberg case is the $M/G/1$ queue. The resolution by recursion for these matrices requires $o(m)$ operations [34].

Property 2 *Let P be an irreducible finite stochastic matrix such that every row of the lower triangle of P contains at least one positive element. Let Q be computed from P by Algorithm 3. Then Q is irreducible, st-monotone, upper-Hessenberg and an upper bound for P.*

The proof is omitted. The algorithm is slightly different of Algorithm 2. The last two instructions create the upper-Hessenberg structure. Note that the generalization to block upper-Hessenberg matrices is straightforward.

Algorithm 3 An upper-Hessenberg st-monotone upper bound Q:
$q_{1,n} = p_{1,n}$;
for $i = 1, 2, \ldots, n$ do $q_{1,i} = p_{1,i}$; $q_{i+1,n} = \max(q_{i,n}, p_{i+1,n})$; od
for $i = 2, 3, \ldots, n$ do
    for $l = n - 1, n - 2, \ldots, i$ do
        $q_{i,l} = \max(\sum_{j=l}^{n} q_{i-1,j}, \sum_{j=l}^{n} p_{i,l}) - \sum_{j=l+1}^{n} q_{i,j}$;
        if $(q_{i,l} = 0)$ and $(p_{i,l} > 0)$ and $(\sum_{j=l+1}^{n} q_{i,j} < 1)$ then
            $q_{i,l} = \epsilon \times (1 - \sum_{j=l+1}^{n} q_{i,j})$
    od
    $q_{i,i-1} = 1 - \sum_{j=i}^{n} q_{i,j}$
    for $l = i - 2, i - 3, \ldots, 1$ do $q_{i,l} = 0$ od
od

The application of this algorithm on matrix $P1$ already defined leads to:

$$Q = \begin{bmatrix} 0.5 & 0.2 & 0.1 & 0.2 & 0.0 \\ 0.1 & 0.6 & 0.1 & 0.1 & 0.1 \\ 0.0 & 0.3 & 0.5 & 0.1 & 0.1 \\ 0.0 & 0.0 & 0.2 & 0.7 & 0.1 \\ 0.0 & 0.0 & 0.0 & 0.5 & 0.5 \end{bmatrix}$$

3.2 Lumpability

Ordinary lumpability is another efficient technique to combine with stochastic bounds [36]. Unlike the former algorithms, lumpability implies a state space reduction. The algorithms are based on Algorithm 1 and on the decomposition of the chain into macro-states. Again we assume that the states are ordered according to the macro-state partition. Let r be the number of macro-states. Let $b(k)$ and $e(k)$ be the indices of the first state and the last state, respectively, of macro-state A_k. First, let us recall the definition of ordinary lumpability.

Definition 9 (ordinary lumpability) *Let Q be the matrix of an irreducible finite DTMC, let A_k be a partition of the states of the chain. The chain is ordinary lumpable according to partition A_k, if and only if for all states e and f in the same arbitrary macro state A_i, we have:*

$$\sum_{j \in A_k} q_{e,j} = \sum_{j \in A_k} q_{f,j} \quad \forall \ macro-state \ A_k$$

Ordinary lumpability constraints are consistent with the st-monotonicity and they provide a simple characterization for matrix Q.

Theorem 6 *Let Q be an st-monotone matrix which is an upper bound for P. Assume that Q is ordinary lumpable for partition A_k and let $Q^{m,l}$ and $P^{m,l}$ be the blocks of transitions from set A_m to set A_l for Q and P respectively, then for all m and l, block $Q^{m,l}$ is st-monotone.*

Indeed, since Q is st-monotone we have:

$$\sum_{j=a}^{n} Q(i,j) \leq \sum_{j=a}^{n} Q(i+1,j) \tag{3}$$

But as Q is ordinary lumpable, if i and $i+1$ are in the same macro-state we have:

$$\sum_{j \in A_r} Q(i,j) = \sum_{j \in A_r} Q(i+1,j) \quad \forall r$$

So we can subtract in both terms of relation 3 partial sums on the macro state which are all equal due to ordinary lumpability. Therefore, assume that a, i and $i+1$ are in the same macro state A_k, we get

$$\sum_{j \geq a, j \in A_k} Q(i,j) \leq \sum_{j \geq a, j \in A_k} Q(i+1,j)$$

The algorithm computes the matrix column by column. Each block needs two steps. The first step is based on Algorithm 1 while second step modifies the first column of the block to satisfy the ordinary lumpability constraint. More precisely, the first step uses the same relations as Algorithm 1 but it has to take into account that the first row of P and Q may now be different due to the second step. The lumpability constraint is only known at the end of the first step. Recall that ordinary lumpability is due to a constant row sum for the block. Thus after the first step, we know how to modify the first column of the block to obtain a constant row sum. Furthermore due to st-monotonicity, we know that the maximal row sum is reached for the last row of the block. In step 2, we modify the first column of the block taking into account the last row sum. Once a block has been computed, it is now possible to compute the block on the left.

Algorithm 4   Construction of an ordinary lumpable st-monotone upper bounding DTMC Q:

$q_{1,n} = p_{1,n}$;
for $x = r, r-1, \ldots, 1$ do
    for $l = e(x)..b(x)$ do $q_{1,l} = \sum_{j=l}^{n} p_{1,l} - \sum_{j=l+1}^{n} q_{1,j}$;
        for $i = 2, 3, \ldots, n$ do
            $q_{i,l} = \max(\sum_{j=l}^{n} q_{i-1,j}, \sum_{j=l}^{n} p_{i,l}) - \sum_{j=l+1}^{n} q_{i,j}$;
        od
        for $y = 1, 2, \ldots, r$ do
            $c = \sum_{j=b(y)}^{e(y)} q_{e(y),j}$;
            for $i = b(y), \ldots, e(y) - 1$ do $q_{i,b(y)} = c - \sum_{j=b(y)+1}^{e(y)} q_{i,j}$; od
        od
    od
od

Let us illustrate the two steps on a simple example using matrix $P1$ formerly defined. Assume that we divide the state-space into two macro-states: $(1, 2)$ and $(3, 4, 5)$. We show the first block after the first step (the matrix on the left) and after the second step.

$$\left[\begin{array}{ccc} 0.1 & 0.2 & 0.0 \\ 0.1 & 0.1 & 0.1 \\ \hline 0.5 & 0.1 & 0.1 \\ \end{array}\right] \qquad \left[\begin{array}{ccc} 0.5 & 0.2 & 0.0 \\ 0.5 & 0.1 & 0.1 \\ \hline 0.5 & 0.1 & 0.1 \\ \end{array}\right]$$

This algorithm is used in the next section for the analysis of a mechanism for high speed networks. Most of the algorithms presented here may be applied but the best results, for this particular problem, were found with this last approach.

3.3   Class C Stochastic Matrices

Some stochastic matrices also have a closed form steady-state solution, for instance, the class C matrices defined in [4].

Definition 10 *A stochastic matrix $Q = (q_{i,j})_{1 \leq i,j \leq n}$ belongs to class C, if for each column j there exists a real constant c_j satisfying the following conditions: $q_{i+1,j} = q_{i,j} + c_j$, $1 \leq i \leq n - 1$. Since Q is a stochastic matrix, the sum of elements in each row must be equal to 1, thus $\sum_{j=1}^{n} c_j = 0$.*

For instance, the matrix $\begin{bmatrix} 0.45 & 0.15 & 0.4 \\ 0.35 & 0.20 & 0.45 \\ 0.25 & 0.25 & 0.5 \end{bmatrix}$ is in class C. It is also st-monotone. These matrices have several interesting properties and we also consider this class for "icx" ordering in section 5. First the steady-state distribution of Q can be computed in linear time:

$$\pi_j = q_{1,j} + c_j \frac{\sum_{j=1}^n j \, q_{1,j} - 1}{1 - \sum_{j=1}^n j \, c_j} \tag{4}$$

The st-monotonicity characterization is also quite simple in this class:

Proposition 2 *Let P be a stochastic matrix belonging to class C. P is st-monotone if and only if $\sum_{k=j}^n c_k \geq 0$, $\forall j \in \{1, \ldots, n\}$.*

The algorithm to obtain a monotone upper bound Q of class C for an arbitrary matrix P has been presented in [4]. First remark that since the upper bounding matrix Q belongs to class C, we must determine its first row $q_{1,j}$, $1 \leq j \leq n$, and the columns coefficients c_j, $1 \leq j \leq n$ rather than all the elements of Q. Within former algorithms the elements of Q are linked by inequalities but now we add the linear relations which define the C class. For instance we have $q_{n,n} = q_{1,n} + n \times c_n$. Therefore we must choose carefully $q_{1,n}$ and c_n to insure that $0 \leq q_{n,n} \leq 1$. Note that x^+ denotes as usual $max(x, 0)$.

Algorithm 5 Construction of a st-monotone upper bounding DTMC Q which belongs to class C:

$$q_{1,n} = \max_{1 \leq i \leq n-1} \left[\frac{(n-1)p_{i,n} - (i-1)}{n-i} \right]$$

$$c_n = \left[\max_{2 \leq i \leq n} \left(\frac{p_{i,n} - q_{1,n}}{i-1} \right) \right]^+$$

for $j = n-1, n-2, \ldots, 2$ do

$$\alpha_j = \max_{2 \leq i \leq n} \left[\frac{\sum_{k=j}^n p_{i,k} - \sum_{k=j}^n q_{1,k}}{i-1} \right]$$

$$g_i = \frac{n-1}{n-i} \left[\sum_{k=j}^n p_{i,k} - \sum_{k=j+1}^n q_{i,k} \right] + \frac{i-1}{n-i} \left[\sum_{k=j+1}^n q_{n,k} - 1 \right]$$

$$q_{1,j} = \left[\max_{1 \leq i \leq n-1} g_i \right]^+$$

$$c_j = \max(\frac{-q_{1,j}}{n-1}, \alpha_j^+ - \sum_{k=j+1}^n c_k)$$

od

$$q_{1,1} = 1 - \sum_{j=2}^n q_{1,j}$$

Again consider an example: let $P5$ be a matrix which does not belong to class C, and Q its upper bounding matrix computed through algorithm 5.

$$P5 = \begin{bmatrix} 0.5 & 0.1 & 0.4 \\ 0.7 & 0.1 & 0.2 \\ 0.3 & 0.2 & 0.5 \end{bmatrix} \qquad Q = \begin{bmatrix} 0.5 & 0.1 & 0.4 \\ 0.4 & 0.15 & 0.45 \\ 0.3 & 0.2 & 0.5 \end{bmatrix}$$

Since $c_3 = 0.05$, $c_2 = 0.05$ $c_1 = -0.1$, Q belongs to class C. The steady-state distributions are :

$$\pi_{P5} = (0.4456, 0.1413, 0.4130) \quad \pi_Q = (0.3941, 0.1529, 0.4529) \quad and \quad \pi_{P5} <_{st} \pi_Q$$

3.4   Partition and Stochastic Complement

The stochastic complement was initially proposed by Meyer in [26] to uncouple Markov chains and to provide a simple approximation for steady-state. Here we propose a completely different idea based on an easy resolution of the stochastic complement. Let us consider a block decomposition of Q: $\begin{pmatrix} A & B \\ C & D \end{pmatrix}$, where A, B, C, and D are matrices of size $n_0 * n_0$, $n_0 * n_1$, $n_1 * n_0$ and $n_1 * n_1$ (with $n_0 + n_1 = n$). We know that $I - D$ is not singular if P is not reducible [26]. We decompose π into two components π_0 and π_1 to obtain the stochastic complement formulation for the steady-state equation:

$$\begin{cases} \pi_0 \ R = 0 \\ \pi_0 \ r = 1 \\ \pi_1 = \pi_0 \ H \end{cases} \tag{5}$$

where $H = B(I - D)^{-1}$, $R = I - A - HC$ and $r = e_0 + He_1$.

Following Quessette [17], we chose to partition the states such that matrix D is upper triangular with positive diagonal elements. It should be clear that this partition is not mandatory for the theory of stochastic complement. However it simplifies the computation of H. Such a partition is always possible, even if for some cases it implies that n_1 is very small [17].

It is quite simple to derive from Algorithm 1 an algorithm which builds a matrix of this form once the partition has been fixed. The algorithm has two steps. The first step is Algorithm 1. Then we remove the transitions in the lower triangle of D and sum up their probabilities in the corresponding diagonal elements of D.

3.5   Single Input Macro State Markov Chain

Feinberg and Chiu [14] have studied chains divided into macro-states where the transition entering a macro-state must go through exactly one node. This node is denoted as the input node of the macro-state. They have developed an algorithm to efficiently compute the steady-state distribution by decomposition. It consists of the resolution of the macro-state in isolation and the analysis of the chain reduced to input nodes. Unlike ordinary lumpability, the assumptions of the theorem are based on the graph of the transitions and do not take into account the real transition rates.

It is very easy to modify Algorithm 1 to create a Single Input Macro State Markov chain. We assume that for every macro state, the input state is the last state of the macro state. Thus the matrix Q looks like this:

$$\left[\begin{array}{c|c|c} A & \begin{array}{c}\cdots\ \ \cdots\\ \cdots 0\cdots\\ \cdots\ \ \cdots\end{array} & \begin{array}{c}\cdots\ \ \cdots\\ \cdots 0\cdots\\ \cdots\ \ \cdots\end{array} \\ \hline \begin{array}{c}\cdots\ \ \cdots\\ \cdots 0\cdots\\ \cdots\ \ \cdots\end{array} & B & \begin{array}{c}\cdots\ \ \cdots\\ \cdots 0\cdots\\ \cdots\ \ \cdots\end{array} \\ \hline \begin{array}{c}\cdots\ \ \cdots\\ \cdots 0\cdots\\ \cdots\ \ \cdots\end{array} & \begin{array}{c}\cdots\ \ \cdots\\ \cdots 0\cdots\\ \cdots\ \ \cdots\end{array} & C \end{array}\right]$$

The algorithm is based on the following decomposition into three types of block : diagonal blocks, upper triangle and lower triangle. The elements of diagonal blocks are computed using the same equalities as in Algorithm 1:

$$\begin{cases} Q_{1,j} &= \sum_{k=j}^{n} P_{1,k} - \sum_{k=j+1}^{n} Q_{1,k} \\ Q_{i+1,j} &= max(\sum_{k=j}^{n} Q_{i,k}, \sum_{k=j}^{n} P_{i+1,k}) - \sum_{k=j+1}^{n} Q_{i+1,k} \end{cases} \tag{6}$$

The elements of blocks in upper and lower triangles have the "single input" structure : several columns of zero followed by a last column which is positive. Furthermore, lower and upper triangles differ because the elements of lower triangle of Q must follows inequalities which take into account the diagonal blocks of Q. Let us denote by $f(i)$ the lower index of the set which contains state i. Then for all i, j in the upper triangle, we just have to sum up the elements of P (take care of the lower index $f(j)$ on the summation of the elements of P):

$$\begin{cases} Q_{1,n} &= \sum_{k=f(n)}^{n} P_{1,k} \\ Q_{1,j} &= \sum_{k=f(j)}^{n} P_{1,k} - \sum_{k=j+1}^{n} Q_{1,k} \\ Q_{i+1,j} &= max(\sum_{k=j}^{n} Q_{i,k}, \sum_{k=f(j)}^{n} P_{i+1,k}) - \sum_{k=j+1}^{n} Q_{i+1,k} \end{cases} \tag{7}$$

And for all i, j in the lower triangle (here the lower index $f(j)$ is also also used in the summation of the elements in the former row of Q):

$$\{ Q_{i+1,j} = max(\sum_{k=f(j)}^{n} Q_{i,k}, \sum_{k=f(j)}^{n} P_{i+1,k}) - \sum_{k=j+1}^{n} Q_{i+1,k} \tag{8}$$

The derivation of the algorithm is straightforward. Again let us apply this algorithm on matrix $P1$ with partition into two sets of size 2 and 3 to obtain matrix Q (we also give the values of f for all the indices):

$$f = (1,1,3,3,3) \quad Q = \left[\begin{array}{cc|ccc} 0.5 & 0.2 & 0.0 & 0.0 & 0.3 \\ 0.1 & 0.6 & 0.0 & 0.0 & 0.3 \\ \hline 0.0 & 0.3 & 0.4 & 0.0 & 0.3 \\ 0.0 & 0.1 & 0.1 & 0.5 & 0.3 \\ 0.0 & 0.2 & 0.0 & 0.3 & 0.5 \end{array}\right]$$

This structure have been used by several authors even if their proofs of comparison are usually based on sample-path theorem [19,24,25].

3.6   Quasi Birth and Death Process

Finally, we have to briefly mention QBD matrices. They have a well-known algorithmic solution [23] but clearly it is not always possible to build an upper bounding st-monotone matrix which is block-tridiagonal. However, it is possible to derive some generalization of Algorithm 1 to get a QBD is the initial matrix has upper bounded transitions to the right (i.e., there exist a small integer k such that for all indices, if $j - i > k$ then $P(i, j) = 0$). The example presented in [24] is partially based on such a structure.

4   A Real Example with Large State Space

As an example, we present the analysis of a buffer policy which combines the PushOut mechanism for the space management and a Head Of Line service discipline. We assume that there exist two types of packets with distinct loss rate requirements. In the sequel, we denote as high priority, the packets which have the highest requirements, i.e., the smallest loss ratio. A low priority packet which arrives in a full buffer is lost. If the buffer is not full, both types of packets are accepted. The PushOut mechanism specifies that when the buffer is full, an arriving high priority packet pushes out of the buffer a low priority one if there is any in the buffer. Otherwise the high priority packet is lost. For the sake of simplicity, we assume that packet size is constant. This is consistent with ATM cells but it is clearly a modeling simplification for other networks. Such a mechanism has been proposed for ATM networks [18]. We further assume that the low priority packets are scheduled before high priority packets (recall that the priority level is based on the access). We assume that the departure due to service completion always takes place just before the arrivals.

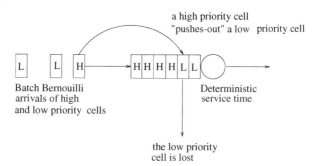

Fig. 1. Push-Out mechanism description

As the buffer size is B, the number of states is $(B + 1)(B + 2)/2$ if the arrivals follow a simple batch process. For the sake of simplicity we assume that the batch size is between 0 and 2. We use the following representation for the state space (T, H) where T is the total number of packets and H is the number of high priority packets. The states are ordered according to a lexicographic non decreasing ordering. It must be clear at this point that the ordering of the state is a very important issue. First, the rewards have to be non decreasing functions of the state indices. Furthermore, as the st-monotone property is based on the state representation and ordering, the accuracy of the results may depend on this ordering. Here, we are interested in the the expected number of lost packet per slot. Let us denote by R^i_M this expectation for type i packets and let $R = R^H + R^L$. The difficult problem here is the computation of R^H. Indeed R can be computed with a smaller chain since the Pushout mechanism does not change the global number of losses. It is sufficient to analyze the global number of packets (i.e without distinction). Such a chain has only $B + 1$ states if we use a simple batch arrival process. For realistic values of buffer size (i.e. 1000), such a chain is very simple to solve with usual numerical algorithms. However for the same value of B, the chain of the HOL+Pushout mechanisms has roughly $5 \cdot 10^5$ states. So, we use Algorithm 4 to get a lumpable bounding matrix. And we analyze the macro-state chain. First let us describe the ordering of the states and the rewards. Let p^H_k be the probability of k arrivals of high priority packets during one slot.

$$R^H = \sum_{(T,H)} \Pi(T, H) \ p^H_2 \ max(0, (H + 2 - B - 1_{T=H}))$$

Where $1_{T=H}$ is an indicator function which states if one high priority packet can leave the buffer at the end of the slot after service completion ($T = H$ that there is no low priority packet). Thus $max(0, (H + 2 - B - 1_{T=H}))$ is the number of packets exceeding the buffer size. For this particular case, due to scheduling of arrivals and service, R^H can be computed in a more simpler expression :

$$R^H = p^H_2 \times \Pi(B, B)$$

Clearly, we have to estimate only one probability and the reward is a non decreasing function which is zero everywhere except for the last state where its value is one. For more general arrival process, the reward function is only slightly different.

The key idea to shorten the state space is to avoid the states with large value of low priority packets. So, we bound the matrix with an ordinary lumpable matrix Q with $o(B \times F)$ macro-states where the parameter F allows a trade-off between the computational complexity and the accuracy of the results. More precisely, we define macro-states (T, Y) where Y is constrained to evolve in the range $T..T - F$. If $Y = T - F$, then the state (T, Y) is a real macro-state which contains all the states (T, X) such that $X \leq T - F$. In this case Y is a upper bound of the number of high priority packets in the states which are aggregated. If $Y > T - F$ then the state contains only one state (T, X) where $Y = X$. So, Y represents exactly the number of high priority packets in the buffer (see figure 2). Clearly, if the value of F is large, we do not reduce the state space but we expect that the bound would be tight.

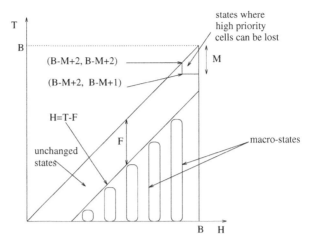

Fig. 2. The aggregated chain

In [16] we have analyzed small buffers to check the accuracy of the bound and large buffers to show the efficiency of the method. Here, we only present a typical comparison of these bounds for a small buffer of size 80 (these small value allows the computation of the exact result for comparison purpose). The load is 0.9 with 2/3 high level packets. With a sufficiently large value for F (typically 10), the algorithm gives accurate results. The exact result for R^H is in this example $8.9 \ 10^{-13}$. The bound with $F = 10$ is $9.5 10^{-13}$. Of course if F is too small, the result is worse and can reach 10^{-6} for $F = 2$. The exact chain has 3321 states while the bound with $F = 10$ is computed with a chain of size 798. The number of states is divided by 4 and we only lost few digits. It is worthy to remark that a reduction by an order on the states space implies a reduction by two or three orders on the computation times for the steady state distribution. And the reduction is much more important if the original chain is bigger. Typically, for a buffer size of 1000 and an aggregation factor F equal to 20, the bounding matrix obtained from Algorithm 5 has roughly 20000 states. The original state space is 25 times larger.

The results shows previously are very accurate. We have found several reasons for that property. First the distribution is skewed. Almost all the probability mass is concentrated on the states with a small number of packets. Moreover the first part of the initial matrix is already st-monotone. This property is due to the ordering of the states we have considered. Again, we have to emphasis that the states ordering is a crucial issue for st-bounds [11].

For instance, consider the matrix of the chain for a small buffer of size 4. The chain has 15 states ordered in a lexicographic way: $\{(0), (1,0), (1,1), (2,0), (2,1), (2,2), (3,0), (3,1), (3,2), (3,3), (4,0), (4,1), (4,2), (4,3), (4,4)\}$. Let us denote by p, q and r respectively the arrival probabilities of arrival for a batch of size 0, 1 or 2. And let a be the probability that an arriving packets is a low priority one. Similarly b is the probability for a high level packet. The distribution of packets types in a size 2 batch are respectively c for 2 low level packets, e for two high level, and d for a mixed batch. Independence assumption on the type of packets entering the queue lead to an important reduction of the number of parameter (for instance $c = a^2$). However, it is not necessary to illustrate the effect of Algorithm 5.

$$
P = \begin{pmatrix}
p|qa\ qb|rc\ rd\ re| & & & & & & & \\
 & p|qa\ qb|rc\ rd\ re| & & & & & & \\
 & p|qa\ qb|rc\ rd\ re| & & & & & & \\
 & p & qa\ qb & rc\ rd\ re & & & & \\
 & & p & qa\ qb & rc\ rd\ re & & & \\
 & & p & qa\ qb & rc\ rd\ re & & & \\
 & & p & qa\ qb & rc & rd & re & \\
 & & & p & qa\ qb & rc & rd & re \\
 & & & & p & qa\ qb & rc & rd & re \\
 & & & & p & qa\ qb & rc & rd & re \\
 & & & & p & qa + rc\ qb + rd & re & \\
 & & & & & p & qa + rc\ qb + rd & re \\
 & & & & & & p & qa + rc\ qb + rd & re \\
 & & & & & & & p & qa + rc\ qb + rd + re \\
 & & & & & & & p & qa + rc\ bq + rd + re
\end{pmatrix}
$$

A careful inspection of matrix P shows that the 10 first rows of the matrix already satisfy the st-monotone property. For a bigger buffer model, this property is still true for the states where the buffer is not full. We assume that $F = 2$, the only one non trivial values for such a small example). Thus, we consider two real macro-states : $\{(3, 2), (3, 3)\}$ and $\{(4, 2), (4, 3), (4, 4)\}$. Note that the initial matrix is already lumpable since the scheduling of service and arrivals imply that some states have similar transitions. For instance states (0), $(1, 0)$ and $(1, 1)$ can be gathered into one macro-state). We use this property in the resolution algorithm but we do not develop here to focus on the bounding algorithm. Algorithm 5 provides a lumpable matrix with the macro-states already defined which can be aggregated to obtain ($f = min(qb, rc)$ and $g = max(qb, rc)$):

$$
\begin{pmatrix}
p|qa\ qb|rc\ rd\ re| & & & & & & \\
 & p|qa\ qb|rc\ rd\ re| & & & & & \\
 & p|qa\ qb|rc\ rd\ re| & & & & & \\
 & p & qa\ qb & rc\ rd & re & & \\
 & & p & qa\ qb & rc\ rd + re & & \\
 & & p & qa\ qb & rc\ rd + re & & \\
 & & & p & qa\ qb & rc & rd & re \\
 & & & & p & qa & qb & rc & rd + re \\
 & & & & & p & qa + qb & & r \\
 & & & & & p & qa + f & g - rc & r \\
 & & & & & & p & qa + f & g + rd + re \\
 & & & & & & & p & q + r
\end{pmatrix}
$$

5   Algorithms for "icx" Comparison

Stoyan's proof in Theorem 4.2.5 of ([35], p.65]) that the monotonicity and the comparability of transition matrices yield sufficient conditions for chain comparison is not restricted to "st" ordering. Similarly, the definitions of the monotonicity and the comparison of stochastic matrices are much more general than the statements presented in section 2. First let us turn back to the definitions for "icx" ordering which is supposed to be more accurate than the st-ordering.

Definition 11 *Let X and Y be two random variables taking values on a totally ordered space. X is said to be less than Y ($X <_{icx} y =$ if and only if $E[f(X)] \leq E[f(Y)]$, for all non decreasing convex functions f, whenever the expectations exist.*

For discrete state space, it is also possible to use a matrix formulation through matrix K_{icx}. Let p and q be respectively the probability distribution vectors of X and Y. $X <_{icx} Y$ if and only if $pK_{icx} \leq qK_{icx}$, where K_{icx} is defined as following :

$$K_{icx} = \begin{bmatrix} 1 & 0 & 0 & \dots & 0 \\ 2 & 1 & 0 & \dots & 0 \\ 3 & 2 & 1 & \dots & 0 \\ \vdots & \vdots & \vdots & \ddots & \vdots \\ n & n-1 & n-2 & \dots & 1 \end{bmatrix}$$

This can be rewritten as follows :

$$X <_{icx} Y \Longleftrightarrow \sum_{k=i}^{n} (k-i+1)\, p_k \leq \sum_{k=i}^{n} (k-i+1)\, q_k, \quad \forall i \in \{1, \dots, n\}$$

Similarly, we can define the increasing concave ordering by the set nondecreasing concave functions. In this case $K_{icv} = -K_{icx}^T$, where A^T denotes the transpose of matrix A.

Clearly, the icx-comparison and the icx-monotonicity of stochastic matrices are defined in the same manner as the st-ordering (see definitions 2 and 3). However, the characterization of the $<_{icx}$-monotonicity through matrix K_{icx} must take into account the finiteness of matrix P. Indeed, the conditions $K_{icx}^{-1} P K_{icx} \geq 0$ provide sufficient conditions for the $<_{icx}$-monotonicity. It is known for a long time time that these conditions are also necessary for infinite chains.

For finite chains, the necessary conditions were unknown until recently. Moreover the conditions $K_{icx}^{-1} P K_{icx} \geq 0$ are very restrictive and they lead to a chain whose first and last states are absorbing. Thus, it was not possible to develop an algorithmic approach without an efficient necessary and sufficient condition for monotonicity. Recently, in [2], Benmammoun has proved such conditions for the icx-monotonicity of finite chains. This characterization is based on matrix Z_{icx} which is slightly different from matrix K_{icx}^{-1}.

$$K_{icx}^{-1} = \begin{bmatrix} 1 & 0 & 0 \ldots 0 \\ -2 & 1 & 0 \ldots 0 \\ 1 & -2 & 1 \ldots 0 \\ \vdots & \vdots & \vdots & \ddots & \vdots \\ 0 & & \ldots & 1 & -2 & 1 \end{bmatrix} \quad Z_{icx} = \begin{bmatrix} 1 & 0 & 0 \ldots 0 \\ -1 & 1 & 0 \ldots 0 \\ 1 & -2 & 1 \ldots 0 \\ \vdots & \vdots & \vdots & \ddots & \vdots \\ 0 & & \ldots & 1 & -2 & 1 \end{bmatrix}$$

5.1 Basic Algorithm

The sufficient conditions to compare Markov chains through the monotonicity and the comparability of matrices (see theorem 1) are also valid for the icx-ordering. Therefore, it is possible to design an algorithm to construct an icx-monotone and upper bounding chain based on Benmammoun's characterization.

Algorithm 6 An icx-monotone upper bound Q:

$q_{1,n} = p_{1,n}$;
$q_{2,n} = max(q_{1,n}, p_{2,n})$;
for $i = 3, \ldots, n$ do $q_{i,n} = max(p_{i,n}, 2q_{i-1,n} - q_{i-2,n})$; od
for $j = n - 1, n - 2, \cdots, 2$ do

$\quad q_{1,j} = \sum_{k=j}^{n}(k - j + 1)p_{1,k} - \sum_{k=j+1}^{n}(k - j + 1)q_{1,k}$;

$\quad q_{2,j} = max \left(\sum_{k=j}^{n}(k - j + 1)p_{2,k}, \sum_{k=j}^{n}(k - j + 1)q_{1,k} \right)$
$\quad\quad - \sum_{k=j+1}^{n}(k - j + 1)q_{2,k}$;

$\quad$ for $i = 3, 4, \cdots, n$ do

$\quad\quad q_{i,j} = max \left(\sum_{k=j}^{n}(k - j + 1)p_{i,k}, \right.$

$\quad\quad\quad 2\sum_{k=j}^{n}(k - j + 1)q_{i-1,k} - \left. \sum_{k=j}^{n}(k - j + 1)q_{i-2,k} \right)$
$\quad\quad\quad - \sum_{k=j+1}^{n}(k - j + 1)q_{i,k}$;
$\quad$ od
od
for $i = 1, 2 \cdots n$ do $q_{i,1} = 1 - \sum_{j=2}^{n} q_{i,j}$; od

---

Unfortunately, the output of this algorithm is not always a stochastic matrix as we may obtain elements larger than 1.0. First, we apply this algorithm to matrix $P6$ and the output is a stochastic upper bound Q:

$$P6 = \begin{bmatrix} 0.5 & 0.15 & 0.35 \\ 0.3 & 0.4 & 0.3 \\ 0.45 & 0.1 & 0.45 \end{bmatrix} \quad Q = \begin{bmatrix} 0.5 & 0.15 & 0.35 \\ 0.35 & 0.3 & 0.35 \\ 0.4 & 0.25 & 0.45 \end{bmatrix}$$

However, for matrix $P7$, the output of Algorithm 6 is not a stochastic matrix since $Q_{3,3} > 1$.

$$P7 = \begin{bmatrix} 0.5 & 0.15 & 0.35 \\ 0.3 & 0.0 & 0.7 \\ 0.45 & 0.1 & 0.45 \end{bmatrix}$$

Indeed, the last column of Q is:

$$Q = \begin{bmatrix} 0.35 \\ 0.7 \\ 1.05 \end{bmatrix}$$

Several heuristics may be used to solve this problem. Further researches are still necessary to obtain a simple and efficient algorithm.

5.2   Class C Matrices

Beside, the closed form solution of the stationary distribution, class C matrices have nice properties about stochastic monotonicity. First, we present the stochastic monotonicity characterization for this class and then we show an algorithm to construct an icx-monotone, upper bounding, class C matrix.

Proposition 3

$$P \ is \ icx - monotone \ \Longleftrightarrow \ \sum_{k=j}^{n}(k - j + 1) \ c_k \geq 0, \quad \forall j \in \{1, \ldots, n\}$$

Proposition 4 *If P is in class C, then*

$$P \ is \ st - monotone \ \Longrightarrow \ P \ is \ icx - monotone$$

Let us emphasize here by an example, that, in general, st-monotonicity does not imply icx-monotonicity:

$$P = \begin{bmatrix} 0.6 & 0.4 & 0 \\ 0.2 & 0.2 & 0.6 \\ 0.1 & 0.3 & 0.6 \end{bmatrix}$$

Clearly, P is st-monotone. On the other hand, if we consider $p = [0.2 \ 0.4 \ 0.4]$ and $q = [0.3 \ 0.1 \ 0.6]$. $pP = [0.24 \ 0.28 \ 0.48]$ and $qP = [0.26 \ 0.32 \ 0.42]$. And $p <_{icx} q$ is true while $pP <_{icx} qP$ is false. Thus P is not icx-monotone.

In the following algorithm we compute an icx-monotone, upper bounding, class C matrix, Q for a given matrix P [4] As in the st-ordering case, this algorithm consists in computing the first row $q_{1,j}$, $1 \leq j \leq n$ and the constant c_j, $1 \leq j \leq n$. In fact, these parameters take values within an interval $([c_j, \overline{c_j}])$ and $[q_{1,j}, \overline{q_{1,j}}])$. Since we construct an upper bound, one must intuitively choose the smallest values for these parameters in order to have elements which are as close as possible to the original ones. Moreover, we define a constant $const$ which is greater than 1, but less than $\overline{c_j}$. By doing so, all entries of Q are positive, thus Q is irreducible.

Algorithm 7 Construction of an icx-monotone upper bounding DTMC Q which belongs to class C:

$$\underline{q_{1,n}} = max_{1\leq i\leq n-1}\left[\frac{(n-1)p_{i,n}-i+1}{n-i}\right]; \; q_{1,n} = \underline{q_{1,n}} + \frac{1-\underline{q_{1,n}}}{const};$$

$$\underline{c_n} = max_{2\leq i\leq n}\left[\frac{p_{i,n}-q_{1,n}}{i-1}\right]; \; \overline{c_n} = \frac{1-q_{1,n}}{n-1};$$

if $\underline{c_n} < 0$ then $c_n = 0$ else $c_n = \underline{c_n} + \frac{\overline{c_n}-\underline{c_n}}{const};$

for $j = n - 1, n - 2, \cdots, 2$ do

$$f(i,j) = \frac{n-1}{n-i}\left[\sum_{k=j}^{n}(k-j+1)p_{i,k} - \sum_{k=j+1}^{n}(k-j+1)q_{i,k}\right]$$
$$- \frac{i-1}{n-i}[1 - \sum_{k=j+1}^{n} q_{n,k}];$$

$$\underline{q_{1,j}} = (max_{1\leq i\leq n-1} \; f(i,j))^{+}; \; q_{1,j} = \underline{q_{1,j}} + \frac{1-\sum_{k=j+1}^{n} q_{1,k}-\underline{q_{1,j}}}{const};$$

$$\alpha_j = max_{2\leq i\leq n}\left(\frac{\sum_{k=j}(k-j+1)p_{i,k}-\sum_{k=j+1}^{n}(k-j+1)q_{i,k}-q_{1,j}}{i-1}\right);$$

$$\underline{c_j} = max(\alpha_j, \frac{-q_{1,j}}{n-1}); \; \overline{c_j} = \frac{1-\sum_{k=j+1}^{n} q_{n,k}-q_{1,j}}{n-1};$$

if $\underline{c_j} < -\sum_{k=j=1}^{n}(k-j+1)c_k$ then $c_j = -\sum_{k=j+1}^{n}(k-j+1)c_k$

      else $c_j = \underline{c_j}\frac{\overline{c_j}-\underline{c_j}}{const};$

od

$$q_{1,1} = 1 - \sum_{j=2}^{n} q_{1,j};$$
$$c_1 = -\sum_{j=2}^{n} c_j;$$

We illustrate the application of this algorithm on matrix $P7$.

$$P7 = \begin{bmatrix} 0.25 & 0.2 & 0.25 & 0.3 \\ 0.15 & 0.1 & 0.65 & 0.1 \\ 0.35 & 0.05 & 0.15 & 0.45 \\ 0.3 & 0.2 & 0.1 & 0.4 \end{bmatrix} \quad Q = \begin{bmatrix} 0.2718 & 0.1962 & 0.162 & 0.37 \\ 0.279 & 0.158 & 0.136 & 0.427 \\ 0.2863 & 0.1199 & 0.1098 & 0.484 \\ 0.2935 & 0.0818 & 0.0837 & 0.541 \end{bmatrix}$$

Matrix Q obtained by this algorithm belongs to class C with $c_1 = 0.00723$, $c_2 = -0.03813$, $c_3 = -0.0261$, $c_4 = 0.057$. Their steady-state distributions are $\pi_P = (0.2755, 0.1497, 0.2354, 0.3393)$ and $\pi_Q = (0.2846, 0.1286, 0.1157, 0.4711)$ and we have $\pi_P <_{icx} \pi_P$.

6   Conclusions

Strong stochastic bounds are not limited to sample-path proofs. It is now possible to compute bounds of the steady-state distribution directly from the chain. This approach may be specially useful for high speed networks modeling where the performance requirements are thresholds. Using the algorithmic approach we survey in this paper, a sample-path proof is not necessary anymore and these algorithms may be integrated into software performance tools based on Markov chains. Generalizations to other orderings or to computation of transient measures are still important problems for performance analysis.

References

1. Abu-Amsha O., VincentJ.-M.: An algorithm to bound functionals of Markov chains with large state space. Int: 4th INFORMS Conference on Telecommunications, Boca Raton, Florida, (1998)
2. Benmammoun M.: Encadrement stochastiques et évaluation de performances des réseaux, PHD, Université de Versailles St-Quentin en Yvelines, (2002)
3. Benmammoun M., Fourneau J.M., Pekergin N., Troubnikoff A.: An algorithmic and numerical approach to bound the performance of high speed networks, Submitted, (2002)
4. Benmammoun M., Pekergin N.: Closed form stochastic bounds on the stationary distribution of Markov chains. To appear in Probability in the Engineering and Informational Sciences, (2002)
5. Boujdaine F., Dayar T., Fourneau J.M., Pekergin N., Saadi S., Vincent J.M.: A new proof of st-comparison for polynomials of a stochastic matrix, Submitted, (2002)
6. Buchholz P.: An aggregation\disaggregation algorithm for stochastic automata networks. In: Probability in the Engineering and Informational Sciences, V 11, (1997) 229–253
7. Buchholz P.: Projection methods for the analysis of stochastic automata networks. In: Proc. of the 3rd International Workshop on the Numerical Solution of Markov Chains, B. Plateau, W. J. Stewart, M. Silva, (Eds.), Prensas Universitarias de Zaragoza, Spain, (1999) pp. 149–168.
8. Courtois P.J., Semal P.: Bounds for the positive eigenvectors of nonnegative matrices and for their approximations by decomposition. In: Journal of ACM, V 31 (1984) 804–825
9. Courtois P.J., Semal P.: Computable bounds for conditional steady-state probabilities in large Markov chains and queueing models. In: IEEE JSAC, V4, N6, (1986)
10. Dayar T., Fourneau J.M., Pekergin N.: Transforming stochastic matrices for stochastic comparison with the st-order, Submitted, (2002)
11. Dayar T., Pekergin, N.: Stochastic comparison, reorderings, and nearly completely decomposable Markov chains. In: Proceedings of the International Conference on the Numerical Solution of Markov Chains (NSMC'99), (Ed. Plateau, B. Stewart, W.), Prensas universitarias de Zaragoza. (1999) 228–246
12. Dayar T., Stewart W. J.: Comparison of partitioning techniques for two-level iterative solvers on large sparse Markov chains. In: SIAM Journal on Scientific Computing V21 (2000) 1691–1705.
13. Donatelli S.: Superposed generalized stochastic Petri nets: definition and efficient solution. In: Proc. 15th Int. Conf. on Application and Theory of Petri Nets, Zaragoza, Spain, (1994)
14. Feinberg B.N., Chiu S.S.: A method to calculate steady-state distributions of large Markov chains by aggregating states. In: Oper. Res, V 35 (1987) 282-290
15. Fernandes P., Plateau B., Stewart W.J.: Efficient descriptor-vector multiplications in stochastic automata networks. In: Journal of the ACM, V45 (1998) 381–414.

16. Fourneau J.M., Pekergin N., Taleb H.: An Application of Stochastic Ordering to the Analysis of the PushOut Mechanism. In Performance Modelling and Evaluation of ATM Networks, Chapman and Hall, (1995) 227–244
17. Fourneau J.M., Quessette F.: Graphs and Stochastic Automata Networks. In: Proceedings of the 2nd Int. Workshop on the Numerical Solution of Markov Chains, Raleigh, USA, (1995)
18. Hébuterne G., Gravey A.: A space priority queueing mechanism for multiplexing ATM channels. In: ITC Specialist Seminar, Computer Network and ISDN Systems, V20 (1990) 37–43
19. Golubchik, L. and Lui, J.: Bounding of performance measures for a threshold-based queuing systems with hysteresis. In: Proceeding of ACM SIGMETRICS'97, (1997) 147–157
20. Hillston J., Kloul L.: An Efficient Kronecker Representation for PEPA Models. In: PAPM'2001, Aachen Germany, (2001)
21. Keilson J., Kester A.: Monotone matrices and monotone Markov processes. In: Stochastic Processes and Their Applications, V5 (1977) 231–241
22. Kijima M.: Markov Processes for stochastic modeling. Chapman & Hall (1997)
23. Latouche G., Ramaswami V.: Introduction to Matrix Analytic Methods in Stochastic Modeling. SIAM, (1999)
24. Lui, J. Muntz, R. and Towsley, D.: Bounding the mean response time of the minimum expected delay routing policy: an algorithmic approach. In: IEEE Transactions on Computers. V44 N12 (1995) 1371–1382
25. Lui, J. Muntz, R. and Towsley, D.: Computing performance bounds of Fork-Join parallel programs under a multiprocessing environment. In: IEEE Transactions on Parallel and Distributed Systems. V9 N3 (1998) 295–311
26. Meyer C.D.: Stochastic complementation, uncoupling Markov chains, and the theory of nearly reducible systems. In: SIAM Review. V31 (1989) 240–272.
27. Pekergin N.: Stochastic delay bounds on fair queueing algorithms. In: Proceedings of INFOCOM'99 New York (1999) 1212–1220
28. Pekergin N.: Stochastic performance bounds by state reduction. In: Performance Evaluation V36-37 (1999) 1–17
29. Plateau B.: On the stochastic structure of parallelism and synchronization models for distributed algorithms. In: Proceedings of the SIGMETRICS Conference on Measurement and Modeling of Computer Systems, Texas (1985) 147–154
30. Plateau B., Fourneau J.-M., Lee K.-H.: PEPS: A package for solving complex Markov models of parallel systems. In: Modeling Techniques and Tools for Computer Performance Evaluation, R. Puigjaner, D. Potier (Eds.), Spain (1988) 291–305
31. Plateau B., Fourneau J.-M.: A methodology for solving Markov models of parallel systems. In: Journal of Parallel and Distributed Computing. V12 (1991) 370–387.
32. Shaked M., Shantikumar J.G.: Stochastic Orders and Their Applications. In: Academic Press, California (1994)
33. Stewart W.J., Atif K., Plateau B.: The numerical solution of stochastic automata networks. In: European Journal of Operational Research V86 (1995) 503–525
34. Stewart W. J.: Introduction to the Numerical Solution of Markov Chains. Princeton University Press, (1994)
35. Stoyan D.: Comparison Methods for Queues and Other Stochastic Models. John Wiley & Sons, Berlin, Germany, (1983)
36. Truffet L.: Reduction Technique For Discrete Time Markov Chains on Totally Ordered State Space Using Stochastic Comparisons. In: Journal of Applied Probability, V37 N3 (2000)

37. Uysal E., Dayar T.: Iterative methods based on splittings for stochastic automata networks. In: European Journal of Operational Research, V 110 (1998) 166–186
38. Van Dijk N.: Error bound analysis for queueing networks" In: Performane 96 Tutorials, Lausanne, (1996)

Dynamic Scheduling via Polymatroid Optimization

David D. Yao

Columbia University, New York, NY 10027, USA,
yao@ieor.columbia.edu,
http://www.ieor.columbia.edu/~yao

Abstract. Dynamic scheduling of multi-class jobs in queueing systems
has wide ranging applications, but in general is a very difficult control
problem. Here we focus on a class of systems for which *conservation laws*
hold. Consequently, the performance space becomes a *polymatroid* — a
polytope with a matroid-like structure, with all the vertices corresponding to the performance under priority rules, and all the vertices are easily
identified. This structure translates the optimal control problem to an
optimization problem, which, under a linear objective, becomes a special
linear program; and the optimal schedule is a priority rule. In a more
general setting, conservation laws extend to so-called generalized conservation laws, under which the performance space becomes more involved;
however, the basic structure that ensures the optimality of priority rules
remains intact. This tutorial provides an overview to the subject, focusing on the main ideas, basic mathematical facts, and computational
implications.

1 Polymatroid

1.1 Equivalent Definitions and Properties

We start with three equivalent definitions of a polymatroid. Definition 1 is the
most standard one; Definition 2 will later motivate the definition for EP; Definition 3 provide a contrast against the structure of the EP in §4 (refer to Definition
7).

Throughout, $E = \{1, ..., n\}$ is a finite set; A^c denotes the complement of set
A: $A^c = E \setminus A$; and the terms, "increasing" and "decreasing" are used in the
non-strict sense, meaning "non-decreasing" and "non-increasing", respectively.

Definition 1. *(Welsh [47], Chapter 18) The following polytope*

$$\mathcal{P}(f) = \{ \ x \geq 0 : \sum_{i \in A} x_i \leq f(A), \ A \subseteq E \ \} \tag{1}$$

*is termed a polymatroid if the function $f : 2^E \mapsto \Re_+$ satisfies the following
properties:*

M.C. Calzarossa and S. Tucci (Eds.): Performance 2002, LNCS 2459, pp. 89–113, 2002.
© Springer-Verlag Berlin Heidelberg 2002

(i)   (normalized) $f(\emptyset) = 0$;
(ii)   (increasing)   if $A \subseteq B \subseteq E$, then $f(A) \leq f(B)$;
(iii) (submodular)   if $A, B \subseteq E$, then $f(A) + f(B) \geq f(A \cup B) + f(A \cap B)$.

In matroid parlance, a function f that satisfies the above properties is termed a "rank function." Also note that a companion to submodularity is *supermodularity*, defined as when the inequality in (iii) holds in the opposite direction ($\leq$).

We now present the second definition for polymatroid. Given a set function $f : 2^E \mapsto \Re_+$, with $f(\emptyset) = 0$, and a permutation π of $\{ 1, 2, \cdots, n \}$, the elements of the set E, we define a vector x^π with the following components (to simplify notation, x_{π_i} below is understood to be $x_{\pi_i}^\pi$):

$$x_{\pi_1} = f(\{\pi_1\})$$
$$x_{\pi_2} = f(\{\pi_1, \pi_2\}) - x_{\pi_1} = f(\{\pi_1, \pi_2\}) - f(\{\pi_1\})$$
$$\vdots$$
$$x_{\pi_n} = f(\{\pi_1, \pi_2, \cdots, \pi_n\}) - f(\{\pi_1, \pi_2, \cdots, \pi_{n-1}\})$$

x^π is termed a "vertex" of the polytope $\mathcal{P}(f)$ in (1). Note, however, that this terminology could be misleading, since *a priori* there is no guarantee that x^π necessarily belongs to the polytope, since we simply do not know, as yet, whether or not x^π defined as above satisfies the set of inequalities that define $\mathcal{P}(f)$ in (1). In fact, this is the key point in the second definition of polymatroid below.

Definition 2. $\mathcal{P}(f)$ *of (1) is a polymatroid if* $x^\pi \in \mathcal{P}(f)$ *for all permutation* π.

Here is a third definition.

Definition 3. $\mathcal{P}(f)$ *of (1) is a polymatroid if for any* $A \subset B \subseteq E$, *there exists a point* $x \in \mathcal{P}(f)$, *such that*

$$\sum_{i \in A} x_i = f(A) \qquad and \qquad \sum_{i \in B} x_i = f(B).$$

Below we show the three definitions are equivalent.

Theorem 1. *The above three definitions for polymatroid are equivalent.*

Proof. (Definition 1 $\Longrightarrow$ Definition 2)
That $x_{\pi_i} \geq 0$ for all i follows directly from the increasing property of f. For any $A \subseteq E$ and $\pi_i \in A$, since f is submodular, we have

$$f(A \cap \{\pi_1, \cdots, \pi_i\}) + f(\{\pi_1, \cdots, \pi_{i-1}\})$$
$$\geq f(A \cap \{\pi_1, \cdots, \pi_{i-1}\}) + f((A \cap \{\pi_1, \cdots, \pi_i\}) \cup \{\pi_1, \cdots, \pi_{i-1}\})$$
$$= f(A \cap \{\pi_1, \cdots, \pi_{i-1}\}) + f(\{\pi_1, \cdots, \pi_i\}),$$

which implies

$$f(\{\pi_1, \cdots, \pi_i\}) - f(\{\pi_1, \cdots, \pi_{i-1}\})$$
$$\leq f(A \cap \{\pi_1, \cdots, \pi_i\}) - f(A \cap \{\pi_1, \cdots, \pi_{i-1}\}).$$

Summing over $\pi_i \in A$, we have

$$\sum_{\pi_i \in A} x_{\pi_i} = \sum_{\pi_i \in A} (f(\{\pi_1, \cdots, \pi_i\}) - f(\{\pi_1, \cdots, \pi_{i-1}\}))$$

$$\leq \sum_{\pi_i \in A} f(A \cap \{\pi_1, \cdots, \pi_i\}) - f(A \cap \{\pi_1, \cdots, \pi_{i-1}\}) = f(A).$$

Hence, $x^\pi \in \mathcal{P}(f)$, and Definition 2 follows.

(Definition 2 $\Longrightarrow$ Definition 3)

For any given $A \subset B \subseteq E$, from Definition 2, it suffices to pick a vertex x^π, such that its first $|A|$ components constitute the set A, and its first $|B|$ components constitute the set B.

(Definition 3 $\Longrightarrow$ Definition 1)

Taking $A = \emptyset$ in Definition 3 yields $f(\emptyset) = 0$. Monotonicity is trivial, since $x_i \geq 0$. For submodularity, take any $A, B \subseteq E$, $A \neq B$; then there exists $x \in \mathcal{P}(f)$ such that

$$\sum_{A \cup B} x_i = f(A \cup B), \quad \text{and} \quad \sum_{A \cap B} x_i = f(A \cap B),$$

since $A \cap B \subset A \cup B$. Therefore,

$$f(A \cup B) + f(A \cap B) = \sum_{A \cup B} x_i + \sum_{A \cap B} x_i = \sum_{i \in A} x_i + \sum_{i \in B} x_i \leq f(A) + f(B),$$

where the inequality follows from $x \in \mathcal{P}(f)$.

1.2   Optimization

Here we consider the optimization problem of maximizing a linear function over the polymatroid $\mathcal{P}(f)$.

$$\text{(P)} \quad \max \sum_{i \in E} c_i \, x_i$$

$$\text{s.t.} \sum_{i \in A} x_i \leq f(A), \quad \text{for all } A \subseteq E,$$

$$x_i \geq 0, \quad \text{for all } i \in E.$$

Assume

$$c_1 \geq c_2 \geq \cdots \geq c_n \geq 0, \tag{2}$$

without loss of generality, since any negative c_i clearly results in the corresponding $x_i = 0$. Let $\pi = (1, 2, \cdots, n)$. Then, we claim that the vertex x^π in Definition 2 is the optimal solution to (P).

To verify the claim, we start with writing down the dual problem as follows:

$$(\mathbf{D}) \quad \min \sum_{A \subseteq E} y_A \, f(A)$$

$$\text{s.t.} \sum_{A \ni i} y_A \geq c_i, \qquad \text{for all } i \in E,$$

$$y_A \geq 0, \qquad \text{for all } A \subseteq E.$$

Define y^π, a candidate dual solution, componentwise as follows:

$$y^\pi_{\{1\}} = c_1 - c_2,$$
$$y^\pi_{\{1,2\}} = c_2 - c_3,$$

$$\vdots$$

$$y^\pi_{\{1,\dots,n-1\}} = c_{n-1} - c_n,$$
$$y^\pi_{\{1,\dots,n\}} = c_n;$$

and set $y^\pi_A = 0$, for all other $A \subseteq E$.

Now the claimed optimality follows from

(1) primal feasibility: x^π is a vertex of the polymatroid $\mathcal{P}(f)$, and hence is feasible by definition (refer to Definition 2);

(2) dual feasibility: that y^π is feasible is easily checked (in particular, non-negativity follows from (2));

(3) complementary slackness: also easily checked, in particular, the n binding constraints in $(\mathbf{P})$ that define the vertex x^π correspond to the n non-zero (not necessarily zero, to be precise) components of y^π listed above.

It is also easy to verify that the primal and the dual objectives are equal: letting $c_{n+1} := 0$, we have

$$\sum_{i \in E} c_i \, x^\pi_i = \sum_{i \in E} c_i \, [f(\{1, \cdots, i\}) - f(\{1, \cdots, i-1\})]$$

$$= \sum_{i=1}^{n} (c_i - c_{i+1}) f(\{1, \cdots, i\}) = \sum_{A \subseteq E} y^\pi_A f(A).$$

To summarize, x^π is optimal for $(\mathbf{P})$ and y^π is optimal for $(\mathbf{D})$. It is important to note that

(a) Primal feasibility is always satisfied, by definition of the polymatroid.

(b) It is the dual feasibility that determines the permutation π, which, by way of complementary slackness, points to a vertex of $\mathcal{P}(f)$ that is optimal.

More specifically, the sum of the dual variables yields the cost coefficients:

$$y^\pi_{\{1,\dots,i\}} + \cdots + y^\pi_{\{1,\dots,n\}} = c_i, \qquad i = 1, \dots, n; \tag{3}$$

the order of which [cf. (2)] decides the permutation π.

2   Conservation Laws

2.1   Polymatroid Structure

To relate to the last section, here $E = \{1, 2, ..., n\}$ denotes the set of all job classes, and x denotes the vector of performance measures of interest. For instance, x_i is the (long-run) average delay or throughput of job class i.

The conservation laws defined below were first formalized in Shanthikumar and Yao [39], where the connection to polymatroid was made. In [39], as well as subsequent papers in the literature, these laws are termed "strong conservation laws." Here, we shall simply refer to these as conservation laws.

Verbally, conservation laws can be summarized into the following two statements:

(i) the total performance (i.e., the sum) over all job classes in E is invariant under any admissible policy;

(ii) the total performance over any given subset, $A \subset E$, of job classes is minimized (or maximized) by offering priority to job classes in this subset over all other classes.

As a simple example, consider a system of two job classes. Each job (of either class) brings a certain amount of "work" (service requirement) to the system. Suppose the server serves (i.e., depletes work) at unit rate. Then it is not difficult to see that (i) the total amount of work, summing over all jobs of both classes that are present in the system, will remain invariant regardless of the actual policy that schedules the server, as long as it is non-idling; and (ii) if class 1 jobs are given preemptive priority over class 2 jobs, then the amount of work in system summing over class 1 jobs is minimized, namely, it cannot be further reduced by any other admissible policy.

We now state the formal definition of conservation laws. For any $A \subseteq E$, denote by $|A|$ the cardinality of A. Let $\mathcal{A}$ denote the space of all *admissible* policies — all non-anticipative and non-idling policies (see more details below), and x^u the performance vector under an admissible policy $u \in \mathcal{A}$. As before, let π denote a permutation of the integers $\{1, 2, ..., n\}$. In particular, $\pi = (\pi_1, ..., \pi_n)$ denotes a priority rule, which is admissible, and in which class π_1 jobs are assigned the highest priority, and class π_n jobs, the lowest priority.

Definition 4. *(Conservation Laws) The performance vector x is said to satisfy conservation laws, if there exists a set function b (or respectively f): $2^E \mapsto \Re_+$, satisfying*

$$b(A) = \sum_{i \in A} x_{\pi_i}, \quad \forall \pi : \{\pi_1, ..., \pi_{|A|}\} = A, \quad \forall A \subseteq E; \tag{4}$$

or respectively,

$$f(A) = \sum_{i \in A} x_{\pi_i}, \quad \forall \pi : \{\pi_1, ..., \pi_{|A|}\} = A, \quad \forall A \subseteq E; \tag{5}$$

(when $A = \emptyset$, by definition, $b(\emptyset) = f(\emptyset) = 0$); such that for all $u \in \mathcal{A}$ the following is satisfied:

$$\sum_{i \in A} x_i^u \geq b(A), \quad \forall A \subset E; \quad \sum_{i \in E} x_i^u = b(E); \tag{6}$$

or respectively,

$$\sum_{i \in A} x_i^u \leq f(A), \quad \forall A \subset E; \quad \sum_{i \in E} x_i^u = f(E). \tag{7}$$

Note that whether the function b or the function f applies in a particular context is determined by whether the performance in question is minimized or maximized by the priority rules. (For instance, b applies to delay, and f applies to throughput.) It is important to note that this minimal (or maximal) performance is required to be independent of the priority assignment among the classes within the subset A on the one hand and the priority assignment among the classes within the subset $E \setminus A$ on the other hand, as long as any class in A has priority over any class in $E \setminus A$. This requirement is reflected in the qualifications imposed on π in defining $b(A)$ and $f(A)$ in (4) and (5). In particular, the definition requires that $b(A)$ and $f(A)$ be respectively, the minimal and the maximal total performance summing over all job classes in the subset A that are given priority over all the other classes.

For the time being, ignore the b part of Definition 4. It is clear that when x satisfies the conservation laws, the performance space, as defined by the polytope in (7), is a polymatroid. This is because following (5) and (7), all the vertices x^π indeed, *by definition*, belong to the polytope. In fact, the polytope in (7) is the polymatroid $\mathcal{P}(f)$ of (1) restricted to the hyperplane $\sum_{i \in E} x_i = f(E)$ (instead of the half-plane $\sum_{i \in E} x_i \leq f(E)$), and is hence termed the *base* of the polymatroid $\mathcal{P}(f)$, denoted $\mathcal{B}(f)$ below. Furthermore, following Theorem 1, we know that when x satisfies conservation laws, the function $f(\cdot)$ as defined in (5) is increasing and submodular.

Next, consider the b part of Definition 4. Note that subtracting the inequality constraint from the equality constraint in (6), we can express these constraints in the same form as in (7), by letting $f(A) := b(E) - b(E \setminus A)$, or equivalently, $b(A) := b(E) - f(E \setminus A)$. Hence, the polytope in (6) is also (the base of) a polymatroid. Furthermore, the increasingness and submodularity of f translate into the increasingness and supermodularity of b.

To sum up the above discussion, we have

Theorem 2. *If the performance vector x satisfies conservation laws, then its feasible space (i.e., the achievable performance region) constitutes the base polytope of a polymatroid, $\mathcal{B}(f)$ or $\mathcal{B}(b)$, of which the vertices correspond to the priority rules. Furthermore, the functions f and b, which are the performance functions corresponding to priority rules, are, respectively, increasing and submodular, and increasing and supermodular.*

2.2 Examples

Consider a queueing system with n different job classes which are denoted by the set E. Let u be the control or scheduling rule that governs the order of service among different classes of jobs. Let $\mathcal{A}$ denote the class of admissible controls, which are required to be non-idling and non-anticipative. That is, no server is allowed to be idle when there are jobs waiting to be served, and the control is only allowed to make use of past history and current state of the system. Neither can an admissible control affect the arrival processes or the service requirements of the jobs. Otherwise we impose no further restrictions on the system. For instance, the arrival processes and the service requirements of the jobs can be arbitrary. Indeed, since the control cannot affect the arrival processes and the service requirements, all the arrival and service data can be viewed as generated *a priori* following any given (joint) distribution and with any given dependence relations. We allow multiple servers, and multiple stages (e.g., tandem queues or networks of queues). We also allow the control to be either preemptive or non-preemptive. (Some restrictions will be imposed on individual systems to be studied below.)

Let x_i^u be a performance measure of class i ($i \in E$) jobs under control u. This need not be a steady-state quantity or an expectation; it can very well be a sample-path realization over a finite time interval, for instance, the delay (sojourn time) of the first m class i jobs, the number of class i jobs in the system at time t, or the number of class i job completions by time t. Let $x^u := (x_i^u)_{i \in E}$ be the performance vector.

For any given permutation $\pi \in \Pi$, let x^π denote the performance vector under a priority scheduling rule that assigns priority to the job classes according to the permutation π, i.e., class π_1 has the highest priority, ..., class π_n has the lowest priority. Clearly any such priority rule belongs to the admissible class.

In all the queueing systems studied below, the service requirements of the jobs are mutually independent, and are also independent of the arrival processes. (One exception to these independence requirements is Example 1 below, where these independence assumptions are not needed.) No independence assumption, however, is required for the arrival processes, which can be arbitrary. When a performance vector satisfies conservation laws, whether its state space is $\mathcal{B}(b)$ (6) or $\mathcal{B}(f)$ (7) depends on whether the performance of a given subset of job classes is minimized or maximized by giving priority to this subset. This is often immediately evident from the context.

Example 1 Consider a $G/G/1$ system that allows preemption. For $i \in E$, let $V_i(t)$ denote the amount of work (processing requirement) in the system at time t due to jobs of class i. (Note that for any given t, $V_i(t)$ is a random quantity, corresponding to some sample realization of the work-load process.) Then it is easily verified that for any t, $x := [V_i(t)]_{i \in E}$ satisfies conservation laws.

Example 2 Continue with the last example. For all $i \in E$, let $N_i(t)$ be the number of class i jobs in the system at time t. When the service times follow exponential distributions, with mean $1/\mu_i$ for class i jobs, we have $\mathsf{E} N_i(t) =$

$\mu_i \mathsf{E} V_i(t)$. Let W_i be the steady-state sojourn time in system for class i jobs. From Little's Law we have $\mathsf{E} W_i = \mathsf{E} N_i / \lambda_i = \mathsf{E} V_i / \rho_i$, where λ_i is the arrival rate of class i jobs, $\rho_i := \lambda_i / \mu_i$, N_i and V_i are the steady-state counterparts of $N_i(t)$ and $V_i(t)$, respectively. Hence, the following x also satisfies conservation laws:

(i)   for any given t, $x := [\mathsf{E} N_i(t)/\mu_i]_{i \in E}$;

(ii) $x := [\rho_i \mathsf{E} W_i]_{i \in E}$.

Example 3 In a $G/M/c$ $(c > 1)$ system that allows preemption, if all job classes follow the same exponential service-time distribution (with mean $1/\mu$), then it is easy to verify that for any t, $x := [\mathsf{E} N_i(t)]_{i \in E}$ satisfies conservation laws. In this case, $\mathsf{E} V_i(t) = \mathsf{E} N_i(t)/\mu$ and $\mathsf{E} W_i = \mathsf{E} N_i/\lambda_i$. Hence, x defined as follows satisfies conservation laws:

(i)   for any given t, $x := [\mathsf{E} N_i(t)]_{i \in E}$, $x := [\mathsf{E} V_i(t)]_{i \in E}$;

(ii) $x := [\lambda_i \mathsf{E} W_i]_{i \in E}$.

(If the control is restricted to be non-preemptive, the results here still hold true. See Example 6 below.)

Example 4 The results in Example 3 still hold when the system is a network of queues, provided all job classes follow the same exponential service-time distribution and the same routing probabilities at each node (service-time distributions and routing probabilities can, however, be node dependent); (external) job arrival processes can be arbitrary and can be different among the classes.

Example 5 Another variation of Example 3 is the queue, $G/M/c/K$, where $K \geq c$ denotes the upper limit on the total number of jobs allowed in the system at any time. In this system, higher priority jobs can preempt lower priority jobs not only in service but also in occupancy. That is, whenever a higher priority job finds (on its arrival) a fully occupied system, a lower priority job within the system (if any) will be removed from the system and its occupancy given to the higher priority job. If there is no lower priority job, then the arrived job is rejected and lost. As in Example 3, all jobs follow the same exponential service-time distribution. Let $R_i(t)$ and $D_i(t)$ $(i \in E)$ denote, respectively, the (cumulated) number of rejected/removed class i jobs and the (cumulated) number of class i departures (service completions) up to time t. Then, for any given t, (i) $x := [\mathsf{E} R_i(t)]_{i \in E}$ and (ii) $x := [\mathsf{E} D_i(t)]_{i \in E}$ satisfy conservation laws.

We next turn to considering cases where the admissible controls are restricted to be non-preemptive.

Example 6 Consider the $G/G/c$ system, $c \geq 1$. If all job classes follow the same service-time distribution, then it is easy to see that the scheduling of the servers will not affect the departure epochs of jobs (in a pathwise sense); although it *will* affect the identity (class) of the departing jobs at those epochs. (See Shanthikumar and Sumita [38], §2, for the $G/G/1$ case; the results there also hold true for the $G/G/c$ case.) Hence, for any given t, $x := [N_i(t)]_{i \in E}$ satisfies conservation laws.

Example 7 Comparing the above with Example 3, we know that the results there also hold for non-preemptive controls. However, in contrast to the extension of Example 3 to the network case in Example 4, the above can only be extended to queues in tandem, where overtaking is excluded. Specifically, the result in Example 6 also holds for a series of $G/G/c$ queues in tandem, where at each node all job classes have the same service-time distribution, which, however, can be node dependent. External job arrival processes can be arbitrary and can be different among classes. The number of servers can also be node dependent.

Example 8 With non-preemptive control, there is a special case for the $G/G/1$ system with only two job classes ($n = 2$) which may follow *different* service-time distributions: for any given t, $x := [V_i(t)]_{i \in E}$ satisfies conservation laws.

For steady-steady measures, from standard results in $GI/G/1$ queues (see, e.g., Asmussen [1], Chapter VIII, Proposition 3.4), we have

$$EV_i = \mu_i^{-1}[EN_i - \rho_i] + \rho_i \mu_i m_i / 2$$

and

$$EV_i = \rho_i[EW_i - \mu_i^{-1} + \mu_i m_i / 2],$$

where m_i is the second moment of the service time of class i jobs. Hence, following the above, we know that $x = [EN_i / \mu_i]_{i \in E}$ and $x = [\rho_i EW_i]_{i \in E}$ also satisfy conservation laws.

Example 9 Two more examples that satisfy conservation laws:

(i)   for the $G/G/1$ system with preemption,

$$x := [\int_0^t \exp(-\alpha \tau) V_i(\tau) d\tau]_{i \in E};$$

(ii)   for the $G/M/1$ system with preemption,

$$x := [E \int_0^t \exp(-\alpha \tau) N_i(\tau) d\tau / \mu_i]_{i \in E},$$

where in both (i) and (ii) $\alpha > 0$ is a discount rate, and t is any given time.

Finally, note that in all the above examples, with the exception of Example 5, whenever $[EN_i(t)]_{i \in E}$ satisfies conservation laws, $[ED_i(t)]_{i \in E}$ also satisfies conservation laws, since in a no-loss system the number of departures is the difference between the number of arrivals (which is independent of the control) and the number in system.

Evidently, based on the above discussions, the state space of the performance vectors in each of the examples above is a polymatroid.

2.3   Optimal Scheduling

Theorem 3. *Consider the optimal control (scheduling) of n jobs classes in the set E:*

$$\max_{u \in \mathcal{A}} \sum_{i \in E} c_i x_i^u \quad [\text{or} \quad \min_{u \in \mathcal{A}} \sum_{i \in E} c_i x_i^u],$$

where x is a performance measure that satisfies conservation laws, and the cost coefficients c_i $(i \in E)$ satisfy, without loss of generality, the ordering in (2). Then, this optimal control problem can be solved by solving the following linear program (LP):

$$\max_{x \in \mathcal{B}(f)} \sum_{i \in E} c_i x_i \quad [\text{or} \quad \min_{x \in \mathcal{B}(b)} \sum_{i \in E} c_i x_i].$$

The optimal solution to this LP is simply the vertex $x^\pi \in \mathcal{B}(f)$, with $\pi = (1, ..., n)$ being the permutation corresponding to the decreasing order of the cost coefficients in (2). And the optimal control policy is the corresponding priority rule, which assigns the highest priority to class 1 jobs, and the lowest priority to class n jobs.

Example 10 ($c\mu$-rule)   Consider one of the performance vectors in Example 2, $x := [\mathsf{E}(N_i)/\mu_i]_{i \in E}$, where N_i is the number of jobs of class i in the system (or, "inventory") in steady state, and μ_i is the service rate. Suppose our objective is to minimize the total inventory cost,

$$\min \sum_{i \in E} c_i \mathsf{E}(N_i),$$

where c_i is the inventory holding cost rate for class i jobs. We then rewrite this objective as

$$\min \sum_{i \in E} c_i \mu_i x_i.$$

(Note that $(N_i)_{i \in E}$ does not satisfy conservation laws; $(x_i)_{i \in E}$ does.) Then, we know from the above theorem that the optimal policy is a priority rule, with the priorities assigned according to the $c_i \mu_i$ values — the larger the value, the higher the priority. This is what is known as the "$c\mu$-rule". When all jobs have the same cost rate, the priorities follow the μ_i values, i.e., the faster the processing rate (or, the shorter the processing time), the higher the priority, which is the so-called SPT (shortest processing time) rule.

The connection between conservation laws and polymatroid, as specified in Theorem 2, guarantees that any admissible control will yield a performance vector that belongs to the polymatroid. Furthermore, the converse is also true: any performance vector that belongs to the polymatroid can be realized by an admissible control. This is because since $\mathcal{B}(f)$ (or $\mathcal{B}(b)$) is a convex polytope, any vector in the performance space can be expressed as a convex combination of the vertices. Following Caratheodory's theorem (refer to, e.g., Chvátal [8]), any vector in the performance space can be expressed as a convex combination of no more than $n+1$ vertices. In other words, any performance vector can be realized by a control that is a *randomization* of at most $n+1$ priority rules, with the convex combination coefficients being the probabilities for the randomization.

In terms of implementation, however, randomization can be impractical. First, computationally, there is no easy way to derive the randomization coefficients. Second, in order to have an unbiased implementation, randomization will have to be applied at the beginning of each regenerative cycle, e.g., a busy period. In heavy traffic, busy periods could be very long, making implementation extremely difficult, and also creating large variance of the performance.

In fact, one can do better than randomization. It is known (e.g., Federgruen and Groenevelt [16]) that any interior point of the performance space can be realized by a particular dynamic scheduling policy, due originally to Kleinrock [30,31], in which the priority index of each job present in the system grows proportionately to the time it has spent waiting in queue, and the server always serves the job that has the highest index. This scheduling policy is completely specified by the proportionate coefficients associated with the jobs classes, which, in turn, are easily determined by the performance vector (provided it is at the interior of the performance space). In terms of practical implementation, there are several versions of this scheduling policy, refer to [18,19].

3   Generalized Conservation Laws

3.1   Motivation and Definition

Although conservation laws apply to the many examples in the last section, there are other interesting and important problems that do not fall into this category. A primary class of such examples includes systems with feedback, i.e., jobs may come back after service completion. For example, consider the so-called Klimov's problem: a multi-class $M/G/1$ queue in which jobs, after service completion, may return and switch to another class, following a Bernoulli mechanism. Without feedback, we know this is a special case of Example 1, and the work in system, $[V_i(t)]_{i \in E}$, satisfies conservation laws. With feedback, however, the conservation laws as defined in Definition 4, need to be modified.

Specifically, with the possibility of feedback, the work of a particular job class, say class i, should not only include the work associated with class i jobs that are present in the system, it should also take into account the *potential* work that will be generated by feedback jobs, which not only include class i jobs but also all other classes that may feedback to become class i. With this modification, the two intuitive principles of conservation laws listed at the beginning of §2.1 will apply.

To be concrete, let us paraphrase here the simple example at the beginning of §2.1 with two job classes, allowing the additional feature of feedback. As before, suppose the server serves at unit rate. Then it is not difficult to see that (i) the total amount of potential work, summing over both classes, will remain invariant regardless of the actual schedule that the server follows, as long as it is a non-idling schedule; and (ii) if class 1 jobs are given (preemptive) priority over class 2 jobs, then the amount of potential work due to class 1 jobs is minimized, namely, it cannot be further reduced by any other scheduling rule. And the same holds for class 2 jobs, if given priority over class 1 jobs.

Another way to look at this example: Let T be the first time there is no class 1 jobs left in the system. Then, T is minimized by giving class 1 jobs (preemptive) priority over class 2 jobs. In particular, T is no smaller than the potential work of class 1 generated by class 1 jobs (only); T is equal to the latter if and only if class 1 jobs are given priority over class 2 jobs.

Therefore, with this modification, the conservation laws in Definition 4 can be generalized. The net effect, as will be demonstrated in the examples below, is that the variables x_i in Definition 4 will have to be multiplied with different coefficients a_i^A that depend on both the job classes (i) and the subsets (A). In particular, when x_i is, for instance, the average number of jobs of class i, a_i^A denotes the rate of potential work of those classes in set A that is generated by class i jobs.

We now state the formal definition of generalized conservation laws (GCL), using the same notation wherever possible as in Definition 4.

Definition 5. *(Generalized Conservation Laws) The performance vector x is said to satisfy generalized conservation laws (GCL), if there exists a set function b (or respectively f): $2^E \mapsto \Re_+$, and a matrix $(a_i^S)_{i \in E, S \subseteq E}$ (which is in general different for b and f, but we will not make this distinction below for notational simplicity) satisfying:*

$$a_i^S > 0, \ i \in S; \quad \text{and} \quad a_i^S = 0, \ i \notin S; \qquad \forall S \subseteq E;$$

such that

$$b(A) = \sum_{i \in A} a_{\pi_i}^A x_{\pi_i}, \quad \forall \pi : \{\pi_1, ..., \pi_{|A|}\} = A, \quad \forall A \subseteq E; \qquad (8)$$

or respectively,

$$f(A) = \sum_{i \in A} a_{\pi_i}^A x_{\pi_i}, \quad \forall \pi : \{\pi_1, ..., \pi_{|A|}\} = A, \quad \forall A \subseteq E; \qquad (9)$$

such that for all $u \in A$ the following is satisfied:

$$\sum_{i \in A} a_i^A x_i^u \geq b(A), \quad \forall A \subset E; \quad \sum_{i \in E} a_i^E x_i^u = b(E); \qquad (10)$$

or respectively,

$$\sum_{i \in A} a_i^A x_i^u \leq f(A), \quad \forall A \subset E; \quad \sum_{i \in E} a_i^E x_i^u = f(E). \qquad (11)$$

It is obvious from the above definition that GCL reduces to the conservation laws if $a_i^A = 1$ for all $i \in A$, and all $A \subseteq E$.

3.2   Examples

Example 11 (Klimov's problem [32]) This concerns the optimal control of a system in which a single server is available to serve n classes of jobs. Class i jobs arrive according to a Poisson process with rate α_i, which is independent of other classes of jobs. The service times for class i jobs are independent and identically distributed with mean μ_i. When the service of a class i job is completed, it either returns to become a class j job, with probability p_{ij}, or leaves the system with probability $1 - \sum_j p_{ij}$. Denote $\alpha = (\alpha_i)_{i \in E}$, $\mu = (\mu_i)_{i \in E}$, and $P = [p_{ij}]_{i,j \in E}$.

Consider the class of non-preemptive policies. The performance measure is

$$x_i^u = \text{long-run average number of class } i \text{ jobs in system under policy } u.$$

The objective is to find the optimal policy that minimizes $\sum_j c_j x_j^u$. Klimov proved that a priority policy is optimal and gave a recursive procedure for obtaining the priority indices.

Tsoucas [42] showed that the performance space of Klimov's problem is the following polytope:

$$\{x \geq 0 : \sum_{i \in S} a_i^S x_i \geq b(S), S \subset E; \sum_{i \in E} a_i^E x_i = b(E)\},$$

where the coefficients are given as $a_i^S = \lambda_i \beta_i^S$, with $\lambda = (\lambda)_{i \in E}$ and $\beta^S = (\beta)_{i \in S}$ obtained as follows:

$$\lambda = (I - P')^{-1} \alpha \quad \text{and} \quad \beta^S = (I - P_{SS})^{-1} \mu_S,$$

where P_{SS} and μ_S are, respectively, the restriction of P and μ to the set S. Note that here, λ_i is the overall arrival rate of class i jobs (including both external arrivals and feedback jobs), β_i^S is the amount of potential work of the classes in S generated by a class i job. (Hence, this potential work is generated at rate α_i in the system.) Summing over $i \in S$ yields the total amount of potential work of the classes in S (generated by the same set of jobs), which is minimized when these jobs are given priority over other classes. This is the basic intuition as to why x satisfies GCL.

Example 12 (Branching bandit process) There are m projects at time 0. They are of K classes, labeled $k = 1, \cdots, K$. Each class k project can be in one of a finite number of states, with E_k denoting the state space. Classifying different project classes or projects of the same class but in different states as different "classes," we denote $E = \cup_k E_k = \{1, \cdots, n\}$ as the set of all project classes. A single server works on the projects one at a time. Each class i project keeps the server busy for a duration of v_i time units. Upon completion, the class i project is replaced by N_{ij} projects of class j. The server then has to decide which next project to serve, following a scheduling rule (control) u. The collection $\{(v_i, N_{ij}), j \in E\}$, follows a general joint distribution, which is independent and identically distributed for all $i \in E$.

Given $S \subseteq E$, the S-descendants of a project of class $i \in S$ refers to all of its immediate descendants that are of classes belonging to S, as well as the immediate descendants of those descendents, and so on. (If a project in S transfers into a class that is not in S, and later transfers back into a class in S, it will not be considered as an S-descendant of the original project.) Given a class i project, the union of the time intervals in which its S-descendants are being served is called an (i, S) period. Let T_i^S denote the length of an (i, S) period. It is the "potential work" of the classes in the set S generated by the class i project. And we use T_m^S to denote the time until the system has completely cleared all classes of projects in S class — under a policy that gives priority to those classes in S over other classes. Note, in particular, that T_m^E represents the length of a busy period.

In the discounted case, the expected reward associated with the control u is $\sum_{i \in E} c_i x_i^u$, where

$$x_i^u = \mathsf{E}_u \left[\int_0^\infty e^{-\alpha t} I_i^u(t) dt \right]$$

$\alpha > 0$ is the discount rate and

$$I_i^u(t) = \begin{cases} 1, & \text{if a class } i \text{ project is being served at time } t \\ 0, & \text{otherwise} \end{cases}$$

Bertsimas and Niño-Mora [3] showed that $x^u = (x_i^u)_{i \in E}$, as defined above, satisfy the GCL, with coefficients

$$a_i^S = \frac{\mathsf{E}[\int_0^{T_i^{S^c}} e^{-\alpha t} dt]}{\mathsf{E}[\int_0^{v_i} e^{-\alpha t} dt]}, \quad i \in S \subseteq E,$$

and

$$b(S) = \mathsf{E}\left[\int_0^{T_m^E} e^{-\alpha t} dt \right] - \mathsf{E}\left[\int_0^{T_m^{S^c}} e^{-\alpha t} dt \right].$$

Intuitively, the GCL here says that the time until all the S^c-descendents of all the projects in S are served is minimized by giving project classes in S^c priority over those in S.

An undiscounted version is also available in [3]. (This includes Klimov's problem, the last example above, as a special case.) The criterion here is to minimize the total expected cost incurred under control u during the first busy period (of the server) $[0, T]$, $\sum_{i \in E} c_i x_i^u$, with

$$x_i^u = \mathsf{E}_u \left[\int_0^\infty t I_i^u(t) dt \right].$$

Following [3], x^u satisfy GCL with coefficients

$$a_i^S = \mathsf{E}[T_i^{S^c}]/\mathsf{E}[v_i], \quad i \in S \subseteq E,$$

and

$$b(S) = \frac{1}{2}\mathsf{E}[(T_m^E)^2] - \frac{1}{2}\mathsf{E}[(T_m^{S^c})^2] + \sum_{i \in S} b_i(S),$$

where

$$b_i(S) = \frac{\mathsf{E}[v_i]\mathsf{E}[v_i^2]}{2} \left(\frac{\mathsf{E}[T_i^{S^c}]}{\mathsf{E}[v_i]} - \frac{\mathsf{E}[(T_i^{S^c})^2]}{\mathsf{E}[v_i^2]} \right), \quad i \in S.$$

The intuition is similar to the discounted case.

4 Extended Polymatroid

4.1 Equivalent Definitions

Recall the space of any performance measure that satisfies conservation laws is a polymatroid. Analogously, one can ask what is the structure of the performance space under GCL, i.e., what is the structure of the following polytopes:

$$\mathcal{EP}(b) = \{ \, x \geq 0 : \sum_{i \in S} a_i^S x_i \geq b(S), \ S \subseteq E \, \}, \tag{12}$$

$$\mathcal{EP}(f) = \{ \, x \geq 0 : \sum_{i \in S} a_i^S x_i \leq f(S), \ S \subseteq E \, \}. \tag{13}$$

The most natural route to approach this issue appears to be mimicking Definition 2 of polymatroid (and this is indeed the route taken in [3]). Similar to the definition of x^π preceding Definition 2, here, given a permutation π (of $\{ 1, 2, \cdots, n \}$), we can generate a vertex x^π as follows.

$$x_{\pi_1} = f(\{\pi_1\})/a_{\pi_1}^{\{\pi_1\}}$$

$$x_{\pi_2} = \left(f(\{\pi_1, \pi_2\}) - a_{\pi_1}^{\{\pi_1, \pi_2\}} x_{\pi_1} \right) \Big/ a_{\pi_2}^{\{\pi_1, \pi_2\}}$$

$$\vdots$$

$$x_{\pi_n} = \left(f(\{\pi_1, \cdots, \pi_n\}) - \sum_{i=1}^{n-1} a_{\pi_i}^{\{\pi_1, \cdots, \pi_n\}} x_{\pi_i} \right) \Big/ a_{\pi_n}^{\{\pi_1, \cdots, \pi_n\}}.$$

Same as in the polymatroid case, we should emphasize here that as yet, x^π does not necessarily belong to the polytope in (13). The vertices for $\mathcal{EP}(b)$ are analogously generated, with $f(\cdot)$ replaced by $b(\cdot)$.

Definition 6. $\mathcal{EP}(f)$ *(respectively $\mathcal{EP}(b)$) is an extended polymatroid (EP) if x^π as generated above (respectively with b replacing f) belongs to the polytope $\mathcal{EP}(f)$, (respectively $\mathcal{EP}(b)$), for any permutation π.*

(The term, "extended polymatroid," was previously used to refer to a polymatroid without the requirement that $x \geq 0$; e.g., see [26], p. 306. Since [3, 42] and other works in the queueing literature, it has been used to refer to the polytopes defined above. Also, in [3], the EP corresponding to the b function is termed "extended contra-polymatroid," with the term "extended polymatroid" reserved for the f function. For simplicity, we do not make such a distinction here and below.)

With the above definition for EP, the right hand side functions b and f are not necessarily increasing and supermodular/submodular. In other words, we do not have a counterpart of Definition 1 for EP (more on this later). On the other hand, the counterpart for Definition 3 does apply.

Definition 7. $\mathcal{EP}(f)$ *is an extended polymatroid if the following is satisfied: for any $A \subset B \subset E$, there exists a point $x \in \mathcal{EP}(f)$, such that*

$$\sum_{i \in A} a_i^A x_i = f(A) \quad \text{and} \quad \sum_{i \in B} a_i^B x_i = f(B).$$

Theorem 4. *The two definitions of EP in 6 and 7 are equivalent.*

Proof. If $\mathcal{EP}(f)$ is EP, then the stated condition in Definition 7 is obviously satisfied: just pick the vertex x^π such that the first $|A|$ components in π constitute the set A, and the first $|B|$ components constitute the set B.

For the other direction, i.e., if the stated condition in Definition 7 holds, then $\mathcal{EP}(f)$ is EP, we use induction on $n = |E|$. That this holds for $n = 1$ is trivial.

Suppose this holds for $n = k$, i.e. for a polytope of the kind in (13) with k variables. Now consider such a polytope with $k + 1$ variables, i.e., $|E| = k + 1$. Without loss of generality, consider the permutation $\pi = (1, 2, ..., k + 1)$. We want to show that the corresponding x^π (i.e., generated from the triangulation above)) is in the polytope $\mathcal{EP}(f)$.

Since $x_1^\pi = f(\{1\})/a_1^{\{1\}}$, we substitute it into the other x_i^π expressions, $i \neq 1$, to arrive at the following polytope of k variables:

$$\mathcal{EP}(\tilde{f}) = \{x \geq 0 : \sum_{i \in S, i \neq 1} a_i^S x_i \leq \tilde{f}(S), \{1\} \in S \subseteq E\},$$

where

$$\tilde{f}(S) := f(S) - \frac{f(\{1\})}{a_1^{\{1\}}} a_1^S.$$

Clearly, since the stated condition in Definition 7 is assumed to hold for $\mathcal{EP}(f)$ (the one with $k+1$ variables), it also holds for $\mathcal{EP}(\tilde{f})$ (the one with k variables), since the equations in question all differ by an amount $f(\{1\})a_1^{\{1\}}/a_1^S$ on both sides. Hence, the induction hypothesis confirms that $\mathcal{EP}(\tilde{f})$ is an EP. This implies that $(x_2^\pi, ..., x_n^\pi) \in \mathcal{EP}(\tilde{f})$, which is equivalent to $x^\pi = (x_1^\pi, x_2^\pi, ..., x_n^\pi)$ satisfying all the constraints in $\mathcal{EP}(f)$ that involve $S \subseteq E$ with $1 \in S$.

We still need to check that x^π satisfies all the other constraints in $\mathcal{EP}(f)$ corresponding to $S \subseteq E$ with $1 \notin S$. To this end, consider the following polytope:

$$\{x \geq 0 : \sum_{i \in S} a_i^S x_i \leq f(S), S \subseteq E \setminus \{1\}\}. \tag{14}$$

The above is another polytope with k variables. Obviously the stated condition in Definition 7, which is assumed to hold for the polytope $\mathcal{EP}(f)$, holds for the above polytope as well (since the defining inequalities in the latter are just part of those in $\mathcal{EP}(f)$). Hence, based on the induction hypothesis, the polytope in (14) is also an EP. This implies that $(x_2^\pi, ..., x_n^\pi)$, and hence x^π, satisfies all the inequalities involved in (14).

Hence, we have established that given the stated condition in Definition 7, x^π does satisfy all the constraints in $\mathcal{EP}(f)$, for each permutation π. Therefore, $\mathcal{EP}(f)$ is an EP.

The above theorem leads immediately to the following:

Corollary 1. *If $\mathcal{EP}(f)$ is an extended polymatroid, then*

$$\mathcal{EP}^-(f) := \{x \geq 0 : \sum_{i \in S} a_i^S x_i \leq f(S), \, S \subseteq E \setminus E_0\}$$

is also an extended polymatroid, for any $E_0 \subset E$.

Proof. Simply verify Definition 7. Since $\mathcal{EP}(f)$ is an EP, we can pick any $A \subset B \subseteq E \setminus E_0 \subset E$, and there exists an $x \in \mathcal{EP}(f)$, such that $\sum_{i \in A} a_i^A x_i = f(A)$ and $\sum_{i \in B} a_i^B x_i = f(B)$. But this is exactly what is required for $\mathcal{EP}^-(f)$ to be EP.

In summary, we have

Theorem 5. *If the performance vector x satisfies GCL, then the performance polytope is an EP, of which the vertices correspond to the performance under priority rules, and the functions $b(A)$ and $f(A)$ correspond to the performance of job classes in set A when A is given priority over all other classes in $E \setminus A$.*

5   Optimization over EP

Here we consider the optimization problem of maximizing a linear function over the EP, $\mathcal{EP}(f)$, defined in (13):

$$\textbf{(PG)} \qquad \max \sum_{i \in E} c_i \, x_i$$

$$\text{s.t.} \sum_{i \in A} a_i^A x_i \leq f(A), \quad \text{for all } A \subseteq E,$$

$$x_i \geq 0, \quad \text{for all } i \in E.$$

The dual problem can be written as follows:

$$\textbf{(DG)} \qquad \min \sum_{A \subseteq E} y_A \, f(A)$$

$$\text{s.t.} \sum_{A \ni i} y_A a_i^A \geq c_i, \quad \text{for all } \in E,$$

$$y_A \geq 0, \quad \text{for all } A \subseteq E.$$

Let us start with $\pi = (1, 2, \cdots, n)$, and consider x^π, the vertex defined at the beginning part of the last section. Below we write out the objective function of **(PG)** at x^π, and use the expression, along with complementary slackness, to identify a candidate for the dual solution. From dual feasibility, we then identify the conditions under which π is the optimal permutation. Collectively, these steps constitute an algorithm that finds the optimal π.

For simplicity, write x for x^π below. We first write out x_n in the objective function:

$$\sum_{i=1}^n c_i x_i = c_n \left(f(\{1, \cdots, n\}) - \sum_{i=1}^{n-1} a_i^{\{1,\cdots,n\}} x_i \right) \bigg/ a_n^{\{1,\cdots,n\}} + \sum_{i=1}^{n-1} c_i x_i$$

$$= y_{\{1,\cdots,n\}} f(\{1, \cdots, n\}) + \sum_{i=1}^{n-1} \left(c_i - y_{\{1,\cdots,n\}} a_i^{\{1,\cdots,n\}} \right) x_i,$$

where we set

$$y_{\{1,\cdots,n\}} = c_n / a_n^{\{1,\cdots,n\}}.$$

Next, we write out x_{n-1} in the summation above, and set

$$y_{\{1,\cdots,n-1\}} = (c_{n-1} - y_{\{1,\cdots,n\}} a_{n-1}^{\{1,\cdots,n\}}) / a_{n-1}^{\{1,\cdots,n-1\}},$$

to reach the following expression:

$$\sum_{i=1}^n c_i x_i = y_{\{1,\cdots,n\}} f(\{1, \cdots, n\}) + y_{\{1,\cdots,n-1\}} f(\{1, \cdots, n-1\})$$

$$+ \sum_{i=1}^{n-2} \left(c_i - y_{\{1,\cdots,n\}} a_i^{\{1,\cdots,n\}} - y_{\{1,\cdots,n-1\}} a_i^{\{1,\cdots,n-1\}} \right) x_i^\pi.$$

This procedure can be repeated to yield the following:

$$\sum_{i=1}^n c_i x_i = y_{\{1,\cdots,n\}} f(\{1, \cdots, n\}) + y_{\{1,\cdots,n-1\}}) f(\{1, \cdots, n-1\})$$

$$+ \cdots + y_{\{1,2\}} f(\{1.2\}) + y_{\{1\}} f(\{1\}), \tag{15}$$

where

$$y_{\{1,\cdots,k\}} = \left(c_k - \sum_{j=k+1}^n y_{\{1,\cdots,j\}} a_k^{\{1,\cdots,j\}} \right) \bigg/ a_k^{\{1,\cdots,k\}}, \tag{16}$$

for $k = 1, ..., n$. (When $k = n$, the vacuous summation in (16) vanishes.) Furthermore, set $y_A := 0$ for all other $A \subseteq E$.

With the above choice of x and y, it is easy to check that complementary slackness is satisfied. Also, primal feasibility is automatic — guaranteed by the definition of EP, since x is a vertex. Hence, we only need to check dual feasibility.

From the construction of y in (16), we have

$$\sum_{j=i}^{n} y_{\{1,\cdots,j\}} a_i^{\{1,\cdots,j\}} = c_i, \qquad i \in E,$$

satisfying the first set of constraints in **(DG)**. So it suffices to show that the n non-zero dual variables in (16) are non-negative. To this end, we need to be specific about the construction of the permutation $\pi = (1, ..., n)$.

Let us start from the last element in π. Note that from (16), we have

$$y_{\{1,\cdots,n\}} = \frac{c_n}{a_n^{\{1,\cdots,n\}}} \geq 0.$$

Next, to ensure $y_{\{1,\cdots,n-1\}} \geq 0$, the numerator of its expression in (16) must be non-negative, i.e.,

$$\frac{c_{n-1}}{a_{n-1}^{\{1,\cdots,n\}}} \geq y_{\{1,\cdots,n\}} = \frac{c_n}{a_n^{\{1,\cdots,n\}}}.$$

Therefore, the index n has to be:

$$n = \arg\min_{i} \frac{c_i}{a_i^{\{1,\cdots,n\}}}.$$

Note that this choice of n guarantees $y_{\{1,\cdots,n-1\}} \geq 0$, independent of the ordering of the other $n-1$ elements in the permutation.

Similarly, to ensure $y_{\{1,\cdots,n-2\}} \geq 0$, from (16), we must have

$$c_{n-2} - y_{\{1,\cdots,n-1\}} a_{n-2}^{\{1,\cdots,n-1\}} - y_{\{1,\cdots,n\}} a_{n-2}^{\{1,\cdots,n\}} \geq 0,$$

or

$$\frac{c_{n-2} - y_{\{1,\cdots,n\}} a_{n-2}^{\{1,\cdots,n\}}}{a_{n-2}^{\{1,\cdots,n-1\}}} \geq y_{\{1,\cdots,n-1\}}.$$

Hence, the choice of $n-1$ has to be:

$$n - 1 = \arg\min_{i \leq n-1} \frac{c_i - y_{\{1,\cdots,n\}} a_i^{\{1,\cdots,n\}}}{a_i^{\{1,\cdots,n-1\}}}.$$

This procedure can be repeated until all elements of the permutation is determined. In general, the index k is chosen in the order of $k = n, n-1, ..., 1$, and it has to satisfy:

$$k = \arg\min_{i \leq k} \frac{c_i - \sum_{j=k+1}^{n} y_{\{1,\cdots,j\}} a_i^{\{1,\cdots,j\}}}{a_i^{\{1,\cdots,k\}}}.$$

Formally, the following algorithm solves the dual problem **(DG)** in terms of generating the permutation π, along with the dual solution y^π. The optimal primal solution is then the vertex, x^π, corresponding to the permutation π.

Algorithm 1 [for **(DG)**]

(i)   Initialization: $S(n) = E$, $k = n$;
(ii) If $k = 1$, stop, and output $\{\pi, S(k); y^\pi(S(k))\}$; else, set

$$\pi_k := \arg \min_i \frac{c_i - \sum_{j=k+1}^n y_{S(j)}^\pi a_i^{S(j)}}{a_i^{S(k)}}$$

$$y_{S(k)}^\pi := \min_i \frac{c_i - \sum_{j=k+1}^n y_{S(j)}^\pi a_i^{S(j)}}{a_i^{S(k)}};$$

(iii) $k \leftarrow k - 1$, $S(k) = S(k+1) \setminus \{\pi_k\}$; goto (ii).

Theorem 6. *Given an extended polymatroid $\mathcal{EP}(f)$, the above algorithm solves the primal and dual LP's, **(PG)** and **(DG)** in $O(n^2)$ steps, with x^π and y^π being the optimal primal-dual solution pair.*

Proof. Following the discussions preceding the algorithm, it is clear that we only need to check $y_{S(k)}^\pi \geq 0$, for $k = 1, \cdots, n$.

When $k = n$, following the algorithm, we have $S(n) = E$, and

$$\pi_n = \arg \min_i \{c_i/a_i^E\}, \qquad y_E^\pi = c_{\pi_n}/a_{\pi_n}^E \geq 0.$$

Inductively, suppose $y_{S(j)}^\pi \geq 0$, for $j = k+1, ..., n$, have all been determined. The choice of π_{k+1} and hence $y_{S(k+1)}^\pi$ in the algorithm guarantees

$$c_k - \sum_{j=k}^n y_{S(j)}^\pi a_k^{S(j)} \geq 0,$$

and hence $y_{S(k)}^\pi \geq 0$.

That the optimal solution is generated in $O(n^2)$ steps is evident from the description of the algorithm.

To summarize, the two remarks at the end of §1.2 for the polymatroid optimization also apply here: (i) primal feasibility is automatic, by way of the definition of EP; and (ii) dual feasibility, along with complementary slackness, identifies the permutation π that defines the (primal) optimal vertex. Furthermore, there is also an analogy to (3), i.e., the sum of dual variables yields the priority index. To see this, for concreteness consider Klimov's problem, with the performance measure x_i being the (long-run) average number of class i jobs in the system. (For this example, we are dealing with a minimization problem over the EP $\mathcal{EP}(b)$. But all of the above discussions, including the algorithm, still apply, mutatis mutandis, such as changing f to b and max to min, etc.) The optimal policy is a priority rule corresponding to the permutation π generated by the above algorithm, with the jobs of class π_1 given the highest priority, and jobs of class π_n, the lowest priority. Let y^* be the optimal dual solution generated by the algorithm. Define

$$\gamma_i := \sum_{S \ni i} y_S^*, \qquad i \in E.$$

Then, we have

$$\gamma_{\pi_i} = y_{\{\pi_1, \cdots, \pi_i\}}^* + \cdots + y_{\{\pi_1, \cdots, \pi_n\}}^*, \quad i \in E. \tag{17}$$

Note that γ_{π_i} is decreasing in i, since the dual variables are non-negative. Hence, the order of γ_{π_i}'s is in the same direction as the priority assignment. In other words, (17) is completely analogous to (3): just like the indexing role played by the cost coefficients in the polymatroid case, in the EP case here $\{\gamma_i\}$ is also a set of indices upon which the priorities are assigned: at each decision epoch, the server chooses to serve, among all waiting jobs, the job class with the highest γ index.

Finally, we can synthesize all the above discussions on GCL and its connection to EP, and on optimization over an EP, to come up with the following generalization of Theorem 3.

Theorem 7. *Consider the optimal control problem in Theorem 3:*

$$\max_{u \in \mathcal{A}} \sum_{i \in E} c_i x_i^u \qquad [\,or \quad \min_{u \in \mathcal{A}} \sum_{i \in E} c_i x_i^u\,].$$

Suppose x is a performance measure that satisfies GCL. Then, this optimal control problem can be solved by solving the following LP:

$$\max_{x \in \mathcal{EP}(f)} \sum_{i \in E} c_i x_i \qquad [\,or \quad \min_{x \in \mathcal{EP}(b)} \sum_{i \in E} c_i x_i\,].$$

The optimal solution to this LP is simply the vertex $x^\pi \in \mathcal{B}(f)$, with π being the permutation identified by Algorithm 1; and the optimal policy is the corresponding priority rule, which assigns the highest priority to class π_1 jobs, and the lowest priority to class π_n jobs.

Applying the above theorem to Klimov's model we can generate the optimal policy, which is a priority rule dictated by the permutation π, which, in turn, is generated by Algorithm 1.

6   Notes and Comments

The materials presented here are drawn from Chapter 11 of the book by Chen and Yao [7], to which the reader is also referred for preliminaries in queueing networks. A standard reference to matroid, as well as polymatroid, is Welsh [47]. The equivalence of the first two definitions of the polymatroid, Definitions 1 and

2, is a classical result; refer to, e.g., Edmonds [13], Welsh [47], and Dunstan and Welsh [12].

The original version of conservation laws, due to Kleinrock [31], takes the form of a single equality constraint, $\sum_{i \in E} x_i = b(E)$ or $= f(E)$. In the works of Coffman and Mitrani [9], and Gelenbe and Mitrani [20], the additional inequality constraints were introduced, which, along with the equality constraint, give a full characterization of the performance space. In a sequence of papers, Federgruen and Groenevelt [15,16,17], established the polymatroid structure of the performance space of several queueing systems, by showing that the RHS (right hand side) functions are increasing and submodular.

Shanthikumar and Yao [39] revealed the *equivalence* between conservations laws and the polymatroid nature of the performance polytope. In other words, the increasingness and submodularity of the RHS functions are not only sufficient but also necessary conditions for conservation laws. This equivalence is based on two key ingredients: On the one hand, the polymatroid Definition 2 asserts that if the "vertex" x^π — generated through a triangular system of n linear equations (made out of a total of $2^n - 1$ inequalities that define the polytope) — belongs to the polytope (i.e., if it satisfies all the other inequalities), for every permutation, π, then the polytope is a polymatroid. On the other hand, in conservation laws the RHS functions that characterize the performance polytope can be defined in such a way that they correspond to those "vertices". This way, the vertices will automatically belong to the performance space, since they are achievable by priority rules.

The direct implication of the connection between conservation laws and polymatroid is the translation of the scheduling (control) problem into an optimization problem. In the case of a linear objective, the optimal solution follows immediately from examining the primal-dual pair: primal feasibility is guaranteed by the polymatroid property — all vertices belong to the polytope, and dual feasibility, along with complementary slackness, yields the priority indices.

Motivated by Klimov's problem, Tsoucas [42], and Bertsimas and Niño-Mora [3] extended conservation laws and related polymatroid structure to GCL and EP. The key ingredients in the conservation laws/polymatroid theory of [39] are carried over to GCL/EP. In particular, EP is defined completely analogous to the polymatroid Definition 2 mentioned above, via the "vertex" x^π; whereas GCL is such that for every permutation π, x^π corresponds to a priority rule, and thereby guarantees its membership to the performance polytope. The equivalent definitions for EP in Definition 7 are due to Lu [34] and Zhang [52] (also see [51]).

Dynamic scheduling of a multi-class stochastic network is a complex and difficult problem that has continued to attract much research effort. A sample of more recent works shows a variety of different approaches to the problem, from Markov decision programming (e.g., Harrison [27], Weber and Stidham [45]), monotone control of generalized semi-Markov processes (Glasserman and Yao [24,25]), to asymptotic techniques via diffusion limits (Harrison [28], and Harrison and Wein [29]). This chapter presents yet another approach, which is based on polymatroid optimization. It exploits, in the presence of conservation laws and GCL, the polymatroid or EP structure of the performance polytope and turns the dynamic control problem into a static optimization problem.

The $c\mu$-rule in Example 10 is a subject with a long history that can be traced back to Smith [40], and the monograph of Cox and Smith [10]; also see, e.g., [5,6]. More ambitious examples of applications that are based on Theorem 3 include: scheduling in a Jackson network ([36]), scheduling and load balancing in a distributed computer system ([37]), and scheduling multi-class jobs in a flexible manufacturing system ([50]).

Klimov's problem generalizes the $c\mu$-rule model by allowing completed jobs to feedback and change classes. Variations of Klimov's model have also been widely studied using different techniques; e.g., Harrison [27], Tcha and Pliska [41]. The optimal priority policy is often referred to as the "Gittins index" rule, as the priority indices are closely related to those indices in dynamic resource allocation problems that are made famous by Gittins ([21,22,23]).

Klimov's model, in turn, belongs to the more general class of branching bandit problems, (refer to §3), for which scheduling rules based on Gittins indices are optimal. There is a vast literature on this subject; refer to, e.g., Lai and Ying [33], Meilijson and Weiss [35], Varaiya et al. [43], Weber [44], Weiss [46], Whittle [48,49]; as well as Gittins [21,22], and Gittins and Jones [23].

GCL corresponds to the so-called "indexable" class of stochastic systems, including Klimov's model and branching bandits as primary examples; refer to [3,4]. Beyond this indexable class, however, the performance space is not even an EP. There have been recent studies that try to bound such performance space by more structured polytopes (e.g., polymatroid and EP), e.g., Bertsimas [2], Bertsimas et al [4], and Dacre et al [11].

References

1. ASMUSSEN, S., *Applied Probability and Queues.* Wiley, Chichester, U.K., 1987.
2. Bertsimas, D., The Achievable Region Method in the Optimal Control of Queueing Systems; Formulations, Bounds and Policies. *Queueing Systems,* **21** (1995), 337–389.
3. Bertsimas, D. and Niño-Mora, J., Conservation Laws, Extended Polymatroid and Multi-Armed Bandit Problems: A Unified Approach to Indexable Systems. *Mathematics of Operations Research,* **21** (1996), 257–306.
4. Bertsimas, D. Paschalidis, I.C. and Tsitsiklis, J.N., Optimization of Multiclass Queueing Networks: Polyhedral and Nonlinear Characterization of Achievable Performance. *Ann. Appl. Prob.,* **4** (1994), 43–75.
5. Baras, J.S., Dorsey, A.J. and Makowski, A.M., Two Competing Queues with Linear Cost: the μc Rule Is Often Optimal. *Adv. Appl. Prob.,* **17** (1985), 186–209.
6. Buyukkoc, C., Varaiya, P. and Walrand, J., The $c\mu$ Rule Revisited. *Adv. Appl. Prob.,* **30** (1985), 237–238.
7. Chen, H. and Yao, D.D., *Fundamentals of Queueing Networks: Performance, Asymptotics and Optimization.* Springer-Verlag, New York, 2001.
8. Chvátal, V., *Linear Programming.* W.H. Freeman, New York, 1983.

9. Coffman, E. and Mitrani, I., A Characterization of Waiting Time Performance Realizable by Single Server Queues. *Operations Research,* **28** (1980), 810–821.
10. Cox, D.R. and Smith, W.L., *Queues.* Methunen, London, 1961.
11. Dacre, K.D., Glazebrook, K.D., and Ninõ-Mora, J., The Achievable Region Approach to the Optimal Control of Stochastic Systems. *J. Royal Statist. Soc.* (1999).
12. Dunstan, F.D.J. and Welsh, D.J.A., A Greedy Algorithm for Solving a Certain Class of Linear Programmes. *Math. Programming,* **5** (1973), 338–353.
13. Edmonds, J., Submodular Functions, Matroids and Certain Polyhedra. *Proc. Int. Conf. on Combinatorics (Calgary)*, Gordon and Breach, New York, 69-87, 1970.
14. Federgruen, A. and Groenevelt, H., The Greedy Procedure for Resource Allocation Problems: Necessary and Sufficient Conditions for Optimality. *Operations Res.,* **34** (1986), 909–918.
15. Federgruen, A. and Groenevelt, H., The Impact of the Composition of the Customer Base in General Queueing Models. *J. Appl. Prob.,* **24** (1987), 709–724.
16. Federgruen, A. and Groenevelt, H., M/G/c Queueing Systems with Multiple Customer Classes: Characterization and Control of Achievable Performance under Non-Preemptive Priority Rules. *Management Science,* **34** (1988), 1121–1138.
17. Federgruen, A. and Groenevelt, H., Characterization and Optimization of Achievable Performance in Queueing Systems. *Operations Res.,* **36** (1988), 733–741.
18. Fong, L.L. and Squillante, M.S., Time-Function Scheduling: A General Approach to Controllable Resource Management. IBM Research Report RC-20155, IBM Research Division, T.J. Watson Research Center, Yorktown Hts., New York, NY 10598, 1995.
19. Franaszek, P.A. and Nelson, R.D., Properties of Delay Cost Scheduling in Time-sharing Systems. IBM Research Report RC-13777, IBM Research Division, T.J. Watson Research Center, Yorktown Hts., New York, NY 10598, 1990.
20. Gelenbe, E. and Mitrani, I., *Analysis and Synthesis of Computer Systems.* Academic Press, London, 1980.
21. Gittins, J.C., Bandit Processes and Dynamic Allocation Indices (with discussions). *J. Royal Statistical Society, Ser. B,* **41** (1979), 148–177.
22. Gittins, J.C., *Multiarmed Bandit Allocation Indices.* Wiley, Chichester, 1989.
23. Gittins, J.C. and Jones, D.M., A Dynamic Allocation Index for the Sequential Design of Experiments. In: *Progress in Statistics: European Meeting of Statisticians, Budapest, 1972,* J. Gani, K. Sarkadi and I. Vince (eds.), North-Holland, Amsterdam, 1974, 241–266.
24. Glasserman, P. and Yao, D.D., *Monotone Structure in Discrete-Event Systems.* Wiley, New York, 1994.
25. Glasserman, P. and Yao, D.D., Monotone Optimal Control of Permutable GSMP's. *Mathematics of Operations Research,* **19** (1994), 449–476.
26. Grötschel, M., Lovász, L and Schrijver, A., *Geometric Algorithms and Combinatorial Optimization*, second corrected edition. Springer-Verlag, Berlin, 1993.
27. Harrison, J.M., Dynamic Scheduling of a Multiclass Queue: Discount Optimality. *Operations Res.,* **23** (1975), 270–282.
28. Harrison, J.M., The BIGSTEP Approach to Flow Management in Stochastic Processing Networks. In: *Stochastic Networks: Theory and Applications,* Kelly, Zachary, and Ziedens (eds.), Royal Statistical Society Lecture Note Series, #4, 1996, 57–90.
29. Harrison, J.M. and Wein, L., Scheduling Networks of Queues: Heavy Traffic Analysis of a Simple Open Network. *Queueing Systems,* **5** (1989), 265–280.
30. Kleinrock, L., A Delay Dependent Queue Discipline. *Naval Research Logistics Quarterly,* **11** (1964), 329–341.

31. Kleinrock, L., *Queueing Systems,* Vol. 2. Wiley, New York, 1976.
32. Klimov, G.P., Time Sharing Service Systems, *Theory of Probability and Its Applications,* **19** (1974), 532–551 (Part I) and **23** (1978), 314–321 (Part II).
33. Lai, T.L. and Ying, Z., Open Bandit Processes and Optimal Scheduling of Queueing Networks. *Adv. Appl. Prob.,* **20** (1988), 447-472.
34. Lu, Y., *Dynamic Scheduling of Stochastic Networks with Side Constraints.* Ph.D. Thesis, Columbia University, 1998.
35. Meilijson, I. and Weiss, G., Multiple Feedback at a Single-Server Station. *Stochastic Proc. and Appl.,* **5** (1977), 195–205.
36. Ross, K.W. and Yao, D.D., Optimal Dynamic Scheduling in Jackson Networks. *IEEE Transactions on Automatic Control,* **34** (1989), 47-53.
37. Ross, K.W. and Yao, D.D., Optimal Load Balancing and Scheduling in a Distributed Computer System. *Journal of the Association for Computing Machinery,* **38** (1991), 676–690.
38. Shanthikumar, J.G. and Sumita, U., Convex Ordering of Sojourn Times in Single-Server Queues: Extremal Properties of FIFO and LIFO Service Disciplines. *J. Appl. Prob.,* **24** (1987), 737–748.
39. Shanthikumar J.G. and Yao D.D., Multiclass Queueing Systems: Polymatroid Structure and Optimal Scheduling Control. *Operation Research,* **40** (1992), Supplement 2, S293–299.
40. Smith, W.L., Various Optimizers for Single-Stage Production. *Naval Research Logistics Quarterly,* **3** (1956), 59–66.
41. Tcha, D. and Pliska, S.R., Optimal Control of Single-Server Queueing Networks and Multiclass M/G/1 Queues with Feedback. *Operations Research,* **25** (1977), 248–258.
42. Tsoucas, P., The Region of Achievable Performance in a Model of Klimov. IBM Research Report RC-16543, IBM Research Division, T.J. Watson Research Center, Yorktown Hts., New York, NY 10598, 1991.
43. Varaiya, P., Walrand, J. and Buyyokoc, C., Extensions of the Multiarmed Bandit Problem: The Discounted Case. *IEEE Trans. Automatic Control,* **30** (1985), 426–439.
44. Weber, R., On the Gittins Index for Multiarmed Bandits. *Annals of Applied Probability,* (1992), 1024–1033.
45. Weber, R. and Stidham, S., Jr., Optimal Control of Service Rates in Networks of Queues. *Adv. Appl. Prob.,* **19** (1987), 202–218.
46. Weiss, G., Branching Bandit Processes. *Probability in the Engineering and Informational Sciences,* **2** (1988), 269–278.
47. Welsh, D., *Matroid Theory,* (1976), Academic Press, London.
48. Whittle, P., Multiarmed Bandits and the Gittins Index. *J. Royal Statistical Society, Ser. B,* **42** (1980), 143–149.
49. Whittle, P., *Optimization over Time: Dynamic Programming and Stochastic Control,* vols. I, II, Wiley, Chichester, 1982.
50. Yao, D.D. and Shanthikumar, J.G., Optimal Scheduling Control of a Flexible Machine. *IEEE Trans. on Robotics and Automation,* **6** (1990), 706–712.
51. Yao, D.D. and Zhang, L., Stochastic Scheduling and Polymatroid Optimization, *Lecture Notes in Applied Mathematics,* **33**, G. Ying and Q. Zhang (eds.), Springer-Verlag, 1997, 333–364.
52. Zhang, L., *Reliability and Dynamic Scheduling in Stochastic Networks.* Ph.D. Thesis, Columbia University, 1997.

Workload Modeling for Performance Evaluation

Dror G. Feitelson

School of Computer Science and Engineering
The Hebrew University, 91904 Jerusalem, Israel
feit@cs.huji.ac.il
http://www.cs.huji.ac.il/~feit

Abstract. The performance of a computer system depends on the characteristics of the workload it must serve: for example, if work is evenly distributed performance will be better than if it comes in unpredictable bursts that lead to congestion. Thus performance evaluations require the use of representative workloads in order to produce dependable results. This can be achieved by collecting data about real workloads, and creating statistical models that capture their salient features. This survey covers methodologies for doing so. Emphasis is placed on problematic issues such as dealing with correlations between workload parameters and dealing with heavy-tailed distributions and rare events. These considerations lead to the notion of structural modeling, in which the general statistical model of the workload is replaced by a model of the process generating the workload.

1 Introduction

The goal of performance evaluation is often to compare different system designs or implementations. The evaluation is expected to bring out performance differences that will allow for an educated decision regarding what design to employ or what system to buy. Thus it is implicitly assumed that observed performance differences indeed reflect important differences between the systems being studied.

However, performance differences may also be an artifact of the evaluation methodology. The performance of a system is not only a function of the system design and implementation. It may also be affected by the workload to which the system is subjected. For example, communication networks have often been analyzed using Poisson-related models of traffic, which indicated that the variance in load should smooth out over time and when multiple data sources are combined. But in 1994 Leland and co-workers showed, based on extensive observations and measurements, that this does not happen in practice [52]. Instead, they proposed a self-similar traffic model that captures the burstiness of network traffic and leads to more realistic evaluations of required buffer space and other parameters [24].

Analyzing network traffic was easy, in a sense, because all packets are of equal size and the only characteristic that required measurement and modeling was

M.C. Calzarossa and S. Tucci (Eds.): Performance 2002, LNCS 2459, pp. 114–141, 2002.
© Springer-Verlag Berlin Heidelberg 2002

the arrival process. But if we consider a complete computer system, the problem becomes more complex [13,11]. For example, a computer program may require a certain amount of CPU time, memory, and I/O, and these resource requirements may be interleaved in various ways during its execution. In addition there are several levels at which we might model the system: we can study the functional units used by a stream of instructions, the subsystems used by a job during its execution, or the requirements of jobs submitted to the system over time. Each of these scales is relevant for the design and evaluation of different parts of the system: the CPU, the hardware configuration, or the operating system.

The main domain used as a source of examples in this survey is that of parallel job scheduling. Workloads in this field are interesting due to the combination of being relatively small and at the same time relatively complex. The size of typical workloads is tens of thousands of jobs, as opposed to millions of packets in communication workloads. These workloads are characterized by a large number of factors, including the job sizes, runtimes, runtime estimates, and arrival patterns. The complexity derives not only from the multiple factors themselves, but from various correlations between them. Research on these issues is facilitated by the availability of data and models in the Parallel Workloads Archive [60]. In addition, there are several documented cases of how workload parameters influence the outcomes of performance evaluation studies [53,57,25].

2   Data Sources

The suggestion that workload modeling should be based on measurements is not new [32,4]. However, for a long time relatively few models based on actual measurements were published. As a result, many performance studies did not use experimental workload models at all (and don't to this day).

It is true that real-world data is not always available, or may be hard to obtain. But not using real data may lead to flawed evaluations [26]. This realization has led to a new wave of workload analyses in various fields of system design in recent years. Maybe the most prominent are the study of Internet traffic patterns [52,62,75] and world-wide web traffic patterns, with the intent of using the knowledge to evaluate server performance and caching schemes [5,18, 6]. Other examples include studies of process arrivals and runtimes [12,37], file systems [36], and video streams [48]. In the area of parallel systems, descriptive studies of workloads have only started to appear in recent years [29,76,58,27, 14]. There are also some attempts at modeling [10,28,21,41,23,54,15] and on-line characterization [34].

But where does the data come from? There are two main options: use data that is available anyway, or collect data specifically for the workload model. The latter can be done in two ways: active or passive instrumentation. Importantly, collected data can and should be made publicly available for use by other researchers [60,33].

2.1 Using Accounting and Activity Logs

The most readily available source of data is accounting or activity logs. Such logs are kept by the system for auditing, and record selected attributes of all activities. For example, many computer systems keep a log of all executed jobs. In large scale parallel systems, these logs can be quite detailed and are a rich source of information for workload studies [60]. Another example is web servers, that are often configured to log all requests.

A good example is provided by the analysis of three months of activity on the 128-node NASA Ames iPSC/860 hypercube supercomputer. This analysis provided the following data [29]:

- The distribution of job sizes (in number of nodes) for system jobs, and for user jobs classified according to when they ran: during the day, at night, or on the weekend.
- The distribution of total resource consumption (node seconds), for the same job classifications.
- The same two distributions, but classifying jobs according to their type: those that were submitted directly, batch jobs, and Unix utilities.
- The changes in system utilization throughout the day, for weekdays and weekends.
- The distribution of multiprogramming level seen during the day, at night, and on weekends. This also included the measured down time (a special case of 0 multiprogramming).
- The distribution of runtimes for system jobs, sequential jobs, and parallel jobs, and for jobs with different degrees of parallelism. This included a connection between common runtimes and the queue time limits of the batch scheduling system.
- The correlation between resource usage and job size, for jobs that ran during the day, at night, and over the weekend.
- The arrival pattern of jobs during the day, on weekdays and weekends, and the distribution of interarrival times.
- The correlation between the time of day a job is submitted and its resource consumption.
- The activity of different users, in terms of number of jobs submitted, and how many of them were different.
- Profiles of application usage, including repeated runs by the same user and by different users, on the same or on different numbers of nodes.
- The dispersion of runtimes when the same application is executed many times.

Note, however, that accounting logs do not always exist at the desired level of detail. For example, even if all communication on a web server is logged, this is at the request level, not at the packet level. To obtain packet-level data, specialized instrumentation is needed.

2.2 Passive and Active Instrumentation

If data is not readily available, it should be collected. This is done by instrumenting the system with special facilities that record its activity. A major problem with this is being unobtrusive, and not modifying the behavior of the system while we measure it.

Passive instrumentation refers to designs in which the system itself is not modified. The instrumentation is done by adding external components to the system, that monitor system activity but do not interfere with it. This approach is commonly used is studies of communication, where it is relatively easy to add a node to a system that only listens to the traffic on the communication network [52,73,35]. A more extreme example is a proposal to add a shadow parallel machine to a production parallel machine, with each shadow node monitoring the corresponding production node, and all of them cooperating to filter and summarize the data [66].

Active instrumentation refers to the modification of the system so that it will collect data about its activity. This can be integrated with the original system design, as was done for example in the RP3 [43]. However, it is more commonly done after the fact, when a need to collect data about a specific system arises. A good example is the Charisma project, which set out to characterize the I/O patterns on parallel machines [59]. This was done by instrumenting the I/O library and requesting users to re-link their applications; when running with the instrumented library, all I/O activity was recorded for subsequent analysis.

Obviously, instrumenting a system to collect data at runtime can affect the systems behavior and performance. This may not be very troublesome in the case of I/O activity, which suffers from high overhead anyway, but may be very problematic for the study of fine grain events related to communication, synchronization, and memory usage. One possible solution to this problem is to model the effect of the instrumentation, thereby enabling it to be factored out of the measurement results [55]. This leads to results that reflect real system behavior (that is, unaffected by the instrumentation), but leaves the problem of performance degradation while the measurements are being taken. An alternative is to selectively activate only those parts of the instrumentation that are needed at each instant, rather than collecting data about the whole system all the time. Remarkably, this can be done efficiently by modifying the system's object code as it runs [38].

2.3 Data Sanitation

Before data can be used to create a workload model, it has to be cleaned up. This has several aspects.

One important aspect is the handling of outliers. Workload logs sometimes include uncommon events that "don't make sense". Examples include

- In the two-year log of jobs run on the LANL CM-5 parallel machine, there is a 10-day stretch in which a single user ran about 5000 instances of a job that executed in 1–2 seconds on 128 nodes.

- In the two-year log of jobs run on the SDSC Paragon parallel machine, there is a large concentration of short jobs that arrive at 3:30 AM on different days. This is probably due to periodic invocation of administrative scripts.
- In the two-year log of jobs run on the SDSC SP2 parallel machine, there is a single hour in which a single user submitted some 580 similar jobs.

Of course, the decision that something is "uncommon" is subjective. The purist approach would be to leave everything in, because in fact it did happen in a real system. But on the other hand, while strange things may happen, it is difficult to argue for a specific one; if we leave it in the workload that is used to analyze systems, we run the risk of promoting systems that specifically cater for a singular unusual condition that is unlikely to ever occur again.

A procedure that was advocated by Cirne and Berman is to use clustering as a means to distinguish between "normal" and "abnormal" data [15]. Specifically, they characterize days in a workload log by an n-valued vector, and cluster these vectors into two clusters in R^n. If the clustering procedure distinguishes a single day and puts it in a cluster by itself, this day is removed and the procedure is repeated with the data that is left. Note, however, that this has its risks: first, abnormal behavior may span more than a single day, as the above examples show; moreover, removing days may taint other data, e.g. when interarrival times are considered.

Another aspect of workload sanitation involves errors. Workload logs may contain data about activities that failed to complete successfully, e.g. jobs that were submitted and either failed or were killed by the user. Should these jobs be included or deleted from the data? On one hand, they represent work that the system had to handle, even if nothing came of it. On the other hand, they do not represent useful work, and may have been submitted again later. An interesting compromise is to keep such data, and explicitly include it in the workload model [15]. This will enable the study of how failed work affects system utilization and the performance of "good" work.

Finally, an important issue is determining the degree to which data is generally representative. One problem is that data may be affected by local procedures and constraints where it was collected. For example, data on programs run on a machine equipped with only 32MB memory will show that programs do not have larger resident sets, but this is probably an artifact of this limit, and not a real characteristic of general workloads. A more striking example is provided by the NASA iPSC log mentioned above. In this log a full 57% of the jobs are invocations of the Unix pwd command on various nodes, which was the technique used by system personnel to verify that the system was working [29]. Another problem is that workloads may evolve with time [39], especially on large and unique installations such as parallel supercomputers. It is therefore important to capture data from a mature system, and not a new (or old) one.

3   Workload Modeling

There are two common ways to use a measured workload to analyze or evaluate a system design [32]: (1) use the traced workload directly to drive a simulation, or (2) create a model from the trace and use the model for either analysis or simulation. For example, trace-driven simulations based on large address traces are often used to evaluate cache designs [45,42]. But models of how applications traverse their address space have also been proposed, and provide interesting insights into program behavior [71,72].

3.1   Why Model

The advantage of using a trace directly is that it is the most "real" test of the system; the workload reflects a real workload precisely, with all its complexities, even if they are not known to the person performing the analysis.

The drawback is that the trace reflects a specific workload, and there is always the question of whether the results generalize to other systems or load conditions. In particular, there are cases where the workload depends on the system configuration, and therefore a given workload is not necessarily representative of workloads on systems with other configurations. Obviously, this makes the comparison of different configurations problematic. In addition, traces are often misleading if we have incomplete information about the circumstances when they were collected. For example, workload traces often contain intervals when the machine was down or part of it was dedicated to a specific project, but this information may not be available.

Workload models have a number of advantages over traces [70].

- It is possible to change model parameters one at a time, in order to investigate the influence of each one, while keeping other parameters constant. This allows for direct measurement of system sensitivity to the different parameters. It is also possible to select model parameters that are expected to match the specific workload at a given site.
  In general it is not possible to manipulate traces in this way, and even when it is possible, it can be problematic. For example, it is common practice to increase the modeled load on a system by reducing the average interarrival time. But this practice has the undesirable consequence of shrinking the daily load cycle as well. With a workload model, we can control the load independent of the daily cycle.
- Using a model, it is possible to repeat experiments under statistically similar conditions that are nevertheless not identical. For example, a simulation can be run several times with different seeds for the random number generator. This is needed in order to compute confidence intervals.
- Logs may not represent the real workload due to various problems: a limit of 4 hours may force users to break long jobs into multiple short jobs, jobs killed by the system may be repeated, etc. If taken at face value this may be misleading, but the problem is that often we do not know about such problems.

Conversely, a modeler has full knowledge of model workload characteristics. For example, it is easy to know which workload parameters are correlated with each other because this information is part of the model.

– Finally, modeling increases our understanding, and can lead to new designs based on this understanding. For example, identifying the repetitive nature of job submittal can be used for learning about job requirements from history. One can design a resource management policy that is parameterized by a workload model, and use measured values for the local workload to tune the policy.

The main problem with models, as with traces, is that of representativeness. That is, to what degree does the model represent the workload that the system will encounter in practice? The answer depends in part on the degree of detail that is included. As noted above, each job is composed of procedures that are built of instructions, and these interact with the computer at different levels. One option is to model these levels explicitly, creating a hierarchy of interlocked models for the different levels [13,10,64]. This has the obvious advantage of conveying a full and detailed picture of the structure of the workload. In fact, it is possible to create a whole spectrum of models spanning the range from condensed rudimentary models to direct use of a detailed trace.

For example, the sizes of a sequence of jobs need not be modeled independently. Rather, they can be derived from a lower-level model of the jobs' structures [30]. Hence the combined model will be useful both for evaluating systems in which jobs are executed on predefined partitions, and for evaluating systems in which the partition size is defined at runtime to reflect the current load and the specific requirements of jobs.

The drawback of this approach is that as more detailed levels are added, the complexity of the model increases. This is detrimental for three reasons. First, more detailed traces are needed in order to create the lower levels of the model. Second, it is commonly the case that there is wider diversity at lower levels. For example, there may be many jobs that use 32 nodes, but at a finer detail, some of them are coded as data parallel with serial and parallel phases, whereas others are written with MPI in an SPMD style. Creating a representative model that captures this diversity is hard, and possibly arbitrary decisions regarding the relative weight of the various options have to be made. Third, it is harder to handle such complex models. While this consideration can be mitigated by automation [70,44], it leaves the problem of having to check the importance and impact of very many different parameters.

3.2 How to Model

The most common approach used in workload modeling is to create a statistical summary of an observed workload. This is applied to all the workload attributes, e.g. computation, memory usage, I/O behavior, communication, etc. [46]. It is typically assumed that the longer the observation period, the better. Thus we can summarize a whole year's workload by analyzing a record of all the jobs that ran on a given system during this year. A synthetic workload can then be generated according to the model, by sampling from the distributions that constitute the model.

The question of what exactly to model, and at what degree of detail, is a hard one. On one hand, we want to fully characterize all important workload attributes. On the other hand a parsimonious model is more manageable, as there are less parameters whose values need to be assessed and whose influence needs to be studied. Also, there is a danger of over-fitting a particular workload at the expense of generality.

Fitting Distributions. The goal of a model is to be able to create a synthetic workload that mimics the original (possibly with certain modifications, according to the effects we wish to study). The statistical summary is therefore a distribution, or collection of distributions for various workload attributes. By sampling from these distributions we then create the model workload [49].

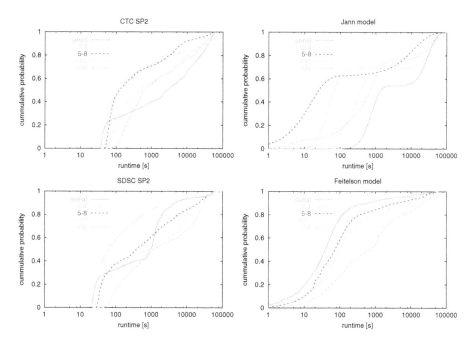

Fig. 1. Distributions of runtimes for different ranges of job sizes, in two workload logs and two models of parallel jobs.

One way to select suitable distributions is based on moments, and especially the mean and the variance of the sample data [23]. For example, these statistics indicate that the distribution of job runtimes has a wide dispersion, leading to a preference for a hyper-exponential model over an exponential one. Jann et al.

have used hyper-Erlang distributions to create models that match the first 3 moments of a distribution [41]. However, such summaries may be misleading, because they may not represent the shape of the distribution correctly. Specifically, in the Jann models, the distributions become distinctly bimodal, whereas the original data is much more continuous (Figure 1). The Feitelson model, which uses a three-stage hyper-exponential distribution, more closely resembles the original data in this respect.

The use of distributions with the right shape is not just an esthetic issue. Some 25 years ago Lazowska showed that using models based on a hyper-exponential distribution with matching moments to evaluate a simple queueing system leads to inaccurate results [50], and advocated the use of distributions with matching percentiles instead. He also noted that a hyper-exponential distribution has three parameters, whereas the mean and standard deviation of data only define two, so many different hyper-exponential distributions that match the first two moments are possible — and lead to different results.

Table 1. Sensitivity of statistics to the largest data points. Data regarding runtimes on the CTC SP2 machine from [23] courtesy of Allen Downey.

Rec's omitted	statistic (% change)		
(% of total)	mean [sec]	CV	median [sec]
0 (0%)	9371	3.1	552
5 (0.01%)	9177 (-2.1%)	2.2 (-29%)	551 (-0.2%)
10 (0.02%)	9094 (-3.0%)	2.0 (-35%)	551 (-0.2%)
20 (0.04%)	9023 (-3.7%)	1.9 (-39%)	551 (-0.2%)
40 (0.08%)	8941 (-4.6%)	1.9 (-39%)	550 (-0.4%)
80 (0.16%)	8834 (-5.7%)	1.8 (-42%)	549 (-0.5%)
160 (0.31%)	8704 (-7.1%)	1.8 (-42%)	546 (-1.1%)

Another problem with using statistics based on high moments of the data is that they are very sensitive to rare large samples [23]. Table 1 shows data based on the runtimes of 50866 parallel jobs from the CTC SP2 machine. Removing just the top 5 values causes the mean to drop by 2%, and the coefficient of variation (the standard deviation divided by the mean) to drop by 29%. The median, as a representative of order statistics, only changes by 0.2%. As the extreme values observed in a sample are not necessarily representative, this implies that the model may be largely governed by a small number of unrepresentative samples.

Finding a distribution that matches given moments is relatively easy, because it can be done based on inverting equations that relate a distribution's parameters to its moments. Finding a distribution that fits a given shape is typically harder [54]. One possibility is to use a maximum likelihood method, which finds the parameters that most likely gave rise to the observed data. Another option is to use an iterative method, in which the goodness of fit at each stage is quantified using the Chi-square test, the Kolmogorov-Smirnov test, or the

Anderson-Darling test (which is like the Kolmogorov-Smirnov test but places more emphasis on the tail of the distribution).

Correlations. Modeling the distribution of each workload attribute in isolation is not enough. An important issue that has to be considered is possible correlations between different attributes.

Correlations are important because they can have a dramatic impact on system behavior. Consider the scheduling of parallel jobs on a massively parallel machine as an example. Such scheduling is akin to 2D bin packing: each job is represented by a rectangle in processors×time space, and these rectangles have to be packed as tightly as possible. Assuming that when each job is submitted we know how many processors it needs, but do not know for how long it will run, it is natural to do the packing according to size. Specifically, packing the bigger jobs first may be expected to lead to better performance [16]. But what if there is a correlation between size and running time? If this is an inverse correlation, we find a win-win situation: the larger jobs are also shorter, so packing them first is statistically similar to using SJF (shortest job first) [47]. But if size and runtime are correlated, and large jobs run longer, scheduling them first may cause significant delays for subsequent smaller jobs, leading to dismal average performance [53].

Table 2. Correlation coefficient of runtime and size for different parallel supercomputer workloads.

System	Correlation
CTC SP2	−0.029
KTH SP2	0.011
SDSC SP2	0.145
LANL CM-5	0.211
SDSC Paragon	0.305

Establishing whether or not a correlation exists is not always easy. The commonly used correlation coefficient only yields high values if a strong linear relationship exists between the variables. In the example of the size and runtime of parallel jobs, the correlation coefficient is typically rather small (Table 2), and a scatter plot shows no significant correlation either (Figure 2). However, these two attributes are actually correlated with each other, as seen from the distributions for the CTC and SDSC logs in Figure 1. In both of these, the distribution of runtimes for ranges of larger job-sizes distinctly favors longer runtimes, whereas smaller jobs sizes favor short runtimes[1].

A coarse way to model correlation, which avoids this problem altogether, is to represent the workload as a set of points in a multidimensional space, and apply

---

[1] The only exception is the serial jobs on the CTC machine, which have very long runtimes; but this anomaly is unique to the CTC workload.

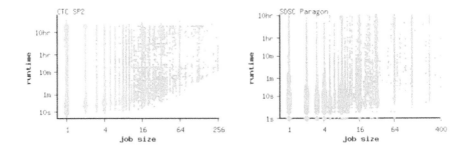

Fig. 2. The correlation between job sizes and runtimes on parallel supercomputers. The scatter-plot data is from the SDSC Paragon parallel machine.

clustering [13]. For example, each job can be represented by a tuple including its runtime, its size, its memory usage, and so on. By clustering we can then select a small number of representative jobs, as use them as the basis of our workload model; each such job comes with a certain (representative) combination of values for the different attributes. However, many workloads do not cluster nicely — rather, attribute values come from continuous distributions, and many different combinations are all possible.

The direct way to model a correlation between two attributes is to use the joint distribution of the two attributes. This suffers from two problems. One is that it may be expected to be hard to find an analytical distribution function that matches the data. The other is that for a large part of the range, the data may be very sparse. For example, most parallel jobs are small and run for a short time, so we have a lot of data about small short jobs. But we may not have enough data about large long jobs to say anything meaningful about the distribution — we just have a small set of unrelated samples.

The typical solution is therefore to divide the range of one attribute into sub-ranges, and model the distribution of the other attribute for each such sub-range. For example, the Jann model of supercomputer workloads divides the job size scale according to powers of two, and creates an independent model of the runtimes for each range of sizes [41]. As can be seen in Figure 1, these models are completely different from each other. An alternative is to use the same model for all subranges, and define a functional dependency of the model parameters on the subrange. For example, the Feitelson model first selects the size of each job according to the distribution of job sizes, and then selects a runtime from a distribution of runtimes that is conditioned on the selected size [28]. Specifically, the runtime is selected from a two-stage hyperexponential distribution, and the probability for using the exponential with the higher mean is linearly dependent on the size:

$$p(n) = 0.95 - 0.2(n/N)$$

Thus, for small jobs (the job size n is small relative to the machine size N) the probability of using the exponential with the smaller mean is 0.95, and for large jobs this drops to 0.75.

Stationarity. A special type of correlation is correlation with time. This means that the workload changes with time: it is not stationary.

On short time scales, the most commonly encountered non-stationary phenomenon is the daily work cycle. In many systems, the workload at night is quite different from the workload during the day. Many workload models ignore this and focus on the daytime workload, assuming that it is stationary. However, when the workload includes items whose duration is on the scale of hours (such as parallel jobs), the daily cycle cannot be ignored. There are two typical ways for dealing with it. One is to divide the day into a number of ranges, and model each one separately assuming that it is stationary [14]. The other is to use parameterized distributions, and model the daily cycle by showing how the parameters change with time of day [54].

Over long ranges, a non-stationary workload can be the result of changing usage patterns as users get to know the system better. It can also result from changing missions, e.g. when one project ends and another takes its place. Such effects are typically not included in workload models, but they could affect the data on which models are based. We return to this issue in Section 5.

Assumptions. An important point that is often overlooked in workload modeling is that everything has to be modeled. It is not good to model one attribute with great precision, but use unbased assumptions for the others.

The problem is that assumptions can be very tempting and reasonable, but still be totally untrue. For example, it is reasonable to assume that parallel jobs are used for speedup, that is, to complete the computation faster. After all, this is the basis for Amdahl's Law. But other possibilities also exist — for example, parallelism can be used to solve the same problem with greater precision rather than faster. The problem is that assuming speedup is the goal leads to a model in which parallelism is inversely correlated with runtime, and this has an effect on scheduling [53,26]. Observations of real workloads indicate that this is not the case, as shown above.

Another reasonable assumption is that users will provide the system with accurate estimates of job runtimes when asked to. At least on large scale parallel systems, users indeed spend significant effort tuning their applications, and may be expected to have this information. Also, backfilling schedulers reward low estimates but penalize underestimates, leading to a convergence towards accurate estimates. Nevertheless, studies of user estimates reveal that they are often highly inaccurate, and often represent an overestimate by a full order of magnitude [57]. Surprisingly, this can sway results comparing schedulers that use the estimates to decide whether to backfill jobs (that is, to use them to fill holes in an existing schedule) [25].

4   Heavy Tails, Self Similarity, and Burstiness

A major problem with applying the techniques described in the previous section occurs when the data is "bad" [3]. This is best explained by an example. If the data fits, say, an exponential distribution, then a running average of growing numbers of data samples quickly converges to the mean of the distribution. But bad data is ill-behaved: it does not converge when averaged, but rather continues to grow and fluctuate. Such effects have received considerable attention lately, as many different data sets were found to display them. For more technical detail on this topic, see [62,61].

4.1   Distributions with Heavy Tails

A very common situation is that distributions have many small elements, and few large elements. For example, there are many small files and few large files; many short processes and few long processes. The question is how dominant are the large elements relative to the small ones. In heavy-tailed distributions, the rare large elements (from the tail of the distribution) dominate.

In general, the relative importance of the tail can be classified into one of three cases [62]. Consider trying to estimate the length of a process, given that we know that it has already run for a certain time, and that the mean of the distribution of process lengths is m.

- If the distribution of process lengths has a *short* tail, than the more we have waited already, the less additional time we expect to wait. The mean of the tail is smaller than m. For example, this would be the case if the distribution was uniform over a certain range.
- If the distribution is *memoryless*, the expected additional time we need to wait for the process to terminate is independent of how long we have waited already. The mean length of the tail is always the same as the mean length of the whole distribution. This is the case for the exponential distribution.
- But if the distribution is *heavy* tailed, the additional time we may expect to wait till the process terminates grows with the time we have already waited. The mean of the tail is larger than m, the mean of the whole distribution. An example of this type is the Pareto distribution.

An important consequence of heavy tailed distributions is the mass disparity phenomenon: a small number of samples account for the majority of mass, whereas all small samples account for negligible mass [17]. Conversely, a typical sample is small, but a typical unit of mass comes from a large sample. Using concrete examples from computers, a typical process is short, but a typical second of CPU activity is part of a long process; a typical file is small, but a typical byte of storage belongs to a large file (Figure 3). This disparity is sometimes referred to as the "mice and elephants" phenomenon. But this metaphor may conjure the image of a bimodal distribution[2], which could be misleading: in most cases, the distribution is continuous.

---

[2] A typical mouse weighs about 28 grams, whereas an elephant weighs 3 to 6 tons, depending on whether it is Indian or African. Cats, dogs, and zebras, which fall in

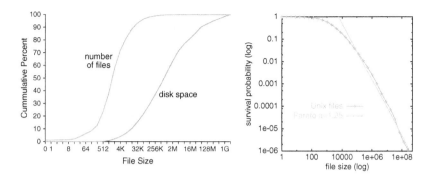

Fig. 3. The distribution of file sizes, from a 1993 survey of 12 million Unix files [40]. Left: 90% of the files are less than 16KB long, and use only some 10% of the total disk space. Half the disk space is occupied by a very small fraction of large files. Right: log-log complementary distribution plot, with possible Pareto model of the tail; see Equation (2).

Formally, it is common to define heavy tailed distributions to be those whose tails decay like a power law — the probability of sampling a value larger than x is proportional to one over x raised to some power [62]:

$$\bar{F}(x) = \Pr[X > x] \sim x^{-a} \qquad\qquad 0 < a < 2 \qquad\qquad (1)$$

where $\bar{F}(x)$ is the survival function (that is, $\bar{F}(x) = 1 - F(x)$), and $\sim$ means "has the same distribution". This is a very strong statement. Consider an exponential distribution. The probability of sampling a value larger than say 100 times the mean is e^{-100}, which is totally negligible for all intents and purposes. But for a Pareto distribution with $a = 2$, this probability is $1/40000$: one in every 40000 samples will be bigger than 100 times the mean. While rare, such events can certainly happen. When the shape parameter is $a = 1.1$, and the tail is heavier, this probability increases to one in 2216 samples.

An important characteristic of heavy tailed distributions is that some of their moments may be undefined. Specifically, using the above definition, if $a \leq 1$ the mean will be undefined, and if $a \leq 2$ the variance will be undefined. But what does this mean? Consider a Pareto distribution with $a = 1$, whose probability density is proportional to x^{-2}. Trying to evaluate its mean leads to

$$E[x] = \int cx \frac{1}{x^2} \mathrm{d}x = c \ln x$$

so the mean is infinite. But for any finite number of samples, the mean obviously exists. The answer is that the mean grows logarithmically with the number of observations. However, this statement is misleading, as the running mean does not actually resemble the log function. In fact, it grows in big jumps every time a

between, are missing from this picture.

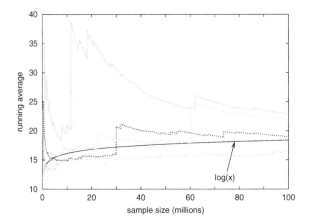

Fig. 4. Examples of the running mean of samples from a Pareto distribution. Four plots using different random number generator seeds are shown.

large observation from the tail of the distribution is sampled, and then it slowly decays again towards the log function (Figure 4).

The definition (1) can also be used to determine if a given data set is heavy tailed. Taking the log from both sides we observe that

$$\log \bar{F}(x) = \log x^{-a} = -a \log x \qquad (2)$$

So plotting $\log \bar{F}(x)$ (the log of the fraction of observations larger than x) as a function of $\log x$ should lead to a straight line with slope $-a$ (this is sometimes called a "log-log complementary distribution plot", or LLCD, see Figure 3).

This technique can be further improved by aggregating successive observations (that is, replacing each sequence of k observations by their sum). Distributions for which such aggregated random variables have the same distribution as the original are called stable distributions. The Normal distribution is the only stable distribution with finite variance. Heavy tailed distributions (according to definition (1)) are also stable, but have an infinite variance. Thus the central limit theorem does not apply, and the aggregated random variables do not have a Normal distribution. Rather, they have the same heavy-tailed distribution. This can be verified by creating LLCD plots of the aggregated samples, and checking that they too are straight lines with the same slope as the original [19, 18]. If the distribution is not heavy tailed, the aggregated samples will tend to be Normally distributed (the more so as the level of aggregation increases), and the slopes of the LLCD plots will increase with the level of aggregation.

Using these and other procedures, the following have been argued to be heavy tailed:

– Process runtimes on general purpose workstations [51,37]. Note that this only applies to the tail of the distribution, i.e. to processes longer than a certain threshold. Measurements show the power to be close to 1.

$$\Pr[T > t] = t^{-k}$$

model	tail	k
[51] ('86)	> 3s	1.05–1.25
[37] ('96)	> 1s	0.78–1.29

- File sizes on a general purpose system (Figure 3), again limited to the tail of the distribution. There has been some discussion on whether this is best modeled by a Pareto or a lognormal distribution, but at least some data sets seem to fit a Pareto model better, and in any case they are highly skewed [22].
- Various aspects of Internet traffic, specifically [62,69]
  - Flow sizes
  - FTP data transfer sizes
  - TELNET packet interarrival times
- Various aspects of web server load, specifically [18,6]
  - The tail of the distribution of file sizes on a server
  - The distribution of request sizes
  - The popularity of the different files (this is a Zipf distribution — see below)
  - The distribution of off times (between requests)
  - The distribution of the number of embedded references in a web page
- The popularity of items (e.g. pages on the web) is often found to follow Zipf's Law [77], which is also a power law [7]. Assume a set of items are ordered according to their popularity counts, i.e. according to how many times each was selected. Zipf's Law is that the count y is inversely proportional to the rank r according to

$$y \approx r^{-b} \qquad\qquad b \approx 1 \qquad\qquad (3)$$

This means that there are r items with count larger than y, or

$$\Pr[Y > y] = r/N \qquad\qquad (4)$$

where N is the total number of items. We can express r as a function of y by inverting the original expression (3), leading to $r \approx y^{-1/b}$; substituting this into (4) gives a power-law tail

$$\Pr[Y > y] = C \cdot y^{-a}$$

moreover, $b \approx 1$ implies $a \approx 1$ [2].

The problem with procedures such as plotting $\log \bar{F}(x)$ as a function of $\log x$ and measuring the slope of the line is that data regarding the tail is sparse by definition. When applying an automatic classification procedure, a single large sample may sway the decision is favor of "heavy". But is this the correct generalization? The question is one of identifying the nature of the underlying distribution, without having adequate data. Claiming a truly heavy tailed distribution is almost always unfounded, because such a claim means that unbounded samples should be expected as more and more samples are generated. In all real cases, samples must be bounded by some number (a process cannot run for longer than the uptime of the computer; a file cannot be larger than the total available disk space).

One simple option is to postulate a certain upper bound on the distribution, but this does not really solve the problem because the question of where to place the bound remains unanswered. Another option is to try fitting alternative distributions for which all moments converge. For example, there have been successful attempts to model file sizes using a lognormal distribution rather than a Pareto distribution [22]. This has the additional benefit of fitting the whole distribution rather than just the tail.

A more general approach is to use phase-type distributions, which employ a mixture of exponentials. Consider a simple example, in which N samples are drawn from an exponential distribution, and one additional sample is a far outlier. This can be modeled as a hyperexponential distribution, with probability $N/(N+1)$ to sample from the main exponential, and probability $1/(N+1)$ to sample from a second exponential distribution with a mean equal to the outlier value. In general, it is possible to construct mixtures of exponentials to fit any observed distribution [9]. This is especially important for analytical modeling, as distributions with infinite moments cause severe problems for such analysis. For simulation the exact definition is somewhat less important, as long as significant mass is concentrated in the tail.

4.2   The Phenomena of Self Similarity

Self similarity refers to situations in which a phenomenon has the same general characteristics at different scales [56,67]. In particular, parts of the whole may be scaled-down copies of the whole, as in well known fractals such as the Cantor set and the Sierpiński triangle. In natural phenomena we cannot expect perfect copies of the whole, but we can expect the same statistical properties. A well known natural fractal is the coast of Britain [56]. Workloads often also display such behavior.

The first demonstrations of self similarity in computer workloads were for Internet traffic, and used a striking visual demonstration. A time series representing the number of packets transmitted during successive time units was recorded. At a fine granularity, i.e. when using small time unites, this was seen to be bursty. But the same bursty behavior persisted also when the time series was aggregated over several orders of magnitude, by using larger and larger time units. This contradicted the common Poisson model of packet arrivals, which predicted that the traffic should average out when aggregated.

Similar demonstrations have since been done for other types of workloads. Figure 5 gives an example from jobs arriving at a parallel supercomputer. Self similarity has also been shown in file systems [36] and in web usage [18].

The mathematical description of self similarity is based on the notion of long-range correlations. Actually, there are correlations at many different time scales: self similarity implies that the workload at a certain instant is similar to the workload at other instants at different scales, starting with a short time scale,

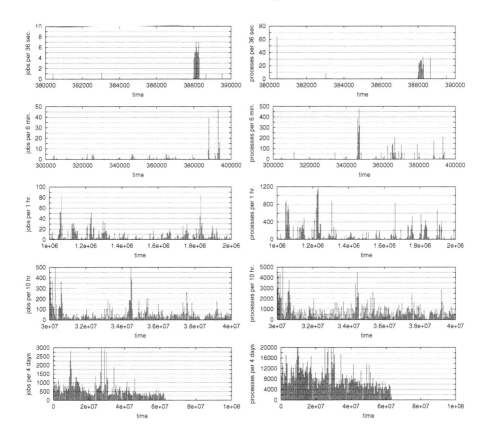

Fig. 5. Burstiness of job arrivals to the SDSC Paragon parallel supercomputer at different time scales. Left: jobs per time unit. Right: processes per time unit (each parallel job is composed of multiple processes). In all the graphs time is in seconds; the duration of the log is two years, which is about 63 million seconds.

through medium time scales, and up to long time scales. But the strength of the correlation decreases as a power law with the time scale.

A model useful for understanding the correlations leading to self similarity is provided by random walks. In a one-dimensional random walk, each step is either to the left or to the right with equal probabilities. It is well known that after n steps the expected distance from the origin is $\sqrt{n}$, or $n^{0.5}$. But what happens if the steps are correlated with each other? If each step has a probability higher than $\frac{1}{2}$ of being in the same direction as the previous step, we can expect slightly longer stretches of steps in the same direction. But this is not enough to change the expected distance from the origin after n steps — is stays $n^{0.5}$. This remains true also if each step is correlated with all previous steps with exponentially decreasing weights. In both these cases, the correlation only has a short range, and the effect of each step decays to zero very quickly.

But if a step is correlated with previous steps with polynomially decreasing weights, meaning that the weight of the step taken k steps back is proportional to k^{-a}, stretches of steps in the same direction become much longer. And the expected distance from the origin is found to behave like n^H, with $0.5 < H < 1$. H is called the Hurst parameter [63]. The closer it is to 1, the more self-similar the walk.

One way of checking whether a process is self similar is directly based on the above: measure the range covered after n steps, and check the exponent that relates it to n. Assume you start with a time series $x_1, x_2, \ldots$. The procedure is as follows [63]:

1. Normalize it subtracting the mean $\bar{x}$ from each sample, giving $z_i = x_i - \bar{x}$. The mean of the new series is obviously 0.
2. Calculate the distance covered after j steps:

$$y_j = \sum_{i=1}^{j} z_i$$

3. The range covered after n steps is the maximum distance that has occurred:

$$R_n = \max_{j=1\ldots n} y_j - \min_{j=1\ldots n} y_j$$

4. Rescale this by dividing by the standard deviation of the original data.
5. The model is that the rescaled range, R/s, should grow like cn^H. To check this take the log leading to

$$\log \left(\frac{R}{s} \right)_n = \log c + H \log n$$

If the process is indeed self similar, we expect to see a straight line, and the slope of the line gives H.

If a long time series is given, the calculation for small values of n is repeated for non-overlapping sub-series of length n each, and the average is used. An example of the results of doing so is given in Figure 6, based on the data shown graphically in Figure 5.

Other ways of checking for self similarity are based on the rate in which the variance decays as observations are aggregated, or on the decay of the spectral density, possibly using wavelet analysis [1]. Results of the Variance-time method are also shown in Figure 6. This is based on aggregating the original time series (that is, replacing each m consecutive values by their average) and calculating the variance of the new series. This decays polynomially with a rate of $-\beta$, leading to a straight line with this slope in log-log axes. The Hurst parameter is then given by

$$H = 1 - (\beta/2)$$

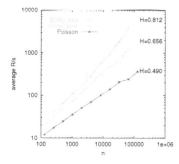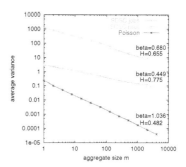

Fig. 6. The $(R/s)_n$ and variance-time methods for measuring self similarity, applied to the data in Figure 5. A Poisson process with no self-similarity is included as reference, as well as linear regression lines.

4.3   Modeling Self-Similarity

Heavy tailed distributions and self similarity are intimately tied to each other, and the modeling of self-similar workloads depends on this. As noted above, self similarity is a result of long-range correlation in the workload. By using heavy tailed distributions to create a workload model with the desired long range correlation, we get a model that also displays self similarity.

The idea is that the workload is not uniform, but rather generated by multiple on-off processes [75,18,36]. "On" periods are active periods, in which the workload arrives at the system at a certain rate (jobs per hour, packets per second, etc). "Off" periods are inactive periods during which no load is generated. The complete workload is the result of many such on-off processes.

The crux of the model is the distributions governing the lengths of the on and off periods. If these distributions are heavy tailed, we get long-range correlation: if a unit of work arrives at time t, similar units of work will continue to arrive for the duration d of the on period to which it belongs, leading to a correlation with subsequent times up to $t + d$. As this duration is heavy tailed, the correlation created by this burst will typically be for a short d; but occasionally a long on period will lead to a correlation over a long span of time. As many different bursts may be active at time t, what we actually get is a combination of such correlations for durations that correspond to the distribution of the on periods. But this is heavy tailed, so we get a correlation that decays polynomially — a long range dependence.

In some cases, this type of behavior is built in, and a direct result of the heavy tailed nature of certain workload parameters. For example, given that web server file sizes are heavy tailed, the distribution of service times will also be heavy tailed (as the time to serve a file is proportional to its size). During the time a file is served, data is transmitted at a constant rate. This is correlated with later transmittals according to the heavy-tailed distribution of sizes and transmission times, leading to long range correlation and self similarity [18].

5   Workload Dynamics and Structural Modeling

The on-off process used for modeling self-similar workloads has another very important benefit. It provides a mechanism for introducing locality into the workload, so that not only the statistics will be modeled, but also the dynamics.

5.1   User Behavior

The procedure for workload modeling outlined in Section 3.2 was to analyze real workloads, recover distributions that characterize them, and then sample from these distributions. The main problem with this procedure is that is loses all structural information.

A real workload is not a random sampling from a distribution. For example, the load on a server used by students at a university changes from week to week, depending on the assignments that are due each time. In each week, everybody is working on the same task, so the workload is composed of many jobs that are statistically similar. The next week all the jobs are similar to each other again, but they are all different from the jobs of the previous week. Over the whole year we indeed observe a wide distribution with many job types, but at any given time we do not see a representative sampling of this distribution. Instead, we only see samples concentrated in a small part of the distribution (Figure 7). The workload displays a "locality of sampling"[3].

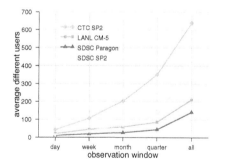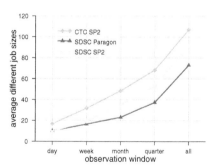

Fig. 7. The dynamics of workloads. Left: the active set of users grows with the observation window. Right: so does the diversity of the workload, in this case represented by the number of different job sizes observed. Note that the x scale is not linear.

The common way to model workload dynamics is with a user behavior graph [31]. This is a graph whose nodes represent states. In each state, the user executes a certain job with characteristics drawn from a certain distribution. The

---

[3] The existence of such local repetitiveness in workloads was suggested to me by Larry Rudolph over ten years ago.

arcs denote the probability of moving from state to state. The graph therefore encodes a Markovian model of the workload dynamics. A random walk on the graph, subject to the model's transition probabilities, creates a random workload sequence such that the probability of each job matches the limiting probability of that job's state, but it also abides by the model of which jobs come after each other, and how many times a job may be repeated (using self-looping arcs in the graph) [64]. However, this needs to be adjusted in order to create heavy tailed distributions.

In a university it may be plausible to argue that all students should be modeled using the same user behavior graph. But in a production environment one would expect different users, with different levels of activity and different behaviors. In addition, the active population changes with time (Figure 7) [23]. Thus what we actually need is not one user behavior graph, but a model of the user population as a whole: how the population of users changes, and what user behavior graph each one should have. Using such a model has two important advantages. First, it has built-in support for generating self-similar workloads (assuming users have long-tailed on and off activity times). Second, it provides a good way to control load without modifying the underlying distributions: simply change the number of users [6].

Another aspect of user behavior, which is not captured by the user behavior graph, is the feedback from the system performance to the generation of new work. Real users are not oblivious to the system's behavior: They typically submit additional work only when existing work is finished. Thus, if the user population is bounded, the system's current performance modulates the offered load, automatically reducing it when congestion occurs, and spreading the load more evenly over time. But adding this integrates the workload model with the system, and prevents the use of an independent workload model.

5.2   Internal Structure

User modeling implants a structure on the workload. But it does not by itself define the basic building blocks of the workload — the jobs that are submitted to the system.

One approach is to use a descriptive model. For example, modeling of parallel applications requires a functional relationship between the number of processors and the runtimes — in short, a speedup function of the application. A model of speedups based on the average parallelism and its variance was proposed by Downey [21]. Another model, based on the parallel and sequential parts of the application and on the overheads of parallelization, was proposed by Sevcik [68].

An alternative is to model the application's internal structure. It is common practice to measure systems using parameterized synthetic applications [8]. Such applications typically involve several nested loops that mimic the behavior of iterative applications, and perform different amounts of computations, I/O operations, and memory accesses. The number of iterations, types of operations, and spread of addresses are all parameters, thus allowing a single simple and generic benchmark to mimic many different applications.

A similar approach can be used to generate a synthetic workload: use a parameterized program, selecting the parameters from suitable distributions in order to create the desired mix of behaviors. For example, Rudolph and Feitelson have proposed a model of parallel applications with relatively few parameters, including the total work done, the average size of work units and its variability, the way in which these work units are partitioned into threads, and the number of barriers by which they are synchronized [30].

The question is what distributions to use. While there has been some work done on characterizing specific applications [20,74,65], there has been little if any work on characterizing the mix of application characteristics in a typical workload. A rather singular example is the Charisma project, in which a whole workload was measured [59]. Interestingly, this requires the same statistical techniques described in Section 3.2, just applied to a different level. Indeed, such hierarchical structuring of workloads has been recognized as an important workload structuring tool [64].

Naturally, all this applies to practically all types of workloads, and not only to jobs on (parallel) machines. For example, web workloads can be viewed as sessions that each include a sequence of requests for pages that each have several embedded components; database workloads include transactions that contain a number of embedded database operations, and so on.

6   Conclusions

Performance evaluation depends on workload modeling. We have outlined the conceptual framework of such modeling, starting with simple statistical characterization, continuing with the handling of self similarity, and ending with the need to also model user behavior. But all this is useless without real measured data from which distributions and parameters can be learned. One of the most important tasks is to collect large amounts of high resolution data about the behavior of workloads, and to share this data to facilitate the creation of better workload models.

Apart from collecting data, there are also many methodological issues that beg for additional work. These include techniques to analyze and characterize workloads, evaluations of the relative importance of different workload parameters, and demonstrations of how workloads affect system performance. In all of these, emphasis should be placed on the dynamics of workloads. And as with the workload data, it is important to share the programs that perform the analysis and implement the models — both to facilitate the dissemination and use of new techniques, and to help ensure that researchers use compatible methodologies.

Acknowledgement. This research was supported by the Israel Science Foundation (grant no. 219/99).

References

1. P. Abry and D. Veitch, *"Wavelet analysis of long-range-dependent traffic"*. *IEEE Trans. Information Theory* **44(1)**, pp. 2–15, Jan 1998.

2. L. A. Adamic, *"Zipf, power-laws, and Pareto – a ranking tutorial"*. 2000. http://www.hpl.hp.com/shl/papers/ranking/.

3. R. J. Adler, R. E. Feldman, and M. S. Taqqu (eds.), *A Practical Guide to Heavy Tails: Statistical Techniques and Applications*. Birkhäuser, 1998.

4. A. K. Agrawala, J. M. Mohr, and R. M. Bryant, *"An approach to the workload characterization problem"*. *Computer* **9(6)**, pp. 18–32, Jun 1976.

5. M. F. Arlitt and C. L. Williamson, *"Web server workload characterization: the search for invariants"*. In *SIGMETRICS Conf. Measurement & Modeling of Comput. Syst.*, pp. 126–137, May 1996.

6. P. Barford and M. Crovella, *"Generating representative web workloads for network and server performance evaluation"*. In *SIGMETRICS Conf. Measurement & Modeling of Comput. Syst.*, pp. 151–160, Jun 1998.

7. L. Breslau, P. Cao, L. Fan, G. Phillips, and S. Shenker, *"Web caching and Zipf-like distributions: evidence and implications"*. In *IEEE Infocom*, pp. 126–134, Mar 1999.

8. W. Buchholz, *"A synthetic job for measuring system performance"*. *IBM Syst. J.* **8(4)**, pp. 309–318, 1969.

9. W. Bux and U. Herzog, *"The phase concept: approximation of measured data and perfrmance analysis"*. In *Computer Performance*, K. M. Chandy and M. Reiser (eds.), pp. 23–38, North Holland, 1977.

10. M. Calzarossa, G. Haring, G. Kotsis, A. Merlo, and D. Tessera, *"A hierarchical approach to workload characterization for parallel systems"*. In *High-Performance Computing and Networking*, pp. 102–109, Springer-Verlag, May 1995. Lect. Notes Comput. Sci. vol. 919.

11. M. Calzarossa, L. Massari, and D. Tessera, *"Workload characterization issues and methodologies"*. In *Performance Evaluation: Origins and Directions*, G. Haring, C. Lindemann, and M. Reiser (eds.), pp. 459–482, Springer-Verlag, 2000. Lect. Notes Comput. Sci. vol. 1769.

12. M. Calzarossa and G. Serazzi, *"A characterization of the variation in time of workload arrival patterns"*. *IEEE Trans. Comput.* **C-34(2)**, pp. 156–162, Feb 1985.

13. M. Calzarossa and G. Serazzi, *"Workload characterization: a survey"*. *Proc. IEEE* **81(8)**, pp. 1136–1150, Aug 1993.

14. S-H. Chiang and M. K. Vernon, *"Characteristics of a large shared memory production workload"*. In *Job Scheduling Strategies for Parallel Processing*, D. G. Feitelson and L. Rudolph (eds.), pp. 159–187, Springer Verlag, 2001. Lect. Notes Comput. Sci. vol. 2221.

15. W. Cirne and F. Berman, *"A comprehensive model of the supercomputer workload"*. In 4th *Workshop on Workload Characterization*, Dec 2001.

16. E. G. Coffman, Jr., M. R. Garey, and D. S. Johnson, *"Approximation algorithms for bin-packing — an updated survey"*. In *Algorithm Design for Computer Systems Design*, G. Ausiello, M. Lucertini, and P. Serafini (eds.), pp. 49–106, Springer-Verlag, 1984.

17. M. E. Crovella, *"Performance evaluation with heavy tailed distributions"*. In *Job Scheduling Strategies for Parallel Processing*, D. G. Feitelson and L. Rudolph (eds.), pp. 1–10, Springer Verlag, 2001. Lect. Notes Comput. Sci. vol. 2221.

18. M. E. Crovella and A. Bestavros, *"Self-similarity in world wide web traffic: evidence and possible causes"*. In *SIGMETRICS Conf. Measurement & Modeling of Comput. Syst.*, pp. 160–169, May 1996.

19. M. E. Crovella and M. S. Taqqu, *"Estimating the heavy tail index from scaling properties"*. *Methodology & Comput. in Applied Probability* **1(1)**, pp. 55–79, Jul 1999.

20. R. Cypher, A. Ho, S. Konstantinidou, and P. Messina, *"A quantitative study of parallel scientific applications with explicit communication"*. *J. Supercomput.* **10(1)**, pp. 5–24, 1996.

21. A. B. Downey, *"A parallel workload model and its implications for processor allocation"*. In *6th Intl. Symp. High Performance Distributed Comput.*, Aug 1997.

22. A. B. Downey, *"The structural cause of file size distributions"*. In 9th *Modeling, Anal. & Simulation of Comput. & Telecomm. Syst.*, Aug 2001.

23. A. B. Downey and D. G. Feitelson, *"The elusive goal of workload characterization"*. *Performance Evaluation Rev.* **26(4)**, pp. 14–29, Mar 1999.

24. A. Erramilli, U. Narayan, and W. Willinger, *"Experimental queueing analysis with long-range dependent packet traffic"*. *IEEE/ACM Trans. Networking* **4(2)**, pp. 209–223, Apr 1996.

25. D. G. Feitelson, *Analyzing the Root Causes of Performance Evaluation Results*. Technical Report 2002-4, School of Computer Science and Engineering, Hebrew University, Mar 2002.

26. D. G. Feitelson, *"The forgotten factor: facts"*. In *EuroPar*, Springer-Verlag, Aug 2002. Lect. Notes Comput. Sci.

27. D. G. Feitelson, *"Memory usage in the LANL CM-5 workload"*. In *Job Scheduling Strategies for Parallel Processing*, D. G. Feitelson and L. Rudolph (eds.), pp. 78–94, Springer Verlag, 1997. Lect. Notes Comput. Sci. vol. 1291.

28. D. G. Feitelson, *"Packing schemes for gang scheduling"*. In *Job Scheduling Strategies for Parallel Processing*, D. G. Feitelson and L. Rudolph (eds.), pp. 89–110, Springer-Verlag, 1996. Lect. Notes Comput. Sci. vol. 1162.

29. D. G. Feitelson and B. Nitzberg, *"Job characteristics of a production parallel scientific workload on the NASA Ames iPSC/860"*. In *Job Scheduling Strategies for Parallel Processing*, D. G. Feitelson and L. Rudolph (eds.), pp. 337–360, Springer-Verlag, 1995. Lect. Notes Comput. Sci. vol. 949.

30. D. G. Feitelson and L. Rudolph, *"Metrics and benchmarking for parallel job scheduling"*. In *Job Scheduling Strategies for Parallel Processing*, D. G. Feitelson and L. Rudolph (eds.), pp. 1–24, Springer-Verlag, 1998. Lect. Notes Comput. Sci. vol. 1459.

31. D. Ferrari, *"On the foundation of artificial workload design"*. In *SIGMETRICS Conf. Measurement & Modeling of Comput. Syst.*, pp. 8–14, Aug 1984.

32. D. Ferrari, *"Workload characterization and selection in computer performance measurement"*. *Computer* **5(4)**, pp. 18–24, Jul/Aug 1972.

33. K. Ferschweiler, M. Calzarossa, C. Pancake, D. Tessera, and D. Keon, *"A community databank for performance tracefiles"*. In *Euro PVM/MPI*, Y. Cotronis and J. Dongarra (eds.), pp. 233–240, Springer-Verlag, 2001. Lect. Notes Comput. Sci. vol. 2131.

34. R. Gibbons, *"A historical application profiler for use by parallel schedulers"*. In *Job Scheduling Strategies for Parallel Processing*, D. G. Feitelson and L. Rudolph (eds.), pp. 58–77, Springer Verlag, 1997. Lect. Notes Comput. Sci. vol. 1291.

35. S. D. Gribble and E. A. Brewer, *"System design issues for internet middleware services: deductions from a large client trace"*. In *Symp. Internet Technologies and Systems*, USENIX, Dec 1997.

36. S. D. Gribble, G. S. Manku, D. Roselli, E. A. Brewer, T. J. Gibson, and E. L. Miller, "*Self-similarity in file systems*". In *SIGMETRICS Conf. Measurement & Modeling of Comput. Syst.*, pp. 141–150, Jun 1998.

37. M. Harchol-Balter and A. B. Downey, "*Exploiting process lifetime distributions for dynamic load balancing*". *ACM Trans. Comput. Syst.* **15(3)**, pp. 253–285, Aug 1997.

38. J. K. Hollingsworth, B. P. Miller, and J. Cargille, "*Dynamic program instrumentation for scalable performance tools*". In *Scalable High-Performance Comput. Conf.*, pp. 841–850, May 1994.

39. S. Hotovy, "*Workload evolution on the Cornell Theory Center IBM SP2*". In *Job Scheduling Strategies for Parallel Processing*, D. G. Feitelson and L. Rudolph (eds.), pp. 27–40, Springer-Verlag, 1996. Lect. Notes Comput. Sci. vol. 1162.

40. G. Irlam, "*Unix file size survey - 1993*". http://www.base.com/gordoni/ufs93.html.

41. J. Jann, P. Pattnaik, H. Franke, F. Wang, J. Skovira, and J. Riodan, "*Modeling of workload in MPPs*". In *Job Scheduling Strategies for Parallel Processing*, D. G. Feitelson and L. Rudolph (eds.), pp. 95–116, Springer Verlag, 1997. Lect. Notes Comput. Sci. vol. 1291.

42. R. E. Kessler, M. D. Hill, and D. A. Wood, "*A comparison of trace-sampling techniques for multi-megabyte caches*". *IEEE Trans. Comput.* **43(6)**, pp. 664–675, Jun 1994.

43. D. N. Kimelman and T. A. Ngo, "*The RP3 program visualization environment*". *IBM J. Res. Dev.* **35(5/6)**, pp. 635–651, Sep/Nov 1991.

44. D. L. Kiskis and K. G. Shin, "*SWSL: a synthetic workload specification language for real-time systems*". *IEEE Trans. Softw. Eng.* **20(10)**, pp. 798–811, Oct 1994.

45. E. J. Koldinger, S. J. Eggers, and H. M. Levy, "*On the validity of trace-driven simulation for multiprocessors*". In 18th *Ann. Intl. Symp. Computer Architecture Conf. Proc.*, pp. 244–253, May 1991.

46. G. Kotsis, "*A systematic approach for workload modeling for parallel processing systems*". *Parallel Comput.* **22**, pp. 1771–1787, 1997.

47. P. Krueger, T-H. Lai, and V. A. Dixit-Radiya, "*Job scheduling is more important than processor allocation for hypercube computers*". *IEEE Trans. Parallel & Distributed Syst.* **5(5)**, pp. 488–497, May 1994.

48. M. Krunz and S. K. Tripathi, "*On the characterization of VBR MPEG streams*". In *SIGMETRICS Conf. Measurement & Modeling of Comput. Syst.*, pp. 192–202, Jun 1997.

49. A. M. Law and W. D. Kelton, *Simulation Modeling and Analysis*. McGraw Hill, 3rd ed., 2000.

50. E. D. Lazowska, "*The use of percentiles in modeling CPU service time distributions*". In *Computer Performance*, K. M. Chandy and M. Reiser (eds.), pp. 53–66, North-Holland, 1977.

51. W. E. Leland and T. J. Ott, "*Load-balancing heuristics and process behavior*". In *SIGMETRICS Conf. Measurement & Modeling of Comput. Syst.*, pp. 54–69, 1986.

52. W. E. Leland, M. S. Taqqu, W. Willinger, and D. V. Wilson, "*On the self-similar nature of Ethernet traffic*". *IEEE/ACM Trans. Networking* **2(1)**, pp. 1–15, Feb 1994.

53. V. Lo, J. Mache, and K. Windisch, "*A comparative study of real workload traces and synthetic workload models for parallel job scheduling*". In *Job Scheduling Strategies for Parallel Processing*, D. G. Feitelson and L. Rudolph (eds.), pp. 25–46, Springer Verlag, 1998. Lect. Notes Comput. Sci. vol. 1459.

54. U. Lublin and D. G. Feitelson, *The Workload on Parallel Supercomputers: Modeling the Characteristics of Rigid Jobs*. Technical Report 2001-12, Hebrew University, Oct 2001.

55. A. D. Malony, D. A. Reed, and H. A. G. Wijshoff, *"Performance measurement intrusion and perturbation analysis"*. IEEE Trans. Parallel & Distributed Syst. **3(4)**, pp. 433–450, Jul 1992.

56. B. B. Mandelbrot, *The Fractal Geometry of Nature*. W. H. Freeman and Co., 1982.

57. A. W. Mu'alem and D. G. Feitelson, *"Utilization, predictability, workloads, and user runtime estimates in scheduling the IBM SP2 with backfilling"*. IEEE Trans. Parallel & Distributed Syst. **12(6)**, pp. 529–543, Jun 2001.

58. T. D. Nguyen, R. Vaswani, and J. Zahorjan, *"Parallel application characterization for multiprocessor scheduling policy design"*. In *Job Scheduling Strategies for Parallel Processing*, D. G. Feitelson and L. Rudolph (eds.), pp. 175–199, Springer-Verlag, 1996. Lect. Notes Comput. Sci. vol. 1162.

59. N. Nieuwejaar, D. Kotz, A. Purakayastha, C. S. Ellis, and M. L. Best, *"File-access characteristics of parallel scientific workloads"*. IEEE Trans. Parallel & Distributed Syst. **7(10)**, pp. 1075–1089, Oct 1996.

60. *Parallel workloads archive*. http://www.cs.huji.ac.il/labs/parallel/workload/.

61. K. Park and W. Willinger, *"Self-similar network traffic: an overview"*. In *Self-Similar Network Traffic and Performance Evaluation*, K. Park and W. Willinger (eds.), pp. 1–38, John Wiley & Sons, 2000.

62. V. Paxon and S. Floyd, *"Wide-area traffic: the failure of Poisson modeling"*. IEEE/ACM Trans. Networking **3(3)**, pp. 226–244, Jun 1995.

63. E. E. Peters, *Fractal Market Analysis*. John Wiley & Sons, 1994.

64. S. V. Raghavan, D. Vasukiammaiyar, and G. Haring, *"Generative workload models for a single server environment"*. In *SIGMETRICS Conf. Measurement & Modeling of Comput. Syst.*, pp. 118–127, May 1994.

65. E. Rosti, G. Serazzi, E. Smirni, and M. S. Squillante, *"Models of parallel applications with large computation and I/O requirements"*. IEEE Trans. Softw. Eng. **28(3)**, pp. 286–307, Mar 2002.

66. R. V. Rubin, L. Rudolph, and D. Zernik, *"Debugging parallel programs in parallel"*. In *Workshop on Parallel and Distributed Debugging*, pp. 216–225, SIG-PLAN/SIGOPS, May 1988.

67. M. Schroeder, *Fractals, chaos, Power Laws*. W. H. Freeman and Co., 1991.

68. K. C. Sevcik, *"Application scheduling and processor allocation in multiprogrammed parallel processing systems"*. Performance Evaluation **19(2-3)**, pp. 107–140, Mar 1994.

69. A. Shaikh, J. Rexford, and K. G. Shin, *"Load-sensitive routing of long-lived IP flows"*. In *SIGCOMM*, pp. 215–226, Aug 1999.

70. A. Singh and Z. Segall, *"Synthetic workload generation for experimentation with multiprocessors"*. In 3rd *Intl. Conf. Distributed Comput. Syst.*, pp. 778–785, Oct 1982.

71. D. Thiébaut, *"On the fractal dimension of computer programs and its application to the prediction of the cache miss ratio"*. IEEE Trans. Comput. **38(7)**, pp. 1012–1026, Jul 1989.

72. D. Thiébaut, J. L. Wolf, and H. S. Stone, *"Synthetic traces for trace-driven simulation of cache memories"*. IEEE Trans. Comput. **41(4)**, pp. 388–410, Apr 1992. (Corrected in *IEEE Trans. Comput.* **42(5)** p. 635, May 1993).

73. J. J. P. Tsai, K-Y. Fang, and H-Y. Chen, *"A noninvasive architecture to monitor real-time distributed systems"*. Computer **23(3)**, pp. 11–23, Mar 1990.

74. J. S. Vetter and F. Mueller, "*Communication characteristics of large-scale scientific applications for contemporary cluster architectures*". In 16th *Intl. Parallel & Distributed Processing Symp.*, May 2002.

75. W. Willinger, M. S. Taqqu, R. Sherman, and D. V. Wilson, "*Self-similarity through high-variability: statistical analysis of Ethernet LAN traffic at the source level*". In *ACM SIGCOMM*, pp. 100–113, 1995.

76. K. Windisch, V. Lo, R. Moore, D. Feitelson, and B. Nitzberg, "*A comparison of workload traces from two production parallel machines*". In 6th *Symp. Frontiers Massively Parallel Comput.*, pp. 319–326, Oct 1996.

77. G. K. Zipf, *Human Behavior and the Principle of Least Effort*. Addison-Wesley, 1949.

Capacity Planning for Web Services
Techniques and Methodology

Virgilio A.F. Almeida

Department of Computer Science,
Federal University of Minas Gerais,
31270-010 Belo Horizonte, Brazil
`virgilio@dcc.ufmg.br`

Abstract. Capacity planning is a powerful tool for managing quality of service on the Web. This tutorial presents a capacity planning methodology for Web-based environments, where the main steps are: understanding the environment, characterizing the workload, modeling the workload, validating and calibrating the models, forecasting the workload, predicting the performance, analyzing the cost-performance plans, and suggesting actions. The main steps are based on two models: a workload model and a performance model. The first model results from understanding and characterizing the workload and the second from a quantitative description of the system behavior. Instead of relying on intuition, ad hoc procedures and rules of thumb to understand and analyze the behavior of Web services, this tutorial emphasizes the role of models, as a uniform and formal way of dealing with capacity planning problems.

1 Introduction

Performance, around-the-clock availability, and security are the most common indicators of quality of service on the Internet. Management faces a twofold challenge. On the one hand, it has to meet customer expectations in terms of quality of service. On the other hand, companies have to keep IT costs under control to stay competitive. Many possible alternative architectures can be used to implement a Web service; one has to be able to determine the most cost-effective architecture and system. This is where the quantitative approach and capacity planning techniques come into play. This tutorial introduces capacity planning [19,1] as an essential tool for managing quality of service on the Web and presents a methodology, where the main steps are: understanding the environment, characterizing the workload, modeling the workload, validating and calibrating the models, predicting the performance, analyzing the cost-performance plans, and suggesting actions. It provides a framework for planning the capacity of Web services and understanding their behavior. The tutorial also discusses a state transition graph called Customer Behavior Model Graph (CBMG), that is used to describe the behavior of groups of users who exhibit similar navigational patterns. The rest of the paper is organized as follows. Section two presents the main steps of the capacity planning methodology. Section three discusses the

M.C. Calzarossa and S. Tucci (Eds.): Performance 2002, LNCS 2459, pp. 142–157, 2002.
© Springer-Verlag Berlin Heidelberg 2002

role of models in capacity planning. Section four describes workload models. Next section discusses issues related to performance models. Finally, section six presents concluding remarks.

2 Capacity Planning as a Management Tool

Planning the capacity of Web services requires that a series of steps be followed in a systematic way. Figure 1 gives an overview of the main steps of the quantitative approach to analyze Web services. The starting point of the process is the business model and its measurable objectives, which are used to establish service level goals and to find out the applications that are central to the goals. Once the business model and its quantitative objectives have been understood, one is able to go through the quantitative analysis cycle. We now cover the various steps of the capacity planning process.

2.1 Understand the Environment

The first step entails obtaining an in-depth understanding of the service architecture. This means answering questions such as: What are the system requirements of the business model? What is the configuration of the site in terms of servers and internal connectivity? How many internal layers are there in the site? What types of servers (i.e., HTTP, database, authentication, streaming media) is the site running? What type of software (i.e., operating system, HTTP server software, transaction monitor, DBMS) is used in each server machine? How reliable and scalable is the architecture? This step should yield a systematic description of the Web environment, its components, and services. This initial phase of the process consists of learning what kind of hardware and software resources, network connectivity, and network protocols, are present in the environment. It also involves the identification of peak usage periods, management structures, and service-level agreements. This information is gathered by various means including user group meetings, audits, questionnaires, help desk records, planning documents, interviews, and other information-gathering techniques [14].

Table 1 summarizes the main elements of a system that must be catalogued and understood before the remaining steps of the methodology can be taken.

2.2 Characterize Workload

Workload characterization is the process of precisely describing the systems's global workload in terms of its main components. Each workload component is further decomposed into basic components. The basic components are then characterized by workload intensity (e.g., transaction arrival rates) and service demand parameters at each resource.

Capacity planning procedures have been used to assure that users receive adequate quality of service as they navigate through the site. A key step of any

Table 1. Elements in Understanding the Environment

Element	Description
Web Server	Quantity, type, configuration, and function.
Application Server	Quantity, type, configuration, and function.
Database Server	Quantity, type, configuration, and function.
Middleware	Type (e.g., TP monitors and DBMS).
Application	Main applications.
Network connectivity	Network connectivity diagram showing LANs, WANs, routers, servers, etc.
Network protocols	List of protocols used.
Service-level agreements	Existing SLAs per application or service.
User Community	Number of potential users, geographic location, etc.
Procurement procedures	Elements of the procurement process, expenditure limits.

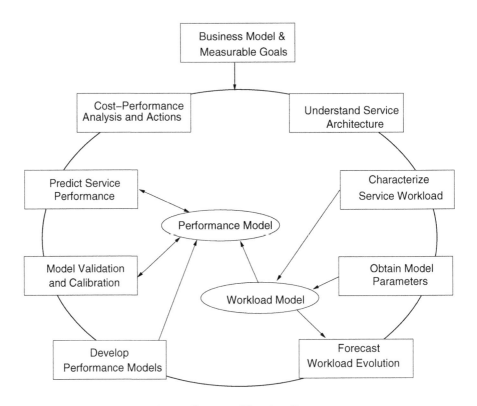

Fig. 1. Capacity Planning Process

performance evaluation and capacity planning study is workload characterization [4,18,3]. Thus, the second step of the methodology aims at characterizing the workload of a Web service. In Web-based environments [3], users interact with the site through a series of consecutive and related requests, called sessions. A session is a sequence of requests to execute e-business functions made by a single customer during a single visit to a Web service. Different navigational patterns can be observed for different groups of users. Examples of e-business functions requested by an online shopper include browse the catalog, search for products or services based on keywords, select products to obtain more detailed information, add to the shopping cart, user registration, and checkout. A customer of an online brokerage site would request different functions, such as enter a stock order, research a mutual fund history, obtain real-time quotes, retrieve company profiles, and compute earning estimates. Web workload is unique in its characteristics and some studies [2,5] identified workload properties and invariants, such as the heavy-tailed distributions (e.g., Pareto distribution) of file sizes in the Web. It has been also observed that Web traffic is bursty in several time scales [20,8].

2.3   Obtain Parameters for the Workload Model

The third step consists of obtaining values for the parameters of the workload models. This step also involves monitoring and measuring the performance of a Web service. It is a key step in the process of guaranteeing quality of service and preventing problems. Performance measurements should be collected from different reference points, carefully chosen to observe and monitor the environment under study. For example, logs of transactions and accesses to servers are the main source of information. Further information, such as page download times from different points in the network may help to track the service level perceived by customers. The information collected should help us answer questions such as: What is the number of user visits per day? What is the average and peak traffic to the site? What characterizes the shoppers of a particular set of products? What are the demands generated by the main requests on the resources (e.g., processors, disks, and networks) of the IT infrastructure? Steps 2 and 3 generate the workload model, which is a synthetic and compact representation of the workload seen by a Web service.

The parameters for a basic component are seldom directly obtained from measurements. In most cases, they must be derived from other parameters that are measured directly. Table 2 shows an example of two basic components, along with examples of parameters that can be measured for each. The last column indicates the type of basic component parameter—workload intensity (WI) or service demand (SD). Values must be obtained or estimated for these parameters, preferably through measurements with performance monitors and accounting systems. Measurements must be made during peak workload periods and for an appropriate monitoring interval.

2.4   Forecast Workload Evolution

The fourth step forecasts the expected workload intensity for a Web service. Forecasting is the art and science of predicting future events. It has been extensively used in many areas, such as the financial market, climate studies and

Table 2. Example of Basic Component Parameters and Types

Basic Component and Parameters	Parameter Type
Order transaction	
Number of transactions submitted per customer	WI
Number of registered customers	WI
Total number of IOs to the Sales DB	SD
CPU utilization at the DB server	SD
Average message size sent/received by the DB server	SD
Web-based training	
Average number of training sessions/day	WI
Average size of image files retrieved	SD
Average size of http documents retrieved	SD
Average number of image files retrieved/session	SD
Average number of documents retrieved/session	SD
Average CPU utilization of the httpd server	SD

production and operations management [12]. For example, one could forecast number and type of employees, volume and type of production, product demand, volume and destination of products. In the Internet, demand forecasting is essential for guaranteeing quality of service. It is critical for the operation of Web services. Let us consider the following scenario [16]. Unprecedented demand for the newest product slows Web servers to a crawl. The company servers were overwhelmed on Tuesday as a wave of customers attempted to download the company's new software product. Web services, in terms of responsiveness and speed, started degrading as more and more customers tried to access the service. And it is clear that many frustrated customers simply stopped trying. This undesirable scenario emphasizes the importance of good forecasting and planning for Web environments.

A good forecast is more than just a single number; it is a set of scenarios and assumptions. Time plays a key role in the forecasting process. The longer the time horizon, the less accurate the forecast will be. Forecasting horizons can be grouped into the classes: short term (e.g., less than three months), intermediate term (e.g., from three months to one year) and long term (e.g., more than 2 years). Demand forecasting in the Web can be illustrated by typical questions that come up very often during the course of capacity planning projects. Can we forecast the number of visitors to the company's Web site in order to plan the adequate capacity to support the load? What is the expected workload for the credit card authorization service during the Christmas season? How will the number of messages processed by the e-mail servers vary over the next year? What will be the number of simultaneous users for the streaming media services six months from now? Implementation of Web services should rely on a careful planning process, a planning process that pays attention to performance and capacity right from the beginning. The goal of this step is to use existing forecasting methods and techniques to predict future workload for Web services.

The literature [12,7] describes several forecasting techniques. In selecting one, some factors need to be considered. The first one is the availability and reliability of historical data. The degree of accuracy and the planning horizon are also factors that determine the forecasting technique. The pattern found in historical data has a strong influence on the choice of the technique. The nature of historical data may be determined through visual inspection of a plot of the data as a function of time. Three patterns of historical data are commomly identified: random, trend, and seasonal. While the trend pattern reflects a workload that tends to increase (or decrease, in some cases), seasonal patterns show the presence of fluctuations. The underlying hypothesis of forecasting techniques is that the information to be forecast is somehow directly related to historical data; this emphasizes the importance of knowing the pattern of historical data. There are many commercial packages (e.g., Matlab, S-PLUS, MS-EXCEL [11]) that perform various methods of forecasting techniques.

2.5   Develop Performance Model

In the fifth step, quantitative techniques and analytical models based on queuing network theory are used to develop performance models of Web services. Performance models are used to predict performance when any aspect of the workload or the site architecture is changed. Two types of models may be used: simulation models and analytical models. Analytical models [6] specify the interactions between the various components of a Web system via formulas. Simulation models [10] mimic the behavior of the actual system by running a simulation program. After model construction and parameterization, the model is solved. That is, the model parameters are manipulated in some fashion to yield performance measures (e.g., throughput, utilization, response time). Many solution techniques have been suggested [13].

Performance models have to consider contention for resources and the queues that arise at each system resource—processors, disks, routers, and network links. Queues also arise for software resources—threads, database locks, and protocol ports. The various queues that represent a distributed system are interconnected, giving rise to a network of queues, called a queuing network (QN). The level of detail at which resources are depicted in the QN depends on the reasons to build the model and the availability of detailed information about the operation and availability of detailed parameters of specific resources.

The input parameters for queuing network models describe the resources of the system, the software, and the workload of the system under study. These parameters include four groups of information:

− servers or components
− workload classes
− workload intensity
− service demands

In order to increase the model's representativeness, workloads are partitioned into classes of somehow similar components. Programs that are alike concerning the resource usage may be grouped into workload classes. Depending on the way a given class is processed by a system, it may be classified as one of two types: *open*, or *closed*.

Servers or service centers, are components of performance models intended to represent the resources of a system. The first step in specifying a model is the definition of the servers that make up the model. The scope of the capacity planning project helps to select which servers are relevant to the performance model. Consider the case of a Web site composed of Web servers, application and database servers connected via a LAN. The capacity planner wants to examine the impact caused on the system by the estimated growth of sales transactions. The specific focus of the project may be used to define the components of a performance model. For example, the system under study could be well represented by an open queueing network model consisting of queues, which correspond to the servers of the site. A different performance model, with other queues, would be required if the planner were interested in studying the effect of a proxy cache on the performance of the system.

2.6   Validate Performance Model

Once the model has been constructed, parameterized, and solved, it should be validated. That is, the performance measures found by solving the model should be compared against actual measurement data of the system being modeled. A performance model is said to be valid if the performance metrics (e.g., response time, resource utilizations, and throughputs) calculated by the model match the measurements of the actual system within a certain acceptable margin of error. For instance, the actual server utilizations should be compared against the server utilizations found by solving the model. This comparison check will be judged to be either acceptable or unacceptable. The choice of what determines acceptable versus unacceptable is left to the modeler. As a rule of thumb, device utilizations within 10%, system throughput within 10%, and response time within 20% are considered acceptable [13]. If the comparison is unacceptable, a series of questions must be addressed to determine the source of the errors.

Errors are possible within each capacity planning step. During workload characterization, measurements are taken for service demands, workload intensity, and for performance metrics such as response time, throughput, and device utilization. The same measures are computed by means of the performance model. If the computed values do not match the measured values within an acceptable level, the model must be calibrated. Even though one can hypothesize the source of possible errors, it is often difficult to pinpoint them and correct them. Therefore, it is normal to iterate among the steps of the methodology until an acceptable model is found. This changing of the model to force it to match the actual system is referred to as the calibration procedure. A calibration is a change to some target parameter of the analytic model. A detailed discussion of calibration techniques is given in [13]. When the model is considered valid it can be used for performance prediction. The sixth step aims at validating the models used to represent performance and workload.

2.7   Predict Service Performance

Prediction is key to capacity planning because one needs to be able to determine how a Web service will react when changes in load levels and customer behavior occur or when new business models are developed. This determination requires predictive models and not experimentation. So, in the seventh step, one uses performance models to predict the performance of Web services under many different scenarios [9].

Performance models aim at representing the behavior of real systems in terms of their performance. In order to use performance models for predicting future scenarios, one needs to obtain the input parameters to feed the model. The input parameters for performance models describe the hardware configuration, the software environment, and the workload of the system under study. The representativeness of a model depends directly on the quality of input parameters. Therefore, a key issue to conduct practical performance prediction is the determination of input parameters for performance models. Two practical questions naturally arise when one thinks of modeling a real system:

– What are the information sources for determining input parameters?
– What techniques are used to calculate input parameters?

The main source of information is the set of performance measurements collected from the observation of the real system under study. Further information can also be obtained from benchmarks and from product specifications provided by manufacturers. However, typical measurement data do not coincide with the kind of information required as input by performance models. For modeling purposes, typical measurement data need to be reworked in order to become useful.

2.8   Analyze Future Scenarios

In the eighth step of the cycle, many possible candidate architectures are analyzed in order to determine the most cost-effective one. Future scenarios should take into consideration the expected workload, the site cost, and the quality of service perceived by customers. Finally, this step should indicate to management what actions should be taken to guarantee that the Web services will meet the business goals set for the future.

The performance model and cost models can be used to assess various scenarios and configurations. Some example scenarios are, "Should we use CDN services to serve images?" " Should we use Web hosting services? " "Should we mirror the site to balance the load, cut down on network traffic and improve global performance?" For each scenario, we can predict what the performance of each system component will be and what the costs are for the scenario. The comparison of the various scenarios yields a configuration plan, an investment plan, and a personnel plan. The configuration plan specifies which upgrades should be made to existing hardware and software resources. The performance model is built and solved and a cost model developed, various analyses can be made regarding cost-performance tradeoffs. The investment plan specifies a timeline

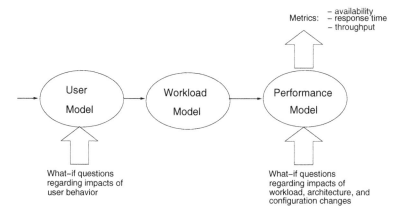

Fig. 2. Customer, Workload, and Resource Models.

for investing in the necessary upgrades. The personnel plan determines what changes in the support personnel size and structure must be made in order to accommodate changes in the system.

3   Models for Capacity Planning

Models play a central role in capacity planning. In the methodology discussed here, we consider two types of models: performance model and workload model. In Web environments, user models are important to provide information to workload models. Figure 2 shows the relationship between user model, workload model, and performance model.

Each Web service request (e.g., a credit card authorization or a search) may exercise the site's resources in different manners. Some services may use large amount of processing time from the application server while others may concentrate on the database server. Other service may demand high network bandwidth, such as requests for streaming media services. Different users exhibit different navigational patterns and, as a consequence, invoke services in different ways with different frequencies. For instance, in an e-business service, some customers may be considered as heavy buyers while others, considered occasional buyers, would spend most of their time browsing and searching the site. Understanding the customer behavior is critical for characterizing the workload as well as to an adequate sizing of the site's resources. Models of user behavior can be quite useful. In addition to characterizing navigational patterns within sessions, one needs to characterize the rate at which sessions of different types are started. This gives us an indication of the workload intensity. Workload models provide input parameters for performance models, that predict the system behavior for that specific workload.

Customer (i.e. user) models capture elements of user behavior in terms of navigational patterns, e-business functions used, frequency of access to the various e-business functions, and times between access to the various services offered by the site. A customer model can be useful for navigational and workload prediction.

- Model User Navigational Patterns for Predictive Purposes. By building models, one can answer what-if questions regarding the effects on user behavior due to site layout changes or content redesign.
- Capture Workload Parameters. If the only purpose of a customer model is to generate a workload model to be used as input to a resource model, then it is not necessary to use a detailed model.

Workload models describe the workload of an Web service in terms of workload intensity (e.g., transaction arrival rates) and service demands on the various resources (e.g., processors, I/O subsystems, networks) that make up the site. The workload model can be derived from the customer model as shown in [16]. Performance models represent the various resources of the site and captures the effects of the workload model on these resources. A performance model can be used for predictive purposes to answer what-if questions regarding performance impacts due to changes in configuration, software and hardware architecture, and other parameters. A performance model is used to compute the values of metrics such as response time, throughput, and business-oriented metrics such as revenue throughput.

4   Workload Models

A workload model is a representation that mimics the real workload under study. Although each system may require a specific approach to characterize and generate a workload model, there are some general guidelines that apply well to all types of systems [4]. The common steps to be followed by any workload characterization include: (1) specification of a point of view from which the workload will be analyzed, (2) choice of the set of parameters that captures the most relevant characteristics of the workload for the purpose of capacity planning, (3) monitoring the system to obtain the raw performance data, (4) analysis and reduction of performance data, (5) construction of a workload model, and (6) verification that the model does capture all the important performance information.

Graphs are also used to represent workloads. For example, a graph-based model can be used to characterize Web sessions and generate information for constructing workload models. This section concentrates on models that represent the behavior of users (i.e, customers). User models capture elements of user behavior in terms of navigational patterns, Web service functions used, frequency of access to the various functions, and times between access to the various services offered by the site. Two different types of models are commonly used in the capacity planning methodology.

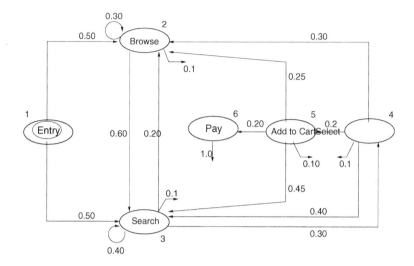

Fig. 3. The Customer Behavior Model Graph

4.1   Customer Graph Behavior Model

In Web-based environments, users interact with the site through a series of consecutive and related requests, called *sessions*. It has been observed that different customers exhibit different navigational patterns. The Customer Behavior Graph Model (CBMG), introduced in [15,17], can be used to capture the navigational pattern of a customer through an e-business site. This pattern includes two aspects: a transitional and a temporal one. The former determines how a customer moves from one state (i.e., an e-business function) to the next. This is represented by the matrix of transition probabilities. The temporal aspect has to do with the time it takes for a customer to move from one state to the next. This time is measured from the server's perspective and is called *server-perceived think time* or just think time. This is defined as the average time elapsed since the server completes a request for a customer until it receives the next request from the same customer during the same session. A think time can be associated with each transition in the CBMG.

So, a CBMG can be defined by a pair (P, Z) where $P = [p_{i,j}]$ is an $n \times n$ matrix of transition probabilities between the n states of the CBMG and $Z = [z_{i,j}]$ is an $n \times n$ matrix that represents the average think times between the states of the CBMG. Recall that state 1 is the Entry state and n is the Exit state.

Consider the CBMG of Figure 3. This CBMG has seven states; the Exit state, state seven, is not explicitly represented in the figure. Let V_j be the average number of times that state j of the CBMG is visited for each visit to the e-business site, i.e., for each visit to the state Entry. Consider the Add to Cart state. We can see that the average number of visits (V_{Add}) to this state is equal to the average number of visits to the state Select (V_{Select}) multiplied by the probability (0.2) that a customer will go from Select to Add Cart. We can then write the relationship

$$V_{\text{Add}} = V_{\text{Select}} \times 0.2. \tag{1}$$

Consider now the Browse state. The average number of visits (V_{Browse}) to this state is equal to the average number of visits to state Search (V_{Search}) multiplied by the probability (0.2) that a customer will go from Search to Browse, plus the average number of visits to state Select (V_{Select}) multiplied by the probability (0.30) that a customer will go from Select to Browse, plus the average number of visits to the state Add to Cart (V_{Add}) multiplied by the probability (0.25) that a customer will go from Add to Cart to Browse, plus the average number of visits to the state Browse (V_{Browse}) multiplied by the probability (0.30) that a Customer will remain in the Browse state, plus the number of visits to the Entry state multiplied by the probability (0.5) of going from the Entry state to the Browse state. Hence,

$$V_{\text{Browse}} = V_{\text{Search}} \times 0.20 + V_{\text{Select}} \times 0.30 + V_{\text{Add}} \times 0.25 +$$
$$V_{\text{Browse}} \times 0.30 + V_{\text{Entry}} \times 0.5. \tag{2}$$

So, in general, the average number of visits to a state j of the CBMG is equal to the sum of the number of visits to all states of the CBMG multiplied by the transition probability from each of the other states to state j. Thus, for any state j ($j = 2, \cdots, n - 1$) of the CBMG, one can write the equation

$$V_j = \sum_{k=1}^{n-1} V_k \times p_{k,j}, \tag{3}$$

where $p_{k,j}$ is the probability that a customer makes a transition from state k to state j. Note that the summation in Eq. (3) does not include state n (the Exit state) since there are no possible transitions from this state to any other state. Since $V_1 = 1$ (because state 1 is the Entry state), we can find the average number of visits V_j by solving the system of linear equations

$$V_1 = 1 \tag{4}$$
$$V_j = \sum_{k=1}^{n-1} V_k \times p_{k,j} \quad j = 2, \cdots, n - 1. \tag{5}$$

Note that $V_n = 1$ since, by definition, the Exit state is only visited once per session.

Useful metrics can be obtained from the CBMG. Once we have the average number of visits (V_j) to each state of the CBMG, we can obtain the average session length as

$$\text{AverageSessionLength} = \sum_{j=2}^{n-1} V_j. \tag{6}$$

Table 3. Using the CVM to Characterize a Session

	Session 1	Session 2	Session 3
Home	1	2	3
Browse	4	8	4
Search	5	5	3
Login	0	1	1
Pay	0	0	1
Register	0	0	1
Add to Cart	0	2	1
Select	3	3	2

For the the visit ratios of Fig. 3, the average session length is

$$\text{AverageSessionLength} = V_{\text{Browse}} + V_{\text{Search}} + V_{\text{Select}} + V_{\text{Add}} + V_{\text{Pay}}$$
$$= 2.498 + 4.413 + 1.324 + 0.265 + 0.053$$
$$= 8.552. \tag{7}$$

The buy to visit Ratio is simply given by V_{Pay}.

Each customer session can be represented by a CBMG, that can be derived from HTTP logs. "Similar" sessions can be clustered to represent each group by a single CBMG. The goal is to characterize the workload by a relatively small and representative number of CBMGs as opposed to having to deal with thousands or even hundreds of thousands of CBMGs. Procedures and algorithms for clustering CBMGs are described in details in [15]

4.2   The Customer Visit Model (CVM)

An alternate and less detailed representation of a session would entail representing a session as a vector of visit ratios to each state of the CBMG. The visit ratio is the number of visits to a state during a session.

Table 3 shows an example of three sessions described by the number of visits to each state of the CBMG. Note that states Entry and Exit are not represented in the CVM since the number of visits to these states is always one. Session 1 in the table represents a session of a customer who browsed through the site, did a few searches, but did not login or buy anything. In Session 2, the customer logged in but did not need to register because it was an already registered customer. This customer abandoned the site before paying even though two items had been added to the shopping cart. Finally, Session 3 represents a new customer who registers with the site, adds one item to the shopping cart, and pays for it.

The CVM is then a set of vectors (columns in Table 3) that indicate the number of times each of the functions supplied by the e-business site are executed. For example, Session 1 would be represented by the vector (1, 4, 5, 0, 0, 0, 0, 3) and Session 2 by the vector (2, 8, 5, 1, 0, 0, 2, 3).

The CBMG is a state transition graph, in which the nodes correspond to states in the session (e.g., browsing, searching, selecting, checking out, and paying) and the arcs correspond to transitions between states. Probabilities are associated with transitions as in a Markov Chain. A Customer Visit Model (CVM) represents sessions as a collection of session vectors, one per session. A session vector $V_j = (v_1, v_2, \cdots v_m)$ for the jth session indicates the number of times, that each of the different functions (e.g., search, browse, add to cart, etc) were invoked during the session. To be able to perform capacity planning studies of a Web service, one needs to map each CBMG or CVM resulting from the workload characterization process described above to IT resources. In other words, one has to associate service demands at the various components (e.g., processors disks and network) with the execution of the functions [16].

5   Performance Models

Performance models represent the way system's resources are used by the workload and capture the main factors determining system performance. These models use information provided by workload models and system architecture description. Performance models are used to compute both traditional performance metrics such as response time, throughput, utilization, and mean queue length as well as innovative business-oriented performance metrics, such as revenue throughput or lost-revenue throughput. Basically, performance models can be grouped into two categories: analytic and simulation models. Performance models help us understand the quantitative behavior of complex systems, such as electronic business applications, e-government, and entertainment. Performance models have been used for multiple purposes in systems.

- In the infrastructure design of Web-based applications, various issues call for the use of models to evaluate system alternatives. For example, a distributed Web server system is any architecture consisting of multiple Web server hosts distributed on a LAN, with some sort of mechanism to distribute incoming requests among the servers. So, for a specific type of workload, what is the most effective scheme for load balancing in a certain distributed Web server system? Models are also useful for analyzing document replacement policies in caching proxies. Bandwidth capacity of certain network links can also be estimated by performance models. In summary, performance models are an essential tool for studying resource allocation problems in the context of Web services.
- Most Web-based applications operate in multi-tiered environments. Models can be used to analyze performance of distributed applications running on three-tiered architectures, composed of Web servers, application servers and database servers.
- Performance tuning of complex applications is a huge territory. When a Web-based application presents performance problems, a mandatory step to solve them is to tune the underlying system. This means to measure the system and try to identify the sources of performance problems: application

design, lack of capacity, excess of load, or problems in the infrastructure (i.e., network, servers, ISP). Performance models can help find performance problems by answering what-if questions as opposed to making changes in the production environment.

Parameters for queuing network (QN) models are divided into the following categories. (1) System parameters specify the characteristics of a system that affect performance. Examples include load-balancing disciplines for Web server mirroring, network protocols, maximum number of connections supported by a Web server, and maximum number of threads supported by the database management system. (2) Resource parameters describe the intrinsic features of a resource that affect performance. Examples include disk seek times, latency and transfer rates, network bandwidth, router latency, and processor speed ratings. (3) Workload parameters that are derived from workload characterization and are divided into types: workload intensity and service demand. Workload intensity parameters provide a measure of the load placed on the system, indicated by the number of units of work that contend for system resources. Examples include the number of requests/sec submitted to the database server and number of sales transactions submitted per second to the credit card service. Workload service demand parameters specify the total amount of service time required by each basic component at each resource. Examples include the processor time of transactions at the database server, the total transmission time of replies from the database server and the total I/O time at the streaming media server.

6   Concluding Remarks

Capacity planning techniques are needed to avoid the pitfalls of inadequate capacity and to meet users' performance expectations in a cost-effective manner. This tutorial provides the foundations required to carry out capacity planning studies. Planning the capacity of Web services requires that a series of steps be followed in a systematic way. This paper gives an overview of the main steps of the quantitative approach to analyze Web services. The main steps are based on two models: a workload model and a performance model. The two models can be used in capacity planning projects to answer typical what-if questions, frequently faced by managers of Web services.

References

1. V. Almeida and D. Menascé, "Capacity Planning: an essential tool for managing Web services", IEEE IT Pro, Vol. 4, Issue 4, July-August, 2002.
2. M. Arlitt and C. Williamson, "Internet Web Servers: workload characterization and performance implication", in *IEEE/ACM Trans. on Networking*, October 1997.
3. M. Arlitt, D. Krishnamurthy, and J. Rolia, "Workload Characterization and Performance Scalability of a Large Web-based Shopping System", in *ACM Transactions on Internet Technologies*, Vol.1, No. 1, Aug. 2001.

4. M. Calzarossa and G. Serazzi, "Workload Characterization: A Survey," *Proceedings of the IEEE*, Vol. 81, No. 8, August 1993.
5. M. Crovella and A. Bestravos, " Self-Similarity in the World Wide Web: evidence possible causes", in *IEEE/ACM Transactions on Networking*, 5(6):835–846, December 1997.
6. P. Denning and J. Buzen, "The operational analysis of queuing network models", *Computing Surveys*, Vol. 10, No. 3 , September 1978, pp. 225-261.
7. R. Jain, *The Art of Computer Systems Performance Analysis*. New York: Wiley, 1991.
8. K. Kant and Y. Won "Server Capacity Planning for Web Traffic Workload", in *IEEE Trans. on Knowledge and Data Engineering*, September 1999.
9. D. Krishnamurthy and J. Rolia, "Predicting the Performance of an E-Commerce Server: Those Mean Percentiles," in *Proc. First Workshop on Internet Server Performance*, ACM SIGMETRICS 98, June 1998.
10. A. Law and W. Kelton, *Simulation Modeling and Techniques*. 2nd ed. New York: McGraw-Hill, 1990.
11. D. Levine, P. Ramsey, R. Smidt, *Applied Statistics for Engineers and Scientists: Using Microsoft Excel & MINITAB*, Upper Saddle River, Prentice Hall, 2001,
12. J. Martinich, *Production and Operations Management : An Applied Modern Approach*, John Wiley & Sons, 1996.
13. D. A. Menascé, V. A. F. Almeida, and L. W. Dowdy, *Capacity Planning and Performance Modeling: From Mainframes to Client-Server Systems*. Upper Saddle River, NJ: Prentice Hall, 1994.
14. D. A. Menascé, D. Dregits, R. Rossin, and D. Gantz, A federation-oriented capacity management methodology for LAN environments, *Proc. 1995 Conf. Comput. Measurement Group*, Nashville, TN, Dec. 3–8, 1995,
15. D. A. Menascé, V. Almeida, R. Fonseca, and M. Mendes, "A Methodology for Workload Characterization for E-Commerce Servers", *Proc. 1999 ACM Conference in Electronic Commerce*, Denver, 1999.
16. D. A. Menascé and V. A. F. Almeida, *Scaling for E-Business: technologies, models, performance and capacity planning*, Prentice Hall, Upper Saddle River, 2000.
17. D. A. Menascé, V. A. F. Almeida, R. Fonseca, and M. A. Mendes, "Business-oriented Resource Management Policies for E-Commerce Servers," *Performance Evaluation*, September 2000.
18. D. A. Menascé, V. Almeida, R. Fonseca, R. Riedi, F. Ribeiro, and W. Meira Jr., "In Search of Invariants for E-Business Workloads ", *Proc. 2000 ACM Conference in Electronic Commerce*, Minneapolis, 2000.
19. D. A. Menascé and V. A. F. Almeida, *Capacity Planning for Web Services: metrics, models and methods*, Prentice Hall, Upper Saddle River, 2002.
20. V. Paxson and S. Floyd, "Wide area traffic: The failure of Poisson modeling," *IEEE/ACM Transactions on Networking* **3**, pp. 226–244, 1995.

End-to-End Performance of Web Services*

Paolo Cremonesi and Giuseppe Serazzi

Dipartimento di Elettronica e Informazione, Politecnico di Milano, Italy,
{cremones, serazzi}@elet.polimi.it

Abstract. As the number of applications that are made available over
the Internet rapidly grows, providing services with *adequate* performance
becomes an increasingly critical issue. The performance requirements of
the new applications span from few milliseconds to hundreds of seconds.
In spite of the continuous technological improvement (e.g., faster servers
and clients, multi-threaded browsers supporting several simultaneous and
persistent TCP connections, access to the network with larger bandwidth
for both servers and clients), the network performance as captured by response time and throughput does not keep up and progressively degrades.
Several are the causes of the poor "Quality of Web Services" that users
very often experience. The characteristics of the traffic (self-similarity
and heavy-tailedness) and the widely varying resource requirements (in
terms of bandwidth, size and number of downloaded objects, processor
time, number of I/Os, etc.) of web requests are among the most important ones. Other factors refer to the architectural complexity of the
network path connecting the client browser to the web server and to the
protocols behavior at the different layers.
In this paper we present a study of the performance of web services.
The first part of the paper is devoted to the analysis of the origins of
the fluctuations in web data traffic. This peculiar characteristic is one of
the most important causes of the performance degradation of web applications. In the second part of the paper experimental measurements
of performance indices, such as end-to-end response time, TCP connection time, transfer time, of several web applications are presented. The
presence of self-similarity characteristics in the traffic measurements is
shown.

1 Introduction

In the last few years, the number of network-based services available on the Internet has grown considerably. Web servers are now used as the ubiquitous interface
for information exchange and retrieval both at enterprise level, via intranets, and
at global level, via the the World Wide Web. In spite of the continuous increase
of the network capacity, in terms of investments in new technologies and in new
network components, the Internet still fails to satisfy the needs of a consistent
fraction of users. New network-based applications require interactive response

---

* This work has been supported by MIUR project COFIN 2001: *High quality Web
systems.*

M.C. Calzarossa and S. Tucci (Eds.): Performance 2002, LNCS 2459, pp. 158–178, 2002.
© Springer-Verlag Berlin Heidelberg 2002

time ranging from few milliseconds to tens of seconds. Traditional best-effort service that characterizes the Internet is not adequate to guarantee strict response time requirements of many new applications. Hence, the need for Quality of Service (QoS) capabilities.

In order to develop techniques that allow to improve performance, it is important to understand and reduce the various sources of delay in the response time experienced by end users. The delays introduced by all the components, both hardware and software, that are involved in the execution of a web service transaction are cumulative. Therefore, in order to decrease the end-to-end response time it is necessary to improve all the individual component response times in the chain, and primarily that of the slowest one.

A first effort should be devoted to the analysis of the workload characteristics with the goal of identifying the causes of traffic fluctuations in the Internet. Such fluctuations contribute to transient congestions in the network components and therefore are the primary sources of the response time increase. At the application level, it is known that the applications that contribute major portions of the network traffic transmit their load in a highly bursty manner, which is a cause of further congestion.

The complexity of the network structure and the behavior of the transport/network protocols play a fundamental role in the propagation of the fluctuations from the application level to the link level.

The complexity of the Internet infrastructure, from the network level up to the application level, results in performance indexes characterized by high variability and long–range dependence. Such features introduce new problems in the analysis and design of networks and web applications, and many of the past assumptions upon which web systems have been built are no longer valid. Usual statistics as average and variance become meaningless in the presence of heavy-tailedness and self-similarity.

The paper is organized as follows. In Sect. 2 we illustrate some of the main sources of web delays: the complexity of the request path browser-server-browser and the origin of the self-similarity property in the Internet traffic are analyzed. In Sect. 3, experimental results concerning the heavy-tailedness properties of end-to-end response times of some web sites are presented. Section 4 describes few case studies that show how to measure and improve web user satisfaction. Section 5 summarizes our contributions and concludes the paper.

2   Sources of Web Delays

One of the typical misconceptions related to the Internet is that the bandwidth is the only factor limiting the speed of web services. Thus, with the diffusion of broadband networks in the next few years, high performance will be guaranteed. This conclusion is clearly *wrong*.

Indeed, although high bandwidth is necessary for the efficient download of large files such as video, audio and images, as more and more services are offered on the Internet, a small *end-to-end response time*, i.e., the overall waiting time that end users experience, is becoming a requirement. The main components that contribute to the end-to-end response time fall into three categories: client side, server side, and network architecture and protocols.

On the client side, the browser parameters, such as the number of simultaneous TCP connections, the page cache size, the memory and computation requirements of the code downloaded from the server (applet, java scripts, plugins, etc.), and the bandwidth of the access network, must be taken into account. On the server side, among the factors that should be carefully analyzed are: the behavior of the server performance with respect to the forecast workload increase, some of the application architecture parameters (e.g., multithreading level, maximum number of opened connections, parallelism level), the CPU and I/O power available (as demand for dynamic content of pages increases, more and more computational power and I/O performance/capacity are required), and the bandwidth of the access network.

The Internet network architecture is characterized by the large number of components that a user request visits along the path between the browser and the web server and back. Each of these components, both hardware and software, introduces some delay that contribute to the creation of the end-to-end response time. The global throughput of a connection between a browser and a web server, and back, corresponds to the throughput of the slowest component in the path. This component, referred to as *bottleneck*, is likely in a congestion state and causes severe performance degradation.

Two are the factors that contribute to the congestion of a component: the frequency of the arriving requests and the service time required for the complete execution of a request. These two factors are related to the characteristics of the workload and to the characteristics of the component. Thus, concentrating only on the bandwidth with the objective of providing a small end-to-end response time it is not enough.

In this section we will analyze some of the most important sources of web delays, namely, the complexity of the path between browsers and servers, and the self-similarity characteristic of Internet traffic.

2.1   The Complexity of the Request Path

A current trend in the infrastructure of the Internet is the increase of the complexity of the chain of networks between a client and a server, that is, the path in both directions between the user browser and the web server, also referred to as *request path*. From the instant a request is issued by a browser, a series of hardware components and software processes are involved in the delivery of the request to the server. Hardware components comprise routers, gateways, intermediate hosts, proxy cache hosts, firewalls, application servers, etc. Software processes involved in the delivery of a request refer to the protocol layers (HTTP, TCP, IP, and those of lower layers), the routing algorithms, the address translation process, the security controls, etc. In Fig. 1, a simplified model of a request path between a user browser and a web server is illustrated.

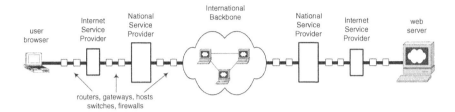

Fig. 1. Simplified model of a request path from a user browser to a web server.

As a consequence, the end-to-end chain of components, or *hops*, between a client browser and a web server (including also the return path) may be very long. They can be subdivided into the hops located in the access networks (ISP and NSP), both on the client and server sides, the hops located in the server farm or the corporate intranet, if not used, and the hops in the Internet infrastructure (mix among national and international carriers, international backbone, routers, etc.). Several statistics collected at business users show that the average number of hops is increasing with the popularity of Internet, reaching an average value of about 15-20. The trend is clearly towards an increase of the number of hops since the architectures of the Internet and of the intranets and server farms are becoming more and more complex due to various new functions to be executed (e.g., security controls, complex back–end applications).

The majority of the components of a request path operate on a store-and-forward basis, i.e., the incoming requests are queued waiting to use the resource, and thus are potential source of delays. The request path browser-server-browser, represented in Fig. 1, can be modeled as an *open queueing network*, i.e., a network of interconnected queues characterized by more sources of arriving requests and by the independence of the arrival processes from the network conditions. Queueing networks are well suited for representing resource contention and queueing for service (see, e.g., [6]). In an open network the number of customers can grow to infinity depending on the saturation condition of the bottleneck resource. Assuming that the distributions of request interarrival times and service times at all resources are exponential and that the scheduling discipline at each resource is FCFS, a typical characteristic of such networks [8] is that each resource behaves like independent M/M/1 queue. In this case the response time tends to a vertical asymptote as the load increases until the resource saturation. The rate of increase of a component response time R, normalized with respect to the square of service time S, as a function of the request arrival rate λ is given by:

$$\frac{dR}{d\lambda}\frac{1}{S^2} = \frac{1}{(1-\lambda S)^2} = \frac{1}{(1-U)^2} \tag{1}$$

where $U = \lambda S$ is the *utilization* of the component, i.e., the proportion of time the component is busy. As it can be seen from Fig. 2, when the arrival rate is such that the utilization is greater than 80%, the rate of increase of the response time is extremely high, i.e., the resource is *congested* and the delay introduced in the packet flow is huge.

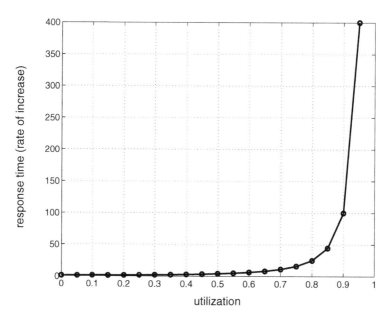

Fig. 2. Rate of increase of response time of a component (normalized with respect to the square of service time) vs component utilization.

The burstiness of Internet traffic produces a variability in the request inter-arrival time much higher than the one exhibited by traffic following exponential assumption, making the actual situation even worse than the one described by (1). As a consequence, the probability of finding a congested component along a request path is much higher than in usual telecommunication environments. Thus, the further away the client browser is from the web server, the greater the likelihood that one, or more, components of the path is found congested. Let p be the probability that a component is in a congestion state and let n be the number of (independent) components along the request path, including the return path, the probability of finding exactly i congested components is

$$\binom{n}{i} p^i (1 - p)^{n-i} , \quad i = 0, 1, 2, ..., n \tag{2}$$

and the probability of finding at least one component congested is $1 - (1 - p)^n$. In Fig. 3, the probability of finding one or more congested components (i.e., of a very high response time experienced by a user) along a request path browser-server-browser as a function of the congestion probability p of a single component and the path length n is reported. The maximum number of components considered in a path is 15, a conservative value if compared to the actual average situation encountered in the Internet. As it can be seen, with a probability of congestion of a component $p = 0.01$, i.e., 1%, and a path length $n = 15$ hops, the probability of finding at least one component congested is 13.9%, a clearly high value.

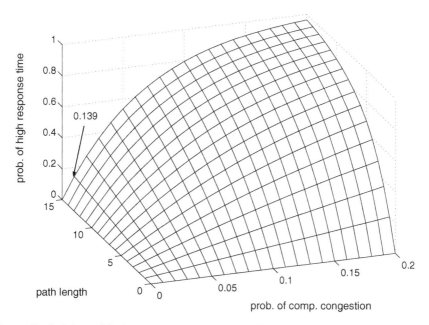

Fig. 3. Probability of finding one or more congested components along a request path browser-web server-browser (i.e., of a very high response time) as a function of the congestion probability p of a single component and the path length n.

2.2   The Self-Similarity of Web Traffic

The World Wide Web is a more variable system than it was expected. Several analyses show that the *limited variability* notion widely used for several decades in telecommunication modelling, i.e., the assumption of the *Poisson nature* of traffic related phenomena, has very little in common with Internet reality. Evidence is provided by the fact that the behavior of the aggregated traffic does not become less bursty as the number of sources increases [12].

More precisely, models in which the exponential distribution of the variables is assumed are not able to describe Internet conditions in which the variables (e.g., duration of the sessions, end-to-end response times, size of downloaded files) show a variability encompassing several time scales. The high temporal variability in traffic processes is captured assuming the *long-term dependence* of the corresponding variables and the *heavy-tail* distribution of their values (i.e., distribution whose tail declines according to a power-law).

A distribution is heavy-tailed (see, e.g., [5]) if its complementary cumulative distribution $1 - F(x)$ decays slower than the exponential, i.e. if

$$\lim_{x \to +\infty} e^{\gamma x} [1 - F(x)] \to +\infty \qquad (3)$$

for all $\gamma > 0$. One of the simplest heavy-tailed distributions is the *Pareto* distribution, whose probability density function $f(x)$ and distribution function $F(x)$ are given by (see, e.g., [15]):

$$f(x) = \alpha \, k^\alpha x^{-\alpha-1}, \qquad F(x) = 1 - k^\alpha x^{-\alpha}, \qquad 0 < k \le x, \quad \alpha > 0 \qquad (4)$$

where k is a positive constant independent of x and α represents the tail index. If $1 < \alpha < 2$, the random variable has infinite variance, if $0 < \alpha \le 1$ the random variable has infinite mean. Note that the first and second moments are infinite only if the tail stretches to infinity, while in practice infinite moments are exhibited as non-convergence of sample statistics.

An interesting property exhibited by the processes whose values follow heavy-tailed distributions is the *self-similar*, or *fractal-like*, behavior, i.e., the behavior of the variables is invariant over all time scales. The autocorrelation function of self-similar time series declines like a power-law for large lags. As a consequence, autocorrelations exist at all time scales, i.e., the high values of the tail of the distribution occur with non-negligible probability and the corresponding traffic is *bursty*.

The probability density functions (in log scale) of several Pareto random variables, with different parameters α and k (4), are compared with the probability density function (dashed line) of an exponential variable in Fig. 4. All the functions have the same mean value equal to one. As it can be seen, the tails of the Pareto random variables are much higher than the one of the exponential random variable.

Evidence of Internet traffic self-similarity is reported in several papers. This type of behavior has been identified in high-speed Ethernet local area networks [9], in Internet traffic [16], in the file sizes of the web servers and in the think time of browsers [4], in the number of bytes in FTP transmissions [12], and in several others variables.

As we showed, the self-similarity property of Internet traffic implies that the values of the corresponding variables exhibit fluctuations over a wide range of time scales, i.e., their variance is infinite. The peculiar nature of the load generated at the application layer, the self-similarity and the heavy-tail characteristics, propagates to lower layers affecting the behavior of the transport and network protocols. This, in turns, induces a self-similarity behavior of the link traffic negatively affecting network performance. The most important causes of such a high variability and of its ubiquitous presence at all layers in the network environment fall into three categories: the *sources* related ones, the *request path* related ones, and the *protocols* related ones.

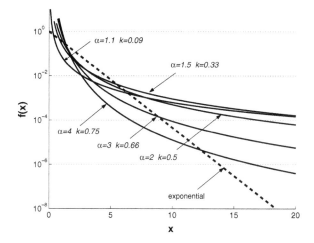

Fig. 4. Probability density functions (in log scale) of several Pareto random variables, with different parameters α and k, compared with the probability density function (dashed line) of an exponential random variable; the mean value of all the functions is one.

The activity of a typical Internet user can be regarded as a sequence of active periods interleaved with idle periods. Observing the usage patterns of the most significant Internet applications, like the retrieval/download/upload cycle of web files using HTTP, the file transfer with FTP, and the send/receive process of SMTP, their execution can be seen as a sequence of activity phases, during which a given amount of data is transferred from one site to another, intermixed with idle phases, when users analyze the downloaded objects (or pages) and type a message or issue a new command, but no load is generated on the network. Such a behavior favors the known burstiness of application data transmission.

Thus, a user can be modeled as a *source of traffic* that alternates between two states identified with ON and OFF, respectively. ON/OFF sources are widely used to model the workload generated by the users of the Internet. During the ON periods, the source is active and data packets are sent on the network, i.e., a burst of load is generated. During the OFF periods, no activity is performed. The characteristics of the ON and OFF periods, e.g., average durations, distributions, traffic generation rates, depend on the application considered. Typically, in the ON periods the traffic is generated at constant rate and the lengths of ON and OFF periods follow known distributions, that may differ from each other, having finite or infinite variance. The very high, or infinite, variance of the input traffic parameters is explained by the results of several empirical studies (see, e.g., [2]) that have shown the presence of self-similarity in the size distribution of web files transferred over the network and thus of their transmission times.

At a more aggegated level than the one of a single source, the traffic generated by a set of users can be modeled considering several ON/OFF sources sharing the network resources. It has been shown [16] [17] that, under certain assumptions, the superposition of many ON/OFF sources generates a process exhibiting the long-term dependency characteristic. Thus, the corresponding model is able to capture the self-similar nature of Internet traffic.

Another phenomenon that influences the origin of fluctuations of Internet traffic (at a more macroscopic level than the one seen at single source level) is related to the amount of correlation existing among the sources. Empirical observations suggest the presence of traffic cycles on a temporal basis, among which the daytime cycle is the most evident. The existence of such a cycle is enough intuitive and is connected to office working hours and availability periods of some on-line services (e.g., typically the traffic peaks during the morning and the afternoon hours). The time difference across the globe may also generate cycles with different periodicity. Other types of source correlations are generated by the occurrence of special events (sport competitions, natural disasters, wars, etc.).

As we have seen, the Internet is a network environment where load fluctuations should be considered physiological rather than exceptional events. The self-similarity characteristic of the load propagates its effects on all the network layers, from the application to the link layer. As a consequence, *transient congestions* may occur with non-negligible probability in each of the components along the *request path* browser-server-browser (Sect.2.1). While the task of performance optimization is relatively straightforward in a network with limited load variability, it becomes significantly more complex in the Internet because of transient congestions. The load imbalance in the resources, usually modeled as an open network of queues (Fig. 1), of a request path will be extreme and will grow as the load increases. Thus, the probability of finding a component subject to transient congestion in a relatively long request path, e.g., of about 15 hops, is consistent (Fig. 3).

When a fluctuation of traffic creates a congestion in a component (e.g., a router) of an open network of queues, the performance degradation due to the overload is huge since the asymptotes of the performance indices are vertical (Fig. 2): the response time increases several orders of magnitude, the throughput reaches saturation, and the number of customers at the congested component tends to infinity.

This unexpected increase of response time triggers the congestion control mechanism implemented in the TCP protocol in order to prevent the source of traffic from overloading the network. Since the source uses a feedback control, directly computed from the network or received from intermediate components, to tune the load sent on the network, the increase of response time (in this context usually referred to as round trip time) beyond a threshold value triggers an immediate reduction of the congestion window size, thus a reduction of the traffic input on the network. The throughput decreases suddenly and will increase slowly according to the algorithm implemented by the TCP version adopted. The various versions of TCP implement different congestion control mechanisms inducing a different impact on network performance [11]. Clearly, this type of behavior introduce further fluctuations in the throughput and, more generally, in the indices capturing the traffic of the Internet.

3   Measurements of End-to-End Performance

In the previous section we have seen that there is a wide evidence of high variability and self-similarity in aggregate Internet traffic. In this section we will see that this property is valid also for end-to-end performance.

3.1   Experiments

The monitoring system used to collect the data consists of a Java–based tool WPET (Web Performance Evaluation Tool) developed at the Politecnico di Milano. WPET is composed by a set of agents for the collection of Internet performance data. Each agent is an automated browser that can be programmed to periodically download web pages and to measure several performance metrics (e.g., download times). Each agent is connected to Internet through a different *connection type* (e.g., ISDN, xDSL, cable, backbone), from different *geographical locations* (e.g., Rome, Milan) and through different *providers*. A WPET agent can surf on a web site performing a set of complex operations, such as fill a form, select an item from a list, follow a link. An agent can handle HTTP and HTTPS protocols, session tracking (url-rewriting and cookies) and plug-ins (e.g., flash animations, applets, activexes). For each visited page, the agent collects performance data for all the objects in the page. For each object, several performance metrics are measured: DNS lookup time, connection time, redirect time, HTTPS handshake time, server response time, object download time, object size, error conditions. All the data collected by the agents are stored in a centralized database and analyzed in order to extract meaningful statistics.

3.2   Evidence of Heavy-Tail Distribution

Figure 5 shows the time required to download the home page of the MIT web site (`www.mit.edu`). Measurements have been collected for 9 days (from March, 20th till March, 28th 2002) downloading the home page every 15 minutes with a WPET agent located in Milan and connected to Internet directly through a backbone. The upper part of the figure shows a sample of the download times. In order to investigate the heavy-tail properties of the download times, a log-log plot of the page time complementary cumulative distribution is shown in the lower left part of Fig. 5.

This plot is a graphical method to check the heavy-tailedness property of a sequence of data. If a good portion of the log-log complementary plot of the distribution is well fitted by a straight line then the distribution hold the heavy-tail property. The plot of Fig. 5 is well approximated by a straight line with slope -3.2, indicating that the distribution is the Pareto one (4) with $\alpha = 3.2$ [17].

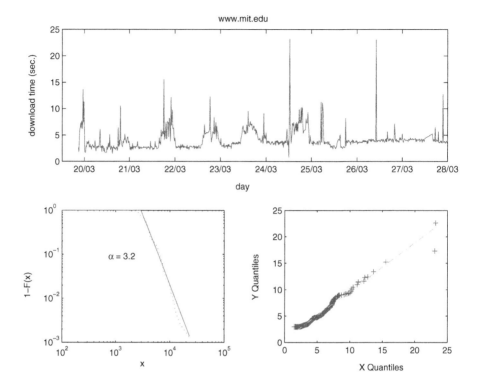

Fig. 5. Download times of the home page of the MIT web site (upper part). Log-Log complementary plot of cumulative distribution $F(x)$ (lower left). Quantile-quantile plot of the estimated Pareto distribution vs. the real distribution (lower right).

While the log-log complementary distribution plot provides solid evidence for Pareto distribution in a given data set, the method described above for producing an estimate for α is prone to errors. In order to confirm the correctness of the estimated parameter α we can use the quantile-quantile plot method (lower right part of Fig. 5). The purpose of this plot is to determine whether two samples come from the same distribution type. If the samples do come from the same distribution, the plot will be linear. The quantile-quantile plot in Fig. 5 shows quantiles of the measured data set (x axis) versus the quantiles of a Pareto distribution with tail parameter $\alpha = 3.2$ (y axis). The plot confirms the correctness of the results.

Figures 6 and 7 extend the analysis by comparing the download times of the home pages of four web servers:

- Massachusetts Institute of Technology (**www.mit.edu**)
- Standford University (**www.standford.edu**)
- Google **www.google.com**)
- Altavista (**www.altavista.com**).

The four plots in both the figures show the log-log complementary cumulative distributions (continuous lines), together with the approximating Pareto distributions (dashed lines). The measurements of Fig. 6 have been collected with a WPET agent running on a system directly connected on a backbone. The measurements of Fig. 7 have been collected with an agent connected to the Internet via an ADSL line. Both the agents were located in Milan. All the figures confirm the heavy-tail property of end-to-end download times.

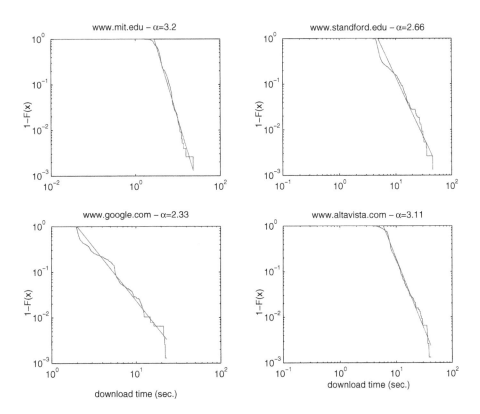

Fig. 6. Log-Log complementary plots of the home page download times distribution of four web sites measured from a *backbone* Internet connection. The real data distribution (continuous line) and the approximated Pareto distribution (dashed line) are shown. The estimated tail index α is reported on each plot.

It is interesting to observe that all the plots in Fig. 7 (ADSL connection) have a lower value of α with respect to the corresponding plots in Fig. 6 (backbone connection). We remember that lower values of α mean higher variability. This suggests that slow client connections are characterized by high variability, because (i) the source of congestion is in the network, not in the client connection, and (ii) the overhead of retransmissions is higher for slower client connections.

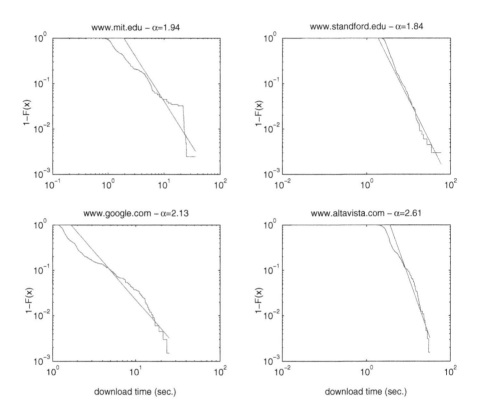

Fig. 7. Log-Log complementary plots of the home page download times distribution of the same four web server of Fig. 6measured from an *ADSL* Internet connection. The real data distribution (continuous line) and the approximated Pareto distribution (dashed line) are shown. The estimated tail index α is reported on each plot.

3.3   Evidence of Self-Similarity

In Fig. 8 we use the wavelet-based method proposed by Abry and Veitch [1] for the analysis of self-similar data and for the estimation of the associated Hurst parameter (for a formal definition of self-similarity see, e.g., [1]). Here we recall that the Hurst parameter H measures the degree of long-range dependence. For self-similar phenomena its value is between 0.5 and 1, and the degree of self-similarity increases as the Hurst parameter approaches 1. For short-range dependent processes, $H \rightarrow 0.5$. Abry and Veitch's method utilizes the ability of wavelets to localize the energy of a signal associated with each time-scale. It is possible to study the scaling of a process by log-plotting the energy associated with several time-scale: a signal which is self-similar will yield a linear plot for the larger times scales. The slope m of the linear portion of the plot is related to the Hurst parameter by the equation

$$H = \frac{m+1}{2} \qquad (5)$$

Figure 8 shows the scaling properties of the MIT home page download times plotted in Fig. 5. The wavelet energy (continuous line) is approximated with a straight line (dashed line) with slope $m = 0.90$. According to (5), the measurements are consistent with a self-similar process with Hurst parameter $H = 0.95$ (very close to 1).

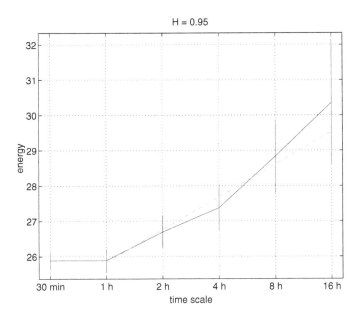

Fig. 8. Scaling analysis of the download times of MIT web site home page. The wavelet energy (continuous line) is approximated with a straight line (dashed line) with slope 0.90.

4   Improving Web Performance

For web sites that need to retain users beyond the first page there is a strong motivation to reduce the delay between the browser click and the delivery of the page content on the user's screen. Although there are many reasons behind poor web performance which are not due to the web server alone (e.g., low bandwidth, high latency, network congestion), in this section we discuss some remedial actions that can be taken in order to reduce the negative influence of such factors on the user end-to-end response time.

In Sect. 4.1 an analysis of how long users are willing to wait for web pages to download is described. Section 4.2 presents some case studies oriented to the detection of performance problems and to the improvement of the end-to-end performance of web sites.

4.1   User Satisfaction

User-perceived response time has a strong impact on how long users would stay at a web site and on the frequency with which they return to the site. Acceptable response times are difficult to determine because people's expectations differ from situation to situation. Users seem willing to wait varying amounts of time for different types of interactions [13]. The amount of time a user is willing to wait appears to be a function of the perceived complexity of the request. For example, people will wait longer:

- for requests that they think are hard or time-consuming for the web site to be performed (e.g. search engines);
- when there are no simple or valid alternatives to the visited web site (e.g., the overhead required to move a bank account increases the tolerance of home banking users).

On the contrary, users will be less tolerant to long delays for web tasks that they consider simple or when they know there are valid alternatives to the web site.

Selvidge and Chaparro [14] conducted a study to examine the effect of download delays on user performance. They used delays of 1 second, 30 seconds, and 60 seconds. They found that users were less frustrated with the one-second delay, but their satisfaction was not affected by the 30 seconds response times.

According to Nielsen, download times greater than 10 seconds causes user discomfort [10]. According to a study presented by IBM researchers, a download time longer than 30 seconds is considered too slow [7].

Studies on how long users would wait for the complete download of a web page have been performed by Bouch, Kuchinsky and Bhatti [3]. They reported good ratings for pages with latencies up to 5 seconds, and poor ratings for pages with delays over 10 seconds. In a second study, they applied the incremental load of web pages (with the banner first, text next and graphics last). Under these conditions, users were much more tolerant of longer latencies. They rated the delay as "good" with latencies up to 30 seconds. In a third study they observed that, as users interact more with a web site, their frustration with downloading delays seems to accumulate. In general, the longer a user interacts with a site (i.e., the longer is the navigation path), the less delay he will tolerate.

In Fig. 9 we have integrated the results of these studies in order to identify two thresholds for the definition of a user satisfaction. The thresholds are function of the navigation step:

- the lower threshold (continuous line) identifies the acceptable experience: users are always satisfied when web pages have a latency up to the lower threshold, independently of the situation;
- the higher threshold (dashed line) identifies the unsatisfactory experience: users will not tolerate longer latencies, independently of the other conditions.

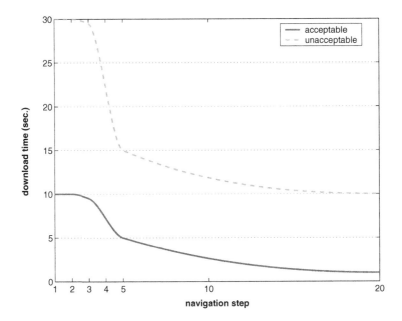

Fig. 9. User satisfaction as a function of the navigation steps. Users are always satisfied with web pages whose download time is below the lower threshold (continuous line). Users will not tolerate latencies longer than the upper threshold (dashed line).

4.2 Optimization Issues

The possible sources of unsatisfactory end-to-end delays fall into three categories:

- *Network problems:* high delays are originated by network problems along the path connecting the user to the web site (such problems can be classified into insufficient bandwidth at the client/web site or congestions in a network component).
- *Site problems:* one or more components of the web site are under-dimensioned (e.g., web server, back-end systems, firewall, load balancer).
- *Complexity problems:* page content and web applications are not optimized (e.g., too many objects in a page, usage of secure protocols with high over-head to deliver non-sensitive information, low-quality application servers).

Figure 10 shows the performance of an Italian web site. Measurements have been collected for two weeks (from December, 23th 2001 to January, 5th 2002) downloading the home page every 30 minutes during work hours (8.00–20.00) with three WPET agents located in Milan. Each agent was connected to the Internet with a 64kbit ISDN line with a different provider. Each bar in the figure is the median of the measurements collected in one day. The three main components of the page download time, namely the connection time (i.e., the round-trip or network latency time), the response time of the server and the transfer time (or transmission time) are reported.

It is evident that the web site has performance problems because the average download time for the home page is higher than 30 seconds (i.e., the maximum tolerance threshold) for all the 14 days. The most probable source of problems resides in the network at the web side. In fact, the average *connection time*, which measures the round-trip time of one packet between the client and the server, is about 10 seconds, while it should be usually smaller than one second.

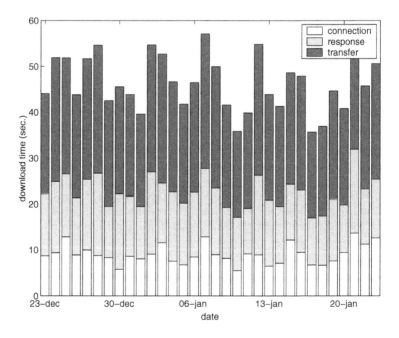

Fig. 10. End-to-end response time for the download of the home page of a web site with network problems. The three basic components, the TCP/IP connection time, the server response time and the page transfer time are shown.

Figure 11 shows the performance of a second web site. Measurements have been collected according to the same scheme of the previous experiment. The performance of this web site are satisfactory, although not excellent. Download time is always lower than 30 seconds but higher than 10 seconds. Connection time is always around 1 second. However, there is still space for optimizations. In fact, the average *response time*, which measures the time required for the web server to load the page from disk (or to generate the page dynamically), is about 10 seconds in most of the cases. By adding new hardware or improving the web application, the response time should be reduced to 1–2 seconds.

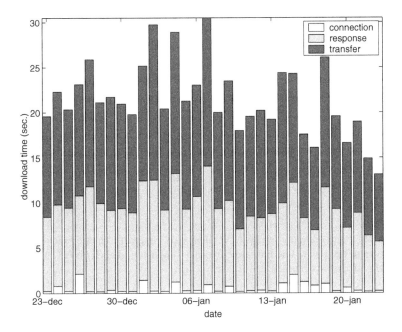

Fig. 11. End-to-end response time for the download of the home page of a web site with server problems. The three basic components, the TCP/IP connection time, the server response time and the page transfer time are shown.

Figure 12 presents an example of a *complexity problem*. The figure shows a *page component* plot. Each vertical bar in the plot represents the download time of a single object in the page. The bar in the lower-left corner is the main HTML document. All the other bars are banners, images, scripts, frames, etc. The time required to download the whole page is measured from the beginning of the first object to the end of the last object to complete the download. Together with the download time, the figure shows the dimension of each object. The measurements have been collected with an agent connected to a backbone. The object pointed out by the arrow is a small one (about 1.5 KByte) but it is the slowest object in the page (it requires almost 20 seconds for its complete download). Without this object the whole page would be received in less than 8 seconds. This object is a banner downloaded from an external ad-server which is poorly connected to the Internet. Because of the banner, the users experience a long delay.

A possible way for the web site to improve the performance experienced by the end user is to download off-line the banners from the ad-server and to cache them locally into the web server.

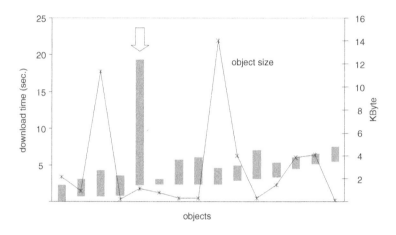

Fig. 12. Page components plot. Vertical bars represent the download times for all the objects in the page. The line indicates the dimension of each object. The object pointed by the arrow is a banner.

Figure 13 is another example of complexity problem. Although the overall size of the page is rather small (less than 100 KBytes) the page is composed of more than 50 small different objects. The overhead introduced with the download of each object (e.g., DNS lookup time, connection time, response time) makes more convenient for a web site to have pages with few big objects than pages with many small objects.

5   Conclusions

In this paper we have analyzed the origins of the high fluctuations in web traffic. The sources of these fluctuations are located into the characteristics of the applications, the complexity of the network path connecting the web user to the web server, the self-similarity of web traffic (file sizes and user think times), and the congestion control mechanism in the TCP/IP protocol. Empirical evidence of self-similar and heavy-tail features in measured end-to-end web site performance is provided. We have integrated this technical knowledge with the results of recent studies aimed at determining the effects of long download delays on users satisfaction. We have showed that users satisfaction can be modelled with

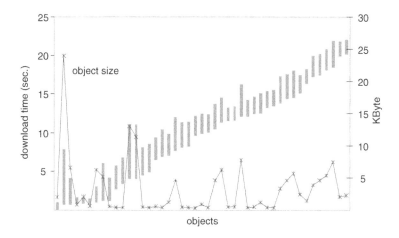

Fig. 13. Page components plot. Vertical bars represent the download times for all the objects in the page. The line indicates the dimension of each object.

two thresholds. Simple guidelines for the detection of web performance problems and for their optimization are also presented.

References

1. Abry, P. and Veitch, D.: Wavelet analysis of long-range dependent traffic. IEEE Trans. on Information Theory **44** (1998) 2–15.
2. Barford, P., Bestavros, A., Bradley, A., Crovella, M.E.: Changes in Web Client Access Patterns: Characteristics and Caching Implications. World Wide Web Journal **2** (1999) 15–28.
3. Bhatti, N., Bouch, A., Kuchinsky, A.: Integrating User–Perceived Quality into Web Server Design. Proc. of the 9th International World-Wide Web Conference. Elsevier (2000) 1–16.
4. Crovella, M.E., Bestavros, A.: Self-Similarity in World Wide Web traffic evidence and possible causes. IEEE/ACM Trans. on Networking **5** (1997) 835–846.
5. Feldmann, A., Whitt. W.: Fitting mixtures of exponentials to long-tail distributions to analyze network performance models. Performance Evaluation **31** (1998) 245–279.
6. Haverkort, B.R.: Performance of Computer Communication System: A Model-based Approach. Wiley, New York (1998).
7. IBM: Designed for Performance.
   `http://www.boulder.ibm.com/wsdd/library/techarticles/hvws/perform.html`
8. Jackson, J.R.: Network of waiting lines. Oper. Res. **5** (1957) 518–521.
9. Leland, W.E., Taqqu, M.S., Willinger, W., Wilson, D.V.: On the Self-Similar Nature of Ethernet Traffic. IEEE/ACM Trans. on Networking **2** (1994), 1–15.
10. Nielsen, J.: Designing Web Usability. New Riders (2000).
11. Park, K., Kim, G., Crovella, M.E.: On the Effect of Traffic Self-similarity on Network Performance. Proc. of the SPIE International Conference on Performance and Control of Network Systems (1997) 296–310.

12. Paxon, V., Floyd, S.: Wide area traffic: The failure of Poisson modeling. IEEE/ACM Trans. on Networking **3** (1995) 226–244.
13. Ramsay, J., Barbesi, A., Preece, J.: A psychological Investigation of Long Retrieval Times on the World Wide Web. Interacting with Computers **10** (1998) 77–86.
14. Selvidge, P.R., Chaparro, B., Bender, G.T.: The World Wide Wait: Effects of Delays on User Performance. Proc. of the IEA 2000/HFES 2000 Congress (2000) 416–419.
15. Trivedi, K.S.: Probability and Statistics with Reliability, Queueing and Computer Science Applications. Wiley, New York (2002).
16. Willinger, W., Paxon, V., Taqqu, M.S.: Self-Similarity and Heavy-Tails: Structural Modeling of Network Traffic. In A Practical Guide To Heavy Tails: Statistical Techniques and Applications. R.Adler, R.Feldman and M.Taqqu Eds., Birkhauser, Boston (1998) 27–53.
17. Willinger, W., Taqqu, M.S., Sherman, R., Wilson, D.V.: Self-Similarity Through High-Variability: Statistical Analysis of Ethernet LAN Traffic at the Source Level. IEEE/ACM Trans. on Networking **5** (1997) 71–86.

Benchmarking

Reinhold Weicker

Fujitsu Siemens Computers, 33094 Paderborn, Germany
reinhold.weicker@fujitsu-siemens.com

Abstract. After a definition (list of properties) of a benchmark, the major benchmarks currently used are classified according to several criteria: Ownership, definition of the benchmark, pricing, area covered by the benchmark. The SPEC Open Systems Group, TPC and SAP benchmarks are discussed in more detail. The use of benchmarks in academic research is discussed. Finally, some current issues in benchmarking are listed that users of benchmark results should be aware of.

1   Introduction: Use, Definition of Benchmarks

A panel discussion on the occasion of the ASPLOS-III symposium in 1989 had the title "Fair Benchmarking – An Oxymoron?" The event looked somewhat strange among all the other, technically oriented presentations at the conference. This anecdotal evidence indicates the unique status that benchmarking has in the computer area: Benchmarking is, on the one hand, a highly technical endeavor. But it also is, almost by definition, related to computer marketing.

We see that benchmarks are used in three areas:
1.   Computer customers as well as the general public use benchmark results to compare different computer systems, be it a vague perception of performance or a specific purchasing decision. Consequently, marketing departments of hardware and software vendors drive to a large degree what happens in benchmarking. After all, the development of good benchmarks is neither easy nor cheap, and it is mostly the computer vendors' marketing departments that in the end, directly or indirectly, pay the bill.
2.   Developers in hardware or software departments use benchmarks to optimize their products, to compare them with alternative or competitive designs. Quite often, design decisions are made on the basis of such comparisons.
3.   Finally, benchmarks are heavily used in computer research papers because they are readily available, and they can be expected to be easily portable. Therefore, when quantitative claims are made in research papers, they are often based on benchmarks.

Although the first usage of benchmarks (comparison of existing computers) is for many the primary usage, this paper tries to touch all three aspects.

What makes a program a benchmark? We can say that a benchmark is a standardized program (or detailed specifications of a program) designed or selected to be run on

M.C. Calzarossa and S. Tucci (Eds.): Performance 2002, LNCS 2459, pp. 179–207, 2002.
© Springer-Verlag Berlin Heidelberg 2002

different computer systems, with the goal of a fair comparison of the performance of those systems. As a consequence, benchmarks are expected to be

1. Portable: It must be possible to execute the program on different computer systems.
2. Fair: Even portable programs may have a certain built-in bias for a specific system, the system that they have been originally written for. Benchmarks are expected to minimize such a bias.
3. Relevant, which typically means "representative for a relevant application area": A performance comparison makes no sense if it is based on some exotic program that may be portable but has no relation to a relevant application area. The benchmark must perform a task that is in some identifiable way representative for a broader area.
4. Easy to measure: It has often been said that the best benchmark is the customer's application itself. However, it often would be prohibitively expensive to port this application to every system one is interested in. The next best thing is a standard benchmark accepted by the relevant players in the field. Both customers and developers appreciate it if benchmark results are available for a large number of systems.
5. Easy to explain: It helps the acceptance of a benchmark if readers of benchmark results have some feeling about the meaning of the result metrics. Similarly, a benchmark is often expected to deliver its result as one "single figure of merit". Experts can and should look at all details of a result but it is a fact of life that many readers only care about one number, a number that somehow characterizes the performance of a particular system.

In his "Benchmark Handbook" [3], Jim Gray lists another property: Scalability, i.e. the benchmark should be applicable to small and large computer systems. While this is a desirable property, some benchmarks (e.g., BAPCo) are limited to certain classes of computers, and still are useful benchmarks.

We will come back to these goals during the following presentations of some important benchmarks. Not surprisingly, some of the goals can be in conflict with each other.

2   Overview, Classification of Benchmarks

The benchmarks that have been or are widely used can be classified according to several criteria. Perhaps the best starting point is "Who owns / administers a benchmark?" It turns out that this also roughly corresponds to a chronological order in the history of benchmarking.

2.1   Classification by Benchmark Ownership, History of Benchmarks

In earlier years, benchmarks were administered by single authors, then industry associations took over. In the last years, benchmarks became popular that are administered by important software vendors.

2.1.1   Individual Authors, Complete Programs

The first benchmarks were published by individual authors and have, after initial publication, spread basically through "word of mouth". Often, their popularity was a surprise for the author. Among those benchmarks are

Table 1. Single-author complete benchmarks

Name and Author(s)	Year	Language	Code size, in byte	Characterization
Whetstone (Curnow/Wichman)	1976	ALGOL 60 / Fortran	2,120	Synthetic Numerical Code, FP-intensive
Linpack (J. Dongarra)	1976	Fortran	(Inner loop:) 230	Package Linear Algebra Numerical Code, FP-intensive
Dhrystone (R. Weicker)	1984	Ada / Pascal / C	1,040	Synthetic System-type code, integer only

A detailed overview of these three benchmarks, written at about the peak of their popularity, can be found in [11]. Among these three benchmarks, only Linpack has retained a certain importance, mainly through the popular "Top 500" list (www.top500.org). It must be stated, and the author, Jack Dongarra, has acknowledged, that it represents just "one application" (solution of a system of linear equations with a dense matrix), resulting in "one number". On the other hand, this weakness can turn into a strength: There is hardly any computer system in the world for which this benchmark has not been run; therefore many results are available. This has lead to the effect that systems are compared on this basis, which will never run, in real life, scientific-numeric code like Linpack.

2.1.2   Individual Authors, Microbenchmarks

The term "microbenchmark" is used for program pieces that intentionally have been constructed to test only one particular feature of the system under test; they do not claim to be representative for a whole application area. However, the feature that they test is important enough that such a specialized test is interesting. The best-known example, and an often-used one, is probably John McCalpin's "Stream" benchmark (www.cs.virginia.edu/stream). It measures "sustainable memory bandwidth and the corresponding computation rate for simple vector kernels" [7]. The once popular "lmbench" benchmark (www.bitmover.com/lmbench), consisting of various small programs executing individual Unix system calls, seems to be no longer actively pursued by its author.

2.1.3   Benchmarks Owned and Administered by Industry Associations

After the success of some small single-author benchmarks in the 1980's, it became evident that small single-author benchmarks like Dhrystone were insufficient to characterize the emerging larger and more sophisticated systems. For example, benchmarks with a small working set cannot adequately measure the effect of memory hierarchies (multi-level caches, main memory). Also, small benchmarks can easily be subject to targeted compiler optimizations. To satisfy the need for benchmarks that are larger and cover a broader area, technical representatives from various computer manufacturers founded industry associations that define benchmarks, set rules for measurements, and review and publish results.

Table 2. Benchmarks owned by industry associations

Benchmark group	Since	URL	Language of bench-marks	Application area	Systems typically tested
GPC / SPEC GPC	1986	www.spec.org/ gpc	C	Graphics programs	Work-stations
Perfect / SPEC HPG	1987	www.spec.org/ hpg	Fortran	Numerical programs	Supercom-puters
SPEC CPU	1988	www.spec.org/ osg/cpu	C, C++, Fortran	Mixed programs	Workstations, Servers
TPC	1988	www.tpc.org	Specifica-tion only	OLTP programs	Database Servers
BAPCo	1991	www.bapco.com	Object Code	PC Applications	PCs
SPEC System	1992	www.spec.org/ osg	C (driver)	Selected system functions	Servers
EEMBC	1997	www.eembc.org	C	Mixed programs	Embedded processors

Among these benchmarking groups, SPEC seems to be some kind of a role model: Some later associations (BAPCo, EEMBC, Storage Performance Council) have followed, to a smaller or larger degree, SPEC's approach in the development and administration of benchmarks. Also, some older benchmarking groups like the "Perfect" or GPC groups decided to use SPEC's established infrastructure for result publication) and to continue their efforts as a subgroup of SPEC. The latest example is the ECPerf benchmarking group, which is currently continuing its effort for a "Java Application Server" benchmark within the SPEC Java subcommittee.

2.1.4 Benchmarks Owned and Administered by Major Software Vendors

During the last decade, benchmarks became popular that were developed by some major software vendors. Often, these vendors are asked about sizing decisions: How many users will be supported on a given system, running a specific application package? Therefore, the vendor typically combined one or more of his application packages with a fixed input and defined this as a benchmark. Later, the major system vendors who run the benchmark cooperate with the software vendor in the evolution of the benchmark, and there is usually some form of organized cooperation around a software vendor's benchmark. Still, the responsibility for result publication typically lies with the software vendor. The attractiveness of these benchmarks for computer customers lies in the fact that they immediately have a feeling for the programs that are executed during the benchmark measurement: Ideally, they are the same programs that customers run in their daily operations.

Table 3. Benchmarks administered by major software vendors

Software vendor	Since	URL	Benchmarks covered	Systems tested
SAP	1993	www.sap.com/ benchmark/	ERP software	Servers
Lotus	1996	www.notesbench. org	Domino and Lotus software, mainly mail	Servers
Oracle Applications	1999	www.oracle.com/ apps_benchmark/	ERP software	Servers

There are more software vendors that have created their own benchmarks, again often as a byproduct of sizing considerations, among them are Baan, Peoplesoft, Siebel, and others. Table 3 only lists those where the external use as a benchmark has become more important than just sizing.

Note that in this group, there is no column "Source Language": Although the application package typically has been developed in a high-level language, the benchmark code is the binary code generated by the software vendor and/or the system vendor for a particular platform.

2.1.5 Result Collections by Third Parties

For completeness, result collections should also be mentioned where a commercial organization does not develop a new benchmark but rather collects benchmark results measured elsewhere. The best-known example is IDEAS International (www.ideasinternational.com). Their web page on benchmarks displays the top results for the TPC, SPEC, Oracle Applications, Lotus, SAP, and BAPCo benchmarks. Such lists or collections of benchmark results from various sources may serve a need of those that just want a short answer to the non-trivial question of performance ranking: "Give me a simple list ranking all systems according to their overall performance", or "Just give me the top 10 systems, without all the details". Often, the media, or high-level managers hard pressed on time, want such a ranking. However, the inevitable danger of such condensed result presentations is that important caveats, important details of a particular result get lost.

2.2   Other Classifications: Benchmark Definition, Pricing, Areas Covered

2.2.1 Benchmark Definition

There are basically three classes of benchmark definitions, with an important additional special case:

1.   Benchmarks that are defined in source code form: This is the "classical" form of benchmarks. They require a compiler for the system under test but this is usually no problem. SPEC, EEMBC, and all older single-author benchmarks listed here belong to this group.

2.   Benchmarks that are defined as binary codes: By definition, these benchmarks cover a limited range of systems only. However, the market of Intel/Windows compatible PCs is large enough that benchmarks covering only this area can be quite popular. The BAPCo benchmarks and other benchmarks often used by the popular PC press (not covered here) belong to this category.

3.   Benchmarks that are defined as specifications only: The TPC benchmarks are defined by a specification document, TPC does not provide source code. Because of the need to provide a level playing field in the absence of source code, and to prevent loopholes, these specification documents are quite voluminous. For example, as of 2002, the current TPC-C definition contains 137 pages, the TPC-W definition even 199 pages.

4.   Benchmarks administered by a software vendor are a somewhat special case: The code running on the system under test is machine code, but it usually is the code sold by the software vendor to his customers, and there is typically a version for every major instruction set architecture / operating system combination. The only problem can be that in the case of a small system vendor, where less systems are sold, the software vendor may not have tuned the code (compilation, use of specific OS features) as well as he does in the case of a big system vendors, where many copies of the software are sold. On the one hand, the software systems sold to customers will also have this property; so one can say that the situation represents real life. On the other hand, the feeling remains that this is somewhat unfair, penalizing smaller system vendors.

In all cases, even in the case where the code executed on the system is given in source or binary form, a benchmark is defined not only by the code that is executed but also by input data and by a document, typically called "Run and Reporting Rules"; it describes the rules and requirements for the measurement environment.

2.2.2 Price / Performance

Some benchmarks include "pricing" rules, i.e. result quotations must contain not only a performance metric but also a price/performance metric. Since its beginnings, TPC results have included such a metric, e.g. "price per tpm-C". Among the other benchmarks, only the Lotus benchmark and the SPEC GPC benchmarks have a price/performance metric.

The value of pricing in benchmarks is often subject to debate, in the benchmark organizations themselves and in the press. Arguments for pricing are:

- Customers naturally are interested in prices, and prices determined according to uniform pricing rules set by the benchmark organization have a chance to be more uniform than, say, prices published by a magazine.
- There is always a tendency among system vendors to aim for the top spot in the performance list. The requirement to provide price information can be a useful corrective against benchmark configurations that degrade into sheer battles of material: If a benchmark scales well, e.g. for clusters, then whoever can accumulate enough hardware in the benchmark lab, wins the competition for performance. The requirement to quote the price of the configuration may prevent such useless battles.

On the other hand, there are the arguments against pricing:

- In the case of systems that are larger than just a single workstation, prices are difficult to determine and have many components: Hardware, software, maintenance. It is hard to find uniform criteria for all components, in particular for maintenance; different companies may have different business models.
- In the computer business, prices get outdated very fast. It is tempting but misleading to compare a price published today with a price published a year ago.
- With the goal to be realistic, some pricing rules (e.g. TPC's rules) allow discounts, provided that they are generally available. On the other hand, this allows system vendors to grant such discounts just for configurations that have been selected with an eye on important benchmark results, making the price less realistic than it appears.
- Experience in benchmark organizations like TPC shows that a large percentage of result challenges have to do with pricing.. This distracts energy from the member organizations that could be better spent in the improvement of benchmarks.

Overall, the arguments against pricing appear to be more convincing. The traditional approach of the SPEC Open Systems Group (OSG) "Have the test sponsor publish, in detail, all components that were used, and encourage the interested reader to get a price quotation directly from vendors' sales offices" seems to work quite well.

2.2.3 Areas Covered by Benchmarks

Finally, an important classification of benchmarks is related to the area the benchmarks intend to cover. One such classification is shown in figure 1.

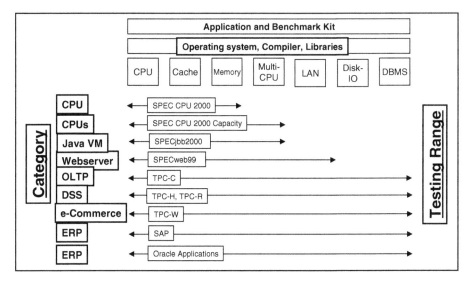

Fig. 1. Areas covered by some major benchmarks (from [10]).

Of course, the benchmark coverage also has some relation to the cost of benchmarking. For example, if networking is involved, the benchmark setup typically includes one or more servers and several (often many) clients. It is not surprising that the number of results for such benchmarks, where measurements take weeks or months, is much smaller than for those that involve only one system.

3   A Closer Look at the More Popular Benchmarks

In this section, the more important benchmarks from SPEC, TPC, and SAP are covered. They are, for large systems (servers), the most widely quoted benchmarks.

3.1   SPEC CPU Benchmarks, Measurement Methods

A CPU benchmark suite, now called CPU89, was SPEC's first benchmark product. When SPEC was founded in 1988, the explicit intention was to provide something better than the small single-author benchmarks that had been used before, and to provide standardized versions of larger programs (e.g. gcc, spice) that were already used by some RISC system vendors.

Since 1989, SPEC has replaced the CPU benchmarks three times, with CPU92, CPU95, and CPU2000. Currently, the SPEC CPU subcommittee is working on CPU2004, intended to replace the current suite CPU2000. On the other hand, the principle of SPEC CPU benchmarking has been remarkably consistent:

- A number of programs are contributed by the SPEC member companies, by the open source community, or by researchers in the academic community. For the CPU2000 suite, and again for CPU2004, SPEC has initiated an award program to encourage such contributions.
- The member companies that are active in the CPU subcommittee port the benchmarks to their various platforms; dependency on I/O or operating system activity is removed, if necessary. Care is taken that all changes are performance-neutral across platforms. If possible, the cooperation of the original program's author(s) is sought for all these activities.
- The benchmarks are tested in a tool harness provided by SPEC. Compilation and execution of the benchmarks is automated as much as possible. The tester supplies a "configuration file" with system-specific parameters (e.g. location of the C compiler, compilation flags, libraries, description of the system under test).

Table 4. SPEC's CPU benchmarks over the years

	CPU89	CPU92	CPU95	CPU2000
Integer programs	4	6	8	12
Floating-point programs	6	14	10	14
Total source lines, Integer	77,100	85,500	275,000	389,300
Total source lines, FP	24,200	44,000	20,600	158,300
Source languages	C, F77	C, F77	C, F77	C, C++, F77, F90
Number of results through Q1/2002	191	1292	1881	1043

SPEC's current CPU2000 suite is described in detail in [5]; this article also describes how SPEC selects its CPU benchmarks, and some problems that have to be solved in the definition of a new benchmark suite. Table 4 summarizes some key data on SPEC's CPU benchmarks (Note: Source line counts do not include comment lines).

The popular "speed" metric typically measures the execution time of each program in the suite when it is executed on one CPU (other CPUs are removed or deactivated), it replaces old "MIPS" metrics that had previously been used. The execution time of each program is set in relation to a "SPEC Reference Time" (execution time on a specific older popular system), and the geometric mean of all these performance ratios is computed as an overall figure of merit (SPECint, SPECfp).

Soon after the introduction of the CPU89 suite, manufacturers of multi-CPU systems wanted to show the performance of their systems with the same benchmarks. In response, SPEC developed rules for a "SPECrate" (throughput) computation: For each benchmark in the suite, several copies are executed simultaneously (typically, as many copies as there are CPUs in the system), and total throughput of this parallel execution (jobs per time period) is computed on a per-benchmark basis. A geometric mean is computed, similar to the "speed" case.

In its official statements, SPEC emphasizes the advice "Look at all the numbers". This means that a customer interested in a particular application area weights benchmarks from this area higher than the rest. Experts can draw even more interesting conclusions, correlating, for example, the working sets for particular benchmarks with the test system's cache architecture and cache sizes [5]. However, such evaluations remained, to a large degree, an area of experts only; customers rarely look at more than the number achieved in the overall metric.

3.2 Evolution of the SPEC CPU Benchmarks, Issues

Despite the consistency of the measurement method, a number of new elements were brought into the suite over the years. Both the SPEC-provided tool harness and the Run Rules regulating conformant executions of the suite grew in complexity. The most important single change was the introduction of the "baseline" metric in 1994.

In the first publications of SPEC CPU benchmark results, the "Notes" section where all compilation parameters (in Unix terminology: "Flags") must be listed, consisted of a few short lines, like

```
Optimization was set to -O3 for all benchmarks except fppp and
spice2g6, which used -O2
```

Over time, this changed drastically; today, one to three small-print lines per benchmark like

```
197.parser: -fast -xprefetch=no%auto -xcrossfile -xregs=syst
           -Wc,-Qgsched-trace_late=1,-Qgsched-T4 -xalias_level=strong
           -Wc,-Qipa:valueprediction -xprofile
```

listing the optimization flags used just for this single benchmark, are not uncommon. Compiler writers had always used internal variables controlling, for example, the tradeoff between the benefit of inlining (elimination of calling sequences etc.) and its negative effects (longer code, more instruction cache misses). Now, these variables were made accessible to the compiler user – an easy and straightforward change in the compiler driver. However, the user often does not have the knowledge to apply the additional command-line parameters properly, nor the time to optimize their use. In addition, sometimes "assertion" flags are used which help a particular benchmark but which would cause other programs to fail. This soon prompted the question whether such excessive optimizations are representative for real programming, or whether it would be better to "burn all flags" [13]. The issue was later discussed in academic publications [1,8] and in the trade press.

After a considerable debate, the final compromise for SPEC, established in January 1994, was that two metrics were established, "baseline" and "peak": Every SPEC CPU benchmark measurement has to measure performance with a restricted "baseline" set of flags (metric name: SPECint_base2000 or similar), and optionally with a more extended "peak" set of flags. In its own publications, on the SPEC web site, SPEC treats them equally. In marketing material, most companies emphasize the higher peak numbers; therefore even the existence of a baseline definition may be unknown to some users of SPEC results. The exact definition of "baseline" can be found in the suite's Run and Reporting Rules. For CPU2000, it can be summarized as follows:

- All benchmarks of a suite must be compiled with the same set of flags (except flags that may be necessary for portability).
- The number of optimization flags is restricted to 4.
- Assertion flags (flags that assert a certain property of the program, one that may not hold for other programs, and that typically allows more aggressive optimizations) are not allowed: This property may not hold for other programs, and one of the basic principles of baseline is that they are "safe", i.e. do not lead to erroneous behavior for any language-compliant program.

The idea is now generally accepted that it makes sense to have, in addition to the "everything goes (except source code changes)" of the "peak" results, a "baseline" result. However, the details are often controversial, they emerge as a compromise in SPEC's CPU subcommittee. The question "What is the philosophy behind baseline?" may generate different answers if different participants are asked. A possible answer could be:

Baseline rules serve to form a "baseline" of performance that takes into account

- reasonable ease of use for developers,
- correctness and safety of the generated code,
- recommendations of the compiler vendor for good performance,
- representativity of the compilation/linkage process for what happens in the production of important software packages.

Again, it cannot be disputed that in some cases, individual points may contradict each other: What if the vendor of a popular compiler sets, for performance reasons, the default behavior to a mode that does not implement all features required by the language definition? This usage mode may be very common – most users lack the expertise to recognize such cases anyway -, but correctness of the generated code, as defined by the language standard, is not guaranteed. Since SPEC releases the CPU benchmarks in source code form, correct implementation of the programming language as defined by the standard is a necessary requirement for a fair comparison.

The baseline topic is probably the most important single issue connected with the SPEC CPU benchmarks. But there are other important issues as well:

- How should a compute-intensive multi-CPU metric be defined? The current SPECrate method takes a simplistic approach: Execute, for example on an n-CPU system, n copies of a given benchmark in parallel, record their start and end times. This introduces some artificial properties into the workload. In a real-life compute-intensive environment, e.g. in a university computing center, batch jobs come and go at irregular intervals and not in lockstep. Typically, there is also an element of overloading: More jobs are in the run queue than CPUs in the system.
- SPEC needs to distribute its CPU benchmarks as source code. For the floating-point suite, it seems possible to get, with some effort, good, state-

of-the-art codes from researchers (engineering, natural sciences). It is more difficult to get similarly good, representative source codes in non-numeric programming. Such programs are typically very large, and the developers, the vendors of such software cannot give them away for free in source code form. Traditionally, SPEC has relied heavily on integer programs from the Open Source community (GNU C compiler, Perl, etc.), but these programs are only one part of the spectrum.

- It has been observed [2] that the SPEC CPU benchmarks, in particular the integer benchmarks, deviate in their cache usage from what is typically observed on "live" systems. The observations in [2] were for the CPU92 benchmarks but the tendency still can be observed today. To some degree, such differences are an unavoidable consequence of the measurement method: For the purpose of benchmarking, with a reasonably long measurement interval, a SPEC CPU benchmark runs for a longer time uninterrupted on one CPU than in real-life environments where jobs often consist of several cooperating processes. Due to the absence of context switches, SPEC CPU measurements show almost no process migration with subsequent instruction cache invalidations.

In particular the last point should be taken by SPEC as a reason to think about other alternatives to measure the raw computing power of a system: In a time when multiple CPUs are placed on a single die, does it make sense to artificially isolate the speed of one CPU for a traditional "speed" measurement?

3.3 SPEC System Benchmarks

SPEC OSG started with CPU benchmarks but very soon also developed benchmarks that measured system performance. The areas that SPEC chose to put efforts in were determined by a perception of the market demands as seen by the SPEC OSG member companies. For example, when the Internet and Java gained popularity, SPEC OSG soon developed its Web and JVM benchmarks. Currently, Java on servers and mail servers are seen as hot topics; therefore, Java server benchmarks and mail server benchmarks are areas where SPEC member companies invest considerable efforts on the development of new benchmarks. There are also areas where SPEC's efforts were unsuccessful: SPEC worked for some time on an I/O benchmark but finally could not find a practical way between raw device measurements and system-specific I/O library calls. (These efforts apparently are taken up now by a separate industry organization, the "Storage Performance Council", see www.storageperformance.org). The only area intentionally left out by SPEC is transaction processing, the traditional domain of the sister benchmarking organization TPC.

It is important to realize that SPEC's system benchmarks are both broader and narrower than the component (CPU) benchmarks:

- They are broader than the CPU benchmarks because they test more components of the system, typically including the OS, networking, and – for some benchmarks – the I/O subsystem.

- They are narrower than the CPU benchmarks because they test the system when it is executing specific, specialized tasks only, e.g. acting as a file server, a web server or a mail server.

This narrower scope of some system benchmarks is not unrelated to real-life practice: Many computers are exclusively used as file servers, web servers, database servers, mail servers, etc. Therefore it makes sense to test them in such a limited scenario only.

Most system benchmarks present results in the form of a table or a curve, giving, for example, the throughput correlated with the response time. This corresponds to SPEC's philosophy "Look at all the numbers", similarly as the CPU benchmark suites gives the results for each individual benchmark. However, SPEC is realistic enough to know that the market often demands a "single figure of merit", and has defined such a number for each benchmark (e.g. maximum throughput, throughput at or below a specific response time). Table 5 lists SPEC's current system benchmarks, with the number of publications over the years.

Table 5. SPEC OSG system benchmark results over the years

	SDM	SFS	SPEC web96	SPEC web99	SPEC jvm98	SPEC jbb2000	SPEC mail2001
1991	51						
1992	17						
1993	5	21					
1994	6	18					
1995	15	21					
1996		14	22				
1997		36	50				
1998		19	80		21		
1999		96	61	5	26		
2000		62	12	49	23	22	
2001		25+34		57	4	57	6
Q1/2002		21		13	3	21	3
Overall	94	215	225	124	77	100	9

Some general differences to the CPU benchmarks are:
- The workload is, almost inevitably, synthetic. Whereas SPEC avoids synthetic benchmarks for the CPU suites, workloads for file server or web server benchmarks cannot be derived from "real life" without extensive trace capturing / replay capabilities that make use in benchmarks impractical. On the other hand, properties that are important for system benchmarks, e.g. file sizes, can be more easily modeled in synthetic workloads.
- The results are more difficult to understand; therefore the benchmarks are possibly not as well known and not as popular as the CPU benchmarks.

- Finally, the measurement effort is much larger. Typically, these benchmarks need clients / workload generators that add considerably to the cost of benchmarking. Therefore, fewer results exist than for the CPU benchmarks.

3.3.1 SDM Benchmark

SPEC's first system benchmark suite, released in 1991, was SDM (System Development Multiuser, released 1991). It consists of two individual benchmarks that differ in some aspects (workload ingredients, think time) but have many properties in common: Both have a mix of general-purpose Unix commands (ls, cd, find, cc, ...) as their workload. Both use scripts or simulated concurrent users that put more and more stress on the system, until the system becomes overloaded and the addition of users results in a decrease in throughput.

After initial enthusiasm, interest in the benchmark died down. Today, SDM results are no longer requested by customers, and therefore not reported by SPEC member companies. This is an interesting phenomenon because we know that many SPEC member companies still use SDM heavily as an internal performance tracking tool: Whenever a new release of the OS is developed, its performance impact is measured with the SDM benchmarks. Why has it then been unsuccessful as a benchmark? It seems that there are several reasons:

- SDM measures typical Unix all-around systems; today, we have more client-server configurations.
- For marketing, the fact that there is not an overall, easy-to-explain single figure of merit (only individual results for sdet and kenbus; no requirement to report both) is probably a severe disadvantage.
- Most important, the ingredients are the system's Unix commands, and several of them (cc, nroff) take a large percentage of time in the benchmark. This opens up possibilities for SDM-specific versions of these commands, e.g. a compiler (cc command) that does little more than syntax checking: Good for great SDM numbers but useless otherwise.

SDM is a good example for the experience that a good performance measurement tool is not yet necessarily a good benchmark: An in-house tool needs no provisions against unintended optimizations ("cheating"); the user would only cheat himself or herself. A benchmark whose results are used in marketing must have additional qualities: It must be tamper-proof against substitution of fast, special-case, benchmark-specific components where normally other software components would be used.

3.3.2 SFS Benchmark

The SFS benchmark (System benchmark, File Server, first release 1993) is SPEC's first client-server benchmark and has established a method that was later used for other benchmarks also: The benchmark code runs solely on the clients, they generate NFS requests like lookup, getattr, read, write, etc. Unix is required for the clients, but the server, the system under test, can be any server capable of accepting NFS requests. SFS tries to be as independent from the clients' performance as possible, concentrating solely on measuring the server's performance.

Despite the large investment necessary for the test sponsor (the setup for a large server may include as many as 480 disks for the server, and as many as 20 load-generating clients), there has been a steady flow of result publications, and SFS is the established benchmark in its area. In 1997, SFS 1.0 was replaced by SFS 2.0. The newer benchmark covers the NFS protocol version 3, and it has a newly designed mix of operations.

In summer 2001, prompted by observations during result reviews, SPEC discovered significant defects in its SFS97 benchmark suite: Certain properties built into the benchmark (periodic changes between high and low file system activities, distribution of files accesses, numeric accuracy of the random process selecting the files that are accessed) were no longer guaranteed with today's fast processors. As a consequence, SPEC has suspended sales of the SFS97 (2.0) benchmark and replaced it by SFS97 R1 V3.0. Result submissions had to start over, since results measured by the defective benchmark cannot be used without considerable care in interpretation.

3.3.3 SPECweb Benchmarks

The SPECweb benchmark (Web server benchmark, first release 1996) was derived from the SFS benchmark, and it has many properties in common with SFS:

- It measures the performance of the server and tries to do this, as much as possible, independently from the clients' performance.
- A synthetic load is generated on the clients, generating HTTP requests. In the case of SPECweb96, these were static GET requests only, the most common type of HTTP requests at that time. SPECweb99 added dynamic requests (dynamic GET, dynamic POST, simulation of an ad rotation scheme based on cookies).
- The file size distribution is based on logs from several large web sites; the file set size is required to scale with the performance

Different from SFS, the benchmark code can run on NT client systems as well as on Unix client systems. Similar to SFS, the server can be any system capable of serving HTTP requests. As apparent from the large number of result publications (see table 5), SPEC's web benchmarks have become very popular.

When it became evident that electronic commerce now constitutes a large percentage of WWW usage, and that this typically involves use of a "Secure Socket Layer" (SSL) mechanism, SPEC responded with a new Web benchmark, SPECweb99_SSL. In the interest of a fast release of the benchmark, SPEC did not change the workload but just added SSL usage to the existing SPECweb99 benchmark. A new SSL handshake is required whenever SPECweb99 terminated a "keepalive" connection (in the average, every tenth request). Of course, it makes no sense to compare SPECweb99_SSL results with (non-SSL) SPECweb99 results. An exception can be results that have been obtained for the same system; they can help to evaluate the performance impact of SSL encryption on the server.

3.3.4 SPEC Java Benchmarks

In the years 1997/1998, when it became clear that Java performance was a hot topic in industry, SPEC felt compelled to produce, during a relatively short time, a suite for Java benchmarking. Previous benchmark collection in this area (Coffeinemark etc.) had known weaknesses that made them vulnerable to specific optimizations. The first SPEC Java benchmark suite followed the pattern of the established CPU benchmarks: A collection of programs, taken from real applications where possible, individual benchmark performance ratios, and the geometric mean over all benchmarks as a "single figure of merit". In the design on the benchmark suite and the run rules for the suite, several new aspects had to be dealt with:

- Garbage collection performance, even though it may occur at unpredictable times, is important for Java performance.
- Just-In-Time (JIT) compilers are typically used with Java virtual machines, in particular for systems for which the manufacturer wants to show good performance.
- During the first years, Java was typically used on small client systems (e.g. within web browsers), and memory size is an important issue for such systems.
- Finally, SPEC had to decide whether benchmark execution needed to follow the strict rules of the official Java definition, or whether some sort of offline compilation should be allowed.

SPEC decided to start with a suite that requires strict compliance with the Java Virtual Machine model. A novel feature of SPECjvm98 results is their grouping into three categories according to the memory size: Under 48 MB, 48 – 256 MB, over 256 MB. The experience seems to show that the test sponsors (mostly hardware manufacturers) followed SPEC's suggestion and produced results not only for big machines but also for "thin" clients.

During the last years, Java became more popular as a programming language not only for small (client) systems, but also for servers. SPEC responded with the SPECjbb2000 Java Business Benchmark which has become quite popular. Manufacturers of server systems now use it to demonstrate the capabilities of their high-end servers. The Java code executed in SPECjbb2000 resembles TPC's TPC-C benchmark (warehouses, processing of orders; see section 3.3) but the realization is different: Instead of real database objects stored on disks, Java objects (in memory) are used to represent the benchmark's data; therefore Java memory administration and garbage collection play an important role for performance. Overall, the intention is to model the middle tier in three-tier software systems; such software is now often written in Java.

Currently, SPEC is working on another benchmark that relies more directly on Java application software. A "Java Application Server" benchmark SPECjAppServer will include the use of program parts that use popular Java application packages (Enterprise JavaBeans ™) and will also involve the use of database software. In this benchmark, client systems drive the server; therefore the cost of benchmarking will be much higher.

3.4 TPC Benchmarks

Like SPEC, the Transaction Processing Performance Council (TPC), founded in 1988, is a non-profit corporation with the mission to deliver objective performance evaluation standards to the industry. However, TPC focuses on transaction processing and data base benchmarks. Another important difference to the SPEC OSG benchmarks is the fact that TPC, from its beginning, included a price/performance metric and made price reporting mandatory (see section 2.2). The most widely used benchmark of this organization, and therefore *the* classic system benchmark, is the TPC-C published in 1992, an OLTP benchmark simulating an order-entry business scenario.

The TPC-C benchmark simulates an environment where virtual users are concurrently executing transactions against a single database. The environment models a wholesale supplier, i.e. a company running a certain number of warehouses, each with an inventory of items on stock. Each warehouse is serving ten sales districts, and each district has 3000 customers. Sales clerks for each district are the virtual users of the benchmark who execute transactions. There are five types of transactions of which the new-order type is the most important, representing the entry of an order on behalf of a customer. The number of order entries per minute the system can handle is the primary performance metric, it is called tpmC (transactions per minute, TPC-C).

The user simulation has to obey realistic assumptions on keying and think times. For the database response times, the benchmark defines permissible upper limits, e.g. five seconds for the new-order transaction type. Further constraints apply to the shares of the transaction types, e.g. only about 45% of all transactions are new order entries, the remaining share is distributed to payments, posting of deliveries, and status checks. To only report the rate of new order entries is motivated by the desire to express a business throughput instead of providing abstract technical quantities. As transactions cannot be submitted to the system at arbitrary speed due to keying and think times, a dependency is enforced between the throughput and the number of emulated users, or the number of configured warehouses and ultimately the size of the database. The warehouse with its ten users is the scaling unit of the benchmark, it comes with customer and stock data and an initial population of orders that occupy physical disk space.

Since TPC does not define its benchmarks via source code, the database vendors, often in cooperation with the major system vendors, typically produce a "benchmark kit" which implements the benchmark for a specific hardware/software configuration. It is then the task of the TPC-certified auditor to check that the kit implements the benchmark correctly, in addition to verifying the performance data (throughput, response times). An important requirement checked by the auditor, which is unique to TPC, are the so-called "ACID properties"

- Atomicity: The entire sequence of actions must be either completed or aborted.
- Consistency: Transactions take the resources from one consistent state to another consistent state.

- Isolation: A transaction's effect is not visible to other transactions until the transaction is committed.
- Durability: Changes made by committed transactions are permanent and must survive system failures.

The rationale for these "ACID properties" is the fundamental requirement that a benchmark must be representative for an application environment, and that therefore, the database used needs to be a "real database". In the case of transaction processing, faster execution could easily be achieved if the implementation would drop one or more of the "ACID property" requirements. But such an environment would not be one into which customers would have enough trust to store their business data in it, and any performance results for such an unstable environment would be meaningless.

Over the years, TPC-C underwent several revisions, the current major revision is 5.0. It differs from revision 3.5 in some aspects only (revised pricing rules); the algorithms remained unchanged. An earlier attempt ("revision 4.0") to make the benchmark easier to handle (e.g. fewer disks required), and at the same time more realistic (e.g. more complex transactions) failed and did not get the necessary votes within TPC. It can be assumed that the investment that companies had made into the existing results (which would then loose their value for comparisons) played a role in this decision.

Complementing TPC-C, TPC introduced, in 1995, its "decision support" benchmark TPC-D. While TPC-C is update-intensive and tries to represent on-line transactions as they occur in real life, TPC-D modeled transactions that change the data base content quite infrequently but perform compute-intensive operations on it, with the goal of supporting typical business decisions. This different task immediately had consequences for practical benchmarking:

- Decision support benchmarks are more CPU-intensive and less I/O intensive than transaction processing benchmarks.
- Decision support benchmarks scale better for cluster systems

In 1999, TPC faced a problem that can be, in a larger sense, a problem for all benchmarks where the algorithm and the input data are known in advance to the implementors: It is possible for the data base implementation to store data not only in the customary form as relations (n-tuples of values, in some physical representation) but to anticipate computations that are likely to be performed on the data later, and to store partial results of such computations. The database can already present "materialized views", as they are called, to the user. It is only a short step from this observation to the construction of materialized views that are designed with an eye towards the requirements of the TPC-D benchmark. Within a short time, such implementations brought a huge increase in reported performance, and TPC was forced to set new rules or to withdraw the benchmark. It decided to replace TPC-D with two successor benchmarks that are different with respect to optimizations based on advance knowledge of the queries: TPC-R allows them, TPC-H does not. It turned out that apparently, the users of TPC benchmark results considered a situation with materialized views as not representative for their environment. After two initial results in 1999/2000, no more TPC-R results were published, and TPC-R can be considered dead. In a broad sense, TPC-R and TPC-H, can be compared with SPEC's "peak" and "baseline" metrics: Similar computations, but in one case, more optimizations are allowed. It is interesting to note that the TPC customers apparently were more interested in the "baseline" version of decision support benchmarks. Realizing that the split into two benchmarks was a temporary solution only, TPC currently works on a common successor benchmark for both TPC-H and TPC-R.

TPC's latest benchmark, TPC-W, covers an important new area; it has been designed to simulate the activities of a business oriented transactional Internet web server, as it might be used in electronic commerce. Correspondingly, the application portrayed by the benchmark is a retail store on the Internet with customer "browse and order" scenario. The figure of merit computed by the benchmark is "Web Interactions Per Second" (WIPS), for a given scale factor (overall item count). The initial problem of TPC-W seems to be its complexity since there are many components that can influence the result:

- Web server, application server, image server, database software, all of which can come from different sources
- SSL implementation
- TCP/IP realization
- Route balancing
- Caching

It could be due to this complexity that there are still relatively few TPC-W results (currently, as of June 2002, 13 results), much less than for TPC-C (79 active results for version 5). This may be an indication that in the necessary tradeoff between representativity (realistic scenarios) and easy of use, TPC might have been too ambitious and might have designed a benchmark that is too costly to measure. Also, the benchmark does not have an easy-to-understand, intuitive result metric. SPEC's "HTTP ops/sec" (in SPECweb96) may be unrealistic if one looks closer at the definition, but it at least *appears* more intuitive than TPC-W's "WIPS" (Web Interactions Per Second). In addition, when the first results were submitted, it became clear that more rules are necessary for the benchmark with respect to the role of the various software layers (web server, application server, database server).

3.5   SAP Benchmarks

Similarly to SPEC and TPC, SAP offers not only a single benchmark but a family of benchmarks; there are various benchmarks for various business scenarios. The SAP Standard Application Benchmarks have accompanied the SAP R/3 product releases since 1993. Since 1995, issues relating to benchmarking, and the public use of results are discussed by SAP and its partners in the SAP Benchmark Council. Benchmark definition and certification of results, however, is at the discretion of SAP. The number of benchmarks in the family is about a dozen, with the majority simulating users in online dialog with SAP R/3.

Two of the benchmarks, Sales and Distribution (SD) and Assemble-to-Order (ATO), cover nearly 90% of all published results. Historically, SD came first and gained its importance by being the tool to measure the SAPS throughput metric (SAP Application Benchmark Performance Standard) that is at the center of all SAP R/3 sizing:

100 SAPS are defined as 2000 fully business processed order line items per hour in the Standard SD benchmark. This is equivalent to 6000 dialog steps and 1600 postings per hour or 2400 SAP transactions per hour.

The SD and ATO business scenario is that of a supply chain: A customer order is placed, the delivery of goods is scheduled and initiated, an invoice in written. In SD, an order comprises five simple and independent items from a warehouse. In ATO, an individually configured and assembled PC is ordered, which explains the differences in complexity. The sequence of SAP transactions consists of a number of dialog steps or screen changes. By means of a benchmark driver the benchmarks simulate concurrent users passing through the respective sequence with 10 seconds think time after each dialog step. After all virtual users have logged into the SAP system and started working in a ramp-up phase, the users repeat the sequence as many times as is necessary to provide a steady state measurement window of at least 15 minutes. It is required that the average response time of the dialog steps is less than two seconds. In case of SD, users, response time, and the throughput expressed as SAPS are the main performance metrics. For ATO where the complete sequence of dialog steps is called *a fully business processed assembly order*, only the throughput in terms of assembly orders per hour is reported.

Looking at SAP benchmark results, it is important to distinguish "two-tier" and "three-tier" results, with the difference lying in the allocation of the different layers for presentation, application and database. The presentation layer is where users are running their front-end tools, typically PCs running a tool called *sapgui* (SAP Graphical User Interface). In the benchmark, this layer is represented by a driver system where for each virtual user a special process is started that behaves like a "sapgui". This driver layer corresponds to the RTE layer in the TPC-C benchmark. It is the location of the SAP application layer software that determines the important distinction between "two-tier" and "three-tier" results:

- If it resides on the same system as the database layer, the result is called a "two-tier" or "central" result. In this case, about 90 % of the CPU cycles are spent in the SAP R/3 application and only 10 % in the data base code.
- If it resides on separate application servers (typically, there are several of them since the application part of the workload is easily distributable), the result is called a "three-tier" result.

Since in result quotations, the number of users is typically related to the database server, the 90-10 relation explains why the same hardware system can have a much higher "three-tier" result than "two-tier" result: In the "three-tier" case, all activities of the SAP application code are offloaded to the second tier. Typically, the benchmarker configures as many application systems as are necessary to saturate the database server. In a large three-tier benchmark installation in November 2000, Fujitsu Siemens used 160 R/3 application servers (4-CPU PRIMERGY N400, Pentium/Xeon-based) in connection with a large 64-CPU PRIMEPOWER2000 as the data base server. Figure 4 shows the impressive scenario of this large SAP three-tier SD measurement.

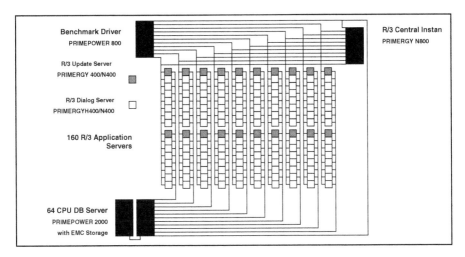

Fig. 2. Example of a large SAP three-tier installation (Fujitsu Siemens, Dec. 2000)

The sponsor of a three-tier SAP benchmark is free how to accommodate the processing needs of the application layer. For example, in another SAP measurement (IBM, with the p680 as database server), the application layer consisted of large p680 systems, too. The benchmarker is free to choose between configurations, based for example on ease of handling, or on the desire to implement a typical implementation for real-life client/server application environments.

It may be of interest to provide some insight into the workload on the database server as the most important factor in the three-tier case. There is a similarity to the TPC-C because both benchmarks deal with database server performance. But while in the TPC-C disk I/O is at the center of interest, it is network I/O in the SAP benchmark. The two workloads are complementing each other in this regard in a very nice way. In the benchmark setup summarized in Figure 4 there were 65000 network roundtrips or 130000 network I/Os per second. Five out of 64 CPUs of the data base server were assigned to handle the interrupt processing for this traffic between application layer and database. The network stack was standard TCP/IP, a mature industry standard.

4 Benchmarking and Computer Research

It is well known that several benchmarks, in particular the SPEC CPU benchmarks, are used extensively in the manufacturers' development labs; we shall discuss this aspect in section 5. A critical look at recent computer science conferences or journals, especially in the area of computer architecture and compiler optimization, shows that this phenomenon is not restricted to manufacturers, it appears in academic research also. Table 6 shows a snapshot for several major conferences in 2000/2001, listing how often benchmarks were used in conference papers (Note that some papers use more than one benchmark program collection).

Table 6. Use of benchmark collections in conference papers

	ASPLOS Nov. 2000	SIGPLAN June 2001	SIGARCH June 2001
Overall number of papers	24	30	24
SPEC CPU (92, 95, 2000)	8	4	17
SPEC JVM98	1	4	1
SPLASH benchmarks (Parallel Systems)	2	-	-
Olden benchmarks (Pointer, Memory)	-	-	3
OLTP / TPC	1	-	1
Various other program collections	11	13	8
No benchmark used	6	9	3

Looking at table 6, we can say:

- Benchmarks that are composed of several individual components (SPEC CPU, SPEC JVM98, Olden, SPLASH) are particularly popular. These are also the benchmarks that are relatively easy to run, compared with others.
- For specific research topics, some benchmark collections that emphasize a particular aspect are popular: SPECJVM98 for Java, the parallelizable SPLASH codes for research on parallel processing, the Olden benchmark collection of pointer- and memory-intensive programs for research on pointers and memory hierarchy.
- The SPEC CPU benchmarks are the most popular benchmark collection overall.
- Very few papers base quantitative data on OLTP workloads.

Given the importance of OLTP, TPC- and SAP-type workloads in commercial computing, one can ask whether academic research neglects to give guidance for computer developers as far as these environments are concerned. Fortunately, specialized workshops like the "Workshop on Computer Architecture Evaluation using Commercial Workloads" held in conjunction with the "Symposium on High Performance Computer Architecture" (www.hpcaconf.org) fill this gap.

"A Quantitative Approach" is the subtitle of one of the most popular and influential books on computer architecture [4]. The underlying thesis is that computer architecture should be driven by ideas whose value can be judged not only by intuition but also by quantitative considerations. A new design principle has to show a quantitative advantage over other designs. Following this approach, there is an apparent trend in Ph.D. dissertations and other research papers:

- A new idea is presented.
- A possible implementation (hardware, software, or a combination of both) is discussed, with operation times for individual operations.
- Simulation results are presented, on the basis of some popular benchmarks, very often some or all of the SPEC CPU benchmarks.
- The conclusion is "We found an improvement of xx to yy percent".

Such a statement is considered proof that the idea has value to it, and is relevant for successor projects, for research grants, and academic promotion.

This tendency, both in manufacturers' development labs and in academic research, places a responsibility on benchmark development groups that can be frightening: Sometimes, aspects of benchmarks become important for such design optimizations that were not yet thought of, or never discussed, when the benchmarks were selected. Suddenly, they develop an influence not only on the comparison of today's computers but also on the design of tomorrow's computers. For example, when the earlier CPU benchmark suites were put together, SPEC looked mainly at the source codes. Now, with techniques like feedback optimization and value prediction becoming more popular in research and possibly also in state-of-the-art compilers, one also has to look much more closely at the input data that are used with the benchmarks: Are they representative for typical problems in the area covered by the benchmarks? Do they encourage optimization techniques that have an over-proportional effect on benchmarks, as opposed to normal programs?

This author once attended an ASPLOS (Architectural Support for Programming Languages and Operating Systems) conference and made a critical remark about some papers that relied, in his opinion, too much on the SPEC CPU benchmarks. He was asked: "Do you mean that we should not use the SPEC benchmarks?" This, of course, would mean to "throw out the child with the bathwater". The result was a short contribution in a newsletter widely read by academic computer architects [12], asking to continue using the SPEC CPU benchmarks, but to use – if possible – all of them, and to report all relevant conditions (e.g. compiler flags). The main request was not to take benchmarks blindly as given, but to include a critical discussion of those properties of the benchmarks that may be relevant for the architectural feature that is studied. For example, in [14] it is shown that the program "HEALTH", one of the often-used "Olden Benchmarks" supposedly representative for linked-list data structures, is algorithmically so inefficient that any performance evaluations based on it are highly questionable. Surprisingly few research papers discuss the value of SPEC's benchmarks from an independent perspective, [2] is one of them (however, discussing the old CPU92 benchmarks). Occasionally, when surprising new results come up, online discussion group are full of statements "Benchmarks, and in particular the SPEC CPU benchmarks, are bogus anyway". But it is hard to find good, constructive criticisms of benchmark programs. More papers that compare benchmarks with other programs that are heavily used would be particularly useful. In one such paper [6], the authors compare the execution characteristics of popular Windows-based desktop applications with that of selected SPEC CINT95 benchmarks and find similarities (e.g., data cache behavior) as well as differences (e.g., indirect branches). Given the large influence – direct or indirect, even in academic research – that benchmarks can have, it would be beneficial for both computer development and computer science research if the benchmarks get the attention and critical scrutiny they deserve.

One has to acknowledge that the three usage areas for benchmarks mentioned in the introduction
1.   Customer information and marketing, goal: Compare today's computers on a fair basis;

2.   Design in manufacturers' labs, goal: Build better computers;
3.   Computer science research, goal: Develop design ideas for the long-term future;
can call for different selection criteria: For goal 1, it makes sense to have
representatives of today's programs in a benchmark suite, including instances of
"dusty deck" code. For goals 2 and 3, it would make much more sense to only have
programs of tomorrow, programs with good coding style, possibly programs of a type
that rarely exists today. For example, it has been observed [6] that object-oriented
programs and programs that make frequent use of dynamically linked libraries
(DLL's) have different execution characteristics than the classical C and Fortran
program in today's SPEC CPU suites.

In addition to its under-representation in academic research, a critical discussion of
benchmarks is also often missing from computer science curricula. In the area of
computer architecture, universities tend to educate future computer designers, not so
much future computer users. On the other hand, it is obvious that many more
graduates will eventually end up making purchase decisions than making design
decisions for computers. They would benefit from a deeper knowledge about the
values and the pitfalls of benchmarks.

5   Use of Benchmarks, Issues, and Opportunities

The presentation of various important benchmarks in section 3 has already shown
some aspects that seem to appear across several benchmarks. Benchmarks as drivers
of optimizations, conflicting goals for benchmarks, and a possible broader use of
benchmarks, for more than just the generation of magical numbers, are some of these
aspects.

5.1   Benchmarks as Drivers of Optimization

It is well known, and intended and encouraged by benchmark organizations, that good
benchmarks drive industry and technology forward. Examples are:

- Advances in compiler optimization encouraged by the SPEC CPU
  benchmarks.
- Advances in database software encouraged by the TPC benchmarks.
- Optimizations in Web servers like caching for static requests, encouraged
  by the SPECweb benchmarks.

It must be emphasized that such advances in performance are a welcome and
intended effect of benchmarks, and that the benchmarking organizations can take
pride in these developments. However, some developments can also be
counterproductive:

- Compiler writers may concentrate on optimizations that are allowed for
  the SPEC CPU benchmarks but that are not used by 80 or 90 % of the
  software developers: Then, the benchmarks lead to a one-sided and
  problematic allocation of resources. SPEC has tried to counter this with
  the requirement to publish "baseline" results. However, this can only be

successful as long as "baseline" optimizations allowed by SPEC are really relevant in the compilation/linkage process of real-life programs.

- Hardware designers may optimize the size of their caches to what the current benchmarks require, irrespective of longer-term needs.
- Database designers may concentrate too much on query situations that occur in benchmarks.

Looking at such issues from a more general point of view, the overall issue is that of the representativity of the benchmark; it tends to appear in several contexts:

- TPC had its problems with materialized views;
- SPEC CPU has its ongoing debates on peak vs. baseline;
- SPEC Web had debates about web server software that was, in one way or another, integrated with the operating system, leading to a sudden increase in performance.

Let us look at the example of the SPEC CPU benchmarks where the component benchmarks are given in source code form. If some aspect of the benchmark turns out to be particularly relevant for the measured performance, but if this property is not shared by important state-of-the-art programs, a particular optimization can suggest to the naive reader a performance improvement that is unreal, i.e. that is based on the specific properties of a particular benchmark only. An issue that seems to come up repeatedly with the SPEC CPU benchmarks is a "staircase" effect of certain single benchmarks with respect to caches. Some programs, together with their input data sets, have a critical working set size: If the working set fits into a cache, performance is a magnitude better than in the case that the working set size makes many memory accesses necessary, possibly connected with "cache thrashing" effects. Several SPEC CPU benchmarks (030.matrix300 in CPU89, 023.eqntott in CPU92, 173.art in CPU2000) apparently had such "magical" working size parameters and, consequently, showed sudden increases in their performance through compiler optimizations that managed to push the working set size below a critical, cache-related boundary. Such optimizations typically generated heated discussions inside and outside of SPEC: "Can such an increase in performance be real?" The optimizations themselves can be "legal", i.e. general enough that they are applicable to other programs also. But the specific performance gain may not be representative; it may come from a particular programming style that SPEC overlooked in its benchmark selection process.

It is not only the compiler and the CPU benchmarks where the question of representativity is relevant. System benchmarks often test the performance of a layered software system. The seven-layer ISO reference model for network architectures is a good example: In the interest of good software engineering practices (modularity, encapsulation, maintainability), software is often organized in layers, each performing a specific task. On the other hand, it is well known that shortcuts through these layers usually result in better performance; the various Web server caches now used in most SPECweb results are a good example. Where should benchmark specifications draw the line when such layer-transgressing optimizations occur for the first time at the occasion of a new benchmark result? What will be seen as an advance in technology, and what will be seen as a "benchmark special", a construct that is outlawed in most benchmarks' rules? Everyone will agree on extreme cases:

- Results where the traditional barrier between system mode and user mode is abandoned in favor of performance do not reflect typical usage and are rightly forbidden.
- On the other hand, the fact that databases running on top of Unix typically omit the Unix file system layer and operate directly on raw devices will be considered standard practice.

It is the cases in between such extremes that often cause lengthy debates in benchmark organizations. Because such optimizations are rarely foreseen at the time when the benchmark, together with its rules, is adopted, these cases typically arise during result reviews, where immediate vendor interests are also involved. TPC has a separate body, the "Technical Advisory Board" (TAB) that makes suggestions in cases of result compliance complaints or when TPC auditors ask for a decision. SPEC leaves these decisions to the appropriate subcommittee, where such discussions often take considerable time away from the committee's technical work, e.g. new benchmark development. But someone has to decide; the alternative that a test sponsor can do anything and remain unchallenged would be even worse.

With its ACID tests, TPC has found an interesting way to enforce the requirement that the software used during the benchmark measurement is "real database software". The ACID tests are a required part of the benchmark; if the system fails them, no result can be submitted. But they are executed separately from the performance measurement, outside the measurement interval. So far, SPEC has not formulated similar tests for its benchmark although one could imagine such tests:

- For the CPU benchmarks, SPEC requires that "hardware and software used to run the CINT2000/CFP2000 programs must provide a suitable environment for running typical C, C++, or Fortran programs" (Run Rules, section 1.2). For baseline, there is the additional requirement that "the optimizations used are expected to be safe" (2.2.1), which is normally interpreted by the subcommittee as a requirement that "the system, as used in baseline, implements the language correctly" (2.2.7). The idea of a "Mhillstone" program that would, outside the measurement interval and with more specialized programs, test for correct implementation, and that would flag illegal over-optimizations, has been debated a few times. However, with its limited resources, SPEC so far has not yet implemented such a test.
- The SPECweb benchmarks are heavily dominated by TCP/IP activity. SPEC requires in the Run Rules that the relevant protocols are followed; but there is no check included in the benchmark. Since the benchmark typically is executed in an isolated local network, an implementation could, theoretically, take a shortcut around requirements like the ability to repeat transmissions that have failed.
- The SPEC SFS benchmark requires stable storage for the file system used in the benchmark measurement. However, the benchmark does not contain code that would test this.

Other aspects of representativity so far have barely been touched by benchmark designers: In [9], Shubhendu Mukherjee points out that future processors might have several modes of operation in relation to cosmic rays: A "fault tolerant" mode where intermittent errors caused by such cosmic rays are compensated by additional circuits (which make the CPU slower), and a "fast execution" mode where such circuitry is not present or not activated. He asks what would be the relevance of benchmark results have that can only be reproduced in the basement of the manufacturer's testing lab where the computer is better shielded from cosmic rays. In the software area, future Shared Memory Processor (SMP) systems may have cache coherency protocols that can switch from "snoopy" to "directory based" and vice versa, with possible performance implications for large vs. small systems. Benchmark results that have been obtained in one environment may not be representative for the other environment.

5.2   Conflicting Goals for Benchmarks

The discussions in the previous sections can be subsumed under the title "Representativity". An obvious way towards achieving this goal is the introduction of new benchmarks (like SPEC's sequence of CPU benchmarks, from CPU89 to CPU2000), or at least the introduction of new rules for existing benchmarks (like TPC's sequence of "major revisions" for its TPC-C benchmark). New benchmarks can make over-aggressive optimizations irrelevant, and the expectation that benchmarks will be retired after a few years can discourage special-case optimizations in the first place. On the other hand, marketing departments and end users want benchmarks to be "stable", to be valid over many years. This leads, for example, to one of the most frequently asked questions to SPEC: "Can I convert SPECint95 ratings to SPECint2000 ratings?" SPEC's official answer "You cannot – the programs are different" is not satisfying for marketing but necessary from a technical point of view.

5.3   More Than Just Generators of Single Numbers: Benchmarks as Useful Tools for the Interested User

Looking at official benchmark result publications, readers will notice that almost all results have been measured and submitted by hardware or software vendors. Given the large costs that are often involved, this is understandable. From a fairness point of view, this can also make sense: Every benchmarker tries to achieve the best result possible; therefore, if all measurements are governed by the same rules, the results should be comparable.

On the other hand, some important questions remain unanswered with this practice: What would be the result if the measurements were performed under conditions that are not optimal but reflect typical system usage better? Examples are:

- What CPU benchmark results would be achieved if the compilation uses a basic "-O" optimization only?
- What would be the result of a Web benchmark that intentionally does not use one of the popular Web cache accelerators?

- What would be the result of a TPC or SAP benchmark measurement if the CPU utilization of the server is at a level recommended for everyday use, and not as close to 100 % as possible?

Manufacturers typically do not publish such measurements because they are afraid of unfair comparisons: Everyone not using a performance-relevant optimization that is legal according to the benchmark's rules would run the risk that the result would let his system appear inferior to competitive systems for which only highly optimized results are published

As a consequence, such measurements under sub-optimal conditions are often performed in the development labs, but the results are never published. The only means to change this would be results published by independent organizations such as technical magazines. For its CPU benchmarks, SPEC has rules stating that if results measured by third parties are submitted to SPEC, a vendor whose products are affected can protest against such a result and hold up result publication for a few weeks but cannot prevent an eventual publication. The idea is that such a publication could be based on really silly conditions ("Let's make this manufacturer's system look bad"), and that the manufacturer should have a fair chance to counter with his own measurement. But in principle, measurements and result submissions by non-vendors are allowed; they just happen very rarely. On the other hand, such measurements, with appropriate accompanying documentation, could have considerable value for an informed and knowledgeable reader.

At least for easy-to-use benchmarks like SPEC's CPU and SPECjbb2000 benchmarks, valuable insights could be gained by the publications of more results that those promoted for marketing purposes. With appropriate documentation, readers could ask for answers to questions like

- What is the performance gain for a new processor architecture if programs are not recompiled? This often happens with important ISV codes.
- What is the performance loss if a PC uses RAM components that are slower but cheaper?
- For different CPU architectures, how much do they depend on sophisticated compilation techniques, how well can they deliver acceptable performance in environments that do not include such techniques?

It would be unrealistic to expect answers to such questions from vendor-published benchmark results; vendors cannot afford to publish anything but the best results. But if benchmarks are well-designed, representative, and portable – as they should be -, then, with some efforts from informed user organizations, researchers, or magazines, they could be used for much more than what is visible today.

Acknowledgments. I want to thank my colleagues in the Fujitsu Siemens Benchmark Center in Paderborn for valuable suggestions, in particular Walter Nitsche, Ludger Meyer, and Stefan Gradek, whose "Performance Brief PRIMEPOWER" [10] provided valuable information on several benchmarks that I have not been pursuing actively myself. In addition, I want to thank my colleagues in the SPEC Open Systems Group; a large part of this paper is based on many years of experience in this group. However, it is evident that it contains a number of statements that reflect the author's personal opinion on certain topics, which may or may not be shared by other SPEC OSG representatives. Therefore, it must be stated that this is a personal account rather than a policy statement of either SPEC or Fujitsu Siemens Computers

References

1. Yin Chan, Ashok Sundarsanam, and Andrew Wolfe: The Effect of Compiler-Flag Tuning in SPEC Benchmark Performance. ACM Computer Architecture News 22,4 (Sept. 1994), 60–70
2. Jeffrey D. Gee, Mark D. Hill, Dionisios N. Pnevmatikos, and Alan Jay Smith: Cache Performance of the SPEC92 Benchmark Suite. IEEE Micro, August 1993, 17–27
3. Jim Gray: The Benchmark Handbook for Database and Transaction Processing Systems. Morgan Kaufmann, San Mateo, 2nd Edition, 1993, 592 pages
4. John Hennessy and David Patterson: Computer Architecture. A Quantitative Approach. 2nd Edition, Morgan Kaufmann, San Francisco 1996, 760 pages plus appendixes
5. John L. Henning: SPEC CPU2000: Measuring CPU Performance in the New Millenium. Computer (IEEE) 33,7 (July 2000), 28–35
6. Dennis C. Lee, et al: Execution Characteristics of Desktop Applications on Windows NT. 25th Annual Symposium on Computer Architecture, = ACM Computer Architecture News 26,3 (June 1998), 27–38
7. John McCalpin: http://www.cs.virginia.edu/stream/ref.html: FAQ list (Frequently Asked Questions) about Stream
8. Nikki Mirghafori, Margret Jacoby, and David Patterson: Truth in SPEC Benchmarks. ACM Computer Architecture News 23,5 (Dec. 1995), 34–42
9. Shubhendu S. Mukherjee: New Challenges in Benchmarking Future Processors. Fifth Workshop on Computer Architecture Evaluation using Commercial Workloads, 2002
10. Performance Brief PRIMEPOWER (PRIMEPOWER Performance Paper). Fujitsu Siemens, LoB Unix, Benchmark Center Paderborn, March 2002. Available, as of June 2002, under http://www.fujitsu-siemens.com/bcc/performance.html
11. Reinhold P. Weicker: An Overview of Common Benchmarks. Computer (IEEE) 23, 12 (Dec. 1990), 65–75
12. Reinhold Weicker: On the Use of SPEC Benchmarks in Computer Architecture Research. ACM Computer Architecture News 25,1 (March 1997), 19–22
13. Reinhold Weicker: Point: Why SPEC Should Burn (Almost) All Flags, and Walter Bays. Counterpoint: Defending the Flag. SPEC Newsletter 7,4, Dec. 1995, 5-6
14. Craig B. Zilles: Benchmark HEALTH Considered Harmful. ACM Computer Architecture News 29,3 (June 2001), 4–5

Benchmarking Models and Tools for Distributed Web-Server Systems

Mauro Andreolini[1], Valeria Cardellini[1], and Michele Colajanni[2]

[1] Dept. of Computer, Systems and Production
University of Roma "Tor Vergata"
Roma I-00133, Italy
{andreolini,cardellini}@ing.uniroma2.it,
[2] Dept. of Information Engineering
University of Modena
Modena I-41100, Italy
colajanni@unimo.it

Abstract. This tutorial reviews benchmarking tools and techniques that can be used to evaluate the performance and scalability of highly accessed Web-server systems. The focus is on design and testing of locally and geographically distributed architectures where the performance evaluation is obtained through workload generators and analyzers in a laboratory environment. The tutorial identifies the qualities and issues of existing tools with respect to the main features that characterize a benchmarking tool (workload representation, load generation, data collection, output analysis and report) and their applicability to the analysis of distributed Web-server systems.

1 Introduction

The explosive growth in size and usage of the Web is causing enormous strain on users, network service, and content providers. Sophisticated software components have been implemented for the provision of critical services through the Web. Consequently, many research efforts have been directed toward improving the performance of Web-based services through caching and replication solutions. A large variety of novel content delivery architectures, such as distributed Web-server systems, cooperative proxy systems, and content distribution networks have been proposed and implemented [35].

One of the key issues is the evaluation of the performance and scalability of these systems under realistic workload conditions. In this tutorial, we focus on the use of benchmarking models and tools during the design, testing, and alternative comparison of locally and geographically distributed systems for highly accessed Web sites. We discuss the properties that should be provided by a benchmarking tool in terms of various parameters: applicability to distributed Web-server systems, realism of workload and significance of the output results. The analysis is also influenced by the availability of the source code and the customizability of the workload model. We analyze popular products that are

M.C. Calzarossa and S. Tucci (Eds.): Performance 2002, LNCS 2459, pp. 208–235, 2002.
© Springer-Verlag Berlin Heidelberg 2002

free or at nominal costs, and provide source code: httperf [32], SPECweb99 (including the version supporting SSL encryption/decryption) [38,39], SURGE [7, 8], S-Clients [6], TPC-W [41], WebBench [45], Web Polygraph [42], and Web-Stone [30]. For this reason, we do not consider commercial tools (e.g., Technovations' Websizr [40], Neal Nelson's Web Server Benchmark [34]) that are more expensive and typically unavailable to the academic community, although they provide richer functionalities. Other benchmarking tools that come from the research (e.g., Flintstone [15], WAGON [24]) have not been included because they are not publicly available.

We can anticipate that none of the observed tools is specifically oriented to testing distributed Web-server systems, and only a minority of them reproduces the load imposed by a modern user session. Many existing benchmarks prefer to test the maximum capacity of a Web server by requesting objects as quickly as possible or at a constant rate. Others with more realistic reproductions of user session behavior (involving multiple requests for Web pages separated by think times) refer to request and delivery of static content only. This result was rather surprising if we think that the variety and complexity of offered Web-based services require system structures that are quite different from the typical browser/server solutions of the early days of the Web. The increasing need for dynamic request, multimedia services, e-commerce transactions, and security are typically based on multi-tier distributed systems. These novel architectures have really complicated the user and client interactions with a Web system, ranging from simple browsing to elaborated sessions involving queries to application and database servers. Not to say about the manipulations to which a user request can be subject, from cookie-based identifications to tunneling, caching, and redirections. Moreover, an increasing amount of Web services and content are subject to security restrictions and secure communication channels involving strong authentication that is becoming a common practice in the e-business world. Since distributed Web-server systems typically provide dynamic and secure services, a modern benchmarking tool should model and monitor the complex interactions occurring between clients and servers. None of them seems publicly available to the academic community.

We illustrate in Fig. 1 the basic structure of a benchmark tool for distributed Web-server systems that we assume based on six main components (benchmarking goal and scope, workload characterization, content mapping on servers, workload generation, data collection, data analysis and report) that will be analyzed in details in the following sections. The clear identification of the characteristics to be evaluated is at the basis of any serious benchmarking study that cannot expect to achieve multiple goals. From this choice, the *workload representation* phase takes as its input the set of parameters representing a given workload configuration and produces a non ambiguous Web workload specification. In the case of a distributed Web-server system, the content is not always replicated among all the servers, hence it is important that the *content mapping* phase decides the assignment of the Web content among multiple front-end and back-end servers. The *workload generation engine* of a benchmark analyzes the workload specification and produces the offered Web workload, issuing the necessary amount of requests to the Web system and handling the server responses. The component responsible for *data collection* considers the metrics of interest that have been chosen in the first phase of the benchmarking study and stores relative data measurements. Often, the whole set of measurements must be aggregated and processed in order to present meaningful results to the benchmark user. The *output analysis and report* component of a benchmark takes the collected data set, computes the desired statistics, and presents them to the benchmark user in a readable form.

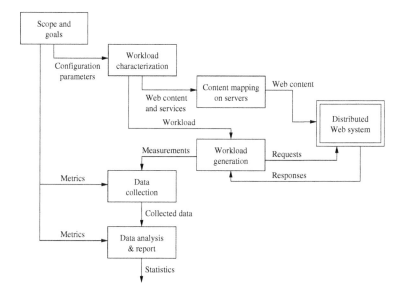

Fig. 1. Main components of a benchmarking tool for distributed Web-server systems.

After a brief description in Sect. 2 of the main architectures for locally and geographically distributed Web-server systems, the remaining sections of this tutorial follows the components outlined in Fig. 1. Finally, Sect. 9 concludes the paper and summarizes some open issues for future research.

2   Distributed Web-Server Systems

In this section we outline the main characteristics of the Web-server systems we consider in this tutorial, by distinguishing *locally* from *geographically* distributed architectures.

Any distributed Web-server system needs to appear as one host to the outside world, so that users need not be concerned about the names or locations of the replicated servers. Although a large system may consist of dozens of nodes, it is publicized with one site name to provide a single interface to users at least at the site name level.

2.1 Locally Distributed Architectures

A locally distributed Web-server system, namely *Web cluster*, is composed by a multi-tier architecture placed at a single location. A typical architecture is shown in Fig. 2. A modern Web cluster has typically a front-end component (called *Web switch*) that is located between the Internet and the first tier of Web server nodes, and it acts as a network representative for the Web site. The Web system comprises also one authoritative Domain Name System (DNS) server for translating the Web site name into one IP address. The role of this name server is easy because a Web cluster provides to the external world a single virtual IP address that corresponds to the IP address of the Web switch.

The HTTP processes running on the Web server nodes listen on some network port for the client requests assigned by the Web switch, prepare the content requested by the clients, send the response back to the clients or to the Web switch depending on the cluster architecture, and finally return to the listen status. The Web server nodes are capable of handling requests for static content, whereas they forward requests for dynamic content to other processes that are interposed between the Web servers and the back-end servers. In less complex architectures these middle-tier processes (e.g., CGI, ASP, JSP) are executed on the same nodes where the HTTP processes run, so to avoid a connection with another server node. These middle-tier processes are activated by and accept requests from the HTTP processes. They interact with database servers or other legacy applications running on the back-end server nodes for providing dynamic content.

In Fig. 2 we evidence the three main flows of interactions of a client with the Web cluster not including secure connections: requests for static files that are served from the disk cache of the Web servers, requests for static files that require the disk access, requests for dynamic content.

The Web switch receives the totality of inbound packets and distributes them among the Web servers. The two main architecture alternatives can be broadly classified according to the OSI protocol stack layer at which the Web switch operates the request assignment, that is *layer-4* and *layer-7* Web switches. The main difference is the kind of information available to the Web switch to perform assignment and routing decision.

Layer-4 Web switches work at TCP/IP layer. They are *content information blind*, because they determine the target server when the client establishes the TCP connection, before sending out the HTTP request. Therefore, the type of information regarding the client is limited to that contained in TCP/IP packets, that is IP source address, TCP port numbers, SYN/FIN flags in the TCP header.

Layer-7 Web switches work at the application layer. They can deploy *content-based* request distribution. The Web switch establishes a complete TCP connection with the client, inspects the HTTP request content, and then relays it to

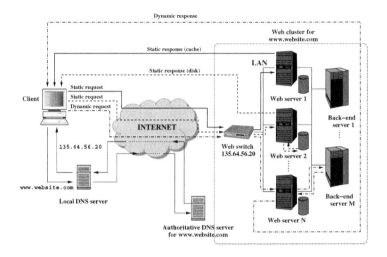

Fig. 2. Flows of interaction in a locally distributed architecture.

the chosen Web server. The selection of the target server can be based on the Web service/content requested, as URL content, SSL identifiers, and cookies.

Another important classification regards the mechanism used by the Web cluster to route outbound packets to the clients. In *two-ways* architectures, both inbound and outbound traffic pass through the Web switch. In *one-way* architectures, only inbound packets flow through the Web switch, while outbound packets use a separate high-bandwidth network connection. A detailed description of request routing mechanisms and dispatching algorithms for locally distributed architectures can be found in [10].

2.2 Geographically Distributed Architectures

A locally distributed system is a powerful and robust architecture from the server point of view, but does not solve the problems related to network delivery, such as first and last mile connectivity, router overload, peering points. An alternative solution is to distribute the server nodes over the Internet. With respect to clusters of nodes that reside at a single location, geographically distributed Web-server systems can reduce network delays experienced by the client, and also provide high availability to face network failures and congestion.

For performance and availability reasons, the distribution take typically place at the granularity of Web clusters that is, each geographically distributed node consists of a cluster of servers as that described in the previous section. We refer to this architectures as to *Web multi-cluster*. It maintains one hostname for the extern as in the Web cluster case, but now each Web cluster has a visible IP address. Hence, the request assignment process can occur in two or more steps. The first request assignment (*inter-cluster*) is typically carried out by the authoritative Domain Name Server (DNS) of the Web site that selects the IP address of the target Web cluster during the address lookup of the client request. The second (*intra-cluster*) dispatching level is executed by the Web switch of the target cluster that distributes the request reaching the cluster among the local Web server nodes. A third (*extra-cluster*) dispatching level based on some request re-routing technique may be integrated with the previous two mechanisms [11, 35].

3   Scope and Goals of the Benchmarking Study

In considering the performance of a Web system we should regard to its software, operating system, and hardware environment, because each of these factors can dramatically influence the results. In a distributed Web-server system, this environment is further complicated by the presence of multiple components, that require connection handoffs, process activations and request dispatching. For example, referring to the Web switch component in Fig. 2, we may be interested to evaluate several alternatives, such as hardware, operating system, network related software, request dispatching policy and request forwarding mechanism. A Web server is characterized by similar hardware and software layers, and besides them by the HTTP software, the data distribution, the software for dynamic requests. A back-end server is also characterized by application and database software. Not to say of the additional complexity that characterizes a geographically distributed system.

A complete performance evaluation of all layers and components of a distributed Web-server system is simply impossible. Hence, any serious benchmarking study should clearly define its goals and limit the scope of the alternatives to be considered. In particular, this tutorial focuses mainly on benchmarking tools used in the design and prototype phase when different architectures must be evaluated and alternative solutions must be compared through experiments in a laboratory. Our main interests do not go to the hardware and operating system that in most cases are simply given. Similarly, we are not interested to evaluate the end-to-end performance of an installed Web system although many considerations can be also used for these purposes.

4   Workload Characterization

The characterization of the workload generated by a Web benchmarking tool represents a central aspect of benchmarking and constitutes a distinguishing core feature of existing tools as on it founds the attempt to mimic the real-world traffic patterns observed by Web-server systems. The generation of synthetic Web traffic is not a trivial task because it aims at reproducing as accurately as possible the characteristics of real traffic patterns, which exhibit some unusual features such as burstiness and self-similarity [4,12]. On the other hand, real world workloads are inherently irreproducible, since it is impossible to replicate the overall conditions under which the performance testing was originally performed.

In this section, we identify the main properties that are at the basis of the process of specifying the workload characterization. Moreover, we analyze the requirements that are specific for the benchmarking of distributed Web-server systems, compare the identified approaches, and discuss how the existing benchmarks realize these properties, providing also directions which we feel should be considered in the realization of benchmarking tools specific to distributed Web-server systems.

4.1   Classification of Alternatives

The workload characterization of a Web benchmark deals with three main aspects:

- the *Web service characterization* defines the types of services requested to the Web-server system;
- the *request stream characterization* defines the characteristics and the methodology used to generate the stream of requests issued to the Web-server system under evaluation;
- the *Web client characterization* defines the behavioral model of the Web client (i.e., the browser) and specifies to which extent the client characteristics support the HTTP specifications.

Characterization of Web-based Services. Let us first examine the characterization of Web-based services. As the variety of services and functions offered over the Web is steadily increasing, and puts dramatic performance demands on Web servers, the workload characterization of a benchmark should attempt to model realistic Web traffic and aim to capture this large variety of services. That is to say, the requests cannot be limited to static resources, but rather the workload should at least include dynamic services, which typically impose higher resource demands on Web servers [2]. Streaming multimedia services provided over the Web are also becoming increasingly popular and should be taken into account in the workload model. Security is a further issue which is often neglected in existing Web server benchmarks. With the increasing number of sensible and private transactions being conducted on the Web, security has raised its importance; therefore, modern workload characteristics should also include encrypted client-server interactions.

In Table 1 we summarize the core parameters that are involved in the specification of the offered workload. The definition of the parameters is oriented to the user session and resembles that described in [7,8,23]. The first set of parameters reviews some basic terminology, the second contains user-oriented parameters, while the third concerns Web object characteristics.

Characterization of the Request Stream. There are several possibilities to generate the stream of Web requests that will reach the tested system. The choice of a methodology impacts on the characteristics of the offered Web workload as

Table 1. Main parameters involved in the specification of Web workload.

Name	Meaning
Web page	A collection of objects constituting a multipart document intended to be rendered simultaneously; the base object is the first fetched from the server, then it is parsed, and all embedded objects are subsequently requested
User session	A sequence of requests for Web pages (clicks) issued by the same user during an entire visit to the Web site
Session length	The number of Web pages constituting a user session
Session interarrival rate	The rate at which new user sessions are generated
User think time	The time between two consecutive Web pages retrievals
Object sizes	The size of the collection of objects stored on the Web system
Request sizes	The size of objects transferred from the Web system
Object popularity	The relative frequency of requests made to individual objects
Embedded objects	The number of objects (not counting the base object) composing a single Web page
Temporal locality	How likely a requested object will be requested again in the near future

well as on the mapping of the synthetic content on the Web-server system that will be analyzed in Sect. 5. As shown in Fig. 3, the generation of the stream of Web requests falls into main four approaches.

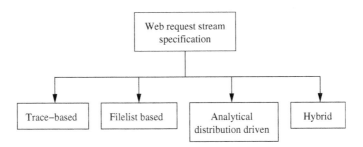

Fig. 3. Possible approaches to generate the stream of Web requests.

In the *trace-based* approach, the characteristics of the Web workload is based on pre-recorded (or synthetically generated) trace logs derived by server access logs [20]. The workload characteristics can be reproduced by replaying (or sampling) the requests as logged in the trace. An alternative is to create an abstract model of the Web site and extract session-oriented high-level information (such as session lengths and inter-arrival times) through a preliminary trace analysis that pre-processes server logs [25]. Some techniques to infer Web session characteristics from trace logs have been described in [1,27]. The trace-based approach allows the benchmark tool to mimic the user behavior in a realistic way. However, the conclusions drawn from the experiments depends on the trace representativeness, as a trace can present workload properties that are strictly peculiar to it and do not have general validity. Furthermore, it can be hard to adjust the workload to imitate future conditions or varying demands.

It should also be remarked that, unlike the early days of the Web, server access logfiles are becoming a precious source of business and marketing information. As a consequence, companies and organizations are not willing to give their traces for free (or even at all), if not after years when the realism of these traces is at least doubtful. A further issue of the trace-based approach regards the reconstruction of the user sessions from the trace logs, which is not a trivial task [1]. For example, as sessions are identified through their IP address, it may happen that clients behind the same proxy are considered as coming from the same machine, which may lead to an improper characterization of the Web workload. Another issue that may complicate the reconstruction of user sessions, especially for highly accessed Web systems, concerns the coarse time resolution at which requests are recorded in server access logs [20].

In the *filelist based* approach, the tool provides a list of Web objects with their access frequencies. The object sizes are typically based upon the analysis of logs from several Web sites. During the workload generation phase, the next object to be retrieved is chosen on the basis of its access frequency. Time characteristics are typically not taken into account, hence the stream of requests depends only on the filelist while the inter-arrival request time is set. The filelist approach lacks of flexibility with respect to the workload specification, and also ignores the concept of user sessions As discussed in [4,3,8,12], Web traffic is bursty, session-oriented, and characterized by heavy-tailed distributions, which have high or even infinite variance and therefore show extreme variability on all time scales. To cmulate these workload characteristics, it is not sufficient to mimic the user activity by requesting a set of files as quickly as possible; it is necessary to provide some support for modeling the session-oriented nature of Web traffic. As a consequence, a benchmark that uses just a filelist is not able to reproduce a realistic Web workload. When using filelists, the only feasible alternative is to provide some support to define the characteristics of a user session (such as user think times) otherwise the workload generator will not be able to emulate a realistic load. Furthermore, the overall size of the file set being used should be checked to ensure that the server caching mechanism is fully exercised.

In the *analytical distribution-driven* approach, the Web workload characteristics are specified by means of mathematical distributions. The requests are issued according to the parameters of the workload model. The probability distributions may be used to generate random values that reproduce all the characteristics of the request stream during the execution of the benchmarking test. An alternative is to pre-generate all user sessions and the resulting sequence of requests, and to store them in a trace file which will be used by the workload generator. The analytical distribution-driven approach allows a tool to define a detailed Web workload characterization because all features are specified through mathematical models. Some can argue about the realism and accuracy of the workload characterization, but changing the parameters of a distribution or a distribution itself to evaluate the performance under different conditions is a really easy task.

The *hybrid* approach is a mix of the *filelist* and *analytical* techniques. For example, the objects to be accessed may be specified through a filelist, while session-oriented parameters, such as session lengths and user think times, are modeled through analytical distributions. In the hybrid method, parameters shaping the main characteristics of session-oriented workload are modeled through stochastic models.

Web Client Characterization. The first important characterization for a Web client regards the alternative between an open and a closed loop model. In a closed model, a pre-determined number of clients sends requests only after having received the previous server responses. Although this model does not give a realistic view of the offered load, it is adopted by several tools that aim to evaluate performance of a Web system subject to constant load. However, this behavior becomes unrealistic and not acceptable for a distributed Web-server system under heavy load conditions. Indeed, as Web traffic increases, clients spend most of their time waiting for responses and, substantially, they issue requests at the response rate imposed by the system responses. This situation is far from reality, in which the clients access a distributed popular Web site concurrently and independently from the server responses. Hence, an open client model, characterized by periodic client interarrival times, is typically preferred when evaluating the performance of a distributed Web-server system.

Another main feature related to the client requests is represented by the HTTP protocol that is supported by the emulated browser. The client should be capable of requesting objects using both HTTP/1.0 and HTTP/1.1. Indeed, the latter provides some interesting features (such as persistent connections, request pipelining, and chunked transfer encoding [20]) which affect the performance of the Web system under testing [8,19]. In particular, persistent connections are used to limit the number of opened TCP connections (thereby reducing resource consumption on the Web-server system) and to avoid slow start each time a new object is requested. It would be also important to have full support for various request methods (GET, POST, HEAD) in the request header. Further issues regard the possibility to allow for session tracking via cookies and to support SSL/TLS encryption in such a way to request secure Web services.

To properly mimic the resource usage of the Web-server system, the emulated client could also use multiple parallel connections for the retrieval of embedded objects in a Web page. Although this is a deprecated technique for its impact on the Web servers, it is commonly employed by modern browsers (together with closing active connection by means of TCP resets) to reduce the latency time experimented by users. This implies that the browser behavior cannot be naively emulated by a simple model in which the client opens a single TCP connection at a time for the retrieval of a single Web object.

4.2   Requirements for Distributed Web-Server Systems

In this section we identify the requirements pertaining to the workload characterization component which are suitable to perform the benchmarking of distributed Web-server systems. Besides the workload characteristics which should mimic at best those of real Web traffic and an open system model for client requests, the distinguishing feature that characterizes the benchmarking of distributed Web-server systems regards the mechanisms supported by the client for request routing.

No particular support is required to the benchmark of Web clusters, as the Web switch completely masks the distributed nature of the architecture to the clients that interact with the Web system as if it were a one server node. On the other hand, some request routing support must be provided for benchmarking geographically distributed Web-server systems in which multiple IP addresses may be visible to client applications. The most important feature to add to the client model is the DNS mechanism with all main steps related to the address lookup phase. This would allow us to test the impact of alternative routing mechanisms, such as DNS-based routing, URL rewriting, and HTTP redirection [13]. To support the last technique, the client should also be able to redirect the request as indicated in the response header.

4.3   Comparison of Selected Tools

In this subsection we analyze how the selected Web benchmarks specify their workload. We appreciate that most benchmark tools allow us to customize and extend the workload model in order to test different scenarios. On the other hand, the option for workload configuration of SPECweb and TCP-W benchmarks are quite limited because their goal is to measure the performance of different systems in a well-defined and standardized scenario. Obviously, we do not penalize these benchmarks for a limit that is intrinsic in their design.

Httperf permits two approaches to generate the request stream that is, hybrid and trace-based [32]. Both methods enable a session-oriented workload characterization and the requests for both static and dynamic services. In the hybrid approach, single or multiple URL sequences may be specified, together with some session oriented parameters, such as user think times. In the trace-based approach, user sessions are defined in a trace file. The requests are issued according to an open model. Both HTTP/1.0 and HTTP/1.1 protocols are fully supported, including cookies (although only one cookie per user session). Primary SSL support is provided, including the possibility of specifying session reuse, which is an important feature as it avoids handshaking every client request. Httperf allows also to specify some realistic browser characteristics, such as the use of multiple concurrent connections.

SURGE relies on a analytically generated workload aimed at dealing with the self-similarity issues of the Web characteristics [7,8]. The workload model derives from empirical analysis of Web server usage to mimic real-world traffic properties. In SURGE, the workload is measured in terms of *User Equivalent*, defined as a single process in an endless loop, alternating between requests and thinking times. Therefore, the user behavior is modeled as a bursty two-state ON/OFF process, where ON periods correspond to the transfer of Web objects, and OFF periods correspond to the silent intervals after that all objects in a Web page have been retrieved. It has been demonstrated that the superposition of a large number of ON/OFF sources results in self-similar traffic, if the durations of ON and OFF phases are described by heavy-tailed distributions [12, 43]. The characteristics of the request stream are specified through heavy-tailed distributions as regarding file size, request size, file popularity, embedded object references, temporal locality, and OFF times. Support for HTTP/1.0 and HTTP/1.1 protocols is provided (the latter with request pipelining), while no security support is provided. The browser activity is emulated using only one connection at time. SURGE remains the most accurate tool for the characterization of static requests. Its main limits, especially for the analysis of multi-tier Web systems, are that the workload model does not take into account request for dynamic services and that the generation of requests follows a closed-loop model.

The S-Clients workload is intentionally not realistic, being characterized by a single file which is requested at a specified fixed rate [6]. This choice provides excellent measurements of the server performance and capacity, but does not exercise other system resources, starting from the disk as the file is always get from the cache. With S-Clients it is not possible to specify any browser behavior, only the plain HTTP/1.0 protocol is supported, and no session encryption is allowed. These aspects make the workload characterization provided by S-Clients inappropriate from the point of view of the workload realism, while it is appreciable its sustained load solution for stress testing distributed Web-server systems, as discussed in Sect. 6.

WebStone denotes the characteristics of the request stream through a file list [30]. The benchmark workload includes both static and dynamic services, the latter generated through CGIs and server APIs. Since the maximum size of the filelist is limited to 100 files, it is difficult to model typical workloads of distributed Web-server systems which consist of thousands of files. Moreover, there is no way of specifying a session-oriented workload, since requests are intended to be issued consecutively. The workload is generated following a closed loop model. The emulation of the browser characteristics is quite limited, as WebStone supports only standard HTTP/1.0 without keep-alive. Support for encryption and authentication is not officially included, although a patched version exists which enables it [31].

WebBench follows a hybrid approach, where the workload characterization is done through test suites that is, appropriate combinations of request streams (which model specific user interactions) along with their reproduction modalities [45]. Static, dynamic (CGI and API), and secure services may be configured. Both HTTP/1.0 and HTTP/1.1 protocols are supported. The two main drawbacks are related to the impossibility to specify the session-oriented nature of client requests and to the closed loop model.

Web Polygraph permits a fairly complete specification of the Web workload, characterized by a session-oriented request stream, Web pages, popularity of files, cacheability at the client, server delays due to network congestion [42]. Many of these propierties may be specified through probability distributions. Requests may be issued through both HTTP/1.0 and HTTP/1.1 protocols, in an open or closed loop model. An interesting feature is the presence of already configured Web workloads oriented to layer-4 and layer-7 Web clusters.

A different common observation is in order about the workload of SPECweb99 and TPC-W benchmarks. They define standardized Web workloads which are not intended to be customized by the user. Hence, they cannot be used to define workloads for different categories of Web sites. The basic workload of SPECweb99 [38] includes both static and dynamically generated content, while an enhanced version supports also secure services [39]. The static workload is characterized by four classes of file sets, modeling different types of Web servers and spread into a precomputed number of directories. Directory access and class access are chosen according to a Zipf distribution. The dynamic workload models two common features of commercial Web servers: advertising and user registration. The client model is closed because a fixed number of clients is executed during each experiment.

The TPC-W benchmark specification (note that it is not a tool) defines the details of the Web services and content at the site and the workload offered by clients [26,41]. It specifies a database structure oriented to e-commerce transactions for an online bookstore together with its Web interface. Clients are characterized by Web interactions that is, well-defined sequences of Web page traversals which pursue particular actions such as browsing, searching, and ordering. Request streams are session-oriented, with think times between Web page retrievals. It also includes secure connections because some client actions (e.g., online buying) require SSL/TLS encryption.

No tool provides explicit support to DNS routing that is of key importance in geographically distributed Web-server systems and Content Delivery Networks. Most benchmarking tools perform only one DNS lookup at the beginning of the test, that is unrealistic since a DNS lookup is needed per each client session. There is no much support even to other (application based) request routing mechanisms, for example only Web Polygraph and WebBench support HTTP redirection.

5   Content Mapping on Servers

An interesting issue of a benchmarking tool for distributed Web-server systems is the replication of the synthetic content among the multiple server nodes. Once the synthetic workload has been specified, it must be replicated on the Web nodes composing the Web-server system prior that the workload generation engine starts to generate the request stream. This constitutes an error-prone operation which should be automated as much as possible. Another peculiarity of distributed Web-server systems is that the replication strategy may differ on the basis of the system architectures, because the content is not always replicated among all the servers.

Let us first examine the problem of mapping the Web site content onto the Web servers in the case of one Web server, for which we identify three alternatives: *full support*, *partial support*, and *no support*.

The most attractive feature to the benchmark user is a full support that is, once the benchmark user provides the specification of the entire Web site content (the tree of static documents as well as the set of data to be placed on the back-end servers), it is automatically generated and uploaded on the Web and back-end server disks. A partial support means that only a portion of the Web site content (that , static documents) is put on the server disk, while other content (that is, dynamic services) is left up to the benchmark user. If the benchmark does not provide any support for the content generation and mapping, the content must be generated and uploaded manually on the server. Manual generation is errore-prone and is often unfeasible due to the large number of involved files. Thus, the presence of a mapping component is strongly encouraged.

Webstone provides a partial support for Web content creation [30]. It is possible to specify and generate a set of static files with given sizes, while dynamic content creation is left to the user. The other Web benchmarking tools, although providing in some cases already predefined Web contents (SPECweb99, WebBench), neither perform content mapping across different Web servers nor install them. Every decision is left to the benchmark user.

The benchmark study of a distributed Web-server system has an additional requirement because the site content may be fully replicated, partially replicated, or partitioned among the multiple server nodes. The two last configurations are typically used to increase the secondary storage scalability [10,44] or to enhance the features of specialized server nodes providing dynamically generated content or streaming media files. It is also important to observe that fully replication can be easily avoided only if we use a layer-7 Web switch that can take content-aware dispatching decisions. An alternative is to use a layer-4 Web switch combined with a distributed file system, because any selected server node should be able to respond to client requests for any part of the Web site content.

We can easily observe that none of the selected benchmarking tools includes any utility for fully or partial content replication among multiple servers.

6   Workload Generation Engine

An important component of a Web benchmarking tool is the workload generation engine, which is responsible for reproducing the specified workload in the most accurate and efficient way.

Distributed Web-server systems are characterized by a huge number of accesses, which have to be emulated with a usually limited amount of resources. This may be obtained by generating and sustaining overload [6] that is, constantly offering a load that exceeds the capacity of the distributed Web system. In this section, we identify the main features of workload generation, analyze the requirements that are specific for distributed Web systems, and discuss how the selected Web benchmarking tools behave with respect to the identified features and requirements.

6.1   Classification of Alternatives

The two main features in a workload generator are the *engine architecture* denoting the computational units used to generate Web traffic (processes or threads) and mutual interactions, and the *coordination scheme* defining the ability of configuring and synchronizing the computational unit executions.

Engine Architectures. We give a possible taxonomy of workload generator architectures in Fig. 4. In a *centralized architecture*, a single instance of the workload generator runs on a single node, whereas in *distributed architectures* the engine is spread across multiple nodes.

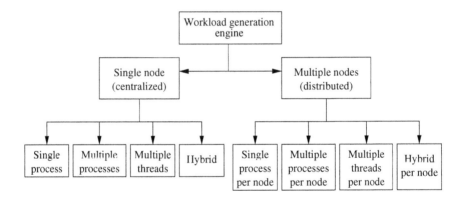

Fig. 4. Architecture of a workload generator.

The architecture characterization defines the nature of the computational units on each client node. In *single-process architectures*, one process is responsible for the generation of the whole workload on the node on which it is running. In *multiple-process architectures*, the task of generating client requests is split up among several user-level processes. The multiple-process approach is relatively straightforward, but suffers from two drawbacks. First, it is CPU-intensive because of frequent context switches, especially when many user processes are spawned on the same machine. Second, since process address spaces are usually separated, most information (e.g., the workload configuration) must be replicated, thus wasting main memory that is an important resource for the scalability of the load generated by the client node.

In *multi-threaded architectures*, light-weight processes sharing the same address space are used to generate the appropriate portion of workload, while in *hybrid architectures* each node runs several user processes, each handling multiple threads. The multi-threaded architecture does not suffer from context switch drawbacks. In general, light-weight processes guarantee for a better scalability, but multi-threaded programming incurs in a higher degree of complexity. Sharing the address space surely leads to a better memory utilization than in the multi-process architecture, at the cost of implementing synchronization primitives which could block client activity. Finally, several threads usually share one set of system resources, which could be exhausted (for example, the file descriptor set used to reference TCP connections).

The hybrid architecture aims to combine the advantages of multi-threaded architectures (lower CPU overhead due to less frequent context switches) with those of multi-process architectures (increase in available system resources such as socket descriptors).

Coordination Schemes. The task of configuring and coordinating the execution of the computational units may be performed manually or automatically. In the latter case, two coordination schemes are possible: *master-client* and *master-collector-client*.

In the master-client scheme (see Fig. 5), the client generation task is delegated to a *master component*, which reads the configuration and performs several operations. First, it decides how many computational units have to be started and how they are distributed among the client nodes, in order to offer the specified workload. Then, it distributes part of the workload specification (for example, the filelist) among all clients. Finally, it synchronizes the start of the benchmarking experiment.

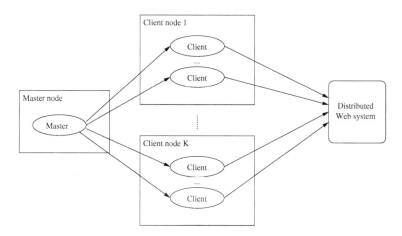

Fig. 5. The master-client coordination scheme.

The master-client approach is further extended in the *master-collector-client* coordination scheme, illustrated in Fig. 6. One or more collector processes are activated on each client node, either manually or automatically through a master process (for clarity of representation, Fig. 6 shows only one collector). The master connects to each collector, distributes the workload configuration, and synchronizes the start of the benchmarking experiment. Each collector reads its portion of configuration from the master, spawns the necessary amount of computational units, and waits for a start signal from the master. Master, collector, and clients are logically separated, but they may reside on the same node.

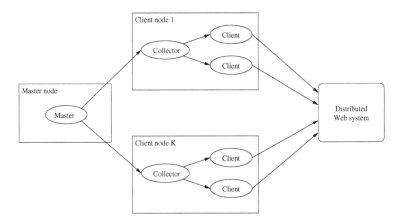

Fig. 6. The master-collector-client coordination scheme.

We can conclude that is clearly preferable to have an automated generation of client emulators among different nodes than referring to manual activations. This is especially true if the coordinator is able to share the Web workload among multiple nodes according to the capacity of each client node.

6.2   Requirements for Distributed Web-Server Systems

Distributed Web-server systems are typically subject to a large amount of traffic, which has to be reproduced somehow to evaluate their performance under realistic conditions. Thus, the *scalability* of the workload generation engine is a strict requirement for a benchmarking tool. Single node architecture is not adequate since operating system resource constraints typically limit the number of concurrent clients. The generation of Web workload should be distributed across as many nodes as possible. The amount of available client nodes for tests is usually limited to few tenths. Thus, it is desirable to generate the maximum amount of workload on a given node. This holds especially when client nodes have heterogeneous capacities. An unbalanced assignment of workload may determine the under-utilization of some nodes and the partial inability to generate requests on others.

Being the scalability of the workload generation engine an important requirement for the performance evaluation of distributed Web systems, we observe that
it is quite difficult to achieve it using a centralized architecture. The only solution to keep one process spawning many concurrent client sessions is to use an
event-driven approach, combined with non-blocking I/O [18]. This single process polls the network for events and reacts accordingly. This approach involves
programming non-blocking I/O, which can be tricky and much more difficult
than in a multi-process or multi-threaded model. Moreover, one process may
run out of file descriptors if the machine is not well tuned. On the other hand,
this approach does not suffer from context switch overheads, provided that the
client node does not execute other resource intensive tasks.

6.3   Comparison of Selected Tools

In this section we analyze how the selected benchmarking tools generate the load
offered to the Web system.

Httperf generates the specified workload through one process, implementing an event-driven approach with non-blocking I/O [32]. As a consequence,
the workload generator keeps a single CPU constantly occupied, so it is recommended not to run more than one httperf process per CPU. Furthermore, the
maximum number of concurrent sessions is bounded by typical process limits
such as the maximum number of open descriptors. As there is no coordination
scheme, several instances of httperf must be executed manually on distinct nodes
to scale to the desired workload; an helper utility can be used to automate this
task [29]. The workload generation engine of httperf is adequate to the performance evaluation of distributed Web systems.

In SURGE the client activity is modeled through a User Equivalent, which
is represented by a thread [7,8]. The benchmarking experiment is activated by
invoking a master which spawns a predefined number of client processes. Each
client process generates a prefixed number of client threads (i.e., User Equiv-
alents). Therefore, SURGE architecture can be defined as being centralized,
multiple-process and multiple-thread. The coordination scheme is a master-
collector-client, although on a single node. Since no support is provided to automatically distribute clients among multiple nodes, several instances of the
SURGE master have to be activated manually on distinct client nodes, in order
to scale the workload.

The workload generator of S-Clients is executed by a single process on one
client node [6]. The engine aims at generating excess load by using non-blocking
connects and closing the socket if no connection was established within a given
interval. There is no means to automatically start different workload generators
on distinct nodes, but this operation has to be performed manually. Furthermore, since timers are implemented using the *rdtsc* primitive [14], the ability to
generate connections with a specified rate depends heavily on the CPU speed of
the client, and the CPU type, which should be a Pentium. The most interesting
feature of S-Clients for the benchmarking of distributed Web systems is the use

of non-blocking connections combined with timeouts, as it allows to guarantee a specified connection rate.

In WebStone, the activity of Web users is emulated through a preconfigured, fixed number of *Web clients* [30]. The architecture of WebStone is distributed and multi-process; each Web client is executed as a distinct user process that requests files continuously. Web clients are distributed over several nodes through another user process, called *Web master*. The workload generator of WebStone is not able to sustain high loads and, consequently, it is not adequate for the performance evaluation of distributed Web-server systems.

In WebBench, Web clients are emulated through client processes running on distinct nodes [45]. The architecture of WebBench is distributed and may be either single-process or multi-threaded. In the first case, each client runs as a user process (called *physical client*), in the latter, multiple clients run as threads (called *logical clients*). A controller on a distinct node coordinates the client execution. The recommended coordination scheme is master-client with one physical client per node. It is also possible to specify a master-collector-client scheme where logical clients are locally coordinated. In both cases, processes residing on client nodes must be started manually. The features of the WebBench workload generation engine are not sufficient for the benchmarking of distributed Web-server systems.

The workload generation engine in Web Polygraph has a centralized, single-process architecture, which is capable of sustaining overload [42]. Optionally, server agents may be used to emulate parts of a distributed Web server system, besides exercising real components. A drawback of Web Polygraph is the lack of some support to automatically distribute the generation of requests across multiple client nodes.

The TPC-W benchmark specification requires that client requests be issued by a given number of "emulated browsers", which remains constant throughout the experiment [26,41]. The number of clients is obtained as a function of the database table size and appropriate scaling factors. As a consequence, it is difficult to generate a considerable amount of traffic without modifying the Web content.

SPECWeb99 distributes clients on several machines in order to achieve workload scalability [38]. If the operating system supports POSIX threads, clients are executed as threads, otherwise as processes. Thus, the architecture of the SPECWeb99 engine is distributed and multi-process or multi-threaded. Clients are executed by processes called *collectors*, which must be manually activated before starting the test. A master process connects to the collectors, sends them the configuration parameters and synchronizes the runs. The workload generation allows for a certain degree of scalability but cannot be sustained when the distributed Web system is under stress.

7 Data Collection and Analysis

The measurement and collection of data during the benchmarking test is of key importance. If done superficially, it leads to improper conclusions about the performance of the resources constituting the system. A first issue concerns the definition of the metrics and the statistics which can yield the most useful information about the components of the distributed Web-server system. Then it is important to investigate the data collection strategies that are somehow related to the previous choices.

7.1 Classification of Alternatives

The most common metrics for Web system performance are reported in Table 2 [28].

Table 2. Typical Web performance metrics.

Name	Meaning
Throughput	The rate at which data is sent through the network
Connection rate	The number of open connections per second
Request rate	The number of client requests per second
Reply rate	The number of server responses per second
Error rate	The percentage of errors of a given type
DNS lookup time	The time to translate the hostname into the IP address
Connect time	The time interval between the initial SYN and the final ACK sent by the client to establish the TCP connection
Latency time	The time interval between the sending of the last byte of a client request and the receipt of the first byte of the corresponding response
Transfer time	The time interval between the receipt of the first response byte and the last response byte
Web object response time	The sum of latency time and transfer time
Web page response time	The sum of Web object response times pertaining to a single Web page, plus the connect time
Session time	The sum of all Web page response times and think times in a user session

As Web workload is characterized by heavy-tailed distributions, most performance metrics may assume highly variable values with non negligible probability. Collecting just minimum, mean, and maximum times, error levels, is not an error, but these metrics may not yield a representative view of the system behavior. The metrics subject to high variability should be represented by means of higher moments, percentiles or cumulative distributions [16,22]. Mean values may be meaningless about peaks due to heavy load. This holds for throughput and response times (specifically, object and page response times), which may exhibit high variations from the mean value.

These performance statistics require more expensive or more sophisticated data collection strategies, because measurements should be collected and stored to allow later creation of histograms. The alternative is to implement techniques to dynamically calculate the median and other percentiles without storing all observations [17]. Let us analyze the main approaches to the *collection strategy* (that is, *record storage*, *data set processing*, and *hybrid*) and *output analysis* that are strictly related.

In the *record storage* approach every record is stored. The generation of meaningful statistics is entirely delegated to the output analysis. This technique allows us to easily compute histograms and percentiles but it requires enormous amount of memory. The main memory is often not sufficient, and the use of secondary memory introduces other problems, such as delays and possible interferences in the experiment. Moreover, the elaboration of great amounts of data tends to be resource expensive even if done post-mortem. Actually, a complete collection and processing of all measurements is seldom necessary, and the use of sampling techniques is the best alternative when we want to use the record storage approach.

In the *data set processing* approach, measurements are not stored directly into some repository, but are used to keep updated the *data set* with the interesting statistics. Data set processing does not use great amounts of system resources such as CPU or memory. This is the standard way for computing performance indexes which do not require sophisticated statistics, such as minimum, maximum, and mean values. It would be also possible to implement techniques that dynamically calculate the median and other percentiles without storing all observations [17], but even these more complex computation may interfere with the experiment. The data set may coincide or not with the set of parameters presented as final statistics. When they do not coincide, the generation of useful statistics is partially delegated to the output analysis component that processes the data set at the end of the benchmarking test.

None of the previous techniques is clearly the best. However, we can observe that sophisticated statistics are really necessary only for those metrics which are subject to high variance. In many other cases, min, max and mean values are acceptable. For this reason, we consider also the *hybrid* approach that is a mix of the previous two techniques. Each measurement may be stored, processed to keep updated a data set, or both. This approach leads to a better trade-off between main memory resource utilization and usefulness of the collected data. The performance indexes that do not require sophisticated statistics may be computed at run time, for the other indexes we can store the relative measurements and postpone the evaluation during the output analysis after the experiment.

When multiple client emulators are used, it is necessary to use the data sets and samples stored by each of them to compute the final metrics which are presented to the benchmark user in a clear form. This operation is mandatory in the case of distributed Web-server systems.

7.2   Requirement for Distributed Web-Server Systems

A typical benchmarking tool for distributed Web-server systems distributes the generation of high volumes of Web traffic across different client nodes. Data collection is usually done at the level of each computational unit. While it is good to have per-process (or per-thread) statistics, it is certainly crucial to have global reports, to understand how well the whole system has performed. To obtain global session statistics, cumulative distributions and percentiles (not only per-node statistics), data sets and records must be aggregated before the computation of global statistics. Therefore, *aggregation of collected data* is a key feature that should characterize all tools for distributed Web-server systems. We also consider important to have *session-oriented statistics* that is, final reports including metrics relative to user sessions, in addition to global statistics, which are quite useful for evaluating the performance of the whole system.

Besides the previous considerations, there is a serious problem that makes traditional benchmarking tools for Web servers not useful to collect important statistics for an accurate performance evaluation of distributed Web-server systems, especially in the design and prototype phase when different alternative architectures and solutions must be evaluated. Indeed, all considered tools have been designed for the interaction of multiple clients with one server and give global metrics that cannot take into account that the server side consists of multiple components usually running on different machines. In a distributed Web-server system, the interaction of the client with this system consists of several steps, such as switching to the right server and invoking the appropriate process for the generation of dynamic content. The delay of each of these phases makes up for the response time seen by the clients. A high response time means a bad system performance, but it does not indicate where the bottleneck is. The associated overhead within each phase of the Web transaction must be measured and evaluated, since bottlenecks in one component make the whole system slower. Some of the phases of a Web transaction in a distributed system are very hard (if not impossible) to measure at run time without making modifications to the system components. For example, in a locally distributed Web system, the time required by the switch to dispatch a client request cannot be measured from the client side. In other cases, the performance of some components may be inferred by the external performance metrics. For example, in one-way Web clusters with a layer-4 Web switch, the initial client SYN is processed by the switch and sent to the appropriate Web server, which establishes the TCP connection. Thus, the *connect time* embodies switch and server latencies, leaving us with the doubt about a potentially overloaded node. Instead, the *latency time* is an approximate measure of server performance, since TCP segments do not pass by the switch once the connection has established with the appropriate server.

In layer-7 one-way Web clusters, the opposite is true. *Connect time* is an approximate measure of switch overload, since it establishes TCP connections with clients prior to assigning requests to the appropriate servers. On the other hand, the *latency time* embodies the Web switch and server delays, since every client TCP segment directed to a server passes through the Web switch. In this case, the latency time does not give sufficient information to localize a possibly overloaded Web system component.

If one-way architectures allow an approximate evaluation of component performance, this estimation is practically impossible in two-way architectures, since both packet flows pass through the switch. Hence, the above mentioned procedure may lead to gross evaluation errors. In general, there is no way for measuring the performance of the Web switch and the single servers through client measurements. Therefore, the right approach is that of enabling logging at every system component and analyzing the resulting logs at the end of the test. Monitor facilities and a *log analyzer* are required to this purpose. They should be highly configurable because different applications may have different logfile formats. Analyzing log outputs may require integration or modifications of the network application software because the standard logs have too coarse granularities (e.g., 1 second in the Apache server). Moreover, the statistics obtained by the internal monitors must be integrated with those of the benchmark reports.

For geographically distributed Web systems, it is necessary to measure the time taken by the request routing mechanism, such as DNS lookup and request redirection times.

7.3   Comparison of Selected Tools

Httperf collects a large variety of metrics, both session- and request-oriented [32]. The most interesting non-session oriented metrics are connect time, latency time, request and reply rate, throughput and error rates. Response time at the granularity of Web objects is not collected; session-oriented metrics include session time and session rate. For each of these metrics, minimum, mean, maximum values and their standard deviations are computed through data sets. Support for record storage through histograms is given only for some metrics such as session length and connection duration. Httperf has a hybrid data collector and a centralized output analyzer. It also performs hybrid processing of the collected data. A final report is presented with global and per-session statistics, thus providing a way for detecting the degree of user concurrency in a distributed Web-server system. However, it requires some extensions. For example, it would be interesting to have the Web page response time as a metric. Moreover, the records should be stored in histograms for later processing to evaluate higher order statistics.

SURGE stores only records of transaction time and Web object size for later processing [7,8]. The output analyzer of SURGE is centralized and oriented to record processing. It operates on server logs (in common log format) and on the log file generated at the end of the benchmarking experiment. Final metrics provided to the benchmark use are session-oriented; a log-log cumulative distribution table of Web page response times is also provided.

S-Clients collects a data set consisting of connection life time sums (which are used to approximate transaction times, since HTTP/1.0 is used) and global counters of opened connections and successfully delivered responses [6]. S-Clients presents only request rate and average response time of the requested URLs.

WebBench keeps at run-time the following data set: a global count of successful requests, a sum of transaction times and a sum of transfer sizes [45]. These data sets are required to compute the final metrics, that is, number of requests per second and throughput. WebBench gives only two overall metrics: interaction times per second and throughput in bytes per second. They are computed locally on each client and centrally gathered by the controller.

Webstone uses a hybrid data collector and output analyzer [30]. The retrieval phases of a Web object (connect latency and transfer times) are marked by timestamps which are all recorded, while global counters are kept through appropriate data sets. WebStone provides a report with global and per Web object connect times, response times, error rates. It also computes a global connection rate and a metric known as *Little's Load Factor* [28]. No session oriented metrics are reported, no response time subdivision in latency and transfer is evaluated, although the collected records allow a successive computation.

The data collector of Web Polygraph is hybrid [42]. It stores records for later computation of reply size and hit/miss response times. It also keeps global counts for error rates, client and server side throughput, cache hit ratio and byte hit ratio. No provision for session oriented metrics is provided. In Web Polygraph, each client and server agent process generates its own log file. They have to be manually concatenated before processing by the report module. Reports include several performance graphs for throughput, cache hits and misses response times, persistent connection usage, error rates.

SPECweb99 uses its own performance metric [38]. Substantially, it is the maximum number of connections supported by the Web server under certain conditions (throughput ranging between 300000 and 400000 bits per second). To this purpose, SPECweb99 collects throughput, request and response times over a single connection. According to online documentation [38], this is done in a data set way. There is no session oriented statistics. In SPECweb99, the output analyzer is centralized: data collected from each client is gathered by the master process which reports test results for that iteration. A report consists of summary, results, overall metric, and configuration information. The SPECweb99 metric is the median of the connection average result over 3 iterations.

The TPC-W benchmark specification defines the collection of the *Web Interaction response time* (WIRT), which is the time interval occurring between the sending of the first byte of a client request that starts a Web interaction and the retrieval of the last byte in the last response of the same Web interaction [26,41]. This is necessary to compute the final metric that is, the throughput of Web interactions per second. The specification also suggests running performance monitors on the servers for monitoring CPU utilization, memory utilization, page/swap activity, database I/O activity, system I/O activity and Web server statistics. The TPC-W benchmark specification defines three performance indexes: WIPS, WIPSb, WIPSo, that are counted as the number of Web interactions per second during shopping, browsing and ordering sessions, respectively.

The TPC-W specification recommends a report including graphs for the following metrics: CPU utilization, memory utilization, page/swap activity, system activity, Web server statistics (number of requests and error rates per second). No session-oriented statistics are planned, but the provided graphs should give an idea about the load conditions of the system.

8   Benchmark Support for Wide Area Networks

Benchmarking experiments of Web-server systems are usually carried out in a closed, isolated, and high-speed local-area network (LAN) environment. These laboratory experiments do not take into consideration network-related factors, such as high and variable delays, transmission errors, packet losses, and network connection limitations [28]. Modeling interactions that occur in the real Web environment using clients machines connected to the Web-server system by a low round-trip time, high-speed LAN may lead to incorrect results, because the provision of Web-based services in the real world involves wide-area network connections in which the presence of network components (such as routers) make the environment noisy and error-prone and have influence on Web server performance [33]. Therefore, to model interactions that occur in the real Web environment using both clients machines connected to the Web-server system by a low round-trip time, high-speed LAN may lead to incorrect results. Indeed, as a result of benchmarking experiments carried out in LAN environments, it occurs that performance aspects of the Web-server system that depend on the network characteristics are not exposed or inaccurately evaluated. As a consequence of WAN delays, Web server resources (such as listen socket's SYN-RCVD queue) remain tied up to clients for much longer periods and therefore the system throughput decreases. Furthermore, in the wide-area Internet, packets are lost or corrupted; this causes performance degradation as these packets have to be retransmitted.

To take into account WAN effect in the benchmarking of distributed Web-server systems two approaches are possible that is, *WAN emulation in a LAN environment* and *WAN environment.* The first consists in emulating the WAN characteristics in a controlled environment, where clients and server machines are interconnected through a LAN network, by incorporating factors such as delays and packet losses into the benchmarking tool. The WAN emulation approach allows to perform the tests in a controllable, configurable, and reproducible environment, allowing easy changes in test conditions and iterative analysis [6,33, 37]. However, incorporating delays and packet losses due to WANs is not a trivial task. On the other hand, experiments performed in a WAN environment allow to identify many problems and causes of delays in Web transfers that do not manifest themselves in a LAN environment [9,5,21]. At the same time, these wide-area benchmarking experiments are hard to reproduce due to the uniqueness of the test environment.

In the WAN environment, the benchmarking experiments are carried out spreading the client machines in a wide area network. This approach suffers from the difficulty in changing the network parameters of interest for different test scenarios. Furthermore, it may be hard to generate a high workload using it as discussed in [9], in which SURGE clients have been spread among different network locations.

The majority of currently available Web benchmarking tools that operate in high-speed LAN environment ignore the emulation of WAN conditions. Some efforts in this direction have been pursued in some already considered benchmarking tools (S-Client [6], WebPolygraph [42], and SpecWeb99 [38], although quite limited in the latter) and also in WASPclient [33].

There are two main approaches that aim to emulate WAN conditions in a LAN environment that is, *centralized* and *distributed*. In the centralized approach, one machine acting as a WAN emulator is interposed between the client machines and the Web-server system to model WAN delays and packet losses by dropping and delaying packets. S-Clients follows this approach, by putting a router between the S-Client machines and the server system aimed at introducing an artificial delay and dropping packets at a controlled rate [6].

In the distributed approach, each client acts as a WAN emulator, by directly delaying and dropping packets. WASPclient implements an interesting distributed approach [33], by using an extended Dummynet layer in the protocol stack of the client machines to drop and delay packets [36]. The centralized approach is transparent to the operating system of both client and server machines; however its scalability is limited [33]. On the contrary, the distributed approach has the advantage that it provides a higher scalability, but it requires modifications to the operating system of the client machines.

9   Conclusions

This study leads us to conclude that many Web benchmark tools work fine when used to analyze a single server system, but none of them is able to address all issues related to the analysis of distributed Web-server systems. Many popular tools, such as SURGE and Webstone, suffer age problems, as they do not support dynamic requests and more recent protocols. Very few of them consider application-level routing of the requests, such as DNS and HTTP redirection, URL rewriting. In summary, we notice the lack of ability to sustain realistic Web traffic under critical load conditions, the difficulty or impossibility of emulating realistic dynamic and secure Web services, the poor support in analyzing collected statistics different from min, max, mean values. Hence, we can conclude that there is a lot of room for further research and implementation in this area.

References

[1] M. Arlitt. Characterizing Web user sessions. *ACM Performance Evaluation Review*, 28(2):50–63, Sept. 2000.

[2] M. Arlitt, D. Krishnamurthy, and J. Rolia. Characterizing the scalability of a large Web-based shopping system. *ACM Trans. on Internet Technology*, 1(1):44–69, Sept. 2001.

[3] M. F. Arlitt and T. Jin. A workload characterization study of the 1998 World Cup Web site. *IEEE Network*, 14(3):30–37, May/June 2000.

[4] M. F. Arlitt and C. L. Williamson. Internet Web servers: Workload characterization and performance implications. *IEEE/ACM Trans. on Networking*, 5(5):631–645, Oct. 1997.

[5] H. Balakrishnan, V. Padmanabhan, S. Seshan, M. Stemm, and R. Katz. TCP behavior of a busy Internet server: Analysis and improvements. In *Proc. of IEEE Infocom 1998*, pages 252–262, San Francisco, CA, Mar. 1998.

[6] G. Banga and P. Druschel. Measuring the capacity of a Web server under realistic loads. *World Wide Web*, 2(1-2):69–89, May 1999.

[7] P. Barford and M. E. Crovella. Generating representative Web workloads for network and server performance evaluation. In *Proc. of ACM Performance 1998/Sigmetrics 1998*, pages 151–160, Madison, WI, July 1998.

[8] P. Barford and M. E. Crovella. A performance evaluation of Hyper Text Transfer Protocols. In *Proc. of ACM Sigmetrics 1999*, pages 188–197, Atlanta, May 1999.

[9] P. Barford and M. E. Crovella. Critical path analysis of TCP transactions. *IEEE/ACM Trans. on Networking*, 9(3):238–248, June 2001.

[10] V. Cardellini, E. Casalicchio, M. Colajanni, and P. S. Yu. The state of the art in locally distributed Web-server systems. *ACM Computing Surveys*, 34(2):263–311, June 2002.

[11] V. Cardellini, M. Colajanni, and P. S. Yu. Geographic load balancing for scalable distributed Web systems. In *Proc. of IEEE MASCOTS 2000*, pages 20–27, San Francisco, CA, Aug./Sept. 2000.

[12] M. E. Crovella and A. Bestavros. Self-similarity in World Wide Web traffic: Evidence and possible causes. *IEEE/ACM Trans. on Networking*, 5(6):835–846, Dec. 1997.

[13] R. T. Fielding, J. Gettys, J. C. Mogul, H. F. Frystyk, L. Masinter, P. J. Leach, and T. Berners-Lee. *Hypertext Transfer Protocol – HTTP/1.1*. RFC 2616, June 1999.

[14] Intel Corp. Using the RDTSC instruction for performance monitoring, July 1998. http://cedar.intel.com/software/idap/media/pdf/rdtscpm1.pdf.

[15] A. K. Iyengar, M. S. Squillante, and L. Zhang. Analysis and characterization of large-scale Web server access patterns and performance. *World Wide Web*, 2(1-2):85–100, Mar. 1999.

[16] R. Jain. *The Art of Computer Systems Performance Analysis: Techniques for Experimental Design, Measurement, Simulation, and Modeling*. Wiley-Interscience, 1991.

[17] R. Jain and I. Chlamtac. The P-Square algorithm for dynamic calculation of percentiles and histograms without storing observations. *ACM Communications*, 28(10), Oct. 1985.

[18] D. Kegel. The C10K problem, 2002. http://www.kegel.com/c10k.html.

[19] B. Krishnamurthy, J. C. Mogul, and D. M. Kristol. Key differences between HTTP/1.0 and HTTP/1.1. *Computer Networks*, 31(11-16):1737–1751, 1999.

[20] B. Krishnamurthy and J. Rexford. *Web Protocols and Practice: HTTP/1.1, Networking Protocols, Caching, and Traffic Measurement*. Addison-Wesley, Reading, MA, 2001.

[21] B. Krishnamurthy and C. E. Wills. Analyzing factors that influence end-to-end Web performance. *Computer Networks*, 33(1-6):17–32, 2000.

[22] D. Krishnamurthy and J. Rolia. Predicting the QoS of an electronic commerce server: Those mean percentiles. In *Proc. of Workshop on Internet Server Performance*, Madison, WI, June 1998.

[23] B. Lavoie and H. F. Frystyk. *Web Characterization Terminology & Definitions Sheet*. W3C Working Draft, May 1999.

[24] Z. Liu, N. Niclausse, and C. Jalpa-Villanueva. Traffic model and performance evaluation of Web servers. *Performance Evaluation*, 46(2-3):77–100, Oct. 2001.

[25] S. Manley, M. Seltzer, and M. Courage. A self-scaling and self-configuring benchmark for Web servers. In *Proc. of ACM Sigmetrics 1998 Conf.*, pages 170–171, Madison, WI, June 1998.

[26] D. A. Menascé. TPC-W: A benchmark for e-commerce. *IEEE Internet Computing*, 6(3):83–87, May/June 2002.

[27] D. A. Menascé and V. A. F. Almeida. *Scaling for E-business. Technologies, Models, Performance and Capacity planning*. Prentice Hall, Upper Saddle River, NJ, 2000.

[28] D. A. Menascé and V. A. F. Almeida. *Capacity Planning for Web Services. Metrics, Models, and Methods*. Prentice Hall, Upper Saddle River, NJ, 2002.

[29] J. Midgley. Autobench, 2002. `http://http://www.xenoclast.org/autobench/`.

[30] Mindcraft. WebStone. `http://www.mindcraft.com/webstone/`.

[31] N. Modadugu. WebStone SSL.
`http://crypto.stanford.edu/~nagendra/projects/WebStone/`.

[32] D. Mosberger and T. Jin. httperf — A tool for measuring Web server performance. *ACM Performance Evaluation Review*, 26(3):31–37, Dec. 1998.

[33] E. M. Nahum, M. Rosu, S. Seshan, and J. Almeida. The effects of wide-area conditions on WWW server performance. In *Proc. of ACM Sigmetrics 2001*, pages 257–267, Cambridge, MA, June 2001.

[34] Neal Nelson. Web Server Benchmark. `http://www.nna.com/`.

[35] M. Rabinovich and O. Spatscheck. *Web Caching and Replication*. Addison Wesley, 2002.

[36] L. Rizzo. Dummynet: A simple approach to the evaluation of network protocols. *ACM Computer Communication Review*, 27(1):31–41, Jan. 1997.

[37] R. Simmonds, C. Williamson, M. Arlitt, R. Bradford, and B. Unger. A case study of Web server benchmarking using parallel WAN emulation. In *Proc. of IFIP Int'l Symposium Performance 2002*, Roma, Italy, Sept. 2002.

[38] Standard Performance Evaluation Corp. SPECweb99.
`http://www.spec.org/osg/web99/`.

[39] Standard Performance Evaluation Corp. SPECweb99_SSL.
`http://www.spec.org/osg/web99ssl/`.

[40] Technovations. Websizr. `http://www.technovations.com/websizr.htm`.

[41] Transaction Processing Performance Council. TPC-W.
`http://www.tpc.org/tpcw/`.

[42] Web Polygraph. `http://www.web-polygraph.org/`.

[43] W. Willinger, M. S. Taqqu, R. Sherman, and D. V. Wilson. Self-similarity through high-variability: Statistical analysis of Ethernet LAN traffic at the source level. *IEEE/ACM Trans. on Networking*, 5(1):71–86, Jan. 1997.

[44] C.-S. Yang and M.-Y. Luo. A content placement and management system for distributed Web-server systems. In *Proceedings of the 20th IEEE International Conference on Distributed Computing Systems*, pages 691–698, Taipei, Taiwan, Apr. 2000.

[45] Ziff Davis Media. WebBench.
`http://www.etestinglabs.com/benchmarks/webbench/webbench.asp`.

Stochastic Process Algebra: From an Algebraic Formalism to an Architectural Description Language

Marco Bernardo[1], Lorenzo Donatiello[2], and Paolo Ciancarini[2]

[1] Università di Urbino, Centro per l'Appl. delle Sc. e Tecn. dell'Inf.
Piazza della Repubblica 13, 61029 Urbino, Italy
bernardo@sti.uniurb.it

[2] Università di Bologna, Dipartimento di Scienze dell'Informazione
Mura Anteo Zamboni 7, 40127 Bologna, Italy
donat, cianca@cs.unibo.it

Abstract. The objective of this tutorial is to describe the evolution of the field of stochastic process algebra in the past decade, through a presentation of the main achievements in the field. In particular, the tutorial stresses the current transformation of stochastic process algebra from a simple formalism to a fully fledged architectural description language for the functional verification and performance evaluation of complex computer, communication and software systems.

1 Introduction

Many computing systems consist of a possibly huge number of components that not only work independently but also communicate with each other. Examples of such systems are communication protocols, operating systems, embedded control systems for automobiles, airplanes, and medical equipment, banking systems, automated production systems, control systems of nuclear and chemical plants, railway signaling systems, air traffic control systems, distributed systems and algorithms, computer architectures, and integrated circuits.

The catastrophic consequences – loss of human lives, environmental damages, and financial losses – of failures in many of these critical systems have compelled computer scientists and engineers to develop techniques for ensuring that these systems are designed and implemented correctly despite of their complexity. The need of formal methods in developing complex systems is becoming well accepted. Formal methods seek to introduce mathematical rigor into each stage of the design process in order to build more reliable systems.

The need of formal methods is even more urgent when planning and implementing concurrent and distributed systems. In fact, they require a huge amount of detail to be taken into account (e.g., interconnection and synchronization structure, allocation and management of resources, real time constraints, performance requirements) and involve many people with different skills in the project (designers, implementors, debugging experts, performance and quality

M.C. Calzarossa and S. Tucci (Eds.): Performance 2002, LNCS 2459, pp. 236–260, 2002.
© Springer-Verlag Berlin Heidelberg 2002

analysts). A uniform and formal description of the system under investigation reduces misunderstandings to a minimum when passing information from one task of the project to another.

Moreover, it is well known that the sooner errors are discovered, the less costly they are to fix. Consequently, it is imperative that a correct design is available before implementation begins. Formal methods are conceived to allow the correctness of a system design to be formally verified. Using formal methods, the design can be described in a mathematically precise fashion, correctness criteria can be specified in a similarly precise way, and the design can be rigorously proved to meet or not the stated criteria.

Although a number of description techniques and related software tools have been developed to support the formal modeling and verification of functional properties of systems, only in recent years temporal characteristics have received attention. This has required extending formal description techniques by introducing the concept of time, represented either in a deterministic way or in a stochastic way.

In the deterministic case, the focus typically is on verifying the satisfaction of real time constraints, i.e. the fact that the execution of specific actions is guaranteed by a fixed deadline after some event has happened. As an example, if a train is approaching a railroad crossing, then bars must be guaranteed to be lowered on due time.

In the stochastic case, instead, systems are considered whose behavior cannot be deterministically predicted as it fluctuates according to some probability distribution. Due to economic reasons, such stochastically behaving systems are referred to as shared resource systems, because there is a varying number of demands competing for the same resources. The consequences are mutual interference, delays due to contention, and varying service quality. Additionally, resource failures significantly influence the system behavior. In this case, the focus is on evaluating the performance of the systems. As an example, if we consider again a railway system, we may be interested in minimizing the average train delay or studying the characteristics of the flow of passengers. The purpose of performance evaluation is to investigate and optimize the time varying behavior within and among individual components of shared resource systems. This is achieved by modeling and assessing the temporal behavior of systems, identifying characteristic performance measures, and developing design rules that guarantee an adequate quality of service.

The desirability of taking account of the performance aspects of shared resource systems in the early stages of their design has been widely recognized [33, 68] and has fostered the development of formal methods for both functional verification and performance evaluation of rigorous system models. The focus of this tutorial is on stochastic process algebra (SPA), a formalism proposed in a seminal work by Ulrich Herzog [46,47] in the early '90s, whose growing interest is witnessed by the annual organization of the international workshop on Process Algebra and Performance Modeling (PAPM) and a number of Ph.D. theses on this subject [48,38,70,67,63,54,62,59,40,53,10,31,24,29,22,25]. With respect to formalisms traditionally used for performance evaluation purposes like Markov chains (MCs) and queueing networks (QNs) [56,58], SPA provides a more complete framework in which also functional verification can be carried out. With respect to previous formal methods for performance evaluation like stochastic Petri nets (SPNs) [1], SPA provides novel capabilities related to compositionality and abstraction that help system modeling and analysis. The first part of this tutorial (Sect. 2) is devoted to the presentation of the main results achieved in the field of SPA since the early '90s.

Although SPA supports compositional modeling via algebraic operators, this feature has not been exploited yet to enforce a more controlled way of describing systems that makes SPA technicalities transparent. By this we mean that in a SPA specification the basic concepts of system component and connection are not clearly elucidated, nor checks are available to detect mismatches when assembling components together. Since nowadays systems are made out of numerous components, in the early design stages it is crucial to be equipped with a formal specification language that permits to reason in terms of components and component interactions and to identify components that result in mismatches when put together. The importance of this activity is witnessed by the growing interest in the field of software architecture and the development of architectural description languages (ADLs) [61,66]. The formal description of the architecture of a complex system serves two purposes. First and foremost is making available a precise document describing the structure of the system to all the people involved in the design, implementation, and maintainance of the system itself. The second one is concerned with the possibility of analyzing the properties of the system at the architectural level, thus allowing for the early detection of design errors. The second part of this tutorial (Sect. 3) is devoted to show how SPA can easily be transformed into a compositional, graphical and hierchical ADL endowed with some architectural checks, which can be profitably employed for both functional verification and performance evaluation at the architectural level of design.

The tutorial finally concludes with some remarks about future directions in the field of SPA based ADLs.

2   SPA: Basic Notions and Main Achievements

SPA is a compositional specification language of algebraic nature that integrates process algebra theory [60,50,5] and stochastic processes. In this section we provide a quick overview of the basic notions about the syntax, the semantics, and the equivalences for SPA, as well as the main results and applications that have been developed in the past decade.

2.1   Syntax: Actions, Operators, and Synchronization Disciplines

SPA is characterized by three main ingredients: the actions modeling the system activities, the algebraic operators whereby composing the subsystem specifications, and the synchronization disciplines.

An action is usually composed of a type a and an exponential rate λ: $<a, \lambda>$ [48,45,27]. The type indicates the kind of activity that is performed by the system at a certain point, while the rate indicates the reciprocal of the average duration of the activity assuming that the duration is an exponentially distributed random variable. A special action type, traditionally denoted by τ, designates a system activity whose functionality cannot be observed and serves for functional abstraction purposes. In order to increase the expressiveness, in [10] prioritized, weighted immediate actions of the form $<a, \infty_{l,w}>$ are proposed, which are useful to model activities whose timing is irrelevant from the performance viewpoint as well as activities whose duration follows a phase type distribution. In alternative to the durational actions considered so far, in [40] a different view is taken according to which an action is either an instantaneous activity a or an exponentially distributed time passage λ.

Several algebraic operators are usually present. The zeroary operator $\underline{0}$ represents the term that cannot execute any action. The action prefix operator $<a, \lambda>.E$ denotes the term that can execute an action with type a and rate λ and then behaves as term E; in the approach of [40], there are the two action prefix operators $a.E$ and $\lambda.E$. The functional abstraction operator E/L, where L is a set of action types not including τ, denotes the term that behaves as term E except that the type a of each executed action is turned into τ whenever $a \in L$. The functional relabeling operator $E[\varphi]$, where φ is a function over action types preserving observability, denotes a term that behaves as term E except that the type a of each executed action becomes $\varphi(a)$. The alternative composition operator $E_1 + E_2$ denotes a term that behaves as either term E_1 or term E_2 depending on whether an action of E_1 or an action of E_2 is executed. The action choice is regulated by the race policy (the fastest one succeeds), so that each action of E_1 and E_2 has an execution probability proportional to its rate. In the approach of [10], immediate actions take precedence over exponentially timed ones and the choice among them is governed by the preselection policy: the lower priority immediate actions are discarded, then each of the remaining immediate actions is given an execution probability proportional to its weight. In the approach of [40], the choice between two instantaneous activities is non-deterministic. The parallel composition operator $E_1 \parallel_S E_2$, where S is a set of action types not including τ, denotes a term that asynchronously executes actions of E_1 or E_2 whose type does not belong to S, and synchronously executes – according to a synchronization discipline – equally typed actions of E_1 and E_2 whose type belongs to S. Finally, a constant A denotes a term that behaves according to the associated defining equation $A \stackrel{\Delta}{=} E$, which allows for recursive behaviors.

There are many different synchronization disciplines. In [45] the rate of the action resulting from the synchronization of two actions is the product of the rates of the two synchronizing actions, where the physical interpretation is that one rate is the formal rate and the other rate acts like a scaling factor. In [48] the bounded capacity assumption is introduced, according to which the rate of an action cannot be increased/decreased due to the synchronization with another action of the same type. In this approach, patient synchronizations are considered, i.e. the rate of the action resulting from the synchronization of two equally typed actions of E_1 and E_2 is given by the minimum of the two total rates with which E_1 and E_2 can execute actions of the considered type, multiplied by the local execution probabilities of the two synchronizing actions. Following the terminology of [36], in [26] a generative-reactive synchronization discipline complying with the bounded capacity assumption is adopted, which is based on the systematic use of prioritized, weighted passive actions of the form $<a, *_{l,w}>$. The idea is that the nonpassive actions probabilistically determine the type of action to be executed at each step, while the passive actions of the determined type probabilistically react in order to identify the subterms taking part in the synchronization. In order for two equally typed actions to synchronize, in this approach one of them must be passive and the rate of the resulting action is given by the rate of the nonpassive action multiplied by the local execution probability of the passive action. Finally, in [40] equal instantaneous activities can synchronize, while time passages cannot. Therefore, when both E_1 and E_2 can let time pass, in this approach the overall time passage is the maximum of the two local, exponentially distributed time passages.

2.2   Semantics: Interleaving and Memoryless Property

The semantics for SPA is defined in an operational fashion by means of a set of axioms and inference rules that formalize the meaning of the algebraic operators. The result of the application of such rules is a labeled transition system (LTS), where states are in correspondence with process terms and transitions are labeled with actions. As an example, the axiom for the action prefix operator

$$<a, \lambda>.E \xrightarrow{a, \lambda} E$$

establishes that term/state $<a, \lambda>.E$ can evolve into term/state E by performing action/transition $<a, \lambda>$. As another example, the inference rule for the functional relabeling operator

$$\frac{E \xrightarrow{a, \lambda} E'}{E[\varphi] \xrightarrow{\varphi(a), \lambda} E'[\varphi]}$$

establishes that, whenever term/state E can evolve into term/state E' by performing action/transition $<a, \lambda>$, term/state $E[\varphi]$ can evolve into term/state $E'[\varphi]$ by performing action/transition $<\varphi(a), \lambda>$.

The most complicated inference rules are those for the alternative composition operator and the parallel composition operator. As far as the alternative composition operator is concerned, the problem is that, in the case of terms like $<a, \lambda>.E + <a, \lambda>.E$, the transition generation process must keep track of the fact that the total rate is $2 \cdot \lambda$ by virtue of the race policy. In [48] it is proposed to use labeled multitransition systems, so that a single transition labeled with $<a, \lambda>$ is generated for the term above, which has multiplicity two. In [45], instead, it is proposed to decorate the transitions with an additional distinguishing label, whose value depends on whether the transitions are due to the left hand side or the right hand side summand of the alternative compositions. As far as the parallel composition operator is concerned, the related inference rules must embody the desired synchronization discipline.

The resulting LTS is an interleaving semantic model, which means that every parallel computation is represented through a choice between all the sequential computations that can be obtained by interleaving the execution of the actions of the subterms composed in parallel. As an example, the parallel term $<a, \lambda>.\underline{0} \|_{\emptyset} <b, \mu>.\underline{0}$ and the sequential term $<a, \lambda>.<b, \mu>.\underline{0}+<b, \mu>.<a, \lambda>.\underline{0}$ are given the same LTS up to state names:

This is correct from the functional viewpoint, because an external observer, who is not aware of the structure of the systems represented by the two terms, sees exactly the same behavior. Moreover, this is correct from the performance viewpoint as well, by virtue of the memoryless property of the exponential distribution. For instance, if in the parallel term action $<a, \lambda>$ is completed before action $<b, \mu>$, then state $\underline{0} \|_{\emptyset} <b, \mu>.\underline{0}$ is reached and the time to the completion of action $<b, \mu>$ is still exponentially distributed with rate μ. In other words, the interleaving style fits well with the fact that the execution of an exponentially timed action can be considered as being started in the state in which it terminates.

The LTS produced by applying the operational semantic rules to a process term represents the integrated semantic model of the process term. It can undergo to integrated analysis techniques, like integrated model checking [8] and integrated equivalence checking (see Sect. 2.3), to detect mixed functional-performance properties, like the probability of executing a certain sequence of activities. From the integrated semantic model, two projected semantic models can be derived. The functional semantic model is a LTS obtained by discarding information about action rates; it can be analyzed through traditional techniques like model checking [30] and equivalence/preorder checking [28]. The performance semantic model is a LTS obtained by discarding information about action types, which happens to be a continuous time Markov chain (CTMC). In the approach of [26], where prioritized, weighted immediate and passive actions are considered, the projected semantic models are generated after pruning the lower priority transitions from the integrated semantic model. Furthermore, the performance semantic model can be generated only if the integrated semantic model is performance closed, i.e. has no passive transitions. If this is the case, the performance semantic model is a CTMC whenever the integrated semantic model has only exponentially timed transitions or both exponentially timed and immediate transitions (in which case states having outgoing immediate transitions are removed as their sojourn time is zero). If instead the integrated semantic model has only immediate transitions, then it is assumed that the execution of each of them takes one time unit so that the performance model turns out to be a discrete time Markov chain (DTMC). CTMCs and DTMCs can then be analyzed through standard techniques [69], mainly based on rewards [52], to derive performance measures.

2.3 Equivalences: Congruence and Lumpability

SPA terms can be equated on the basis of their functional and performance behavior. The mostly used method is that, inspired by [57], of the Markovian bisimulation equivalence [48,45,27], based on the ability of two terms of simulating each other behavior. The idea is that, given an equivalence relation $\mathcal{B}$ over process terms, $\mathcal{B}$ is a Markovian bisimulation if, for each pair $(E_1, E_2) \in \mathcal{B}$, action type a, and equivalence class C of $\mathcal{B}$, the total rate with which E_1 reaches states in C by executing actions of type a is equal to the total rate with which E_2 reaches states in C by executing actions of type a. The Markovian bisimulation equivalence is then defined as the union of all the Markovian bisimulations.

The Markovian bisimulation equivalence enjoys several properties. First, it is a congruence w.r.t. all the operators as well as recursive constant defining equations [48,45,27,26]. This ensures substitutivity, i.e. compositionality at the semantic level: given a term, if any of each subterms is replaced by a Markovian bisimulation equivalent subterm, the new term is Markovian bisimulation equivalent to the original one. Second, the Markovian bisimulation equivalence complies with the ordinary lumping for MCs [64], thus ensuring that equivalent terms possess the same performance characteristics [48,27]. Third, the Markovian bisimulation equivalence is the coarsest congruence contained in the intersection of the bisimulation equivalence [60] and the ordinary lumping, which means that it is the best Markovian equivalence we can hope for in a bisimulation setting [10]. Fourth, the Markovian bisimulation equivalence has a sound and complete axiomatization – with $<a, \lambda_1>.E + <a, \lambda_2>.E - <a, \lambda_1 + \lambda_2>.E$ as typical axiom besides the usual expansion law for the parallel composition operator – which provides an alternative characterization easier to understand [45].

There are some variants of the Markovian bisimulation equivalence. In the approach of [26], the Markovian bisimulation equivalence is extended to deal with prioritized, weighted immediate and passive actions. In the approach of [40], a weak Markovian bisimulation equivalence is defined that abstracts from instantaneous τ activities. In [48], a different weak Markovian bisimulation equivalence is proposed that, in some cases, abstracts from exponentially timed τ actions. Finally, an alternative view is taken in [17]: following the testing approach of [32], it is proposed of equating two terms whenever they have the same probability to pass the same tests within the same average time. The resulting equivalence, called Markovian testing equivalence, is coarser than the Markovian bisimulation equivalence, abstracts from internal immediate actions and in some cases from internal exponentially timed actions, and possesses an alternative characterization in terms of extended traces. The congruence property, the axiomatization, and the relationship with the ordinary lumping for the Markovian testing equivalence are still under investigation. As far as ordinary lumping is concerned, it is known that in some cases the Markovian testing equivalence produces a more compact exact aggregation.

2.4   Performance Properties: Algebraic and Logic Approaches

SPA provides the capability of expressing the performance aspects of the behavior of complex systems, but not the performance properties of interest. In a Markovian framework, stationary and transient performance measures (system throughput, resource utilization, average buffer occupation, mean response time, etc.) are usually described as weighted sums of state probabilities and transition frequencies, where state weights are called yield rewards and transition weights are called bonus rewards [52].

In [13,12] it is proposed to reuse the classical technique of rewards by extending the action format to include as many pairs of yield and bonus rewards as there are performance measures of interest. In this framework, at semantic model construction time every state is given a yield reward that is equal to the sum of the yield rewards of the actions it can execute. The Markovian bisimulation equivalence is then extended to take rewards into account, in a way that preserves compositionality as well as the performance measures of interest.

In [29] an alternative reward based approach is proposed, which associates certain rewards with those states satisfying certain formulas of a Markovian modal logic that characterizes the Markovian bisimulation equivalence. This approach is implemented through a high level language for enquiring about the stationary performance characteristics possessed by a process term. Such a language, whose formal underpinning is constituted by the Markovian modal logic, relies on the combination of the standard mathematical notation, a notation based on the Markovian bisimulation equivalence to focus queries directly on states, and a notation expressing the potential to perform an action of a given type.

Finally, in [8,7,6] it is proposed to directly express the performance properties of interest through logical formulas, whose validity is verified through an integrated model checking procedure. The continuous stochastic logic is used in this framework to inquiry about the value of stationary and transient performability measures of a system. According to the observation that the progress of time can be regarded as the earning of reward, a reward based variant of such a logic is then introduced, where yield rewards are assumed to be already attached to the states.

2.5   General Distributions

When introducing generally distributed durations in SPA, the memoryless property can no longer be exploited to define the semantics in the plain interleaving style. The reason is that the actions can no more be thought of as being started in the states where they are terminated; the underlying performance models are no longer MCs. Therefore, we have to keep track of the sequence of states in which an action started and continued its execution.

There are several approaches in the literature, among which we mention below those for which a notion of equivalence (in the bisimulation style) is developed. In [70] the problem of identifying the start and the termination of an action is solved at the syntactic level by means of suitable operators that represent the random setting of a timer and the expiration of a timer, respectively. Semantic models are infinite LTSs from which performance measures can be derived via simulation.

In [31] the problem is again solved at the syntax level through suitable clock related operators, with the difference that the semantic models are finitely represented through stochastic automata equipped with clocks.

In [25], instead, the problem of identifying the start and the termination of an action is addressed at the semantic level through the ST approach of [37]. At semantic model construction time, the start and the termination of each action are distinguished and kept connected to each other. This framework naturally supports action refinement, which can be exploited to replace a generally timed action with a process term composed only of exponentially timed actions resulting in a phase type duration that approximates the original duration.

2.6   State Space Explosion

The semantic models for SPA are state based, hence suffer from the state space explosion problem, i.e. the fact that the size of the state space grows exponentially with the number of subterms composed in parallel. In general, this problem can be tackled with traditional congruence based techniques. For instance, it is wise to build the state space underlying a process term in a stepwise fashion, along the structure imposed by the occurrences of the parallel composition operator, and minimize the state space obtained at every step according to the Markovian bisimulation equivalence. An alternative strategy is to operate at the syntactical level using the axioms of the Markovian bisimulation equivalence as rewriting rules.

More specific techniques to fight the state space explosion problem are present in the literature. Among them we mention those based on Kronecker representation [27,67], time scale decomposition [59], product form solution [39,65,49], symbolic representation [44], stochastic Petri net semantics [14], and queueing network representation [9].

2.7   Tools and Case Studies

A few tools are under distribution for the modeling and analysis of systems with SPA. Among them we mention the PEPA Workbench [34], the TIPPtool [55], and TwoTowers [18].

With such tools several case studies have been conducted, which are concerned with computer systems, communication protocols, and distributed algorithms. Among such case studies we mention those related to CSMA/CD [10], token ring [10], electronic mail system [41], multiprocessor mainframe [42], industrial production cell [51], robot control [35], plain old telephone system [43], multimedia stream [23], adaptive mechanisms for transmitting voice over IP [21, 3], ATM switches [2], replicated web services [11], Lehmann-Rabin randomized algorithm for dining philosophers [10], and comparison of six mutual exclusion algorithms [13].

3   Turning SPA into an ADL

SPA supports the compositional modeling of complex systems via algebraic operators. However, this feature has not been exploited yet to enforce an easier and more controlled way of describing systems that makes SPA technicalities transparent to the designer. As an example, if a system is made out of a certain number of components, with SPA the system is simply described as the parallel composition of a certain number of subterms, each representing the behavior of a single component, with suitable synchronization sets to represent the component interactions. It is desirable to be able to describe the same system at a higher level of abstraction, where the parallel composition operators and the related synchronization sets do not come into play. It is more natural to separately define the behavior of each type of component, to indicate the actions through which each component type interacts with the others, to declare the instances of each component type that form the system, and to specify the way in which the interacting actions are attached to each other in order to make the component instances interact. This view brings the advantage that the system components and the component interactions are clearly elucidated, with the synchronization mechanism being hidden (e.g. interacting actions must not necessarily have the same type). Another strength is the capability of defining the behavior – possibly parametrized w.r.t. action rates – and the interactions of a component type just once and subsequently reusing it as many times as there are instances of that component type in the system. Additionally, it is desirable that composite systems can be described in a hierachical way, and that a graphical support is provided for the whole modeling process.

Besides this useful syntactical sugar, checks are needed to detect possible mismatches when assembling components together and to identify the components that cause such mismatches. A typical example is deadlock freedom. If we put together some components that we know to be deadlock free, we would like that their combination is still deadlock free. In order to investigate that, we need suitable checks that allow deadlock to be quickly detected and some diagnostic information to be obtained for localizing the source of deadlock. As another example, in order to evaluate the performance of a system, its model must be performance closed. In this case, a check at the syntax level is helpful to easily detect and pinpoint possible violations of the performance closure.

In this section we show how SPA can be enhanced to work with at the architectural level of design. Based on ideas contained in [4,16,19,20], we illustrate how SPA can be turned into a fully fledged ADL for the modeling, functional verification, and performance evaluation of complex systems. Recalled that the transformation is largely independent of the specific SPA, we concentrate on

EMPA$_{gr}$ [26] – which includes prioritized, weighted immediate and passive actions and the generative-reactive synchronization discipline – and we exhibit the resulting SPA based ADL called Æmilia [15,9]. The description of a system with Æmilia can be done in a compositional, hierachical, graphical and controlled way. First, we have to define the behavior of the types of components in the system and their interactions with the other components. The functional and performance aspects of the behavior are described through a family of EMPA$_{gr}$ terms or the invocation of the specification of a previously modeled system, while the interactions are described through actions occurring in the behavior. Second, we have to declare the instances of each type of component present in the system and the way in which their interactions are attached to each other in order to allow the instances to communicate. This process is supported by a graphical notation. Then, the whole behavior of the system is a family of EMPA$_{gr}$ terms transparently obtained by composing in parallel the behavior of the declared instances according to the specified attachments. From the whole behavior, integrated, functional and performance semantic models can be automatically derived, which can undergo to the analysis techniques mentioned in Sect. 2. In addition to that, Æmilia comes equipped with some architectural checks for ensuring deadlock freedom and performance closure.

3.1   Components and Topology: Textual and Graphical Notations

A description in Æmilia represents an architectural type. As shown in Table 1, the description of an architectural type starts with the name of the architectural type and its numeric parameters, which often are values for exponential rates and weights. Each architectural type is defined as a function of its architectural element types (AETs) and its architectural topology. An AET is defined as a function of its behavior, specified either as a family of sequential [1] EMPA$_{gr}$ terms or through an invocation of a previously defined architectural type, and its interactions, specified as a set of EMPA$_{gr}$ action types occurring in the behavior that act as interfaces for the AET. The architectural topology is specified through the declaration of a set of architectural element instances (AEIs) representing the system components, a set of architectural (as opposed to local) interactions given by some interactions of the AEIs that act as interfaces for the whole architectural type, and a set of directed architectural attachments among the interactions of the AEIs. Every interaction is declared to be an input interaction or an output interaction and the attachments must respect such a classification: every attachment must involve an output interaction and an input interaction of two different AEIs. An AEI can have different types of interactions (input/output, local/architectural); it must have at least one local interaction. Every local interaction must be involved in at least one attachment, while every architectural interaction must not be involved in any attachment. In order to allow several AEIs to synchronize, every local interaction can be involved in

---

[1] Including only $\underline{0}$, constants, action prefix operators, and alternative composition operators.

several attachments provided that no autosynchronization arises, i.e. no chain of attachments is created that starts from a local interaction of an AEI and terminates on a local interaction of the same AEI. On the performance side, we require that, for the sake of modeling consistency, all the occurrences of an action type in the behavior of an AET have the same kind of rate (exponential, immediate with the same priority level, or passive with the same priority level) and that, to comply with the generative-reactive synchronization discipline of EMPA_{gr}, every chain of attachments contains at most one interaction whose associated rate is exponential or immediate.

Table 1. Structure of an Æmilia textual description

archi_type	⟨name and numeric parameters⟩
archi_elem_types	⟨architectural element types: behaviors and interactions⟩
archi_topology	
archi_elem_instances	⟨architectural element instances⟩
archi_interactions	⟨architectural interactions⟩
archi_attachments	⟨architectural attachments⟩
end	

We now illustrate the textual notation of Æmilia by means of an example concerning a pipe-filter system. The system is composed of three identical filters and one pipe. Each filter acts as a service center of capacity two that is subject to failures and subsequent repairs, which is characterized by a service rate σ, a failure rate ϕ, and a repair rate ρ. For each item processed by the upstream filter, the pipe instantaneously forwards it to one of the two downstream filters according to the availability of free positions in their buffers. If both have free positions, the choice is resolved probabilistically based on $p_{routing}$. The Æmilia textual description is provided in Table 2. [2] Such a description establishes that there are three instances F_0, F_1, and F_2 of *FilterT* as well as one instance P of *PipeT*, connected in such a way that the items flow from F_0 to P and from P to F_1 or F_2. It is worth observing that the system components are clearly elucidated and easily connected to each other, and that the numeric parameters allow for a good degree of specification reuse: e.g., the behavior of the filters is defined only once. Additionally, the *accept_item* input interaction of F_0 and the *serve_item* output interactions of F_1 and F_2 are declared as being architectural. Therefore, they can be used for hierchical modeling, e.g. to describe a client-server system where the server structure is like the pipe-filter organization above.

Æmilia comes equipped with a graphical notation as well, in order to provide a visual help during the architectural design of complex systems. Such a graphical notation is based on flow graphs [60]. In a flow graph representing an architec-

---

[2] Wherever omitted, priority levels and weights are taken to be 1.

Table 2. Textual description of *PipeFilter*

archi_type	$PipeFilter(\textbf{exp\_rate }\sigma_0,\sigma_1,\sigma_2,\phi_0,\phi_1,\phi_2,\rho_0,\rho_1,\rho_2;$
	$\qquad\textbf{weight }p_{routing})$
archi_elem_types	
elem_type	$FilterT(\textbf{exp\_rate }\sigma,\phi,\rho)$
behavior	$Filter \stackrel{\Delta}{=} <accept\_item,*>.Filter' +$
	$\qquad <fail,\phi>.<repair,\rho>.Filter$
	$Filter' \stackrel{\Delta}{=} <accept\_item,*>.Filter'' +$
	$\qquad <serve\_item,\sigma>.Filter +$
	$\qquad <fail,\phi>.<repair,\rho>.Filter'$
	$Filter'' \stackrel{\Delta}{=} <serve\_item,\sigma>.Filter' +$
	$\qquad <fail,\phi>.<repair,\rho>.Filter''$
interactions	**input** $accept\_item$
	output $serve\_item$
elem_type	$PipeT(\textbf{weight }p)$
behavior	$Pipe \stackrel{\Delta}{=} <accept\_item,*>.(<forward\_item_1,\infty_{1,p}>.Pipe +$
	$\qquad\qquad <forward\_item_2,\infty_{1,1-p}>.Pipe)$
interactions	**input** $accept\_item$
	output $forward\_item_1, forward\_item_2$
archi_topology	
archi_elem_instances	$F_0 : FilterT(\sigma_0,\phi_0,\rho_0)$
	$F_1 : FilterT(\sigma_1,\phi_1,\rho_1)$
	$F_2 : FilterT(\sigma_2,\phi_2,\rho_2)$
	$P : PipeT(p_{routing})$
archi_interactions	**input** $F_0.accept\_item$
	output $F_1.serve\_item, F_2.serve\_item$
archi_attachments	**from** $F_0.serve\_item$ **to** $P.accept\_item$
	from $P.forward\_item_1$ **to** $F_1.accept\_item$
	from $P.forward\_item_2$ **to** $F_2.accept\_item$
end	

tural description in Æmilia, the boxes denote the AEIs, the black circles denote the local interactions, the white squares denote the architectural interactions, and the directed edges denote the attachments. As an example, the architectural type *PipeFilter* can be pictorially represented through the flow graph of Fig. 1. From a methodological viewpoint, when modeling an architectural type with Æmilia, it is convenient to start with the flow graph representation of the architectural type and then to textually specify the behavior of each AET.

3.2   Translation Semantics

The semantics of an Æmilia specification is given by translation into $EMPA_{gr}$. While only the dynamic operators (action prefix and alternative composition) of $EMPA_{gr}$ can be used in the syntax of an Æmilia specification, the more complicated static operators (functional abstraction, functional relabeling, and parallel composition) of $EMPA_{gr}$ are transparently used in the semantics of an Æmilia specification. The translation into $EMPA_{gr}$ is accomplished in two steps.

In the first step, the semantics of all the instances of each AET is defined to be the behavior of the AET projected onto its interactions. Such a projected

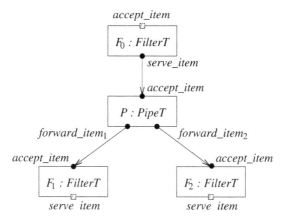

Fig. 1. Flow graph of *PipeFilter*

behavior is obtained from the family of sequential EMPA$_{\text{gr}}$ terms representing the behavior of the AET by applying a functional abstraction operator on all the actions that are not interactions. In this way, we abstract from all the internal details of the behavior of the instances of the AET. For the pipe-filter system of Table 2 we have

$$[\![FilterT]\!] = [\![F_0]\!] = [\![F_1]\!] = [\![F_2]\!] = Filter/\{fail, repair\}$$
$$[\![PipeT]\!] = \qquad\qquad [\![P]\!] \qquad\qquad = Pipe$$

thus abstracting from the internal activities *fail* and *repair*.

In the second step, the semantics of an architectural type is obtained by composing in parallel the semantics of its AEIs according to the specified attachments. Recalled that the parallel composition operator is left associative, for the pipe-filter system we have

$$[\![PipeFilter]\!] = [\![F_0]\!][serve\_item \mapsto a] \parallel_\emptyset$$
$$[\![F_1]\!][accept\_item \mapsto a_1] \parallel_\emptyset$$
$$[\![F_2]\!][accept\_item \mapsto a_2] \parallel_{\{a,a_1,a_2\}}$$
$$[\![P]\!][accept\_item \mapsto a,$$
$$forward\_item_1 \mapsto a_1,$$
$$forward\_item_2 \mapsto a_2]$$

The use of the functional relabeling operator is necessary to make the AEIs interact. As an example, F_0 and P must interact via *serve_item* and *accept_item*, which are different from each other. Since the parallel composition operator allows only equally typed actions to synchronize, in $[\![PipeFilter]\!]$ each *serve_item* action executed by $[\![F_0]\!]$ and each *accept_item* action executed by $[\![P]\!]$ is relabeled to an action with the same type a. In order to avoid interferences, it is important that a be a fresh action type, i.e. an action type occurring neither in $[\![F_0]\!]$ nor in $[\![P]\!]$. Then a synchronization on a is forced between the relabeled versions of $[\![F_0]\!]$ and $[\![P]\!]$ by means of operator $\parallel_{\{a,a_1,a_2\}}$. It is worth reminding that the transformation of *PipeFilter* into $[\![PipeFilter]\!]$, which can be analyzed through the techniques mentioned in Sect 2, is completely transparent to the designer.

The interested reader is referred to [9,16] for a formal definition of the translation semantics.

3.3   Architectural Checks

Æmilia is equipped with some architectural checks that the designer can use to verify the well formedness of the architectural types and, in case a mismatch is detected, to identify the components that cause it. Most of such checks are based on the weak bisimulation equivalence [60], which captures the ability of the functional semantic models of two terms to simulate each other behaviors up to internal actions.

The first two checks take care of verifying whether the deadlock free AEIs of an architectural type fit together well, i.e. do not lead to system blocks. The first check (compatibility) is concerned with architectural types whose topology is acyclic. For an acyclic architectural type, if we take an AEI K and we consider all the AEIs $C_1, \ldots, C_n$ attached to it, we can observe that they form a star topology whose center is K, as the absence of cycles prevents any two AEIs among $C_1, \ldots, C_n$ from communicating via an AEI different from K. It can easily be recognized that an acyclic architectural type is just a composition of star topologies. An efficient compatibility check based on the weak bisimulation equivalence (together with a simple constraint on action priorities) ensures the absence of deadlock within a star topology whose center K is deadlock free, and this check scales to the whole acyclic architectural type. The basic condition to check is that every C_i is compatible with K, i.e. the functional semantics of their parallel composition is weakly bisimulation equivalent to the functional semantics of K itself. Intuitively, this means that attaching C_i to K does not alter the behavior of K, i.e. K is designed in such a way that it suitably coordinates with C_i.

Since the compatibility check is not sufficient for cyclic architectural types, the second check (interoperability) deals with cycles. A suitable interoperability check based on the weak bisimulation equivalence (together with a simple constraint on action priorities) ensures the absence of deadlock within a cycle $C_1, \ldots, C_n$ of AEIs in the case that at least one of such AEIs is deadlock free. The basic condition to check is that at least one deadlock free C_i interoperates with the other AEIs in the cycle, i.e. the functional semantics of the parallel composition of the AEIs in the cycle projected on the interactions with C_i only is weakly bisimulation equivalent to the functional semantics of C_i. Intuitively, this means that inserting C_i into the cycle does not alter the behavior of C_i, i.e. that the behavior of the cycle assumed by C_i matches the actual behavior of the cycle. In the case in which no deadlock free AEI is found in the cycle that interoperates with the other AEIs, a loop shrinking procedure can be used to single out the AEIs in the cycle responsible for the deadlock.

On the performance side, there is a third check to detect architectural mismatches resulting in performance underspecification. This check (performance closure) ensures that the performance semantic model underlying an architectural type exists in the form of a CTMC or DTMC. In order for an architectural type to be performance closed, the basic condition to check is that no AET behavior contains a passive action whose type is not an interaction, and that every set of attached local interactions contains one interaction whose associated rate is exponential or immediate.

We conclude by referring the interested reader to [9,16] for a precise definition and examples of application of the architectural checks outlined in this section.

3.4 Families of Architectures and Hierarchical Modeling

An Æmilia description represents a family of architectures called an architectural type. An architectural type is an intermediate abstraction between a single architecture and an architectural style [66]. An important goal of the software architecture discipline is the creation of an established and shared understanding of the common forms of software design. Starting from the user requirements, the designer should be able to identify a suitable organizational style, in order to capitalize on codified principles and experience to specify, analyze, plan, and monitor the construction of a system with high levels of efficiency and confidence. An architectural style defines a family of systems having a common vocabulary of components as well as a common topology and set of contraints on the interactions among the components. As examples of architectural styles we mention main program-subroutines, pipe-filter, client-server, and the layered organization. Since an architectural style encompasses an entire family of software systems, it is desirable to formalize the concept of architectural style both to have a precise definition of the system family and to study the architectural properties common to all the systems of the family. This is not a trivial task because there are at least two degrees of freedom: variability of the component topology and variability of the component internal behavior.

An architectural type is an approximation of an architectural style, where the component topology and the component internal behavior can vary from instance to instance of the architectural type in a controlled way, which preserves the architectural checks. More precisely, all the instances of an architectural type must have the same observable functional behavior and conforming topologies, while the internal behavior and the performance characteristics can freely vary. An instance of an architectural type can be obtained by invoking the architectural type and passing actual AETs preserving the observable functional behavior of the formal AETs, an actual topology (actual AEIs, actual architectural interactions, and actual attachments) that conforms to the formal topology, actual names for the architectural interactions, and actual values for the numeric parameters.

The simplest form of architectural invocation is the one in which the actual parameters coincide with the formal ones, in which case the actual parameters are omitted for the sake of conciseness. The possibility of defining the behavior of an AET through an architectural invocation as well as declaring architectural interactions can be exploited to model a system architecture in a hierarchical way. As an example, consider the pipe-filter organization of Table 2 and suppose that it is the architecture of the server of a client-server system.

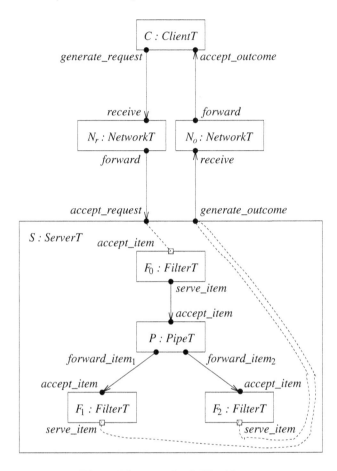

Fig. 2. Flow graph of *ClientServer*

The flow graph description of the resulting client-server system is depicted in Fig. 2, while its textual description is reported in Table 3. The client description is parametrized w.r.t. the request generation rate λ, while the communication link description is parametrized w.r.t. the communication speed δ. As can be observed, the behavior of the server is defined through an invocation of the previously defined architectural type *PipeFilter*, where the actual names *accept_request*, *generate_outcome*, and *generate_outcome* substitute for the formal architectural interactions $F_0.accept\_item$, $F_1.serve\_item$, and $F_2.serve\_item$, respectively.

A more complex form of architectural invocation is the one in which actual AETs are passed that are different from the corresponding formal AETs. In this case, we have to make sure that the actual AETs preserves the functional behavior determined by the formal ones. To this purpose, Æmilia is endowed with an efficient behavioral conformity check based on the weak bisimulation equiv-

Table 3. Textual description of *ClientServer*

archi_type	$ClientServer(\mathbf{exp\_rate}\ \lambda, \delta_r, \delta_o,$
	$\qquad\qquad\qquad \sigma_0, \sigma_1, \sigma_2, \phi_0, \phi_1, \phi_2, \rho_0, \rho_1, \rho_2;$
	$\qquad\qquad \mathbf{weight}\ p_{routing})$
archi_elem_types	
elem_type	$ClientT(\mathbf{exp\_rate}\ \lambda)$
behavior	$Client \stackrel{\Delta}{=}\ <generate\_request, \lambda>.$
	$\qquad\qquad <accept\_outcome, *>.Client$
interactions	**output** $generate\_request$
	input $accept\_outcome$
elem_type	$NetworkT(\mathbf{exp\_rate}\ \delta)$
behavior	$Network \stackrel{\Delta}{=}\ <receive, *>.<forward, \delta>.Network$
interactions	**input** $receive$
	output $forward$
elem_type	$ServerT(\mathbf{exp\_rate}\ \sigma_0, \sigma_1, \sigma_2, \phi_0, \phi_1, \phi_2, \rho_0, \rho_1, \rho_2;$
	$\qquad\qquad \mathbf{weight}\ p_{routing})$
behavior	$Server \stackrel{\Delta}{=} PipeFilter(;\quad /*$ actual AETs $*/$
	$\qquad\qquad ;\quad /*$ actual AEIs $*/$
	$\qquad\qquad ;\quad /*$ actual arch. interactions $*/$
	$\qquad\qquad ;\quad /*$ actual attachments $*/$
	$\qquad\qquad accept\_request,$
	$\qquad\qquad\quad generate\_outcome,$
	$\qquad\qquad\quad generate\_outcome;$
	$\qquad\qquad \sigma_0, \sigma_1, \sigma_2, \phi_0, \phi_1, \phi_2, \rho_0, \rho_1, \rho_2,$
	$\qquad\qquad\quad p_{routing})$
interactions	**input** $accept\_request$
	output $generate\_outcome$
archi_topology	
archi_elem_instances	$C : ClientT(\lambda)$
	$N_r : NetworkT(\delta_r)$
	$N_o : NetworkT(\delta_o)$
	$S : ServerT(\sigma_0, \sigma_1, \sigma_2, \phi_0, \phi_1, \phi_2, \rho_0, \rho_1, \rho_2, p_{routing})$
archi_interactions	
archi_attachments	**from** $C.generate\_request$ **to** $N_r.receive$
	from $N_r.forward$ **to** $S.accept\_request$
	from $S.generate\_outcome$ **to** $N_o.receive$
	from $N_o.forward$ **to** $C.accept\_outcome$
end	

alence (together with a simple constraint on action rates) to verify whether an architectural type invocation conforms to an architectural type definition, in the sense that the architectural type invocation and the architectural type definition have the same observable functional semantics up to some relabeling. The basic condition to check is that the functional semantics of each actual AET is weakly bisimulation equivalent to the functional semantics of the corresponding formal AET up to some relabeling. This behavioral conformity check ensures that all the correct instances of an architectural type possess the same compatibility, interoperability, and performance closure properties. In other words, the outcome of the application of the compatibility, interoperability, and performance closure checks to the definition of an architectural type scales to all the behaviorally conforming invocations of the architectural type.

The most complete form of architectural invocation is the one in which both actual AETs and an actual topology are passed that are different from the corresponding formal AETs and formal topology, respectively. In this case, we have to additionally make sure that the actual topology conforms to the formal topology. There are three kinds of admitted topological extensions, all of which preserve the compatibility, interoperability, and performance closure properties under some general conditions.

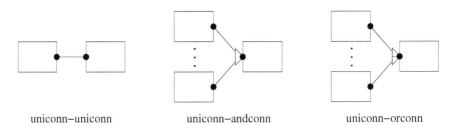

uniconn–uniconn   uniconn–andconn   uniconn–orconn

Fig. 3. Legal attachments in case of extensible and/or connections

The first kind of topological extension is given by the extensible and/or connections. As an example, consider the client-server system of Table 3. Every instance of such an architectural type can admit a single client and a single server, whereas it would be useful to allow for an arbitrary number of clients (to be instantiated when invoking the architectural type) that can connect to the server. From the syntactical viewpoint, the extensible and/or connections are introduced in Æmilia by further typing the interactions of the AETs. Besides the input/output qualification, the interactions are classified as uniconn, andconn, and orconn, with only the three types of attachments shown in Fig. 3 considered legal. A uniconn interaction is an interaction to which a single AEI can be attached; e.g., all the interactions of *ClientServer* are of this type. An andconn interaction is an interaction to which a variable number of AEIs can be attached, such that all the attached AEIs must synchronize when that interaction takes place; e.g., a broadcast transmission. An orconn interaction is an interaction to which a variable number of AEIs can be attached, such that only one of the attached AEIs must synchronize when that interaction takes place; e.g., a client-server system with several clients. Every output orconn interaction must be declared to depend on one input orconn interaction, with the occurrences of the two interactions alternating in the behavior of the AET that contains them. On the semantic side, the treatment of uniconn and orconn interactions is trivial. Instead, every occurrence of an input orconn interaction must be replaced by a choice among as many indexed occurrences of that interaction as there are attached AEIs, while every occurrence of an output orconn interaction must be augmented with the same index given to the occurrence of the preceding input orconn interaction on which it depends. Such modifications, which are completely transparent to the designer, are necessary to reflect the fact that an orconn interaction expresses a choice among different attached AEIs whenever the interaction takes place.

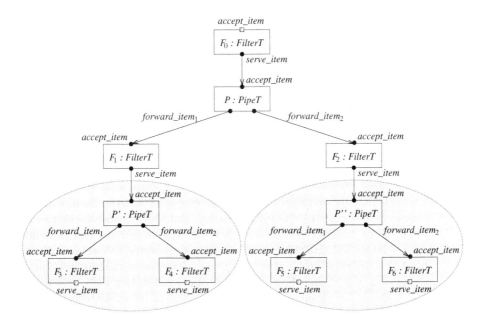

Fig. 4. Flow graph of an exogenous extension of *PipeFilter*

The second kind of topological extension is given by the exogenous one. As an example, consider the pipe-filter system of Table 2. Every instance of such an architectural type can admit a single pipe connected to one upstream filter and two downstream filters, whereas it would be desirable to be able to express by means of that architectural type any pipe-filter system with an arbitrary number of filters and pipes, such that every pipe is connected to one upstream filter and two downstream filters. E.g., the flow graph in Fig. 4 should be considered as a legal extension of the flow graph in Fig. 1. The idea behind the exogenous extensions is that, since the architectural interactions of an architectural type are the frontier of the whole architectural type, it is reasonable to extend the architectural type at some of its architectural interactions with instances of the already defined AETs, in a way that follows the prescribed topology.

The third kind of topological extension is given by the endogenous one. As an example, consider the Æmilia description of a ring of stations each following the same protocol: wait for a message from the previous station in the ring, process the received message, and send the processed message to the next station in the ring. Since such a protocol guarantees that only one station can transmit at a given instant, the protocol can be considered as an abstraction of the IEEE 802.5 standard medium access control protocol for local area networks known as token ring. One of the stations is designated to be the initial one, in the sense that it is

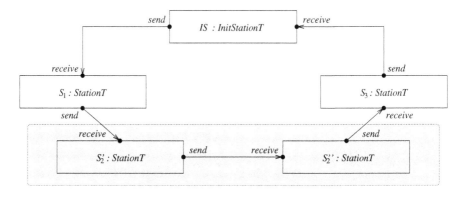

Fig. 5. Flow graph of an endogenous extension of *Ring*

the first station allowed to send a message. Suppose that the Æmilia description declares one instance of the initial station and three instances of the normal station. Every instance of the architectural type, say *Ring*, can thus admit a single initial station and three normal stations connected to form a ring, whereas it would be desirable to be able to express by means of that architectural type any ring system with an arbitrary number of normal stations. E.g., the flow graph in Fig. 5 should be considered as a legal extension of the architectural type *Ring*. The idea behind the endogenous extensions is that of replacing a set of AEIs with a set of new instances of the already defined AETs, in a way that follows the prescribed topology. In this case, we consider the frontier of the architectural type w.r.t. one of the replaced AEIs to be the set of interactions previously attached to the local interactions of the replaced AEI. On the other hand, all the replacing AEIs that will be attached to the frontier of the architectural type w.r.t. one of the replaced AEIs must be of the same type as the replaced AEI.

We conclude by referring the interested reader to [9,16,19,20] for a precise definition of the behavioral and topological conformity checks outlined in this section.

4   Conclusion

In this paper we have recalled the basic notions and the main achievements in the field of SPA and we have stressed its current transformation into a fully fledged ADL for the compositional, graphical, hierarchical and controlled modeling of complex systems as well as their functional verification and performance evaluation. Such a transformation eases the modeling process and provides an added value given by some architectural checks for detecting deadlock as well as performance underspecification, which scale over families of architectures.

Concerning future work in the area of SPA based ADLs, first of all we mention the importance of devising additional architectural checks on the performance side, that provide diagnostic information like in the case of the compatibility and interoperability checks. At the architectural level of design, it is extremely useful to be able to reinterpret the performance results in terms of components and their interactions. In order to achieve that, the performance must be calculated not on a flat model like a MC, but on a model that maintains some correspondence with the system structure, so that there is the possibility to localize bottlenecks. Some work in this direction can be found in [9], where Æmilia descriptions are translated into queueing network models.

Furthermore, SPA based ADLs should be viewed in the context of the whole software life cycle. A link should be established from higher level notations like UML, where requirements are expressed in a less formal way, as well as to object oriented programming languages, aiming at the automatic generation of code that possesses the functional and performance properties formally proved at the architectural level.

References

1. M. Ajmone Marsan, G. Balbo, G. Conte, S. Donatelli, G. Franceschinis, *"Modelling with Generalized Stochastic Petri Nets"*, John Wiley & Sons, 1995
2. A. Aldini, M. Bernardo, R. Gorrieri, *"An Algebraic Model for Evaluating the Performance of an ATM Switch with Explicit Rate Marking"*, in Proc. of the *7th Int. Workshop on Process Algebra and Performance Modelling (PAPM 1999)*, Prensas Universitarias de Zaragoza, pp. 119-138, Zaragoza (Spain), 1999
3. A. Aldini, M. Bernardo, R. Gorrieri, M. Roccetti, *"Comparing the QoS of Internet Audio Mechanisms via Formal Methods"*, in ACM Trans. on Modeling and Computer Simulation 11:1-42, 2001
4. R. Allen, D. Garlan, *"A Formal Basis for Architectural Connection"*, in ACM Trans. on Software Engineering and Methodology 6:213-249, 1997
5. J.C.M. Baeten, W.P. Weijland, *"Process Algebra"*, Cambridge University Press, 1990
6. C. Baier, B. Haverkort, H. Hermanns, J.-P. Katoen, *"On the Logical Characterisation of Performability Properties"*, in Proc. of the *27th Int. Coll. on Automata, Languages and Programming (ICALP 2000)*, LNCS 1853:780-792, Geneve (Switzerland), 2000
7. C. Baier, B. Haverkort, H. Hermanns, J.-P. Katoen, *"Model Checking Continuous-Time Markov Chains by Transient Analysis"*, in Proc. of the *12th Int. Conf. on Computer Aided Verification (CAV 2000)*, LNCS 1855:358-372, Chicago (IL), 2000
8. C. Baier, J.-P. Katoen, H. Hermanns, *"Approximate Symbolic Model Checking of Continuous Time Markov Chains"*, in Proc. of the *10th Int. Conf. on Concurrency Theory (CONCUR 1999)*, LNCS 1664:146-162, Eindhoven (The Netherlands), 1999
9. S. Balsamo, M. Bernardo, M. Simeoni, *"Combining Stochastic Process Algebras and Queueing Networks for Software Architecture Analysis"*, to appear in Proc. of the *3rd Int. Workshop on Software and Performance (WOSP 2002)*, Rome (Italy), 2002
10. M. Bernardo, *"Theory and Application of Extended Markovian Process Algebra"*, Ph.D. Thesis, University of Bologna (Italy), 1999
11. M. Bernardo, *"A Simulation Analysis of Dynamic Server Selection Algorithms for Replicated Web Services"*, in Proc. of the *9th Int. Symp. on Modeling, Analysis and Simulation of Computer and Telecommunication Systems (MASCOTS 2001)*, IEEE-CS Press, pp. 371-378, Cincinnati (OH), 2001

12. M. Bernardo, M. Bravetti, *"Reward Based Congruences: Can We Aggregate More?"*, in Proc. of the *1st Joint Int. Workshop on Process Algebra and Performance Modelling and Probabilistic Methods in Verification (PAPM/PROBMIV 2001)*, LNCS 2165:136-151, Aachen (Germany), 2001

13. M. Bernardo, M. Bravetti, *"Performance Measure Sensitive Congruences for Markovian Process Algebras"*, to appear in Theoretical Computer Science, 2002

14. M. Bernardo, N. Busi, M. Ribaudo, *"Integrating TwoTowers and GreatSPN through a Compact Net Semantics"*, to appear in Performance Evaluation, 2002

15. M. Bernardo, P. Ciancarini, L. Donatiello, *"ÆMPA: A Process Algebraic Description Language for the Performance Analysis of Software Architectures"*, in Proc. of the *2nd Int. Workshop on Software and Performance (WOSP 2000)*, ACM Press, pp. 1-11, Ottawa (Canada), 2000

16. M. Bernardo, P. Ciancarini, L. Donatiello, *"Architecting Software Systems with Process Algebras"*, Tech. Rep. UBLCS-2001-07, University of Bologna (Italy), 2001

17. M. Bernardo, W.R. Cleaveland, *"A Theory of Testing for Markovian Processes"*, in Proc. of the *11th Int. Conf. on Concurrency Theory (CONCUR 2000)*, LNCS 1877:305-319, State College (PA), 2000

18. M. Bernardo, W.R. Cleaveland, W.S. Stewart, *"TwoTowers 1.0 User Manual"*, `http://www.sti.uniurb.it/bernardo/twotowers/`, 2001

19. M. Bernardo, F. Franzè, *"Architectural Types Revisited: Extensible And/Or Connections"*, in Proc. of the *5th Int. Conf. on Fundamental Approaches to Software Engineering (FASE 2002)*, LNCS 2306:113-128, Grenoble (France), 2002

20. M. Bernardo, F. Franzè, *"Exogenous and Endogenous Extensions of Architectural Types"*, in Proc. of the *5th Int. Conf. on Coordination Models and Languages (COORDINATION 2002)*, LNCS 2315:40-55, York (UK), 2002

21. M. Bernardo, R. Gorrieri, M. Roccetti, *"Formal Performance Modelling and Evaluation of an Adaptive Mechanism for Packetised Audio over the Internet"*, in Formal Aspects of Computing 10:313-337, 1999

22. H. Bohnenkamp, *"Compositional Solution of Stochastic Process Algebra Models"*, Ph.D. Thesis, RWTH Aachen (Germany), 2001

23. H. Bowman, J.W. Bryans, J. Derrick, *"Analysis of a Multimedia Stream using Stochastic Process Algebra"*, in Proc. of the *6th Int. Workshop on Process Algebra and Performance Modelling (PAPM 1998)*, pp. 51-69, Nice (France), 1998

24. J.T. Bradley, *"Towards Reliable Modelling with Stochastic Process Algebras"*, Ph.D. Thesis, University of Bristol (UK), 1999

25. M. Bravetti, *"Specification and Analysis of Stochastic Real-Time Systems"*, Ph.D. Thesis, University of Bologna (Italy), 2002

26. M. Bravetti, M. Bernardo, *"Compositional Asymmetric Cooperations for Process Algebras with Probabilities, Priorities, and Time"*, in Proc. of the *1st Int. Workshop on Models for Time Critical Systems (MTCS 2000)*, Electronic Notes in Theoretical Computer Science 39(3), State College (PA), 2000

27. P. Buchholz, *"Markovian Process Algebra: Composition and Equivalence"*, in Proc. of the *2nd Int. Workshop on Process Algebra and Performance Modelling (PAPM 1994)*, pp. 11-30, Erlangen (Germany), 1994

28. W.R. Cleaveland, J. Parrow, B. Steffen, *"The Concurrency Workbench: A Semantics-Based Tool for the Verification of Concurrent Systems"*, in ACM Trans. on Programming Languages and Systems 15:36-72, 1993

29. G. Clark, *"Techniques for the Construction and Analysis of Algebraic Performance Models"*, Ph.D. Thesis, University of Edinburgh (UK), 2000

30. E.M. Clarke, O. Grumberg, D.A. Peled, *"Model Checking"*, MIT Press, 1999

31. P. D'Argenio, *"Algebras and Automata for Timed and Stochastic Systems"*, Ph.D. Thesis, University of Twente (The Netherlands), 1999
32. R. De Nicola, M.C.B. Hennessy, *"Testing Equivalences for Processes"*, in Theoretical Computer Science 34:83-133, 1983
33. D. Ferrari, *"Considerations on the Insularity of Performance Evaluation"*, in IEEE Trans. on Software Engineering 12:678-683, 1986
34. S. Gilmore, *"The PEPA Workbench User Manual"*, http://www.dcs.ed.ac.uk/pepa/tools.html, 2001
35. S. Gilmore, J. Hillston, D.R.W. Holton, M. Rettelbach, *"Specifications in Stochastic Process Algebra for a Robot Control Problem"*, in Journal of Production Research 34:1065-1080, 1996
36. R.J. van Glabbeek, S.A. Smolka, B. Steffen, *"Reactive, Generative and Stratified Models of Probabilistic Processes"*, in Information and Computation 121:59-80, 1995
37. R.J. van Glabbeek, F.W. Vaandrager, *"Petri Net Models for Algebraic Theories of Concurrency"*, in Proc. of the *Conf. on Parallel Architectures and Languages Europe (PARLE 1987)*, LNCS 259:224-242, Eindhoven (The Netherlands), 1987
38. N. Götz, *"Stochastische Prozeßalgebren – Integration von funktionalem Entwurf und Leistungsbewertung Verteilter Systeme"*, Ph.D. Thesis, University of Erlangen (Germany), 1994
39. P.G. Harrison, J. Hillston, *"Exploiting Quasi-Reversible Structures in Markovian Process Algebra Models"*, in Computer Journal 38:510-520, 1995
40. H. Hermanns, *"Interactive Markov Chains"*, Ph.D. Thesis, University of Erlangen (Germany), 1998
41. H. Hermanns, U. Herzog, J. Hillston, V. Mertsiotakis, M. Rettelbach, *"Stochastic Process Algebras: Integrating Qualitative and Quantitative Modelling"*, Tech. Rep. 11/94, University of Erlangen (Germany), 1994
42. H. Hermanns, U. Herzog, V. Mertsiotakis, *"Stochastic Process Algebras as a Tool for Performance and Dependability Modelling"*, in Proc. of the *1st IEEE Int. Computer Performance and Dependability Symp. (IPDS 1995)*, IEEE-CS Press, pp. 102-111, Erlangen (Germany), 1995
43. H. Hermanns, J.-P. Katoen, *"Automated Compositional Markov Chain Generation for a Plain-Old Telephone System"*, in Science of Computer Programming 36:97-127, 2000
44. H. Hermanns, J. Meyer-Kayser, M. Siegle, *"Multi Terminal Binary Decision Diagrams to Represent and Analyse Continuous Time Markov Chains"*, in Proc. of the *3rd Int. Workshop on the Numerical Solution of Markov Chains (NSMC 1999)*, Zaragoza (Spain), 1999
45. H. Hermanns, M. Rettelbach, *"Syntax, Semantics, Equivalences, and Axioms for MTIPP"*, in Proc. of the *2nd Int. Workshop on Process Algebra and Performance Modelling (PAPM 1994)*, pp. 71-87, Erlangen (Germany), 1994
46. U. Herzog, *"Formal Description, Time and Performance Analysis – A Framework"*, in *Entwurf und Betrieb verteilter Systeme*, Informatik Fachberichte 264, Springer, 1990
47. U. Herzog, *"EXL: Syntax, Semantics and Examples"*, Tech. Rep. 16/90, University of Erlangen (Germany), 1990
48. J. Hillston, *"A Compositional Approach to Performance Modelling"*, Cambridge University Press, 1996
49. J. Hillston, N. Thomas, *"Product Form Solution for a Class of PEPA Models"*, in Performance Evaluation 35:171-192, 1999

50. C.A.R. Hoare, *"Communicating Sequential Processes"*, Prentice Hall, 1985

51. D.R.W. Holton, *"A PEPA Specification of an Industrial Production Cell"*, in Computer Journal 38:542-551, 1995

52. R.A. Howard, *"Dynamic Probabilistic Systems"*, John Wiley & Sons, 1971

53. K. Kanani, *"A Unified Framework for Systematic Quantitative and Qualitative Analysis of Communicating Systems"*, Ph.D. Thesis, Imperial College (UK), 1998

54. J.-P. Katoen *"Quantitative and Qualitative Extensions of Event Structures"*, Ph.D. Thesis, University of Twente (The Netherlands), 1996

55. U. Klehmet, V. Mertsiotakis, *"TIPPtool – User's Guide"*, http://www7.informatik.uni-erlangen.de/tipp/tool.html, 1998

56. L. Kleinrock, *"Queueing Systems"*, John Wiley & Sons, 1975

57. K.G. Larsen, A. Skou, *"Bisimulation through Probabilistic Testing"*, in Information and Computation 94:1-28, 1991

58. S.S. Lavenberg editor, *"Computer Performance Modeling Handbook"*, Academic Press, 1983

59. V. Mertsiotakis, *"Approximate Analysis Methods for Stochastic Process Algebras"*, Ph.D. Thesis, University of Erlangen (Germany), 1998

60. R. Milner, *"Communication and Concurrency"*, Prentice Hall, 1989

61. D.E. Perry, A.L. Wolf, *"Foundations for the Study of Software Architecture"*, in ACM SIGSOFT Software Engineering Notes 17:40-52, 1992

62. M. Rettelbach, *"Stochastische Prozeßalgebren mit zeitlosen Aktivitäten und probabilistischen Verzweigungen"*, Ph.D. Thesis, University of Erlangen (Germany), 1996

63. M. Ribaudo, *"On the Relationship between Stochastic Process Algebras and Stochastic Petri Nets"*, Ph.D. Thesis, University of Torino (Italy), 1995

64. P. Schweitzer, *"Aggregation Methods for Large Markov Chains"*, in Mathematical Computer Performance and Reliability, North Holland, pp. 275-286, 1984

65. M. Sereno, *"Towards a Product Form Solution for Stochastic Process Algebras"*, in Computer Journal 38:622-632, 1995

66. M. Shaw, D. Garlan, *"Software Architecture: Perspectives on an Emerging Discipline"*, Prentice Hall, 1996

67. M. Siegle, *"Beschreibung und Analyse von Markovmodellen mit grossem Zustandsraum"*, Ph.D. Thesis, University of Erlangen (Germany), 1995

68. C.U. Smith, *"Performance Engineering of Software Systems"*, Addison-Wesley, 1990

69. W.J. Stewart, *"Introduction to the Numerical Solution of Markov Chains"*, Princeton University Press, 1994

70. B. Strulo, *"Process Algebra for Discrete Event Simulation"*, Ph.D. Thesis, Imperial College (UK), 1994

Automated Performance and Dependability Evaluation Using Model Checking

Christel Baier[1], Boudewijn Haverkort[2], Holger Hermanns[3]*, and
Joost-Pieter Katoen[3]

[1] Institut für Informatik I, University of Bonn
Römerstraße 164, D-53117 Bonn, Germany
[2] Dept. of Computer Science, RWTH Aachen
Ahornstraße 55, D-52056 Aachen, Germany
[3] Faculty of Computer Science, University of Twente
P.O. Box 217, 7500 AE Enschede, The Netherlands

Abstract. Markov chains (and their extensions with rewards) have been widely used to determine performance, dependability and performability characteristics of computer communication systems, such as throughput, delay, mean time to failure, or the probability to accumulate at least a certain amount of reward in a given time.

Due to the rapidly increasing size and complexity of systems, Markov chains and Markov reward models are difficult and cumbersome to specify by hand at the state-space level. Therefore, various specification formalisms, such as stochastic Petri nets and stochastic process algebras, have been developed to facilitate the specification of these models at a higher level of abstraction. Up till now, however, the specification of the measure-of-interest is often done in an informal and relatively unstructured way. Furthermore, some measures-of-interest can not be expressed conveniently at all.

In this tutorial paper, we present a logic-based specification technique to specify performance, dependability and performability measures-of-interest and show how for a given finite Markov chain (or Markov reward model) such measures can be evaluated in a fully automated way. Particular emphasis will be given to so-called path-based measures and hierarchically-specified measures. For this purpose, we extend so-called model checking techniques to reason about discrete- and continuous-time Markov chains and their rewards. We also report on the use of techniques such as (compositional) model reduction and measure-driven state-space generation to combat the infamous state space explosion problem.

1 Introduction

Over the last decades many techniques have been developed to specify and solve performance, dependability and performability models. In many cases, the models addressed possess a continuous-time Markov chain as their associated stochastic process. To avoid the specification of performance models directly at the state

---

* Corresponding author; `hermanns@cs.utwente.nl`, phone: +31 53 489-4661.

M.C. Calzarossa and S. Tucci (Eds.): Performance 2002, LNCS 2459, pp. 261–289, 2002.
© Springer-Verlag Berlin Heidelberg 2002

level, high-level specification methods have been developed, most notably those based on stochastic Petri nets, stochastic process algebras, and stochastic activity networks. With appropriate tools supporting these specification methods, such as, for instance, provided by TIPPtool [36], the PEPA workbench [23], GreatSPN [13], UltraSAN [56] or SPNP [14], it is relatively comfortable to specify performance models of which the associated CTMCs have millions of states. In combination with state-of-the-art numerical means to solve the resulting linear system of equations (for steady-state measures) or the linear system of differential equations (for time-dependent or transient measures) a good workbench is available to construct and solve dependability models of complex systems.

However, whereas the specification of performance and dependdability models has become very comfortable, the specification of the measures of interest most often has remained fairly cumbersome. In particular, most often only simple state-based measures can be defined with relative ease.

In contrast, in the area of formal methods for system verification, in particular in the area of model checking, very powerful logic-based methods have been developed to express properties of systems specified as finite state automata (note that we can view a CTMC as a special type of such an automaton). Not only are suitable means available to express state-based properties, a logic like CTL [16] (Computational Tree Logic; see below) also allows one to express properties over state sequences. Such capabilities would also be welcome in specifying performance and dependability measures.

To fulfil this aim, we have introduced the so-called *continuous stochastic logic* (CSL) that provides us ample means to specify state- as well as path-based performance measures for CTMCs in a compact and flexible way [1,2,3,4,5]. Moreover, due to the formal syntax and semantics of CSL, we can exploit the structure of CSL-specified measures in the subsequent evaluation process, such that typically the size of the underlying Markov chains that need to be evaluated can be reduced considerably.

To further strengthen the applicability of the stochastic model checking approach we recently considered Markov models involving costs or rewards, as they are often used in the performability context. We extended the logic CSL to the *continuous stochastic reward logic* CSRL in order to specify steady-state, transient and path-based measures over CTMCs extended with a reward structure (Markov reward models) [4]. We showed that well-known performability measures, most notably also the *performability distribution* introduced by Meyer [51, 52,53], can be specified using CSRL. However, CSRL allows for the specification of new measures that have not yet been addressed in the performability literature. For instance, when rewards are interpreted as costs, we can express the probability that, given a starting state, a certain goal state is reached within t time units, thereby deliberately avoiding or visiting certain immediate states, and with a total cost (accumulated reward) below a certain threshold.

We have introduced CSL and CSRL (including its complete syntax and formal semantics) in a much more theoretical context as we do in this tutorial paper (cf. [2,3,4,5,33]).

The rest of the paper is organised as follows. In Section 2 and Section 3 we present the two system evaluation techniques that will be merged in this paper: performance and dependability evaluation and formal verification by means of model checking. We then proceed with the specification of performance measures using CSL in Section 4, and of performability measures using CSRL in Section 5. Section 6 addresses lumpability to combat the state space explosion problem; Section 7 concludes the paper.

2   Performance Modelling with Markov Chains

2.1   Introduction

Performance and dependability evaluation aim at forecasting system behaviour in a quantitative way by trying to answer questions related to the performance and dependability of systems. Typical problems that are addressed are: how many clients can this file server adequately support, how large should the buffers in a router be to guarantee a packet loss of at most 10^{-6}, or how long does it take before 2 failures have occurred? Notice that we restrict ourselves to model-based performance and dependability evaluation, as opposed to measurement-based evaluation.

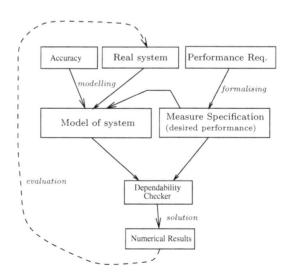

Fig. 1. The model-based performance evaluation cycle

The basic idea of model-based performance and dependability evaluation is to construct an abstract (and most often approximate) model of the system under consideration that is just detailed enough to evaluate the measures of interest (such as time-to-failure, system throughput, or number of failed components) with the required accuracy (mean values, variances or complete distributions). The generated model is "solved" using either analytical, numerical or simulation techniques. We focus on numerical techniques as they pair a good modelling flexibility with still reasonable computational requirements. Due to the ever increasing size and complexity of real systems, performance and dependability models that are directly amenable for a numerical solution, i.e., typically continuous-time Markov chains (CTMCs), are awkward to specify "by hand" and are therefore generated automatically from high-level description/modelling languages such as stochastic Petri nets, stochastic process algebras or queueing networks [30]. The steps in the process from a system to a useful dependability or performance evaluation are illustrated in the model-based performance and dependability evaluation cycle in Fig. 1.

It remains to be stated at this point that even though good support exists for the actual model description, the specification of the measures of interest is mostly done in an informal or less abstract way.

2.2 Discrete and Continuous-Time Markov Chains

This section recalls the basic concepts of discrete- and continuous-time Markov chains with finite state space. The presentation is focused on the concepts needed for the understanding of the rest of this paper; for a more elaborate treatment we refer to [21,43,47,48,59]. We slightly depart from the standard notations by representing a Markov chain as an ordinary finite transition system where the edges are equipped with probabilistic information, and where states are labelled with atomic propositions, taken from a set AP. Atomic propositions identify specific situations the system may be in, such as "acknowledgement pending", "buffer empty", or "variable X is positive".

Discrete-time Markov chains. A DTMC is a triple $\mathcal{M} = (S, \mathbf{P}, L)$ where S is a finite set of *states*, $\mathbf{P} : S \times S \to [0,1]$ is the *transition probability matrix*, and $L : S \to 2^{AP}$ is the *labelling function*. Intuitively, $\mathbf{P}(s, s')$ specifies that probability to move from state s to s' in a single step, and function L assigns to each state $s \in S$ the set $L(s)$ of atomic propositions $a \in AP$ that are valid in s. One may view a DTMC as a finite state automaton equipped with transition probabilities and in which time evolves in discrete steps.

Continuous-time Markov chains. A CTMC is a tuple $\mathcal{M} = (S, \mathbf{R}, L)$ where state space S and labelling function L are as for DTMCs, and $\mathbf{R} : S \times S \to \mathbb{R}_{\geq 0}$ is the *rate matrix*. Intuitively, $\mathbf{R}(s, s')$ specifies that the probability of moving from state s to s' within t time-units (for positive t) is $1 - e^{-\mathbf{R}(s,s') \cdot t}$. Alternatively, a CTMC can be viewed as a finite state automaton enhanced with transition labels specifying (in a certain way) the time it takes to proceed along them. It should be noted that this definition does not require $\mathbf{R}(s, s) = -\sum_{s' \neq s} \mathbf{R}(s, s')$, as is usual for CTMCs. In the traditional interpretation, at the end of a stay in state s, the system will move to a different state. In our setting, self-loops at state s are possible and are modelled by having $\mathbf{R}(s, s) > 0$. We thus allow the system to occupy the same state before and after taking a transition.

Let $\underline{E}(s) = \sum_{s' \in S} \mathbf{R}(s, s')$, the total rate at which any transition emanating from state s is taken.[1] More precisely, $\underline{E}(s)$ specifies that the probability of leaving s within t time-units (for positive t) is $1 - e^{-\underline{E}(s) \cdot t}$. The probability of eventually moving from state s to s', denoted $\mathbf{P}(s, s')$, is determined by the probability that the delay of going from s to s' finishes before the delays of other outgoing edges from s; formally, $\mathbf{P}(s, s') = \mathbf{R}(s, s')/\underline{E}(s)$ (except if s is an absorbing state, i.e. if $\underline{E}(s) = 0$; in this case we define $\mathbf{P}(s, s') = 0$). The matrix $\mathbf{P}$ describes an embedded DTMC of the CTMC.

Example 1. As a running example we address a *triple modular redundant system* (TMR) taken from [28], a fault-tolerant computer system consisting of three processors and a single (majority) voter. We model this system as a CTMC where state $s_{i,j}$ models that i ($0 \leqslant i < 4$) processors and j ($0 \leqslant j \leqslant 1$) voters are operational. As atomic propositions we use $AP = \{ up_i \mid 0 \leqslant i < 4 \} \cup \{ down \}$. The processors generate results and the voter decides upon the correct value by taking a majority vote. The failure rate of a single processor is λ and of the voter ν failures per hour (fph). The expected repair time of a processor is $1/\mu$ and of the voter $1/\delta$ hours. It is assumed that one component can be repaired at a time. The system is operational if at least two processors and the voter are functioning correctly. If the voter fails, the entire system is assumed to have failed, and after a repair (with rate δ) the system is assumed to start "as good as new". The details of the CTMC modelling this system are (with a clock-wise ordering of states for the matrix/vector-representation, starting with $s_{3,1}$):

$$\mathbf{R} = \begin{pmatrix} 0 & 3\lambda & 0 & 0 & \nu \\ \mu & 0 & 2\lambda & 0 & \nu \\ 0 & \mu & 0 & \lambda & \nu \\ 0 & 0 & \mu & 0 & \nu \\ \delta & 0 & 0 & 0 & 0 \end{pmatrix} \quad \text{and } \underline{E} = \begin{pmatrix} 3\lambda+\nu \\ 2\lambda+\mu+\nu \\ \lambda+\mu+\nu \\ \mu+\nu \\ \delta \end{pmatrix}$$

States are represented by circles and there is an edge between state s and state s' if and only if $\mathbf{R}(s, s') > 0$. The labelling is defined by $L(s_{i,1}) = \{ up_i \}$ for $0 \leqslant i < 4$ and $L(s_{0,0}) = \{ down \}$, and is indicated near the states (set braces are omitted for singletons). For the transition probabilities we have, for instance, $\mathbf{P}(s_{2,1}, s_{3,1}) = \mu/(2\lambda+\mu+\nu)$ and $\mathbf{P}(s_{0,1}, s_{0,0}) = \nu/(\mu+\nu)$.

State sequences. A *path* σ through a CTMC is a (finite or infinite) sequence of states where the time spent in any of the is recorded. For instance,

---

[1] Note that $\mathbf{R}$ and $\underline{E}$ just form an alternative representation of the usual infinitesimal generator matrix $\mathbf{Q}$; more precisely, $\mathbf{Q} = \mathbf{R} - diag(\underline{E})$. Note that this alternative representation does not affect the transient and steady-state behaviour of the CTMC, and is used for technical convenience only.

$\sigma = s_0, t_0, s_1, t_1, s_2, t_2, \ldots$ is an infinite path with for natural i, state $s_i \in S$ and time $t_i \in \mathbb{R}_{>0}$ such that $\mathbf{R}(s_i, s_{i+1}) > 0$. We let $\sigma[i] = s_i$ denote the $(i{+}1)$-st state along a path, $\delta(\sigma, i) = t_i$, the time spent in s_i, and $\sigma@t$ the state of σ at time t. (For finite paths these notions have to be slightly adapted so as to deal with the end state of a path.) Let $Path(s)$ be the set of paths starting in s. A Borel space (with probability measure Pr) can be defined over the set $Path(s)$ in a straightforward way; for details see [2].

Steady-state and transient measures. For CTMCs, two major types of state probabilities are normally considered: steady-state probabilities where the system is considered "in the long run", i.e., when an equilibrium has been reached, and transient probabilities where the system is considered at a given time instant t. Formally, the transient probability

$$\pi(s, s', t) \;=\; \Pr\{\sigma \in Path(s) \mid \sigma@t = s'\},$$

stands for the probability to be in state s' at time t given the initial state s. We denote with $\underline{\pi}(s, t)$ the vector of state probabilities (ranging over states s') at time t, when the starting state is s. The transient probabilities are then computed from a system of linear differential equations:

$$\underline{\pi}'(s, t) = \underline{\pi}(s, t) \cdot \mathbf{Q},$$

which can be solved by standard numerical methods or by specialised methods such as *uniformisation* [45,26,25]. With uniformisation, the transient probabilities of a CTMC are computed via a uniformised DTMC which characterises the CTMC at discrete state transition epochs. Steady-state probabilities are defined as

$$\pi(s, s') = \lim_{t \to \infty} \pi(s, s', t),$$

This limit always exists for finite CTMCs. In case the steady-state distribution does not depend on the starting state s we often simply write $\pi(s')$ instead of $\pi(s, s')$. For $S' \subseteq S$, $\pi(s, S') = \sum_{s' \in S'} \pi(s, s')$ denotes the steady-state probability for the set of states S'. In this case, steady-state probabilities are computed from a system of linear equations:

$$\underline{\pi}(s) \cdot \mathbf{Q} = \underline{0} \text{ with } \sum_{s'} \pi(s, s') = 1,$$

which can be solved by direct methods (such as Gaussian elimination) or iterative methods (such as SOR or Gauss-Seidel).

Notice that the above two types of measures are truly *state based*; they consider the probability for particular states. Although this is interesting as such, one can image that for many performance and dependability questions, there is an interest in the occurrence probability of certain state *sequences*. Stated differently, we would also like to be able to express measures that address the probability on particular paths through the CTMC. Except for the recent work by Obal and Sanders [54], we are not aware of suitable mechanisms to express such measures. In the sequel, we will specifically address this issue.

3   Formal Verification with Model Checking

Whereas performance and dependability evaluation focusses on answering questions concerning quantitative system issues, traditional formal verification techniques try to answer questions related to the *functional* correctness of systems. Thus, formal verification aims at forecasting system behaviour in a qualitative way. Typical problems that are addressed by formal verification are: (i) safety, e.g., does a given mutual exclusion algorithm guarantee mutual exclusion? (ii) liveness, e.g., does a routing protocol eventually transfer packets to the correct destination? and (iii) fairness, e.g., will a repetitive attempt to carry out a transaction be eventually granted?

Prominent formal verification techniques are theorem proving and model checking, as well as (but to a less formal extent) testing [17,50,55,8]. Important to note at this point is that for an ever-increasing class of systems, their "formal correctness" cannot be separated anymore from their "quantitative correctness", e.g., in real-time systems, multi-media communication protocols and many embedded systems.

3.1   Model Checking

The model checking approach requires a *model* of the system under consideration together with a desired *property* and systematically checks whether the given model satisfies this property. The basic technique of model checking is a systematic, usually exhaustive, state-space search to check whether the property is satisfied in each state of the system model, thereby using effective methods to combat the infamous state-space explosion problem.

Using model checking, the user specifies a model of the system (the "possible behaviour") and a specification of the requirements (the "desirable behaviour") and leaves the verification up to the model checker. If an error is found, the model checker provides a counter-example showing under which circumstance the error can be generated. The counter-example consists of an example scenario in which the model behaves in an undesired way, thus providing evidence that the system (or the model) is faulty and needs to be revised, cf. Fig. 2. This allows the user to locate the error and to repair the system (or model specification). If no errors are found, the user can refine the model description and continue the verification process, e.g., by taking more design decisions into account, so that the model becomes more concrete and realistic.

Typically, models of systems are finite-state automata, where transitions model the evolution of the system while moving from one state to another. These automata are usually generated from a high-level description language such as Petri nets, Promela [41] or Statecharts [27]. At this point, notice the similarities with the models used for performance and dependability evaluation.

Computational Tree Logic. Required system properties can be specified in an extension of propositional logic called *temporal logic*. Temporal logics allow the formulation of properties that refer to the dynamic behaviour of a system;

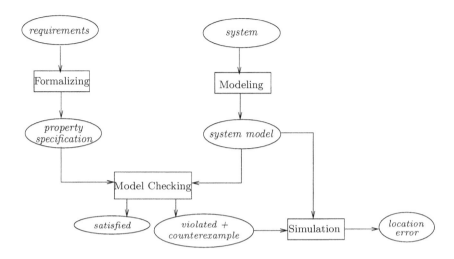

Fig. 2. The model checking approach

it allows to express for instance the temporal ordering of events. Note that the term "temporal" is meant in a qualitative sense, not in a quantitative sense. An important logic for which efficient model checking algorithms exist is CTL [16] (Computational Tree Logic). This logic allows to state properties over *states*, and over *paths* using the following syntax:

State-formulas

$$\Phi ::= a \ \Big| \ \neg\Phi \ \Big| \ \Phi \lor \Phi \ \Big| \ \exists\varphi \ \Big| \ \forall\varphi$$

a : atomic proposition
$\exists\varphi$: there *Exists* a path that fulfils φ
$\forall\varphi$: *All* paths fulfil φ

Path-formulas

$$\varphi ::= X\,\Phi \ \Big| \ \Phi\mathcal{U}\,\Phi$$

$X\,\Phi$: the *neXt* state fulfils Φ
$\Phi\mathcal{U}\Psi$: Φ holds along the path, *Until* Ψ holds
$\Diamond\Phi$: true $\mathcal{U}\,\Phi$, i.e., eventually Φ
$\Box\Phi$: $\neg\Diamond\neg\Phi$, i.e., invariantly Φ

The meaning of atomic propositions, negation ($\neg$) and disjunction ($\lor$) is standard; note that using these operators, other boolean operators such as conjunction ($\land$), implication ($\Rightarrow$), and so forth, can be defined. The state-formula $\exists\varphi$ is valid in state s if there *exists* some path starting in s and satisfying φ. The formula $\exists\Diamond deadlock$, for example, expresses that for some system run eventually a deadlock can be reached (potential deadlock). On the contrary, $\forall\varphi$ is valid if *all* paths satisfy φ; $\forall\Diamond deadlock$ thus means that a deadlock is inevitable. A path satisfies an until-formula $\Phi\mathcal{U}\Psi$ if the path has an initial finite prefix (possibly only containing state s) such that Φ holds at all states along the path until a state for which Ψ holds is encountered along the path.

Example 2. Considering the TMR system example as a finite-state automaton, some properties one can express with CTL are:

- $up_3 \Rightarrow \exists\Diamond down$:
  if the system is fully operational, it may eventually go down.
- $up_3 \Rightarrow \forall\mathsf{X}\,(up_2 \lor down)$:
  if the system is fully operational, any next step involves the failure of a component.
- $\exists\Box\neg\,down$:
  it is possible that the voter never fails.
- $\exists((up_3 \lor up_2)\,\mathcal{U}\,down)$:
  it is possible to have two or three processors continuously working until the voter fails.

Model checking CTL. A model, i.e., a finite-state automaton where states are labelled with atomic propositions, is said to satisfy a property if and only if all its initial states satisfy this property. In order to check whether a model satisfies a property Φ, the set $Sat(\Phi)$ of states that *satisfy* Φ is computed recursively, after which it is checked whether the initial states belong to this set. For atomic propositions this set is directly obtained from the above mentioned labelling of the states; $Sat(\Phi \land \Psi)$ is obtained by computing $Sat(\Phi)$ and $Sat(\Psi)$, and then intersecting these sets; $Sat(\neg\Phi)$ is obtained by taking the complement of the entire state space with respect to $Sat(\Phi)$. The algorithms for the temporal operators are slightly more involved. For instance, for $Sat(\exists\mathsf{X}\,\Phi)$ we first compute the set $Sat(\Phi)$ and then compute those states from which one can move to this set by a single transition. $Sat(\exists(\Phi\,\mathcal{U}\,\Psi))$ is computed in an iterative way: (i) as a precomputation we determine $Sat(\Phi)$ and $Sat(\Psi)$; (ii) we start the iteration with $Sat(\Psi)$ as these states will surely satisfy the property of interest; (iii) we extend this set by the states in $Sat(\Phi)$ from which one can move to the already computed set by a single transition; (iv) if no new states have been added in step (iii), we have found the required set, otherwise we repeat (iii). As the number of states is finite, this procedure is guaranteed to terminate. The worst case time complexity of this algorithm (after an appropriate treatment of the $\exists\Box$-operator [16]) is linear in the size of the formula and the number of transitions in the model.

Applications. Although the model checking algorithms are conceptually relatively simple, their combination with clever techniques to combat the state-space explosion problem (such as binary decision diagrams, bit-state hashing and partial-order reduction) make model checking a widely applicable and successful verification technique. This is illustrated by the success of model checkers such as SPIN, SMV, Uppaal and Murφ, and their successful application to a large set of industrial case studies ranging from hardware verification (VHDL, Intel P7 Processor), software control systems (traffic collision avoidance and alert system

TCAS-II, storm surge barrier), and communication protocols (ISDN-User Part and IEEE Futurebus+); see for an overview [18].

4   Stochastic Model Checking CTMCs

As has become clear from the previous section, the existing approaches for formal verification using model checking and performance and dependability evaluation have a lot in common. Our aim is to integrate these two evaluation approaches even more, thereby trying to combine the best of both worlds.

4.1   A Logic for Performance and Dependability

To specify and evaluate performance and dependability measures as logical formulas over CTMCs, we describe in this section CSL [1,2], a stochastic variant of CTL, and explain how model checking this logic can be performed, summarising work reported in [2,3,46].

Syntax. CSL extends CTL with two probabilistic operators that refer to the steady-state and transient behaviour of the system being studied. Whereas the steady-state operator refers to the probability of residing in a particular set of *states* (specified by a state-formula) in the long run, the transient operator allows us to refer to the probability of the occurrence of particular *paths* in the CTMC. In order to express the time-span of a certain path, the path-operators until $\mathcal{U}$ and next X are extended with a parameter that specifies a time-interval. Let I be an interval on the real line, p a probability and $\trianglelefteq$ a comparison operator, i.e., $\trianglelefteq \in \{\leqslant, \geqslant\}$. The syntax of CSL now becomes:

State-formulas
$$\Phi ::- a \ \Big| \ \neg\Phi \ \Big| \ \Phi \vee \Phi \ \Big| \ \mathcal{S}_{\trianglelefteq p}(\Phi) \ \Big| \ \mathcal{P}_{\trianglelefteq p}(\varphi)$$

$\mathcal{S}_{\trianglelefteq p}(\Phi)$: prob. that Φ holds in steady state $\trianglelefteq p$
$\mathcal{P}_{\trianglelefteq p}(\varphi)$: prob. that a path fulfils $\varphi \trianglelefteq p$

Path-formulas
$$\varphi ::= X^I\,\Phi \ \Big| \ \Phi\,\mathcal{U}^I\,\Phi$$

$X^I\,\Phi$: the next state is reached at time $t \in I$ and fulfils Φ
$\Phi\,\mathcal{U}^I\,\Psi$: Φ holds along the path until Ψ holds at time $t \in I$

The state-formula $\mathcal{S}_{\trianglelefteq p}(\Phi)$ asserts that the steady-state probability for the set of Φ-states meets the bound $\trianglelefteq p$. The operator $\mathcal{P}_{\trianglelefteq p}(.)$ replaces the usual CTL path quantifiers $\exists$ and $\forall$. In fact, for most cases $\exists\varphi$ can be written as $\mathcal{P}_{>0}(\varphi)$ and $\forall\varphi$ as $\mathcal{P}_{\geqslant 1}(\varphi)$. These rules are not generally applicable due to fairness considerations [6]. $\mathcal{P}_{\trianglelefteq p}(\varphi)$ asserts that the probability measure of the paths satisfying φ meets the bound $\trianglelefteq p$. Temporal operators like $\Diamond$, $\Box$ and their realtime variants $\Diamond^I$ or $\Box^I$ can be derived, e.g., $\mathcal{P}_{\trianglelefteq p}(\Diamond^I\,\Phi) = \mathcal{P}_{\trianglelefteq p}(\text{true }\mathcal{U}^I\,\Phi)$ and $\mathcal{P}_{\geqslant p}(\Box^I\,\Phi) = \mathcal{P}_{\leqslant 1-p}(\Diamond^I\,\neg\Phi)$. The untimed next- and until-operators are obtained by $X\Phi = X^I\Phi$ and $\Phi_1\,\mathcal{U}\,\Phi_2 = \Phi_1\,\mathcal{U}^I\,\Phi_2$ for $I = [0, \infty)$.

Semantics. State-formulas are interpreted over the states of a CTMC. Let $\mathcal{M} = (S, \mathbf{R}, L)$ with labels in AP. The meaning of CSL-formulas is defined by means of a so-called satisfaction relation (denoted by $\models$) between a CTMC $\mathcal{M}$, one of its states s, and a formula Φ. For simplicity the CTMC identifier $\mathcal{M}$ is often omitted as it is clear from the context. The pair (s, Φ) belongs to the relation $\models$, usually denoted by $s \models \Phi$, if and only if Φ is valid in s. For CSL state-formulas we have:

$$
\begin{aligned}
s &\models a & &\text{iff } a \in L(s), \\
s &\models \neg\Phi & &\text{iff } s \not\models \Phi, \\
s &\models \Phi_1 \vee \Phi_2 & &\text{iff } s \models \Phi_1 \vee s \models \Phi_2, \\
s &\models \mathcal{S}_{\trianglelefteq p}(\Phi) & &\text{iff } \pi(s, Sat(\Phi)) \trianglelefteq p, \\
s &\models \mathcal{P}_{\trianglelefteq p}(\varphi) & &\text{iff } Prob(s, \varphi) \trianglelefteq p,
\end{aligned}
$$

where $Prob(s, \varphi)$ denotes the probability of all paths $\sigma \in Path(s)$ satisfying φ when the system starts in state s, i.e.,

$$
Prob(s, \varphi) = \Pr\{\sigma \in Path(s) \mid \sigma \models \varphi\}.
$$

The satisfaction relation for the path-formulas is defined by a satisfaction relation (also denoted by $\models$) between paths and CSL path-formulas as follows. We have that $\sigma \models X^I \Phi$ iff

$$
\sigma[1] \text{ is defined and } \sigma[1] \models \Phi \wedge \delta(\sigma, 0) \in I,
$$

and that $\sigma \models \Phi_1 \mathcal{U}^I \Phi_2$ iff

$$
\exists t \in I. \, (\sigma@t \models \Phi_2 \wedge \forall u \in [0, t). \, \sigma@u \models \Phi_1).
$$

Note that the formula $\Phi_1 \mathcal{U}^\varnothing \Phi_2$ cannot be satisfied.

4.2 Expressing Measures in CSL

What types of performance and dependability measures can be expressed using CSL? As a first observation, we remark that by means of the logic one does not specify a measure but in fact a constraint (or: bound) on a performance or dependability measure. Four types of measures can be identified: steady-state measures, transient-state measures, path-based measures, and nested measures. Assume that for each state s, we have a characteristic atomic proposition $in(s)$ valid in state s and invalid in any other state.

Steady-state measures. The formula $\mathcal{S}_{\trianglelefteq p}(in(s))$ imposes a requirement on the steady-state probability to be in state s. For instance, $\mathcal{S}_{\leqslant 10^{-5}}(in(s_{2,1}))$ is valid in state $s_{0,0}$ (cf. the running example) if the steady-state probability of having a system configuration in which a single processor has failed is at most 0.00001 (when starting in state $s_{0,0}$). This can be easily generalized towards selecting sets of states by using more general state-formulas. The formula $\mathcal{S}_{\trianglelefteq p}(\Phi)$ imposes a constraint on the probability to be in some Φ-state on the long run. For instance, the formula $\mathcal{S}_{\geqslant 0.99}(up_3 \vee up_2)$ states that on the long run, for at least 99% of the time at least 2 processors are operational.

Transient measures. The combination of the probabilistic operator with the temporal operator $\Diamond^{[t,t]}$ can be used to reason about transient probabilities since

$$\pi(s, s', t) = Prob(s, \Diamond^{[t,t]} \; in(s')).$$

More specifically, $\mathcal{P}_{\trianglelefteq p}(\Diamond^{[t,t]} \; in(s'))$ is valid in state s if the transient probability at time t to be in state s' satisfies the bound $\trianglelefteq p$. For instance, $\mathcal{P}_{\leqslant .2}(\Diamond^{[t,t]} \; in(s_{2,1}))$ is valid in state $s_{0,0}$ if the transient probability of state $s_{2,1}$ at time t is at most 0.2 when starting in state $s_{0,0}$. In a similar way as done for steady-state measures, the formula $\mathcal{P}_{\geqslant 0.99}(\Diamond^{[t,t]} \; up_3 \vee up_2)$ requires that the probability to have 3 or 2 processors running at time t is at least 0.99. For specification convenience, a transient-state operator

$$\mathcal{T}_{\trianglelefteq p}^{@t}(\varPhi) = \mathcal{P}_{\trianglelefteq p}(\Diamond^{[t,t]} \; \varPhi)$$

could be defined. It states that the probability for a $\varPhi$-state at time t meets the bound $\trianglelefteq p$.

Path-based measures. The standard transient measures on (sets of) states are expressed using a specific instance of the $\mathcal{P}$-operator. However, by the fact that this operator allows an arbitrary path-formula as argument, much more general measures can be described. An example is the probability of reaching a certain set of states provided that all paths to these states obey certain properties. For instance,

$$\mathcal{P}_{\leqslant 0.01}((up_3 \vee up_2)\,\mathcal{U}^{[0,10]} \; down)$$

is valid for those states where the probability of the system going *down* within 10 time-units after having continuously operated with at least 2 processors is at most 0.01.

Nested measures. By nesting the $\mathcal{P}$- and $\mathcal{S}$-operators more complex measures of interest can be specified. These are useful to obtain a more detailed insight into the system's behaviour. We provide two examples. The property

$$\mathcal{S}_{\leqslant 0.9}(\mathcal{P}_{\geqslant 0.8}(\Box^{[0,10]}\neg down))$$

is valid in those states that guarantee that in equilibrium with probability at least 0.9 the probability that the system will not go down within 10 time units is at least 0.8. Conversely,

$$\mathcal{P}_{\geqslant 0.5}((\neg down)\,\mathcal{U}^{[10,20]} \; \mathcal{S}_{\geqslant 0.8}((up_3 \vee up_2)))$$

is valid for those states that with probability at least 0.5 will reach a state s between 10 and 20 time-units, which guarantees the system to be operational with at least 2 processors when the system is in equilibrium. Besides, prior to reaching state s the system must be operational continuously.

To put it in a nutshell, we believe that there are two main benefits by using CSL for specifying constraints on measures-of-interest. First, the specification is completely formal such that the interpretation is unambiguous. Whereas this is also the case for standard transient and steady-state measures, this often does not apply to measures that are derived from these elementary measures. Such measures are typically described in an informal manner. A rigorous specification of such more intricate measures is of utmost importance for their automated analysis (as proposed in the sequel). Furthermore, an important aspect of CSL is the possibility to state performance and dependability requirements over a selective set of paths through a model, which was not possible previously. Finally, the possibility to nest steady-state and transient measures provides a means to specify complex, though important measures in a compact and flexible way.

4.3   Model Checking CSL-Specified Measures

Once we have formally specified the (constraint on the) measure-of-interest in CSL by a formula Φ, and have obtained our model, i.e., CTMC $\mathcal{M}$, of the system under consideration, the next step is to adapt the model checking algorithm for CTL to support the automated validation of Φ over a given state s in $\mathcal{M}$. The basic procedure is as for model checking CTL: in order to check whether state s satisfies the formula Φ, we recursively compute the set $Sat(\Phi)$ of states that satisfy Φ, and check whether s is a member of that set. For the non-probabilistic state-operators this procedure is the same as for CTL. The main problem we have to face is how to compute $Sat(\Phi)$ for the $\mathcal{S}$ and $\mathcal{P}$-operators. We deal with these operators separately.

Steady-state measures. For an ergodic (strongly connected) CTMC:

$$s \in Sat(\mathcal{S}_{\trianglelefteq p}(\Phi)) \text{ iff } \sum_{s' \in Sat(\Phi)} \pi(s, s') \trianglelefteq p.$$

Thus, checking whether state s satisfies $\mathcal{S}_{\trianglelefteq p}(\Phi)$, a standard steady-state analysis has to be carried out, i.e., a system of linear equations has to be solved.

In case the CTMC $\mathcal{M}$ is not strongly-connected, the approach is to determine the so-called bottom strongly-connected components (BSCCs) of $\mathcal{M}$, i.e., the set of strongly-connected components that cannot be left once they are reached. Then, for each BSCC (which is an ergodic CTMC) the steady-state probability of a Φ-state (determined in the standard way) and the probability to reach any BSCC B from state s is determined. To check whether state s satisfies $\mathcal{S}_{\trianglelefteq p}(\Phi)$ it then suffices to verify

$$\sum_{B} \left(Prob(s, \Diamond B) \cdot \sum_{s' \in B \cap Sat(\Phi)} \pi^B(s') \right) \trianglelefteq p,$$

where $\pi^B(s')$ denotes the steady-state probability of s' in BSCC B, and $Prob(s, \Diamond B)$ is the probability to reach BSCC B from state s. To compute these probabilities, standard methods for steady-state and graph analysis can be used.

Path-based measures. In order to understand how the model checking of the path-based operators is carried out it turns out to be helpful to give (recursive) characterisations of $Prob(s, \varphi)$:

$$s \in Sat(\mathcal{P}_{\unlhd p}(\varphi)) \text{ iff } Prob(s, \varphi) \unlhd p.$$

- **Timed Next:** For the timed next-operator we obtain that $Prob(s, X^I \, \Phi)$ equals

$$\left(e^{-\underline{E}(s) \cdot \inf I} - e^{-\underline{E}(s) \cdot \sup I}\right) \cdot \sum_{s' \in Sat(\Phi)} \mathbf{P}(s, s'), \tag{1}$$

  i.e., the probability to leave state s in the interval I times the probability to reach a Φ-state in one step. Thus, in order to compute the set $Sat(X^I \, \Phi)$ we first recursively compute $Sat(\Phi)$ and add state s to $Sat(X^I \, \Phi)$ if it fulfils (1); this check boils down to a matrix-vector multiplication.
- **Time-Bounded Until:** For the sake of simplicity, we only treat the case $I = [0, t]$; the general case is a bit more involved, but can be treated in a similar way [3]. The probability $Prob(s, \Phi \, \mathcal{U}^{[0,t]} \, \Psi)$ is the least solution of the following set of equations: (i) 1, if $s \in Sat(\Psi)$, (ii) 0, if $s \notin Sat(\Phi) \cup Sat(\Psi)$, and

$$\int_0^t \sum_{s' \in S} \mathbf{R}(s, s') \cdot e^{-\underline{E}(s) \cdot x} \cdot Prob(s', \Phi \, \mathcal{U}^{[0,t-x]} \, \Psi) \, dx \tag{2}$$

  otherwise. The first two cases are self-explanatory; the last equation is explained as follows. If s satisfies Φ but not Ψ, the probability of reaching a Ψ-state from s within t time-units equals the probability of reaching some direct successor state s' of s within x time-units ($x \leqslant t$), multiplied by the probability to reach a Ψ-state from s' in the remaining time-span $t-x$.
  It is easy to check that for the untimed until-operator (i.e., $I = [0, \infty)$) equation (2) reduces to

$$\sum_{s' \in S} \mathbf{P}(s, s') \cdot Prob(s', \Phi \, \mathcal{U} \, \Psi).$$

Thus, for the standard until-operator, we can check whether a state satisfies $\mathcal{P}_{\unlhd p}(\Phi \, \mathcal{U} \, \Psi)$ by first computing recursively the sets $Sat(\Phi)$ and $Sat(\Psi)$ followed by solving a linear system of equations.

Solution for time-bounded until. We now concentrate on numerical techniques for solving the so-called Volterra integral equation system (2) arising in the time-bounded until case.

As a first approach, numerical integration techniques can be applied. Experiments with integration techniques based on equally-sized abscissas have shown that the computation time for solving (2) is rapidly increasing when the state space becomes larger (above 10,000 states), or when the required accuracy becomes higher, e.g., between 10^{-6} and 10^{-9}. Numerical stability is another issue of concern when using this method [37].

An alternative method is to reduce the problem of computing $Prob(s, \Phi\,\mathcal{U}^{[0,t]}\,\Psi)$ to a transient analysis problem for which well-known and efficient computation techniques do exist. This idea is based on the earlier observation that for a specific instance of the time-bounded until-operator we know that it characterises a standard transient probability measure:

$$\mathcal{T}^{@t}_{\trianglelefteq p}(\Phi) = \mathcal{P}_{\trianglelefteq p}(\text{true}\,\mathcal{U}^{[t,t]}\,\Phi)$$

Thus, for computing $Prob(s, \text{true}\,\mathcal{U}^{[t,t]}\,\Phi)$ standard transient analysis techniques can be exploited. This raises the question whether we might be able to reduce the general case, i.e., $Prob(s, \Phi\,\mathcal{U}^{[0,t]}\,\Psi)$, to an instance of transient analysis as well. This is indeed possible: the idea is to transform the CTMC $\mathcal{M}$ under consideration into another CTMC $\mathcal{M}'$ such that checking $\varphi = \Phi\,\mathcal{U}^{[0,t]}\,\Psi$ on $\mathcal{M}$ amounts to checking $\varphi' = \text{true}\,\mathcal{U}^{[t,t]}\,\Psi$ on $\mathcal{M}'$; a transient analysis of $\mathcal{M}'$ (for time t) then suffices. The question then is, how do we transform $\mathcal{M}$ in $\mathcal{M}'$? Two simple observations form the basis for this transformation. First, we observe that once a Ψ-state in $\mathcal{M}$ has been reached (along a Φ-path) before time t, we may conclude that φ holds, regardless of which states will be visited after having reached Ψ. Thus, as a first transformation we make all Ψ-states absorbing. Secondly, we observe that φ is violated once a state has been reached that neither satisfies Φ nor Ψ. Again, this is regardless of the states that are visited after having reached $\neg(\Phi \wedge \Psi)$. Thus, as a second transformation, all the $\neg(\Phi \wedge \Psi)$-states are made absorbing. It then suffices to carry out a transient analysis on the resulting CTMC $\mathcal{M}'$ for time t and collect the probability mass to be in a Ψ-state (note that $\mathcal{M}'$ typically is smaller than $\mathcal{M}$):

$$Prob^{\mathcal{M}}(s, \Phi\,\mathcal{U}^{[0,t]}\,\Psi) = Prob^{\mathcal{M}'}(s, \text{true}\,\mathcal{U}^{[t,t]}\,\Psi).$$

In fact, by similar observations it turns out that also verifying the general $\mathcal{U}^I$-operator can be reduced to instances of (nested) transient analysis [3]. As mentioned above, the transient probability distribution can be computed via a *uniformised* DTMC which characterises the CTMC at discrete state transition epochs. A direct application of uniformisation to compute $Prob^{\mathcal{M}}(s, \Phi\,\mathcal{U}^{[0,t]}\,\Psi)$ requires to perform this procedure for each state s. An improvement suggested in [46] cumulates the entire vector $\underline{Prob}^{\mathcal{M}}(\Phi\,\mathcal{U}^I\,\Psi)$ for all states simultaneously.

For a single operator $\mathcal{U}^I$ this yields a time complexity of $\mathcal{O}(|\mathbf{R}| \cdot N_\varepsilon)$, where $|\mathbf{R}|$ is the number of non-zero entries in $\mathbf{R}$, and N_ε is the number of iterations within the uniformisation algorithm needed to achieve a given accuracy ε. The value N_ε can be computed a priori, it linearly depends on the maximal diagonal entry of the generator matrix $\underline{E}_{\max}$, and on the maximal time bound $t_{\max}$ occuring in Φ.

In total, the time complexity to decide the validity of a CSL fomula Φ on a CTMC $(S, \mathbf{R}, L)$ is $\mathcal{O}(|\Phi| \cdot (|\mathbf{R}| \cdot \underline{E}_{\max} \cdot t_{\max} + |S|^{2.81}))$, and the space complexity is $\mathcal{O}(|\mathbf{R}|)$ [5].

5   Stochastic Model Checking Markov Reward Models

5.1   Introduction

With the advent of fault-tolerant gracefully-degradable computer systems, the separation between performance and dependability aspects of a system does not make sense anymore. Indeed, fault-tolerant systems can operate "correctly" at various levels of performance, and the dependability of a system might be expressed in terms of providing a minimum performance level, rather then in terms of a certain amount of operational hardware resources. These considerations lead, in the late 1970'a and the early 1980's, to the concept of performability [51,52], in which it is investigated how well a system performs over a finite time horizon, provided (partial) system failures and repair actions are taken into account. As it turned out later, the notion of performability also fits quite naturally to the notion of quality of service as specified in ITU-T Recommendation G.106 [12]. Furthermore, as natural model for performability evaluations, so-called Markov reward models have been adopted, as will be explained below; for further details on performability evaluation, see [29].

Markov reward models. An MRM is a CTMC augmented with a *reward structure* assigning a real-valued reward to each state in the model. Such reward can be interpreted as bonus, gain, or conversely, as cost. Typical measures of interest express the amount of gain accumulated by the system, over a finite or infinite time-horizon. Formally, an MRM is a tuple $\mathcal{M} = (S, \mathbf{R}, L, \rho)$ where $(S, \mathbf{R}, L)$ is a CTMC, and $\rho : S \to \mathbb{R}_{\geqslant 0}$ is a *reward structure* that assigns to each state s a reward $\rho(s)$, also called gain or bonus, or dually, cost.

Example 3. For the TMR example, the reward structure can be instantiated in different ways so as to specify a variety of performability measures. The simplest reward structure (leading to an availability model) divides the states into operational and non-operational ones: $\rho_1(s_{0,0}) = 0$ and $\rho_1(s_{i,0}) = 1$ for the remaining states. A reward structure in which varying levels of trustworthiness are represented is for instance based on the number of operational processors: $\rho_2(s_{0,0}) = 0$ and $\rho_2(s_{i,1}) = i$. As a third reward structure, one may consider the maintenance costs of the system, by setting: $\rho_3(s_{0,0}) = c_2$ and $\rho_3(s_{i,1}) = c_1 \cdot (3 - i)$, where c_1 is the cost to replace a processor, and c_2 the cost to renew the entire system. As a fourth option (which we do not further consider here) one can also imagine a reward structure quantifying the power consumption in each state.

Accumulating reward along a path. The presence of a reward structure allows one to reason about (at least) two different aspects of system cost/reward. One either may refer to the instantaneous reward at a certain point in time (even in steady-state), or one may refer to the reward accumulated in a certain interval of time. For an MRM $(S, \mathbf{R}, L, \rho)$, and $\sigma = s_0, t_0, s_1, t_1, s_2, t_2, \ldots$ an infinite path (through the corresponding CTMC $(S, \mathbf{R}, L)$) the instantaneuos reward at time t is given by $\rho(\sigma@t)$. The cumulated reward $y(\sigma, t)$ along σ up to time t can be formalised as follows. For $t = \sum_{j=0}^{k-1} t_j + t'$ with $t' \leqslant t_k$ we define $y(\sigma, t) = \sum_{j=0}^{k-1} t_j \cdot \rho(s_j) + t' \cdot \rho(s_k)$. For finite paths ending at time point t the cumulated reward definition is slightly adapted, basically replacing t' by $t - \sum_{j=0}^{l-1} t_j$.

Measure specification. The specification of the measure-of-interest for a given MRM can not always be done conveniently, nor can all possible measures-of-interest be expressed conveniently. In particular, until recently it has not been possible to directly express measures where state *sequences* or paths matter, nor to accumulate rewards only in certain subsets of states, if the rewards outside these subsets are non-zero. Such measures are then either "specified" informally, with all its negative implications, or require a manual tailoring of the model so as to address the right subsets of states. Below we will address a rigorous but flexible way of expressing performability measures.

Finally, note that Obal and Sanders recently proposed a technique to specify so-called path-based reward variables [54] by which the specification of measures over state sequences becomes more convenient, because it avoids the manual tailoring of the model. In the context of the stochastic process algebra PEPA, Clark *et al.* recently proposed the use of a probabilistic modal logic to ease the specification of reward *structures* of MRM [15], as opposed to the specification of reward-based *measures*, as we do.

5.2 A Logic for Performability

The addition of rewards on the model level raises the question how they can be reflected on the measure specification level, i.e., on the level of the logic. We restrict ourselves for the moment to consider the accumulation of reward, because this turns out to be a conceptually interesting extension that fits very well to the temporal logic approach. We shall later (in Section 5.6) return to the question how to support other forms of reward quantification, such as instantaneuos reward.

Since rewards are accumulated along a path, it appears wise to extend the *path* formulas of CSL to account for the earning of reward, and this is what distinguishes CSRL from CSL. The state formulas of CSRL are unchanged relative to CSL (until Section 5.6), whereas path formulas φ now become

$$\varphi ::= X_J^I \Phi \mid \Phi \mathcal{U}_J^I \Phi,$$

for intervals $I, J \subseteq \mathbb{R}_{\geqslant 0}$. In a similar way as before, we define $\Diamond_J^I \Phi = \text{true } \mathcal{U}_J^I \Phi$ and $\mathcal{P}_{\trianglelefteq p}(\Box_J^I \Phi) = \neg \mathcal{P}_{\trianglelefteq p}(\Diamond_J^I \neg \Phi)$. Interval I can be considered as a timing constraint whereas J represents a bound for the cumulative reward. The path-formula $X_J^I \Phi$ asserts that a transition is made to a Φ-state at time point $t \in I$ such that the earned cumulative reward r until time t meets the bounds specified by J, i.e., $r \in J$. The semantics of $\Phi_1 \mathcal{U}_J^I \Phi_2$ is as for $\Phi_1 \mathcal{U}^I \Phi_2$ with the additional constraints that earned cumulative reward r at the time of reaching some Φ_2-state lies in J, i.e., $r \in J$.

Example 4. As an example property for the TMR system, $\mathcal{P}_{\geqslant 0.95}(\Diamond_{[0,200]}^{[60,60]}\mathsf{true})$ denotes that with probability of at least 0.95 the cumulative reward, e.g., the incurred costs of the system for reward structure ρ_3, at time instant 60 is at most 200. Given that the reward of a state indicates the power consumed per time-unit, property $\mathcal{P}_{<0.08}(up_3\,\mathcal{U}_{[7,\infty)}^{[0,30]}\,(down \vee up_2))$ expresses that with probability less than 0.08 within 30 time units at least 7 units of power have been consumed in full operational mode before some component fails. A simpler property, that only refers to reward accumulation, $\mathcal{P}_{>0.5}(\Diamond_{[0,10]}^{[0,\infty)}down)$ would say that it is likely (probability > 0.5) to spend less than 10 units of energy before a voter failure.

The semantics of the CSRL path-formulas is an extension of the CSL semantics we introduced in Section 4.1. It differs from the latter in that additional constraints are imposed reflecting that the accumulated reward on the path must be in the required interval. We have that $\sigma \models X_J^I\,\varPhi$ iff

$$\sigma[1] \text{ is defined and } \sigma[1] \models \varPhi \wedge \delta(\sigma,0) \in I \ \wedge \ y(\sigma,\delta(\sigma,0)) \in J$$

and that $\sigma \models \varPhi_1\,\mathcal{U}_J^I\,\varPhi_2$ iff

$$\exists t \in I.\,(\sigma@t \models \varPhi_2 \ \wedge \ (\forall u \in [0,t).\,\sigma@u \models \varPhi_1) \ \wedge \ y(\sigma,t) \in J).$$

For the X_J^I case, the definition refines the one for CSL by demanding that the reward accumulated during the time $\delta(\sigma,0)$ of staying in the first state of the path lies in J, while for $\mathcal{U}_J^I$ the reward accumulated until the time t when touching a $\varPhi_2$-state must be in J.

5.3   Expressing Measures in CSRL

MRMs are an extension of CTMCs, and so is CSRL an extension of CSL. Since CSL does not allow any reference to rewards, it is obtained by putting no constraint on the reward accumulated, i.e., by setting $J = [0,\infty)$ for all sub-formulas:

$$X^I\,\varPhi \ = \ X_{[0,\infty)}^I\,\varPhi \qquad \text{and} \qquad \varPhi_1\,\mathcal{U}^I\,\varPhi_2 \ = \ \varPhi_1\,\mathcal{U}_{[0,\infty)}^I\,\varPhi_2.$$

Similarly, we can identify a new logic CRL (continuous reward logic) in case $I = [0,\infty)$ for all sub-formulas. In CRL it is only possible to refer to the cumulation of rewards, but not to the advance of time. The formula $\mathcal{P}_{>0.5}(\Diamond_{[0,10]}^{[0,\infty)}down)$ is an example property of the CRL subset of CSRL. The CRL logic will play a special role when describing the model checking of CSRL, and therefore we will first discuss how model checking CRL can be performed, before turning our attention to CSRL. Before doing so, we list in Table 1 a variety of standard performance, dependability, and performability measures and how they can be phrased in CSRL. Here F is a generic formula playing the role of an identifier of the failed system states of the model under study (in the TMR example, F would be $down \vee up_0$). These measures correspond to basic formulas in the logic,

Table 1. Some typical performability measures

performability measure	formula	logic
steady-state availability	$\mathcal{S}_{\trianglelefteq p}(\neg F)$	**CSL**
instantaneous availability at time t	$\mathcal{P}_{\trianglelefteq p}(\Diamond^{[t,t]}\neg F)$	**CSL**
distribution of time to failure	$\mathcal{P}_{\trianglelefteq p}(\neg F \mathcal{U}^{[0,t]} F)$	**CSL**
distribution of reward until failure	$\mathcal{P}_{\trianglelefteq p}(\neg F \mathcal{U}_{[0,r]} F)$	**CRL**
distribution of cumulative reward until t	$\mathcal{P}_{\trianglelefteq p}(\Diamond^{[t,t]}_{[0,r]} \text{true})$	**CSRL**

and it is worth to highlight that much more involved and nested measures are easily expressible in CSRL, such as

$$\mathcal{S}_{>0.3}\left(\mathcal{P}_{<0.3}(\Diamond^{[0,85]}_{[3,5]} up_2) \Rightarrow \mathcal{P}_{>0.1}((\neg down)\,\mathcal{U}^{[5,\infty)} up_3)\right).$$

5.4 Model Checking CRL-Specified Measures

This section discusses how model checking can be performed for CRL properties, i.e., formulas which do only refer to the cumulation of rewards, but not to the advance of time. We will explain how a duality result can be used to reduce model checking of such formulas to the CSL model checking algorithm described above.

The basic strategy is the same as for CSL, and only the path operators X_J, $\mathcal{U}_J$ need specific considerations. To calculate the probability of satisfiying such a path formula we rely on a general duality result for MRMs and CSRL [4].

Duality. Assume an MRM $\mathcal{M} = (S, \mathbf{R}, L, \rho)$ with positive reward structure, i.e., $\rho(s) > 0$ for each state s. The basic idea behind the duality phenomenon is that the progress of time can be regarded as the earning of reward and vice versa. This observation is inspired by [7]. To make it concrete, we define an MRM $\mathcal{M}^{-1} = (S, \mathbf{R}', L, \rho')$ that results from $\mathcal{M}$ by

- rescaling the transition rates by the reward of their originating state, i.e., $\mathbf{R}'(s, s') = \mathbf{R}(s, s')/\rho(s)$ and,
- inverting the reward structure, i.e., $\rho'(s) = 1/\rho(s)$.

Intuitively, the transformation of $\mathcal{M}$ into $\mathcal{M}^{-1}$ stretches the residence time in state s with a factor that is proportional to the reciprocal of its reward $\rho(s)$ if $\rho(s) > 1$, and it compresses the residence time by the same factor if $0 < \rho(s) < 1$. The reward structure is changed similarly. Note that $\mathcal{M} = (\mathcal{M}^{-1})^{-1}$.

One might interpret the residence of t time units in $\mathcal{M}^{-1}$ as the earning of t reward in state s in $\mathcal{M}$, or (reversely) an earning of a reward r in state s in $\mathcal{M}$ corresponds to a residence of r in $\mathcal{M}^{-1}$. As a consequence, the rôles of time and reward in $\mathcal{M}$ are reversed in $\mathcal{M}^{-1}$. In terms of the logic CSRL, this corresponds to swapping reward and time intervals inside a CSRL formula, and allows one to establish that

$$Prob^{\mathcal{M}}(s, X^I_J \Phi) = Prob^{\mathcal{M}^{-1}}(s, X^J_I \Phi), \text{ and}$$

$$Prob^{\mathcal{M}}(s, \Phi_1 \mathcal{U}^I_J \Phi_2) = Prob^{\mathcal{M}^{-1}}(s, \Phi_1 \mathcal{U}^J_I \Phi_2).$$

As a consequence, one can obtain the set $Sat^{\mathcal{M}}(\Phi)$ (comprising the states in $\mathcal{M}$ satisfying Φ) by computing instead $Sat^{\mathcal{M}^{-1}}(\Phi^{-1})$, i.e.,

$$Sat^{\mathcal{M}}(\Phi) \;=\; Sat^{\mathcal{M}^{-1}}(\Phi^{-1}),$$

where Φ^{-1} is defined as Φ where for each sub-formula in Φ of the form X^I_J or $\mathcal{U}^I_J$ the intervals I and J are swapped. For the TMR example, for $\Phi = \mathcal{P}_{\geqslant 0.9}(\neg F \mathcal{U}^{[50,50]}_{[10,\infty)} F)$ we have $\Phi^{-1} = \mathcal{P}_{\geqslant 0.9}(\neg F \mathcal{U}^{[10,\infty)}_{[50,50]} F)$. We refer to [4] for a proof of this property, and to extensions of this result to some cases with zero rewards. Note that we excluded zero rewards here, since otherwise the model inversion would imply divisions by zero.

The duality result is the key to model check CRL on MRMs (satisfying the above restriction), since the swapping of formula implies that X_J turns into X^J, and $\mathcal{U}_J$ into $\mathcal{U}^J$. Hence, any CRL formula corresponds to a CSL formula interpreted on the dual MRM. As a consequence, model checking CRL can proceed via the algorithm for CSL, with some overhead (linear in the model size plus the formula length) needed to swap the model and swap the formula.

5.5   Model Checking CSRL-Specified Measures

For the general case of CSRL, model checking algorithms are more involved, and research on their effectiveness is ongoing [32,33]. In this section we describe the basic strategy and sketch three algorithms implementing this strategy. A more detailed comparison of the algorithmic intricacies can be found in [33].

Given an MRM $\mathcal{M} = (S, \mathbf{R}, L, \rho)$ the model checking algorithm proceeds as in the earlier considered cases: in order to check whether state s satisfies the formula Φ, we recursively compute the set $Sat(\Phi)$ of states that satisfy Φ, and check whether s is a member of that set. Most of the cases have been discussed before in this paper, except for the handling of path operators with both time and reward intervals. For the sake of simplicity, we do not consider the next operator X, and we (again) restrict to formulas where all occurring intervals are of the form $[0, x]$, i.e., they impose upper bounds on the time or the cumulated reward, but no lower bound.

So, the question is how to compute $Prob(s, \Phi \mathcal{U}^{[0,t]}_{[0,r]} \Psi)$. Recall that in the CSL case, the crucial step has been to reduce the computation to instances of transient analysis. Indeed, it is possible to proceed in a similar way. In analogy to the CSL strategy, we can show that the above probability agrees with the probability $Prob(s, \mathsf{true}\,\mathcal{U}^{[t,t]}_{[0,r]} \Psi)$ on a transformed MRM where all Ψ-states and

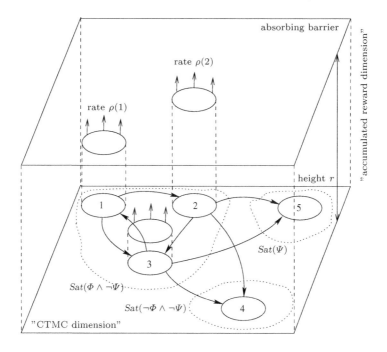

Fig. 3. Two-dimensional stochastic process $((X_t, Y_t), t \geq 0)$ for model checking $Prob(s, \Phi\, \mathcal{U}^{[0,t]}_{[0,r]}\, \Psi)$.

all $\neg\,(\Phi \wedge \Psi)$-states are made absorbing, and have reward 0 assigned to them. The intuitive justification is as in the CSL setting. The rewards are set to 0 since once a path reaches a Ψ-state at time $t' < t$, while not having accumulated more than r reward, it suffices to be trapped in that state until time t provided no reward will be earned anymore, i.e., $\rho(s) = 0$ for Ψ-state s. Note that we can amalgamate all states satisfying Ψ and all states satisfying $\neg\,(\Phi \wedge \Psi)$, thereby making the MRM considerably smaller.

Thus, we can restrict our attention to the computation of $Prob(s, \text{true}\, \mathcal{U}^{[t,t]}_{[0,r]}\, \Psi)$. This probability, in turn, can be derived from the *transient accumulated reward distribution* of the MRM. (Compare this to the *transient distribution* used in the CSL case at this point.) To explain why this is the case, we consider a two-dimensional stochastic process $((X_t, Y_t), t \geq 0)$ on $S \times \mathbb{R}_{\geq 0}$, as illustrated in Figure 3. Informally speaking, this stochastic process has a discrete component that describes the transition behaviour in the original MRM, combined with a continuous component that describes the accumulated reward gained over time. For $t = 0$ we have $Y_t = 0$, and for $t > 0$ the value of Y_t increases continuously with rate $\rho(X_t)$. Hence, the discrete states of the original CTMC become "columns" of which the height models the accumulated reward. To take into account the reward bound ($\leq r$), we introduce an absorbing barrier in the process whenever Y_t reaches the level r. Actually, we are interested in $\Pr\{Y_t \leqslant r, X_t \in S'\}$, i.e., the probability of being in a certain subset S' of states at time t, having accumulated a reward smaller than r. For our purposes, S' shall be chosen to be the set $Sat(\Psi)$ of states satisfying Ψ and we start the process in state s under consideration. We have that

$$Prob(s, \text{true } \mathcal{U}_{[0,r]}^{[t,t]} \Psi) = \Pr\{Y_t \leqslant r, X_t \in Sat(\Psi)\}$$

for the transformed MRM described above. This allows us to decide the satisfaction of time- and reward-bounded until formulas via numerical recipes for calculating $\Pr\{Y_t \leqslant r, X_t \in S'\}$ on the two dimensional stochastic process (X_t, Y_t). It is worth to remark that similar processes (with mixed discrete-continuous state spaces) also emerge in the analysis of non-Markovian stochastic Petri nets (when using the supplementary variable approach, cf. [22]), Markov-regenerative stochastic Petri nets [9], and in fluid-stochastic Petri nets [42]. We briefly sketch three other approaches to compute $\Pr\{Y_t \leqslant r, X_t \in S'\}$ here, which are more directly applicable to the problem.

An Erlangian approximation. A first approach to compute $\Pr\{Y_t \leqslant r, X_t \in S'\}$ is to approximate the fixed reward bound r by a reward bound that is Erlang-k distributed with mean r. One may view this as some kind of discretisation of the continuous reward dimension into k steps. The main advantage of this approach is that the resulting model is both discrete-space and completely Markovian, and hence the techniques developed for CSL properties (cf. Section 4.3) can be used to approximate the required probabilities; reaching the reward bound in the original model corresponds to reaching a particular set of states in the approximated model. As a disadvantage we mention that an appropriate value for k (the number of phases in the Erlangian approximation) is not known *a priori*. Furthermore, when CSRL expressions are nested, it is yet unclear how the error in the approximation propagates. Furthermore, the resulting Markov chain becomes substantially larger, especially if k is large. On the other hand, the MRM can be described as a tensor product of two smaller MRMs, which can be exploited in the solution procedure (as far as the storage of the generator matrix is concerned).

With an Erlang-k distributed approximation of the reward bound together with uniformisation, the space complexity of this method is $\mathcal{O}(|S|^2 \cdot k^2)$, and the time complexity is $\mathcal{O}(N_\varepsilon \cdot |S|^2 \cdot k^2)$, where N_ε equals the number of steps required to reach a certain accuracy ε (which can be computed a priori). Note that N_ϵ determines the accuracy of only the transient analysis; it does *not* account for the (in-)accuracy of the approximation itself.

Discretisation. Recently, Tijms and Veldman [60] proposed a discretisation method for computing the transient distribution of the accumulated reward in an MRM. Their algorithm is a generalisation of an earlier algorithm by Goyal and Tantawi [24] for MRMs with only 0- and 1-rewards. The basic idea is to discretise both the time and the accumulated reward as multiples of the same step size d, where d is chosen such that the probability of more than one transition in the MRM in an interval of length d is negligible. The algorithm allows only natural number rewards, but this is no severe restriction since rational rewards can be scaled to yield natural numbers.

The time complexity of this method is $\mathcal{O}(|S|\cdot t\cdot|(t-r)|/d^2)$ and the space complexity is $\mathcal{O}(|S|\cdot r/d)$. As the computational effort is proportional to d^{-2}, the computation time grows rapidly when a higher accuracy is required.

Occupation time distributions. In 2000, Sericola [57] derived a result for the distribution of occupation times in CTMCs prior to a given point in time t. The approach is based on uniformisation, and (as with uniformisation) it is possible to calculate an a priori error bound for the computed values. The distribution of this occupation time can be used to derive $\Pr\{Y_t \leqslant r, X_t \in S'\}$, based on the observation that if $O(s,t)$ is the occupation time of state s prior to t then $\rho(s) \cdot O(s,t)$ is the accumulated reward for this state prior to t. Summing over all states leads to the accumulated reward required.

The computation of the occupation time distribution is an iterative procedure, which in each iteration updates a linearly growing set of matrices. The computational and storage requirements of the approach are therefore considerable. If we truncate after the N_ε-th iteration, we obtain an overall time complexity of $\mathcal{O}(N_\varepsilon^3|S|^3)$ and an overall space complexity of $\mathcal{O}(N_\varepsilon^2|S|^3)$. Contrary to the Erlangian approximation, N_ϵ determines the accuracy of the entire computation procedure in this approach.

General observations. We have implemented all three algorithms, and experimented with them on a case study analysing the power consumption in ad-hoc mobile networks [33]. We can report the following observations:

- The three computational procedures converge to the same value, however, only for the occupation time distribution approach an a priori error bound (and hence a stopping criterion) is available.
- The method based on occupation time distributions is fast and accurate. In the current case study (which is small) we did not run into storage problems, however, the cubic storage requirements will limit this method to relatively small case studies.
- The discretisation method is slow when a fine-grain discretisation is used. Unfortunately, we have no method available (yet) to get a hold on the required step size to achieve a certain accuracy.
- The Erlangian approach is fast (where we did not even exploit the tensor structure in the generator matrix), but also here, we have to guess a reasonable number of phases for the approximation.
- The discretisation method suffers particularly from large time-bounds and large state spaces, as these make the number of matrices to be computed larger.
- The method based on occupation time distributions becomes less attractive when the time bound is large in comparison to the uniformisation rate. We

are currently investigating whether some kind of steady-state detection can be employed to shorten the computation in these cases.

5.6   Extending CSRL with Further Reward Operators

So far we have considered the accumulation of reward along paths, because as this is the basic novelty we support via the enriched path operators X_J^I and $\mathcal{U}_J^I$. In an orthogonal manner, it is possible to support further reward-based measures, namely by allowing further state operators.

To do so, consider state s in MRM $\mathcal{M}$. For time t and set of states S', the *instantaneous reward* $\rho^{\mathcal{M}}(s, S', t)$ equals $\sum_{s' \in S'} \pi^{\mathcal{M}}(s, s', t) \cdot \rho(s')$ and denotes the rate at which reward is earned in some state in S' at time t. The *expected (or long run) reward rate* $\rho^{\mathcal{M}}(s, S')$ equals $\sum_{s' \in S'} \pi^{\mathcal{M}}(s, s') \cdot \rho(s')$. We can now add the following state operators to our framework:

Expected reward rate $\mathcal{E}_J$: The operator $\mathcal{E}_J(\Phi)$ is true if the expected (long run) reward rate is in the interval J, if starting in state s:

$$s \models \mathcal{E}_J(\Phi) \quad \text{iff} \quad \rho^{\mathcal{M}}(s, Sat^{\mathcal{M}}(\Phi)) \in J.$$

Expected instantaneous reward rate $\mathcal{E}_J^t$: The operator $\mathcal{E}_J^t(\Phi)$ states that the expected instantaneous reward rate at time t lies in J:

$$s \models \mathcal{E}_J^t(\Phi) \quad \text{iff} \quad \rho^{\mathcal{M}}(s, Sat^{\mathcal{M}}(\Phi), t) \in J.$$

Expected cumulated reward $\mathcal{C}_J^I$: The operator $\mathcal{C}_J^I(\Phi)$ states that the expected amount of reward accumulated in Φ-states during the interval I lies in J:

$$s \models \mathcal{C}_J^I(\Phi) \quad \text{iff} \quad \int_I \rho^{\mathcal{M}}(s, Sat^{\mathcal{M}}(\Phi), u) \; du \in J.$$

The inclusion of these operators in CSRL is possible because their model checking is rather straightforward. The first two formulas require the summation of the Φ-conforming steady-state or transient state probabilities multiplied with the corresponding rewards. The operator $\mathcal{C}_J^I(\Phi)$ can be evaluated using a variant of uniformisation [28,58]. Some example properties are now: $\mathcal{E}_J(\neg F)$, which expresses the expected reward rate, e.g., the system's capacity, for an operational system, $\mathcal{E}_J^t(\text{true})$ expresses the expected instantaneous reward rate at time t and $\mathcal{C}_J^{[0,t]}(\text{true})$ expresses the amount of accumulated reward up to time t.

The suggestion to include these operators into CSRL exemplifies how a pragmatic approach (providing new algorithms for new measures) can be combined with our logical approach, and can profit from the latter due to the ability of nesting state and path formulas in an arbitrary manner.

6   Stochastic Model Checking and Lumpability

This section is devoted to an important property that the CSRL logic family possesses. The property relates the well-known concepts of lumpability and bisimulation to the distinguishing power of the logic. We exemplify this property for CSRL, since this includes the other logics as subsets.

Bisimulation (lumping) equivalence. Lumpability enables the aggregation of CTMCs and MRMs without affecting performance properties [47,10,40,35]. We adapt the standard notion slightly in order to deal with MRMs with state-labellings. We only sketch the concepts here, and refer to the papers [4,5] for more details. For some MRM $\mathcal{M} = (S, \mathbf{R}, L, \rho)$ we say that an equivalence relation R on S is a *bisimulation* if whenever $(s, s') \in R$ then

$$L(s) = L(s') \text{ and } \rho(s) = \rho(s') \text{ and } \mathbf{R}(s, C) = \mathbf{R}(s', C) \text{ for all } C \in S/R,$$

where S/R denotes the quotient space under R and $\mathbf{R}(s, C) = \sum_{s' \in C} \mathbf{R}(s, s')$. States s and s' are said to be *bisimilar* iff there exists a bisimulation R that contains (s, s'). Thus, any two bisimilar states are equally labelled and the cumulative rate of moving from these states to any equivalence class C is equal. Since R is an equivalence relation, we can construct the quotient $\mathcal{M}/R$, often called the lumped Markov model of $\mathcal{M}$.

Example 5. The reflexive, symmetric and transitive closure of the relation

$$R = \{ (0111, 1011), (1011, 1101), (0011, 0101), (0101, 1001) \}$$

is a bisimulation on the set of states of the MRM depicted in Fig. 4. For convenience, double arrows are used to indicate that there exists a transition from a state to another state and vice versa. The lumped MRM $\mathcal{M}/R$ consists of five aggregated states, yielding, in fact, the MRM of the TMR system discussed in Example 1. For instance, state $s_{2,1}$ of the original model can be considered as the lumped state representing the three possible configurations in which, out of three, a single processor has failed. These configurations are represented in the detailed version of Fig. 4 by the states 0111, 1011, and 1101.

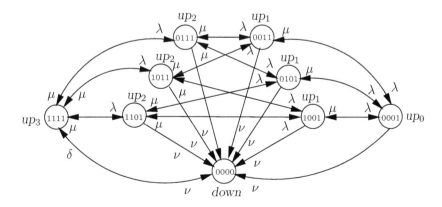

Fig. 4. A detailed version of the TMR model

It is well known that the measures derived from $\mathcal{M}$ and its quotient $\mathcal{M}/R$ are strongly related if R is a bisimulation. Without going into details, it is possible to compute transient as well as steady state probabilities on the lumped MRM $\mathcal{M}/R$ if one is only interested in probabilities of equivalence classes. For a given MRM it is therefore possible to establish the following property [4,19,5]:

$$s \models \Phi \quad \text{iff} \quad s' \models \Phi \quad \text{for all CSRL formulas } \Phi$$
$$\text{if and only if} \quad s \text{ and } s' \text{ are bisimilar.}$$

In other words, CSRL cannot distinguish between lumping equivalent states, but non-equivalent states can always be distinguished by some CSRL formula. This looks like a theoretical result, but it also has practical implications: it allows one to carry out model checking of CSRL (and CSL, and CRL) on the quotient state space with respect to lumpability. This lumped state space is often much smaller than the original one. It can be computed by a partition refinement algorithm [39,20].

7   Conclusions and Future Outlook

In this paper we have tried to give a tutorial style overview on the model checking approach to continuous time Markov chains and Markov reward models. While the logics CSL and CRL can be model checked using well-known numerical techniques to analyse Markov chains, more work is needed in the context of model checking performability properties expressible with CSRL to make the analysis effective.

Since the first paper on algorithms for CSL model checking has been published in 1999 [2] the approach has been implemented in (at least) three research tools, namely the ETMCC model checker [37], the model checker Prism, and the APNN toolbox [11]. While ETMCC is a dedicated CSL model checker based on sparse matrix data structures, Prism employs BDD based techniques to combat the state space explosion problem. The APNN toolbox uses Kronecker representations to achieve better space efficiency.

So far, we (and others) have applied stochastic model checking to various small and medium size case studies, including the analysis of a dependable workstation cluster [31], the verification of the performance of the plain ordinary telephone system protocol [3], the estimation of power consumption in mobile ad hoc networks [33], and the assessment of the survivability of the Hubble space telescope [34]. Among work that extends the basic stochastic model checking approach to a broader context, we are aware of the extension of CSL to process algebra specifications [38], to semi-Markov chains [44] and to random time bounds [49].

More work is foreseen in many exciting areas extending what has been described in this tutorial paper, ranging from research on the inclusion of nondeterminism, to efforts to improve the effectiveness of the algorithms described, to the application of stochastic model checking to realistic case studies.

Acknowledgements. The authors thank Joachim Meyer-Kayser, Markus Siegle and Lucia Cloth for valuable discussions and contributions. Holger Hermanns is partially supported by the Netherlands Organization for Scientific Research (NWO) and Joost-Pieter Katoen is partially supported by the Dutch Technology Foundation (STW). The cooperation between the research groups in Aachen, Bonn, and Twente takes place as part of the Validation of Stochastic Systems (VOSS) project, funded by the Dutch NWO and the German Research Council DFG.

References

1. A. Aziz, K. Sanwal, V. Singhal, and R. Brayton. Model checking continuous time Markov chains. *ACM Transactions on Computational Logic*, **1**(1): 162–170, 2000.

2. C. Baier, J.-P. Katoen, and H. Hermanns. Approximate symbolic model checking of continuous-time Markov chains. In *Concurrency Theory*, LNCS 1664: 146–162, Springer-Verlag, 1999.

3. C. Baier, B.R. Haverkort, H. Hermanns, and J.-P. Katoen. Model checking continuous-time Markov chains by transient analysis. In *Computer Aided Verification*, LNCS 1855: 358–372, Springer-Verlag, 2000.

4. C. Baier, B.R. Haverkort, H. Hermanns, and J.-P. Katoen. On the logical characterisation of performability properties. In *Automata, Languages, and Programming*, LNCS 1853: 780–792, Springer-Verlag, 2000.

5. C. Baier, B.R. Haverkort, H. Hermanns, and J.-P. Katoen. Model checking algorithms for continuous-time Markov chains. Technical report TR-CTIT-02-10. Centre for Telematics and Information Technology, University of Twente. 2001.

6. C. Baier and M. Kwiatkowska. On the verification of qualitative properties of probabilistic processes under fairness constraints. *Information Processing Letters*, **66**(2): 71–79, 1998.

7. M.D. Beaudry. Performance-related reliability measures for computing systems. *IEEE Transactions on Computers*, **C-27**: 540–547, 1978.

8. B. Bérard, M. Bidoit, A. Finkel, F. Laroussine, A. Petit, L. Petrucci, and Ph. Schnoebelen. *Systems and Software Verification*. Springer-Verlag, 2001.

9. A. Bobbio and M. Telek. Markov regenerative SPN with non-overlapping activity cycles. In *Proc. Int'l IEEE Performance and Dependability Symposium*: 124–133, 1995.

10. P. Buchholz. Exact and ordinary lumpability in finite Markov chains. *Journal of Applied Probability*, **31**: 59–75, 1994.

11. P. Buchholz, J.-P. Katoen, P. Kemper, and C. Tepper. Model checking large structured Markov chains. *Journal of Logic and Algebraic Programming*, to appear, 2001.

12. *CCITT Blue Book, Fascicle III.1*, International Telecommunication Union, Geneva, 1989.

13. G. Chiola, G. Franceschinis, R. Gaeta, and M. Ribaudo. GreatSPN 1.7: graphical editor and analyzer for timed and stochastic Petri nets. *Performance Evaluation*, **24** (1-2):47-68, 1995.

14. G. Ciardo, J.K. Muppala, and K.S. Trivedi. SPNP: stochastic Petri net package. In *Proc. 3rd Int. Workshop on Petri Nets and Performance Models*, pp. 142–151, IEEE CS Press, 1989.

15. G. Clark, S. Gilmore, and J. Hillston. Specifying performance measures for PEPA. In *Formal Methods for Real-Time and Probabilistic Systems*, LNCS 1601: 211–227, Springer-Verlag, 1999.

16. E. Clarke, E. Emerson, and A. Sistla. Automatic verification of finite-state concurrent systems using temporal logic specifications. *ACM Transactions on Programming Languages and Systems*, **8**: 244–263, 1986.
17. E. Clarke, O. Grumberg, and D. Peled. *Model Checking*. MIT Press, 1999.
18. E. Clarke and R. Kurshan. Computer-aided verification. *IEEE Spectrum*, **33**(6): 61–67, 1996.
19. J. Desharnais and P. Panangaden. Continuous stochastic logic characterizes bisimulation of continuous-time Markov processes. *Journal of Logic and Algebraic Programming*, to appear, 2001.
20. S. Derisavi, H. Hermanns, and W.H. Sanders. Optimal state space lumping in Markov models. 2002. submitted for publication.
21. W. Feller. *An Introduction to Probability Theory and its Applications*. John Wiley & Sons, 1968.
22. R. German. *Performance Analysis of Communication Systems: Modeling with Non-Markovian Stochastic Petri Nets*. John Wiley & Sons, 2000.
23. S. Gilmore and J. Hillston. The PEPA workbench: a tool to support a process algebra-based approach to performance modelling. In *Computer Performance Evaluation, Modeling Techniques and Tools*, LNCS 794: 353-368, Springer-Verlag, 1994.
24. A. Goyal and A.N. Tantawi. A measure of guaranteed availability and its numerical evaluation. *IEEE Transactions on Computers*, 37: 25–32, 1988.
25. W.K. Grassmann. Finding transient solutions in Markovian event systems through randomization. In *Numerical Solution of Markov Chains*, pp. 357–371, Marcel Dekker Inc, 1991.
26. D. Gross and D.R. Miller. The randomization technique as a modeling tool and solution procedure for transient Markov chains. *Operations Research* **32**(2): 343–361, 1984.
27. D. Harel. Statecharts: a visual formalism for complex systems. *Science of Computer Programming*, **8**: 231–274, 1987.
28. B.R. Haverkort. *Performance of Computer Communication Systems: A Model-Based Approach*. John Wiley & Sons, 1998.
29. B.R. Haverkort, R. Marie, G. Rubino, and K.S. Trivedi (editors). *Performability Modelling: Techniques and Tools*. John Wiley & Sons, 2001.
30. B.R. Haverkort and I. Niemegeers. Performability modelling tools and techniques. *Performance Evaluation*, **25**: 17–40, 1996.
31. B.R. Haverkort, H. Hermanns, and J.-P. Katoen. The use of model checking techniques for quantitative dependability evaluation. In *IEEE Symposium on Reliable Distributed Systems.*, pp. 228–238. IEEE CS Press, 2000.
32. B.R. Haverkort, L. Cloth, H. Hermanns, J.-P. Katoen, and C. Baier. Model checking CSRL-specified performability properties. In *5th Int. Workshop on Performability Modeling of Computer and Communication Systems*, Erlangen, *Arbeitsberichte des IMMD*, **34** (13), 2001. 2001.
33. B.R. Haverkort, L. Cloth, H. Hermanns, J.-P. Katoen, and C. Baier. Model checking performability properties. In *Proc. IEEE Int'l Conference on Dependable Systems and Networks*, IEEE CS press, 2002.
34. H. Hermanns. Construction and verfication of performance and reliability models. *Bulletin of the EATCS*, **74**:135-154, 2001.
35. H. Hermanns, U. Herzog, and J.-P. Katoen. Process algebra for performance evaluation. *Theoretical Computer Science*, 274(1-2):43–87, 2002.
36. H. Hermanns, U. Herzog, U. Klehmet, V. Mertsiotakis, and M. Siegle. Compositional performance modelling with the TIPPTOOL. *Performance Evaluation*, **39**(1-4): 5–35, 2000.

37. H. Hermanns, J.-P. Katoen, J. Meyer-Kayser, and M. Siegle. A Markov chain model checker. In *Tools and Algorithms for the Construction and Analysis of Systems*, LNCS 1785: 347–362, Springer-Verlag, 2000.
38. H. Hermanns, J.-P. Katoen, J. Meyer-Kayser, and M. Siegle. Towards model checking stochastic process algebra. In *Integrated Formal Methods*, LNCS 1945: 420–439, Springer-Verlag, 2000.
39. H. Hermanns and M. Siegle. Bisimulation algorithms for stochastic process algebras and their BDD-based implementation. In *Formal Methods for Real-Time and Probabilistic Systems*, LNCS 1601: 244–265, Springer-Verlag, 1999.
40. J. Hillston. *A Compositional Approach to Performance Modelling.* Cambridge University Press, 1996.
41. G.J. Holzmann. The model checker SPIN. *IEEE Transactions on Software Engineering*, **23**(5): 279–295, 1997.
42. G. Horton, V. Kulkarni, D. Nicol, K. Trivedi. Fluid stochastic Petri nets: Theory, application and solution techniques. *Eur. J. Oper. Res.*, 105(1): 184–201,1998.
43. R.A. Howard. *Dynamic Probabilistic Systems; Volume 1: Markov Models.* John Wiley & Sons, 1971.
44. G.G. Infante-Lopez, H. Hermanns, and J.-P. Katoen. Beyond memoryless distributions: Model checking semi-Markov chains. In *Process Algebra and Probabilistic Methods*, LNCS 2165: 57–70, Springer-Verlag, 2001.
45. A. Jensen. Markov chains as an aid in the study of Markov processes. *Skandinavisk Aktuarietidskrift* **36**: 87–91, 1953.
46. J.-P. Katoen, M.Z. Kwiatkowska, G. Norman, and D. Parker. Faster and symbolic CTMC model checking. In *Process Algebra and Probabilistic Methods*, LNCS 2165: 23–38, Springer-Verlag, 2001.
47. J.G. Kemeny and J.L. Snell. *Finite Markov Chains.* Van Nostrand, 1960.
48. V.G. Kulkarni. *Modeling and Analysis of Stochastic Systems.* Chapman & Hall, 1995.
49. M.Z. Kwiatkowska, G. Norman, and A. Pacheco. Model checking CSL until formulae with random time bounds. In *Process Algebra and Probabilistic Methods*, LNCS 2399, Springer-Verlag, 2002.
50. K.L. McMillan. *Symbolic Model Checking.* Kluwer Academic Publishers, 1993.
51. J.F. Meyer. On evaluating the performability of degradable computing systems. *IEEE Transactions on Computers*, **29**(8): 720–731, 1980.
52. J.F. Meyer. Closed-form solutions of performability, *IEEE Transactions on Computers*, 31(7): 648–657, 1982.
53. J.F. Meyer. Performability: a retrospective and some pointers to the future. *Performance Evaluation*, 14(3-4): 139–156, 1992.
54. W.D. Obal II and W.H. Sanders. State-space support for path-based reward variables. *Performance Evaluation*, **35**: 233–251, 1999.
55. D. Peled. *Software Reliability Methods.* Springer-Verlag, 2001.
56. W.H. Sanders, W.D. Obal II, M.A. Qureshi, and F.K. Widnajarko. The UltraSAN modeling environment. *Performance Evaluation*, **24**: 89–115, 1995.
57. B. Sericola. Occupation times in Markov processes. *Stochastic Models*, 16(5): 339–351, 2000.
58. E. de Souza e Silva and H.R. Gail. Performability analysis of computer systems: from model specification to solution. *Perf. Ev.*, **14**: 157–196, 1992.
59. W.J. Stewart. *Introduction to the Numerical Solution of Markov Chains.* Princeton University Press, 1994.
60. H.C. Tijms, R. Veldman. A fast algorithm for the transient reward distribution in continuous-time Markov chains, *Operation Research Letters*, 26: 155–158, 2000.

Measurement-Based Analysis of System Dependability Using Fault Injection and Field Failure Data

Ravishankar K. Iyer and Zbigniew Kalbarczyk

Center for Reliable and High-Performance Computing
University of Illinois at Urbana-Champaign
1308 W. Main St., Urbana, IL 61801-2307
{iyer, kalbar}@crhc.uiuc.edu

Abstract. The discussion in this paper focuses on the issues involved in analyzing the availability of networked systems using fault injection and the failure data collected by the logging mechanisms built into the system. In particular we address: (1) *analysis in the prototype phase using physical fault injection to an actual system.* We use example of fault injection-based evaluation of a software-implemented fault tolerance (SIFT) environment (built around a set of self-checking processes called ARMORS) that provides error detection and recovery services to spaceborne scientific applications and (2) *measurement-based analysis of systems in the field.* We use example of LAN of Windows NT based computers to present methods for collecting and analyzing failure data to characterize network system dependability. Both, fault injection and failure data analysis enable us to study naturally occurring errors and to provide feedback to system designers on potential availability bottlenecks. For example, the study of failures in a network of Windows NT machines reveals that most of the problems that lead to reboots are software related and that though the average availability evaluates to over 99%, a typical machine, on average, provides acceptable service only about 92% of the time.

1 Introduction

The dependability of a system can be experimentally evaluated at different phases of its lifecycle. In the *design phase*, computer-aided design (CAD) environments are used to evaluate the design via simulation, including simulated fault injection. Such fault injection tests the effectiveness of fault-tolerant mechanisms and evaluates system dependability, providing timely feedback to system designers. Simulation, however, requires accurate input parameters and validation of output results. Although the parameter estimates can be obtained from past measurements, this is often complicated by design and technology changes. In the *prototype phase*, the system runs under controlled workload conditions. In this stage, controlled physical fault injection is used to evaluate the system behavior under faults, including the detection coverage and the recovery capability of various fault tolerance mechanisms. Fault injection on the real system can provide information about the failure process, from fault occurrence to system recovery, including error latency, propagation, detection, and recovery (which may involve reconfiguration). In the *operational phase*, a direct measurement-based approach can be used to measure systems in the

M.C. Calzarossa and S. Tucci (Eds.): Performance 2002, LNCS 2459, pp. 290–317, 2002.
© Springer-Verlag Berlin Heidelberg 2002

field under real workloads. The collected data contain a large amount of information about naturally occurring errors/failures. Analysis of this data can provide understanding of actual error/failure characteristics and insight into analytical models. Although measurement-based analysis is useful for evaluating the real system, it is limited to detected errors. Further, conditions in the field can vary widely, casting doubt on the statistical validity of the results. Thus, all three approaches – simulated fault injection, physical fault injection, and measurement-based analysis – are required for accurate dependability analysis.

In the design phase, simulated fault injection can be conducted at different levels: the electrical level, the logic level, and the function level. The objectives of simulated fault injection are to determine dependability bottlenecks, the coverage of error detection/recovery mechanisms, the effectiveness of reconfiguration schemes, performance loss, and other dependability measures. The feedback from simulation can be extremely useful in cost-effective redesign of the system. For thorough discussion of different techniques for simulated fault injection can be found in [10].

In the prototype phase, while the objectives of physical fault injection are similar to those of simulated fault injection, the methods differ radically because real fault injection and monitoring facilities are involved. Physical faults can be injected at the hardware level (logic or electrical faults) or at the software level (code or data corruption). Heavy-ion radiation techniques can also be used to inject faults and stress the system. The detailed treatment of the instrumentation involved in fault injection experiments using real examples, including several fault injection environments is given in [10].

In the operational phase, measurement-based analysis must address issues such as how to monitor computer errors and failures and how to analyze measured data to quantify system dependability characteristics. Although methods for the design and evaluation of fault-tolerant systems have been extensively researched, little is known about how well these strategies work in the field. A study of production systems is valuable not only for accurate evaluation but also for identifying reliability bottlenecks in system design. In [10] the measurement-based analysis is based on over 200 machine-years of data gathered from IBM, DEC, and Tandem systems (note that these are not networked systems).

In this paper we discuss the current research in the area of experimental analysis of computer system dependability in the context of methodologies suited for measurement-based dependability analysis of networked systems. In particular we focus on:

- *Analysis in the prototype phase using physical fault injection to an actual system.* We use example of fault injection-based evaluation of a software-implemented fault tolerance (SIFT) environment (built around a set of self-checking processes called ARMORS, [13]) that provides error detection and recovery services to spaceborne scientific applications.
- *Measurement based analysis of systems in the field.* We use example of LAN of Windows NT based computers to present methods for collecting and analyzing failure data to characterize network system dependability.

2   Fault/Error Injection Characterization of the SIFT Environment for Spaceborne Applications

Fault/error injection is an attractive approach to the experimental validation of dependable systems. The objective of fault injection is to mimic the existence of faults and errors and hence to enable studying the failure behavior of the system. Fault\error injection can be employed to conduct detailed studies of the complex interactions between fault and fault handling mechanisms, e.g., [1] and [10]. In particular fault injection aims at (1) exposing deficiencies of fault tolerance mechanisms (i.e., fault removal), e.g., [3], and (2) evaluating coverage of fault tolerance mechanisms (i.e., fault forecasting, e.g., [2]. Number of tools were proposed to support fault injection analysis and evaluation of systems, e.g., FERRARI [14], FIAT [5], and NFTAPE [22].

This section presents an example of applying fault/error injection in assessing fault tolerance mechanisms of software implemented fault tolerance environment for spaceborne applications. In traditional spaceborne applications, onboard instruments collect and transmit raw data back to Earth for processing. The amount of science that can be done is clearly limited by the telemetry bandwidth to Earth. The Remote Exploration and Experimentation (REE) project at NASA/JPL intends to use a cluster of commercial off-the-shelf (COTS) processors to analyze the data onboard and send only the results back to Earth. This approach not only saves downlink bandwidth, but also provides the possibility of making real-time, application-oriented decisions.

While failures in the scientific applications are not critical to the spacecraft's health in this environment (spacecraft control is performed by a separate, trusted computer), they can be expensive nonetheless. The commercial components used by REE are expected to experience a high rate of radiation-induced transient errors in space (ranging from one per day to several per hour), and downtime directly leads to the loss of scientific data. Hence, a fault-tolerant environment is needed to manage the REE applications.

The missions envisioned to take advantage of the SIFT environment for executing MPI-based [19] scientific applications include the Mars Rover, the Orbiting Thermal Imaging Spectrometer (OTIS). More details on the applications and the full dependability analysis can be found in [31] and [32], respectively.

The remaining of this section presents a methodology for experimentally evaluating a distributed SIFT environment executing an REE texture analysis program from the Mars Rover mission. Errors are injected so that the consequences of faults can be studied. The experiments do not attempt to analyze the cause of the errors or fault coverage. Rather, the error injections progressively stress the detection and recovery mechanisms of the SIFT environment:

1. SIGINT/SIGSTOP injections. Many faults are known to lead to crash and hang failures . SIGINT/SIGSTOP injections reproduce these first-order effects of faults in a controlled manner that minimizes the possibility of error propagation or checkpoint corruption.
2. Register and text-segment injections. The next set of error injections represent common effects of single-event upsets by corrupting the state in the register set and text segment memory. This introduces the possibility of error propagation and checkpoint corruption.

3. Heap injections. The third set of experiments further broaden the failure scenarios by injecting errors in the dynamic heap data to maximize the possibility of error propagation. The results from these experiments are especially useful in evaluating how well intraprocess self-checks limit error propagation.

REE computational model. The REE computational model consists of a trusted, radiation-hardened (rad-hard) Spacecraft Control Computer (SCC) and a cluster of COTS processors that execute the SIFT environment and the scientific applications. The SCC schedules applications for execution on the REE cluster through the SIFT environment.

REE testbed configuration. The experiments were executed on a 4-node testbed consisting of PowerPC 750 processors running the Lynx real-time operating system. Nodes are connected through 100 Mbps Ethernet in the testbed. Between one and two megabytes of RAM on each processor were set aside to emulate local nonvolatile memory available to each node. The nonvolatile RAM is expected to store temporary state information that must survive hardware reboots (e.g., checkpointing information needed during recovery). Nonvolatile memory visible to all nodes is emulated by a remote file system residing on a Sun workstation that stores program executables, application input data, and application output data.

2.1   SIFT Environment for REE

The REE applications are protected by a SIFT environment designed around a set of self-checking processes called ARMORS (Adaptive Reconfigurable Mobile Objects of Reliability) that execute on each node in the testbed. ARMORs control all operations in the SIFT environment and provide error detection and recovery to the application and to the ARMOR processes themselves. We provide a brief summary of the ARMOR-based SIFT environment as implemented for the REE applications; additional details of the general ARMOR architecture appear in [13].

SIFT Architecture

An ARMOR is a multithreaded process internally structured around objects called elements that contain their own private data and provide elementary functions or services (e.g., detection and recovery for remote ARMOR processes, internal self-checking mechanisms, or checkpointing support). Together, the elements constitute the functionality that defines an ARMOR's behavior. All ARMORs contain a basic set of elements that provide a core functionality, including the ability to (1) implement reliable point-to-point message communication between ARMORs, (2) communicate with the local daemon ARMOR process, (3) respond to heartbeats from the local daemon, and (4) capture ARMOR state. Specific ARMORs extend this core functionality by adding extra elements.

Types of ARMORs. The SIFT environment for REE applications consists of four kinds of ARMOR processes: a Fault Tolerance Manager (FTM), a Heartbeat ARMOR, daemons, and Execution ARMORs

- *Fault Tolerance Manager (FTM).* A single FTM executes on one of the nodes and is responsible for recovering from ARMOR and node failures as well as interfacing with the external Spacecraft Control Computer (SCC).
- *Heartbeat ARMOR.* The Heartbeat ARMOR executes on a node separate from the FTM. Its sole responsibility is to detect and recover from failures in the FTM through the periodic polling for liveness.
- *Daemons.* Each node on the network executes a daemon process. Daemons are the gateways for ARMOR-to-ARMOR communication, and they detect failures in the local ARMORs.
- *Execution ARMORs.* Each application process is directly overseen by a local Execution ARMOR.

Executing REE Applications
Fig. 1 illustrates a configuration of the SIFT environment with two MPI applications (from the Mars Rover and OTIS missions) executing on a four-node testbed. Arrows in the figure depict the relationships among the various processes (e.g., the application sends progress indicators to the Execution ARMORs, the FTM is responsible for recovering from failures in the Heartbeat ARMOR, and the FTM heartbeats the daemon processes).

Each application process is linked with a SIFT interface that establishes a one-way communication channel with the local Execution ARMOR at application initialization. The application programmer can use this interface to invoke a variety of fault tolerance services provided by the ARMOR.

Error Detection Hierarchy
The top-down error detection hierarchy consists of:
- *Node and daemon errors.* The FTM periodically exchanges heartbeat messages with each daemon (every 10 s in our experiments) to detect node crashes and hangs. If the FTM does not receive a response by the next heartbeat round, it assumes that the node has failed. A daemon failure is treated as a node failure.
- *ARMOR errors.* Each ARMOR contains a set of assertions on its internal state, including range checks, validity checks on data (e.g., a valid ARMOR ID), and data structure integrity checks. Other internal self-checks available to the ARMORs include preemptive control flow checking, I/O signature checking, and deadlock/livelock detection [4]. In order to limit error propagation, the ARMOR kills itself when an internal check detects an error. The daemon detects crash failures in the ARMORs on the node via operating system calls. To detect hang failures, the daemon periodically (every 10 s in the experiments) sends "Are-you-alive?" messages to its local ARMORs.
- *REE applications.* All application crash failures are detected by the local Execution ARMOR. Crash failures in the MPI process with rank 0 can be detected by the Execution ARMOR through operating system calls (i.e., waitpid). The other Execution ARMORs periodically check that their MPI processes (ranks 1 through n) are still in the operating system's process table. If not, it concludes that the application has crashed. An application process notifies the local Execution ARMOR through its communication channel before exiting normally so that the ARMOR does not misinterpret this exit as an abnormal termination.

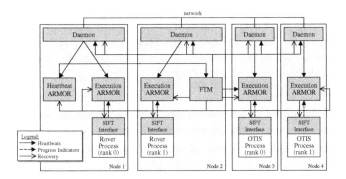

Fig. 1. SIFT Architecture for Executing two MPI Applications on a Four-Node Network.

A polling technique is used to detect application hangs in which the Execution ARMOR periodically checks for *progress indicator* updates sent by the application. A progress indicator is an "I'm-alive" message containing information that denotes application progress (e.g., a loop iteration counter). If the Execution ARMOR does not receive a progress indicator within an application-specific time period, the ARMOR concludes that the application process has hung.

Error Recovery

Nodes. The FTM migrates the ARMOR and application processes that were executing on the failed node to other working nodes in the SIFT environment.

ARMORs. ARMOR state is recovered from a checkpoint. To protect the ARMOR state against process failures, a checkpointing technique called *microcheckpointing* is used [30]. Microcheckpointing leverages the modular element composition of the ARMOR process to incrementally checkpoint state on an element-by-element basis.

REE Applications. On detecting an application failure, the Execution ARMOR notifies the FTM to initiate recovery. The version of MPI used on the REE testbed precludes individual MPI processes from being restarted within an application; therefore, the FTM instructs all Execution ARMORs to terminate their MPI processes before restarting the application. The application executable binaries must be reloaded from the remote disk during recovery.

2.2 Injection Experiments

Error injection experiments into the application and SIFT processes were conducted to: (1) stress the detection and recovery mechanisms of the SIFT environment, (2) determine the failure dependencies among SIFT and application processes, (3) measure the SIFT environment overhead on application performance, (4) measure the overhead of recovering SIFT processes as seen by the application.
  1. Study the effects of error propagation and the effectiveness of internal self-checks in limiting error propagation.

The experiments used NFTAPE, a software framework for conducting injection campaigns [22].

Error Models

The error models used the injection experiments represent a combination of those employed in several past experimental studies and those proposed by JPL engineers.

- *SIGINT/SIGSTOP.* These signals were used to mimic "clean" crash and hang failures as described in the introduction.
- *Register and text-segment errors.* Fault analysis has predicted that the most prevalent faults in the targeted spaceborne environment will be single-bit memory and register faults, although shrinking feature sizes have raised the likelihood of clock errors and multiple-bit flips in future technologies. Several error injections were uniformly distributed within each run since each injection was unlikely to cause an immediate failure, and only the most frequently used registers and functions in the text segment were targeted for injection.
- *Heap errors.* Heap injections were used to study the effects of error propagation. One error was injected per run into non-pointer data values only, and the effects of the error were traced through the system.

Errors were not injected into the operating system since our experience has shown that kernel injections typically led to a crash, led to a hang, or had no impact. Maderia et al. [18] used the same REE testbed to examine the impact of transient errors on LynxOS.

Definitions and Measurements

System, experiment, and run. We use the term *system* to refer to the REE cluster and associated software (i.e., the SIFT environment and applications). The system does not include the radiation-hardened SCC or communication channel to the ground. An error injection *experiment* targeted a specific process (application process, FTM, Execution ARMOR, or Heartbeat ARMOR) using a particular error model. For each process/error model pair, a series of *runs* were executed in which one or more errors were injected into the target process.

Activated errors and failures. An injection causes an error to be introduced into the system (e.g., corruption at a selected memory location or corruption of the value in a register). An error is said to be *activated* if program execution accesses the erroneous value. A *failure* refers to a process deviating from its expected (correct) behavior as determined by a run without fault injection. The application can also fail by producing output that falls outside acceptable tolerance limits as defined by an external application-provided verification program.

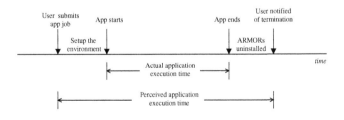

Fig. 2. Perceived vs. Actual Execution Time

A *system failure* occurs when either (1) the application cannot complete within a predefined timeout or (2) the SIFT environment cannot recognize that the application has completed successfully. System failures require that the SCC reinitialize the SIFT environment before continuing, but they do not threaten the SCC or spacecraft integrity[1].

Recovery time. Recovery time is the interval between the time at which a failure is detected and the time at which the target process restarts. For ARMOR processes, this includes the time required to restore the ARMOR's state from checkpoint. In the case of an application failure, the time lost to rolling back to the most recent application checkpoint is accounted for in the application's total execution time, not in the recovery time for the application.

Perceived application execution time. The perceived execution time is the interval between the time at which the SCC submits an application for execution and the time at which the SIFT environment reports to the SCC that the application has completed.

Actual application execution time. The actual execution time is the interval between the start and the end of the application. The difference between perceived and actual execution time accounts for the time required to install the Execution ARMORs before running the application and the time required to uninstall the Execution ARMORs after the application completes (see Fig. 2). This is a fixed overhead independent of the actual application execution time.

Baseline application execution time. In the injection experiments, the perceived and actual application execution times are compared to a baseline measurement in order to determine the performance overhead added by the SIFT environment and recovery. Two measures of baseline application performance are used: (1) the application executing without the SIFT environment and without fault injection and (2) the application executing in the SIFT environment but without fault injection. The difference between these two measures provides the overhead that the SIFT processes impose on the application. Table 1 shows that the SIFT environment adds less than two seconds to the perceived application execution time. The mean application execution time and recovery time are calculated for each fault model. Ninety-five percent confidence intervals (t-distribution) are also calculated for all measurements.

Table 1. Baseline Application Execution Time

	Perceived	Actual
Without SIFT	75.71 ± 0.65	75.71 ± 0.65
With SIFT	77.97 ± 0.48	75.74 ± 0.48

2.3 Crash and Hang Failures

This section presents results from SIGINT and SIGSTOP injections into the application and SIFT processes, which were used to evaluate the SIFT environment's

---

[11] While the vast majority of failures in the SIFT environment will not affect the trusted SCC, in reality there exists a nonzero probability that the SCC can be impacted by SIFT failures. We discount this possibility in the paper because there is not a full-fledged SCC available for conducting such an analysis.

ability to handle crash and hang failures. We first summarize the major findings from over 700 crash and hang injections:

- All injected errors into both the application and SIFT processes were recovered.
- Recovering from errors in SIFT processes imposed a mean overhead of 5% to the application's actual execution time. This 5% overhead includes 25 cases out of roughly 700 runs in which the application was forced to block or restart because of the unavailability of a SIFT process. Neglecting those cases in which the application must redo lost computation, the overhead imposed by a recovering SIFT process was insignificant.
- Correlated failures involving a SIFT process and the application were observed. In 25 cases, crash and hang failures caused a SIFT process to become unavailable, prompting the application to fail when it did not receive a timely response from the failed SIFT process. All correlated failures were successfully recovered.

Results for 100 runs per target are summarized in Table 2. In some cases, the injection time (used to determine when to inject the error) occurred after the application completed. For these runs, no error was injected. The row "Baseline" reports the application execution time with no fault injection. One hundred runs were chosen in order to ensure that failures occurred throughout the various phases of an application's execution (including an idle SIFT environment before application execution, application submission and initialization, application execution, application termination, and subsequent cleanup of the SIFT environment).

Application Recovery
Hangs are the most expensive application failures in terms of lost processing time. Application hangs are detected using a polling technique in which the Execution ARMOR executes a thread that wakes up every 20 seconds to check the value of a counter incremented by progress indicator messages sent by the application. Because the counter is polled at fixed intervals, the error detection latency for hangs can be up to twice the checking period.

Table 2. SIGINT/SIGSTOP Injection Results

Target	Failures	Successful Recoveries	App. Exec. Time (s)		Recovery Time (s)
			Perceived	Actual	
SIGINT					
Baseline	-	-	74.78 ± 0.55	72.68 ± 0.49	-
Application	100	100	89.80 ± 1.50	87.88 ± 1.50	0.48 ± 0.05
FTM	81	81	79.60 ± 1.61	73.89 ± 0.25	0.64 ± 0.16
Execution ARMOR	100	100	77.91 ± 1.01	75.98 ± 1.00	0.61 ± 0.07
Heartbeat ARMOR	97	97	75.26 ± 0.92	74.39 ± 0.96	0.47 ± 0.12
SIGSTOP					
Baseline	-	-	71.96 ± 0.32	70.03 ± 0.27	-
Application	84	84	112.21 ± 1.87	110.21 ± 1.87	0.47 ± 0.05
FTM	97	97	76.20 ± 1.94	70.09 ± 0.88	0.79 ± 0.15
Execution ARMOR	98	98	85.01 ± 4.41	82.21 ± 4.28	0.63 ± 0.15
Heartbeat ARMOR	77	77	71.88 ± 0.24	70.24 ± 0.24	0.56 ± 0.21

SIFT Environment Recovery

FTM recovery. The perceived execution time for the application is extended if (1) the FTM fails while setting up the environment before the application execution begins or (2) the FTM fails while cleaning up the environment and notifying the Spacecraft Control Computer that the application terminated. The application is decoupled from the FTM's execution after starting, so failures in the FTM do not affect it. The only overhead in actual execution time originates from the network contention during the FTM's recovery, which lasts for only 0.6-0.7 s.

An FTM-application correlated failure. The error injections also revealed a correlated failure in which the FTM failure caused the application to restart in 2 of the 178 runs (see [32] for description of correlated failure scenarios).

The SIFT environment is able to recover from this correlated failure because the components performing the detection (Heartbeat ARMOR detecting FTM failures and Execution ARMOR detecting application failures) are not affected by the failures.

Execution ARMOR. Of the 198 crash/hang errors injected into the Execution ARMORs, 175 required recovery only in the Execution ARMOR. For these runs, the application execution overhead was negligible. The overhead reported in Table 2 (up to 10% for hang failures) resulted from the remaining 23 cases in which the application was forced to restart.

An Execution ARMOR-application correlated failure. If the application process attempted to contact the Execution ARMOR (e.g., to send progress indicator updates or to notify the Execution ARMOR that it is terminating normally) while the ARMOR was recovering, the application process blocked until the Execution ARMOR completely recovered. Because the MPI processes are tightly coupled, a correlated failure is possible if the Execution ARMOR overseeing the other MPI process diagnosed the blocking as an application hang and initiated recovery.

This correlated failure occurred most often when the Execution ARMOR hung (i.e., due to SIGSTOP injections): 22 correlated failures were due to SIGSTOP injections as opposed to 1 correlated failure resulting from an ARMOR crash (i.e., due to SIGINT injections). This is because an Execution ARMOR crash failure is detected immediately by the daemon through operating system calls, making the Execution ARMOR unavailable for only a short time. Hangs, however, are detected via a 10-second heartbeat.

2.4   Register and Text-Segment Injections

This section expands the scope of the injections to further stress the detection and recovery mechanisms by allowing for the possibility of checkpoint corruption and error propagation to another process. Results from approximately 9,000 single-bit errors into the register set and text segment of the application and SIFT processes show that:

- Most register and text-segment errors led to crash and hang failures that were recovered by the SIFT environment.
- Eleven of the approximately 700 observed failures led to system failures in which either the application did not complete or the SIFT environment did not detect that the application successfully completed. These 11 system failures resulted from

injected errors that corrupted an ARMOR's checkpoint or propagated outside the injected process.

• Text-segment errors were more likely than register errors to lead to system failures. This was because values in registers typically had a shorter lifetime (i.e., they were either never used or quickly overwritten) when compared to information stored in the text segment.

Table 3 summarizes the results of approximately 6,000 register injections and 3,000 text-segment injections into both the application and ARMOR processes. Failures are classified into four categories: segmentation faults, illegal instructions, hangs, and errors detected via assertions. The second column in Table 3 gives the number of successful recoveries vs. the number of failures for each set of experiments. Errors that were not successfully recovered led to system failures (4 due to FTM failures, 5 due to Execution ARMOR failures, and 2 due to Heartbeat ARMOR failures).

FTM recovery. Table 3 shows that the FTM successfully recovered from all register injections. Two text-segment injections were detected through assertions on the FTM's internal data structures, and both of these errors were recovered.

Table 3 also shows that the FTM could not recover from four text-segment errors. In each case, the error corrupted the FTM's checkpoint prior to crashing. Because the checkpoint was corrupted, the FTM crashed shortly after being recovered. This cycle of failure and recovery repeated until the run timed out.

There were seven cases of a correlated failure in which the FTM failed during the application's initialization: three from text-segment injections and four from register injections. Both the FTM and the application recovered from all seven correlated failures.

Table 3. Register and Text-Segment Injection Results

Target	Recoveries/ Failures	Failure Classification				App. Exec. Time (s)		Recoverry Time (s)
		Seg. fault	Illegal instr.	Hang	Assert-ion	Perceived	Actual	
Baseline	-	-	-	-	-	71.96 ± 0.32	70.03 ± 0.27	-
Register Injections								
Application	95 / 95	71	4	20	0	90.70 ± 2.57	88.81 ± 2.57	0.70 ± 0.21
FTM	84 / 84	58	6	16	4	75.65 ± 1.54	73.42 ± 1.28	0.71 ± 0.03
Execution ARMOR	77 / 80	56	6	15	3	76.19 ± 1.82	73.56 ± 1.83	0.45 ± 0.08
Heartbeat ARMOR	77 / 77	62	6	8	1	73.00 ± 0.22	70.66 ± 0.21	0.31 ± 0.04
Text-segment Injections								
Application	82 / 82	41	23	18	0	89.47 ± 2.87	87.49 ± 2.88	1.05 ± 0.33
FTM	84 / 88	53	28	5	2	76.47 ± 2.87	71.00 ± 2.31	0.51 ± 0.05
Execution ARMOR	93/ 95	45	31	11	8	77.48 ± 1.93	74.83 ± 1.86	0.43 ± 0.04
Heartbeat ARMOR	95 / 97	53	33	11	0	73.23 ± 0.37	71.21 ± 0.36	0.30 ± 0.01

Execution ARMOR recovery. Three register injections and two text-segment injections into the Execution ARMOR led to system failure. In each of these cases, the error propagated to other ARMOR processes or to the Execution ARMOR's checkpoint.

One text-segment injection and three register injections caused errors in the Execution ARMOR to propagate to the FTM (i.e., the error was not fail-silent). Although the Execution ARMOR did not crash, it sent corrupted data to the FTM when the application terminated, causing the FTM to crash. The FTM state in its checkpoint was not affected by the error, so the FTM was able to recover to a valid state. Because the FTM did not complete processing the Execution ARMOR's notification message, the FTM did not send an acknowledgment back to the Execution ARMOR. The missing acknowledgment prompted the Execution ARMOR to resend the faulty message, which again caused the FTM to crash. This cycle of recovery followed by the retransmission of faulty data continued until the run timed out.

One of the text-segment injections caused the Execution ARMOR to save a corrupted checkpoint before crashing. When the ARMOR recovered, it restored its state from the faulty checkpoint and crashed shortly thereafter. This cycle repeated until the run timed out.

In addition to the system failures described above, three text-segment injections into the Execution ARMOR resulted in the restarting of the texture analysis application. All three of these correlated failures were successfully recovered.

Heartbeat ARMOR recovery. The Heartbeat ARMOR recovered from all register errors, while text-segment injections brought about two system failures. Although no corrupted state escaped the Heartbeat ARMOR, the error prevented the Heartbeat ARMOR from receiving incoming messages. Thus, the Heartbeat ARMOR falsely detected that the FTM had failed, since it did not receive a heartbeat reply from the FTM. The ARMOR then began to initiate recovery of the FTM by (1) instructing the FTM's daemon to reinstall the FTM process, and (2) instructing the FTM to restore its state from checkpoint after receiving acknowledgment that the FTM has been successfully reinstalled.

Among the successful recoveries from text-segment errors shown in Table 3, four involved corrupted heartbeat messages that caused the FTM to fail. Although faulty data escaped the Heartbeat ARMOR, the corrupted message did not compromise the FTM's checkpoint. Thus, the FTM was able to recover from these four failures.

2.5 Heap Injections

Careful examination of the register injection experiments showed that crash failures were most often caused by segmentation faults raised from dereferencing a corrupted pointer. To maximize the chances for error propagation, only data (not pointers) were injected on the heap. Results from targeted injections into FTM heap memory were grouped by the element into which the error was injected. Table 4 shows the number of system failures observed from 100 error injections per element, classified as to the their effect on the system. One hundred targeted injections were sufficient to observe either escaped or detected errors given the amount of state in each element; overall, 500 heap injections were conducted on the FTM.

Table 4. System Failures Observed Through Heap Injections

Legend (Effect on system): (A) unable to register daemons, (B) unable to install Execution ARMORs,   (C) unable to start applications, (D) unable to uninstall Execution ARMORs after application completes.
Legend (System failure/assertion check classification): (2) system failure without assertion firing, (3) system failure with assertion firing, (4) successful recoveries after assertion fired.

Element	Effect on System				System Failures			#4
	A	B	C	D	Total	#2	#3	
mgr_armor_info. Stores information about subordinate ARMORs such as location and element composition.	4	1	5	4	14	6	8	19
exec_armor_info. Stores information about each Execution ARMOR such as status of subordinate application.	0	0	5	4	9	4	5	9
app_param. Stores information about application such as executable name, command-line arguments, and number of times application restarted.	0	0	0	0	0	0	0	2
agr_app_detect. Used to detect that all processes for MPI application have terminated and to initiate recovery if necessary.	0	0	0	0	0	0	0	4
node_mgmt. Stores information about the nodes, including the resident daemon and hostname.	0	14	0	0	14	0	14	3
TOTAL	4	15	10	8	37	10	27	37

Many data errors were detectable through assertions within the FTM, but not all assertions were effective in preventing system failures. One of four scenarios resulted after a data error was injected (the last three columns in Table 4 are numbered to refer to scenarios 2-4):

1. The data error was not detected by an assertion and had no effect on the system. The application completed successfully as if there were no error.
2. The data error was not detected by an assertion but led to a system failure. None of the system failures impacted the application while it was executing.
3. The data error was detected by an assertion check, but only after the error had propagated to the FTM's checkpoint or to another process. Rolling back the FTM's state in these circumstances was ineffective, and system failures resulted from which the SIFT environment could not recover. These cases show that error latency is a factor when attempting to recover from errors in a distributed environment.
4. The data error was detected by an assertion check before propagating to the FTM's checkpoint or to another process. After an assertion fired, the FTM killed itself and recovered as if it had experienced an ordinary crash failure.

The injection results in Table 4 show that the least sensitive elements (*app_param* and *mgr_app_detect*) were those modules whose state was substantially read-only after being written early within the run. With assertions in place, none of the data errors led to system failures. At the other end of the sensitivity spectrum, 28 errors in two elements caused system failures. In contrast with the elements causing no system failures, the data in *mgr_armor_info* and *node_mgmt* were repeatedly written during the initialization phases of a run.

Table 4 also shows the efficiency of assertion checks in preventing system failures. The rightmost two columns in the table represent the total number of runs in which assertions detected errors. For example, assertions in the *mgr_armor_info* element detected 27 errors, and 19 of those errors were successfully recovered. The data also show that assertions coupled with the incremental microcheckpointing were able to prevent system failures in 58% of the cases (27 of 64 runs in which assertions fired).

On the other hand, assertions detected the error too late to prevent system failures in 27 cases. For example, 14 of the 17 runs in which assertions detected errors in the node_mgmt element resulted in system failures. This problem was rectified by adding checks to the translation results before sending the message.

2.6 Lessons Learned

SIFT overhead should be kept small. System designers must be aware that SIFT solutions have the potential to degrade the performance and even the dependability of the applications they are intended to protect. Our experiments show that the functionality in SIFT can be distributed among several processes throughout the network so that the overhead imposed by the SIFT processes is insignificant while the application is running.

SIFT recovery time should be kept small. Minimizing the SIFT process recovery time is desirable from two standpoints: (1) recovering SIFT processes have the potential to affect application performance by contending for processor and network resources, and (2) applications requiring support from the SIFT environment are affected when SIFT processes become unavailable. Our results indicate that fully recovering a SIFT process takes approximately 0.5 s. The mean overhead as seen by the application from SIFT recovery is less than 5%, which takes into account 10 out of roughly 800 failures from register, text-segment and heap injections that caused the application to block or restart because of the unavailability of a SIFT process. The overhead from recovery is insignificant when these 10 cases are neglected.

SIFT/application interface should be kept simple. In any multiprocess SIFT design, some SIFT processes must be coupled to the application in order to provide error detection and recovery. The Execution ARMORs play this role in our SIFT environment. Because of this dependency, it is important to make the Execution ARMORs as simple as possible. All recovery actions and those operations that affect the global system (e.g., job submission and detecting remote node failures) are delegated to a remote SIFT process that is decoupled from the application's execution. This strategy appears to work, as only 5 of 373 observed Execution ARMOR failures led to system failures.

SIFT availability impacts the application. Low recovery time and aggressive checkpointing of the SIFT processes help minimize the SIFT environment downtime, making the environment available for processing application requests and for recovering from application failures.

System failures are not necessarily fatal. Only 11 of the 10,000 injections resulted in a system failure in which the SIFT environment could not recover from the error. These system failures did not affect an executing application.

3   Error and Failure Analysis of a LAN of Windows NT-Based Servers

Direct monitoring, recording, and analysis of naturally occurring errors and failures in the system can provide valuable information on actual error/failure behavior, identify system bottlenecks, quantify dependability measures, and verify assumptions made in analytical models. In this section we provide an example of system dependability analysis using failure data collected from a Local Area Networks (LAN) of Windows NT servers.

In most commercial systems, information about failures can be obtained from the manual logs maintained by administrators or from the automated event-logging mechanisms in the underlying operating system. Manual logs are very subjective and often unavailable. Hence they are not typically suited for automated analysis of failures. In contrast, the event logs maintained by the system have predefined formats, provide contextual information in case of failures (e.g., a trace of significant events that precede a failure), and are thus conducive to automated analysis. Moreover, as failures are relatively rare events, it is necessary to meticulously collect and analyze error data for many machine-months for the results of the data analysis to be statistically valid. Such regular and prolonged data acquisition is possible only through automated event logging. Hence most studies of failures in single and networked computer systems are based on the error logs maintained by the operating system running on those machines.

This section presents methodology and results from an analysis of failures found in a network of about 70 Windows NT based mail servers (running Microsoft Exchange software). The data for the study is obtained from event logs (i.e., logs of machine events that are maintained and modified by the Windows NT operating system) collected over a six-month period from the mail routing network of a commercial organization. In this study we analyze only machine reboots because they constitute a significant portion of all logged failure data and are the most severe type of failure. As a starting point, a preliminary data analysis is conducted to classify the nature of observed failure events. This failure categorization is then used to examine the behavior of individual machines in detail and to derive a finite state model. The model depicts the behavior of a typical machine. Finally, a domain-wide analysis is performed to capture the behavior of the domain in a finite state model. The thorough failure data analysis, the reader can find in [12].

Related Work. Analysis of failures in computer systems has been the focus of active research for quite some time. Studies of failures occurring in commercial systems (e.g., VAX/VMS, Tandem/GUARDIAN) are based primarily on failure data collected from the field. The focus of such studies is on categorizing the nature of failures in the systems (e.g., software failures, hardware failures), identifying availability bottlenecks, and obtaining models to estimate the availability of the systems being analyzed. Lee [15], [16] analyzed failures in Tandem's GUARDIAN operating system. Tang [25] analyzed error logs pertaining to a multicomputer environment based on VAX/VMS cluster. Thakur [27] presented an analysis of failures in the Tandem Nonstop-UX operating system.

Hsueh [9] explored errors and recovery in IBM's MVS operating system. Based on the error logs collected from MVS systems, a semi-Markov model of multiple errors (i.e. errors that manifest themselves in multiple ways) was constructed to analyze system failure behavior. Measurement-based software reliability models were also presented in [15], [16] (for the GUARDIAN system) and [25], [26] (for the VAX cluster).

The impact of workload on system failures was also extensively studied. Castillo [6] developed a software reliability prediction model that took into account the workload imposed on the system. Iyer [11] examined the effect of workload on the reliability of the IBM 3081 operating system. Mourad [21] performed a reliability study on the IBM MVS/XA operating system and found that the error distribution is heavily dependent on the type of system utilization. Meyer [20] presented an analysis of the influence of workload on the dependability of computer systems.

Lin [17] and Tsao [28] focused on trend analysis in error logs. Gray [8] presented results from a census of Tandem systems. Chillarege [7] presented a study of the impact of failures on customers and the fault lifetimes. Sullivan [23], [24] examined software defects occurring in operating systems and databases (based on field data). Velardi [29] examined failures and recovery in the MVS operating system.

3.1   Error Logging in Windows NT

Windows NT operating system offers capabilities for error logging. This software records information on errors occurring in the various subsystems, such as memory, disk, and network subsystems, as well as other system events, such as reboots and shutdowns. The reports usually include information on the location, time, type of the error, the system state at the time of the error, and sometimes error recovery (e.g., retry) information. The main advantage of on-line automatic logging is its ability to record a large amount of information about transient errors and to provide details of automatic error recovery processes, which cannot be done manually. Disadvantages are that an on-line log does not usually include information about the cause and propagation of the error or about off-line diagnosis. Also, under some crash scenarios, the system may fail too quickly for any error messages to be recorded.

An important question to be asked here is: How accurate are event logs in characterizing failure behavior of the system? While event logs provide valuable insight into understanding the nature and dynamics of typical problems observed in a network system, in many cases the information in event logs is not sufficient to precisely determine a nature of a problem (e.g., whether it was a software or hardware component failure). The only reliable way to improve accuracy of logs is (1) to perform more frequent, detailed logging by each component and (2) instrument the Windows NT code with new (more precise) logging mechanisms. However, there is always a trade-off between accuracy and intrusiveness of measurements. No commercial organization will permit someone to install an untested tool to monitor the network. Consequently, we use existing logs not only to characterize failure behavior of the network (presented in this paper), but also to determine how the logging system could be improved (e.g., by adding to the operating system a query mechanism to remotely probe system components about their status). It should be noted that in many commercial operating systems (e.g., MVS) event logs are accurate enough to document failures.

3.2   Classification of Data Collected from a LAN of Windows NT-Based Servers

The initial breakup of the data on a system reboot is primarily based on the events that preceded the current reboot by no more than an hour (and that occurred after the previous reboot). For each instance of a reboot, the most severe and frequently occurring events (hereafter referred to as prominent events) are identified. The corresponding reboot is then categorized based on the source and the id of these prominent events. In some cases, the prominent events are specific enough to identify the problem that caused the reboot. In other cases, only a high-level description of the problem can be obtained based on the knowledge of the prominent events. Table 5 shows the breakup of the reboots by category.

Hardware or firmware related problems: This category includes events that indicate a problem with hardware components (network adapter, disk, etc.), their associated drivers (typically drivers failing to load because of a problem with the device), or some firmware (e.g., some events indicated that the Power On Self Test had failed).

Connectivity problems: This category denotes events that indicated that either a system component (e.g., redirector, server) or a critical application (e.g., MS Exchange System Attendant) could not retrieve information from a remote machine. In these scenarios, it is not possible to pinpoint the actual cause of the connectivity problem. Some of the connectivity failures result from network adapter problems and hence are categorized as hardware related.

Table 5. Breakup of Reboots Based on Prominent Events

Category	Frequency	Percentage
Total reboots	1100	100
Hardware or firmware problems	105	9
Connectivity problems	241	22
Crucial application failures	152	14
Problems with a software component	42	4
Normal shutdowns	63	6
Normal reboots/power-off (no indication of any problems)	178	16
Unknown	319	29

Crucial application failure: This category encompasses reboots, which are preceded by severe problems with, and possibly shutdown of, critical application software (such as Message Transfer Agent). In such cases, it wasn't clear why the application reported problems. If an application shutdown occurs as a result of connectivity problem, then the corresponding reboot is categorized as connectivity-related.

Problems with a software component: Typically these reboots are characterized by startup problems (such as a critical system component not loading or a driver entry point not being found). Another significant type of problem in this category is the machine running out of virtual memory, possibly due to a memory leak in a software component. In many of these cases, the component causing the problem is not identifiable.

Normal shutdowns: This category covers reboots, which are not preceded by warnings or error messages. Additionally, there are events that indicate shutting down of critical application software and some system components (e.g., the BROWSER). These represent shutdowns for maintenance or for correcting problems not captured in the event logs.

Normal reboots/power-off: This category covers reboots which are typically not preceded by shutdown events, but do not appear to be caused by any problems either. No warnings or error messages appear in the event log before the reboot.

Based on data in Table 5, the following observations can be made about the failures:

1. 29% of the reboots cannot be categorized. Such reboots are indeed preceded by events of severity 2 or lesser, but there is not enough information available to decide (a) whether the events were severe enough to force a reboot of the machine or (b) the nature of the problem that the events reflect.
2. A significant percentage (22%) of the reboots have reported connectivity problems. Connectivity problems suggest that there could be propagated failures in the domain. Furthermore, it is possible that the machines functioning as the master browser and the Primary Domain Controller (PDC)[2], respectively are potential reliability bottlenecks of the domain.
3. Only a small percentage (10%) of the reboots can be traced to a system hardware component. Most of the identifiable problems are software related.
4. Nearly 50% of the reboots are *abnormal* reboots (i.e., the reboots were due to a problem with the machine rather than due to a normal shutdown).
5. In nearly 15% of the cases, severe problems with a crucial mail server application force a reboot of the machine.

3.3 Analysis of Failure Behavior of Individual Machines

After the preliminary investigation of the causes of failures, we probe failures from the perspective of an individual machine as well as the whole network. First we focus on the failure behavior of individual machines in the domain to obtain (1) estimates of machine up-times and down-times, (2) an estimate of the availability of each machine, and (3) a finite state model to describe the failure behavior of a typical machine in the domain. Machine up-times and down-times are estimated as follows:

- For every reboot event encountered, the timestamp of the reboot is recorded.
- The timestamp of the event immediately preceding the reboot is also recorded. (This would be the last event logged by the machine before it goes down.)
- A smoothing factor of one hour is applied to the reboots (i.e., for multiple reboots that occurred within an period of one hour, except the last one, are disregarded).
- Each up-time estimate is generated by calculating the time difference between a reboot timestamp and the timestamp of the event preceding the next reboot.

---

[2] In the analyzed network, the machines belonged to a common Windows NT domain. One of the machines was configured as the Primary Domain Controller (PDC). The rest of the machines functioned as Backup Domain Controllers (BDCs).

- Each down-time estimate is obtained by calculating the time difference between a reboot timestamp and the timestamp of the event preceding it.

Machine uptimes and machine downtimes are presented in Table 6. As the standard deviation suggests, there is a great degree of variation in the machine uptimes. The longest uptime was nearly three months. The average is skewed because of some of the longer uptimes. The median is more representative of the typical uptime.

Table 6. Machine Uptime & Downtime Statistics

Item	Machine Uptime Statistics	Machine Downtime Statistics
Number of entries	616	682
Maximum	85.2 days	15.76 days
Minimum	1 hour	1 second
Average	11.82 days	1.97 hours
Median	5.54 days	11.43 minutes
Standard Deviation	15.656 days	15.86 hours

As the table shows, 50% of the downtimes last about 12 minutes. This is probably too short a period to replace hardware components and reconfigure the machine. The implication is that majority of the problems are software related (memory leaks, misloaded drivers, application errors etc.). The maximum value is unrealistic and might have been due to the machine being temporarily taken off-line and put back in after a fortnight.

Since the machines under consideration are dedicated mail servers, bringing down one or more of them would potentially disrupt storage, forwarding, reception, and delivery of mail. The disruption can be prevented if explicit rerouting is per-formed to avoid the machines that are down. But it is not clear if such rerouting was done or can be done. In this context the following observations would be causes for concern: (1) average downtime measured was nearly 2 hours or (2) 50% of the measured uptime samples were about 5 days or less.

Availability

Having estimated machine uptime and downtime, we can estimate the availability of each machine. The availability is evaluated as the ratio:

[<average uptime> / (<average uptime> + <average downtime>)]*100

Table 7 summarizes the availability measurements. As the table depicts, the majority of the machines have an availability of 99.7% or higher. Also there is not a large variation among the individual values. This is surprising considering the rather large degree of variation in the average uptimes. It follows that machines with smaller average up-times also had correspondingly smaller average downtimes, so that the ratios are not very different. Hence, the domain has two types of machines: those that reboot often but recover quickly and those that stay up relatively longer but take longer to recover from a failure.

Table 7. Machine Availability

Item	Value
Number of machines	66
Maximum	99.99
Minimum	89.39
Median	99.76
Average	99.35
Standard Deviation	1.52

Fig. 3 shows the *unavailability distribution* across the machines (unavailability was evaluated as: *100 – Availability*). Less than 20% of the machines had an availability of 99.9% or higher. However, nearly 90% of the machines had an availability of 99% or higher. It should be noted that these numbers indicate the fraction of time the machine is alive. They do not necessarily indicate the ability of the machine to provide useful service because the machine could be alive but still unable to provide the service expected of it. To elaborate, each of the machines in the domain acts as a mail server for a set of user machines. Hence, if any of these mail servers has problems that prevent it from receiving, storing, forwarding, or delivering mail, then that server would effectively be unavailable to the user machines even though it is up and running. Hence, to obtain a better estimate of machine availability, it is necessary to examine how long the machine is actually able to provide service to user machines.

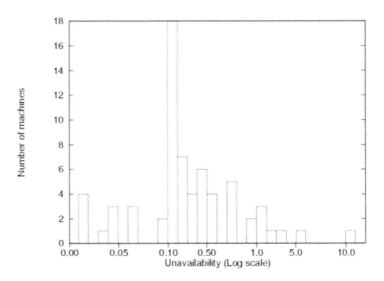

Fig. 3. Unavailability Distribution

Modeling Machine Behavior

To obtain more accurate estimates of machine availability, we modeled the behavior of a typical machine in terms of a *finite state model*. The model was based on the events that each machine logs. In the model, each state represents a level of functionality of the machine. A machine is either in a fully functional state, in which it logs events that indicate normal activity, or in a partially functional state, in which it logs events that indicate problems of a specific nature.

Selection and assignment of states to a machine was performed as follows. The logs were split into time-windows of one hour each. For each such window, the machine was assigned a state, which it occupied throughout the duration of the window. The assignment was based on the events that the machine logged in the window. Table 8 describes the states identified for the model.

Table 8. Machine States

State Name	Main Events (id/source/severity)	Explanation
Reboot	6005/EventLog/4	Machine logs reboot and other initialization events
Functional	5715/NETLOGON/4 1016/MSExchangeIS Private/8	Machine logs successful communication with PDC
Connectivity problems	3096/NETLOGON/1 5719/NETLOGON/1	Problems locating the PDC
Startup problems	7000/Service Control Manager/1 7001/Service Control Manager/1	Some system component or application failed to startup
MTA problems	2206/MSExchangeMTA/2 2207/MSExchangeMTA/2	Message Transfer Agent has problems with some internal databases
Adapter problems	4105/CpqNF3/1 4106/CpqNF3/1	The NetFlex Adapter driver reports problems
Temporary MTA problems	9322/MSExchangeMTA/4 9277/MSExchangeMTA/2 3175/MSExchangeMTA/2 1209/MSExchangeMTA/2	Message Transfer Agent reports problems of a temporary (or less severe) nature
Server problems	2006/Srv/1	Server component reports having received badly formatted requests
BROWSER problems	8021/BROWSER/2 8032/BROWSER/1	Browser reports inability to contact the master browser
Disk problems	11/Cpq32fs2/1 5/Cpq32fs2/1 9/Cpqarray/1 11/Cpqarray/1	Disk drivers report problems
Tape problems	15/dlttape/1	Tape driver reports problems
Snmpelea problems	3006/Snmpelea/1	Snmp event log agent reports error while reading an event log record
Shutdown	8033/BROWSER/4 1003/MSExchangeSA/4	Application/machine shutdown in progress

Each machine (except the Primary Domain Controller (PDC) whose transitions were different from the rest) in the domain was modeled in terms of the states mentioned in the table. A hypothetical machine was created by combining the transitions of all the individual machines and filtering out transitions that occurred less frequently. Fig. 4 describes this hypothetical machine. In the figure, the weight on each outgoing edge represents the fraction of all transitions from the originating state (i.e., tail of the arrow) that end up in a given terminating state (i.e., head of the arrow). For example, if there is an edge from state A to state B with a weight of 0.5, then it would indicate that 50% of all transitions from state A are to state B. From Fig. 4 the following observations can be made:

- Only about 40 % of the transitions out of the *Reboot* states are to the *Functional* state. This indicates that in the majority of the cases, either the reboot is not able to solve the original problem, or it creates new ones.
- More than half of the transitions out of the *Startup problems* are to the *Connectivity problems* state. Thus, the majority of the startup problems are related to components that participate in network activity.
- Most of the problems that appear when the machine is functional are related to network activity. Problems with the disk and other components are less frequent.

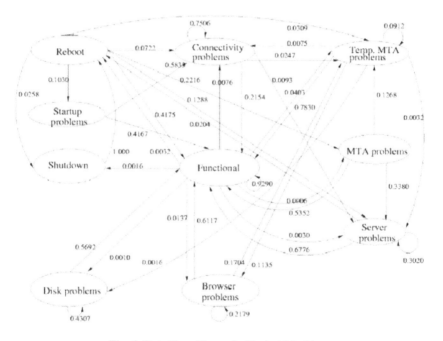

Fig. 4. State Transitions of a Typical Machine

- More than 50% of the transitions out of *Disk problems* state are to the *Functional* state. Also, we do not observe any significant transitions from the *Disk problems* state to other states. This could be due to one or more of the following:
  1. The machines are equipped with redundant disks so that even if one of them is down, the functionality is not disrupted in a major way.
  2. The disk problems, though persistent, are not severe enough to disrupt normal activity (maybe retries to access the disk succeed).
  3. The activities that are considered to be representative of the *Functional* state may not involve much disk activity.

- Over 11% of the transitions out of the *Temporary MTA problems* state are to the *Browser problems* state. We suspect that there was a local problem that caused RPCs to timeout or fail and caused problems for the MTA and BROWSER. Another possibility is that, in both cases, it was the same remote machine that could not be contacted. Based on the available data, it was not possible to determine the real cause of the problem.

To view the transitions from a different perspective, we computed the weight of each outgoing edge as a fraction of all the transitions in the finite state machine. Such a computation provided some interesting insights, which are enumerated below:

1. Nearly 10% of all the transitions are between the *Functional* and *Temporary MTA* problems states. These MTA problems are typically problems with some RPC calls (either failing or being canceled).
2. About 0.5% (1 in 200) of all transitions are to the *Reboot* state.
3. The majority of the transitions into the *MTA problems* state are from the *Reboot* state. Thus, MTA problems are primarily problems that occur at startup. In contrast, the majority of the transitions into the *Server problems* state and the *Browser problems* state (excluding the self loops) are from the *Functional* state. So, these problems (or at least a significant fraction of them) typically appear after the machine is functional.
4. About 92% of all transitions are into the *Functional* state. This figure is approximately a measure of the average time the hypothetical machine spends in the functional state. Hence it is a measure of the average availability of a typical machine. In this case, availability measures the ability of the machine to provide service, not just to stay alive.

3.4 Modeling Domain Behavior

Analyzing system behavior from the perspective of the whole domain (1) provides a macroscopic view of the system rather than a machine-specific view, (2) helps to characterize the nature of interactions in the network, and (3) aids in identifying potential reliability bottlenecks and suggests ways to improve resilience to operational faults.

Inter-reboot Times. An important characteristic of the domain is how often reboots occur within it. To examine this, the whole domain is treated as a black box, and every reboot of every machine in the domain is considered to be a reboot of the black box. Table 9 shows the statistics of such inter-reboot times measured across the whole domain.

Table 9. Inter-reboot Time Statistics for the Domain

Item	Value
Number of samples	882
Maximum	2.46 days
Minimum	Less than 1 second
Median	2402 seconds
Average	4.09 hours
Standard Deviation	7.52 hours

Finite State Model of the Domain

The proper functioning of the domain relies on the proper functioning of the PDC and its interactions with the Backup Domain Controllers (BDCs). Thus it would seem useful to represent the domain in terms of how many BDCs are alive at any given moment and also in terms of the PDC being functional or not. Accordingly, a finite state model was constructed as follows:

1. The data collection period was broken up into time windows of a fixed length,
2. For each such time window, the state of the domain was computed, and
3. A transition diagram was constructed based on the state information.

The state of the domain during a given time window was computed by evaluating the number of machines that rebooted during that time window. More specifically, the states were identified as shown in Table 10. Fig. 5 shows the transitions in the domain. Each time window was one hour long.

Table 10. Domain States and their Interpretation

State Name	Meaning
PDC	Primary Domain Controller (PDC) rebooted
BDC	1 Backup Domain Controller (BDC) rebooted
MBDC	Many BDCs rebooted
PDC+BDC	PDC and One BDC rebooted
PDC+MBDC	PDC and Many BDCs rebooted
F	Functional (no reboots observed)

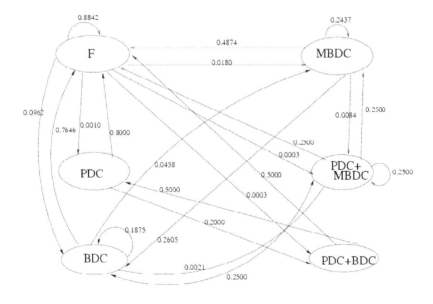

Fig. 5. Domain State Transitions

Fig. 5 reveals some interesting insights.

1. Nearly 77% of all transitions from the *F* state, excluding the self-loops, are to the *BDC* state. If these transitions do indeed result in disruption in service, then it is possible to improve the overall availability significantly just by tolerating single machine failures.
2. A non-negligible number of transitions are between the *F* state and the *MBDC* state and between states *BDC* and *MBDC*. This would indicate potentially correlated failures and recovery (see [12] for more details).
3. Majority of transitions from state *PDC* are to state *F*. This could be explained by one of the following:
   - Most of the problems with the *PDC* are not propagated to the BDCs,
   - The PDC typically recovers before any such propagation takes effect on the BDCs, or
   - The problems on the PDC are not severe enough to bring it down, but they might worsen as they propagate to the BDCs and force a reboot.
- However, 20% of the transitions from the *PDC* state are to the *PDC+BDC* state. So there is a possibility of the propagation of failures.

4   Conclusions

The discussion in this paper focused on the issues involved in analyzing the availability of networked systems using fault injection and the failure data collected by the logging mechanisms built into the system. To achieve accurate and comprehensive system dependability evaluation the analysis must span the three phases of system life: design phase, prototype phase, and operational phase.

For example the presented fault injection study of the ARMOR-based SIFT environment demonstrated that:

1. Structuring the fault injection experiments to progressively stress the error detection and recovery mechanisms is a useful approach to evaluating performance and error propagation.
2. Even though the probability for correlated failures is small, its potential impact on application availability is significant.
3. The SIFT environment successfully recovered from all correlated failures involving the application and a SIFT process because the processes performing error detection and recovery were decoupled from the failed processes.
4. Targeted injections into dynamic data on the heap were useful in further investigating system failures brought about by error propagation. Assertions within the SIFT processes were shown to reduce the number of system failures from data error propagation by up to 42%.

Similarly analysis of failure data collected in a network of Windows NT machines provides insights into network system failure behavior.

1. Most of the problems that lead to reboots are software related. Only 10% are attributable to specific hardware components.
2. Rebooting the machine does not appear to solve the problem in many cases. In about 60% of the reboots, the rebooted machine reported problems within a hour or two of the reboot.

3. Though the average availability evaluates to over 99%, a typical machine in the domain, on average, provides acceptable service only about 92% of the time.
4. About 1% of the reboots indicate memory leaks in the software.
5. There are indications of propagated or correlated failures. Typically, in such cases, multiple machines exhibit identical or similar problems at almost the same time.

Moreover, the failure data analysis also provides insights into the error logging mechanism. For example, event-logging features that are absent, but desirable, in Windows NT can be suggested:

1. The presence of a Windows NT shutdown event will improve the accuracy in identifying the causes of reboots. It will also lead to better estimates of machine availability.
2. Most of the events observed in the logs were either due to applications or to high-level system components, such as file-system drivers. It is not evident if this is due to a genuine absence of problems at the lower levels or it is just because the lower-level system components log events sparingly or resort to other means to report events. If the latter is true, then improved event logging by the lower-level system components (protocol drivers, memory managers) can enhance the value of event logs in diagnosis.

Acknowledgments. This manuscript is based on a research supported in part by NASA under grant NAG-1-613, in cooperation with the Illinois Computer Laboratory for Aerospace Systems and Software (ICLASS), by Tandem Computers, and in part by a NASA/JPL contract 961345, and by NSF grants CCR 00-86096 ITR and CCR 99-02026.

References

1. J.Arlat, et al., "Fault Injection for Dependability Validation – A Methodology and Some Applications," *IEEE Trans. On Software Engineering*, Vol. 16, No. 2, pp. 166-182, Feb. 1990.
2. J.Arlat, et al., "Fault Injection and Dependability Evaluation of Fault-Tolerant Systems," *IEEE Trans. On Computers*, Vol. 42, No. 8, pp.913-923, Aug. 1993.
3. D. Avresky, et al., "Fault Injection for the Formal Testing of Fault Tolerance," *Proc. 22nd Int. Symp. Fault-Tolerant Computing*, pp. 345-354, June 1992.
4. S. Bagchi, "Hierarchical error detection in a software-implemented fault tolerance (SIFT) environment," Ph.D. Thesis, University of Illinois, Urbana, IL, 2001.
5. J.H. Barton, E.W. Czeck, Z.Z. Segall, and D.P. Siewiorek, "Fault injection experiments using FIAT," *IEEE Trans. Computers*, Vol.39, pp.575-582, Apr. 1990.
6. X. Castillo and D.P. Siewiorek, "A Workload Dependent Software Reliability Prediction Model," *Proc. 12th Int. Symp. Fault-Tolerant Computing*, pp.279-286, 1982.
7. R. Chillarege,S. Biyani, and J. Rosenthal, "Measurement Of Failure Rate in Widely Distributed Software," *Proc. 25th Int. Symp. Fault-Tolerant Computing*, pp. 424-433, 1995.
8. J. Gray, "A Census of Tandem System Availability between 1985 and 1990," *IEEE Trans. Reliability*," Vol. 39, No. 4, pp. 409-418, 1990.

9. M.C. Hsueh, R.K. Iyer, and K.S. Trivedi, "Performability Modeling Based on Real Data: A Case Study," *IEEE Trans. Computers*, Vol. 37, No.4, pp. 478-484, April 1988.
10. R. Iyer, D. Tang, "Experimental Analysis of Computer System Dependability," *Chapter 5 in Fault Tolerant Computer Design*, D.K. Pradhan, Prentice Hall, pp.282-392, 1996.
11. R.K. Iyer and D.J. Rossetti, "Effect of System Workload on Operating System Reliability: A Study on IBM 3081," *IEEE Trans. Software Engineering*, Vol. SE-11, No. 12, pp. 1438-1448, 1985.
12. M. Kalyanakrishnam, "Failure Data Analysis of LAN of Windows NT Based Computers," *Proc. 18th Symp. on Reliable Distributed Systems*, pp.178-187, October 1999.
13. Z. Kalbarczyk, R. Iyer, S. Bagchi, K. Whisnant, "Chameleon: A software infrastructure for adaptive fault tolerance," *IEEE Trans. on Parallel and Distributed Systems*, vol. 10, no. 6, pp. 560-579, 1999.
14. G.A. Kanawati, N.A. Kanawati, and J.A. Abraham, "FERRARI: A flexible software-based fault and error injection system," *IEEE Trans. Computers*, Vol.44, pp.248-260, Feb. 1995.
15. I. Lee and R.K. Iyer, "Analysis of Software Halts in Tandem System," *Proc. 3rd Int. Symp. Software Reliability Engineering*, pp. 227-236, 1992.
16. I. Lee and R.K. Iyer, "Software Dependability in the Tandem GUARDIAN Operating System," *IEEE Trans. on Software Engineering*, Vol. 21, No. 5, pp. 455-467, 1995.
17. T.T. Lin, D.P. Siewiorek, "Error Log Analysis: Statistical Modeling and Heuristic Trend Analysis," *IEEE Trans. Reliability*, Vol. 39, No. 4, pp.419-432, 1990.
18. H. Maderia, R. Some, F. Moereira, D. Costa, D. Rennels, "Experimental evaluation of a COTS system for space applications," *Proc. Of Int. Conf. On Dependable Systems and Networks (DSN '02)*, Washington DC, pp. 325-330, June 2002.
19. Message Passing Interface Forum, "MPI-2: Extensions to the Message Passing Interface," *http://www.mpi-forum.org/docs/mpi-20.ps*.
20. J.F. Meyer and L. Wei, "Analysis of Workload Influence on Dependability" *Proc. 18th Int. Symp. Fault-Tolerant Computing*, pp.84-89, 1988.
21. S. Mourad and D. Andrews, "On the Reliability of the IBM MVS/XA Operating System," *IEEE Trans. on Software Engineering*, October 1987.
22. D. Stott, B. Floering, Z. Kalbarczyk, and R. Iyer, "Dependability assessment in distributed systems with lightweight fault injectors in NFTAPE," *Proc. Int. Performance and Dependability Symposium, IPDS-00*, pp. 91-100, 2000.
23. M.S. Sullivan, R. Chillarege,"Software Defects and Their Impact on System Availability — A Study of Field Failures in Operating Systems," *Proc. 21st Int. Symp. Fault-Tolerant Computing*, pp. 2-9, 1991.
24. M.S. Sullivan and R. Chillarege, "A Comparison of Software Defects in Database Management Systems and Operating Systems," *Proc. 22nd Int. Symp. Fault-Tolerant Computing*, pp.475-484, 1992.
25. D. Tang and R.K. Iyer, "Analysis of the VAX/VMS Error Logs in Multicomputer Environments — A Case Study of Software Dependability," *Proc. 3rd Int. Symp. Software Reliability Engineering*, Research Triangle Park, North Carolina, pp. 216-226, October 1992.
26. D. Tang and R.K. Iyer, "Dependability Measurement and Modeling of a Multicomputer Systems," *IEEE Trans. Computers*, Vol. 42, No. 1, pp.62-75, January 1993.
27. A.Thakur, R.K.Iyer, L. Young, I. Lee, "Analysis of Failures in the Tandem NonStop-UX Operating System," *Proc. Int'l Symp. Software Reliability Engineering*, pp. 40-49, 1995.
28. M.M. Tsao and D.P. Siewiorek, "Trend Analysis on System Error files," *Proc. 13th Int. Symp. Fault-Tolerant Computing*, pp. 116-119, June 1983.
29. P. Velardi and R.K. Iyer, "A Study of Software Failures and Recovery in the MVS Operating System'" *IEEE Trans. On Computers*, Vol. C-33, No. 6, pp.564-568, June 1984.
30. K. Whisnant, Z. Kalbarczyk, and R. Iyer, "Micro-checkpointing: Checkpointing for multithreaded applications," *in Proceedings of the 6th International On-Line Testing Workshop*, July 2000.

31. K. Whisnant, R. Iyer, Z. Kalbarczyk, P. Jones, "An Experimental Evaluation of the ARMOR-based REE Software-Implemented Fault Tolerance Environment," pending technical report, University of Illinois, Urbana, IL, 2001.
32. K. Whisnant, et al., "An Experimental Evaluation of the REE SIFTEnvironment for Spaceborne Applications," *Proc. Of Int. Conf. On Dependable Systems and Networks (DSN '02)*, Washington DC, pp. 585-594, June 2002.

Software Reliability and Rejuvenation: Modeling and Analysis

Kishor S. Trivedi and Kalyanaraman Vaidyanathan

Dept. of Electrical & Computer Engineering
Duke University
Durham, NC 27708-0291, USA
{kst,kv}@ee.duke.edu

Abstract. Several recent studies have established that most system outages are due to software faults. Given the ever increasing complexity of software and the well-developed techniques and analysis for hardware reliability, this trend is not likely to change in the near future. In this paper, we classify software faults and discuss various techniques to deal with them in the testing/debugging phase and the operational phase of the software. We discuss the phenomenon of software aging and a preventive maintenance technique to deal with this problem called software rejuvenation. Stochastic models to evaluate the effectiveness of preventive maintenance in operational software systems and to determine optimal times to perform rejuvenation for different scenarios are described. We also present measurement-based methodologies to detect software aging and estimate its effect on various system resources. These models are intended to help develop software rejuvenation policies. An automated online measurement-based approach has been used in the software rejuvenation agent implemented in a major commercial server.

1 Introduction

Outages in computer systems consist of both hardware and software failures. While hardware failures have been studied extensively and varied mechanisms have been presented to increase system availability with regard to such failures, software failures and the corresponding reliability/availability analysis has not drawn much attention from researchers. The study of software failures has now become more important since it has been recognized that computer systems outages are more due to software faults than to hardware faults [19,35,40]. Therefore, software reliability is one of the weakest links in system reliability.

In this paper, we attempt to classify software faults based on an extension of Gray's classification [17] and discuss the various techniques to deal with these faults in the testing/debugging and operational phase of the software. We then describe the phenomenon of software aging, where the state of the software system gradually degrades with time. This might eventually cause a performance degradation of the system or result in a crash/hang failure. Particular attention is given to software rejuvenation - a proactive form of environment diversity

M.C. Calzarossa and S. Tucci (Eds.): Performance 2002, LNCS 2459, pp. 318–345, 2002.
© Springer-Verlag Berlin Heidelberg 2002

to deal with software aging, explaining its various approaches and methods in practice.

1.1 What Is a Software Failure?

According to Laprie et al. [29], "a system failure occurs when the delivered service no longer complies with the specifications, the latter being an agreed description of the system's expected function and/or service". This definition applies to both hardware and software system failures. Faults or bugs in a hardware or a software component cause errors. An error is defined as that part of the system which is liable to lead to subsequent failure, and an error affecting the service is an indication that a failure occurs or has occurred. If the system comprises of multiple components, errors can lead to a component failure. As various components in the system interact, failure of one component might introduce one or more faults in another.

1.2 Classification of Software Faults

Gray [17] classifies software faults into *Bohrbugs* and *Heisenbugs*. Bohrbugs are essentially permanent design faults and hence almost deterministic in nature. They can be identified easily and weeded out during the testing and debugging phase (or early deployment phase) of the software life cycle. Heisenbugs, on the other hand, are essentially permanent faults whose conditions of activation occur rarely or are not easily reproducible. Hence, these faults result in transient failures, i.e., failures which may not recur if the software is restarted. Some typical situations in which Heisenbugs might surface are boundaries between various software components, improper or insufficient exception handling and interdependent timing of various events. It is for this reason that Heisenbugs are extremely difficult to identify through testing. Hence, a mature piece of software in the operational phase, released after its development and testing stage, is more likely to experience failures caused by Heisenbugs than due to Bohrbugs. Most recent studies on failure data have reported that a large proportion of software failures are transient in nature [17,18], caused by phenomena such as overloads or timing and exception errors [9,40]. The study of failure data from Tandem's fault tolerant computer system indicated that 70% of the failures were transient failures, caused by faults like race conditions and timing problems [30].

1.3 Software Aging

The phenomenon of *software aging* has been reported by several recent studies [16,25]. It was observed that once the software was started, potential fault conditions gradually accumulated with time leading to either performance degradation or transient failures or both. Failures may be of crash/hang type or those resulting from data inconsistency because of aging. Typical causes of aging, i.e., slow degradation, are memory bloating or leaking, unreleased file-locks, data corruption, storage space fragmentation and accumulation of round off errors.

Popular and widely used software like the web browser *Netscape* is known to suffer from serious memory leaks which lead to occasional crash/hang of the application. This problem is particularly pronounced in systems with low swap space. The newsreader software *xrn* also experiences problems due to memory leaks. Software aging has not only been observed in software used on a mass scale but also in specialized software used in high availability and safety-critical applications. This phenomenon has been observed in general purpose UNIX applications [25]. The applications experienced a crash/hang failure over time which resulted in unplanned and expensive downtime. Avritzer and Weyuker [4] report aging manifesting as gradual performance degradation in an industrial telecommunication software system. They deal with *soft failures*, i.e, a type of failure where the system may enter a faulty state in which the system is still available for service but has degraded to unacceptable performance levels, losing users or packets. A similar kind of gradual performance degradation in file systems leading to a soft failure is discussed by Smith and Seltzer [39]. Their study shows that in a degraded file system caused by normal usage and filling up of storage space, the read throughput may be as much as 40% lower than that in an empty file system. The reason behind this is the fragmentation of storage space over time which results in non-sequential allocation of blocks. The most glaring example of software aging in recent times is reported by Marshall [32]. In this case, software aging resulted in loss of human life. The software system in the US Patriot missiles deployed during the Gulf War accumulated numerical roundoff error. This led to the interpretation of an incoming Iraqi Scud missile as a false alarm which cost the lives of 28 US soldiers.

We designate faults attributed to software aging, which are quite different from Bohrbugs and Heisenbugs, as *aging-related* faults. These faults are similar to Heisenbugs in that they are activated under certain conditions (for example, lack of OS resources) which may not be easily reproducible. However, as discussed later, their modes and methods of recovery differ significantly. Figure 1 shows our extended classification and treatment strategies for each class.

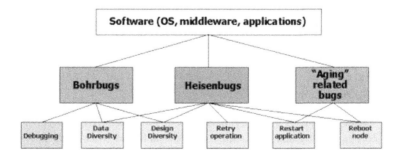

Fig. 1. Classification and treatment of software faults

1.4 Software Fault Tolerance

Techniques for tolerating faults in software have been divided into three classes:

- **Design diversity:** Design diversity techniques are specifically developed to tolerate design faults in software arising out of wrong specifications and incorrect coding. Two or more variants of a software developed by different teams, but to a common specification are used. These variants are then used in a time or space redundant manner to achieve fault tolerance. Popular techniques which are based on the design diversity concept for fault tolerance in software are N-version programming [3], recovery block [23] and N-self checking programming [28]. The design diversity approach was developed mainly to deal with Bohrbugs, but can to some extent deal with Heisenbugs.
- **Data diversity:** Data diversity, a technique for fault tolerance in software, was introduced by Amman and Knight [2]. While the design diversity approaches to provide fault tolerance rely on multiple versions of the software written to the same specifications, the data diversity approach uses only one version of the software. This approach relies on the observation that software sometime fails for certain values in the input space and this failure could be averted if there is a minor perturbation of input data which is acceptable to the software. Data diversity can work well with Bohrbugs and is cheaper to implement than design diversity techniques. To some extent, data diversity can also deal with Heisenbugs since different input data is presented and by definition, these bugs are non-deterministic and non-repeatable.
- **Environment diversity** Environment diversity is the newest approach to fault tolerance in software. Although this technique has been used for long in an *ad hoc* manner, only recently has it gained recognition and importance. Having its basis on the observation that most software failures are transient in nature, the environment diversity approach requires reexecuting the software in a different environment [27]. Environment diversity deals effectively with Heisenbugs by exploiting their definition and nature. Adams [1] has proposed restarting the system as the best approach to masking software faults. Environment diversity, a generalization of restart [24,27], is a cheap but effective technique for fault tolerance in software. Examples of environment diversity techniques include operation retry operation, application restart and node reboot. The retry and restart operations can be done on the same node or on another spare (cold/warm/hot) node [30]. A specific form of environment diversity, called *software rejuvenation* [25,47], which forms the crux of this paper is discussed in detail in the following sections.

1.5 Software Rejuvenation

To counteract software aging, a proactive technique called *software rejuvenation* has been proposed [25,47]. It involves stopping the running software occasionally, "cleaning" its internal state and restarting it. Garbage collection, flushing operating system kernel tables, reinitializing internal data structures are some examples of what cleaning the internal state of a software might involve. An extreme, but well known example of rejuvenation is a hardware reboot. It has been implemented in the real-time system collecting billing data for most telephone exchanges in the United States [5]. A very similar technique called *software capacity restoration*, has been used by Avritzer and Weyuker in a large telecommunications switching software [4], where the switching computer is rebooted occasionally upon which its service rate is restored to the peak value. Grey [20] proposed performing operations solely for fault management in SDI (Strategic Defense Initiative) software which are invoked whether or not the fault exists and called it operational redundancy. Tai et al. [41] have proposed and analyzed the use of on-board preventive maintenance for maximizing the probability of successful mission completion of spacecrafts with very long mission times. The necessity of performing preventive maintenance in a safety critical environment is evident from the example of aging in Patriot's software [32]. The failure which resulted in loss of human lives could have been prevented if the computer was restarted after each 8 hours of running time. Rejuvenation has been implemented in various other kinds of systems - transaction processing systems [7], web servers [46] and cluster servers [8].

Software rejuvenation (preventive maintenance) incurs an overhead (in terms of performance, cost and downtime) which should be balanced against the loss incurred due to unexpected outage caused by a failure. Thus, an important research issue is to determine the optimal times to perform rejuvenation. In this paper, we present two approaches for analyzing software aging and studying aging-related failures.

The rest of this paper is organized as follows. Section 2 describes various analytical models for software aging and to determine optimal times to perform rejuvenation. Measurement-based models are dealt with in Section 3. The implementation of a software rejuvenation agent in a major commercial server is discussed in Section 4. Section 5 describes various approaches and methods of rejuvenation and Section 6 concludes the paper with pointers to future work.

2   Analytic Models for Software Rejuvenation

The aim of the analytic modeling is to determine optimal times to perform rejuvenation which maximize *availability* and minimize the *probability of loss* or the *response time of a transaction* (in the case of a transaction processing system). This is particularly important for business-critical applications for which adequate response time can be as important as system uptime. The analysis is done for different kinds of software systems exhibiting varied failure/aging characteristics.

The accuracy of a modeling based approach is determined by the assumptions made in capturing aging. In [12,13,14,25,41] only the failures causing unavailability of the software are considered, while in [34] only a gradually decreasing service rate of a software which serves transactions is assumed. Garg et al. [15], however, consider both these effects of aging together in a single model. Models proposed in [12,13,25] are restricted to hypo-exponentially distributed time to failure. Those proposed in [14,34,41] can accommodate general distributions but only for the specific aging effect they capture. Generally distributed time to failure, as well as the service rate being an arbitrary function of time are allowed in [15]. It has been noted [40] that transient failures are partly caused by overload conditions. Only the model presented by Garg et al. [15] captures the effect of load on aging. Existing models also differ in the measures being evaluated. In [14,41] software with a finite mission time is considered. In the [12,13,15,25] measures of interest in a transaction based software intended to run forever are evaluated.

Bobbio et al.[6] present fine grained software degradation models, where one can identify the current degradation level based on the observation of a system parameter, are considered. Optimal rejuvenation policies based on a risk criterion and an alert threshold are then presented. Dohi et al. [10,11] present software rejuvenation models based on semi-Markov processes. The models are analyzed for optimal rejuvenation strategies based on cost as well as steady-state availability. Given a sample data of failure times, statistical non-parametric algorithms based on the total time on test transform are presented to obtain the optimal rejuvenation interval.

2.1   Basic Model for Rejuvenation

Figure 2 shows the basic software rejuvenation model proposed by Huang et al. [25]. The software system is initially in a "robust" working state, 0. As time progresses, it eventually transits to a "failure-probable" state 1. The system is still operational in this state but can fail (move to state 2) with a non-zero probability. The system can be repaired and brought back to the initial state 0. The software system is also rejuvenated at regular intervals from the failure probable state 1 and brought back to the robust state 0.

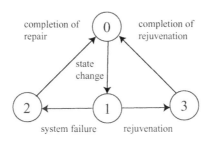

Fig. 2. State transition diagram for rejuvenation

Huang et al. [25] assume that the stochastic behavior of the system can be described by a simple continuous-time Markov chain (CTMC) [43]. Let Z be the random time interval when the highly robust state changes to the failure probable state, having the exponential distribution $\Pr\{Z \le t\} = F_0(t) = 1 - \exp(-t/\mu_0)$ $(\mu_0 > 0)$. Just after the state becomes the failure probable state, a system failure may occur with a positive probability. Without loss of generality, we assume that the random variable Z is observable during the system operation. Define the failure time X (from state 1) and the repair time Y, having the exponential distributions $\Pr\{X \le t\} = F_f(t) = 1 - \exp(-t/\lambda_f)$ and $\Pr\{Y \le t\} = F_a(t) = 1 - \exp(-t/\mu_a)$ $(\lambda_f > 0, \ \mu_a > 0)$. If the system failure occurs before triggering a software rejuvenation, then the repair is started immediately at that time and is completed after the random time Y elapses. Otherwise, the software rejuvenation is started. Note that the software rejuvenation cycle is measured from the time instant just after the system enters state 1. Define the distribution functions of the time to invoke the software rejuvenation and of the time to complete software rejuvenation by $F_r(t) = 1 - \exp(-t/\mu_r)$ and $F_c(t) = 1 - \exp(-t/\mu_c)$ $(\mu_c > 0, \ \mu_r > 0)$, respectively. The CTMC is then analyzed and the expected system down time and the expected cost per unit time in the steady state is computed. An optimal rejuvenation interval which minimizes expected downtime (or expected cost) is obtained.

It is not difficult to introduce the periodic rejuvenation schedule and to extend the CTMC model to the general one. Dohi et al. [10,11] developed semi-Markov models with the periodic rejuvenation and general transition distribution functions. More specifically, let Z be the random variable having the common distribution function $\Pr\{Z \le t\} = F_0(t)$ with finite mean μ_0 (> 0). Also, let X and Y be the random variables having the common distribution functions $\Pr\{X \le t\} = F_f(t)$ and $\Pr\{Y \le t\} = F_a(t)$ with finite means λ_f (> 0) and μ_a (> 0), respectively. Denote the distribution function of the time to invoke the software rejuvenation and the distribution of the time to complete software rejuvenation by $F_r(t)$ and $F_c(t)$ (with mean μ_c (> 0)), respectively. After completing the repair or the rejuvenation, the software system becomes as good as new, and the software age is initiated at the beginning of the next highly robust state. Consequently, we define the time interval from the beginning of the system operation to the next one as one cycle, and the same cycle is repeated again and again. The time to software rejuvenation (the rejuvenation interval) is a constant, t_0, i.e., $F_r(t) = U(t - t_0)$, where $U(\cdot)$ is the unit step function.

The underlying stochastic process is a semi-Markov process with four regeneration states. If the sojourn times in all states are exponentially distributed, this model is the CTMC in Huang et al. [25]. Using the renewal theory [36], the steady-state system availability is computed as

$$A(t_0) = \Pr\Big\{\text{software system is operative in the steady state}\Big\}$$

$$= \frac{\mu_0 + \int_0^{t_0} \overline{F}_f(t)dt}{\mu_0 + \mu_a F_f(t_0) + \mu_c \overline{F}_f(t_0) + \int_0^{t_0} \overline{F}_f(t)dt}$$

$$= S(t_0)/T(t_0), \tag{1}$$

where in general $\overline{\phi}(\cdot) = 1 - \phi(\cdot)$ The problem is to derive the optimal software rejuvenation interval t_0^* which maximizes the system availability in the steady state $A(t_0)$. We make the following assumption that the mean time to repair is strictly larger than the mean time to complete the software rejuvenation (i.e., $\mu_a > \mu_c$). This assumption is quite reasonable and intuitive. The following result gives the optimal software rejuvenation schedule for the semi-Markov model.

Assume that the failure time distribution is strictly IFR (increasing failure rate) [43]. Define the following non-linear function:

$$q(t_0) = T(t_0) - \left\{(\mu_a - \mu_c)r_f(t_0) + 1\right\}S(t_0), \tag{2}$$

where $r_f(t) = (dF_f(t)/dt)/\overline{F}_f(t)$ is the failure rate.

(i) If $q(0) > 0$ and $q(\infty) < 0$, then there exists a finite and unique optimal software rejuvenation schedule t_0^* $(0 < t_0^* < \infty)$ satisfying $q(t_0^*) = 0$, and the maximum system availability is

$$A(t_0^*) = \frac{1}{(\mu_a - \mu_c)r_f(t_0^*) + 1}. \tag{3}$$

(ii) If $q(0) \leq 0$, then the optimal software rejuvenation schedule is $t_0^* = 0$, i.e. it is optimal to start the rejuvenation just after entering the failure probable state, and the maximum system availability is $A(0) = \mu_0/(\mu_0 + \mu_c)$.

(iii) If $q(\infty) \geq 0$, then the optimal rejuvenation schedule is $t_0^* \to \infty$, i.e. it is optimal not to carry out the rejuvenation, and the maximum system availability is $A(\infty) = (\mu_0 + \lambda_f)/(\mu_0 + \mu_a + \lambda_f)$.

If the failure time distribution is DFR (decreasing failure rate), then the system availability $A(t_0)$ is a convex function of t_0, and the optimal rejuvenation schedule is $t_0^* = 0$ or $t_0^* \to \infty$ [10,11].

Garg et al. [12] have developed a Markov Regenerative Stochastic Petri Net (MRSPN) model where rejuvenation is performed at deterministic intervals assuming that the failure probable state 1 is not observable.

2.2 Preventive Maintenance in Transactions Based Software Systems

In [15], Garg et al. consider a transaction-based software system whose macro-states representation is presented in Figure 3. The state in which the software is available for service (albeit with decreasing service rate) is denoted as state A. After failure a recovery procedure is started. In state B the software is recovering from failure and is unavailable for service. Lastly, the software occasionally undergoes preventive maintenance (PM), denoted by state C. PM is allowed only from state A. Once recovery from failure or PM is complete, the software is reset to state A and is as good as new. From this moment, which constitutes a renewal, the whole process stochastically repeats itself.

The system consists of a server type software to which transactions arrive at a constant rate λ. Each transaction receives service for a random period. The service rate of the software is an arbitrary function measured from the

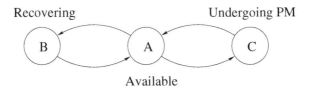

Fig. 3. Macro-states representation of the software behavior

last renewal of the software (because of aging) denoted by $\mu(\cdot)$. Therefore, a transaction which starts service at time t_1, occupies the server for a time whose distribution is given by $1 - e^{-\int_{t_1}^{t} \mu(\cdot)\, dt}$. If the software is busy processing a transaction, arriving customers are queued. Total number of transactions that the software can accommodate is K (including the one being processed) and any more arriving when the queue is full are lost. The service discipline is FCFS. The software fails with a rate $\rho(\cdot)$, that is, the *CDF* of the time to failure X is given by $F_X(t) = 1 - e^{-\int_0^t \rho(\cdot)\, dt}$. Times to recover from failure Y_f and to perform PM Y_r are random variables with associated general *CDFs* F_{Y_f} and F_{Y_r} respectively. The model does not require any assumptions on the nature of F_{Y_f} and F_{Y_r}. Only the respective expectations $\gamma_f = E[Y_f]$ and $\gamma_r = E[Y_r]$ are assumed to be finite. Any transactions in the queue at the time of failure or at the time of initiation of PM are assumed to be lost. Moreover, any transactions which arrive while the software is recovering or undergoing PM are also lost.

The effect of aging in the model may be captured by using decreasing service rate and increasing failure rate, where the decrease or the increase respectively can be a function of time, instantaneous load, mean accumulated load or a combination of the above.

Two policies which can be used to determine the time to perform PM are considered. Under policy I which is purely time-based, PM is initiated after a constant time δ has elapsed since it was started (or restarted). Under policy II, which is based on instantaneous load and time, a constant waiting period δ must elapse before PM is attempted. After this time PM is initiated if and only if there are no transactions in the system. Otherwise, the software waits until the queue is empty upon which PM is initiated. The actual PM interval under Policy II is determined by the sum of PM wait δ and the time it takes for the queue to get empty from that point onwards B. Since the latter quantity is dependent on system parameters and can not be controlled, the actual PM interval has a range $[\delta, \infty)$.

Given the above behavioral model the following measures are derived for each policy: steady state availability of the software A_{SS}, long run probability of loss of a transaction P_{loss}, and expected response time of a transaction given that it is successfully served T_{res}. The goal is to determine optimal values of δ (PM interval under policy I and PM wait under policy II) based on the constraints on one or more of these measures.

According to the model described above at any time t the software can be in any one of three states: up and available for service (state A), recovering from a failure (state B) or undergoing PM (state C). Let $\{Z(t), t \geq 0\}$ be a stochastic process which represents the state of the software at time t. Further, let the sequence of random variables $S_i, i > 0$ represent the times at which transitions among different states take place. Since the entrance times S_i constitute renewal points $\{Z(S_i), i > 0\}$ is an embedded discrete time Markov chain (DTMC) with a transition probability matrix P given by:

$$P = \begin{bmatrix} 0 & P_{AB} & P_{AC} \\ 1 & 0 & 0 \\ 1 & 0 & 0 \end{bmatrix}. \tag{4}$$

The steady state probability π_i of the DTMC being in state $i, i \in \{A, B, C\}$ is:

$$\pi = [\pi_A, \pi_B, \pi_C] = \left[\frac{1}{2}, \frac{1}{2} P_{AB}, \frac{1}{2} P_{AC}\right]. \tag{5}$$

The software behavior is modeled via the stochastic process $\{(Z(t), N(t)), t \geq 0\}$. If $Z(t) = A$, then $N(t) \in \{0, 1, \ldots, K\}$ as the queue can accommodate up to K transactions. If $Z(t) \in \{B, C\}$, then $N(t) = 0$, since by assumption all transactions arriving while the software is either recovering or undergoing PM are lost. Further, the transactions already in the queue at the transition instant are also discarded. It can be shown that the process $\{(Z(t), N(t)), t \geq 0\}$ is a Markov regenerative process (MRGP). Transition to state A from either B or C constitutes a regeneration instant.

Let U be a random variable denoting the sojourn time in state A, and denote its expectation by $E[U]$. Expected sojourn times of the MRGP in states B and C are already defined to be γ_f and γ_r. The steady state availability is obtained using the standard formulae from MRGP theory: $A_{SS} = Pr\{software\ is\ in\ state\ A\}$

$$= \frac{\pi_A E[U]}{\pi_B \gamma_f + \pi_C \gamma_r + \pi_A E[U]}. \tag{6}$$

The probability that a transaction is lost is defined as the ratio of expected number of transactions which are lost in an interval to the expected total number of transactions which arrive during that interval. Since the evolution of $\{Z(t), N(t)), t > 0\}$ in the intervals comprising of successive visits to state A is stochastically identical it suffices to consider just one such interval. The number of transactions lost is given by the summation of three quantities: (1) transactions in the queue when the system is exiting state A because of the failure or initiation of PM (2) transactions that arrive while failure recovery or PM is in progress and (3) transactions that are disregarded due to the buffer being full. The last quantity is of special significance since the probability of buffer being full will increase due to the degrading service rate. It follows that the probability of loss is given by

$$P_{loss} = \frac{\pi_A E[N_l] + \lambda \left(\pi_B \gamma_f + \pi_C \gamma_r + \pi_A \int_0^\infty p_K(t)dt \right)}{\lambda \left(\pi_B \gamma_f + \pi_C \gamma_r + \pi_A E[U] \right)} \tag{7}$$

where $E[N_l]$ is the expected number of transactions in the buffer when the system is exiting state A. Equation 7 is valid only for policy II. Under policy I sojourn time in state A is limited by δ, so the upper limit in the integral $\int_0^\infty p_K(t)dt$ is δ instead of ∞.

Next an upper bound on the mean response time of a transaction given that it is successfully served, T_{res}, is derived. The mean number of transactions, denoted by E, which are accepted for service while the software is in state A is given by the mean number of transactions which are not accepted due to the buffer being full, subtracted from the mean total number of transactions which arrive while the software is in state A, that is, $E = \lambda \left[E[U] - \int_{t=0}^\infty p_K(t)dt \right]$. Out of these transactions, on the average, $E[N_l]$ are discarded later because of failure or initiation of PM. Therefore, the mean number of transactions which actually receive service given that they were accepted is given by $E - E[N_l]$. The mean total amount of time the transactions spent in the system while the software is in state A is $W = \int_{t=0}^\infty \sum_i i p_i(t) \, dt$. This time is composed of the mean time spent by the transactions which were served as well as those which were discarded, denoted as W_S and W_D, respectively. Therefore, $W = W_S + W_D$. The response time we are interested in is given by $T_{res} = W_S/(E - E[N_l])$, which is upper bounded by $T_{res} < \frac{W}{E - E[N_l]}$.

$p_i(t)$ is the probability that there are i transactions queued for service, which is also the probability of being in state i of the subordinated process at time t. $p_{i'}(t)$ is the probability that the system failed when there were i transactions queued for service. These transient probabilities for both policies can be obtained by solving the systems of forward differential-difference equations given in [15]. In general they do not have a closed-form analytical solution and must be evaluated numerically. Once these probabilities are obtained, the rest of the quantities P_{AB}, P_{AC}, $E[U]$ and $E[N_l]$ can be easily computed [15] and then used to obtain the steady state availability A_{SS}, the probability of transaction lost P_{loss} and the upper bound on the response time of a transaction T_{res}.

Examples are presented to illustrate the usefulness of the presented model in determining the optimum value of δ (PM interval in the case of policy I and PM wait in the case of policy II). First, the service rate and failure rate are assumed to be functions of real time, where $\rho(t)$ is defined to be the hazard function of Weibull distribution, while $\mu(t)$ is defined to be a monotone non-increasing function that approximates the service degradation. Figure 4 shows A_{ss} and P_{loss} for both policies plotted against δ for different values of the mean time to perform PM γ_r. Under both policies, it can be seen that for any particular value of δ, higher the value of γ_r, lower is the availability and higher is the corresponding loss probability. It can also be observed that the value of δ which minimizes probability of loss is much lower than the one which maximizes availability. In

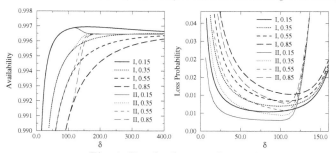

Fig. 4. Results for experiment 1

fact, the probability of loss becomes very high at values of δ which maximize availability. For any specific value of γ_r, policy II results in a lower minima in loss probability than that achieved under policy I. Therefore, if the objective is to minimize long run probability of loss, such as in the case of telecommunication switching software, policy II always fares better than policy I.

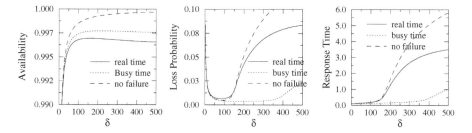

Fig. 5. Results of experiment 2

Figure 5 shows A_{SS}, P_{loss} and upper bound on T_{res} plotted against δ under policy I. Each of the figures contains three curves. $\mu(\cdot)$ and $\rho(\cdot)$ in the solid curve are functions of real time $\mu(t)$ and $\rho(t)$, whereas in the dotted curve they are functions (with the same parameters) of the mean total processing time $\mu(L(t))$ and $\rho(L(t))$. The dashed curve represents a third system in which no crash/hang failures occur $\rho(\cdot) = 0$, but service degradation is present with $\mu(\cdot) = \mu(t)$. This experiment illustrates the importance of making the right assumptions in capturing aging because as seen from the figure, depending on the forms chosen for $\mu(\cdot)$ and $\rho(\cdot)$, the measures vary in a wide range.

2.3   Software Rejuvenation in a Cluster System

Software rejuvenation has been applied to cluster systems [8,45]. This is a novel application, which significantly improves cluster system availability and productivity. The Stochastic Reward Net (SRN) model of a cluster system employing simple time-based rejuvenation is shown in Figure 6. The cluster consists of n nodes which are initially in a "robust" working state, P_{up}. The aging process is modeled as a 2-stage hypo-exponential distribution (increasing failure rate) [43] with transitions T_{fprob} and $T_{noderepair}$. Place P_{fprob} represents a "failure-probable" state in which the nodes are still operational. The nodes then can eventually transit to the fail state, $P_{nodefail1}$. A node can be repaired through the transition $T_{noderepair}$, with a coverage c. In addition to individual node failures, there is also a common-mode failure (transition T_{cmode}). The system is also considered down when there are a ($a \leq n$) individual node failures. The system is repaired through the transition $T_{sysrepair}$.

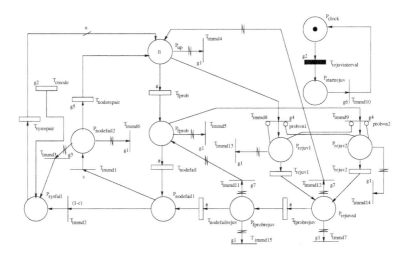

Fig. 6. SRN model of a cluster system employing simple time-based rejuvenation

In the simple time-based policy, rejuvenation is done successively for all the operational nodes in the cluster, at the end of each deterministic interval. The transition $T_{rejuvinterval}$ fires every d time units depositing a token in place $P_{startrejuv}$. Only one node can be rejuvenated at any time (at places P_{rejuv1} or P_{rejuv2}). Weight functions are assigned such that the probability of selecting a token from P_{up} or P_{fprob} is directly proportional to the number of tokens in each. After a node has been rejuvenated, it goes back to the "robust" working state, represented by place $P_{rejuved}$. This is a duplicate place for P_{up} in order to distinguish the nodes which are waiting to be rejuvenated from the nodes which have already been rejuvenated. A node, after rejuvenation, is then allowed to fail with the same rates as before rejuvenation even when another node is being rejuvenated. Duplicate places for P_{upb} and P_{fprob} are needed to capture this. Node repair is disabled during rejuvenation. Rejuvenation is complete when the sum of nodes in places $P_{rejuved}$, $P_{fprobrejuv}$ and $P_{nodefail2}$ is equal to the total number of nodes, n. In this case, the immediate transition T_{immd10} fires, putting back all the rejuvenated nodes in places P_{up} and P_{fprob}. Rejuvenation stops when there are $a-1$ tokens in place $P_{nodefail2}$, to prevent a system failure. The clock resets itself when rejuvenation is complete and is disabled when the system is undergoing repair. Guard functions ($g1$ through $g7$) are assigned to express complex enabling conditions textually.

In condition-based rejuvenation (Figure 7), rejuvenation is attempted only when a node transits into the "failure probable" state. In practice, this degraded state could be predicted in advance by means of analyses of some observable system parameters [16]. In case of a successful prediction, assuming that no other node is being rejuvenated at that time, the newly detected node can be rejuvenated. A node is allowed to fail even while waiting for rejuvenation.

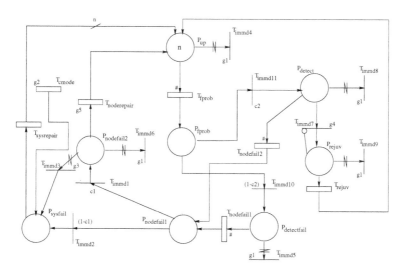

Fig. 7. SRN model of a cluster system employing condition-based rejuvenation

For the analyses, the following values are assumed. The mean times spent in places P_{up} and P_{fprob} are 240 hrs and 720 hrs respectively. The mean times to repair a node, to rejuvenate a node and to repair the system are 30 min, 10 min and 4 hrs respectively. In this analysis, the common-mode failure is disabled and node failure coverage is assumed to be perfect. All the models were solved using the SPNP (Stochastic Petri Net Package) tool [22]. The measures computed were expected unavailability and the expected cost incurred over a fixed time interval. It is assumed that the cost incurred due to node rejuvenation is much less than the cost of a node or system failure since rejuvenation can be done at predetermined or scheduled times. In our analysis, we fix the value for $cost_{nodefail}$ at \$5,000/hr, the $cost_{rejuv}$ at \$250/hr. The value of $cost_{sysfail}$ is computed as the number of nodes, n, times $cost_{nodefail}$.

Figure 8 shows the plots for an 8/1 configuration (8 nodes including 1 spare) system employing simple time-based rejuvenation. The upper plot and lower plots show the expected cost incurred and the expected downtime (in hours) respectively in a given time interval, versus rejuvenation interval (time between successive rejuvenation) in hours. If the rejuvenation interval is close to zero, the system is always rejuvenating and thus incurs high cost and downtime. As the rejuvenation interval increases, both expected unavailability and cost incurred decrease and reach an optimum value. If the rejuvenation interval goes beyond the optimal value, the system failure has more influence on these measures than rejuvenation. The analysis was repeated for 2/1, 8/2, 16/1 and 16/2 configurations. For time-based rejuvenation, the optimal rejuvenation interval was 100 hours for the 1-spare clusters, and approximately 1 hour for the 2-spare clusters. In our analysis of condition-based rejuvenation, we assumed 90% prediction coverage. For systems that have one spare, time-based rejuvenation can reduce downtime by 26% relative to no rejuvenation. Condition-based rejuvenation does somewhat better, reducing downtime by 62% relative to no rejuvenation. However, when the system can tolerate more than one failure at a time, downtime is reduced by 98% to 95% via time-based rejuvenation, compared to a mere 85% for condition-based rejuvenation.

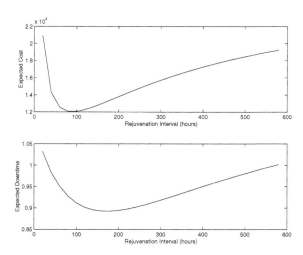

Fig. 8. Results for an 8/1 cluster system employing time-based rejuvenation

3   Measurement Based Models for Software Rejuvenation

While all the analytical models are based on the assumption that the rate of software aging is known, in the measurement based approach, the basic idea is to monitor and collect data on the attributes responsible for determining the health of the executing software. The data is then analyzed to obtain predictions about possible impending failures due to resource exhaustion.

In this section we describe the measurement-based approach for detection and validation of the existence of software aging. The basic idea is to periodically monitor and collect data on the attributes responsible for determining the health of the executing software, in this case the UNIX operating system. Garg et al. [16] propose a methodology for detection and estimation of aging in the UNIX operating system. An SNMP-based distributed resource monitoring tool was used to collect operating system resource usage and system activity data from nine heterogeneous UNIX workstations connected by an Ethernet LAN at the Department of Electrical and Computer Engineering at Duke University. A central monitoring station runs the manager program which sends *get* requests periodically to each of the agent programs running on the monitored work-stations. The agent programs in turn obtain data for the manager from their respective machines by executing various standard UNIX utility programs like *pstat, iostat* and *vmstat*. For quantifying the effect of aging in operating system resources, the metric *Estimated time to exhaustion* is proposed. The earlier work [16] uses a purely time-based approach to estimate resource exhaustion times, whereas the the work presented in [44] takes into account the current system workload as well.

A methodology based on time-series analysis to detect and estimate resource exhaustion times due to software aging in a web server while subjecting it to an artificial workload, is proposed in [31]. Avritzer and Weyuker [4] monitor production traffic data of a large telecommunication system and describe a rejuvenation strategy which increases system availability and minimizes packet loss. Cassidy et al. [7] have developed an approach to rejuvenation for large online transaction processing servers. They monitor various system parameters over a period of time. Using pattern recognition methods, they come to the conclusion that 13 of those parameters deviate from normal behavior just prior to a crash, providing sufficient warning to initiate rejuvenation.

3.1 Time-Based Estimation

In the time-based estimation method presented by Garg et al. [16], data was collected from the UNIX machines at intervals of 15 minutes for about 53 days. Time-ordered values for each monitored object are obtained, constituting a time series for that object. The objective is to detect aging or a long term trend (increasing or decreasing) in the values. Only results for the data collected from the machine *Rossby* are discussed here.

First, the trends in operating system resource usage and system activity are detected using *smoothing* of observed data by *robust locally weighted regression*, proposed by Cleveland [16]. This technique is used to get the global trend between outages by removing the local variations. Then, the slope of the trend is estimated in order to do prediction. Figure 9 shows the smoothed data super-imposed on the original data points from the time series of objects for Rossby. Amount of *real memory free* (plot 1) shows an overall decrease, whereas *file table size* (plot 2) shows an increase. Plots of some other resources not discussed here also showed an increase or decrease. This corroborates the hypothesis of aging with respect to various objects.

The seasonal Kendall test [16] was applied to each of these time series to detect the presence of any global trends at a significance level, α, of 0.05. With Z_α=1.96, all values are such that the null hypothesis (H_0) that no trend exists

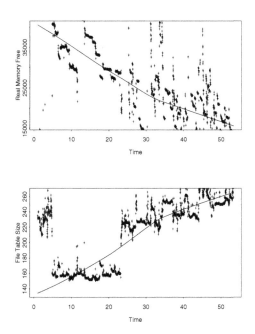

Fig. 9. Non-parametric regression smoothing for Rossby objects

is rejected for the variables considered. Given that a global trend is present and that its slope is calculated for a particular resource, the time at which the resource will be exhausted because of aging only, is estimated. Table 1 refers to several objects on Rossby and lists an estimate of the slope (change per day) of the trend obtained by applying Sen's slope estimate for data with seasons [16]. The values for real memory and swap space are in Kilobytes. A negative slope, as in the case of *real memory*, indicates a decreasing trend, whereas a positive slope, as in the case of *file table size*, is indicative of an increasing trend. Given the slope estimate, the table lists the estimated time to failure of the machine due to aging only with respect to this particular resource. The calculation of the time to exhaustion is done by using the standard linear approximation $y = mx + c$.

A comparative effect of aging on different system resources can be obtained from the above estimates. Overall, it was found that *file table size* and *process table size* are not as important as *used swap space* and *real memory free* since they have a very small slope and high estimated times to failure due to exhaustion. Based on such comparisons, we can identify important resources to monitor and manage in order to deal with aging related software failures. For example, the resource *used swap space* has the highest slope and *real memory free* has the second highest slope. However, *real memory free* has a lower time to exhaustion than *used swap space*.

Table 1. Estimated slope and time to exhaustion for Rossby, Velum and Jefferson objects

Resource Name	Initial Value	Max Value	Sen's Slope Estimation	95% Confidence Interval	Estimated Time to Exh. (days)
Rossby					
Real Memory Free	40814.17	84980	-252.00	-287.75 : -219.34	161.96
File Table Size	220	7110	1.33	1.30 : 1.39	5167.50
Process Table Size	57	2058	0.43	0.41 : 0.45	4602.30
Used Swap Space	39372	312724	267.08	220.09 : 295.50	1023.50
Jefferson					
Real Memory Free	67638.54	114608	-972.00	-1006.81 : -939.08	69.59
File Table Size	268.83	7110	1.33	1.30 : 1.38	5144.36
Process Table Size	67.18	2058	0.30	0.29 : 0.31	6696.41
Used Swap Space	47148.02	524156	577.44	545.69 : 603.14	826.07

3.2 Time and Workload-Based Estimation

The method discussed in the previous subsection assumes that accumulated use of a resource over a time period depends only on the elapsed time. However, it is intuitive that the rate at which a resource is consumed is dependent on the current workload. In this subsection, we discuss a measurement-based model to estimate the rate of exhaustion of operating system resources as a function of both time and the system workload [44]. The SNMP-based distributed resource monitoring tool described previously was used for collecting operating system resource usage and system activity parameters (at 10 min intervals) for over 3 months. Only results for the data collected from the machine Rossby are discussed here. The *longest* stretch of sample points in which no reboots or failures occurred were used for building the model. A semi-Markov reward model [42] is constructed using the data. First different workload states are identified using statistical cluster analysis and a state-space model is constructed. Corresponding to each resource, a reward function based on the rate of resource exhaustion in the different states is then defined. Finally the model is solved to obtain trends and the estimated exhaustion rates and time to exhaustion for the resources.

The following variables were chosen to characterize the system workload - *cpuContextSwitch, sysCall, pageIn,* and *pageOut. Hartigan's k-means clustering algorithm* [21] was used for partitioning the data points into clusters based on workload. The statistics for the eleven workload clusters obtained are shown in Table 2. Clusters whose centroids were relatively close to each other and those with a small percentage of data points in them, were merged to simplify computations. The resulting clusters are $W_1 = \{1, 2, 3\}$, $W_2 = \{4, 5\}$, $W_3 = \{6\}$, $W_4 = \{7\}$, $W_5 = \{8\}$, $W_6 = \{9\}$, $W_7 = \{10\}$ and $W_8 = \{11\}$.

Transition probabilities from one state to another were computed from data, resulting in transition probability matrix P of the embedded discrete time Markov chain The sojourn time distribution for each of the workload states was fitted to either 2-stage hyper-exponential or 2-stage hypo-exponential dis-

Table 2. Statistics for the workload clusters

No.	Cluster Center				% of pts.
	cpuConSw	sysCall	pgOut	pgIn	
1	48405.16	94194.66	5.16	677.83	0.98
2	54184.56	122229.68	5.39	81.41	0.76
3	34059.61	193927.00	0.02	136.73	0.93
4	20479.21	45811.71	0.53	243.40	1.89
5	21361.38	37027.41	0.26	12.64	7.17
6	15734.65	54056.27	0.27	14.45	6.55
7	37825.76	40912.18	0.91	12.21	11.77
8	11013.22	38682.46	0.03	10.43	42.87
9	67290.83	37246.76	7.58	19.88	4.93
10	10003.94	32067.20	0.01	9.61	21.23
11	197934.42	67822.48	415.71	184.38	0.93

tribution functions. The fitted distributions were tested using the Kolmogorov-Smirnov test at a significance level of 0.01.

Two resources, *usedSwapSpace* and *realMemoryFree*, are considered for the analysis, since the previous time-based analysis suggested that they are critical resources. For each resource, the reward function is defined as the rate of corresponding resource exhaustion in different states. The true slope (rate of increase/decrease) of a resource at every workload state is estimated by using Sen's non-parametric method [44]. Table 3 shows the slopes with 95% confidence intervals.

It was observed that slopes in a given workload state for a particular resource during different visits to that state are almost the same. Further, the slopes across different workload states are different and generally higher the system activity, higher is the resource utilization. This validates the assumption that resource usage *does* depend on the system workload and the rates of exhaustion vary with workload changes. It can also be observed from Table 3 that the slopes for *usedSwapSpace* in all the workload states are non-negative, and the slopes for *realMemoryFree* are non-positive in all the workload states except in one. It follows that *usedSwapSpace* increases whereas *realMemoryFree* decreases over time which validates the software aging phenomenon.

The semi-Markov reward model was solved using the SHARPE tool [37] developed by researchers at Duke University. The slope for the workload-based estimation is computed as the expected reward rate in steady state from the model. The times to resource exhaustion is computed as the job completion time (mean time to accumulate x amount of reward) of the Markov reward model. Table 4 gives the estimates for the slope and time to exhaustion for *usedSwapSpace* and *realMemoryFree*. It can be seen that workload based estimations gave a lower time to resource exhaustion than those computed using time based estimations. Since the machine failures due to resource exhaustion were observed much before

Table 3. Slope estimates (in KB/10 min)

| State | usedSwapSpace | | realMemoryFree | |
	Slope Est.	95 % Conf. Interval	Slope Est.	95 % Conf. Interval
W_1	119.3	5.5 - 222.4	-133.7	-137.7 - -133.3
W_2	0.57	0.40 - 0.71	-1.47	-1.78 - -1.09
W_3	0.76	0.73 - 0.80	-1.43	-2.50 - -0.62
W_4	0.57	0.00 - 0.69	-1.23	-1.67 - -0.80
W_5	0.78	0.75 - 0.80	0.00	-5.65 - 6.00
W_6	0.81	0.64 - 1.00	-1.14	-1.40 - -0.88
W_7	0.00	0.00 - 0.00	0.00	0.00 - 0.00
W_8	91.8	72.4 - 111.0	91.7	-369.9 - 475.2

the times to resource exhaustion estimated by the time based method, it follows that the workload based approach results in better estimations.

Table 4. Estimates for slope (in KB/10 min) and time to exhaustion (in days) for *usedSwapSpace* and *realMemoryFree*

| Method of Estimation | usedSwapSpace | | | realMemoryFree | | |
	Slope Estimate	95 % Conf. Interval	Est. Time to Exh.	Slope Estimate	95 % Conf. Interval	Est. Time to Exh.
Time based	0.787	0.786 - 0.788	2276.46	-2.806	-3.026 - -2.630	60.81
Workload based	4.647	1.191 - 7.746	490.50	-4.1435	-9.968 - 2.592	41.38

3.3   Time Series and ARMA Models

In this section, a measurement-based approach based on time-series analysis to detect software aging and to estimate resource exhaustion times due to aging in a web server is described [31]. The experiments are conducted on an Apache web server running on the Linux platform. Before carrying out other experiments, the capacity of the web server is determined so that the appropriate workload to use in the experiments can be decided. The capacity of the web server was found to be around 390 requests/sec. In the next part of the experiment, the web server was run without rejuvenation for a long time until the performance degraded or until the server crashed. The requests were generated by *httperf* [33] to get one of five specified files from the server of sizes 500 bytes, 5KB, 50KB, 500KB and 5MB. The corresponding probabilities that a given file is requested are: 0.35, 0.5, 0.14, 0.009 and 0.001, respectively. During the period of running, the performance measured by the workload generator and system parameters collected by the Linux system monitoring tool, *procmon*, were recorded.

The first data set was collected in a 7-day period with a connection rate of 350 requests/sec. The second set was collected in a 25-day period with connection rate of 400 request/sec. During the experiment, we recorded more than 100 parameters, but for our modeling purposes, six representative parameters pertaining to system resources were selected (Table 5). In addition to the six system status parameters, the response time of the web server, recorded by *httperf* on the client machine, is also included in the model as a measure of performance of the web server.

Table 5. Analyzed parameters and their physical meaning

Parameter	Physical meaning
PhysicalMemoryFree	Free physical memory
SwapSpaceUsed	Used swap space
LoadAvg5Min	Average CPU load in the last five minutes
NumberDiskRequests	Number of disk requests in the last five minutes
PageOutCounter	Number of pages paged out in the last five minutes
NewProcesses	Number of newly spawned processes in the last five minutes
ResponseTime	The interval from the time *httperf* sends out the first byte of request until it receives the first byte of reply

After collecting the data, it needs to be analyzed to determine if software aging exists, which is indicated by degradation in performance of the web server and/or exhaustion of system resources. The performance of the web server is measured by response time which is the interval from the time a client sends out the first byte of request until it receives the first byte of reply. Figure 10(a) shows the plot of the response time in data set I. To identify the trend, the range of y-axis is magnified (Figure 10(b)). The response time becomes longer with the running time of the experiment. To determine whether the trend is just a fluctuation due to noise or an essential characteristic of the data, a linear regression model is used to fit the time series of the response time. The least squares solution is $r = 15.5655 + 0.027t$, where r is response time in milliseconds, t is the time from the beginning of the experiment. The 95% confidence interval for the slope is $(0.019, 0.036)$ ms/hour. Since the slope is positive, it can be concluded that the performance of the web server is degrading.

Performing the same analysis to the parameters related to system resources, it was found that the available resources are decreasing. Estimated slopes of some of the parameters using linear regression model are listed in Table 6.

The parameters in data set II are used as the modeling objects since the duration of data set II is longer than that of data set I. In this case, there are seven parameters to be analyzed. The analysis can be done using two different approaches: (1) building a univariate model for each of the outputs or, 2) building only one multivariate model with seven outputs. In this case, seven univariate models are built and then combined into a single multivariate model. First, the parameters are determined to determine their characteristics and build an ap-

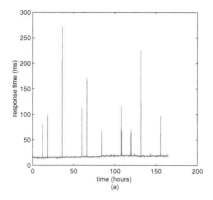
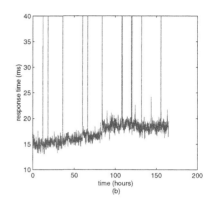

Fig. 10. Response time of the web server

Table 6. Estimated slope of parameters

Data Set	Parameter	Slope	95% confidence interval
	response time	0.027 ms/hour	(0.019, 0.036) ms/hour
I	free physical memory	-88.472 KB/hour	(-93.337, -83.607) KB/hour
	used swap space	29.976 KB/hour	(29.290, 30.662) KB/hour
	response time	0.063 ms/hour	(0.057, 0.068) ms/hour
II	free physical memory	15.183 KB/hour	(14.094, 16.271) KB/hour
	used swap space	7.841 KB/hour	(7.658, 8.025) KB/hour

propriate model with one output and four inputs for each parameter - connection rate, linear trend, periodic series with a period of one week, and periodic series with a period of one day. The autocorrelation function (ACF) and the partial autocorrelation function (PACF) for the output are computed. The ACF and the PACF help us decide the appropriate model for the data [38]. For example, from the ACF and PACF of *used swap space* it can be determined that an autoregressive model of order 1 [AR(1)] is suitable for this data series. Adding the inputs to the AR(1) model, we get the ARX(1) model for used swap space:

$$Y_t = aY_{t-1} + b_1X_t + b_2L_t + b_3W_t + b_4D_t, \tag{8}$$

where Y_t is the used swap space, X_t is the connection rate, L_t is the time step which represents the linear trend, W_t is the weekly periodic series and D_t is the daily periodic series. After observing the ACF and PACF of all the parameters, we find that all of the PACFs cut off at certain lags. So all the multiple input single output (MISO) models are of the ARX type, only with different orders. This gives great convenience in combining them into a multiple input multiple output (MIMO) ARX model which is described later.

In order to combine the MISO ARX models into a MIMO ARX model, we need to choose the order between different outputs. This is done by inspecting the CCF (cross-correlation function) between each pair of the outputs to find out the leading relationship between them. If the CCF between parameter A and

B gets its peak value at a positive lag k, we say that A leads B by k steps and it might be possible to use A to predict B. In our analysis, there are 21 CCFs that need to be computed. And in order to reduce the complexity, we only use the CCFs that exhibit obvious leading relationship with lags less than 10 steps. The next step after determination of the orders is to estimate the coefficients of the model by the least squares method. The first half of the data is used to estimate the parameters and the rest of the data is then used to verify the model. Figure 11 shows the two-hour-ahead (24-step) predicted used swap space which

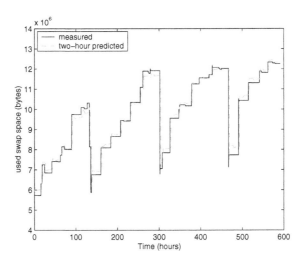

Fig. 11. Measured and two-hour ahead predicted used swap space

is computed using the established model and the data measured up to two hours before the predicted time point. From the plots, we can see that the predicted values are very close to the measured values.

4   Implementation of a Software Rejuvenation Agent

The first commercial version of a software rejuvenation agent (SRA) for the IBM xSeries line of cluster servers has been implemented with our collaboration [8, 26,45]. The SRA was designed to monitor consumable resources, estimate the time to exhaustion of those resources, and generate alerts to the management infrastructure when the time to exhaustion is less than a user-defined notification horizon. For Windows operating systems, the SRA acquires data on exhaustible resources by reading the registry performance counters and collecting parameters such as available bytes, committed bytes, non-paged pool, paged pool, handles, threads, semaphores, mutexes, and logical disk utilization. For Linux, the agent accesses the /proc directory structure and collects equivalent parameters such as memory utilization, swap space, file descriptors and inodes. All collected parameters are logged on to disk. They are also stored in memory preparatory to time-to-exhaustion analysis.

In the current version of the SRA, rejuvenation can be based on elapsed time since the last rejuvenation, or on prediction of impending exhaustion. When using Timed Rejuvenation, a user interface is used to schedule and perform rejuvenation at a period specified by the user. It allows the user to select when to rejuvenate different nodes of the cluster, and to select "blackout" times during which no rejuvenation is to be allowed. Predictive Rejuvenation relies on curve-fitting analysis and projection of the utilization of key resources, using recently observed data. The projected data is compared to prespecified upper and lower exhaustion thresholds, within a notification time horizon. The user specifies the notification horizon and the parameters to be monitored (some parameters believed to be highly indicative are always monitored by default), and the agent periodically samples the data and performs the analysis. The prediction algorithm fits several types of curves to the data in the fitting window. These different curve types have been selected for their ability to capture different types of temporal trends. A model-selection criterion is applied to choose the "best" prediction curve, which is then extrapolated to the user-specified horizon. The several parameters that are indicative of resource exhaustion are monitored and extrapolated independently. If any monitored parameter exceeds the specified minimum or maximum value within the horizon, a request to rejuvenate is sent to the management infrastructure. In most cases, it is also possible to identify which process is consuming the preponderance of the resource being exhausted, in order to support selective rejuvenation of just the offending process or a group of processes.

5   Approaches and Methods of Software Rejuvenation

Software rejuvenation can be divided broadly into two approaches as follows:

- **Open-loop approach:** In this approach, rejuvenation is performed without any feedback from the system. Rejuvenation in this case, can be based just on elapsed time (periodic rejuvenation) [25,12] and/or instantaneous/cumulative number of jobs on the system [15].
- **Closed-loop approach:** In the closed-loop approach, rejuvenation is performed based on information on the system "health". The system is monitored continuously (in practice, at small deterministic intervals) and data is collected on the operating system resource usage and system activity. This data is then analyzed to estimate time to exhaustion of a resource which may lead to a component or an entire system degradation/crash. This estimation can be based purely on time, and workload-independent [16,8] or can be based on both time and system workload [44].

  The closed-loop approach can be further classified based on whether the data analysis is done off-line or on-line. Off-line data analysis is done based on system data collected over a period of time (usually weeks or months).

The analysis is done to estimate time to rejuvenation. This off-line analysis approach is best suited for systems whose behavior is fairly deterministic. The on-line closed-loop approach, on the other hand, performs on-line analysis of system data collected at deterministic intervals. Another approach to estimate the optimal time to rejuvenation could be based on system failure data [11]. This approach is more suited for off-line data analysis.

This classification of approaches to rejuvenation is shown in Figure 12.

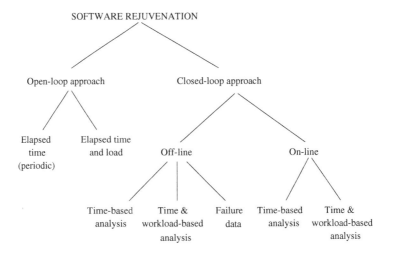

Fig. 12. Approaches to software rejuvenation

Rejuvenation is a very general proactive fault management approach and can be performed at different levels - the system level or the application level. An example of a system level rejuvenation is a hardware-reboot. At the application level, rejuvenation is performed by stopping and restarting a particular offending application, process or a group of processes. This is also known as a *partial rejuvenation*. The above rejuvenation approaches when performed on a single node can lead to undesired and often costly downtime. Rejuvenation has been recently extended for cluster systems, in which two or more nodes work together as a single system [8,45]. In this case, rejuvenation can be performed by causing no or minimal downtime by failing over applications to another spare node.

6 Conclusions

In this paper, we classified software faults based on an extension of Gray's classification and discussed the various techniques to deal with them. Attention was devoted to software rejuvenation, a proactive technique to counteract the phenomenon of software aging. Various analytical models for software aging and to determine optimal times to perform rejuvenation were described. Measurement-based models based on data collected from operating systems were also discussed. The implementation of a software rejuvenation agent in a major commercial server was then briefly described. Finally, various approaches to rejuvenation and rejuvenation granularity were discussed.

In the measurement-based models presented in this paper, only aging due to each individual resource has been captured. In the future, one could improve the algorithm used for aging detection to involve multiple parameters simultaneously, for better prediction capability and reduced false alarms. Dependences between the various system parameters could be studied. The best statistical data analysis method for a given system is also yet to be determined.

References

1. E. Adams. Optimizing Preventive Service of the Software Products. *IBM Journal of R&D*, 28(1):2-14, January 1984.
2. P. E. Amman and J. C. Knight. Data Diversity: An Approach to Software Fault Tolerance. In *Proc. of 17th Int. Symp. on Fault Tolerant Computing*, pages 122-126, June 1987.
3. A. Avizienis and L. Chen. On the Implementation of N-version Programming for Software Fault Tolerance During Execution. In *Proc. IEEE COMPSAC 77*, pp 149-155, November 1977.
4. A. Avritzer and E.J. Weyuker. Monitoring Smoothly Degrading Systems for Increased Dependability. *Empirical Software Eng. Journal*, Vol 2, No. 1, pp 59-77, 1997.
5. L. Bernstein. Text of seminar delivered by Mr. Bernstein. In *University Learning Center*, George Mason University, January 29 1996.
6. A. Bobbio, A. Sereno and C. Anglano. Fine Grained Software Degradation Models for Optimal rejuvenation policies. *Performance Evaluation*, Vol. 46, pp 45-62, 2001.
7. K. Cassidy, K. Gross and A. Malekpour. Advanced Pattern Recognition for Detection of Complex Software Aging in Online Transaction Processing Servers. In *Proc. Dependable Systems and Networks, DSN 2002*, Washington D.C., June 2002.
8. V. Castelli, R. E. Harper, P. Heidelberger, S. W. Hunter, K. S. Trivedi, K. Vaidyanathan and W. Zeggert. Proactive Management of Software Aging. *IBM Journal of R&D*, Vol. 45, No.2, March 2001.
9. R. Chillarege, S. Biyani and J. Rosenthal. Measurement of Failure Rate in Widely Distributed Software. In *Proc. of 25th IEEE Int. Symp. on Fault Tolerant Computing*, pp 424-433, Pasadena, CA, July 1995.
10. T. Dohi, K. Goševa–Popstojanova and K. S. Trivedi. Analysis of Software Cost Models with Rejuvenation. In *Proc. of the 5th IEEE Int. Symp. on High Assurance Systems Engineering, HASE 2000*, Albuquerque, NM, November 2000.
11. T. Dohi, K. Goševa–Popstojanova and K. S. Trivedi. Statistical Non-Parametric Algorithms to Estimate the Optimal Software Rejuvenation Schedule. *Proc. of the 2000 Pacific Rim Int. Symp. on Dependable Computing, PRDC 2000*, Los Angeles, CA, December 2000.
12. S. Garg, A. Puliafito, M. Telek and K. S. Trivedi. Analysis of Software Rejuvenation Using Markov Regenerative Stochastic Petri Net. In *Proc. of the Sixth Int. Symp. on Software Reliability Engineering*, pp 180-187, Toulouse, France, October 1995.

13. S. Garg, Y. Huang, C. Kintala and K. S. Trivedi. Time and Load Based Software Rejuvenation: Policy, Evaluation and Optimality. In *Proc. of the First Fault-Tolerant Symposium*, Madras, India, December 1995.
14. S. Garg, Y. Huang and C. Kintala, K.S. Trivedi, Minimizing Completion Time of a Program by Checkpointing and Rejuvenation. *Proc. 1996 ACM SIGMETRICS* Philadelphia, PA, pp 252-261, May 1996.
15. S. Garg, A. Puliafito, M. Telek and K. S. Trivedi. Analysis of Preventive Maintenance in Transactions Based Software Systems. *IEEE Trans. on Computers*, pp 96-107, Vol.47, No.1, January 1998.
16. S. Garg, A. van Moorsel, K. Vaidyanathan and K. S. Trivedi. A Methodology for Detection and Estimation of Software Aging. In *Proc. of the Ninth Int. Symp. on Software Reliability Engineering*, pp 282-292, Paderborn, Germany, November 1998.
17. J. Gray. Why do Computers Stop and What Can be Done About it? In *Proc. of 5th Symp. on Reliability in Distributed Software and Database Systems*, pp 3-12, January 1986.
18. J. Gray. A Census of Tandem System Availability Between 1985 and 1990. *IEEE Trans. on Reliability*, 39:409-418, October 1990.
19. J. Gray and D. P. Siewiorek. High-Availability Computer Systems. *IEEE Computer*, pages 39-48, September 1991.
20. B. O. A. Grey. Making SDI Software Reliable through Fault-tolerant Techniques. *Defense Electronics*, pp 77–80,85–86, August 1987.
21. J. A. Hartigan. *Clustering Algorithms*. New York:Wiley, 1975.
22. C. Hirel, B. Tuffin and K. S. Trivedi. SPNP: Stochastic Petri Net Package. Version 6.0. B. R. Haverkort et al. (eds.): TOOLS 2000, Lecture Notes in Computer Science 1786, pp 354-357, Springer-Verlag Heidelberg, 2000.
23. J. J. Horning, H. C. Lauer, P. M. Melliar-Smith and B. Randell. A Program Structure for Error Detection and Recovery. *Lecture Notes in Computer Science*, 16:177-193, 1974.
24. Y. Huang, P. Jalote and C. Kintala. Two Techniques for Transient Software Error Recovery. *Lecture Notes in Computer Science, Vol. 774*, pp 159-170. Springer Verlag, Berlin, 1994.
25. Y. Huang, C. Kintala, N. Kolettis and N. D. Fulton. Software Rejuvenation: Analysis, Module and Applications. In *Proc. of 25th Symp. on Fault Tolerant Computing*, pp 381-390, Pasadena, CA, June 1995.
26. IBM Netfinity Director Software Rejuvenation - White Paper. IBM Corporation, Research Triangle Park, NC, January 2001.
27. P. Jalote, Y. Huang and C. Kintala. A Framework for Understanding and Handling Transient Software Failures. In *Proc. 2nd ISSAT Int. Conf. on Reliability and Quality in Design*, Orlando, FL, 1995.
28. J. C. Laprie, J. Arlat, C. Béounes, K. Kanoun and C. Hourtolle. Hardware and Software Fault Tolerance: Definition and Analysis of Architectural Solutions. In *Proc. of 17th Symp. on Fault Tolerant Computing*, pp 116-121, Pittsburgh, PA,1987.
29. J. C. Laprie (Ed.). *Dependability: Basic Concepts and Terminology*. Springer-Verlag, Wien, New York, 1992.
30. I. Lee and R. K. Iyer. Software Dependability in the Tandem GUARDIAN System. *IEEE Trans. on Software Engineering*, pp 455-467, Vol. 21, No. 5, May 1995.
31. L. Li, K. Vaidyanathan and K. S. Trivedi. An Approach to Estimation of Software Aging in a Web Server. In *Proc. of the Int. Symp. on Empirical Software Engineering, ISESE 2002*, Nara, Japan, October 2002 (to appear).

32. E. Marshall. Fatal Error: How Patriot Overlooked a Scud. *Science*, pp 1347, March 13 1992.
33. D. Mosberger and T. Jin. Httperf - A Tool for Measuring Web Server Performance *In First Workshop on Internet Server Performance, WISP*, Madison, WI, pp.59-67, June 1998.
34. A. Pfening, S. Garg, A. Puliafito, M. Telek and K. S. Trivedi. Optimal Rejuvenation for Tolerating Soft Failures. *Performance Evaluation*, 27 & 28, pp 491-506, October 1996.
35. D. K. Pradhan. *Fault-Tolerant Computer System Design*. Prentice Hall, Englewood Cliffs, NJ, 1996.
36. S. M. Ross. *Stochastic Processes*. John Wiley & Sons, New York, 1983.
37. R. A. Sahner, K. S. Trivedi, A. Puliafito. *Performance and Reliability Analysis of Computer Systems - An Example-Based Approach Using the SHARPE Software Package*. Kluwer Academic Publishers, Norwell, MA, 1996.
38. R. H. Shumway and D. S. Stoffer. *Time Series Analysis and Its Applications*, Springer-Verlag, New York, 2000.
39. K. Smith and M. Seltzer. File System Aging - Increasing the Relevance of File System Benchmarks In *Proc. of ACM SIGMETRICS*, June 1997.
40. M. Sullivan and R. Chillarege. Software Defects and Their Impact on System Availability - A Study of Field Failures in Operating Systems. In *Proc. 21st IEEE Int. Symp. on Fault Tolerant Computing*, pages 2–9, 1991.
41. A. T. Tai, S. N. Chau, L. Alkalaj, and H. Hecht. On-board Preventive Maintenance: Analysis of Effectiveness and Optimal Duty Period. In *Proc. of 3rd Int. Workshop on Object-oriented Real-time Dependable Systems*, Newport Beach, California, February 1997.
42. K. S. Trivedi, J. Muppala, S. Woolet and B. R. Haverkort. Composite Performance and Dependability Analysis. *Performance Evaluation*, Vol. 14, Nos. 3-4, pp 197-216, February 1992.
43. K. S. Trivedi. *Probability and Statistics, with Reliability, Queuing and Computer Science Applications*, 2nd edition. John Wiley, 2001.
44. K. Vaidyanathan and K. S. Trivedi. A Measurement-Based Model for Estimation of Resource Exhaustion in Operational Software Systems. In *Proc. of the Tenth IEEE Int. Symp. on Software Reliability Engineering*, pp 84-93, Boca Raton, FL, November 1999.
45. K. Vaidyanathan, R. E. Harper, S. W. Hunter, K. S. Trivedi. Analysis and Implementation of Software Rejuvenation in Cluster Systems. In *Proc. of the Joint Int. Conf. on Measurement and Modeling of Computer Systems, ACM SIGMETRICS 2001/Performance 2001*, Cambridge, MA, June 2001.
46. http://www.apache.org
47. http://www.software-rejuvenation.com

Performance Validation of Mobile Software Architectures

Vincenzo Grassi[1], Vittorio Cortellessa[2], Raffaela Mirandola[1]

[1] Dipartimento di Informatica, Sistemi e Produzione
Università di Roma "Tor Vergata", Italy
grassiv@acm.org, mirandola@info.uniroma2.it
[2] Dipartimento di Informatica
Università de L'Aquila, Italy
cortelle@univaq.it

Abstract. Design paradigms based on the idea of code mobility have been recently introduced, where components of an application may (autonomously or upon request) move to different locations, during the application execution. Besides, software technologies are readily available (e.g. Java-based), that provide tools to implement these paradigms. Based on mobile code paradigms and technologies, different but functionally equivalent software architectures can be defined and it is widely recognized that, in general, the adoption of a particular architecture can have a large impact on quality attributes such as modifiability, reusability, reliability, and performance. Hence, validation against specific attributes is necessary and claims for a careful planning of this activity. Within this framework, the goal of this tutorial is twofold: to provide a general methodology for the validation of software architectures, where the focus is on the transition from the modeling of software architectures to the validation of non-functional requirements; to substantiate this general methodology into the specific case of software architectures exploiting mobile code.

1 Introduction

The pervasive deployment of large-scale networking infrastructures is vastly changing the architecture of software systems and applications, leading to more and more applications designed to operate in distributed wide area environments, thus introducing new challenges to architects of scalable distributed applications. Indeed, the large number of available hosts with very different capabilities, connected by networks with varying capacities and loads, implies that the designer is unlikely to know a priori how to structure the application in a way that best leverages the available infrastructure, and that any assumption regarding the underlying physical system, which is made early at the design time, is unlikely to hold later.

This highly heterogeneous and dynamic environment rises problems that could be considered negligible in local area environments. As a consequence, technologies, architectures and methodologies traditionally used to develop distributed applications in local area environments, usually based on the notion of *location transparency*, exhibit several limitations in wide area environments, and often fail in providing the desired quality level. On the contrary, *location awareness* has been suggested as an innovative approach in the design of software applications for wide area environments, to deal since the early design phases with the characteristics and constraints of the different locations. Explicitly considering components location at the application level straightforwardly leads to exploit the location change as a new dimension in the design and implementation of distributed applications. Indeed, *mobile code* design paradigms, based on the ability of moving code across the nodes of a network, have been recently

M.C. Calzarossa and S. Tucci (Eds.): Performance 2002, LNCS 2459, pp. 346–373, 2002.
© Springer-Verlag Berlin Heidelberg 2002

introduced. Besides, software technologies are readily available (e.g. Java-based), that provide tools to implement these paradigms, so that both have become a central part of the toolset supporting the design of applications for wide area environments

Code mobility, as it is intended in this perspective, should not be confused with the well known concept of process migration, even if the adopted mechanisms to implement them may be similar. Process migration is a (distributed) OS issue, realized transparently to the application (usually to get load balancing), and hence does not represent a tool in the hands of the application designer; on the contrary, code mobility is intended to bring the ability of changing location under the control of the designer, so representing a new tool he/she can exploit to accomplish quality requirements, laying the foundation for a new generation of technologies, architectures, models, and applications.

Using mobile code paradigms and technologies, different but functionally equivalent software architectures can be designed and implemented, and it is widely recognized that, in general, the adoption of a particular architecture can have a large impact on quality attributes of a distributed application such as modifiability, reusability, reliability, and performance [33]. In particular, with respect to performance, code mobility offers to application designers new latitudes in using the systems resources. No longer remote resources must be accessed remotely; instead, (part of) the application can move to use the resources locally. Under the right circumstances, this can reduce both network traffic and network protocol overhead, so reducing the total amount of work done by the system, and improving the performance of the entire system. On the other hand, under the wrong circumstances, the entire system slows down, e.g. because of excessive migration traffic, or increased load at already congested nodes. Hence, validation of mobility-based architectures against specific performance attributes is necessary, and calls for a careful planning of this activity.

The goal of this tutorial is twofold: to provide a general methodology for the validation of software architectures, where the focus is on the transition from the modeling of software architectures to the validation of non-functional requirements; to show how this general methodology can be substantiated in the specific case of software architectures exploiting mobile code. We emphasize the former point in section 2, where we provide a taxonomy of the parameters every approach to software architecture validation should depend on. Then, for the latter point, we review approaches for the validation of mobile software architectures, presenting them in the framework of the above mentioned taxonomy. To provide a basic understanding of the features and performance related costs of different mobile code styles, we first give in section 3 a basic taxonomy of these styles, and then, in section 4, we survey methodologies for performance validation of mobile software architectures. We classify these methodologies as *ad-hoc* and *general-purpose* methodologies. Ad-hoc methodologies consider code mobility "in isolation", lacking of features to model a whole software application. General-purpose methodologies overcome this limitation by embedding code mobility modeling into some formalism for the specification of software applications. Finally, section 5 concludes the paper and provides hints for future research.

2 Non Functional Requirements Validation

The validation of software architectures can be performed versus functional and/or non-functional requirements (NFR). Approaches basically differ in the two cases, as the former are statements of services the software system should provide, how it should react to particular inputs and behave in particular situations, whereas NFR are constraints on the services offered by the software system that affect the software quality.

Although validation is being accepted as a crucial activity in software development, yet NFR are often neglected. Economic reasons (such as short time to market and special skills required) and practical reasons (non-functional software aspects are often determined by the latest decisions in the lifecycle, such as the hardware configuration hosting the software system) contribute to the reluctance from the world of software development to adopt an engineered approach to the validation of NFR. A consistent effort has been spent in the last few years in order to fill this gap between software development and validation versus NFR. Beyond every particular approach to the problem, a common ground to work on can be envisaged in the following two issues: (i) determining the amount and the type of information to embed in a software architecture in order to enable its validation versus NFR, (ii) introducing algorithms to translate architecture description languages/notation (augmented with additional information) into a model ready to be validated. Various approaches have been recently introduced for both the issues (see [3] for an overview on this topic). Two attributes appear today crucial to make any approach to the validation of NFR realistically accepted by the software community, that are: transparency, i.e., minimal affection on the software notation and the software process adopted (to cope with issue (i)), and effectiveness, i.e., low complexity algorithms to annotate and transform software models (to cope with issue (ii)).

We propose here a classification of the parameters that all these approaches have to deal with, (mainly aimed at providing guidelines for a structured approach to NFR validation), and we show how a NFR validation approach can be seen as an instantiation from this framework. From section 4 on we focus on a particular class of instances, that are the approaches to the performance validation of mobile software architectures.

The parameters of a methodology to validate a software architecture versus non-functional requirements can be expressed as follows:

architectural style (**AS**) – the style, if any, adopted to build the software architecture (e.g., client-server, mobile code, etc.[1]);

original notation (**ON**) – the architectural description language/notation used to model the software architecture, as it is from the software development process (e.g., UML, a Process Algebra, etc.);

non-functional attribute (**NFA**) – the non-functional attribute that is concerned with the set of requirements that the software architecture must fulfill (e.g., reliability, performance, safety, etc.);

missing information (**MI**) – the information that is lacking in the software architecture description, which is rather crucial for the type of validation that is pursued

---

[1] Note that an architectural style is defined as a set of construction rules that a developer has to follow while building a software architecture. Depending on the style, those rules can spread over different aspects, such as: types of interactions among components, roles of components, types of connectors, etc. In our case, we focus on architectural styles defined on the capability of components to move.

(e.g., number of invocations of a component within a certain scenario, mapping of components to platform sites, etc.[2]);

collection technique (**CT**) – the technique adopted to collect the missing information (e.g., prototype execution, retrieving from a repository of projects);

target model notation (**TMN**) – the notation adopted for representing the model whose solution provides the non-functional attribute values useful for the validation task (e.g., Petri Nets, Queuing Networks, etc.);

solution technique (**ST**) – the technique adopted to process the target model and obtain a numerical solution (e.g., simulation, analytical, etc.).

Every validation approach can be reduced to an assignment of values to the above parameters, therefore it may be intended as an instance of the framework that we are outlining. For example, in a Bayesian approach to the reliability validation of a UML-based software architecture, in which the operational profile and the failure probabilities are missing, the following values for the above parameters may be devised:

architectural style (**AS**) = "don't care";

original notation (**ON**) = Unified Modeling Language;

non-functional attribute (**NFA**) = reliability;

missing information (**MI**) = operational profile, failure probabilities;

collection technique (**CT**) = repository (operational profile), unit testing (failure probabilities);

target model notation (**TMN**) = Bayesian stochastic model;

solution technique (**ST**) = numerical simulation.

Obviously the choice of a parameter value is not always independent from the choices of the other ones. In many cases the domain of a choice is restricted to a subset of potential values as a consequence of another parameter assignment. For example, in case a reliability validation has to be performed (i.e., NFA=reliability), it is quite inconvenient to choose a Queuing Model as target (i.e., TMN=Queueing Model), because queues are suitable to represent delays and contentions, and they badly work to combine failure probabilities. Therefore, although a potential domain for every parameter can be defined, in practice limitations may reciprocally induce restrictions of domains while the choices are progressively performed.

In figure 1 we propose a dependency graph, where each node represents one of the above parameters. Two types of edges *(i,j)* are introduced, both representing a dependency between parameters *i* and *j*, with the following semantics:

weak dependency (dashed arrow) – it would be better choosing the value of *j* after choosing the value of *i*; this means that the value assigned to *i* helps the validation team to better understand which would be the more appropriate choice for *j*;

strong dependency (continuous arrow) – a value must be assigned to *j* after assigning a value to *i*; this means that, without knowing the value of *i*, the validation team cannot perform the choice of *j*.

---

[2] Usually the missing information appears (in the whole approach) either as annotations on the available software architecture description or as an integration of the description itself (in the latter case, for example, as an extension of a software connector).

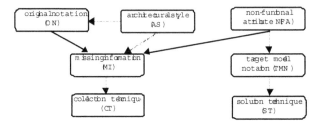

Figure 1. Graph of dependencies among parameters for NFR validation

Between ON and MI in figure 1 there is a strong dependency as the software model notation determines the set of items and relationships that are available to model the architecture, hence determines also the set of missing items and relationships, depending on the type of validation to perform (NFA). The same type of dependency occurs between NFA and MI, as the information lacking in the architectural design may heavily differ depending on the type of non-functional attribute to validate. As seen in the example above, instead, the dependency between AS and MI can be considered as a weak one, because knowing the architectural style may help to determine the missing information but, in some cases, cannot affect at all this selection (e.g., the architectural style has almost no relationship with the information to be added to UML diagrams in order to perform a reliability analysis of a component based software system). In a similar way it can be considered the weak dependency between AS and ON, because the architectural style may drive software developers to choose the most appropriate notation that better suits that style constraints.

On the other hand, the dependency between TMN and ST has been represented as a weak one because a certain type of model can be solved (almost in all cases) by different techniques with different solution process complexity. Therefore, in the latter case, it would be better to delay the choice of a solution technique after the selection of the model notation, in order to be able to use the technique with lowest complexity. Analogous considerations can be made around the dependency of CT from MI, as if we know what type of information has to be collected then we can devise a much effective technique for the CT task. And, finally, there is a weak dependency between NFA and TMN, derived from the consideration that the same non-functional attribute can be validated using different types of model (e.g. Petri Nets and Queuing Models are suitable models for performance evaluation), but the complexity of the validation process may heavily change if using a notation rather than another, and this depends on the specific non-functional requirements under validation.

For any pair of parameters (i,j) without a connecting path in the graph of figure 1, no evident dependency occurs, namely they can be concurrently chosen because one value does not bring any information on the other one. For example, there is no dependency between CT and TMN, as the way we collect the missing information is not affected by the type of target model notation, which affects, instead, the way we represent that information.

With this classification we have introduced a partial order in the choices that a validation team has to perform in order to accomplish its validation task. Essentially three primary parameters have been identified in figure 1, that are AS, NFA and ON (note that the dependency between AS and ON, being weak, does not always hold). This matches with almost all the practical situations where, starting from an architectural language/notation ON (whose choice should be influenced by the architectural style

AS), and having in mind a non-functional attribute to validate (NFA), all the remaining choices about the target model and the software annotations have to be made.

Once all the parameters have been determined, what remains to do is to introduce a methodology for the translation of the architecture description language/notation, with additional information annotated on it, into the target model ready to be validated. In the framework of the classification scheme of figure 1 such type of translation algorithm can be seen as ON+MI → TMN. Any translation methodology should match the attributes remarked at the beginning of this section, that is minimal affection on the software process and effectiveness. Several proposals have been formulated in the last few years for translating widely used software notations into target models, but there is still considerable room for further improvements and extensions.

The track of this tutorial is to look, within the framework introduced in this section, at the software validation approaches having AS in the domain of mobile software architectures and NFA in the domain of performance (see section 4).

3 Mobile Code Paradigms

The definition of the *software architecture* of an application, that is its coarse-grained organization in terms of components and interactions among them, represents one of the first and crucial steps in the design stage [5]. Software architectures can be classified according to the adopted *design paradigms* (or *architectural styles*), each of them characterized by specific architectural abstractions/rules and reference structures, that can then be instantiated into actual architectures. Client-server is a traditional example of design style. In this perspective, different mobile code styles can be identified, each characterized by different interaction patterns among components located at different sites, and the available technologies for code mobility provides the *mechanisms* to instantiate them. A review of these technologies is out of the scope of this paper (see [13, 17] for a review of notable examples of them), whereas in this section we present a taxonomy of mobile code styles, aimed at providing a basic understanding of their features and performance related costs, that will be exploited in the subsequent presentation of performance validation methodologies for mobile architectures[3].

The taxonomy is largely inspired to the ones presented in [13, 29], and is based on the decomposition of distributed applications into *code components* (the know-how to perform a computation), *resources components* (references to resources needed to perform a computation), *state components* (comprising private data as well as control information that identify a thread of execution, such as the call stack and instruction pointer), *interactions* (events involving two or more components, like exchanging a message), *sites* (locations where processing takes place).

All the basic mobile code styles included in this taxonomy consider a single interaction between components residing at two different sites, aimed at carrying out a given operation. They differ in the distribution of components at the two sites at the beginning of the interaction, in the interaction pattern, and in the distribution of components at the end of the interaction, as shown in table 1, where **A** and **B** denote the components that participate in the interaction, C and R denote the code and

---

[3] Of course, knowledge of the characteristics of a particular mobile code technology would be necessary to finely tune, in the late phases of the development cycle, the performance model of mobile software architecture.

resources (parameters) needed to perform the operation, while L_1 and L_2 are two different sites.

The styles identified are: *remote execution* (REX), *code on demand* (COD), and *mobile agent* (MA). In all the styles, component **A** initiates the interaction.

Table 1. Mobile code styles

Style	before interaction		after interaction	
	L_1	L_2	L_1	L_2
REX	A, C, R	B	A, C, R	B, C, R
COD	A, R	B, C	A, C, R	B, C
(weak/strong) MA	A, C, R	B	-	A, C, B, R

In the REX style[4], both the code and the parameters needed to perform the operation are present at the **A** site, that ships both of them to the **B** site, requesting **B** to perform on its behalf the operation (exploiting also other code and resource components already present at site L_2). In general, a reply could be sent to **A** at the completion of the operation. Java *servlets* ("push" case) [37] and the REV scheme [34] are implementations of this style. The COD style is somehow the complementary of REX, since in this case it is **B** that owns the code C and ships it to **A** on its request. Java *applets* [36] are an implementation of this style.

In the two styles examined so far only data and "passive" pieces of code are sent from one location to another one, to re-direct the location of processing, while the location of the active components (in particular, their state component that identifies their thread of execution), remain fixed. On the other hand, in the MA style, an active component moves itself (i.e. its state component) together with needed code and parameters to the **B** site, to exploit locally the resources of that site. A further distinction can be made between a *weak* and a *strong* MA style, where in the former only data state (i.e., private variables) is transferred, while in the latter also the execution state (i.e., instruction pointer and control stack) is transferred. In the case of strong MA, the transferred component can immediately resume its execution at the new site from the exact point where it was stopped, at the expense of freezing, packing and transferring all the computation state, which could be quite heavy. In the case of weak MA, the amount of transferred information (and the work done to capture it) may be much smaller, but some method must be devised to decide, on the basis of the encoded information, where to restart execution after migration. Several technologies that implement weak and strong MA paradigms are reviewed in [13, 17].

4 Performance Validation of Mobile Software Architectures

In this section we propose a classification of those performance validation approaches proposed in the literature that apply to mobile software architectures. In the perspective of the framework in section 2, these are the approaches spreading AS over the mobility-based styles and NFR over the performance requirements. All the remaining parameters

---

[4] We prefer to call this style "remote execution (REX)"as in [29] instead of the often used denomination "remote evaluation (REV)" to avoid ambiguity with the REV scheme proposed in [34], which is a particular *mechanism* that implements this style.

may freely vary among different approaches, and we push this classification to show, where feasible, values they assume in each approach instance.

The approaches here presented are partitioned into two main classes: *ad-hoc* and *general-purpose* methodologies.

The contribution of ad-hoc methodologies consists of cost models for a single interaction between components, for different mobile code paradigms. The cost models are provided either as closed-form analytic expressions, or as dynamic models (Petri net) which are numerically evaluated.

General-purpose methodologies can be further classified as methodologies based on formal specifications of the software behavior (process algebras), and methodologies based on semi-formal specifications (Unified Modeling Language). For both cases we highlight the advantages and present some methodologies proposed in the literature to generate a performance model starting from different notations for mobility-based architectural models.

4.1 Ad-hoc Models

Ad-hoc models consider code mobility "in isolation", providing cost models for a single interaction between components, for different mobile code styles. From our validation framework viewpoint, they consider NFA $\in$ {total network load, total processing time}, while the adopted TMN consists of either closed-form analytic expressions, or dynamic models that can be numerically evaluated. Because of the lack of features to model a whole application, ad-hoc models cannot be considered as general validation methodologies. However, they contribute to clarify the dependencies between (AS, NFA) and MI, when AS spreads over mobility-based styles, by giving insights about the quantities that affect the selected NFAs, and hence about the information that should be collected in any validation methodology for these attributes.

We review ad-hoc models proposed in the literature[5], presenting all of them in a unified scenario, consisting of a single "interaction session" between two partners (**A** and **B**) residing at different locations, with **A** requesting to **B** the execution of an operation that can be articulated in N "low level" requests, and corresponding (intermediate) results.

Closed-Form Models. We present all the models reviewed in this section as special instances of general closed-form expressions for the average total network load, and the average total processing time, denoted as L^X and T^X respectively, with $X \in$ {REX, COD, MA}.

Common parameters used in all the closed-forms (hence representing the missing information MI for the considered measures) are:

    req : average size (in bytes) of a "low level" operation request

    rep : average size (in bytes) of a "low level" result

    α^X : communication overhead[6]; B_{req}^X : average size of a single request;

---

[5] Most of the papers considered in this section also present models for the client-server style, for the sake of comparison with code mobility styles.

[6] This coefficient takes into account the overhead caused by additional information needed for connection setup and message encapsulation; in general, the α^X coefficient, $X \in$ {COD,

B_{rep}^X : average size of a single reply;

τ : network throughput (in bytes/sec); Δ^X : average network latency;

M^X : average marshalling/unmarshalling time of a request/reply;

T_{req}^X : average processing time (for **A**) of a request;

T_{rep}^X : average processing time (for **B**) of a reply;

φ^X : semantic compression factor for replies ($0 < \varphi^X \le 1$).

Other parameters, used only in some closed forms, are listed in the following.

REX style. **A** assembles the original requests into less than N "high-level" operations requests (at most, they are all assembled in a single operation), sends them together with the corresponding code to **B**, and gets the corresponding replies. Closed-form expressions for the network load and the processing time are:

$$L^{REX} = R^{REX} \alpha^{REX} \left(B_{code}^{REX} + \varphi^{REX} B_{rep}^{REX} \right)$$

$$T^{REX} = \frac{1}{\tau} L^{REX} + R^{REX} \left(\Delta^{REX} + M^{REX} + T_{req}^{REX} + T_{rep}^{REX} \right)$$

where: R^{REX} : number of "high level" operation requests needed to complete the interaction

B_{code}^{REX} : average size of the code of a high level operation sent to **B** for remote evaluation

Table 2. Proposed parameters instantiations in closed-forms for the REX style

	R^{REX}	α^{REX}	B_{code}^{REX}	B_{rep}^{REX}	φ^{REX}	Δ^{REX}	M^{REX}	T_{req}^{REX}	T_{rep}^{REX}
[2]	1	> 1	> 0	N rep	1, $1/N$	-	-	-	-
[21]	$\geq 1, < N$	> 1	> 0 $(req \cdot N/R^{REX})$	> 0 $(rep \cdot N/R^{REX})$	1	0	> 0	> 0	> 0

COD style. The scenario modeled by the following closed-forms assumes that **A** requests the execution of less than N high-level operations to **B**; to model a COD-based interaction, we assume that **B**, if the needed code is present at its site, executes the operations, otherwise fetches the code from some other site. Closed-form expressions for the network load and the processing time are:

$$L^{COD} = R^{COD} \alpha^{COD} \left(B_{req}^{COD} + P_{code}^{COD} (B_{fetch}^{COD} + B_{code}^{COD}) + \varphi^{COD} B_{rep}^{COD} \right)$$

$$T^{COD} = \frac{1}{\tau} L^{COD} + R^{COD} \left(\Delta^{COD} + M^{COD} + T_{req}^{COD} + T_{rep}^{COD} \right)$$

REX, MA} may be dependent on the size of the data exchanged in the communication, that is the overhead coefficient for data of size Y is: $\alpha^X = \alpha^X(Y)$.

[7] The authors in [21] calls the REX style as "stationary agent access" (SA) style.

where:

R^{COD} : average number of "high level" operations needed to complete the interaction;

P_{code}^{COD} : probability that the code for a high level operatio is not already present at the location of **B**;

B_{fetch}^{COD} : average size of the request for the code of a high level operation sent by **B**;

B_{code}^{COD} : average size of the code of a high level operation.

Table 3. Proposed parameters instantiations in closed-forms for the COD style

	R^{COD}	α^{COD}	B_{req}^{COD}	P_{code}^{COD}	B_{code}^{COD}	B_{fetch}^{COD}	B_{rep}^{COD}	φ^{COD}	Δ^{COD}	M^{COD}	T_{req}^{COD}	T_{req}^{COD}
[2]	1	> 1	> 0	≥0, ≤1	> 0	> 0	$N\,rep$	1, $1/N$	-	-	-	-

We point out that the model for the processing time of the COD style has been extrapolated from the models for other styles, since no explicit model for the processing time of this style is present in the literature. For this reason no specific instantiation of parameters in the latter four columns of table 3 is given.

MA style. **A** moves to the **B** site, to interact locally with **B**. Then, it can go back to the starting site, or move to some other site, carrying with it the information accumulated at the **B** site; in the latter case, it can optionally send back the collected information to the starting site. Closed-form expressions for the network load and the processing time are:

$$L^{MA} = \alpha^{MA} \left(\left(P_{code}^{MA} + \beta_{back}\beta_{code} \right) B_{code}^{MA} \right.$$
$$\left. + (1 + \beta_{back})\left(B_{state}^{MA} + B_{data}^{MA} \right) + (1 - \beta_{back})\beta_{rep}\varphi^{MA} B_{rep}^{MA} \right)$$

$$T^{MA} = \frac{1}{\tau} L^{MA} + \Delta^{MA} + M^{MA} + T_{req}^{MA} + T_{rep}^{MA}$$

where: P_{code}^{MA} : probability that the code of the mobile agent is not already present at the location of **B**;

B_{code}^{MA} : average size of the mobile agent code;

B_{state}^{MA} : average size of the mobile agent execution state;

B_{data}^{MA} : average size of the mobile agent data (before the interaction starts);

$\beta_{back} = \begin{cases} 1 & \text{if the agent goes back to the starting locatio} \\ 0 & \text{otherwise} \end{cases}$;

$$\beta_{code}^{\ 8} = \begin{cases} 1 \text{ if the agent code is not retained at the return locatio} \\ 0 \text{ otherwise} \end{cases} ;$$

$$\beta_{rep} = \begin{cases} 1 \text{ if a "high level" reply is sent to the starting locatic} \\ 0 \text{ otherwise} \end{cases} .$$

Table 4. Proposed parameters instantiations in closed-forms for the MA style

	[35]	[9]	[2]	[22]	[21]
α^{MA}	1	1	> 1	> 1	> 1
P_{code}^{MA}	$\geq 0, \leq 1$	$\geq 0, \leq 1$	1	1	1
B_{code}^{MA}	$> 0 \ (\geq N \cdot req)$	> 0	> 0	> 0	> 0
B_{state}^{MA}	> 0	> 0	> 0	> 0	> 0
B_{data}^{MA}	≥ 0	≥ 0	≥ 0	≥ 0	0
φ^{MA}	$> 0, \leq 1$	1	1, 1/N	$> 0, \leq 1$	1
B_{rep}^{MA}	$N \cdot rep$	$N \cdot rep$	$N \cdot rep$	$N \cdot rep$	> 0
β_{back}	0	0, 1	0	0	1
β_{code}	-	1	-	-	0
β_{rep}	0, 1	0	0, 1	1	1
Δ^{MA}	$(1+\beta_{rep})\delta^{\ 9}$	-	-	0	0
M^{MA}	$2\mu(B_{data}^{MA} + B_{state}^{MA} + \beta_{rep} B_{rep}^{MA})^{10}$	-	-	> 0	> 0
T_{req}^{MA}	0	-	-	0	> 0
T_{rep}^{MA}	0	-	-	> 0	> 0

In all the considered models for the MA style (with the exception of [22], where it is unspecified) it is assumed that, after the completion of the interaction, the agent data grow as follows: $B_{data}^{MA} \leftarrow B_{data}^{MA} + \varphi^{MA} B_{rep}^{MA}$. In this way it is modeled the (possible) accumulation of information collected by the mobile agent as it visits new sites.

With regard to the parameters instantiations shown in table 4, it should be noted that the marshalling/unmarshalling overhead of [35] is calculated under the assumption that the agent code is already available in transport format. [22] analyzes a broadcast

---

[8] If the agent goes back to the starting **A** location, then $\beta_{code} = 0$ means that only its data (the original data plus the ones collected at **B** location) and execution state actually go back, since a copy of the (immutable) code has been retained there; the term $(1-\beta_{back})$ that multiplies β_{rep} means that only if the agent does not go back to the starting location, a reply could be sent there.

[9] δ denotes the average roundtrip time (in secs.).

[10] $\mu > 0$ represents a marshalling/unmarshalling factor (in secs/byte); this factor is multiplied by 2 to take into account both marshalling and unmarshalling of a message.

data filtering application, where the MA paradigm (with filtering at the server) is compared against broadcast filtering at the client (hence no other mobile code style is modeled, while closed-forms are presented for network load and processing time in the broadcast case). Moreover, [4] builds on the model presented in [2] to derive closed-forms expressing the network load caused by the MA style in conjunction with multicast protocols to deliver the agent to multiple destinations.

Dynamic models. The interaction scenario modeled by the models considered in this section is the same considered before, but, differently from the models of the previous section, here they adopt TMN = {Petri net} and are limited to NFA = { total processing time } [27]. Moreover, these models refer only to AS $\in$ { REX, MA }, whereas no model is provided in [27] for the COD style. We do not present details of these models. Anyway, the parameters are basically the same as the ones in the previous section, except for the fact that many of them are instantiated as random variables with a given probability distribution, rather than as constant (average) values, and can be listed as follows (with $X \in$ {REX, MA}):

$\alpha^X = 1;$ $\qquad P^X_{code} = 1;$ $\qquad B^X_{rep}$: uniformly distributed in $[rep_{min}, rep_{max}]$

$B^{MA}_{data} = 0;$ $\qquad \beta_{back} = 0;$ $\qquad \beta_{rep} = 0$ or $\beta_{rep} = 1;$

$\Delta^X = 0;$ $\qquad M^X = 0;$ $\qquad T^X_{req}$ and T^X_{rep}: exponentially distributed.

The only remarkable difference with the previous closed-form models concerns the semantic compression that in [27] is modeled only for the MA paradigm as a constraint on the growth of the B^{MA}_{data} parameter, as follows: $B^{MA}_{data} \leftarrow B^{MA}_{data} + D^{MA}_{rep}$, with D^{MA}_{rep} uniformly distributed in $[rep_{min}, n \cdot rep_{max}]$, where $n > 1$ is a parameter independent of the agent history. Hence, differently from the closed-form models of the previous section, the agent data do not grow linearly with the number of visited locations, if the agent visits more than one location.

4.2 General-Purpose Formal Models: Process Algebras

The validation methodologies considered in this section are based on the selection of ON = { Process Algebras}, and do not focus on specific NFAs. Hence, the adopted TMN is general enough to allow the evaluation of different NFAs, and consists of TMN = {Stochastic Process Algebras + associated Markov Processes}; correspondingly, possible STs consist of any solution technique suitable for this TMN. From these choices it results that MI includes at least the (exponential) completion rates of all the activities that are modeled in the adopted Process Algebra.

Process algebras are well-known formalisms for the modelling and analysis of parallel and distributed systems. What makes them attractive as ON for the evaluation of large and complex systems, are mainly their compositional and abstraction features, that facilitate building complex system models from smaller ones. Moreover, they are equipped with a formal semantics, that allows a non ambiguous system specification, and a calculus that allows to prove rigorously whether some functional properties hold. Stochastic process algebras are an extension of these formalisms with stochastic features for the specification of system activities duration, that allow the analysis of quantitative non-functional properties. We defer to the vast available literature for details about the general characteristics of these formalisms (e.g., [14]), and focus in this section on process algebras for the modeling of mobile software architectures. We only provide their (partial) formal syntax and informal descriptions of the corresponding semantics, aimed at illustrating the salient features of different approaches to formal modeling of code mobility. Then, we illustrate a proposed methodology for the translation of this formalism into a TMN for the analysis of NFAs, with TMN consisting of Markov processes (and stochastic process algebras as intermediate TMN).

A process algebra is a formal language, whose syntax basically appears like this:

$$P ::= \mathbf{0} \mid \pi.P \mid P + P \mid P \parallel P \mid \dots \text{ }^{11}$$

where $\mathbf{0}$ denotes the "null" (terminated) process that cannot perform any action, $+$ and $\parallel$ denote process composition by non-deterministic alternative or parallelism, respectively, and $\pi.P$ denotes the process that performs action $\pi \in Act$, and then behaves as P (where Act is a set of possible actions). Process algebras for mobility modeling basically differ in the set Act of actions the defined processes can perform. We group them into two sections, based on the way used to model the location of components.

Example 1. To illustrate some of the modeling approaches reviewed in this and next section, we will use a simple application example based on a traveling agency scenario, where a travel agency periodically contacts K flying companies to get information about the cost of a ticket for some itinerary. The agency exchanges a sequence of N messages with each company, to collect the required information. Using a traditional client-server approach, this means that the agency should explicitly establish N RPCs with each company to complete the task. On the other hand, with a REX approach, the agency could send a code encompassing all the N messages along with some gluing operations, to be executed by each company, getting only the final reply. Within a COD approach, we could think that the agency makes an overall request to each company, and that it is the responsibility of each company to possibly get somewhere the needed code to fulfill the request. Finally, in an MA approach, the agency could deliver an agent that travels along all the K companies getting locally the information, and then reports it back to the agency. *EndOfExample1*

Models with "Indirect" Location Specification. Algebras listed in this section can be considered as a direct derivation from CCS-like algebras [23], and are characterized by the modeling of mobility as a change in the links that connect processes. Before reviewing them, we briefly illustrate a basic CCS-like algebra. In this case, we have $\pi \in \{\tau_i (i = 1, 2, \dots), \mathbf{in}x, \mathbf{out}x\}$, where τ_i denotes a "silent" (internal) action of a process[12], while **in** and **out** are input and output actions, respectively, along the link named x, that can be used to synchronize a process with another parallel process that executes their output or input counterparts along the same link. For example, if two processes are specified as follows:

$$P := \mathbf{out}a.P_1 \qquad\qquad Q := \mathbf{in}a.Q_1$$

from these definitions we get that $P \parallel Q$ evolves into $P_1 \parallel Q_1$, that is, processes P and Q synchronize (i.e., wait for each other) thanks to a communication along link a, and

---

[11] Note that, for the sake of simplicity, this syntax is incomplete, since we are omitting constructs to define abstraction mechanisms, or recursive behavior, etc.

[12] Subscript i is used to distinguish different internal actions, which is useful for modeling purposes.

then prosecute in parallel (possibly independently of each other, if no other synchronizing communication takes place in their following behavior).

π-*calculus* [24]. This algebra, besides synchronization between parallel processes, allows also link names communication, so that we can change the links a process uses to communicate with other processes. The possible system actions are $\pi \in \{\tau_i \ (i = 1, 2, \ldots),$ **in**x, **out**x, **in**$x(y)$, **out**$x(Y)\}$, where in addition to the above definitions, Y (y) is a "link name" (link variable), sent (received) over the link named x. For example, with the following specifications:

$$P_1 := \mathbf{out}a(b).P_3 \qquad\qquad P_2 := \mathbf{out}a(c).P_3 \qquad\qquad Q := \mathbf{in}\ a(y).\mathbf{out}y.Q_1$$

we get that $P_1 \parallel Q$ evolves into $P_3 \parallel \mathbf{out}b.Q_1$, while $P_2 \parallel Q$ evolves into $P_3 \parallel \mathbf{out}c.Q_1$. In this example, the parallel composition of Q with P_1 or P_2 gives rise to the evolution of Q into a process that communicates along the link b or c, respectively, and then behaves as process Q_1.

HOπ-calculus [30]. Besides the operations of π-calculus, this algebra allows also the communication of process names, so that we can change the behavior of the receiving process. The possible system actions are again $\pi \in \{\tau_i \ (i = 1, 2, \ldots),$ **in**x, **out**x, **in**$x(y)$, **out**$x(Y))\}$, but, in addition to the above definitions, Y (y) may also be a "process name" (process variable) besides a link name (variable), sent (received) over the link named x. For example, with the following specifications:

$$P_1 := \mathbf{out}\ a(R).P_3 \qquad\qquad P_2 := \mathbf{out}\ a(S).P_3 \qquad\qquad Q := \mathbf{in}\ a(z).z.Q_1$$

we get that $P_1 \parallel Q$ evolves into $P_3 \parallel R.Q_1$, while $P_2 \parallel Q$ evolves into $P_3 \parallel S.Q_1$. In other words, the parallel composition of Q with P_1 or P_2 gives rise to the evolution of Q into a process that behaves like process R or S, respectively, and then as process Q_1.

Example 2[13]. Let us consider the system of example 1 in the case of K=2 flying companies, with Fi and ai ($i=1, 2$) denoting a company and the channel used to communicate with it, C denoting the overall code corresponding to the N "low level" interactions, and Ri the overall response collected at company Fi. Using HOπ-calculus, this application could be modeled as follows, in case of REX paradigm (where *Sys* models the overall application):
$TravAg = \mathbf{out}a1(C).\mathbf{in}a1(x).\mathbf{out}a2(C).\mathbf{in}a2(x).TravAg$
$Fi = \mathbf{in}ai(z).z.\mathbf{out}ai(Ri).Fi$
$Sys = TravAg \parallel F1 \parallel F2$
EndOfExample2.

Models with "Direct" Location Specification. The above approaches suggest as ON for the modeling of mobile architectures a process algebra where the location of a process is indirectly defined in terms of its connectivity, i.e. the link names it sees and the identity of the processes it can communicate with at a given instant of time using those links; hence, the location of a process can be changed by changing the links it sees (by sending it new link names, as in the π-calculus , or by sending the process itself, i.e., its name, as in the HOπ-calculus to a receiving process that has a

---

[13] Adapted from [25].

different location (again, defined by its connectivity)). Other process algebras approaches have been defined where the location of processes is directly and explicitly defined, giving it a first class status, so allowing for a more direct modeling and reasoning about problems related to locations, such as access rights or code mobility, thus making these algebras somewhat more appealing as ON for mobile architectures. Two of these approaches are the *ambient* calculus and *KLAIM*. In the following we briefly outline some of their features. As before, the presentation is far from complete, with the main goal of only giving some flavor of the way they adopt to model process location and mobility in a process algebras setting.

Ambient calculus [7]. In this formalism the concept of *ambient* is added to the basic constructs for processes definition and composition described above. An ambient has a *name* that specifies its identity, and can be thought of as a sort of boundary that encloses a set of running processes. Ambients, denoted as $n[P]$, where n is the ambient name and P is the enclosed process, can be entered, exited or opened (i.e., dissolved) by appropriate operations executed by a process, so allowing to model movement as the crossing of ambient boundaries. Ambients are hierarchically nested, and a process can only enter an ambient which is sibling of its ambient in the hierarchy, and can exit only into the parent ambient of its ambient; hence, moving to a "far" ambient in the ambients hierarchy requires, in this formalism, the explicit crossing of multiple ambients. The mobility operations for an ambient $n[.]$ are denoted by **inamb**n, **outamb**n, **open**n, respectively[14]. In general, a process cannot forge them by itself, but receives them thanks to the communication operations **in** and **out**. Hence, a process receiving one of such operations through a communication actually receives a capability for it, being allowed to execute the corresponding operation on the named ambient. The (partial) formal syntax of this algebra is then as follows:

$$P ::= \mathbf{0} \mid \pi.P \mid P + P \mid P \parallel P \mid n[P] \mid \ldots$$

with $\pi \in \{\tau_i \, (i = 1, 2, \ldots), \mathbf{in}(x), \mathbf{out}(M), \mathbf{inamb}n, \mathbf{outamb}n, \mathbf{open}n\}$, where x is a variable and M stands for either an ambient name (n), or a capability for an ambient (either **inamb**n, or **outamb**n, or **open**n). Communication is restricted to be local, i.e. only between processes enclosed in the same ambient. Communication between non local processes requires the definition of some sort of "messenger" agent that explicitly crosses the required ambient boundaries bringing with itself the information to be communicated. Alternatively, a process can move itself to the ambient of its partner before (locally) communicating with it. In both cases, the messenger or the moving process must possess the needed capabilities.

KLAIM (Kernel Language for Agents Interaction and Mobility) [11]. This formalism allows to define a net of locations that are basically not nested into each other, with direct communication possible, in principle, between processes located at any location, differently from the ambient calculus (anyway, the extension to nested location is possible). Another remarkable difference with the ambient calculus, and with all the previously mentioned algebras, consists of the adoption of a *generative* (rather than message passing) style of communication, based on the use of *tuple spaces* and the

---

[14] Note that the ambient operations are named **in**, **out** and **open** in the original paper [7]; we have renamed them to avoid confusion with the names used in this paper to denote the mesage passing communication operations.

communication primitives of the *Linda* coordination language [8]. Tuple spaces are linked to locations, and interaction between processes located at different locations can happen by putting or retrieving the opportune tuple into the tuple space at a given location. Again, the (partial) formal syntax of this algebra is as follows:

$$P ::= \mathbf{0} \mid \pi.P \mid P + P \mid P \parallel P \mid \dots$$

with $\pi \in \{\tau_i\ (i = 1, 2, \dots),\ \mathbf{in\_t}(t)@l,\ \mathbf{read\_t}(t)@l,\ \mathbf{out\_t}(t)@l,\ \mathbf{eval\_t}(t)@l,$ $\mathbf{newloc}(u)\}$, where the indicated operations are the usual Linda-like operations on a tuple t, restricted to operate on the tuple space associated to the l location[15]. Moreover, the $\mathbf{newloc}(u)$ operation allows a process to create a new (initially private) location that can be accessed through the name u. Note that the fields of a tuple may be either values, or processes, or localities, or variables of the previous types. This allows a simple modelling of all the mobile code styles (namely REX, COD and MA), as shown in [11].

Other formal models. Other approaches to mobility modeling (and formal verification of functional requirements for mobile systems) have been proposed, not based on a process algebras framework: Mobile UNITY [26], Mob$_{adtl}$ [12], COMMUNITY [38]. The former two have a temporal logic based semantics, and the latter has a category theory based semantics. We do not consider explicitly these approaches since the translation methodology from ON to TMN described in the following section has been presented in the framework of process algebras.

From Process Algebras to Performance Models. In this section we present a methodology for the translation from ON to a suitable TMN, when the application model is built using ON={Process Algebra}. This approach has been presented in the framework of π-calculus and HOπ-calculus, but it is applicable to any formalism with an operational semantics, like all the process algebras presented above. We start with a brief review of operational semantics, and then outline the approach, presented in [25].

The operational semantics of a process specified using the syntax of a given process algebra is given by a *labeled transition system*, i.e. (informally) a graph that represents all the possible system evolutions; each node of the graph represents a particular system state, while a transition represents a state change, and the label associated to a transition provides information about the "activities" that cause the corresponding state change. The transition relation (i.e. which are the states reachable in one step from a given state, and the associated labels) is specified by giving a set of syntax-driven rules, in the sense that they are associated to the syntactic rules of the algebra. Each rule takes the form $\dfrac{Premises}{Conclusion}$ whose meaning is that whenever the premises (that can be interpreted as a given computational step) occur, then the conclusion will occur as well. (Simplified) examples of such rules are the following:

$$\frac{}{\pi.P \xrightarrow{\pi} P}, \quad \frac{P \xrightarrow{\pi} P}{P + Q \xrightarrow{\pi} P'}, \quad \frac{P \xrightarrow{\pi} P'}{P \parallel Q \xrightarrow{\pi} P \parallel Q}, \quad \frac{P \xrightarrow{out x} P', Q \xrightarrow{in x} Q}{P \parallel Q \xrightarrow{\tau} P' \parallel Q'}$$

---

[15] Note that the tuple operations are named **in**, **out**, **read** and **eval** in the original paper [11]; we have renamed them to avoid confusion with the names used in this paper to denote the message passing communication operations.

Note that the third rule specifies a transition relation for parallel independent processes, while the fourth rule specifies a transition relation for parallel processes that synchronize themselves through a communication operation[16].

Example 3. The labeled transition system obtained applying rules as the ones specified above to the *Sys* model of example 2 (using HOπ-calculus) is given by (assuming C = $(\tau_1 + \tau_2).\mathbf{0}$):

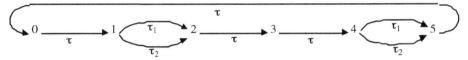

EndOfExample3

In general, methodologies for the translation of process algebras into a TMN suitable for the analysis of NFAs are based on the association of a stochastic duration, that hence represent a MI for these methodologies, to the activities specified in the process algebra, so obtaining, as a first step, a stochastic process algebra that, in our framework, can be considered as an intermediate notation toward the final TMN. Then, starting from a stochastic process algebra model, a stochastic duration can be associated to each label in the labeled transition system that represents the operational semantic of the original model. If this duration is exponentially distributed (hence expressed by an exponential rate), then we get a continuous time Markov chain. A fundamental problem to make practically usable these approaches is how giving a meaningful value to the exponential rates associated to the transitions, since, in a realistic system, their number is very high. The idea of [25], is to associate to each transition a label that does not merely register the action associated to that transition (e.g., τ_1, as in example 3), but also the inference rules used during the deduction of the transition, so to keep trace of the "underlying operations" that lead to the execution of that action. For instance, in example 3 the operation underlying the execution of action τ_1 is a selection operation between the two concurrently enabled operation τ_1 and τ_2. These "enhanced" labels can be used to define a systematic way for deriving the rates to be associated to the system transitions. The enhanced labels are built using symbols from a suitable alphabet (e.g., $\{+, \|, \ldots\}$), to record the inference rules used during the derivation of the transitions. For example, the transition rules given above would be rewritten as follows to get enhanced labels[17]:

$$\frac{}{\pi.P\xrightarrow{\pi}P}, \quad \frac{P\xrightarrow{\theta}P'}{P+Q\xrightarrow{+\theta}P}, \quad \frac{P\xrightarrow{\theta}P'}{P\|Q\xrightarrow{\|\theta}P'\|Q}, \quad \frac{P\xrightarrow{\vartheta\text{out }x}P', Q\xrightarrow{\vartheta'\text{in }x}Q'}{P\|Q\xrightarrow{\{\|\vartheta\text{out }x, \vartheta'\text{ in }x\}}P'\|Q}$$

---

[16] In the "standard" semantics of process algebras [24], the label of this latter rule is equal to τ, that is an invisible action, since the two matching input and output operations "consume" each other, making them unobservable for an external "observer" (e.g. a process running in parallel).

[17] Again, we are introducing a simplification: in a complete specification different symbols should be used to distinguish the selection of the left or right alternative in a parallel or alternative choice composition (see [25]).

where an enhanced label is, in general, given by $\theta = \vartheta\pi$, with π denoting, as before, a particular system action, and $\vartheta \in \{+, \|, ...\}^*$ denoting the sequence of inference rules followed to fire that action.

Example 4. The transition system of example 3 would be enhanced as follows:

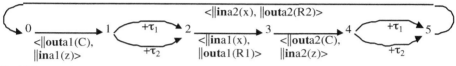

EndOfExample4

Using the enhanced labels, the rate of a transition can be calculated by defining suitable functions, as follows:

$$\$_b : Act \rightarrow \Re^+, \qquad \$_s : \{+, \|, ...\} \rightarrow \Re^+, \qquad \$: \{+, \|, ...\}^* \bullet Act \rightarrow \Re^+$$

where $\bullet$ denotes the concatenation operator, $\$_b$ defines the basic exponential rate of an action in a reference architecture dedicated only to the execution of that action without any interference, while $\$_s$ defines a slowing factor in the execution of an action due to the execution of some underlying operation in the target architecture where the action is actually executed. $\$$ is the function that calculates the actual exponential rate of the transition, taking into account all possible interferences, and can be basically recursively defined using $\$_b$ and $\$_s$, as follows [18]:

$$\$(\pi) = \$_b(\pi), \qquad \$(\sigma\vartheta\pi) = \$_s(\sigma)\$(\vartheta\pi), \qquad \sigma \in \{+, \|, ...\}, \vartheta \in \{+, \|, ...\}^*$$

By suitably defining the functions $\$_b$ and $\$_s$, we can limit the problem of calculating meaningful transition rates to the problem of defining only the cost of the "primitive" system actions, and of the slowing factors caused by a particular target architecture. Note that, with respect to our validation framework, this means that the methodology of [25], besides defining a method for the translation from ON to TMN, also gives strong indication about what MI should be collected. Having this information, the calculation of the actual transition rates can be completely automated (but it should be remarked that the definition of the above functions is, in general, quite an ambitious task). It should be noted also that, by changing the definition of $\$_s$, we can also analyze the impact on performance of different target architectures.

Once the rates of all the possible transitions from a given state (representing the system behaving like process P_i) have been determined, the overall rate from state P_i to another state P_j which is one-step successor of state P_i is given by:

$$q(P_i, P_j) = \sum_{P_i \xrightarrow{\vartheta\pi} P_j} \$(\vartheta\pi)$$

(note that, in general, more than one transition from state P_i to state P_j may be present in the graph of the transition system). The process so obtained gives us information about the rate at which the system actions are performed. In general, to carry out a

---

[18] Note that in this presentation we do not have explicitly considered the problem of how calculating the rate of synchronization (i.e., communication) operations; for a discussion of this topic, see [18].

performance evaluation, we need also a *reward structure*, that associates to each state of the process a performance-related reward (or cost), that constitutes another possible MI that should be collected. In the described approach, these rewards could be calculated using a procedure similar to the one followed to calculate the transition rates. Besides being added to the Markov process derived from a process algebra specification, rewards could also be formally included in a stochastic process algebra, to allow formal reasoning about them. For a discussion about this topic, which is beyond the scope of this paper, see [18].

4.3 General-Purpose Semi-Formal Models: UML

The advantage of using process algebras as ON mainly consists in the possibility of a rigorous and non ambiguous modeling activity. However, the use of these formal notations does not have yet gained widespread acceptance in the practice of software development. On the contrary, a semi-formal notation, the Unified Modeling Language (UML) [6], that lacks some of the formal rigor of the notations considered in the previous section, has quickly become a de-facto standard in the industrial software development process. UML recent success is mainly due to the following reasons [1]:

- It allows to embed into the model static and dynamic aspects of the software by using different diagrams, each representing a different view of the software system. Each view captures a different set of concerns and aspects regarding the subject. Therefore it is broadly applicable to different types of domains or subject areas.
- The same conceptual framework and the same notation can be used from specification through design to implementation.
- In UML, more than in classical object oriented approaches, the boundaries between analysis, design and implementation are not clearly stated. As a consequence, there is more freedom in software development process, even if the Rational Unified Process [19] has been proposed as a guideline for software process development based on UML.
- UML is not a proprietary and closed language but an open and fully extensible language. The extensibility mechanisms and the potential for annotations of UML allow it to be customized and tailored to particular system types, domains, and methods/processes. It can be extended to include constructs for working within a particular context (e.g., performance requirement validation) where even very specialized knowledge can be captured.
- It is widely supported by a broad set of tools. Various tool vendors intend to support UML in order to facilitate its application throughout an organization. By having a set of tools that support UML, knowledge may be more readily captured and manipulated to meet an organization's objectives.

UML consists of two parts: a *notation*, used to describe a set of diagrams (also called the syntax of the language) and a *metamodel* (also called the semantics of the language) that specifies the abstract integrated semantics of UML modeling concepts. The UML notation encompasses several kinds of diagrams, most of them belonging to previous methodologies, that provide specific views of the system. UML diagrams can be distinguished into four main types:

1. Static diagrams: Use Case, Class and Object Diagrams
2. Behavioral diagrams: Activity and State Diagrams
3. Interaction diagrams: Sequence and Collaboration Diagrams

4.   Implementation diagrams: Component and Deployment Diagrams

"Standard" UML as ON for mobile architecture. Standard UML can be used as ON for mobile architectures, since UML already provides some mechanisms for this goal. They are mainly based on the use of a tagged value `location` within a component to express its location, and of the `copy` and `become` stereotypes to express the location change of a component. The former stereotype can be used to specify the creation of an independent component copy at a new location (like in the COD and REX styles), and the latter to specify a location change of a component that preserves its identity (like in the MA style). In [6] it is shown how to use these mechanisms within a Collaboration Diagram to model the location change of a mobile component interleaved with interactions among components.

Example 5. The travel agency application can be modeled by the following Collaboration Diagram, based on standard UML, in case of MA paradigm.

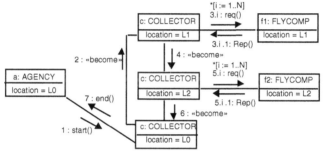

EndOfExample5

However, this modelling approach presents some drawbacks, since it mixes together two different views, one concerning the architectural style (e.g. the fact that a component behaves according to some mobility style), and the other one concerning the actual sequence of messages exchanged between components during a particular interaction. Moreover, this approach may lead to a proliferation of objects in the diagrams, that actually represent the same object at different locations. Both these drawbacks can lead to quite obscure models of the application behavior.

"Extended" UML as ON for mobile architecture. To overcome the drawbacks of standard UML as ON for mobile architectures, the dependency between the modeled AS and the chosen ON can be made explicit by adopting a different approach based on the use of both Collaboration and Sequence Diagrams (CD and SD), with a clear separation of concerns between them, as proposed in [15]. The SD describes the actual sequence of interactions between components, which is basically independent of the adopted style and obeys only to the intrinsic logic of the application, while the CD only models the interaction structure (i.e. who interacts with whom) and style, without showing the actual sequence of exchanged messages.

The interaction logic is described using the standard UML notation for SD. The interaction structure is modeled by the links that connect components in CD, with arrows specifying unidirectional or bidirectional interactions. For the interaction style, the main goal is to distinguish a style where components location is statically assigned, from a style where components do change location to adapt to environment change. To this purpose, the standard location tagged value can be used to specify the component location, while it is necessary to extend the UML semantics by introducing a new stereotype moveTo that applies to messages in the CD. Where present, moveTo indicates that the source component moves to the location of its target before starting a sequence of consecutive interactions with it. If no other information is present, this style applies to each sequence of interactions shown in the associated SD, between the source and target components of the moveTo message; otherwise a condition can be added to restrict this style to a subset of interactions between two components. It should be noted that this approach appears suitable to model only mobile architectures where the architecture style is AS={MA}.

Example 6 According to the adopted modeling framework, the travel agency example application can be modeled as shown in figure 2.

Figure 2. Travel agency example: (a) interaction logic, (b) architectural style

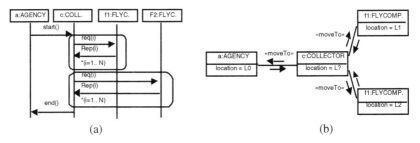

(a)   (b)

Figure 2.a shows a SD that describes in detail the "logic" of the interaction, i.e. the sequence of messages exchanged among the components. In this diagram no information is present about the adopted style, that is whether or not some component changes location during the interactions. This information is provided by the CD in figure 2.b, that models a style where component mobility is considered. More precisely, the diagram shows that only c can change location, and according to the moveTo semantics described above, it moves to the location of a, f1 or f2 before interacting with them. Note that in figure 2.b the location of c is left unspecified (L?), since it can dynamically change. In general, it is possible to give it a specified value in the diagram, that would show the "initial" location of the mobile object in an initial deployment configuration. *EndOfExample6*

In general, there could be uncertainty about the convenience of adopting a mobile code style in the design of an application. To model this uncertainty about the architecture (i.e. location and possible mobility of components), a new stereotype moveTo? has been proposed in [15], that extends the semantics of the moveTo stereotype described above. When a message between two components in a CD is labeled with moveTo?, this means that the source component "could" move to the location of its target at the beginning of a sequence of interactions with it. In a sense, this means that, based on the information the designer has at that stage, he/she considers acceptable both a static and a mobile architecture. Hence, a general UML support to model a (possibly) mobile architectural style consists of a CD where some messages are unlabeled, some can be labeled with the (possibly constrained) moveTo stereotype, and some with the moveTo? stereotype. The former two cases correspond to a situation where the designer feels confident enough to decide about the best architectural style, while the latter to a situation where the designer lacks such a confidence. In the next section, we illustrate methodologies for the translation from a model defined using the extended UML as ON, to suitable TMNs for the analysis of different NFAs.

From extended UML models to performance models. The goal is to build a stochastic model that describes the system dynamics, whose evaluation provides information about the performance one can expect by adopting an MA or "static" architectural style, as described in the previous section. In terms of the extended UML presented above, the gained insights should allow the designer to substitute the moveTo? messages in the preliminary CD with (possibly constrained) moveTo messages, or with no such message at all, if the obtained insights provide evidence that a static architectural style is more advantageous. Specifically two different methodologies have been proposed [15, 16] that, starting from a set of annotated UML diagrams derive two different TMNs, namely, a Markov model or a queueing network model. In the following we briefly present these two methodologies.

The first one is suitable for cases when the NFAs of interest are mainly interaction-related measures (e.g., generated network traffic) without considering possible contention with other applications. In this approach, the TMN is a Markov Reward Process (MRP) [28] when the CDs modeling the architectural style only use the moveTo stereotype, and a Markov Decision Process (MDP) [28] when the CDs modeling the architectural style also use the moveTo? stereotype.

The second one, based on classic SPE technique [32, 33], is suitable for cases where the NFAs of interest are measures like throughput or response time and we are possibly interested in considering contention with other applications on the use of system resources. Two different TMNs are taken into account, namely, Execution Graphs [32] and Extended Queueing Network Models [20] for NFAs with and without consideration to the impact of contention, respectively.

In both cases, it is assumed that the diagrams described in the previous section are augmented with appropriate annotations expressing the "cost" of each interaction with respect to a given performance measure (see, for example, [31] and papers in [39]), to represent the needed MI. For example, if we are interested in the generated network traffic, MI includes at least the size of each exchanged message.

Markov models. In general, a MRP models a state transition system, where the next state is selected according to a transition probability that only depends on the current state. Moreover, each time a state is visited or a transition occurs, a reward is accumulated, that depends on the involved state or transition. Typical measures that can be derived from such a model are the reward accumulated in a given time interval, or the reward accumulation rate in the long period. A MDP extends the MRP model by associating to each state a set of alternative *decisions*, where both the rewards and the transitions associated to that state are decision dependent. A *policy* for a MDP consists in a selection, for each state, of one of the associated decisions, that will be taken each time that state is visited. Hence, different policies lead to different system behaviors and to different accumulated rewards. In other words, a MDP defines a family of MRPs, one for each different policy that can be determined. Algorithms exist to determine the optimal policy with respect to some optimality criterion (e.g. minimization of the accumulated reward) [28].

In the translation methodology adopted in [15], a MRP/MDP state corresponds to a possible configuration of the components location, while a state transition models the occurrence of an interaction between components or a location change, and the associated reward is the cost of that interaction. In case of MDP, the decisions associated to states model the alternative choices of mobility or no mobility as architectural style, for those components that are the source of a moveTo? message.

The translation method from the extended UML to this TMN consists of the definition of some elementary generation rules, and then in the use of these rules to define a MDP generation algorithm [15].

Once the MDP has been generated, it can be solved to determine the optimal policy, that is the selection of a decision in each state that optimizes the reward accumulated in the corresponding MRP. Of course, the optimal policy depends on the values given to the system parameters (e.g., the size of the messages and of the possibly mobile component). Different values for these parameters model different scenarios.

Queueing Network models. A different methodology for the derivation of performance models from extended UML diagrams has been proposed in [16], based on SPE techniques, having queueing network models as basic TMN.

The SPE basic concept is the separation of the software model (SM) from its execution environment model (i.e., hardware platform model or machinery model, MM). The SM captures the essential aspects of software behavior; and is usually represented by means of Execution Graphs (EG). An EG is a graph whose nodes represent software workload components and whose edges represent transfers of control. Each node is weighted by a demand vector that represents the resource usage of the node (i.e., the demand for each resource).

The MM models the hardware platform and is based on the Extended Queueing Network Model (EQNM). To specify an EQNM, we need to define: the components (i.e., service centers), the topology (i.e., the connections among centers) and some relevant parameters (such as job classes, job routing among centers, scheduling discipline at service centers, service demand at service centers). Component and topology specification is performed according to the system description, while parameters specification is obtained from information derived by EGs and from knowledge of resource capabilities. Once the EQNM is completely specified, it can be analyzed by use of classical solution techniques (simulation, analytical technique, hybrid simulation) to obtain performance indices such as the mean network response time or the utilization index.

To cope with mobility, in the methodology proposed in [16], well-known formalisms such as EG and EQNM have been extended by defining the *mob?*-EG and *mob?*-EQNM formalisms with the goal of modelling code mobility and the uncertainty about its possible adoption, within a model of the system dynamics.

To include the information about possible component mobility expressed in the CDs by moveTo? messages, a new kind of EG called *mob?*–EG is derived [16]. The *mob?*-EG modifies the original EG by introducing *mv* nodes that model the cost of code mobility. Moreover, the *mob?*-EG extends the EG formalism by introducing a new kind of node, called *mob?*, characterized by two different outcomes, "*yes*" and "*no*", that can be non-deterministically selected, followed by two possible EGs. The EG corresponding to branch "*yes*" models the selection of component mobility style, while the EG of the branch "*no*" models the static case.

Example 7. The structure (without labels showing performance related information) of the *mob?*-EG derived from the SD and CD of example 6 is illustrated in the following figure.

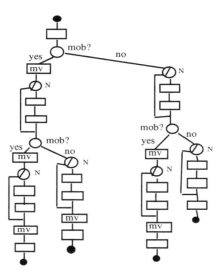

EndOfExample7

Mob?-EG can be considered by itself as the TMN for a first kind of performance evaluation corresponding to the special case of a stand-alone application where the application under study is the unique in the execution environment (therefore there is no resource contention). In this case performance evaluation can be carried out by standard graph analysis techniques [32] to associate an overall "cost" to each path in the *mob?*-EG as a function of the cost of each node that belongs to that path. Note that each path in the *mob?*–EG corresponds to a different mobility strategy, concerning when and where components move. Hence these results provide an optimal bound on the expected performance for each strategy, and can help the designer in selecting a subset of the possible mobility strategies that deserve further investigation in a more realistic setting of competition with other applications.

The complete application of SPE techniques implies the definition of a target performance model obtained from the merging of the *mob?*-EG with a QN modeling the executing platform. The merging leads to the complete specification of a EQNM by defining job classes and routing, using information from the blocks and parameters of the *mob?*-EG. However, well known translation methodologies [10, 32] are not sufficient to perform this merging because of the presence of the *mob?* nodes with non-deterministic semantics in the *mob?*-EG; hence it is necessary to give a new translation rule to cope with this kind of nodes. To this end an extension of classical EQNMs has been proposed [16], to be used as TMN when the ON is the extended UML defined in the previous section. The extension is based on the definition of new service centers, called *r?(outing)*, that model the possibility, after the visit of a service center (and therefore the completion of a software block) to choose, in a non-deterministic way, which is the routing to follow: the one modelling the static strategy or the one modelling the mobile strategy.

In such a way, a job visiting center *r?* generates two different mutually exclusive paths: one path models the job routing when the component changes its location, the other one models the routing of a static component. Note that, as node *mob?* in the EG, nodes *r?* are characterized by a null service time, since they only represent a routing selection point. The obtained model is called *mob?*-EQNM and is characterized by different routing chains starting from nodes *r?*. Note that these different routing chains are mutually exclusive; in other words a *mob?*-EQNM actually models a family of EQNMs, one for each different path through the *r?* nodes, corresponding to a different mobility policy.

Example 8. The following figure illustrates an example of *mob?*-EQNM derived from the *mob?*-EG of example 7, exploiting also information about the execution platform (e.g., obtained from a UML Deployment Diagram). The figure evidences the mutually exclusive routing chains.

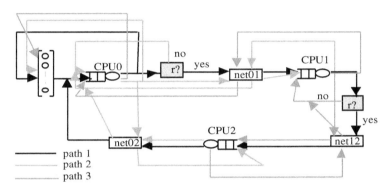

EndOfExample8

When the *mob?*-EQNM is the TMN, the ST suggested in [16] for contention based analysis is based on solving the *mob?*-EQNM through well assessed techniques [20, 32], separately considering each different EQNM belonging to the family modeled by the *mob?*-EQNM. When the number of different EQNMs is high, this solution approach could result in a high computation complexity. This problem can be alleviated by exploiting results from the stand-alone analysis. However, more efficient solution methods deserve further investigation. Starting from the obtained results it is possible to choose the mobility strategy which is *optimal* according to the selected criterion, for example the one that minimizes the response time.

5 Conclusions

The primary goal of this tutorial has been to provide a structured view within the domain of performance validation of mobile software architectures. The classification of the approaches presented in section 4 has been supported by a general framework (section 2) classifying the parameters each approach has to deal with. In table 5 we summarize the values (in some cases the classes of values) assumed by the parameters introduced in section 2 in all the types of approaches reviewed in section 4.

Besides ad-hoc models, whose merits and limitations have been outlined in section 4.1, two kinds of approaches for the systematic modeling and analysis of NFA in mobile software architectures emerge from our review, based on the use of formal or semi-formal languages as ON. We would like to remark here that our review is probably not complete, but we believe it is representative of existing approaches.

The merit of formal languages comes primarily from their lack of ambiguity, and their precise compositional features. However, as it can also be inferred from table 5, their use in NFA validation requires the assignment of reward and exponential duration to all the modelled actions, that could be quite a difficult task. The method presented in section 4.2 provides guidelines about how building meaningful rates, but leaves open the problem of how collecting the required detailed information. One way to overcome this drawback could be based on bridging the gap between process algebras and other formalisms (like UML) used by software designers, to facilitate the extraction of the detailed information required by process algebras from artifacts produced by the designers.

On the other hand, the use of UML as ON from which to derive performance models is not immune from problems as well, so the general problem of deriving meaningful performance models from UML artifacts deserves further investigation by itself. Also UML modeling of mobile software architectures still appears not completely satisfactory, because of the lack of widely accepted models for all the mobile code styles reviewed in section 3.

Table 5. Summary of parameters instantiation in the reviewed approaches to non functional requirements validation of mobile software architectures

O N		AS	NFA	TMN	MI	ST
none		REX, COD, MA	processing time, network load	closed-form	model parameters	analytic
		REX, MA	processing time	Petri net		numerical
Formal (P.A.)	"indirect location"	REX, COD, MA	"any"	stochastic P. A. and MRP	transition and reward rates	mainly numerical
	"direct location"					
Semi-Formal (UML)	standard					
	with mobility-oriented extensions	MA	interaction related (stand-alone applications)	MRP, MDP	performance annotations in the SDs	mainly numerical
			throughput, response time (stand-alone and contention-based measures)	Execution Graph, EQNM	performance annotations in the UML diagrams	analytic, numerical, simulation

Besides the primary goal of reviewing non functional requirements validation approaches for mobile software architectures, another goal of this tutorial has been to promote the identification of instances of the proposed general validation framework in other areas, such as reliability validation of real-time systems, just to name one. We do not claim this classification as being "the right one", but with this tutorial we rather would like to solicit feedback, extensions and new instances to come out.

Everybody involved in modern (distributed, embedded, mobile) software systems design, is concerned about "software quality", but still very few of them take into account the actual possibility of introducing methodologies/techniques/tools to systematically improve this attribute. Therefore we believe that in the area of non-functional requirements validation much work should be done in the direction of schematization to make it an acceptable activity from the software designer side.

Acknowledgements

Work partially supported by MURST project "SAHARA: Software Architectures for heterogeneous access network infrastructures".

Bibliography

1. S. Alhir, "The true value of the Unified Modeling Language", *Distributed Computing*, 29-31, July 1998.
2. M. Baldi, G.P. Picco "Evaluating the tradeoffs of mobile code design paradigms in network management applications" in Proc. *20th Int. Conf. on Software Engineering (ICSE 98)*, (R. Kemmerer and K. Futatsugi eds.), Kyoto, Japan, Apr. 1998.
3. S.Balsamo, M.Simeoni "Deriving Performance Models from Software Architecture Specifications" *Res. Rep. CS-2001-04,* Dip. di Informatica, Università di Venezia, Feb. 2001; *ESM 2001, SCS, European Simulation Muticonference 2001*, Prague, 6-9 June 2001.
4. M. Barbeau "Transfer of mobile agents using multicast: why and how to do it on wireless mobile networks" *Tech. Rep. TR-00-05*, School of Computer Science, Carleton University, July 2000.
5. L. Bass, P. Clements, R. Kazman, *Software Architectures in Practice*, Addison-Wesley, New York, NY, 1998.
6. G. Booch, J. Rumbaugh, and I.Jacobson, *The Unified Modeling Language User Guide*, Addison Wesley, New York, 1999.
7. L. Cardelli, A.D. Gordon "Mobile ambients" *Foundations of Software Science and Computational Structures* (M. Nivat ed.), LNCS 1378, Springer-Verlag, 1998, pp. 140-155
8. N. Carriero, D. Gelernter "Linda in context" *Communications of the ACM*, vol. 32, no.4, 1989, pp. 444-458.
9. T.-H. Chia, S. Kannapan "Strategically mobile agents" in Proc. *1st Int. Conf. on Mobile Agents (MA '97)*, Springer-Verlag, 1997.
10. V. Cortellessa, R. Mirandola "PRIMA-UML: a performance validation incremental methodology on early UML diagrams" *Science of Computer Programming*, Elsevier Science, vol 44, n.1, pp 101-129, July 2002.
11. R. De Nicola, G. Ferrari, R. Pugliese, B. Venneri "KLAIM: a kernel language for agents interaction and mobility" *IEEE Trans. on Software Engineering*, vol. 24, no. 5, May 1998, pp. 315-330
12. G. Ferrari, C. Montangero, L. Semini, S. Semprini "Mobile agents coordination in Mob$_{adtl}$" Proc. of *4th Int. Conf. on Coordination Models and Languages (COORDINATION'00)*, (A. Porto and G.-C. Roman eds.), Springer-Verlag, Limassol, Cyprus, Sept. 2000.
13. A. Fuggetta, G.P. Picco, G. Vigna "Understanding code mobility" *IEEE Trans. on Software Engineering*, vol. 24, no. 5, May 1998, pp. 342-361.
14. N. Gotz, U. Herzog, M. Rettelbach "Multiprocessor system design: the integration of functional specification and performance analysis using stochastic process algebras" in *Performance Evaluation of Computer and Communication Systems* (L. Donatiello and R. Nelson eds.), LNCS 729, Springer-Verlag, 1993.
15. V. Grassi, R. Mirandola, "Modeling and performance analysis of mobile software architectures in a UML framework" in *<<UML2001>> Conference Proceedings*, LNCS 2185, Springer Verlag, October 2001.
16. V. Grassi, R. Mirandola, "PRIMAmob-UML: a Methodology for Performance analysis of Mobile Software Architecture", in *WOSP 2002, Third International Conference on Software and Performance*, ACM, July 2002.
17. R. Gray, D. Kotz, G. Cybenko, D. Rus "Mobile agents: motivations and state-of-the-art systems" in *Handbook of Agent Technology*, AAAI/MIT Press, 2001.
18. H. Hermanns, U. Herzog, J.-P. Katoen "Process algebras for performance evaluation", *Theoretical Computer Science*, vol. 274, no. 1-2, 2002, pp. 43-87.
19. I. Jacobson, G. Booch, J. Rumbaugh, *The Unified Software Development Process*, Addison-Wesley Object Technology Series, 1999.
20. R. Jain, *Art of Computer Systems Performance Analysis*, Wiley, New York, 1990.

21. T. Kawamura, S. Joseph, A. Ohsuga, S. Honiden "Quantitative evaluation of pairwise interactions between agents" in *Joint Symp. on Agent Systems and Applications and Symp. on Mobile Agents (ASA/MA 2000)*, Springer LNCS 1882, pp. 192-205, 2000.
22. D. Kotz, G. Jiang, R. Gray, G. Cybenko, R.A. Peterson "Performance analysis of mobile agents for filtering data streams on wireless networks" in 3rd *ACM Workshop on Modeling, Analysis and Simulation of Wireless and Mobile Systems (MSWiM 2000)*, Aug. 2000.
23. R. Milner, *Communication and Concurrency*, Prentice Hall, 1989.
24. R. Milner, *Communicating and Mobile Systems: the π-calculus*, Cambridge Univ. Press, 1999.
25. C. Nottegar, C. Priami, P. Degano "Performance evaluation of mobile processes via abstract machines" *IEEE Trans. on Software Engineering*, vol. 27, no. 10, Oct. 2001, pp. 867-889
26. G.P. Picco, G.-C. Roman, P.J. McCann "Reasoning about code mobility in Mobile UNITY" *ACM Transactions on Software Engineering and Methodology*, vol. 10, no. 3, July 2001, pp. 338-395.
27. A. Puliafito, S. Riccobene, M. Scarpa "An analytical comparison of the client-server, remote evaluation and mobile agent paradigms" in *1st Int. Symp. on Agent Systems and Applications and 3rd Int. Symp. on Mobile Agents (ASA/MA 99)*, Oct. 1999.
28. M.L. Puterman, *Markov Decison Processes*, J. Wiley and Sons, 1994.
29. K. Rothermel, F. Hohl, N. Radouniklis "Mobile agent systems: what is missing?" in *Distributed Applications and Interoperable Systems (DAIS 1997)*, 1997.
30. D. Sangiorgi "Expressing mobility in process algebras: first-order and higher-order paradigms" PhD thesis, Univ. of Edinburgh, 1992.
31. B. Selic, "Response to the omg rfp for schedulability, performance and time", OMG document number ad/2001-06-14, June 2001.
32. C. Smith, *Performance Engineering of Software Systems*, Addison-Wesley, Reading, MA, 1990.
33. C. Smith, L. Williams, *Performance solutions: A Practical Guide to Creating Responsive, Scalable Software*, Addison Wesley, 2002.
34. J.W. Stamos, D.K. Gifford "Implementing remote evaluation" *IEEE Trans. on Software Engineering*, vol. 16, no. 7, July 1990, pp. 710-722.
35. M. Strasser, M. Schwehm "A performance model for mobile agent systems" in *Int. Conference on Parallel and Distributed Processing Techniques and Applications* (PDPTA 97), vol. II, (H.R. Arabnia ed.), Las Vegas 1997, pp. 1132-1140.
36. Sun Microsystems "The Java language", White Paper, 1994.
37. Sun Microsystems "The Java servlet API", White Paper, 1997.
38. M. Wermelinger, J.L. Fiadeiro "Connectors for mobile programs" *IEEE Trans. on Software Engineering*, vol. 24, no. 5, May 1998, pp. 331-341.
39. WOSP 2000, Proc. of the *2nd Int. Workshop on Software and Performance*, ACM, 2000.

Performance Issues of Multimedia Applications*

Edmundo de Souza e Silva[1], Rosa M. M. Leão[1], Berthier Ribeiro-Neto[2], and
Sérgio Campos[2]

[1] Federal University of Rio de Janeiro
COPPE/PESC, Computer Science Department {rosam, edmundo}@land.ufrj.br
[2] Federal University of Minas Gerais
Computer Science Department {berthier,scampos}@dcc.ufmg.br

Abstract. The dissemination of the Internet technologies, increasing
communication bandwidth and processing speeds, and the growth in demand for multimedia information gave rise to a variety of applications.
Many of these applications demand the transmission of a continuous
flow of data in real time. As such, continuous media applications may
have high storage requirements, high bandwidth needs and strict delay
and loss requirements. These pose significant challenges to the design
of such systems, specially since the Internet currently provides no QoS
guarantees to the data it delivers. An extensive range of problems have
been investigated in the last years from issues on how to efficiently store
and retrieve continuous media information in large systems, to issues on
how to efficiently transmit the retrieved information via the Internet.
Although broad in scope, the problems under investigation are tightly
coupled. The purpose of this chapter is to survey some of the techniques
proposed to cope with these challenges.

1 Introduction

The fast development of new technologies for high bandwidth networks, wireless
communication, data compression, and high performance CPUs has made it
technically possible to deploy sophisticated communication infrastructures for
supporting a variety of multimedia applications. Among these we can distinguish,
for instance, quality audio and video on demand (to the home), virtual reality
environments, digital libraries, and cooperative design.

Multimedia objects, such as movies, voice extracts, texts, and pictures, are
usually stored in compressed (encoded) form on the disks of a multimedia server.
Since the encoded objects might be long, the playing of an object should not be
delayed until the whole object is transmitted. Instead, the playing of the object
should be initiated as early as possible.

A common characteristic among multimedia applications is the so-called *continuous* nature of their generated data. In continuous media (CM), strict timing
relationships exist that define the schedule by which CM data must be rendered

---

* This work is supported in part by grants from CNPq/ProTeM. E. de Souza e Silva
is also supported by additional grants from CNPq/PRONEX and FAPERJ.

M.C. Calzarossa and S. Tucci (Eds.): Performance 2002, LNCS 2459, pp. 374–404, 2002.
© Springer-Verlag Berlin Heidelberg 2002

(e.g., a video displayed, 3D graphics rendered, or audio played out). These timing relationships coupled with the high aggregate bandwidth needs, the high individual application bandwidth needs, and the high storage requirements pose significant challenges to the design of such systems. This is particularly troublesome in the scenario of the Internet, which is beginning to be used to convey multimedia data but which was not designed for this purpose.

In this work, we discuss the main technical issues involved in the design and implementation of practical (distributed) multimedia systems. We take a particular view, which divides the system in three main components: the multimedia server, the resource sharing techniques for transmitting data across the network, and methods for improving the utilization of network bandwidth and buffers. We look at each of these components, reviewing the related literature, introducing the key underlying technical issues, and providing insights on how each of them impacts the performance of the multimedia system.

2   The Multimedia Server

The *multimedia server* is a key component of a distributed multimedia system. Its performance (in terms of the number of clients supported) affects the overall cost of the system and might be decisive for determining economical viability. As a result, studying the performance of multimedia servers is an important problem which has received wide attention lately [8,42,19,18,17,28,30,34,33,45, 46,54,63]. The server is a computer system containing one or more processors, a finite amount of memory M, and a number D of disks. The disks are used to store compressed multimedia objects, which are retrieved by the clients.

Compressed video objects are composed of frames, where a *frame* is a snapshot of the state of all bits in the screen. To decode the frames in a stream, the client has to store them in memory which requires some level of buffering. The frames are consumed at a constant rate. Since the number of bits in each component frame varies, the input *bit rate* and the output *bit rate* for the buffer at the client side are variable (VBR).

It is common to implement the server such that it always sends data to the client in blocks of fixed size. When it is possible to always send the same number of blocks in the unit of time, we say that the traffic flows at a constant bit rate (CBR). Keeping a CBR (or nearly CBR) traffic implies that the frame rate varies at the input of the client buffer. To avoid interruption of the display, a much larger buffer might be required at the client to compensate for variations in the frame arrival rate. In Sec. 3 we discuss traffic smoothing techniques to compensate for these rate variations. Several proposals in the literature are then based on CBR assumptions [9,14,53,55,67].

Due to disk seek and rotational delays, one or more sectors need to be retrieved from the server during each disk access to attain good performance. The set of disk sectors that the server sends to the client at one time is here called a *data block*. Each data block is stored in the buffer of the client and consumed from there. While the client decodes a data block, other clients can be served. This way the server is able to multiplex the disk bandwidth among various clients, which are served concurrently. The approach works because the total disk bandwidth available at the server far exceeds the display rate with which each client consumes bytes.

Let O_i be a reference to the ith multimedia object in the server and b_i be a reference to any data block of the object O_i. Consistently with several prototype implementations, we assume that the data blocks of each object O_i are all of the same size. The data blocks of distinct objects, however, might be of different sizes (i.e., $size(b_i) \neq size(b_j)$).

A client makes a request for an object O_i. If this request is admitted into the system, the server starts sending blocks of the object O_i to the client machine. The client might have to wait until the buffer fills up to a pre-defined threshold before starting to play the object. The time interval between the client request and the beginning of the display is called *startup latency*. To send the blocks to the client, the server first retrieves them from disk into main memory. Thus, *buffers* are also required at the server side.

A client gets a block of data and starts consuming it. Before consuming all the data in that block, the client must get the next block of data for the object it is playing. Otherwise, interruption in the service will occur. In the case of a movie, this means that the motion picture might suddenly freeze in front of the user (also called *hiccup*). Thus, each client must get the blocks of data in a timely fashion.

2.1   The Size of the Multimedia Server

The size of a multimedia server installation is a direct function of the number D of disks in the system. Given the server size, the maximum load that can be imposed to the system is determined, as we now discuss.

The number of disks used in a multimedia server is related to the bandwidth demand, to the storage requirements, and to the amount of capital available for investing in the system. Consider, for instance, movie objects encoded in MPEG-2 (320×240 screen). The typical bandwidth requirement for such objects is 1.5 Mbps (mega bits per second). Thus, to support the display of 1500 MPEG-2 movie objects, a total net bandwidth of 2250 Mbps is required. The scenario 1 below illustrates this situation.

Scenario 1: SCSI Technology: effective disk bandwidth: 60 MBps = 480 Mbps[1]; disk storage capacity: 73.4 GB; maximum number of concurrent customers: 1500; bandwidth requirement of 1 MPEG-2 object: 1.5 Mbps; storage requirement of 1 MPEG-2 object: 1 GB; effective server bandwidth required: 1500 * 1.5 = 2250 Mbps; rough number of disks required in the server: $\lceil 2250/480 \rceil = 5$; number of distinct MPEG-2 objects in storage: $\lfloor 5 * 73.4 \rfloor = 367$; number of disks with 20% redundancy: 6.

---

[1] Estimated bandwidth in mega bits per second (Mbps), including seek time, for current disk technology.

Thus, to provide 1500 customers with real-time MPEG-2 streams we need a total of 5 SCSI disks (current technology). This computation is quite rough, since it does not consider memory and bus bandwidth bottlenecks, and redundancy for fault tolerance. With a 20% degree of redundancy, a total of 6 disks would be required.

Besides bandwidth, the storage requirements need also to be taken into account. Since the storage capacity of each SCSI disk considered above is 73.4 GB (giga bytes) and each MPEG-2 object of 1 hour and 40 minutes takes roughly 1 GB, with 5 disks we can store up to 367 MPEG-2 objects.

However, 367 is not really the number of movies one would expect to find in a video store. Typically, at least a few thousand movies should be available. One alternative is to use cheaper technology, such as IDE, to provide plenty of storage capacity with good bandwidth delivery. For instance, consider the scenario 2 immediately below.

Scenario 2: IDE Technology: effective disk bandwidth: 16 MBps = 128 Mbps; disk storage capacity: 80 GB; maximum number of concurrent customers: 1500; bandwidth requirement of 1 MPEG-2 object: 1.5 Mbps; storage requirement of 1 MPEG-2 object: 1 GB; effective server bandwidth required: 1500 * 1.5 = 2250 Mbps; rough number of disks required in the server: $\lceil 2250/128 \rceil = 18$; number of distinct MPEG-2 objects in storage: $\lfloor 18 * 80 \rfloor = 1440$; number of disks with 50% redundancy: 27.

Thus, we can now store up to 1440 distinct MPEG-2 objects in 18 IDE disks of 80 GB each. And this is accomplished while attending up to 1500 concurrent customers as before. Notice that we now use a degree of redundancy of 50%, because disks based on IDE technology are not as reliable as disks based on SCSI technology. Since each IDE disk in scenario 2 costs about 1/6 of an SCSI disk in scenario 1, the configuration in scenario 2 is either cheaper or price equivalent to the configuration in scenario 1. Most important, replacing IDE disks is easier because they can be bought everywhere at any time (i.e., IDE technology is really ubiquitous nowadays).

The data block size, contrary to the number of disks, is related more to the design of the system itself. Given a number of disks and a memory space for buffers, usually an optimal block size can be determined. The block size can be chosen to minimize the cost per stream or to maximize the number of streams that can be supported concurrently. One primary constraint has to be met: the block size must be large enough to amortize the delays due to seek and rotational latency. Block sizes ranging from 512 Kbytes to 1 Mbytes are usually large enough to accomplish this effect.

2.2   The Layout

The blocks which compose the various multimedia objects are laid out across the disks in the system. A simplistic approach is to store all blocks of the same object on a single disk. The main advantage of this approach is simplicity and ease of maintenance. However, there is a considerable disadvantage. If a popular video is heavily requested, the disk that stores that video will be overloaded. Thus, severe load imbalance might result, which limits the number of clients that can be served. More sophisticated strategies involve spreading the blocks of the same object across multiple disks (the so called *striping* techniques).

Layout Using Striping. The key idea of striping is to spread out the data blocks of each object across the disks of the server. This way, during the service time of an object, each client request is continuously moved from one disk to another and shares the bandwidth of all the disks in the system. We say that the object storage has been decoupled from the disks and call this effect *object decoupling* (see Figure 1). Object decoupling provides a load balancing effect which allows a higher number of clients in the system and a better utilization of disk bandwidth.

Usually, when a striped layout is used, the server operates in cycles. At each cycle of duration T, the server retrieves one data block for each client in the system (this retrieval incurs in three delays: seek time, rotational latency, and transfer time). While that client consumes the block, other clients can be served. Discontinuities in the service are avoided by guaranteeing that each client is served in every cycle. When all clients in the system have been served, the server *sleeps* if there is still time available in the current cycle of duration T.

To accommodate objects with distinct bandwidth requirements, we can simply allow the sizes of the storage units to vary. For instance, objects O_i and O_j will have blocks sizes b_i and b_j ($b_i \neq b_j$), respectively. Each block is stored as a separate storage unit. For a same object O_i, however, the block sizes are all the same (i.e., $b_i[j] = b_i[j+1]$). At the disk level, one can keep the storage unit size constant to avoid fragmentation. For an object that has higher bandwidth requirements, two or more storage units can be combined to compose a data block, as illustrated in Figure 1. Each data block of the object O_i is composed of a single storage unit while each data block of the object O_j is composed of two storage units. We see that two or more disks might now be involved in the retrieval of a unique data block. Since the storage unit size is kept constant, storage and bandwidth fragmentation problems are minimized.

Random Data Allocation Layout. Striping layouts are good because they provide object decoupling. However, in general, all striping strategies impose a tight coupling between the layout itself and the block access pattern as a way to balance the load among the various disks. To avoid this tight coupling, an alternative is to employ a random data allocation. It can be shown that a random layout is as good as striping in terms of performance [64], but presents important advantages as we briefly point out here.

A *random data allocation* layout uses storage units that are all of the same size. However, contrary to the striping approach, each storage unit is stored in a disk position that is determined according to the following procedure: (a) select a disk at random; (b) within that disk, select a free position at random.

As a result, storage units are placed randomly across the disks of the system. Objects with higher bandwidth requirements are served by combining several

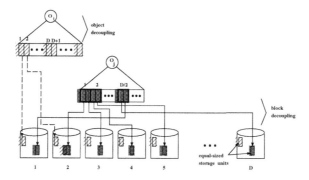

Fig. 1. Hybrid layout with equal-sized stripe units and block sizes which vary from one object to the other.

storage units to form a data block. Also, the physical location of the data blocks is now independent of the block access pattern.

A random data allocation layout provides the following characteristics: object decoupling; access pattern decoupling; no disk storage fragmentation; small probability of prolonged bandwidth fragmentation; good performance. The good performance is attained because the load tends to be statistically balanced among the various disks. Random data allocation is the only layout scheme that provides all these features together. Because of this, it simplifies the overall design and implementation of the system. Therefore, we argue that it is the paradigm of choice for the design and implementation of multimedia servers in general.

Comparative Performance Analysis: Striping versus Random Layout. In [64] a detailed comparison between a server based on striping and a server based on a random layout is presented. The experimental results show that system performance with a random layout is competitive or superior to the performance obtained with a striping layout. This is the case not only for unpredictable access patterns generated by sophisticated interactive applications such as virtual worlds and scientific visualizations, but also for sequential access patterns generated by more standard video applications.

To illustrate, let us focus on the case of standard video applications. When only a small amount of buffer is allowed at the server (say, 1.5 MBytes per stream), a striping layout performs slightly superior to a random layout providing an increase in the maximum number of streams sustained of roughly 5%. If the amount of buffer per stream is allowed to increase to 3.5 MBytes per stream, both layouts lead to the same overall performance. Additional increments in buffer space per stream favor the random layout, whose performance becomes superior.

Assume now that more disk space is made available, such that data blocks can be replicated. This is useful, for instance, to improve reliability against disk failure. Consider a 25% degree of replication of video data blocks. This is good for a random layout because replicated blocks can be used to alleviate the load of momentarily overloaded disks. In this case, with a buffer space of 3.5 MBytes per stream, a server based on a random layout presents performance (maximum number of streams sustained by the server) that is 10-15% higher than the performance of a server based on a striping layout.

2.3   Staging, Reconfiguration, and Fault Tolerance

In practical installations, there are other important issues that have to be considered for proper operation of a multimedia server. Among these, we distinguish the staging of new videos, the reconfiguration of the server to improve performance, and fault tolerance against failures of service in the disks of the server. In this section, we discuss these issues in more detail and compare their relative performance considering random-based and striping-based servers.

The Staging Mechanism. Since multimedia objects might be quite large (particularly movie objects), the number of objects that can be stored on the disks of the system might be quite limited. This implies that the objects in the system need to be replaced by new ones from time to time. Since the new objects are usually loaded from tape, we call this process the *staging mechanism*. This is an issue which has not received much attention in the specialized literature but which is critically important in any practical system.

For offline staging, the use of block decoupling provides an efficient solution. If online staging is desired, the admission control and the scheduling processes are affected because a new stream has to be admitted and scheduled. This type of stream might require higher bandwidth because redundant data (such as copies of the data to support fault tolerance) have also to be updated. For a striped layout under heavy load, it might be the case that two fragmented pieces of bandwidth are available but cannot be used for staging because a coalesced bandwidth is required. For instance, this might be the case of a new stream which is been fed live to the server. If the new stream is not live, then there is no problem because the staging can proceed in non real-time mode.

Staging has similar costs both for a striped and for a random layout, whenever the staging is offline. For online staging, a random layout is advantageous. For instance, a random layout makes it easier to deal with the staging of a new stream which is been fed live. Also, a random layout allows the staging of a new object at a rate which is different from its playout rate which is often more difficult to do with a striped layout.

Disk Reconfiguration. In practical situations, it is reasonable to expect that the demand on a given server system might eventually exceed its planned capacity. For instance, it might be the case that the demand for disk bandwidth exceeds the total disk bandwidth currently available in the server. This problem can be fixed by adding new disks to the system and copying data blocks (of the objects already in the system and of new objects) into the new disks. This is what we call *disk reconfiguration*. We would like to be able to reconfigure the system while maintaining the server fully operational.

Consider that we have D disks in the system and that we want to add K new disks. For simplicity, we consider here that the new disks are of the same capacity and of the same bandwidth as the disks already installed in the server. Consider also that no new objects will be added to the system. With current disk technology, the extra K disks can be "hot" inserted into the system while it is running. Thus, no interruption in service is required. However, the storage units need to be remapped to take advantage of the newly available bandwidth.

To exemplify, assume an installation with 8 disks to which 2 new disks are added. We have that $D = 8$ and $K = 2$. In this case, it can be shown that 80% of all storage units need to be moved if the layout is done with striping, while only 20% of all storage units need to be moved if the layout is random. Thus, we conclude that it is much cheaper to reconfigure an installation when the layout is random.

Fault Tolerance. Maintaining the integrity of the data and its accessibility are crucial aspects of a multimedia server. Particularly critical are failures of the disks of the system. While each individual disk is fairly reliable, a large set of disks presents a considerably higher likelihood of failure of a component. With a multimedia server, it is particularly important to provide tolerance to this type of failure because failure of a single disk might disrupt the service to all clients in the system. Basically, fault tolerance is provided by the maintenance of redundant information about the data. Two basic schemes can be used: full replication and parity encoding.

With parity encoding, the D disks of the system are divided in n_g groups. Let g, $g = D/n_g$, be the number of disks per group. For each group, one of the disks is reserved for storing parity information while the remaining $g - 1$ are used for storing data. The parity information is computed as the *exclusive-or* of the storage units in the $g - 1$ disks. We use storage units instead of data blocks because, in case block decoupling is used, data blocks are not confined to a single disk. Let $su_i[k]$, $su_i[k+1]$, ..., $su_i[k+g-2]$ be $g - 1$ consecutive storage units (belonging to data blocks of object O_i) which appear each in a separate disk (assume this for now). Then, the parity information $p_i[k]$ for this set of storage units is computed as $p_i[k] = su_i[k] \oplus su_i[k+1] \oplus \dots \oplus su_i[k+g-2]$. The set composed of the parity storage unit $p[k]$ and of the $g - 1$ storage units from $su_i[k]$ to $su_i[k+g-2]$ is called a *parity group* of size g. If the disk that contains $su_i[k+1]$ is lost, this storage unit can be rebuilt by the following computation $su_i[k+1] = su_i[k] \oplus p_i[k] \oplus \dots \oplus su_i[k+g-2]$. Thus, the disk with the parity information takes the place of the disk which was lost.

The idea of fault tolerance with full replication is to use additional space which is of the same size of the space occupied by the whole set of data blocks. Thus, all data blocks are duplicated. While more expensive in terms of space, this approach allows recovering from some types of catastrophic failures and improving the performance of the system. Gains in performance are possible because any request for a data block can now be served by two different disks and thus, we can always select the disk with a smaller queue.

Full replication can also be useful in situations where a parity-based scheme is not the most appropriate one. For instance, consider a distributed server composed of multiple machines which contain themselves multiple disks. Assume that we stripe the data across the multiple disks. In case a parity-based scheme is adopted for fault tolerance, parity groups should be confined to individual machines to avoid overheads in buffer, networking, and synchronization. This provides tolerance to a disk failure but not to the failure of a machine. To provide tolerance to a machine failure, a full replication scheme can be adopted instead in which each data block and its copy reside on separate machines. This is in fact the approach adopted in [9].

It can be shown that a random layout allows using a parity-based scheme as well as any random layout. Further, full replication can be better taken advantage of with the adoption of a random layout (instead of a striped layout). In fact, the design and implementation of recovery and load balancing algorithms is simplified because one can rely on the randomness of the data block allocation to even out the load.

3   Transmitting Information

There are several performance issues that need to be addressed in order to transmit continuous real-time streams over the Internet with acceptable quality. For instance, real time video encoded in MPEG2 typically requires an average bandwidth of approximately 1-4 Mbps, and a voice stream approximately from 6-64Kbps, depending on the encoding scheme. However, so far the Internet does not allow bandwidth reservation as needed. In addition congestion in the network may cause significant variability on the interval between the arrival of successive packets (jitter). Since real time streams must be decoded and played following strict time constraints, large jitter values will cause the playout process to be interrupted. Packet losses may also severely degrade the quality of the multimedia presentation, depending on the loss pattern. Yet another problem is network heterogeneity and client heterogeneity. Client heterogeneity means that the receivers have different network requirements, due to different capabilities to present the received multimedia information. For multicast applications, the heterogeneity imposes an additional challenge since a stream being transmitted would have to be multicast through several networks and clients (with possibly drastic different characteristics) and somehow adapt to the needs of each client. In this section we discuss a few mechanisms used to mitigate the effects of random delay and losses in the network.

3.1   How to Cope with Network Jitter and the Rate Variability

We start by considering an audio stream encoded with PCM, say with silence detection. The audio stream is sampled at $125\mu sec$ interval and usually 160 samples are collected in a single packet generating a CBR stream of one IP packet per $20msec$ [47] at each active interval. The client consumes the 160 samples at every $20msec$, and thus it is vulnerable to random delays in the network. If the expected information does not arrive on time, annoying distortions may occur in the decoded audio signal. Let T be the packet generation interval and X the corresponding segment interarrival time. The random variable $J = X - T$ is called *jitter*.

One simple mechanism to reduce the jitter is to use a *playout buffer* at the client, where a given number of packets are stored. At the beginning of each *active* period, where packets are generated, the client stores packets till a given threshold is reached before starting to decode the received samples. The threshold value may be fixed at the beginning of the connection or be adjusted dynamically during the duration of the session. Figure 2 illustrates the basic idea. In

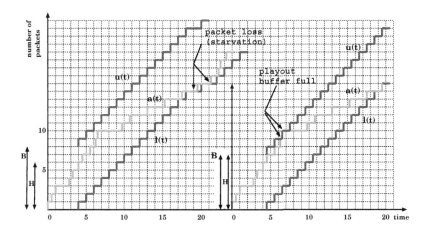

Fig. 2. The playout buffer

that figure, the curve $l(t)$ is equal to the number of packets consumed by the application by time t. (In this example, it is assumed PCM encoding and thus the packet consumption rate is constant.) The upper curve is simply $u(t) = l(t) + B$ where B is the playout buffer space. The curve labeled $a(t)$ is equal to the number of packets that have arrived by time t. Note that the arrival instants are not equally spaced due to the jitter introduced by the network. In the leftmost part of Fig. 2, $B = 8$ and $H = 6$, and so the decoding starts immediately after the arrival of the 6-th packet. The amount of packets stored in the playout buffer as a function of time is $a(t) - l(t)$, while $u(t) - a(t)$ quantifies the buffer space available at t. Buffer starvation occurs if the lower curve touches the bottom curve and buffer overflow occurs when the middle curve crosses the top curve. As shown in the figure, the buffer empties at $t = 18$. Thus, at $t = 19$ there is no packet to be decoded (buffer starvation). When this occurs, some action must be taken perhaps re-playing the last information in the buffer, as an approximation of the data carried by the missing packet at that time. In the right hand part of Fig. 2 the threshold value H is increased to $H = 7$. As a consequence, $l(t)$

is shifted to the right. In this example, this change prevents buffer starvation during the observation period. The value of B is also decreased to 7, and $u(t)$ is moved downwards with respect to the preceding curve.

It is easy to see that this simple technique eliminates any negative jitter. From Fig. 2, it is also clear that larger threshold values decrease the jitter variability. However, latency increases with increasing threshold values. But interactive applications, such as a live conversation, do not tolerate latencies larger than $200 - 300$ msec. This imposes a constrain of 20-25 packets on H. An issue is the choice of H and the amount of buffer space necessary to minimize the loss of packets in case a long burst of packets arrive at the receiver.

Diniz and de Souza e Silva [22] calculate the distribution of the jitter as seen by the client, when a playout buffer is used. The packet interarrival time is modeled by a phase-type distribution that matches the first and second moments of this measure obtained from actual network measurements. Packets are consumed at constant rate (PCM), similar to the example of Fig. 2. Silent periods are included in the model. The goal is to study the tradeoffs between latency and probability of a positive jitter. It was concluded that the probability of a positive jitter can be significantly reduced, while maintaining an acceptable latency for real time traffic.

In addition to the delay variability imposed by the network, compressed audio/video streams exhibit non-negligible burstiness on several time scales, due to the encoding schemes and scene variations. Sharp variations on traffic rates have a negative impact on resource utilization. For instance, more bandwidth may be necessary to maintain the necessary QoS for the application. The issue is to develop control algorithms to smooth the CM traffic before transmission to the clients.

Smoothing techniques can be applied at the traffic source or at another intermediate node (e.g., a proxy) in the path to the client. Sen et al [65] address the issue of online bandwidth smoothing. To better understand the problem consider Fig. 3, where it is assumed that there is no variable delay imposed by the network when a compressed video stream is sent to a client.

Due to the compression encoding, the rate of bit consumption at the client node varies with time. Video servers however, read fixed size blocks of information from the storage server (each block may be fragmented into packets to fit the network maximum transfer unit (MTU) before transmission). Then in Fig. 3, the interval between the consumption of constant size data blocks at the client varies with time. The jumps in the y-axis (a block of data) are of constant size. This contrasts with the usual representation of variable frame size consumed at fixed intervals of time (e.g. $1/30sec$).

In Fig. 3, a controller at the server site schedules the transmission of video blocks after they are retrieved from the storage server and queued in a FIFO buffer. Two sets of curves are shown in the figure. In set 1, let $l_c(t)$ be the number of bits consumed by the client by time t, and $u_c(t) = l_c(t) + B_c$, where B_c is the size of the playout buffer. Similarly, let $a_s(t)$ (in set 2) be the accumulated number of bits that are read from the server disks during $(0, t)$ according to the

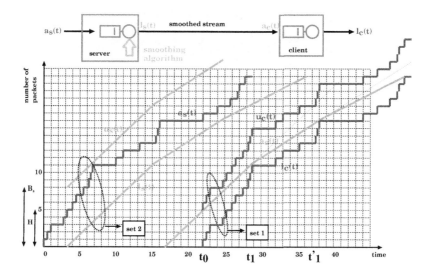

Fig. 3. The concept of smoothing

demand of the client, and $l_s(t)$ be the smoothed stream curve, i.e. the number of bits effectively dispatched by t. Note that: (a) $a_c(t) = l_s(t - \tau)$ where τ is a (assumed constant) network delay from the server to the client; (b) $a_s(t - \tau') = l_c(t)$ where τ' is the constant network delay plus the delay to fill the playout buffer; (c) the jumps of $l_c(t)$ occur at the instants of consumption of a block of data. If we assume that the playout buffer is filled until its capacity before the continuous stream is played back, the number of bits in the playout buffer is given by the difference between the top and the middle curves in set 1.

The server seeks to transmit data to the client as smooth as possible that is, $l_s(t)$ in the figure should resemble a straight line with the smallest possible right angle. Since the shape of $l_c(t)$ and consequently $u_c(t)$ and $a_s(t)$ is determined by the encoding algorithm applied to the video to be transmitted, the issue is how to plan the transmission of the data so that $u_c(t) \leq a_c(t) \leq l_c(t)$, and yet the maximum transmission rate is kept as close as possible to the average consumption rate.

In [62] Salehi *et al* obtained an efficient algorithm that can generate a transmission schedule given the complete knowledge of $a_c(t)$. This is referred to as an *offline* algorithm. Roughly, from a initial time t_i (start from $i = 0$), one should construct the longest possible line that does not violate the constraints imposed by $u_c(t)$ and $l_c(t)$ in Fig. 3. Clearly, by construction, this straight line intersects one of the boundary curves at a time point $t'_{i+1} > t_i$, (and so the rate would have to be changed at this point), and touches one of these curves at a time $t_{i+1} < t'_{i+1}$. To avoid sudden rate changes one should vary the previous rate as soon as possible. Consequently a new starting point is chosen at t_{i+1}. The process is repeated (setting $i = i + 1$) until the end of the stream is reached, and $a_c(t)$ is obtained which determines the scheduling algorithm.

The set 2 in Fig. 3 shows the arrival and transmission curves at the server. Note that the server starts its transmission as soon as a threshold H is reached (in the figure the threshold is equal to 5 blocks). $u_s(t) = l_s(t) + B_s$, where B_s is the FIFO buffer available at the server. One should note that, once $l_s(t)$ is determined, B_s and the threshold can be calculated to avoid overflow and underflow.

We can represent the curves $u_c(t)$, $l_c(t)$ and $a_c(t)$ as vectors $\mathbf{u}$, $\mathbf{l}$, $\mathbf{a}$ respectively, each with dimension N, where N is the number of data blocks in the video stream, and the i-th entry in one of the vectors, say vector $\mathbf{l}$, is the amount of time to consume the i-th block. In [62] majorization is used as a measure of smoothness of the curves. Roughly, if a vector $\mathbf{x}$ is majorized by $\mathbf{y}$ ($\mathbf{x} \prec \mathbf{y}$) then $\mathbf{x}$ represents a smoother curve than $\mathbf{y}$. It is shown in [62] that if $\mathbf{x} \prec \mathbf{y}$ then $var(\mathbf{x}) = \sum_i (x_i - \bar{x})^2$ and since, by definition, the maximum entry in $\mathbf{x}$ is less or equal than the corresponding entry in $\mathbf{y}$, a vector $\mathbf{x}$ that is majorized by $\mathbf{y}$ has smaller maximum rate and smaller variance than $\mathbf{y}$. The schedule algorithm outlined above is shown to be optimum and unique in [62]. Furthermore the optimal schedule minimizes the effective bandwidth requirements.

This algorithm is the basis for the *online* smoothing problem [65]. It is assumed that, at any time τ, the server has the knowledge of the time to consume each of the next P blocks. This is called the *lookahead interval* and is used to compute the optimum smoothing schedule using the algorithm of [62]. Roughly, blocks that are read from the storage server are delayed by w units and passed to the server buffer that implements the smoothing algorithm which is invoked every $1 \leq \alpha \leq w$ blocks.

Further work in the topic include [50] where it is shown that, given a buffer space of size B at the server queue, a maximum delay jitter J can be achieved by an off-line algorithm (similar to the above algorithm). Furthermore, an on-line algorithm can achieve a jitter J using buffer space $2B$ at the server FIFO queue. While the smoothing techniques described above are suitable for video applications, interactive visualization applications pose additional problems. This subject was studied in [73].

In summary, the amount of buffer space in the playout buffer of Fig. 3 is a key parameter that determines how smooth the transmission of a CM stream can be. It also serves to reduce the delay variability introduced by the network. The queue at the server site in Fig. 3 implements the smoothing algorithm and the amount of buffer used is also a design parameter. As mentioned above, jitter reduction and smoothness are achieved at expense of the amount of buffer space. But the larger these buffers the larger the latency to start playing the stream.

3.2   How to Cope with Losses

In the previous subsection we are concerned with random delays introduced by the network as well as the ability to reduce sudden rate chains in the coded data stream to lower the demand for network resources. Besides random delays, the Internet may drop packets mainly due to congestion at the routers. Furthermore, packet delays may be so large that they may arrive too late to be played at the receiver, in a real time application.

A common method to recover from a packet loss is retransmission. However, a retransmitted packet will arrive at the receiver at least one round-trip-time (RTT) later than the original copy and this delay may be unacceptable for real time applications. Therefore, retransmission strategies are only useful if the RTT between the client and the server is very small compared with amount of time to empty the playout buffer.

A number of retransmission strategies have been proposed in the context of multicast streaming. For example, receiver-initiated recovery schemes may obtain the lost data from neighboring nodes which potentially have short RTTs with respect to the node that requested the packet [69].

The other methods to cope with packet loss in CM applications are *error concealment*, *error resilience*, interleaving and *FEC* (forward error correction). Error resilience and error concealment are techniques closely coupled with the compression scheme used. Briefly error resilience schemes attempt to limit the error propagation due to the loss, for instance via re-synchronization. An error propagation occurs when the decoder needs the information contained in one frame to decode other frames. Error concealment techniques attempt to reconstruct the signal from the available information when part of it is lost. This is possible if the signal exhibits short term self-similarities. For instance, in voice applications the decoder could simply re-play the last packet received when the current packet is not available. Another approach is to interpolate neighboring signal values. Several other error concealment techniques exist (see [57,74] for more details and references on the subject).

Interleaving is an useful technique for reducing the effect of loss bursts. The basic idea is to separate adjacent packets of the original stream by a given distance, and re-organize the sequence at the receiver. This scheme introduces no redundancy (and so does not consume extra bandwidth), but introduces latency to re-order the packets at the receiver.

FEC techniques add sufficient redundancy in the CM stream so that the received bit stream can be reconstructed at the receiver even when packet losses occur. The main advantage of FEC schemes is the small delay to recover from losses in comparison with recovery using retransmission. However, this advantage comes at the expense of increasing the transmission rate. The issue is to develop FEC techniques that can recover most of the *common* patterns of losses in the path from the sender to the receiver without much increase in the bandwidth requirements to transmit the continuous stream.

A number of FEC techniques have been proposed in the literature [57,74]. The simplest approach is as follows. The stream of packets is divided into groups of size $N - 1$, and a XOR operation is performed on the $N - 1$ packets of each group. The resulting "parity packet" is transmitted after each group. Clearly, if a single packet is lost in a group of N packets the loss can be recovered.

Three issues are evident from this simple scheme. First, since a new packet is generated for every $N - 1$ packets the bandwidth requirements increases by a factor of $1/(N-1)$. As an example, considering voice PCM transmission, if $N = 5$ the new necessary bandwidth to transmit the stream would be 80 Kbps instead of 64 Kbps. Second, it is necessary to characterize the transmission losses to evaluate how effective is the FEC scheme. If losses come into bursts of length $B > 1$, then this simple scheme is evidently not effective. Third, a block of N packets must be entirely received in order to recover from a loss. Consequently, N must be smaller than the receiver playout buffer which is in turn limited by the latency that can be tolerated in an interactive application. Furthermore, suppose a loss occurs at position n in a block. Then $N-n$ should be smaller than the number of packets in the playout buffer at the arrival time of the $(n-1)$-th packet in the block. This indicates that the probability that the queue length of playout buffer is smaller than N should be small for the method to be effective. In summary, to avoid a substantial increase in the bandwidth requirements the block size should be larger, but a large block size implies a large playout buffer which in turn increase latency.

Measures in the Internet have shown that loss probabilities are little sensitive to packet sizes [10,29]. Therefore, another scheme to protect against losses is to transmit a sample of the audio stream in multiple packets [12]. For instance, piggybacking the voice sample carried by packet n in packet $n+1$ as well. This technique allows the recovery of single losses with minimum latency, but at the expense of doubling the throughput. A clever way to reduce the bandwidth requirements is to include in packet $n+1$ the original (voice) sample sent in packet n, but further compressed using a smaller bit rate codec than the primary encoding. As an example, suppose the primary (voice) sample of each packet is replicated twice. If we use PCM codec for the primary sample (64k Kbps), GSM for the first copy (13.2 Kbps) and LPC for the second copy (≈ 5 Kpbs) burst sizes of length 2 can be recovered at the expense of increasing the throughput from 64 Kbps to ≈ 82 Kbps. Therefore, with only a 20.8% increase in the throughput, and an increase in latency of 40 msec (2×20 msec packet delay), bursts of length 2 can be recovered in this example.

Packet losses occur mostly due to congestion in the network and so it can be argued that increasing the throughput rate of a stream transmission to recover from losses is unfair with respect to flow controlled sessions such as TCP. Therefore, it is evident that FEC schemes should be optimized for the type of loss incurred by the network in order to have the smallest impact in the consumed bandwidth. The work in [29] was aimed at studying the packet loss process in the Internet and at proposing a new efficient XOR-FEC mechanism extending previous work. Several measures were calculated from traces between Brazil and the USA such as: the distribution of the number of consecutive losses and the distribution of the number of packets received between two losses. These two measures are particularly important for determining the efficiency of a recovery XOR-FEC based algorithm. The approach proposed in [29] can be briefly described as follows. The CM stream is divided into groups each called a *window* and the packets in a window is sub-divided into non-overlapping sets, each protected by an XOR operation. Figure 4(a) illustrates an example with 6 packets

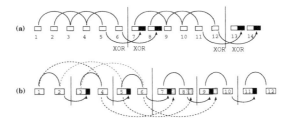

Fig. 4. The FEC scheme of [29]

per window and two subsets, and we call this a 2:6 class of algorithm. The result of the XOR operation for a set of packets is sent piggybacked in a packet of the next window. Clearly we can use codecs of smaller transmission rate as in [12] for saving in bandwidth. Note that burst errors of size at most equal to 2 packets can be recovered, and efficiency in bandwidth is gained at expense of latency to recover from losses. Furthermore, the scheme in Fig. 4(a) has the practically same overhead as the simple XOR scheme first described, but can recover from consecutive losses of size two. Another class of schemes can be obtained by merging two distinct $k : n$ class of algorithms, such that all packets belong to at least two different subsets and therefore are covered by two different XORs. Figure 4(b) illustrates an example where schemes 1:2 and 3:6 are overlapped. In this case, all losses of size one in the larger window can be recovered. Furthermore, complex loss patterns can also be protected. For example, if packets 2, 3, 4, and 5 were lost, they can all be recovered. The overhead of this mixed scheme is clearly obtained by adding the overhead of the individual schemes.

In [29] the algorithm is applied in the real data obtained from measures and the efficiency of different FEC-based algorithms are evaluated. The conclusions show the importance of adapting to different networks conditions. (This issue was also addressed by Bolot *et al* [11], in the context of the scheme of [12].) Furthermore, in all the tests performed, the class of schemes that mixed two windows provided better results than the class with a single window under the same overhead.

Altman *et al* developed an analytical model to analyze the FEC scheme of [12] and other related schemes. The loss process was modeled using a simple M/M/K queue. The aim is to assess the tradeoffs between increased loss protection from the FEC algorithm and the adverse impact from the resulting increase in the network resources usage due to the redundancy added to the original stream. The results show that the scheme studied may not always result in performance gains, in particular if a non-negligible fraction of the flows implements the same FEC scheme. It would be interesting to evaluate the performance of other FEC approaches.

To conclude the subsection we refer to a recent proposed approach to mitigate the effect of losses. As is evident from above, short term loss correlations have an adverse effect on the efficiency of the recovery algorithms. One way to reduce the possible correlations is to split the continuous stream sent from a source to a given destination into distinct paths. For instance, we could split a video stream in two and sent the even packets in the sequence via one path and the odd packets via another path to the destination. This is called *path diversity* [76]. In [6] it is assumed that the loss characteristics in a path can be represented by a 2-state Markov chain (Gilbert model) and a Markov model was developed to access the advantages of the approach. Clearly a number of tradeoffs exists, depending on the loss characteristics of each path, if the different paths share or not a set of links, etc.

3.3   Characterizing the Packet Loss Process and the Continuous Media Traffic Stream

Packet losses is one of the main factors that influence the quality of the signal received. Therefore, understanding and modeling the loss process is imperative to analyze the performance of the loss recovery algorithms. In general, measurements are obtained from losses seen by packet probes sent according to the specific traffic under study (for instance at regular intervals of 20 msec), and models are obtained to match the collected statistics. However, queueing models with finite buffer have also been used.

Bolot [10] characterize the burstiness of packet losses by the conditional probability that a packet is lost given that a previous packet is also lost, and analyze data from probes sent at constant intervals between several paths in the Internet. A simple finite buffer single server queueing model (fed by two streams, one representing the probes and the other representing the Internet traffic) was used as the basis for interpreting the results obtained from the measures.

The most commonly used model for representing error bursts is a 2-state discrete time Markov chain, usually called the Gilbert model. The Gilbert model assumes that the size of consecutive losses is a geometric random variable. However, these models may not capture with accuracy the correlation structure of the loss process. The work in [75] use a 2^k-state Markov chain to model the loss process, aimed at capturing temporal dependencies in the traces they collected. They analyze the accuracy of the models against several traces collected by sending probes at regular intervals. Salamatian and Vaton [61] propose the use of Hidden Markov models (HMM) to model the loss sequence in the Internet, due to their capability to represent dependencies in the observed process. In an HMM each state can output a subset of symbols according to some distribution. The states and transitions between states are not observable, but only the output symbols. In [61] it is shown that HMM models are more appropriate to represent the loss sequence than the 2^k-state Markov chain model used in [75], with less states. However, one disadvantage of the method is the cost of estimating the Markov chain parameters. More recently, the authors of [43] compare four models to represent the loss process in wireless channels, including the 2^k-state Markov model, a HMM with 5 states and a proposed On-Off model where the holding times at each state are characterized by a mixture of geometric phases which are determined by using the Baum-Welch algorithm. The conclusion indicates that the extended On-Off model better captures first and second order statistics of the traces studied. A recent study done by Markopoulou *et al* [51] evaluates the quality of voice in the Internet. In this work a methodology is developed that takes into account delay and loss measurements for assessing the quality of a call. The measures were obtained by sending regularly spaced probes to measurement facilities in different cities. The results indicate the need of carefully evaluating the CM traffic and properly designing the playout buffers.

Traffic characterization is one important topic for understanding the influence of CM streams in the network resources. The topic is related to loss characterization and the main goals are to obtain concise descriptions of the flow under study and to capture in the model relevant statistics of the flow. The objective is to predict, with sufficient accuracy, the impact of the traffic generated by applications on the resources being utilized (both in the network and in the servers), and evaluate the QoS perceived by the applications. The amount of work done on traffic characterization is sufficient vast to deserve surveys and books on the area [31,1,52,56]. Our interest in this chapter is to introduce a few issues on the topic.

In order to build a model of the traffic load, the proper traffic *descriptors* that capture important characteristics of the flows competing for resources have to be chosen. Examples of traffic descriptors are: the mean traffic rate, the peak-to-mean ratio, the autocovariance, the index of dispersion and the Hurst parameter. The issue is to select a set of descriptors such that traces and models with matching descriptors produce similar performance metrics.

A large number of models have been proposed in the literature. They include models in which the autocorrelation function decays exponentially (for instance, the Markovian models), and models in which the autocorrelation function decays at a slower rate, that is, hyperbolically (in this case the corresponding stationary process is called long-range dependent [56]). Although not possessing the long-range dependence property Markov models are attractive due to several reasons. First, they are mathematically tractable. Second, long-range correlations can be approximately obtained from certain kind of models. Third, it may be argued that long-range dependency is not a crucial property for some performance measures and Markov models can be used to accurately predict performance metrics (e.g. see [38,37]). Usually, a traffic model is built (or evaluated) by matching the descriptors calculated from the model against those obtained from measurement data. For Markovian models it is not difficult to calculate first and second order statistics [49].

As can be inferred from the above discussion, Markovian models are a useful tool for the performance evaluation of CM applications. They can be used to model the traffic stream, generate artificial loads, model the loss process and evaluate techniques to efficiently transmit CM streams.

4 Resource Sharing Techniques

Conventional multimedia servers provide each client with a separate stream. As a consequence, the resources available in the multimedia system, particularly network bandwidth, can be quickly exhausted. Consider, for instance, the scenarios 1 and 2 discussed in Sec. 2. To maintain 1500 concurrent streams live, with a separate bandwidth allocated to each of them, it is necessary to sustain a total bandwidth of 2,25 Gbps at the output channel of the multimedia server. While technically feasible, this is quite expensive nowadays and prohibitive from a commercial point of view.

A common approach for dealing with this problem is to allow several clients to share a common stream. This is accomplished through mechanisms, here called *resource sharing techniques*, which allow the clients to share streams and buffers. The goal is to reduce the demand for network bandwidth, disk bandwidth, and storage space. While providing the capability of stream sharing, these techniques have also to provide QoS to the clients.

As is Sec. 3 client QoS is affected by the server characteristics, such as latency and available disk bandwidth, and by the network characteristics, such as bandwidth, loss, jitter, and end-to-end delay. The challenge is to provide very short startup latency and jitter for all client requests and to be able to serve a large number of users at minimum costs.

The bandwidth sharing mechanisms proposed in the literature fall into two categories: *client request oriented* and *periodic broadcast*. *Client request oriented* techniques are based on the transmission, by the server, of a CM stream in response to multiple requests for its data blocks from the client. *Periodic broadcast* techniques are based on the periodic transmission by the server of the data blocks.

Besides these sharing mechanisms, one can also use proxy servers to reduce network load. Proxy servers are an orthogonal technique to bandwidth sharing protocols, but one which is quite popular because it can be easily implemented and can be managed at low costs.

We partition our presentation in three topics. We first describe *client request oriented* techniques. Then, *periodic broadcast* mechanisms are presented, followed by a discussion on proxy-based strategies.

4.1   Client Request Oriented Techniques

The simplest approach for allowing the sharing of bandwidth is to batch new clients together whenever possible. This is called *batching* [2,20,21] and works as follows. Upon the request of a new media stream s_i by an arriving client c_k, a batching window is initiated. Every new client that arrives within the bounds of this window and requests the stream s_i is inserted in a waiting queue i.e., it is batched together with the client c_k. When the window expires, a single transmission for the media stream s_i is initiated. This transmission is shared by all clients, as in standard broadcast television. Batching policies reduce bandwidth requirements at the expense of introducing an additional delay to the users (i.e., client startup latency increases).

Stream tapping [15], patching [13,40], and controlled multicast [32] were introduced to avoid the latency problems of batching. They are very similar techniques. They can provide immediate service to the clients, while allowing clients arriving at different instants to share a common stream.

In the basic patching scheme [40], the server maintains a queue with all pending requests. Whenever a server channel becomes available, the server admits all the clients that requested a given video at once. These clients compose a new batch. Assume, that this new batch of clients requested a CM stream s_i which is already being served. Then, all clients in this new batch immediately join this on-going multicast transmission of s_i and start buffering the arriving data. To obtain the initial part of the stream s_i, which is called a *patch* because it is no longer being multicasted, a new channel is opened with the multimedia server. Data arriving through this secondary channel is immediately displayed. Once the initial part of s_i (i.e., the patch) has been displayed, the client starts consuming data from its internal buffer. Thus, in this approach, the clients are responsible for maintaining enough buffer space to allow merging the patch portion of the stream with its main part. They also have to be able to receive data in two channels.

Stream tapping, optimal patching [13], and controlled multicast differ from the basic patching scheme in the following way: they define an optimal patching window w_i for each CM stream s_i. This window is the minimum interval between the initial instants of two successive complete transmissions of the same stream s_i. The size of w_i can improve the performance of patching. If w_i is set too large, most of the server channels are used to send patches. On the other hand, if w_i is too small no stream merging will occur. The patching window size is optimal if it minimizes the requirements of server and network bandwidth. The algorithm works as follows. Clients which requested the stream s_i prefetch data from an on-going multicast transmission, if they arrive within w_i units of time from the beginning of the previous complete transmission. Otherwise, a new multicast transmission of stream s_i is initiated. A mathematical model which captures the relation between the patching window size and the required server bandwidth is proposed in [13]. In [32] an expression for the optimal patching window is obtained.

Figure 5 illustrates batching and patching techniques. In Fig. 5(a), three new clients requesting the stream s_i arrive within the batching window. They are served by the same multicast transmission of s_i. Figure 5(b) shows the patching mechanism. We assume that the three requests arrive within a patching window. The request r_0 triggers the initial multicast transmission of stream s_i, r_1 triggers the transmission of the patch interval $(t_1 - t_0)$ of s_i for r_1, and r_2 starts a transmission of the $(t_2 - t_0)$ missing interval of s_i for r_2.

A study of the bandwidth required by optimal patching, stream tapping, and controlled multicast is presented in [27]. It is assumed that the arrivals of client requests are Poisson with mean rate equal to λ_i for stream s_i. The required server bandwidth for delivery of stream s_i is given by [27] as: $B_{OP,ST,CM} = (1 + w_i^2 N_i/2)/(w_i + 1/N_i)$, where $N_i = \lambda_i T_i$, T_i is the total length of stream s_i and w_i is the patching window.

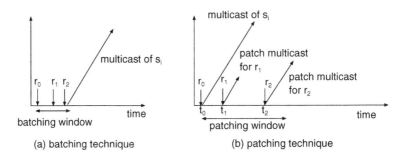

Fig. 5. Batching and patching techniques.

The expression presented above is very similar to the results obtained in [13, 32]. The value of the optimal patching window can be obtained differentiating the expression for $B_{\mathrm{OP,ST,CM}}$. It is equal to $(\sqrt{2N_i+1}-1)/N_i$. The server bandwidth for an optimal patching window is given by [32]: $B_{\mathrm{optimal\_window}} = \sqrt{2N_i+1}-1$.

A second approach to reduce server and network bandwidth requirements, called *Piggybacking*, was introduced in [4,35,48]. The idea is to change dinamically the display rates of on-going stream transmissions to allow one stream to catch up and merge with the other. Suppose that stream s_i is currently being transmitted to a client. If a new request for s_i arrives, then a new transmission of s_i is started. At this point in time, the server slows down the data rate of the first transmission and speeds up the data rate of the second transmission of s_i. As soon as the two transmissions become identical, they can be merged and one of the two channels can be released. One limitation of this technique is that it requires a specialized hardware to support the change of the channel speed dinamically.

In the hierarchical stream merging (HSM) techniques [7,25,27] clients that request the same stream are hierarchically merged into groups. The client receives simultaneously two streams: the one triggered by its own request and a second stream which was initiated by an earlier request from a client. With time, the client is able to join the latter on-going multicast transmission and the delivery of the stream initiated by it can be aborted. The merged clients also start listening on the next most recently initiated stream. Figure 6 shows a scenario where four client requests arrive for stream s_1 during the interval (t_1, t_3). The server initiates a new multicast transmission of s_1 for each new client. At time t_2, client c_2, who is listening to the stream for c_1, can join this on-going multicast transmission. At time t_3, client c_4 joins the transmission of c_3. Thus, after t_3, client c_4 can listen to the multicast transmission initiated at t_1. At t_5, client c_4 will be able to join the transmission started for client c_1. Bandwidth skimming (BS) [26] is similar to HSM. In this technique, policies are defined to reduce the user bandwidth requirements to less than twice the stream playback rate.

In [27], an expression for the required bandwidth of a server operating with the HSM and BS techniques was obtained. Suppose that the transmission rate needed by a client is equal to b units of the media playback rate ($b = 2$ for HSM and $b < 2$ for bandwidth skimming) and that the request arrivals are Poisson with mean rate equal to λ_i for stream s_i. The required server bandwidth for delivery of stream s_i can be approximated by: $B_{\text{HSM,BS}} \approx \eta_b ln(N_i/\eta_b + 1)$, where N_i is defined as above and η_b is the positive real constant that satisfies: $\eta_b[1 - (\eta_b/(\eta_b + 1))^b] = 1$

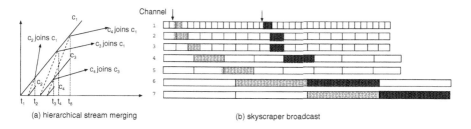

Fig. 6. Hierarchical stream merging and skyscraper broadcasting

Most of the studies in the literature have evaluated the required server bandwidth for the proposed sharing techniques. One key question is how the performance of a multimedia system is affected when the server bandwidth is limited by the equations previously presented. In a recent work [68] analytical models for HSM, BS and patching techniques are proposed to evaluate two performance metrics of a multimedia system: the mean time a client request is delayed if the server is overloaded (it is called the mean client waiting time) and the fraction of clients who renege if they are not served with low delay (it is called the *balking rate*). The models assumptions are: client request arrivals are Poisson, each client requests the entire media stream and all media streams have the same length and require the same playout rate. The model proposed to evaluate the balking rate is a closed two-center queueing network with C clients (C is the server bandwidth capacity in number of channels). The mean client waiting time is obtained from a two-center queueing network model with K users (There are one user per class and each class represents one stream.) Each user models the *first request for a stream* s_i, the others requests that batch with the *first* are not represented in the model. Results obtained from the analytical models show that the client balking rate may be high and the mean client waiting time is low when the required server bandwidth is defined as in the equations presented above. Furthermore the two performance parameters are very sensitive to the increase in the client load.

4.2   Periodic Broadcast Techniques

The idea behind periodic broadcast techniques is that each stream is divided into segments that can then be simultaneously broadcast periodically on a set of k

different channels. A channel c_1 delivers only the first segment of a given stream and the other $(k-1)$ channels deliver the remainder of the stream. When a client wants to watch a video, he must wait for the beginning of the first segment on channel c_1. A client has a schedule for tuning into each of the $(k-1)$ channels to receive the remaining segments of the video. The broadcasting schemes can be classified into three categories [39]. The first group of periodic broadcast techniques divides the stream into increasing sized segments and transmits them in channels of the same bandwidth. Smaller segments are broadcast more frequently than larger segments and the segments follow a size progression $(l_1, l_2, ..., l_n)$. In the Pyramid Broadcasting (PB) protocol [70], the sizes of the segments follow a geometric distribution and one channel is used to transmit different streams. The transmission rate of the channels is high enough to provide on time delivery of the stream. Thus, client bandwidth and storage requirements are also high.

To address the problem of high resource requirements at the client side, a technique called Permutation-based Pyramid Broadcasting (PPB) was proposed in [3]. The idea is to multiplex a channel into k subchannels of lower rate. In the Skyscraper broadcast technique [41] each segment is continuously transmitted at the video playback rate on one channel as shown in Fig. 6. The series of segments sizes is 1,2,2,5,5,12,12,25,25,52,52,... with a largest segment size equal to W. Figure 6 shows two client request arrival times: one just prior the third segment and the other before the 18th segment broadcast on channel 1. The transmission schedules of both clients are represented by the gray shaded segments. The schedule is such that a client is able to continuous playout the stream receiving data in no more than two channels. The required maximum client buffer space is equal to the largest segment size.

For all techniques described above the required server bandwidth is equal to the number of channels and is independent of the client request arrival rate. Therefore, these periodic broadcast techniques are very bandwidth efficient when the client request arrival rate is high. A dynamic skyscraper technique was proposed in [24] to improve the performance of the skyscraper. It considered the dynamic popularity of the videos and assumed lower client arrival rates. It dynamically changes the video that is broadcast on the channels. A set of segments of a video are delivered in transmission clusters. Each cluster starts every W slots on channel 1 and broadcasts a different video according to the client requests. Client requests are scheduled to the next available transmission cluster using a FIFO discipline, if there is no transmission cluster already been assigned to the required video. A new segment size progression is proposed in [27] to provide immediate service to client. Server bandwidth requirements for transmitting a stream s_i considering Poisson arrivals with mean rate λ_i are given by [27]: $B_{Dyn\_Sky} = 2U\lambda_i + (K-2)/(1+1/\lambda_i WU)$, where U is the duration of a unit-segment, W is the largest segment size and K is the number of segments in the segment size progression.

Another group, the harmonic broadcast techniques, divide the video in equal sized segments and transmit them into channels of decreasing bandwidth. The third group combines the approaches described above. They are a hybrid scheme of pyramid and harmonic broadcasting.

4.3   Proxy Based Strategies

The use of proxies in the context of CM applications has several advantages. Server and network bandwidth requirements can be reduced and the client startup latency can be very low. In Sec. 4.1 and 4.2 the models to evaluate the scalability of the bandwidth sharing techniques are based on the assumption that client request arrivals are sequential (i.e., clients request a stream and playout it from the beginning to the end). The required server bandwidth for these techniques varies logarithmically with the client request arrivals (for stream merging) and logarithmically with the inverse of the start-up delay (for periodic broadcasting) [44]. In a recent work [44], tight lower bounds on the required server bandwidth for multicast delivery techniques when the client request arrivals are not sequential were derived. The results obtained suggested that for non-sequential access the scalability of these techniques is not so high as for sequential access. Thus, the use of proxies is a complementary strategy that can reduce resource requirements and client latency of large scale CM applications.

Provisioning a multimedia application with proxy servers involves determining which content should be stored at each proxy. Several studies are based on the storage of data accessed most frequently. Distinct approaches exist in the literature. One idea is to divide the compressed video in layers that can be cached at the proxy. An alternative is to cache a portion of a video file at the proxy. Recent work combines the use of proxies with bandwidth sharing mechanisms such as periodic broadcast and client request oriented techniques. In the last approach, not only the popularity of the video should be considered to decide which portion of the stream have to be stored at the proxy. The data staged at the proxy depends also on the mechanisms used to share the transmission of data. In most of the bandwidth sharing mechanisms, the server delivers the initial portion of a stream more frequently than the latter part. Therefore, the storage of a prefix can reduce more significantly the transmission costs than the storage of the suffix.

Caching of Video Layers. In a video layer encoding technique, the compressed video stream is divided into layers: a base layer and enhancement layers. The base layer contains essential low quality encoding information, while the enhancement layers provide optional information that can be used to improve the video stream quality.

The approach used in [72] is to divide a video stream in two parts and to store the bursts of the stream in a proxy. A *cut-off rate* C_{rate} is defined, where $0 \leq C_{rate} \leq P_{rate}$ (P_{rate} is the peak rate). The first part of the stream (the *upper part*) exceeds the *cut-off rate*, and the remaider of the stream is the *lower part*. The upper part is staged at a proxy server and the lower part is retrieved from the server. The stream transmitted from the server to the clients approaches to a CBR stream as C_{rate} decreases. Two heuristic algorithms are presented to determine which video and what percentage of it has to be cached at the proxy. The first stores hot videos i.e., popular videos, entirely at the proxy. The second stores a portion of a video so as to minimize the bandwidth requirements on the server-proxy path. Results shown that the second heuristic performs better than the first.

Another approach is presented in [59]. A mechanism for caching video layers is used in conjunction with a congestion control and a quality adaptation mechanism. The number of video layers cached at the proxy is based on the popularity of the video. The more popular is a video, the more layers are stored in the proxy. Enhancement layers of cached streams are added according to a quality adaptation mechanism [60]. One limitation of this approach is that it requires the implementation of a congestion control and of a quality adaptation mechanism in all the transmissions between clients and proxies and between proxies and servers.

Partial Caching of the Video File. The scheme proposed in [66] is based on the storage of the initial frames of a CM stream in a proxy cache. It is called proxy prefix caching. It was motivated by the observation that the performance of CM applications can be poor due to the delay, throughput and loss characteristics of the Internet. As presented in Sec. 3 the use of buffers can reduce network bandwidth requirements and allow the application to tolerate larger variations in the network delay. However, the buffer size is limited by the maximum startup latency a client can tolerate. Proxy prefix caching allows reducing client startup latency, specially when buffering techniques are used. The scheme work as follows. When a client requests a stream, the proxy immediately delivers the prefix to the client and asks the server to initiate the transmission of the remaining frames of the stream. The proxy uses two buffers during the transmission of stream s_i: the prefix buffer B_p and a temporary buffer B_t. Initially, frames are delivered from the B_p buffer while frames coming from the server are stored in the B_t buffer.

Caching with Bandwidth Sharing Techniques. When using a proxy server in conjunction with scalable delivery mechanisms several issues have to be addressed. The data to be stored at each proxy depends on the relative cost of streaming a video from the server and from the proxy, the number of proxies, the client arrival rate and the path from the server to the proxy (unicast or multicast enabled).

Most of the studies in the literature [23,58,16,36,71,5] define a system cost function which depends on the fraction of the stream stored at the proxy (w_i), the bandwidth required for a stream (b_i), the client arrival rate (λ_i) and the length of the stream (T_i). The cost for delivering a stream s_i is given by $C_i(w_i, b_i, \lambda_i, T_i) = B_{server}(w_i, b_i, \lambda_i, T_i) + B_{proxy}(w_i, b_i, \lambda_i, T_i)$ where B_{server} is the cost of the server-proxy required bandwidth and B_{proxy} is the cost of the proxy-client required bandwidth. Then, an optimization problem is formulated. The goal is to minimize the transmission costs subject to bounds on the total storage and/or bandwidth available at the proxy. The solution of the problem gives the proxy cache allocation that minimizes the aggregate transmission cost.

The work of [71] combines proxy prefix caching with client request oriented techniques for video delivery between the proxy and the client. It is assumed that the transmission between the server and the proxy is unicast and the network paths from the proxy to the clients are either multicast/broadcast or unicast. Two scenarios are evaluated: (a) the proxy-client path is unicast and (b) the proxy-client path is multicast. For the scenario (a) two transmission strategies are proposed. In the first a batching technique is used to group the client request arrivals within a window w_{p_i} (equal to the length of the prefix stored at the proxy). Each group of clients is served from the same unicast transmission from the server to the proxy. The second is an improvement of the first. It is similar to the patching technique used in the context of unicast. If a client request arrives at time t after the end of w_{p_i}, the proxy schedules a patch for the transmission of the missing part from the server. The $(T_i - t)$ (T_i is the length of the stream s_i) remaining frames of the stream are delivered from the on-going transmission of stream s_i. The client will receive data from at most two channels: the patch channel and the on-going transmission channel. For the scenario (b), two transmission schemes are presented: the multicast patching technique [13] implemented at the proxy and the multicast merging which is similar to the stream merging technique [25]. A dynamic programming algorithm is used to solve the optimization problem. Results show that the transmission costs when a prefix cache is used are lower compared to caching the entire stream, and that significant transmissions savings can be obtained with a small proxy size.

The work in [36] studies the use of proxy prefix caching with periodic broadcast techniques. The authors propose the use of patching to deliver the prefix from the proxy to the client and periodic broadcast to deliver the remaining frames (the suffix) from the server to the client. Clients will temporarily receive both the prefix from the proxy and the suffix from the server. Therefore, the number of channels a client needs is the sum of the channels to obtain the suffix and the prefix. A slight modification in periodic broadcast and patching is introduced such that the maximum number of simultaneous channels required by a client is equal to two. Proxy buffer allocation is based on a three steps algorithm aimed at minimizing server bandwidth in the path from the server to the proxy. Results show that the optimal buffer allocation algorithm outperforms a scheme where the proxy buffer is evenly divided among the streams without considering the length of each stream.

In [5] the following scenarios are considered: (a) the bandwidth skimming protocol is used in the server-proxy and proxy-client paths, (b) the server-proxy path is unicast capable and the bandwidth skimming technique is used in the proxy-client path, and (c) scenarios (a) and (b) combined to proxy prefix caching. In the scenario (a) the proxy can store an arbitrary fraction of each stream s_i. Streams are merged at the proxy and at the server using the closest target bandwidth skimming protocol [25]. In the scenario (b) the server-proxy path is unicast, thus only streams requested from the same proxy can be merged at the server. Several results are obtained from a large set of system configuration parameters. They show that the use of proxy servers is cost effective in the following cases: the server-proxy path is not multicast enabled or the client arrival rate is low or the cost to deliver a stream from the proxy to the client is very small when compared to the cost to deliver a stream from the server to the client.

5 Conclusions

In this chapter we have surveyed several performance issues related to the design of real time voice and video applications (such as voice transmission tools and multimedia video servers). These include issues from continuous media retrieval to transmission. Since the topic is too broad to be covered in one chapter we trade deepness of exposition to broadness, in order to cover a wide range of inter-related problems.

As can be seen in the material covered, an important aspect in the design of multimedia servers is the storage strategy. We favor the use of the random I/O technique due to its simplicity of implementation and comparable performance with respect to other schemes. This technique is particularly attractive when different types of data are placed in the server, for instance mixture of voice, video, transparencies, photos, etc. Furthermore, the same technique can be easily employed in proxies. To evaluate the performance of the technique, queueing models constructed from real traffic streams traces can be used. It is clear the importance of accurate traffic models to feed the overall server model.

A multimedia server should try to send the requested streams as smooth as possible (or as close as possible to CBR traffic) to minimize the impact of sudden rate changes in the network resource. Large buffers at the receiver imply better smoothing, but at the expense of increasing latency to start displaying a stream. The receiver playout buffer is also used to reduce the packet delay variability imposed by the network and to help in the recovery process when a packet loss occur. We have surveyed a few packet recovery techniques, and presented the main tradeoffs such as error correction capability and increase in the transmission rate, efficiency versus latency, etc. Modeling the loss process is an important problem and many issues remain open. Although some of the conclusions in the chapter were drawn based on the study of voice traffic the issues are not different for video traffic.

Due to the high speed of modern disk systems, presently the bottleneck to delivery the continuous media stream to clients is mainly at the local network where the server is attached, and not at the storage server. Therefore, an issue that has drawn attention in recent years is the development of algorithms to conserve bandwidth, when a large number of clients submit requests to the server. Since multicast is still far from been widely deployed, we favor schemes that use unicast transmission from the storage server to proxy servers. Between the proxy and the clients multicast is more likely to be feasible, and therefore multicast-based techniques to reduce bandwidth requirements are most likely to be useful in the path from the proxy to the clients.

To conclude, we stress the importance of developing multimedia applications and perform tests on prototypes, collect statistics, develop models based on the data obtained. Modeling tools are an important part of the evaluation process, and this includes not only simulation but analytical tools, traffic generators, etc. Several tools and prototypes have been developed in recent years. Our own tools include: video servers, implementing different storage techniques; voice transmission tool implementing FEC recovery mechanisms; distributed whiteboard (with multicast library), TANGRAM-II that includes a modeling environment with analytical as well as simulation solvers, traffic modeling environment and traffic generator and analyzer. (Most of the tools can be download from www.land.ufrj.br and/or www.dcc.ufmg.br.)

References

1. A. Adas. Traffic Models in Broadband Networks. *IEEE Communications Magazine*, (7):82–89, 1997.
2. C. C. Aggarwal, J. L. Wolf, and P. S. Wu. On optimal batching policies for video-on-demand storage server. In *Proc. of the IEEE Conf. on Multimedia Systems*, 1996.
3. C. C. Aggarwal, J. L. Wolf, and P. S. Wu. A permutation-based pyramid broadcasting scheme for video-on-demand systems. In *Proc. of the IEEE Conf. on Multimedia Systems*, 1996.
4. C.C. Aggarwal, J.L. Wolf, and P.S. Wu. On optimal piggyback merging policies. In *Proc. ACM Sigmetrics'96*, pages 200–209, May 1996.
5. J. Almeida, D. Eager, M. Ferris, and M. Vernon. Provisioning content distribution networks for streaming media. In *Proc. of IEEE/Infocom'02*, June 2002.
6. J. Apostolopoulos, T. Wong, W. Tan, and S. Wee. On multiple description streaming with content delivery networks. In *Proc. of IEEE/Infocom'02*, NY, June 2002.
7. A. Bar-Noy, G. Goshi, R. E. Ladner, and K. Tam. Comparison os stream merging algorithms for media-on-demand. In *Proc. MMCN'02*, January 2002.
8. S. Berson, R.Muntz, S. Ghandeharizadeh, and X. Ju. Staggered striping in multimedia information systems. In *ACM SIGMOD Conference*, 1994.
9. W. Bolosky, J.S. Barrera, R. Draves, R. Fitzgerald, G. Gibson, M. Jones, S. Levi, N. Myhrvold, and R. Rashid. The Tiger video fileserver. In *Proc. NOSSDAV'96*. 1996.
10. J-C. Bolot. Characterizing end-to-end packet delay and loss in the Internet. In *Proc. ACM Sigcomm'93*, pages 289–298, September 1993.
11. J-C. Bolot, S. Fosse-Parisis, and D. Towsley. Adaptive FEC-based error control for Internet telephony. In *Proc. of IEEE/Infocom'99*, pages 1453–1460, 1999.
12. J-C. Bolot and A. Vega-García. The case for FEC-based error control for packet audio in the Internet. *ACM Multimedia Systems*, 1997.
13. Y. Cai, K. Hua, and K. Vu. Optimizing patching performance. In *Proc. SPIE/ACM Conference on Multimedia Computing and Networking*, 1999.
14. S. Campos, B. Ribeiro-Neto, A. Macedo, and L. Bertini. Formal verification and analysis of multimedia systems. In *ACM Multimedia Conference*. Orlando, November 1999.
15. S. W. Carter and D. D. E. Long. Improving video-on-demand server efficiency through stream tapping. In *Sixth International Conference on Computer Communications and Networks*, pages 200–207, 1997.

16. S.-H.G. Chan and F. Tobagi. Tradeoff between system profit and user delay/loss in providing near video-on-demand service. *IEEE Transactions on Circuits and Systems for Video Technology*, 11(8):916–927, August 2001.

17. E. Chang and A. Zakhor. Cost analyses for VBR video servers. *IEEE Multimedia*, 3(4):56–71, 1996.

18. A.L. Chervenak, D.A. Patterson, and R.H. Katz. Choosing the best storage system for video service. In *ACM Multimedia Conf.*, pages 109–119. SF, 1995.

19. T. Chua, J. Li, B. Ooi, and K. Tan. Disk striping strategies for large video-on-demand servers. In *ACM Multimedia Conf.*, pages 297–306, 1996.

20. A. Dan, D. Sitaram, and P. Shahabuddin. Scheduling policies for an on-demand video server with batching. In *Proc. of the 2nd ACM Intl. Conf. on Multimedia*, pages 15–23, 1994.

21. A. Dan, D. Sitaram, and P. Shahabuddin. Dynamic batching policies for an on-demand video server. *Multimedia Systems*, (4):112–121, 1996.

22. M.C. Diniz and E. de Souza e Silva. Models for jitter control at destination. In *Proc., IEEE Intern. Telecomm. Symp.*, pages 118–122, 1996.

23. D. Eager, M. Ferris, and M. Vernon. Optimized caching in systems with heterogenous client populations. *Performance Evaluation*, (42):163–185, 2000.

24. D. Eager and M. Vernon. Dynamic skyscraper broadcasts for video-on-demand. In 4th *International Workshop on Multimedia Information Systems*, September 1998.

25. D. Eager, M. Vernon, and J. Zahorjan. Optimal and efficient merging schedules for video-on-demand servers. In *Proc. ACM Multimedia'99*, November 1999.

26. D. Eager, M. Vernon, and J. Zahorjan. Bandwidth skimming: A technique for cost effective video-on-demand. In *Proc. Multimedia Computing and Networking*, January 2000.

27. D. Eager, M. Vernon, and J. Zahorjan. Minimizing bandwidth requirements for on-demand data delivery. *IEEE Transactions on Knowledge and Data Engineering*, 13(5):742–757, September 2001.

28. F. Fabbrocino, J.R. Santos, and R.R. Muntz. An implicitly scalable, fully interactive multimedia storage server. In *DISRT'98*, pages 92–101. Montreal, July 1998.

29. D.R. Figueiredo and E. de Souza e Silva. Efficient mechanisms for recovering voice packets in the Internet. In *Proc. of IEEE/Globecom'99, Global Internet Symp.*, pages 1830–1837, December 1999.

30. C.S. Freedman and D.J. DeWitt. The SPIFFI scalable video-on-demand system. In *ACM Multimedia Conf.*, pages 352–363, 1995.

31. V.S. Frost and B. Melamed. Traffic Modeling for Telecommunications Networks. *IEEE Communications Magazine*, 32(3):70–81, 1994.

32. L. Gao and D. Towsley. Supplying instantaneous video-on-demand services using controlled multicast. In *IEEE International Conference on Multimedia Computing and Systems*, pages 117–121, 1999.

33. S. Ghandeharizadeh, R. Zimmermann, W. Shi, R. Rejaie, D. Ierardi, and T.-W. Li. Mitra: a scalable continuous media server. *Multimedia Tools and Applications*, 5(1):79–108, July 1997.

34. L. Golubchick, J.C.S. Lui, E. de Souza e Silva, and R.Gail. Evaluation of performance tradeoffs in scheduling techniques for mixed workload multimedia servers. *Journal of Multimedia Tools and Applications*, to appear, 2002.

35. L. Golubchick, J.C.S. Lui, and R. Muntz. Reducing i/o demand in video-on-demand storage servers. In *Proc. ACM Sigmetrics'95*, pages 25–36, May 1995.

36. Y. Guo, S. Sen, and D. Towsley. Prefix caching assisted periodic broadcast: Framework and techniques to support streaming for popular videos. In *Proc. of ICC'02*, 2002.

37. D. Heyman and D. Lucantoni. Modeling multiple ip traffic with rate limits. In J.M. de Souza, N. da Fonseca, and E. de Souza e Silva, editors, *Teletraffic Engineering in the Internet Era*, pages 445–456. 2001.

38. D.P. Heyman and T.V. Lakshman. What are the Implications of Long-Range Dependence for VBR-Video Traffic Engineering. *IEEE/ACM Transactions on Networking*, 4(3):301–317, June 1996.

39. Ailan Hu. Video-on-demand broadcasting protocols: A comprehensive study. In *Proc. IEEE Infocom*, pages 508–517, 2001.

40. K. A. Hua, Y. Cai, and S. Sheu. Patching: A multicast technique for true video-on demand services. In *Proceedings of ACM Multimedia*, pages 191–200, 1998.

41. K.A. Hua and S. Sheu. Skyscraper broadcasting: a new broadcasting scheme for metropolitan video-on-demand systems. In *Proc. of ACM Sigcomm'97*, pages 89–100. ACM Press, 1997.

42. J.Chien-Liang, D.H.C. Du, S.S.Y. Shim, J. Hsieh, and M. Lin. Design and evaluation of a generic software architecture for on-demand video servers. *IEEE Transactions on Knowledge and Data Engineering*, 11(3):406–424, May 1999.

43. P. Ji, B. Liu, D. Towsley, and J. Kurose. Modeling frame-level errors in gsm wireless channels. In *Proc. of IEEE/Globecom'02 Global Internet Symp.*, 2002.

44. S. Jin and A. Bestavros. Scalability of multicast delivery for non-sequential streaming access. In *Proc. of ACM Sigmetrics'02*, June 2002.

45. K. Keeton and R. Kantz. Evaluating video layout strategies for a high-performance storage server. In *ACM Multimedia Conference*, pages 43–52, 1995.

46. J. Korst. Random duplicated assignment: An alternative to striping in video servers. In *ACM Multimedia Conference*, pages 219–226. Seattle, 1997.

47. J.F. Kurose and K.W. Ross. *Computer Networking: A Top-Down Approach Featuring the Internet*. Addison-Wesley, 2001.

48. S.W. Lau, J.C.S. Lui, and L. Golubchik. Merging video streams in a multimedia storage server: Complexity and heuristics. *ACM Multimedia Systems Journal*, 6(1):29–42, January 1998.

49. R.M.M. Leão, E. de Souza e Silva, and Sidney C. de Lucena. A set of tools for traffic modelling, analysis and experimentation. In *Lecture Notes in Computer Science 1786 (TOOLS'00)*, pages 40–55, 2000.

50. Y. Mansour and B Patt-Shamir. Jitter control in QoS networks. *IEEE/ACM Transactions on Networking*, 2001.

51. A.P. Markopoulou, F.A. Tobagi, and M.J. Karam. Assessment of VoIP quality over Internet backbones. In *Proc. of IEEE/Infocom'02*, June 2002.

52. H. Michiel and K. Laevens. Traffic Engineering in a Broadband Era. *Proceedings of the IEEE*, pages 2007–2033, 1997.

53. R.R. Muntz, J.R. Santos, and S. Berson. A parallel disk storage system for real-time multimedia applications. *Intl. Journal of Intelligent Systems*, 13(12):1137–1174, December 1998.

54. B. Ozden, R. Rastogi, and A. Silberschatz. Disk striping in video server environments. In *IEEE Intl. Conference on Multimedia Computing and Systems*, 1996.

55. B. Ozden, R. Rastogi, and A. Silberschatz. On the design of a low-cost video-on-demand storage system. In *ACM Multimedia Conference*, pages 40–54, 1996.

56. K. Park and W. Willinger. *Self-Similar Network Traffic: an Overview*, pages 1–38. John Wiley and Sons, INC., 2000.

57. C. S. Perkins, O. Hodson, and V. Hardman. A survey of packet-loss recovery techniques for streaming audio. *IEEE Network Magazine*, pages 40–48, Sep. 1998.

58. S. Ramesh, I. Rhee, and K. Guo. Multicast with cache (mcache): An adaptative zero-delay video-on-demand service. *IEEE Transactions on Circuits and Systems for Video Technology*, 11(3):440–456, March 2001.
59. R. Rejaie, H. Yu, M. Handley, and D. Estrin. Multimedia proxy caching mechanism for quality adaptive streaming applications in the Internet. In *Proc. IEEE Infocom*, pages 980–989, 2000.
60. Reza Rejaie, Mark Handley, and Deborah Estrin. Quality adaptation for congestion controlled video playback over the Internet. In *Proc. ACM Sigcomm'99*, pages 189–200, August 1999.
61. K. Salamatian and S. Vaton. Hidden Markov Modeling for network communication channels. In *Proc. of Sigmetrics/Performance'01*, pages 92–101, Cambridge, Massachusetts, USA, June 2001.
62. J.D. Salehi, Z.L.Zhang, J.F. Kurose, and D. Towsley. Supporting stored video: reducing rate variability and end-to-end resource requirements through optimal smoothing. *IEEE/ACM Transactions on Networking*, 6(4):397–410, 1998.
63. J.R. Santos and R. Muntz. Performance analysis of the RIO multimedia storage system with heterogeneous disk configurations. In *ACM Multimedia Conf.*, 1998.
64. J.R. Santos, R. Muntz, and B. Ribeiro-Neto. Comparing random data allocation and data striping in multimedia servers. In *Proc. ACM Sigmetrics'00*, pages 44–55. Santa Clara, 2000.
65. S. Sen, J. Rexford, J. Dey, J. Kurose, and D. Towsley. Online smoothing of variable-bit-rate streaming video. *IEEE Transactions on Multimedia*, 2000.
66. S. Sen, J. Rexford, and D. Towsley. Proxy prefix caching for multimedia streams. In *Proc. IEEE Infocom*, pages 1310–1319, 1999.
67. P.J. Shenoy and H.M. Vin. Efficient striping techniques for multimedia file servers. In *Proc. NOSSDAV'97*, pages 25–36. 1997.
68. H. Tan, D. Eager, M. Vernon, and H. Guo. Quality of service evaluations of multicast streaming protocols. In *Proc. of ACM Sigmetrics 2002*, June 2002.
69. D. Towsley, J. Kurose, and S. Pingali. A comparison of sender-initiated and receiver-initiated reliable multicast protocols. *IEEE Journal on Selected Areas in Communications*, 15(3):398–406, April 1997.
70. S. Viswanathan and T. Imielinski. Pyramid broadcasting for video on demand service. In *Proc. IEEE Multimedia Computing and Networking*, volume 2417, pages 66–77, 1995.
71. B. Wang, S. Sen, M. Adler, and D. Towsley. Optimal proxy cache allocation for efficient streaming media distribution. In *Proc. IEEE Infocom*, 2002.
72. Y. Wang, Z. Zhang, D. Du, and D. Su. A network-conscious approach to end-to-end video delivery over wide area networks using proxy servers. In *Proc. of IEEE Infocom 98*, pages 660–667, Abril 1998.
73. W.R. Wong. *On-time Data Delivery for Interactive Visualization Apploications*. PhD thesis, UCLA/CS Dept., 2000.
74. D. Wu, Y.T. Hou, and Y. Zhang. Transporting real-time video over the Internet: Challenges and approaches. *Proceedings of the IEEE*, 88(12):1855–1875, December 2000.
75. M. Yajnik, S. Mon, J. Kurose, and D. Towsley. Measurement and modeling of the temporal dependence in packet loss. In *Proc. of IEEE/Infocom'99*, 1999.
76. E. Steinbach Yi J. Liang and B. Girod. Real-time voice communication over the Internet using packet path diversity. In *Proc. ACM Multimedia 2001*, Ottawa, Canada, Sept./Oct. 2001.

Markovian Modeling of Real Data Traffic: Heuristic Phase Type and MAP Fitting of Heavy Tailed and Fractal Like Samples*

András Horváth and Miklós Telek

Dept. of Telecommunications, Budapest University of Technology and Economics,
{horvath,telek}@webspn.hit.bme.hu

Abstract. In order to support the effective use of telecommunication infrastructure, the "random" behavior of traffic sources has been studied since the early days of telephony. Strange new features, like fractal like behavior and heavy tailed distributions were observed in high speed packet switched data networks in the early '90s. Since that time a fertile research aims to find proper models to describe these strange traffic features and to establish a robust method to design, dimension and operate such networks.

In this paper we give an overview of methods that, on the one hand, allow us to capture important traffic properties like slow decay rate, Hurst parameter, scaling factor, etc., and, on the other hand, makes possible the quantitative analysis of the studied systems using the effective analysis approach called matrix geometric method.

The presentation of this analysis approach is associated with a discussion on the properties and limits of Markovian fitting of the typical non-Markovian behavior present in telecommunication networks.

1 Introduction

In the late 80's, traffic measurement of high speed communication networks indicated unexpectedly high variability and burstiness over several time scales, which indicated the need of new modeling approaches capable to capture the observed traffic features. The first promising approach, the fractal modeling of high speed data traffic [28], resulted in a big bum in traffic theory. Since that time a series of traffic models were proposed to describe real traffic behavior: fractional Gaussian noises [30,37], traditional [7] and fractional ARIMA processes [18], fractals and multifractals [49,13], etc.

A significant positive consequence of the new traffic engineering wave is that the importance of traffic measurement and the proper statistical analysis of measured datasets became widely accepted and measured datasets of a wide range of real network configurations became publicly available [52].

In spite of the intensive research activity, there are still open problems associated with these new traffic models:

---

* This work is supported by the OTKA-T34972 grant of the Hungarian Research Found.

M.C. Calzarossa and S. Tucci (Eds.): Performance 2002, LNCS 2459, pp. 405–434, 2002.
© Springer-Verlag Berlin Heidelberg 2002

- None of the traffic models is evidently verified by the physical behavior of the networks. The proposed models allow us to represent some of the features of data traffic, but some other features are not captured. Which are the important traffic features?
- The traffic features of measured data are checked via statistical tests and the traffic features of the models are checked using analysis and simulation methods. Are these tests correct enough? Is there enough data available for reliable tests?
- The majority the proposed traffic models has important asymptotic properties, but all tests are based on finite datasets. Shall we draw consequence on the asymptotic properties based on finite datasets? And vice-versa, shall we draw consequence from the asymptotic model behavior on the performance of finite systems.
- Having finite datasets the asymptotic properties extracted from tests performed on different time scales often differ. Which is the dominant time scale to consider?

The above listed questions refer to the correctness of traffic models. There is an even more important issue which determines the utility of a traffic model, which is computability. The majority of the mentioned traffic models are not accompanied with effective analysis tools which would allow us to use them in practical traffic engineering.

In this paper we discuss the application of Markovian models for traffic engineering. The most evident advantage of this modeling approach with respect to the above mentioned ones is that it is supported with a set of effective analysis techniques called matrix geometric methods [34,35,27,29]. The other features of Markovian models with respect to the answers of the above listed questions are subjects to discussion. By the nature of Markovian models, non-exponential asymptotic behavior cannot be captured, and hence, they are not suitable for that purpose. Instead, recent research results show that Markovian models are able to approximate arbitrary non-Markovian behavior for an arbitrary wide range of scales.

The paper summarizes a traffic engineering procedure composed by the following steps:

- statistical analysis of measured traffic data,
- Markovian approximation of traffic processes,
- analysis of performance parameters based on the Markovian model.

All steps of this procedure are supported with a number of numerical example and the results are verified against simulation and alternative analysis methods.

The paper is organized as follows. Section 2 discusses some relevant characteristics of traffic processes and describe models that exhibit these features. Statistical tests for identifying these characteristics in datasets are described in Section 3. A short introduction to Markovian models is given in 4. An overview of the existing fitting methods with connected application examples is given in 5. The survey is concluded in 6.

2   Traffic Models and Their Properties

The traffic process at a given point of a telecommunication network is characterized by the data packet arrival instances (or equivalently by the interarrival times) and the associated data packet sizes. Any of these two processes can be composed by dependent or independent samples. In case of identically distributed independent samples the process modeling simplifies to capturing a distribution, while in case of dependent samples the whole stochastic process (with its intrinsic dependency structure) has to be captured as well.

2.1   Heavy Tailed Distributions

One of the important new observations of the intensive traffic measurement of high speed telecommunication networks is the presence of heavy tailed distributions. Marginal distributions of specific traffic processes, file size distribution on HTTP servers, etc, were found to be "heavy tailed". The random variable Y, with cumulative distribution function (cdf) $F_Y(x)$, is said to be heavy tailed if

$$1 - F_Y(x) = x^{-\alpha}L(x),$$

where $L(x)$ is slowly varying as $x \to \infty$, i.e., $lim_{x\to\infty}L(ax)/L(x) = 1$ for $a > 0$. (There are several different naming conventions applied in this field. Heavy tailed distributions are called regularly varying or power tail distributions also.) Typical member of this distribution class is the Pareto family.

There is an important qualitative property of the moments of heavy tailed distributions. If Y is heavy tailed with parameter α then its first $n < \alpha$ moments $E(Y^n)$ are finite and its all higher moments are infinite.

There are other classes of distributions whose tail decay slower than the exponential. The random variable Y, with distribution $F_Y(x)$, is said to be long tailed if

$$\lim_{x\to\infty} e^{\gamma x}(1 - F_Y(x)) = \infty, \qquad \forall \gamma > 0$$

The Weibull family ($F(x) = 1 - e^{-(t/a)^c}$) with $c < 1$ is long tailed, even if all moments of the Weibull distributed random variables are finite. The heavy tailed distributions form a subclass of the long tailed class.

A characteristic property of the heavy tailed class is the asymptotic relation of the distribution of the sum of n samples, $S_n = Y_1+\ldots+Y_n$, and the maximum of n samples, $M_n = \max_{1\le i\le n} Y_i$:

$$Pr(S_n > x) \sim Pr(M_n > x) \tag{1}$$

where the notation $g(x) \sim f(x)$ denotes $lim_{x\to\infty}\frac{f(x)}{g(x)} = 1$. In words, the sum of heavy tailed random variables is dominated by a *single* large sample and the rest of the samples are negligible small compare to the dominant one for large values of x. The probability that S_n is dominated by more than one "large" samples or it is obtained as the sum of number of small samples is negligible for "large" values of S_n. This interpretation gives an intuitive explanation for a set of complex results about the waiting time of queuing models with heavy tailed service time distribution [6].

2.2   Processes with Long Range Dependence

The definition of long range dependence of traffic arrival processes is as follows. Let us divide the time access into equidistant intervals of length Δ. The number of arrivals in the ith interval is denoted by X_i. $\mathcal{X} = \{X_i, i = 0, 1, \dots\}$ is a stochastic process whose aggregated process is defined as follows:

$$\mathcal{X}^{(m)} = \{X_i^{(m)}\} = \left\{ \frac{X_1 + \dots + X_m}{m}, \dots, \frac{X_{mk+1} + \dots + X_{(m+1)k}}{m}, \dots \right\}$$

The autocorrelation function of $\mathcal{X}^{(m)}$ is:

$$r^{(m)}(k) = \frac{E\{(X_n^{(m)} - E(X^{(m)})) \cdot (X_{n+k}^{(m)} - E(X^{(m)}))\}}{E\{(X_n^{(m)} - E(X^{(m)}))^2\}}$$

The process $\mathcal{X}$ exhibits long-range dependence (LRD) of index β if its autocorrelation function can be realized as

$$r(k) \sim A(k)k^{-\beta}, \quad k \to \infty$$

where A(k) is a slowly varying function.

Self-similar processes. Using the above definition of the aggregated process, $\mathcal{X}$ is

a) exactly self-similar if $\mathcal{X} \stackrel{d}{=} m^{1-H}\mathcal{X}^{(m)}$, i.e., if $\mathcal{X}$ and $\mathcal{X}^{(m)}$ are identical within a scale factor in finite dimensional distribution sense.
b) exactly second-order self-similar if $r^{(m)}(k) = r(k), \quad \forall m$, $k \geq 0$
c) asymptotically second-order self-similar if $r^{(m)}(k) \to r(k), \quad (k, m \to \infty)$

where H is the Hurst parameter, also referred to as the self-similarity parameter.

For exactly self-similar processes the scaling behavior, which is characterized by the Hurst parameter (H), can be checked based on any of the absolute moments of the aggregated process:

$$log(E(|X^{(m)}|^q)) = log(E(|m^{H-1}X|^q)) = q(H-1)log(m) + log(E(|X|^q)). \quad (2)$$

According to (2), in case of a self-similar process, plotting $log(E(|X^{(m)}|^q))$ against $log(m)$ for fixed q results in a straight line. The slope of the line is $q(H-1)$. Based on the above observations the test is performed as follows. Having a series of length N, the moments may be estimated as

$$E(|X^{(m)}|^q) = \frac{1}{\lfloor N/m \rfloor} \sum_{i=1}^{\lfloor N/m \rfloor} |X_i^{(m)}|^q,$$

where $\lfloor x \rfloor$ denotes the largest integer number smaller or equal to x. To test for self-similarity $log(E(|X^{(m)}|^q))$ is plotted against $log(m)$ and a straight line is fitted to the curve. If the straight line shows good correspondence with the curve, then the process is self-similar and its Hurst-parameter may be calculated by the slope of the straight line. This approach assumes that the scaling behavior of all absolute moments, q, are the same and it is captured by the Hurst-parameter. If it is the case we talk about mono-fractal behavior. The variance-time plot, which is used widespread to gain evidence of self-similarity, is the special case with $q = 2$. It depicts the behavior of the 2nd moments for the centered data.

It is worth to point out that self-similarity and stationarity imply that either $E(X) = 0$, or $E(X) = \pm\infty$, or $H = 1$. But $H = 1$ implies as well that $X_i = X_j$, $\forall i, j$ almost surely. As a consequence, to test for statistical self-similarity makes sense only having zero-mean data, i.e., the data has to be centered before the analysis.

Multi-fractal processes. Statistical tests of self-similarity try to gain evidence through examining the behavior of the absolute moments $E(|X^{(m)}|^q)$. In case of monofractal processes the scaling behavior of all absolute moments is characterized by a single number, the Hurst parameter. Multifractal processes might exhibit different scaling for different absolute moments. Multifractal analysis looks at the behavior of $E(|X^{(m)}|^q)$ for different values q and results in a *spectrum* that illustrates the behavior of the absolute moments. This analysis procedure is detailed in Section 3.3.

Fractional Gaussian noise. By now we provided the definition of the large class of self-similar stochastic processes, but we did not provide any specific member of this class. The two simplest self-similar processes that are often used in validation of self-similar modeling assumptions are the fractional Gaussian noise and the ARIMA process.

Fractional Gaussian noise, $X_i, i \geq 1$, is the increment process of fractional Brownian motion, $B(t), t \in \mathbb{R}^+$:

$$X_i = B(i + 1) - B(i),$$

Fractional Brownian motion with Hurst parameter H ($0.5 < H < 1$) is characterized by the following properties: i) $B(t)$ has stationary increment, ii) $E(B(t)) = 0$, iii) $E(B^2(t)) = t^{2H}$ (assuming the time unit is such that $E(B^2(1)) = 1$), iv) $B(t)$ has continuous path, v) $B(t)$ is a Gaussian process, i.e., all of its finite dimensional distributions are Gaussian. The covariance of fractional Brownian motion is $E(B(t) \cdot B(s)) = 1/2(s^{2H} + t^{2H} - |s-t|^{2H})$, and hence, the auto-covariance function of fractional Gaussian noise $\gamma(h) = E(X_i X_{i+h}) \sim H(2H - 1)h^{2H-2}$ is positive and exhibits long-range dependence.

ARIMA process. An other simple self-similar process is the fractional ARIMA(0,d,0) process. It is defined as:

$$X_i = \sum_{j=0}^{\infty} c_j \epsilon_{i-j}$$

where ϵ_i are i.i.d. standard normal random variables and the c_j coefficients implement moving average with parameter d according to $c_j = \frac{\Gamma(j+d)}{\Gamma(d)\Gamma(j+1)}$. For large values of j the coefficients $c_j \sim \frac{j^{d-1}}{\Gamma(d)}$. The asymptotic behavior of the auto-covariance function is

$$\gamma(h) = E(X_i X_{i+h}) \sim C_d h^{2d-1}$$

with coefficient $C_d = \pi^{-1}\Gamma(1-2d)\sin(\pi d)$. For $0 < d < 1/2$ the auto-covariance function has the same polynomial decay as the auto-covariance function of fractional Gaussian noise with $H = d + 1/2$.

The better choice among these two processes depends on the applied analysis method. The fractional Gaussian noise is better in exhibiting asymptotic properties based on finite number of samples, while the generation of fractional ARIMA process samples is easier since it is based on an explicit expression.

3   Statistical Analysis of Measured Traffic Datasets

3.1   Estimation of the Heavy Tail Index

In this section we discuss methods for identifying the heavy tail index of datasets. Application of the methods is illustrated on the dataset EPA_HTTP which can be downloaded from [52] and contains a day of HTTP logs with about 40000 entries. The experimental complementary cumulative distribution function (ccdf) of the length of the requests is depicted in Figure 1.

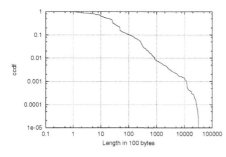

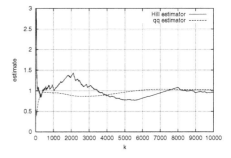

Fig. 1. Experimental ccdf of the length of requests arriving to the server

Fig. 2. The Hill- and the dynamic qq-plot for the EPA trace

Hill estimator. A possible approach to estimate the index of the tail behavior α is the Hill estimator [20]. This estimator provides the index as a function of the k largest elements of the dataset and is defined as

$$\alpha_{n,k} = \left(\frac{1}{k} \sum_{i=0}^{k-1} \left(\log X_{(n-i)} - \log X_{(n-k)} \right) \right)^{-1} \tag{3}$$

where $X_{(1)} \leq \dots \leq X_{(n)}$ denotes the order statistics of the dataset. In practice, the estimator given in (3) is plotted against k and if the plot stabilizes to a constant value this provides an estimate of the index. The Hill-plot (together with the dynamic qq-plot that will be described later) for the EPA trace is depicted in Figure 2.

The idea behind the procedure and theoretical properties of the estimator are discussed in [39]. Applicability of the Hill estimator is reduced by the fact that

- its properties (e.g. confidence intervals) are known to hold only under conditions that often cannot be validated in practice [39],
- the point at which the power-law tail begins must be determined and this can be difficult because often the datasets do not show clear border between the power-law tail and the non-power-low body of the distributions.

By slight modifications in the way the Hill plot is displayed, the uncertainty of the estimation procedure can be somewhat reduced, see [39,40].

Quantile-quantile regression plot. The above described Hill estimator performs well if the underlying distribution is close to Pareto. With the quantile-quantile plot (qq-plot), which is a visual tool for assessing the presence of heavy tails in distributions, one can check this. The qq-plot is commonly used in various forms, see for example [8,41]. Hereinafter, among the various forms, we follow the one presented in [25].

Having the order statistics $X_{(1)} \leq \dots \leq X_{(n)}$ plot

$$\left\{ \left(-\log \left(1 - \frac{j}{k+1} \right), \log X_{(j)} \right), n - k + 1 \leq j \leq n \right\} \tag{4}$$

for a fixed value of k. (As one can see only the k upper order statistics is considered in the plot, the other part of the sample is neglected.) The plot, if the data is close to Pareto, should be a straight line with slope $1/\alpha$. By determining the slope of the straight line fitted to the points by least squares, we obtain the so-called qq-estimator [25].

The qq-estimator can be visualized in two different ways. The *dynamic* qq-plot, depicted in Figure 2, plots the estimate of α as the function of k (this plot is similar to the Hill-plot). The *static* qq-plot, given in Figure 3, depicts (4) for a fixed value of k and shows its least square fit. As for the Hill-plot, when applying the qq-estimator, the point at which the tail begins has to be determined.

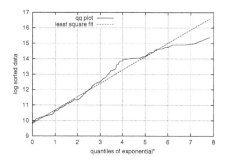
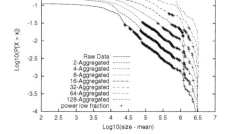

Fig. 3. Static qq-plot for the EPA trace

Fig. 4. Complementary distribution function for different aggregation levels for the EPA trace

Estimation based on the scaling properties. Another method is proposed in [9] which, in contrast to the Hill- and qq-estimator, does not require to determine where the tail begins. The procedure is based on the scaling properties of sums of heavy tailed distribution. The estimator, which is implemented in the tool *aest*, determines the heavy tail index by exploring the complementary distribution function of the dataset at different aggregation levels. For the EPA trace, the index estimated by *aest* is 0.97. In order to aid further investigation, the tool produces a plot of the complementary distribution function of the dataset at different aggregation levels indicating the segments where heavy tailed behavior is present. This plot for the considered dataset is depicted in Figure 4.

3.2   Tests for Long Range Dependency

Recently, it has been agreed [28,36,37] that when one studies the long-range dependence of a traffic trace the most significant parameter to be estimated is the degree of self-similarity, usually given by the so-called Hurst-parameter. The aim of the statistical approach, based on the theory of self-similarity, is to find the Hurst-parameter.

In this section methods for estimating the long-range dependence of datasets are recalled. Beside the procedures described here, several other can be found in the literature. See [3] for an exhaustive discussion on this subject.

It is important to note that the introduced statistical tests of self-similarity, based on a finite number of samples, provides an approximate value of H only for the considered range of scales. Nothing can be said about the higher scales and the asymptotic behavior based on these tests.

Throughout the section, we illustrate the application of the estimators on the first trace of the well-known Bellcore dataset set that contains local-area network (LAN) traffic collected in 1989 on an Ethernet at the Bellcore Morristown Research and Engineering facility. It may be downloaded from the WEB site collecting traffic traces [52]. The trace was first analyzed in [16].

Variance-time plot. One of the tests for *pseudo* self-similarity is the variance-time plot. It is based on the fact that for self-similar time series $\{X_1, X_2, \dots\}$

$$\text{Var}(X^{(m)}) \sim m^{-\beta} \quad, \quad \text{as } m \to \infty, \quad 0 < \beta < 1.$$

The variance-time plot depicts $Log(\text{Var}(X^{(m)}))$ versus $Log(m)$. For *pseudo* self-similar time series, the slope of the variance-time plot $-\beta$ is greater than -1. The Hurst parameter can be calculated as $H = 1 - (\beta/2)$. A traffic process is said to be *pseudo* self-similar when the empirical Hurst parameter is between 0.5 and 1.

The variance-time plot for the analyzed Bellcore trace is depicted in Figure 5. The Hurst-parameter given by the variance-time plot is 0.83.

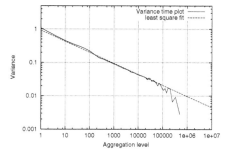

Fig. 5. Variance-time plot and its least square fit for the Bellcore trace

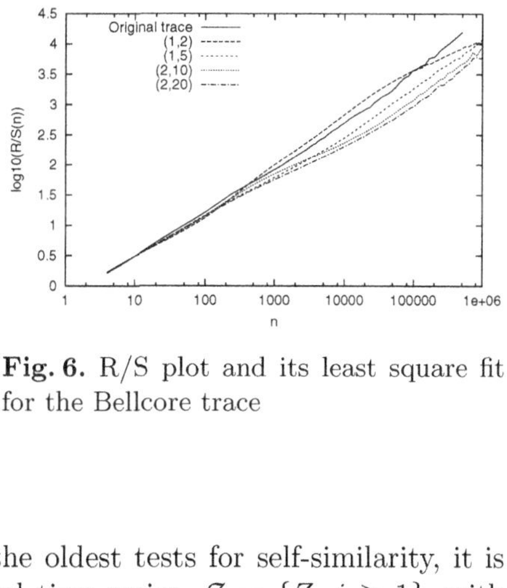

Fig. 6. R/S plot and its least square fit for the Bellcore trace

R/S plot. The R/S method is one of the oldest tests for self-similarity, it is discussed in detail in [31]. For interarrival time series, $\mathcal{Z} = \{Z_i, i \geq 1\}$, with partial sum $Y_n = \sum_{i=1}^{n} Z_i$, and sample variance

$$S^2(n) = \frac{1}{n} \sum_{i=1}^{n} Z_i^{\,2} - \frac{1}{n^2} \cdot Y_n^2,$$

the R/S statistic, or the rescaled adjusted range, is given by:

$$R/S(n) = \frac{1}{S(n)} \left[\max_{0 \leq k \leq n} \left(Y(k) - \frac{k}{n} Y(n) \right) - \min_{0 \leq k \leq n} \left(Y(k) - \frac{k}{n} Y(n) \right) \right].$$

$R/S(n)$ is the scaled difference between the fastest and the slowest arrival period considering n arrivals. For stationary LRD processes $R/S(n) \approx (n/2)^H$. To determine the Hurst parameter based on the R/S statistic the dataset is divided into blocks, $\log[R/S(n)]$ is plotted versus $\log n$ and a straight line is fitted on the points. The slope of the fitted line is the estimated Hurst parameter.

The R/S plot for the analyzed Bellcore trace is depicted in Figure 6. The Hurst-parameter determined based on the R/S plot is 0.78.

Whittle estimator. The Whittle estimator is based on the maximum likelihood principle assuming that the process under analysis is Gaussian. The estimator, unlike the previous ones, provides the estimate through a non-graphical method. This estimation takes more time to perform but it has the advantage of providing confidence intervals as well. For details see [17,3]. For the Bellcore trace, the estimated value of the Hurst parameter is 0.82 and its 95% confidence interval is $[0.79, 0.84]$.

3.3   Multifractal Framework

In this section we introduce two techniques to analyze multifractal processes.

Legendre spectrum. Considering a continuous-time process $\mathcal{Y} = \{Y(t), t > 0\}$ the scaling of the absolute moments of the increments is observed through the *partition function*

$$T(q) = \lim_{n \to \infty} \frac{1}{-n} \log_2 E \left[\sum_{k=0}^{2^n - 1} |Y((k+1)2^{-n}) - Y(k2^{-n})|^q \right]. \tag{5}$$

Then, a multifractal spectrum, the so-called *Legendre spectrum* is given as the *Legendre transform* of (5)

$$f_L(\alpha) = T^*(\alpha) = \inf_q (q\alpha - T(q))$$

Since $T(q)$ is always concave, the Legendre spectrum $f_L(\alpha)$ may be found by simple calculations using that

$$T^*(\alpha) = q\alpha - T(q), \text{ and } (T^*)'(\alpha) - q \text{ at } \alpha = T'(q). \tag{6}$$

Let us mention here that there are also other kinds of fractal spectrum defined in the fractal world (see for example [42]). The Legendre spectrum is the most attractive one from numerical point of view, and even though in some cases it is less informative than, for example, the large deviation spectrum, it provides enough information in the cases considered herein.

In case of a discrete-time process $\mathcal{X}$ we assume that we are given the increments of a continuous-time process. This way, assuming that the sequence we examine consists of $N = 2^L$ numbers, the sum in (5) becomes

$$S_n(q) = \sum_{k=0}^{N/2^n - 1} |X_k^{(2^n)}|^q, \ 0 \le n \le L, \tag{7}$$

where the expectation is ignored. Ignoring the expectation is accurate for small n, i.e., for the finer resolution levels. In order to estimate $T(q)$, we plot $\log_2(S_n(q))$ against $(L - n)$, $n = 0, 1, ..., L$, then $T(q)$ is found by the slope of the linear line fitted to the curve. If the linear line shows good correspondence with the

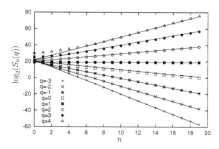

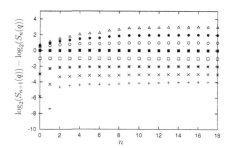

Fig. 7. Scaling of log-moments with linear fits for the interarrival times of the Bellcore *pAug* trace

Fig. 8. Increments of log-moments for the interarrival times of the Bellcore *pAug* trace

curve, i.e., if $\log_2(S_n(q))$ scales linearly with $\log(n)$, then the sequence $\mathcal{X}$ can be considered a multifractal process.

Figure 7, 9, 8 and 10 illustrate the above described procedure to obtain the Legendre spectrum of the famous Bellcore *pAug* traffic trace (the trace may be found at [52]). Figure 7 depicts the scaling behavior of the log moments calculated through (7). With q in the range $[-3, 4]$, excluding the finest resolution levels $n = 0, 1$ the moments show good linear scaling. For values of q outside the range $[-3, 4]$ the curves deviate more and more from linearity. As, for example, in [43] one may look at non-integer values of q as well, but, in general, it does not provide notably more information on the process. To better visualize the deviation from linearity Figure 8 depicts the increments of the log-moment curves of Figure 7. Completely horizontal lines would represent linear log-moment curves.

The partition function $T(q)$ is depicted in Figure 9. The three slightly different curves differ only in the considered range of the log-moments curves, since different ranges result in different linear fitting. The lower bound of the linear fitting is set to 3, 5 and 7, while the upper bound is 18 in each cases. (In the rest of this paper the fitting range is 5 - 18 and there are 100 moments evaluated in the range $q \in [-5, +5]$.) Since the partition function varies only a little (its derivative is in the range $[0.8, 1.15]$), it is not as informative as its Legendre transform is (Figure 10). According to (6) the Legendre spectrum is as wide as wide the range of derivatives of the partition function is, i.e., the more the partition function deviates from linearity the wider the Legendre spectrum is. The Legendre transform significantly amplifies the scaling information, but it is also sensitive to the considered range of the log-moments curves.

See [43] for basic principles of interpreting the spectrum. We mention here only that a curve like the one depicted in Figure 10 reveals a *rich multifractal spectrum*. On the contrary, as it was shown in [51], the fractional Brownian motion (fBm) has a trivial spectrum. The partition function of the fBm is a straight line which indicates that its spectrum consists of one point, i.e., the behavior of its log-moments is identical for any q.

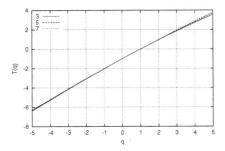
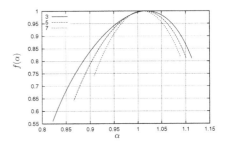

Fig. 9. Partition function estimated through the linear fits shown in Figure 7

Fig. 10. The Legendre transform of the partition function (Figure 9) results in the Legendre spectrum

Haar wavelet. Another way to carry out multiscale analysis is the Haar wavelet transform. The choice of using the *unnormalized* version of the Haar wavelet transform is motivated by the fact that it suits more the analysis of the Markovian point process introduced further on.

The multiscale behavior of the finite sequence $X_i, 1 \leq i \leq 2^L$ will be represented by the quantities $c_{j,k}, d_{j,k}, j = 0, \ldots, L$ and $k = 1, \ldots, 2^L/2^j$. The finest resolution is described by $c_{0,k}, 1 \leq k \leq 2^L$ which gives the finite sequence itself, i.e., $c_{0,k} = X_k$. Then the multiscale analysis based on the unnormalized Haar wavelet transform is carried out by iterating

$$c_{j,k} = c_{j-1,2k-1} + c_{j-1,2k}, \tag{8}$$

$$d_{j,k} = c_{j-1,2k-1} - c_{j-1,2k}, \tag{9}$$

for $j = 1, \ldots, L$ and $k = 1, \ldots, 2^L/2^j$. The quantities $c_{j,k}, d_{j,k}$ are the so-called scaling and wavelet coefficients of the sequence, respectively, at scale j and position k. At each scale the coefficients are represented by the vectors $c_j = [c_{j,k}]$ and $d_j = [d_{j,k}]$ with $k = 1, \ldots, 2^L/2^j$. For what concerns c_j, the higher j the lower the resolution level at which we have information on the sequence. The information that we lost as a result of the step from c_{j-1} to c_j, is conveyed by the sequence of wavelet coefficients d_j. It is easy to see that c_{j-1} can be perfectly reconstructed from c_j and d_j. As a consequence the whole $X_i, 1 \leq i \leq 2^L$ sequence can be constructed (in a top to bottom manner) based on a normalizing constant, $c_L = c_{L,1} = \sum_{i=1}^{2^L} X_i$, and the $d_j, j = 1, \ldots, L$ vectors.

By taking the expectation of the square of (8) and (9)

$$E[c_{j,k}^2] = E[c_{j-1,2k-1}^2] + 2E[c_{j-1,2k-1}c_{j-1,2k}] + E[c_{j-1,2k}^2], \tag{10}$$

$$E[d_{j,k}^2] = E[c_{j-1,2k-1}^2] - 2E[c_{j-1,2k-1}c_{j-1,2k}] + E[c_{j-1,2k}^2], \tag{11}$$

Let us assume that the series we analyze are stationary; then, by summing (10) and (11) and rearranging the equation, we have

$$E[c_{j-1}^2] = \frac{1}{4}\left(E[d_j^2] + E[c_j^2]\right). \tag{12}$$

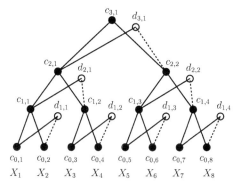

Fig. 11. Haar wavelet transform

Similarly, by consecutive application of (12) from one scale to another, the $E[d_j^2], j = 1, \ldots, L$ series completely characterize the variance decay of the $X_i, 1 \le i \le 2^L$ sequence apart of a normalizing constant ($c_L = c_{L,1} = \sum_{i=1}^{2^L} X_i$). This fact allows us to realize a series with a given variance decay if it is possible to control the 2nd moment of the scaling coefficient with the chosen synthesis procedure. In Section 5 we will briefly discuss a method that attempts to capture the multifractal scaling behavior via the series $E[d_j^2], j = 1, \ldots, L$.

4   Markovian Modeling Tools

Markovian modeling tools are stochastic processes whose stochastic behavior depends only on the state of a "background" Markov chain. The research and application of these modeling tools through the last 20 years resulted in a widely accepted standard notation. The two classes of Markovian processes considered in this paper are Phase type distributions and Markovian arrival processes. Here, we concentrate our attention mainly on continuous time Markovian models, but it is also possible to apply Markovian models in discrete time [33,5,27].

4.1   Phase Type Distribution

$Z(t)$ is a continuous time Markov chain with n transient state and one absorbing state. Its initial probability distribution is $\hat{\alpha}$ and generator matrix is $\hat{\mathbf{B}}$. The time to reach the absorbing state, T, phase type distributed with representation $\alpha, \mathbf{B}$, where α is the sub-vector of $\hat{\alpha}$ and $\mathbf{B}$ is the sub-matrix of $\hat{\mathbf{B}}$ associated with the transient states. The cumulative distribution function (cdf), the probability density function (pdf), and the moments of this distribution are:

$$F_T(t) = 1 - \alpha e^{\mathbf{B}t} h, \quad f_T(t) = \alpha \mathbf{B} e^{\mathbf{B}t} h, \quad E[X^i] = i! \, \alpha \, (-\mathbf{B})^{-i} h,$$

where h is the column vector of ones. The number of unknown in the $\alpha, \mathbf{B}$ representation of a PH distribution is $\mathcal{O}(n^2)$.

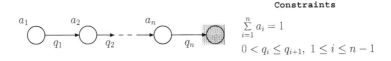

Fig. 12. Canonical form for Acyclic continuous-time PH distributions

When $Z(t)$ is an acyclic Markov chain the associated PH distribution is referred to as Acyclic PH (APH) distribution. The popularity of APH distributions (specially in PH fitting) lies in the fact that all APH distributions can be uniquely transformed into a canonical from (Figure 12) which has only $\mathcal{O}(n)$ parameters [10] and the flexibility of the PH and the APH class of the same order is very close. E.g., the 2nd order PH and APH classes exhibit the same moments bounds [50].

4.2   Markovian Arrival Process

Let $Z(t)$ be an irreducible Markov chain with finite state space of size m and generator $\mathbf{Q}$. An arrival process is associated with this Markov chain in the following way:

– while the Markov chain stays in state i arrival occurs at rate λ_i,
– when the Markov chain undergoes a state transition from i to j arrival occurs with probability p_{ij}.

The standard description of MAPs is given with matrices $\mathbf{D_0}$ and $\mathbf{D_1}$ of size $(m \times m)$, where $\mathbf{D_0}$ contains the transition rates of the Markov chain which are not accompanied with arrivals and $\mathbf{D_1}$ contains the transition rates which are accompanied with arrivals, i.e.:

– $\mathbf{D_0}_{ij} = (1 - p_{ij})\mathbf{Q}_{ij}$, for $i \neq j$ and $\mathbf{D_0}_{ii} = \mathbf{Q}_{ii} - \lambda_i$;
– $\mathbf{D_1}_{ij} = p_{ij}\mathbf{Q}_{ij}$ for, $i \neq j$ and $\mathbf{D_1}_{ii} = \lambda_i$.

Many familiar arrival processes represent special cases of MAPs:

– the Poisson process (MAP with a single state),
– interrupted Poisson process: a two-state MAP in which arrivals occur only in one of the states and state jumps do not cause arrival,
– Markov modulated Poisson process: state jumps do not give rise to arrivals.

The class of MAPs is closed for superposition and Markovian splitting.

5   Fitting Markovian Models to Datasets

Fitting a Markovian model to a measured dataset is to find a Markovian model which exhibits a stochastic behavior as close to the one of the measured dataset as possible. In practice, the order of approximate Markov models should kept low, both, for having few model parameters to evaluate and for obtaining computable models. The presence of slow decay behavior (heavy tail or long range correlation) in measured datasets makes the fitting more difficult. Typically a huge number of samples needed to obtain a fairly reliable view on the stochastic behavior over a range of several orders of magnitude, and, of course, the asymptotic behavior can not be checked based on finite datasets. A class of fitting methods approximates the asymptotic behavior based on the reliably known ranges (e.g., based on 10^6 i.i.d. samples the cdf. can be approximated up to the $1 - F(x) \sim 10^{-4} - 10^{-5}$ limit). The asymptotic methods are based on the assumption that the dominant parameters (e.g., tail decay, correlation decay) of the known ranges remain unchanged in the unknown region up to the asymptotic limit.

Unfortunately, Markovian models can not exhibit any complex asymptotic behavior. In the asymptotic region Markovian models have exponential tail decay or autocorrelation. Due to this dominant property Markovian models were not considered for fitting datasets with slow decaying features for a long time. Recently, in spite of the exponential asymptotic decay behavior, Markovian models with slow decay behavior for several orders of magnitude were introduced. These results broaden the attention from asymptotically slow decay models to models with slow decay in given predefined range. The main focus of this paper is on the use of Markovian models with slow decay behavior in applied traffic engineering.

A finite dataset provides only a limited information about the stochastic properties of traffic processes. Especially, the long range and the asymptotic behavior cannot be extracted from finite dataset. To overcome the lack of these important model properties the set of information provided by the dataset is often accompanied by engineering assumptions in practice. One of the most commonly applied traffic engineering assumptions is that the decay trends of a known region continuous to infinity.

The use of engineering assumptions has a significant role in model fitting as well. With this respect there are two major classes of fitting methods:

- fitting based on al the samples,
- fitting based on information extracted from the samples,

Naturally, there are methods which combines these two approaches.

The fitting methods based on extracted information find their roots in traffic engineering assumptions. It is a common goal in traffic engineering to find a simple (characterized by few parameters), but robust (widely applicable) traffic model which is based on few representative traffic parameters of network traffic. The traffic models discussed in Section 2 are completely characterized by very few parameters. E.g., the tail behavior of a power tail distribution is characterized by the heavy tail index α, fractional Gaussian noise is characterized by parameter H and the variance over a natural time unit. Assuming that there is representative information of the dataset, it is worth to complete the model fitting based on this compact description of the traffic properties instead of using all the very large dataset. Unfortunately, a commonly accepted, accurate and compact traffic characterization is not available up to now. This way, when the fitting is based on extracted information, the goodness of fitting strongly depend on the descriptive power of the selected characteristics to be fitted.

In this section we introduce a selected set of fitting methods from both classes. The fitting methods that are based on extracted information are composed by two mains steps: the statistical analysis of the dataset to extract representative properties and the fitting itself based on these properties. The first step of this procedure is based on the methods presented in the previous section, and only the second step is considered here.

5.1   PH Fitting

General PH fitting methods minimizes a *distance measure* between the experimental distribution and the approximate PH one. The most commonly applied distance measure is the relative entropy: $\int_0^\infty f(t) \ \log \left(\dfrac{f(t)}{\hat{f}(t)} \right) \ dt$ where $f(t)$ and $\hat{f}(t)$ denote the pdf of the distribution to be fitted and that of the fitting distribution, respectively. The number of parameters to minimize in this procedure depends on the order of the approximate PH model. The required order of PH models can be approximated based on the dataset [48], but usually small models are preferred in practice for computational convenience. It is a common feature of the relative entropy and other distance measures that the distance is a non-linear function of the PH parameters.

General PH fitting methods might perform poorly in fitting slow decaying tail behavior [22]. As an alternative, heuristic fitting procedures can be applied that focus on capturing the tail decay behavior. In case of heuristic fitting methods, the goal is not to minimize a properly defined distance measure, but to construct a PH distribution which fulfills a set of heuristic requirements.

According to the above classification of fitting procedures general fitting methods commonly belong to the *fitting based on samples* class and heuristic fitting methods to the *fitting to extracted model properties* class.

The literature of general PH fitting methods is quite large. A set of methods with a comparison of their fitting properties are presented in [26]. Here we consider only those methods which were applied for fitting slowly decaying behavior in [11] and [22]. Among the heuristic methods we discuss the one proposed in [14] and its extension in [22].

EM method. The *expectation maximization* (EM) method was proposed to apply for PH fitting in [2]. It is a statistical method which performs an iterative optimization over the space of the PH parameters to minimize the relative entropy. It differs from other relative entropy minimizing methods in the way it searches for the minimum of the non-linear distance measure. Based on the fact that hyper-exponential distributions can capture slow decay behavior ([14]), a specialized version of the EM algorithm, which fits the dataset with hyper-exponential distributions, is applied for fitting measured traffic datasets in [11].

Starting from an initial guess $\alpha^{(0)}$, $\lambda^{(0)}$ and denoting the pdf of the hyper-exponential distribution with initial probability vector α and intensity vector λ by $\hat{f}(t|\alpha, \lambda)$, the iterative procedure calculates consecutive hyper-exponential distributions based on the samples $t_1, \ldots, t_N$ as:

$$\alpha_i^{(k+1)} = \frac{1}{N} \sum_{n=1}^{N} \frac{\alpha_i^{(k)} \hat{f}(t_n|e_i, \lambda^{(k)})}{\hat{f}(t_n|\alpha^{(k)}, \lambda^{(k)})}, \quad \alpha_i^{(k+1)} = \frac{\dfrac{1}{N} \sum_{n=1}^{N} \dfrac{\alpha_i^{(k)} \hat{f}(t_n|e_i, \lambda^{(k)})}{\hat{f}(t_n|\alpha^{(k)}, \lambda^{(k)})}}{\dfrac{1}{N} \sum_{n=1}^{N} t_n \dfrac{\alpha_i^{(k)} \hat{f}(t_n|e_i, \lambda^{(k)})}{\hat{f}(t_n|\alpha^{(k)}, \lambda^{(k)})}}$$

where e_i is the vector of zeros with a one at the ith position.

The computational complexity of this simplified method using hyper-exponential distributions is much less than the one for the whole PH class. Nevertheless, a reliable view on the (slow decaying) tail behavior requires very large number of samples. The complexity of the simplified fitting method is still proportional to the size of the dataset, hence the applicability of this approach is limited by computational complexity ($\sim 10^7$ samples were reported in [11]). On the other hand, due to the strict structure of hyper-exponential distributions (e.g., there is no fork in the structure), less iterations are required to reach a reasonable accuracy ($5 - 10$ iterations were found to be sufficient in [11]).

This simplified EM fitting method is a potential choice for model fitting when we have a large dataset, but we do not have or do not want to apply any engineering assumption on the properties of the dataset.

Tail fitting based on the ccdf. The method proposed by Feldmann and Whitt [14] is a recursive fitting procedure that results in a hyper-exponential distribution whose cumulative distribution function (ccdf) at a given set of points is "very close" to the ccdf of the original distribution. This method was successfully applied to fit Pareto and Weibull distributions.

Combined fitting method. In [22] a PH fitting method is proposed that handles the fitting of the body and the fitting of the tail in a separate manner. This is done by combining the method proposed by Feldmann and Whitt [14] and a general method to.

The limitation of this combined method comes from the limitation of the method of Feldmann and Whitt. Their method is applicable only for fitting distributions with monotone decreasing density function. Hence the proposed combined method is applicable when the tail of the distribution is with monotone decreasing density. In the case of the combined method, this restriction is quite loose since the border of the main part and the tail of the distribution is arbitrary, hence the restriction of applicability is to have a positive number C such that the density of the distribution is monotone decreasing above C.

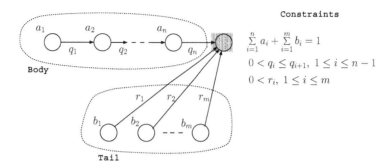

Fig. 13. Structure of approximate Phase type distribution

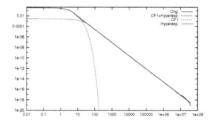

Fig. 14. Different parts of the pdf are approximated by different parts of the PH structure

The result of this fitting algorithm is a Phase type distribution of order $n+m$, where n is the number of phases used for fitting the body and m is the number of phases used for fitting the tail. The structure of this Phase type distribution is depicted in Figure 13 where we have marked the phases used to fit the body and those to fit the tail. The parameters $\beta_1, \ldots, \beta_m, \mu_1, \ldots, \mu_m$ are computed by considering the tail while the parameters $\alpha_1, \ldots, \alpha_m, \lambda_1, \ldots, \lambda_2$ are determined considering the main part of the distribution.

To illustrate the combined fitting method, we consider the following Pareto-like distributions [45]:

$$\text{Pareto I:} \quad f(t) = \begin{cases} \alpha B^{-1} e^{-\frac{\alpha}{B} t} & \text{for } t \leq B \\ \alpha B^\alpha e^{-\alpha} t^{-(\alpha+1)} & \text{for } t > B \end{cases}$$

$$\text{Pareto II:} \quad f(t) = \frac{b^\alpha e^{-b/t}}{\Gamma(\alpha)} x^{-(\alpha+1)}$$

For both ditributions α is the heavy tail index.

Figure 14 pictures how different parts of the PH structure (Figure 13) contributes to the pdf when fitting distribution Pareto I with parameters $\alpha = 1.5, B = 4$. In this case 8 phases are used to fit the body and 10 to fit the tail.

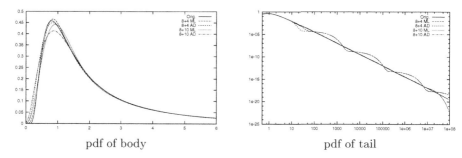

pdf of body   pdf of tail

Fig. 15. Pareto II distribution and its PH approximation with the combined method

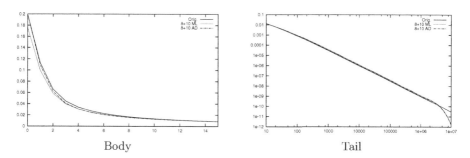

Body   Tail

Fig. 16. Queue length distribution of an M/G/1 queue and its approximate M/PH/1 queue

Figure 15 illustrates the fitting of distribution Pareto II with parameters $\alpha = 1.5, b = 2$. In the legend of the figure ML indicates that the relative entropy measure was applied to fit the main part (corresponding to the maximum likelihood principle), while AD stands for area difference of the pdf. Still in the legend, X+Y means that X phases was used to fit the body, while Y to fit the tail. Figures 16 shows the effect of Phase type fitting on the M/G/1 queue behaviour with Pareto II service (utilization is 0.8). Exact result of the M/G/1 queue was computed with the method of [45].

At this point we take detour to discrete-time models. Discrete-time counterpart of the fitting method, i.e. when discrete-time PH distributions are applied, is given in [24]. We apply discrete PH distributions to fit the EPA trace. The ccdf of the body and the tail of the resulting discrete PH distribution are shown in Figure 17 and 18. In Figure 18 we depicted the polynomial fit of the tail behaviour as well.

5.2 MAP Fitting Based on Samples

Similarly to the case of PH fitting, MAP fitting methods can be classified as general and heuristic ones. General methods utilize directly the data samples, and hence they do not require any additional engineering knowledge. Our numerical experiences show that MAP fitting is a far more difficult task than PH fitting.

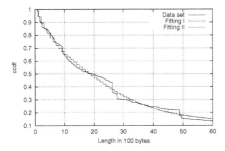
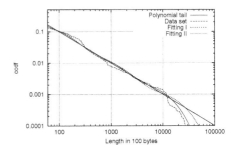

Fig. 17. Body of the approximating distributions

Fig. 18. Tail of the approximating distributions

A simple explanation is that fitting a process is more difficult than fittign a distribution. Capturing slow decaying behaviour with general MAP fitting seems impossible.

Anyhow, there are numerical methods available for fitting low order MAPs directly to datasets. In [32,15,46] a fitting method based on maximum likelihood estimate is presented, and in [47] the EM method is used for maximizing the likelihood estimate.

Simple numerical tests (like taking a MAP, drawing samples from it, and fitting a MAP of the same order to these samples) often fail for MAPs of higher order (≥ 3) and the accuracy of the method does not necessarily improve with increasing number of samples.

5.3   Heuristic MAP Fitting

An alternative to general MAP fitting is to extract a set of (hopefully) dominant properties of the traffic process from the dataset and to create a MAP (of particular structure) that exhibits the same properties. This kind of heuristic methods fail to satisfy the above mentioned "self test" by their nature, but if the selected set of parameters are really dominant with respect to the goal of the analysis we can achieve "sufficient" fitting. [19] proposed to fit the following parameters: mean arrival rate, variance to mean ratio of arrivals in $(0, t)$, and its asymptotic limit. After the notion of long range dependence in traffic processes the Hurst parameter was added to this list. The following subsections introduces heuristic fitting methods with various properties to capture and various fitting MAP structures.

MAP structures approximating long range dependent behaviour. An intuitive way to provide long range dependent behaviour for several time scales with Markovian models is to compose a combined model from small pieces each of which represents the model behaviour at a selected range of the time scales. One of the first models of this kind was proposed in [44]. The same approach was applied for traffic fitting in [38], but recently this approach is criticized in [12]. Renewal processes with heavy tailed interarrival times also exhibit self-similar properties. Using this fact the approximate heavy tailed PH distributions can be used to create a MAP with PH renewal process. In [1] superposition of 2 state MMPPs are used for approximating 2nd order self-similarity. The proposed procedure fits the mean arrival rate, the 1-lag correlation, the Hurst parameter and the required range of fitting.

Fitting based on separate handling of long- and short-range dependent behavior. In [21] a procedure is given to construct a MAP such a way that some parameters of the traffic generated by the model match predefined values. The following parameters are set:

- The fundamental arrival rate describes the expected number of arrivals in a time unit.
- In order to describe the burstiness of the arrival stream, the index of dispersion for counts $I(t) = \mathrm{Var}(N_t)/E(N_t)$ is set for two different values of time: $I(t_1)$ and $I(t_2)$. The choice of these two time points significantly affects the goodness of fitting.
- A higher order descriptor, the third centralized moment of the number of arrivals in the interval $(0, t_3)$, $M(t_3) = E[(N_{t_3} - E(N_{t_3}))^3]$ is set.
- The degree of *pseudo* self-similarity is defined by the Hurst parameter H. The Hurst parameter is realized in terms of the variance-time behavior of the resulting traffic, i.e., the straight line fitted by regression to the variance-time curve in a predefined interval has slope $2(H - 1)$.

The MAP resulting from the procedure is the superposition of a PH arrival process and a two-state MMPP. In the following we sketch how to construct a PH arrival process with *pseudo* self-similar behavior and describe the superposition of this PH arrival process with a two-state MMPP. Detailed description of the procedure is given in [21].

Let us consider an arrival process whose interarrival times are independent random variables with heavy tail probability density function (pdf) of Pareto type

$$f(x) = \frac{c \cdot a^c}{(x + a)^{c+1}}, \quad x \geq 0. \tag{13}$$

The process X_n ($n > 0$) representing the number of arrivals in the nth time-slot is asymptotically second-order self-similar with Hurst parameter $H = (3 - c)/2$ ([49]).

Using the method of Feldman and Whitt [14] one may build an arrival process whose interarrival times are independent, identically distributed PH random variables with pdf approximating (13). To check *pseudo* self-similarity of this PH renewal processes Figure 19 plots $Var(X^{(m)})$ of PH arrival processes whose interarrival time is a 6 phase PH approximation of the pdf given in (13) for different values of c. As it can be observed $Var(X^{(m)})$ is close through several orders of magnitude to the straight line corresponding to the self-similar case with slope $2(H-1)$. The aggregation level where $Var(X^{(m)})$ drops compared to the straight line may be increased by changing the parameters of the PH fitting algorithm.

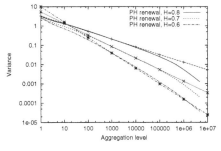

Fig. 19. Variance-time plot of *pseudo* self-similar arrival processes with i.i.d. PH interarrival

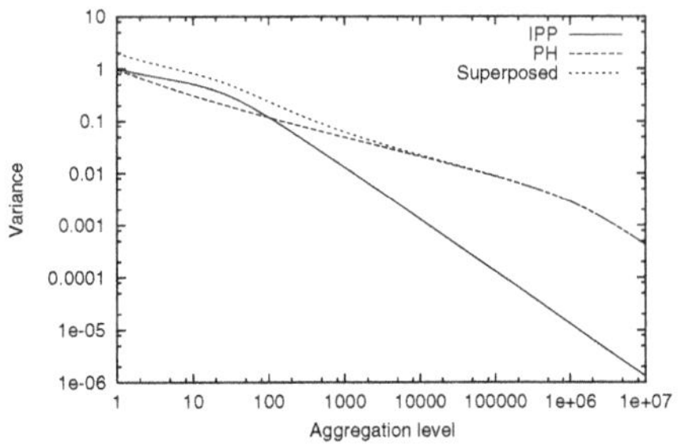

Fig. 20. Superposition of the PH arrival process with an MMPP

The parameters of the two-state MMPP with which the PH arrival process is superposed are calculated in two steps:

1. At first we calculate the parameters of an Interrupted Poisson Process (IPP). The IPP is a two-state MMPP that has one of its two arrival rates equal to 0. The calculated parameters of the IPP are such that the superposition of the PH arrival process and the IPP results in a traffic source with the desired first and second order parameters $E(N_1)$, $I(t_1)$ and $I(t_2)$.
2. In the second step, based on the IPP we find a two-state MMPP that has the same first and second order properties as the IPP has (recalling results from [4]), and with which the superposition results in the desired third centralized moment.

If the MMPP is "less long-range dependent" than the PH arrival process, the *pseudo* self-similarity of the superposed traffic model will be dominated by the PH arrival process. This fact is depicted in Figure 20. It can be observed that if the Hurst parameter is estimated based on the variance-time plot the Hurst parameter of the superposed model is only slightly smaller than the Hurst parameter of the PH arrival process. In numbers, the Hurst parameter of the PH arrival process is 0.8 while it is 0.78 for the superposed model (based on the slope in the interval $(10, 10^6)$). This behavior is utilized in the fitting method to approximate the short and long range behavior in a separate manner.

We illustrate the procedure by fitting the Bellcore trace. Variance-time plots of the traffic generated by the MAPs resulted from the fitting are depicted in Figure 21. The curve signed by (x_1, x_2) belongs to the fitting when the first (second) time point of fitting the IDC value, t_1 (t_2), is x_1 (x_2) times the expected interarrival time. R/S plots for both the real traffic trace and the traffic generated by the approximating MAPs are given in Figure 22. The fitting of the traces

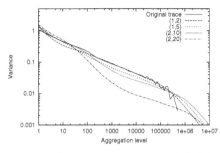

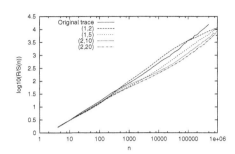

Fig. 21. Variance-time plots of MAPs with different time points of IDC matching

Fig. 22. R/S plots of MAPs with different time points of IDC matching

were tested by a •/D/1 queue, as well. The results are depicted in Figure 23. The •/D/1 queue was analyzed by simulation with different levels of utilization of the server. As one may observe the lower t_1 and t_2 the longer the queue length distribution follows the original one.

The fitting method provides a MAP whose some parameters are the same as those of the original traffic process (or very close). Still, the queue length distribution does not show a good match. This means that the chosen parameters do not capture all the important characteristics of the traffic trace.

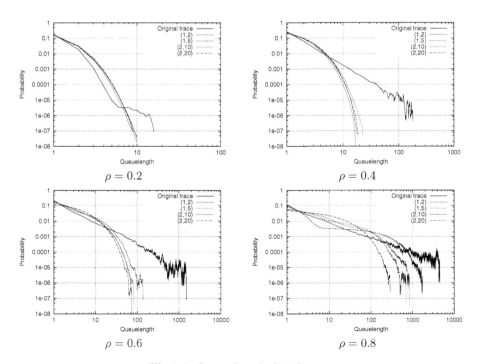

Fig. 23. Queue-length distribution

MMPP Exhibiting Multifractal Behavior. In [23] a special MMPP structure is proposed to exhibit multifractal behavior. The background CTMC of the MMPP has a symmetric n-dimensional cube structure and the arrival intensities are set according to the variation of the arrival process at the different time scales. The special choice of the structure is motivated by the generation of the Haar wavelet transform. Basically the Haar wavelet transform evaluates the variation of the dataset at different aggregation levels (time scales), and similarly, the proposed MMPP structure provide different variation of the arrival rate at different time scales.

The composition of the proposed MMPP structure is similar to the generation of the Haar wavelet transform (a procedure for traffic trace generation based on this transform is introduced in [43]). Without loss of generality, we assume that the time unit is such that the long term arrival intensity is one. A MMPP of one state with arrival rate 1 represents the arrival process at the largest (considered) time scale.

At the next time scale, $1/\lambda$, an MMPP of two states with generator

$$\begin{array}{|cc|} \hline -\lambda & \lambda \\ \lambda & -\lambda \\ \hline \end{array}$$

and with arrival rates $1 - a_1$ and $1 + a_1$ $(-1 \leq a_1 \leq 1)$ represents the variation of the arrival process. This composition leaves the long term average arrival rate unchanged.

In the rest of the composition we perform the same step. We introduce a new dimension and generate the n-dimensional cube such that the behavior at the already set time scales remains unchanged. E.g., considering also the $1/\gamma\lambda$ time scale an MMPP of four states with generator

$$\begin{array}{|cc|cc|} \hline \bullet & \lambda & \gamma\lambda & \\ \lambda & \bullet & & \gamma\lambda \\ \hline \gamma\lambda & & \bullet & \lambda \\ & \gamma\lambda & \lambda & \bullet \\ \hline \end{array}$$

and with arrival rates $(1-a_1)(1-a_2)$, $(1+a_1)(1-a_2)$, $(1-a_1)(1+a_2)$ and $(1+a_1)(1+a_2)$ $(-1 \leq a_1, a_2 \leq 1)$ represents the variation of the arrival process. With this MMPP, parameter a_1 (a_2) determines the variance of the arrival process at the $1/\lambda$ $(1/\gamma\lambda)$ time scale. If γ is large enough $(>\sim 30)$ the process behavior at the $1/\lambda$ time scale is independent of a_2. The proposed model is also applicable with a small γ. In this case, the only difference is that the model parameters and the process behavior of different time scales are dependent.

A level n MMPP of the proposed structure is composed by 2^n states and it has $n + 2$ parameters. Parameters γ and λ defines the considered time scales, and parameters $a_1, a_2, \ldots, a_n$ determines the variance of the arrival process at the n considered time scales. It can be seen that the ratio of the largest and the smallest considered time scales is γ^n. Having a fixed n (i.e., a fixed cardinality of the MMPP), any large ratio of the largest and the smallest considered time scales can be captured by using a sufficiently large γ.

A simple numerical procedure can be applied to fit a MMPP of the given structure to a measured dataset. This heuristic approach is composed by "engineering considerations" based on the properties of the measured dataset and a parameter fitting method.

First, we fix the value of n. According to our experience a "visible" multiscaling behavior can be obtained from $n = 3 \sim 4$. The computational complexity of the fitting procedure grows exponentially with the dimension of the MMPP. The response time with $n = 6$ (MMPP of 64 states) is still acceptable (in the order of minutes).

Similarly to [43], we set γ and the λ based on the inspection of the dataset. Practically, we define the largest, T_M, and the smallest, T_m, considered time scales and calculate γ and λ from

$$T_M = \frac{1}{\lambda} \; ; \quad T_m = \frac{1}{\gamma^n \lambda}.$$

The extreme values of T_M and T_m can be set based on simple practical considerations. For example when the measured dataset is composed by N arrival instances, T_M can be chosen to be less than the mean time of $N/4$ arrivals, and T_m can be chosen to be greater than the mean time of 4 arrivals. A similar approach was applied in [43]. These boundary values can be refined based on a detailed statistical test of the dataset. E.g., if the scaling behavior disappears beyond a given time scale, T_M can be set to that value.

Having γ and λ, we apply a downhill simplex method to find the optimal values of the variability parameters $a_1, a_2, \ldots, a_n$. The goal function that our parameter fitting method minimizes is the sum of the relative errors of the second moment of Haar wavelet coefficients up to a predefined time scale S:

$$\min_{a_1, \ldots, a_n} \sum_{j=1}^{S} \frac{|E(d_j^2) - E(\hat{d}_j^2)|}{E(d_j^2)} \; .$$

The goal function can be calculated analytically as it is described in [23].

Application of the fitting procedure is illustrated on the Bellcore trace. We applied the fitting method with $n = 5$ and several different predefined setting of γ, λ. We found that the goodness of the fitting is not very sensitive to the predefined parameters around a reasonable region. The best "looking" fit is obtained when T_m is the mean time of 16 arrivals and $\gamma = 8$. In this case T_M is the mean time of $16*8^5 = 2^{19}$ arrivals which corresponds to the coarsest time scale we can analyze in the case of the Bellcore trace. The simplex method minimizing the sum of the relative error of the second moments of the Haar wavelet coefficients over $S = 12$ time scales resulted in: $a_1 = 0.144, a_2 = 0.184, a_3 = 0.184, a_4 = 0.306, a_5 = 0.687$. The result of fitting the second moment of the Haar wavelet transform at different aggregation levels is plotted in Figure 24. At small time scales the fitting seems to be perfect, while at larger time scales the error enlarges. The slope of the curves are almost equal in the depicted range.

The multiscaling behavior of the obtained MAP and of the original dataset are illustrated via the log-moment curves in Figure 25. In the figure, the symbols

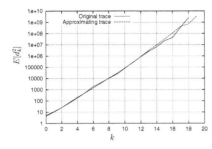

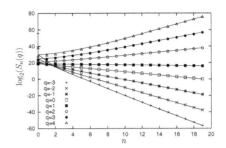

Fig. 24. The second moment of the Haar wavelet transform at different aggregation levels

Fig. 25. Scaling of log-moments of the original trace and the fitting MMPP

represent the log-moment curves of the fitting MAP and the solid lines indicate the corresponding log-moment curves of the Bellcore trace. In the range of $n \in (3, 19)$ the log-moment curves of the fitting MAP are very close to the ones of the original trace. The log-moment curves of the approximate MAP are also very close to linear in the considered range.

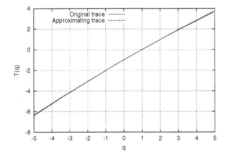

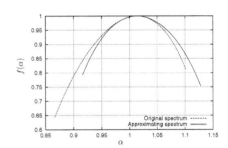

Fig. 26. Partition function estimated through the linear fits shown in Figure 25

Fig. 27. The Legendre transform of the original dataset and the one of the approximate MMPP

The partition functions of the fitting MAP and of the original trace are depicted in Figure 26. As it was mentioned earlier, the visual appearance of the partition function is not very informative about the multifractal scaling behavior. Figure 27 depicts the Legendre transform of the partition functions of the original dataset and the approximating MAP. The visual appearance of the Legendre transform significantly amplifies the differences of the partition functions. In Figure 27, it can be seen that both processes exhibit multifractal behavior but the original dataset has a bit richer multifractal spectrum.

We also compared the queuing behavior of the original dataset with that of the approximate MAP assuming deterministic service time and different levels of utilization, ρ. Figure 28 depicts the queue length distribution resulting from the

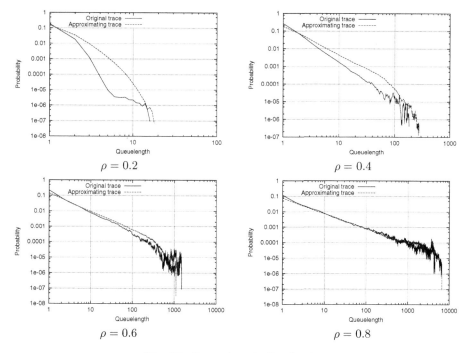

Fig. 28. Queue-length distribution

original and the approximate arrival processes. The queue length distribution curves show a quite close fit. The probability of an empty queue, which is not displayed in the figures, is the same for the MAP as for the original trace since the MAP has the same average arrival intensity as the original trace. The fit is better with a higher queue utilization, which might mean that different scaling behaviors play a dominant rule at different utilizations, and the ones that are dominant at high utilization are better approximated by the proposed MAP.

6   Conclusions

This paper collects a set of methods which can be used in practice for measurement based traffic engineering. The history of traffic theory of high speed communication networks is summarized together with a short introduction to the mathematical foundation of the applied concepts. The common statistical methods for the analysis of data traces and the practical problems of their application is discussed.

The use of Markovian methods is motivated by the fact that an effective analysis technique, the matrix geometric method, is available for the evaluation of Markovian queuing systems. To obtain the Markovian approximation of measured traffic data a variety of heuristic fitting methods are applied. The properties and abilities of these methods are also discussed.

The presented numerical examples provide insight to the qualitative understanding of the strange traffic properties of high speed networks.

References

1. A. T. Andersen and B. F. Nielsen. A markovian approach for modeling packet
   traffic with long-range dependence. *IEEE Journal on Selected Areas in Communications*, 16(5):719–732, 1998.
2. S. Asmussen and O. Nerman. Fitting Phase-type distributions via the EM algorithm. In *Proceedings: "Symposium i Advent Statistik"*, pages 335–346, Copen-
   hagen, 1991.
3. J. Beran. *Statistics for long-memory processes*. Chapman and Hall, New York,
   1994.
4. A. W. Berger. On the index of dispersion for counts for user demand modeling. In
   ITU, Madrid, Spain, June 1994. Study Group 2, Question 17/2.
5. A. Bobbio, A. Horváth, M. Scarpa, and M. Telek. Acyclic discrete phase type
   distributions: Properties and a parameter estimation algorithm. submitted to Performance Evaluation, 2000.
6. S. C. Borst, O. J. Boxma, and R. Nunez-Queija. Heavy tails: The effect of the service discipline. In *Tools 2002*, pages 1–30, London, England, April 2002. Springer,
   LNCS 2324.
7. G. E. P. Box, G. M Jenkins, and C. Reinsel. *Time Series Analysis: Forecasting
   and Control*. Prentice Hall, Englewood Cliff, N.J., third edition, 1994.
8. E. Castillo. *Extreme Value Theory in Engineering*. Academic Press, San Diego,
   California, 1988.
9. M. E. Crovella and M. S. Taqqu. Estimating the heavy tail index from scaling
   properties. *Methodology and Computing in Applied Probability*, 1(1):55–79, 1999.
10. A. Cumani. On the canonical representation of homogeneous Markov processes
    modelling failure-time distributions. *Microelectronics and Reliability*, 22:583–602,
    1982.
11. R. El Abdouni Khayari, R. Sadre, and B. Haverkort. Fitting world-wide web
    request traces with the EM-algorithm. In *Proc. of SPIE*, volume 4523, pages 211–
    220, Denver, USA, 2001.
12. R. El Abdouni Khayari, R. Sadre, and B. Haverkort. A valiadation of the pseudo
    self-similar traffic model. In *Proc. of IPDS*, Washington D.C., USA, 2002.
13. A. Feldman, A. C. Gilbert, and W. Willinger. Data networks as cascades: Investi-
    gating the multifractal nature of internet WAN traffic. *Computer communication
    review*, 28/4:42–55, 1998.
14. A. Feldman and W. Whitt. Fitting mixtures of exponentials to long-tail distribu-
    tions to analyze network performance models. *Performance Evaluation*, 31:245–
    279, 1998.
15. W. Fischer and K. Meier-Hellstern. The Markov-modulated Poisson process
    (MMPP) cookbook. *Performance Evaluation*, 18:149–171, 1992.
16. H. J. Fowler and W. E. Leland. Local area network traffic characteristics, with im-
    plications for broadband network congestion management. *IEEE JSAC*, 9(7):1139–
    1149, 1991.
17. R. Fox and M. S. Taqqu. Large sample properties of parameter estimates for
    strongly dependent stationary time series. *The Annals of Statistics*, 14:517–532,
    1986.

18. C. W. J. Granger and R. Joyeux. An introduction to long-memory time series and fractional differencing. *Journal of Time Series Analysis*, 1:15–30, 1980.

19. H. Heffes and D. M. Lucantoni. A Markov-modulated characterization of packetized voice and data traffic and related statistical multiplexer performance. *IEEE Journal on Selected Areas in Communications*, 4(6):856–868, 1986.

20. B. M. Hill. A simple general approach to inference about the tail of a distribution. *The Annals of Statistics*, 3:1163–1174, 1975.

21. A. Horváth, G. I. Rózsa, and M. Telek. A map fitting method to approximate real traffic behaviour. In *8th IFIP Workshop on Performance Modelling and Evaluation of ATM & IP Networks*, pages 32/1–12, Ilkley, England, July 2000.

22. A. Horváth and M. Telek. Approximating heavy tailed behavior with phase type distributions. In *3rd International Conference on Matrix-Analytic Methods in Stochastic models*, Leuven, Belgium, 2000.

23. A Horváth and M. Telek. A markovian point process exhibiting multifractal behaviour and its application to traffic modeling. In *Proc. of MAM4*, Adelaide, Australia, 2002.

24. A. Horváth and M. Telek. Phfit: A general phase-type fitting tool. In *Proc. of 12th Performance TOOLS*, volume 2324 of *Lecture Notes in Computer Science*, pages 82–91, Imperial College, London, April 2002.

25. M. Kratz and S. Resnick. The qq–estimator and heavy tails. *Stochastic Models*, 12:699–724, 1996.

26. A. Lang and J. L. Arthur. Parameter approximation for phase-type distributions. In S. R. Chakravarty and A. S. Alfa, editors, *Matrix-analytic methods in stochastic models*, Lecture notes in pure and applied mathematics, pages 151–206. Marcel Dekker, Inc., 1996.

27. G. Latouche and V. Ramaswami. *Introduction to Matrix-Analytic Methods in Stochastic Modeling*. Series on statistics and applied probability. ASA-SIAM, 1999.

28. W. E. Leland, M. Taqqu, W. Willinger, and D. V. Wilson. On the self-similar nature of ethernet traffic (extended version). *IEEE/ACM Transactions in Networking*, 2:1–15, 1994.

29. D. M. Lucantoni. New results on the single server queue with a batch Markovian arrival process. *Commun. Statist.-Stochastic Models*, 7(1):1–46, 1991.

30. B. B. Mandelbrot and J. W. Van Ness. Fractional Brownian motions, fractional noises and applications. *SIAM Review*, 10:422–437, 1969.

31. B. B. Mandelbrot and M. S. Taqqu. Robust R/S analysis of long-run serial correlation. In *Proceedings of the 42nd Session of the International Statistical Institute*, volume 48, Book 2, pages 69–104, Manila, 1979. Bulletin of the I.S.I.

32. K.S. Meier. A fitting algorithm for Markov-modulated Poisson processes having two arrival rates. *European Journal of Operations Research*, 29:370–377, 1987.

33. M. Neuts. Probability distributions of phase type. In *Liber Amicorum Prof. Emeritus H. Florin*, pages 173–206. University of Louvain, 1975.

34. M.F. Neuts. *Matrix Geometric Solutions in Stochastic Models*. Johns Hopkins University Press, Baltimore, 1981.

35. M.F. Neuts. *Structured stochastic matrices of M/G/1 type and their applications*. Marcel Dekker, 1989.

36. I. Norros. A storage model with self-similar imput. *Queueing Systems*, 16:387–396, 1994.

37. I. Norros. On the use of fractional brownian motion in the theorem of connectionless networks. *IEEE Journal on Selected Areas in Communications*, 13:953–962, 1995.

38. A. Ost and B. Haverkort. Modeling and evaluation of pseudo self-similar traffic with infinite-state stochastic petri nets. In *Proc. of the Workshop on Formal Methods in Telecommunications*, pages 120–136, Zaragoza, Spain, 1999.
39. S. Resnick. Heavy tail modeling and teletraffic data. *The Annals of Statistics*, 25:1805–1869, 1997.
40. S. Resnick and C. Starica. Smoothing the hill estimator. *Advances in Applied Probability*, 29:271–293, 1997.
41. J. Rice. *Mathematical Statistics and Data Analysis*. Brooks/Cole Publishing, Pacific Grove, California, 1988.
42. R. H. Riedi. An introduction to multifractals. Technical report, Rice University, 1997. Available at http://www.ece.rice.edu/~riedi.
43. R. H. Riedi, M. S. Crouse, V. J. Ribeiro, and R. G. Baraniuk. A multifractal wavelet model with application to network traffic. *IEEE Transactions on Information Theory*, 45:992–1018, April 1999.
44. S. Robert and J.-Y. Le Boudec. New models for pseudo self-similar traffic. *Performance Evaluation*, 30:1997, 57-68.
45. M. Roughan, D. Veitch, and M. Rumsewicz. Numerical inversion of probability generating functions of power-law tail queues. tech. report, 1997.
46. T. Rydén. Parameter estimation for Markov Modulated Poisson Processes. *Stochastic Models*, 10(4):795–829, 1994.
47. T. Ryden. An EM algorithm for estimation in Markov modulated Poisson processes. *Computational statist. and data analysis*, 21:431–447, 1996.
48. T. Rydén. Estimating the order of continuous phase-type distributions and markov-modulated poisson processes. *Stochastic Models*, 13:417–433, 1997.
49. B. Ryu and S. B. Lowen. Point process models for self-similar network traffic, with applications. *Stochastic models*, 14, 1998.
50. M. Telek and A. Heindl. Moment bounds for acyclic discrete and continuous phase-type distributions of second order. In *in proc. of Eighteenth Annual UK Performance Engineering Workshop (UKPEW)*, Glasgow, UK, 2002.
51. J. Lévy Véhel and R. H. Riedi. Fractional brownian motion and data traffic modeling: The other end of the spectrum. In C. Tricot J. Lévy Véhel, E. Lutton, editor, *Fractals in Engineering*, pages 185–202. Springer, 1997.
52. The internet traffic archive. http://ita.ee.lbl.gov/index.html.

Optimization of Bandwidth and Energy Consumption in Wireless Local Area Networks

Marco Conti and Enrico Gregori

Consiglio Nazionale delle Ricerche
IIT Institute, Via G. Moruzzi, 1
56124 Pisa, Italy
{marco.conti, enrico.gregori}@iit.cnr.it

Abstract. In the recent years the proliferation of portable computers, handheld digital devices, and PDAs has led to a rapid growth in the use of wireless technologies for the Local Area Network (LAN) environment. Beyond supporting wireless connectivity for fixed, portable and moving stations within a local area, the wireless LAN (WLAN) technologies can provide a mobile and ubiquitous connection to the Internet information services. The design of WLANs has to concentrate on bandwidth consumption because wireless networks deliver much lower bandwidth than wired networks, e.g., 2-11 Mbps [1] versus 10-150 Mbps [2]. In addition, the finite battery power of mobile computers represents one of the greatest limitations to the utility of portable computers [3], [4]. Hence, a relevant performance-optimization problem is the balancing between the minimization of battery consumption, and the maximization of the channel utilization. In this paper, we study bandwidth and energy consumption of the IEEE 802.11 standard, i.e., the most mature technology for WLANs. Specifically, we derived analytical formulas that relate the protocol parameters to the maximum throughput and to the minimal energy consumption. These formulas are used to define an effective method for tuning at run time the protocol parameters.

1 Introduction

In IEEE802.11 WLANs [1], the Medium Access Control (MAC) protocol is the main element that determines the efficiency in sharing the limited resources of the wireless channel. The MAC protocol coordinates the transmissions of the network stations and, at the same time, manages the congestion situations that may occur inside the network. The congestion level in the network negatively affects both the channel utilization (i.e. the fraction of channel bandwidth used from successfully transmitted messages), and the energy consumed to successfully transmit a message. Specifically, each collision reduces the channel bandwidth and the battery capacity available for successful transmissions. To decrease the collision probability, the IEEE 802.11 protocol uses a CSMA/CA protocol based on a truncated binary exponential backoff scheme that doubles the backoff window after each collision [1], [2]. However, the

M.C. Calzarossa and S. Tucci (Eds.): Performance 2002, LNCS 2459, pp. 435–462, 2002.
© Springer-Verlag Berlin Heidelberg 2002

time spreading of the accesses that the standard backoff procedure accomplishes has a negative impact on both the channel utilization, and the energy consumption. Specifically, the time spreading of the accesses can introduce large delays in the message transmissions, and energy wastages due to the carrier sensing. Furthermore, the IEEE 802.11 policy has to pay the cost of collisions to increase the backoff time when the network is congested.

In [5], [6] and [7], given the binary exponential backoff scheme adopted by the standard, solutions have been proposed for a better uniform distribution of accesses. The most promising direction for improving the backoff protocols is to adopt feedback-based tuning algorithms that exploit the information retrieved from the observation of the channel status [8], [9], [10]. For the IEEE 802.11 MAC protocol, some authors have proposed an adaptive control of the network congestion by investigating the number of users in the system [11], [12], [13]. This investigation could result expensive, difficult to obtain, and subject to significant errors, especially in high contention situations [12]. Distributed (i.e. independently executed by each station) strategies for power saving have been proposed and investigated in [14], [15]. Specifically, in [14] the authors propose a power controlled wireless MAC protocol based on a fine-tuning of network interface transmitting power. [15] extends the algorithm presented in [7] with power saving features.

This paper presents and evaluates a distributed mechanism for the contention control in IEEE 802.11 WLANs that extends the standard access mechanism without requiring any additional hardware. Our mechanism dynamically adapts the backoff window size to the current network contention level, and guarantees that an IEEE 802.11 WLAN *asymptotically* achieves its optimal channel utilization and/or the minimum energy consumption. For this reason we named our mechanism Asymptotical Optimal Backoff (*AOB*). To tune the parameters of our mechanism we analytically studied the bandwidth and energy consumption of the IEEE 802.11 standard, and we derived closed formulas that relate the protocol backoff parameters to the maximum throughput and to the minimal energy consumption.

Our analytical study of IEEE 802.11 performance is based on a p-persistent model of the IEEE 802.11 protocol [11], [15]. This protocol model differs from the standard protocol only in the selection of the backoff interval. Instead of the binary exponential backoff used in the standard, the backoff interval of the p-persistent IEEE 802.11 protocol is sampled from a geometric distribution with parameter p. In [11], it was shown that a p-persistent IEEE 802.11 closely approximates the standard protocol.

In this paper, we use the p-persistent model to derive analytical formulas for the IEEE802.11 protocol capacity and energy consumption. From these formulas we compute the p value (i.e., the average backoff window size) corresponding to maximum channel utilization (*optimal capacity p*, also referred to as p_{opt}^{C}), and the p value corresponding to minimum energy consumption (*optimal energy p*, also referred to as p_{opt}^{E}). The properties of the optimal operating points (both from the efficiency and power saving standpoint) are deeply investigated. In addition, we also provide closed formulas for the optimal p values. These formulas are used by AOB to dynamically tune the WLAN backoff parameters either to maximize WLAN efficiency, or to minimize WLAN energy consumption.

Via simulation, we compared the performance figures of the IEEE 802.11 protocol with or without our backoff tuning algorithm. Results obtained indicate that the enhanced protocol significantly improves the standard protocol, and (in all the configurations analyzed) produces performance figures very close to the theoretical limits.

2. IEEE 802.11

The IEEE 802.11 standard defines a MAC layer and a Physical Layer for WLANs. The MAC layer provides both contention-based and contention-free access control on a variety of physical layers. The standard provides 2 Physical layer specifications for radio (Frequency Hopping Spread Spectrum, Direct Sequence Spread Spectrum), operating in the 2,400 - 2,483.5 MHz band (depending on local regulations), and one for infrared. The Physical Layer provides the basic rates of 1 Mbit/s and 2 Mbit/s. Two projects are currently ongoing to develop higher-speed PHY extensions to 802.11 operating in the 2.4 GHz band (project 802.11b, handled by TGb) and in the 5 GHz band (project 802.11a handled by TGa), see [16] and [17].

The basic access method in the IEEE 802.11 MAC protocol is the *Distributed Coordination Function* (DCF) which is a *Carrier Sense Multiple Access with Collision Avoidance* (CSMA/CA) MAC protocol. In addition to the DCF, the IEEE 802.11 also incorporates an alternative access method known as the *Point Coordination Function* (PCF) - an access method that is similar to a polling system and uses a point coordinator to determine which station has the right to transmit. In this section we only present the aspects of the DCF access method relevant for the scope of this paper. For the detailed explanation of the IEEE 802.11 standard we address interested readers to [1], [2], [18].

The DCF access method is based on a CSMA/CA MAC protocol. This protocol requires that every station, before transmitting, performs a Carrier Sensing activity to determine the state of the channel (idle or busy). If the medium is found to be idle for an interval that exceeds the *Distributed InterFrame Space* (DIFS), the station continues with its transmission. If the medium is busy, the transmission is deferred until the ongoing transmission terminates, and a Collision Avoidance mechanism is adopted. The IEEE 802.11 Collision Avoidance mechanism is a *Binary Exponential Backoff* scheme [1], [19], [20], [21]. According to this mechanism, a station selects a random interval, named *backoff interval,* that is used to initialize a *backoff counter.*

The backoff counter is decreased as long as the channel is sensed idle, stopped when a transmission is detected on the channel, and reactivated when the channel is sensed idle again for more than a DIFS. A station transmits when its backoff counter reaches zero.

When, the channel is idle the time is measured in constant length units (*Slot_Time*) indicated as slots in the following. The backoff interval is an integer number of slots and its value is uniformly chosen in the interval (0, *CW_Size*-1), where *CW_Size* is, in each station, a local parameter that defines the current station *Contention Window* size. Specifically, the backoff value is defined by the following expression [1]:

$$Backoff\_Counter = INT\big(Rnd(\ )\cdot CW\_Size\big) \quad ,$$

where $Rnd()$ is a function which returns pseudo-random numbers uniformly distributed in $[0..1]$.

The Binary Exponential Backoff is characterized by the expression that gives the dependency of the CW_Size parameter by the number of *unsuccessful transmission attempts* (N_A) already performed for a given frame. In [1] it is defined that the first transmission attempt for a given frame is performed adopting CW_Size equal to the minimum value CW_Size_min (assuming low contention). After each unsuccessful (re)transmission of the same frame, the station doubles CW_Size until it reaches the maximal value fixed by the standard, i.e. CW_Size_MAX, as follows:

$$CW\_Size(N\_A) = \min\big(CW\_Size\_MAX, CW\_Size\_\min \cdot 2^{(N\_A-1)}\big) \quad .$$

Positive acknowledgements are employed to ascertain a successful transmission. This is accomplished by the receiver (immediately following the reception of the data frame) which initiates the transmission of an acknowledgement frame (ACK) after a time interval *Short Inter Frame Space* (SIFS), which is less than DIFS.

If the transmission generates a collision[1], the CW_Size parameter is doubled for the new scheduling of the retransmission attempt thus obtaining a further reduction of contention.

The increase of the CW_Size parameter value after a collision is the reaction that the 802.11 standard DCF provides to make the access mechanism adaptive to channel conditions.

2.1 IEEE 802.11 Congestion Reaction

Fig. 1 shows simulation data regarding the channel utilization of a standard 802.11 system running in DCF mode, with respect to the contention level, i.e. the number of active stations with continuous transmission requirements. The parameters adopted in the simulation, presented in Table 1, refer to the Frequency Hopping Spread Spectrum implementation [1].

Fig. 1 plots the channel utilization versus the number of active stations obtained assuming asymptotic conditions, i.e. all the stations have always a frame to transmit. By analyzing the behavior of the 802.11 DCF mechanism some problems could be identified. Specifically, the results presented in the figure show that the channel utilization is negatively affected by the increase in the contention level.

These results can be explained as, in the IEEE 802.11 backoff algorithm, a station selects the initial size of the Contention Window by assuming a low level of congestion in the system. This choice avoids long access delays when the load is light. Unfortunately, this choice causes efficiency problems in bursty arrival scenarios, and in

---

[1] A collision is assumed whenever the ACK from the receiver is missing

congested systems, because it concentrates the accesses in a reduced time window, and hence it may cause a high collision probability.

Table 1: System's physical parameters

parameter	value
Number of Stations (M)	variable from 2 to 200
CW_Size_min	16
CW_Size_MAX	1024
Channel transmission rate	2 Mb/s
Payload size	Geometric distribution (parameter q)
Acknowledgement size	200 μ sec (50 Bytes)
Header size	136 μ sec (34 Bytes)
SlotTime (t_{slot})	50 μ sec
SIFS	28 μ sec
DIFS	128 μ sec
Propagation time	< 1 μ sec

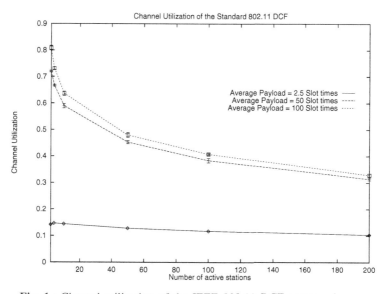

Fig. 1.: Channel utilization of the IEEE 802.11 DCF access scheme

In high-congestion conditions each station reacts to the contention on the basis of the collisions so far experienced while transmitting a frame. Every station performs its attempts blindly, with a late collision reaction performed (increasing *CW_Size*). Each increase of the *CW_Size* is obtained paying the cost of a collision. It is worth noting that, as a collision detection mechanism is not implemented in the IEEE 802.11, a collision implies that the channel is not available for the time required to transmit the longest colliding packet. Furthermore, after a successful transmission the *CW_Size* is set again to the minimum value without maintaining any knowledge of the current contention level. To summarize the IEEE 802.11 backoff mechanism has two main drawbacks: *i*) the increase of the *CW_Size* is obtained paying the cost of a collision, and *ii*) after a successful transmission no state information indicating the actual contention level is maintained.

3. Low-Cost Dynamic Tuning of the Backoff Window Size

The drawbacks of the IEEE 802.11 backoff algorithm, explained in the previous section, indicate the direction for improving the performance of a random access scheme, by exploiting the information on the current network congestion level that is already available at the MAC level. Specifically, the utilization rate of the slots (*Slot Utilization*) observed on the channel by each station is used as a simple and effective estimate of the channel congestion level. The estimate of the Slot Utilization must be frequently updated. For this reason in [7] it was proposed an estimate that has to be updated by each station in every *Backoff interval*, i.e., the defer phase that precedes a transmission attempt.

A simple and intuitive definition of the slot utilization estimate is then given by:

$$Slot\_Utilization = \frac{Num\_Busy\_Slots}{Num\_Available\_Slots} \quad ,$$

where *Num_Busy_Slots* is the number of slots, in the backoff interval, in which a transmission attempt starts, hereafter referred as *busy slots*. A transmission attempt can be either a successful transmission, or a collision; and *Num_Available_Slots* is the total number of slots available for transmission in the backoff interval, i.e. the sum of idle and busy slots.

In the 802.11 standard mechanism every station performs a Carrier Sensing activity and thus the proposed slot utilization (S_U) estimate is simple to obtain. The information required to estimate S_U is already available to an IEEE 802.11 station, and no additional hardware is required.

The current S_U estimate can be utilized by each station to evaluate (before trying a "blind" transmission) the opportunity to perform, or to defer, its scheduled transmission attempt. If a station knows that the probability of a successful transmission is low, it should defer its transmission attempt. Such a behavior can be achieved in an IEEE 802.11 network by exploiting the DCC mechanism proposed in [7]. According to DCC, each IEEE 802.11 station performs an additional control (beyond carrier sensing and backoff algorithm) before any transmission attempt. This control is based on a new parameter named *Probability of Transmission P_T(...)* whose value is dependent on the current contention level of the channel, i.e., S_U. The heuristic formula proposed in [7] for $P\_T(...)$ is:

$$P\_T(S\_U,\ N\_A) = 1 - S\_U^{N-A} \quad ,$$

where, by definition, S_U assumes values in the interval [0,1], and N_A is the number of attempts already performed by the station for the transmission of the current frame.

The N_A parameter is used to partition the set of active stations in such a way that each subset of stations is associated with a different level of privilege to access the channel. Stations that have performed several unsuccessful attempts have the highest transmission privilege [7].

The P_T parameter allows to filter the transmission accesses. When, according to the standard protocol, a station is authorized to transmit (i.e., backoff counter is zero and channel is idle) in the protocol extended with the Probability of Transmission, a station will perform a real transmission with probability P_T, otherwise (i.e. with probability $1-P\_T$) the transmission is re-scheduled as a collision would have occured, i.e. a new backoff interval is sampled.

To better understand the relationship between the P_T definition and the network congestion level, we can observe the Fig. 2.

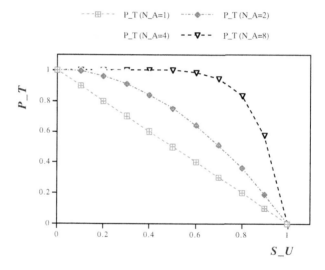

Fig. 2: DCC Probability of Transmission

In the figure we show the P_T curves (for users with different N_A) with respect to the estimated S_U values. Assuming a slot utilization near to zero, we can observe that each station, independently by its number of performed attempts, obtains a Probability of Transmission near to 1. This means that the proposed mechanism has no effect on the system, and each user performs its accesses just like in the standard access scheme, without any additional contention control. This point is significant as it implies the absence of overhead introduced in low-load conditions. The differences in the users behavior as a function of their levels of privilege (related to the value of the N_A parameter) appear when the slot utilization grows. For example, assuming a slot utilization near to 1, say 0.8, we observe that the stations with the highest N_A value obtains a Probability of Transmission close to 1 while stations at the first transmission attempt transmit with a probability equal to 0.2.

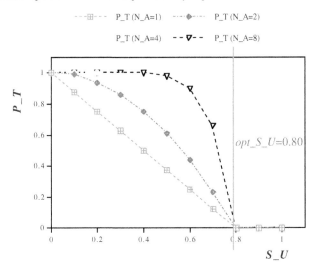

Fig. 3: Generalized Probability of Transmission

It is worth noting a property of the DCC mechanism: the slot utilization of the channel never reaches the value 1. Assuming S_U near or equal to 1, the DCC mechanism reduces the Probabilities of Transmission for all stations close to zero thus reducing the network contention level. This effect was due to the P_T definition, and in particular to the explicit presence of the upper bound 1 for the slot utilization estimate. The DCC choice to use 1 as the asymptotical limit for the S_U is heuristic, and it is induced by the lack of the knowledge of which is the optimal upper bound for the S_U value *(opt_S_U)* to guarantee the maximum channel utilization. It is worth noting that, if opt_S_U is known, the P_T mechanism can be easily tuned to guarantee that the maximum channel utilization is achieved. Intuitively, if the slot-utilization boundary value (i.e. the value one for DCC) would be replaced by the opt_S_U value, we reduce all the probabilities of transmission to zero in correspondence of slot utilization values greater or equal to the opt_S_U. This can be achieved by generalizing the definition for the Probability of Transmission:

$$P\_T\left(opt\_S\_U, S\_U, N\_A\right) = 1 - \min\left(1, \frac{S\_U}{opt\_S\_U}\right)^{N\_A} \qquad (1)$$

Specifically, by applying this definition of the transmission probability we obtain the P_T curves shown in Fig. 3. These curves have been obtained by applying the generalized P_T definition with $opt\_S\_U=0.80$. As expected the curves indicate the effectiveness of the generalized P_T definition in providing a S_U bounding that changes with the opt_S_U value.

The generalized Probability of Transmission provides an effective tool for controlling, in an optimal way, the congestion inside a IEEE 802.11 WLAN provided that the *opt_S_U* value is known. In the next section we will show how this optimal value can be computed. The computation is based on the exploitation of the results derived in [11].

4. Protocol Model

Consider a system with M active stations accessing a slotted multiple-access channel. The random access protocols for controlling this channel can be either a S-Aloha or a *p*-persistent CSMA algorithm. In the first case (Aloha) the stations transmit constant-length messages with length l that exactly fits in a slot. In the latter case (CSMA), the message length is a random variable L, with average l. Hereafter, to simplify the presentation we will assume that L values always correspond to an integer number of slots. In both cases, when a transmission attempt is completed (successfully or with a collision), each network station with packets ready for transmission (hereafter *back-logged station*) will start a transmission attempt with probability p.

To derive a closed formula of the channel utilization, say ρ, for the p-persistent CSMA protocols we observe the channel between two consecutive successful transmissions. Let us denote with t_i the time between the $(i\text{-}1)$th successful transmission and the ith successful transmission, and with s_i the duration of the ith successful transmission. Hence, the channel utilization is simply obtained:

$$\rho = \lim_{n \to \infty} \frac{s_1 + s_2 + \mathrm{L} + s_n}{t_1 + t_{i2} + \mathrm{L} + t_n}. \tag{2}$$

By dividing both numerator and denominator of Equation (3) by n, after some algebraic manipulations, it follows that:

$$\rho = \frac{E[S]}{E[T]} \quad , \tag{3}$$

where $E[S]$ is the average duration of a successful transmission, and $E[T]$ is the average time between two successful transmissions. The $E[T]$ formula is straightforwardly obtained by considering the behavior of a CSMA protocol. Specifically, before successfully transmitting a message, a station will experience $E[N_c]$ collisions, on average. Furthermore, each transmission is preceded by an idle time, say $E[Idle]$, during which a station listens to the channel. Therefore, we can write:

$$E[T] = \left(E[N_c] + 1\right) \cdot E[Idle] + E[N_c] \cdot E[Coll \mid Coll] + E[S] \quad , \tag{4}$$

where $E[Coll \mid Coll]$ is the average duration of a collision, given that a collision occurs. Finally, the unknown quantities in Equation(4) are derived in Lemma 1 under the following assumptions: *i)* the channel idle time is divided in fixed time lengths, say t_{slot}; *ii)* all the stations adopt a *p*-persistent CSMA algorithm to access the channel; *iii)* all the stations operate in saturation conditions, i.e., they have always a message waiting to be transmitted; *iv)* the message lengths, say l_i, are random variables identically and independently distributed.

Lemma 1. In a network with M stations operating according to assumptions i) to iv) above, by denoting with $\Pr\{L \le h\}$ the probability that the time occupied by the transmission of the message L is less or equal to $h \cdot t_{slot}$:

$$E[Idle] = \frac{(1-p)^M}{1-(1-p)^M} \quad , \tag{5}$$

$$E[N_c] = \frac{1-(1-p)^M}{Mp(1-p)^{M-1}} - 1 \quad , \tag{6}$$

$$E[Coll \mid Coll] = \tag{7}$$

$$= \frac{t_{slot}}{1-\left[(1-p)^M + Mp(1-p)^{M-1}\right]} \cdot \sum_{h=1}^{\infty} h \Big\{ \left[1-(1-\Pr\{L \le h\})p\right]^M -$$

$$\left[1-(1-\Pr\{L < h\})p\right]^M - M\left[\Pr\{L \le h\} - \Pr\{L < h\}\right]p(1-p)^{M-1} \Big\}$$

Proof. The proof is obtained with standard probabilistic considerations (see [11]).

◊

$E[S]$ is a constant independent of the p value, but dependent only on the message length distribution. As it appears from Equation (4) and Lemma 1, the channel utilization is a function of the protocol parameter p, the number M of active stations and the message length distribution. The protocol capacity, say ρ_{MAX}, is obtained by finding the p value, say p_{opt}^C, that maximizes Equation (3). Since $E[S]$ is a constant, the utilization-maximization problem is equivalent to the following minimization problem:

$$\min_{p \in [0,1]} \left\{ \left(E[N_c]+1\right) \cdot E[Idle] + E[N_c] \cdot E[Coll \mid Coll] \right\} \quad , \tag{8}$$

For instance, for the Slotted-ALOHA access scheme the p_{opt}^C value is calculated by considering in Equation (8) constant messages with length 1 t_{slot}. By solving Equation (8) we obtain that $p_{opt}^C = 1/M$ and $\rho_{MAX} \underset{M \gg 1}{\to} e^{-1}$. However, from Equation (8), it is not possible to derive a general exact closed formula for the p_{opt}^C value in the general message-length distribution case.

Due to the choice of $l = 1$, collisions and successful transmissions always last a single t_{slot}. However, for a *p-persistent* CSMA protocol with a general message-length distribution, the protocol capacity depends on the message length, hence, the p_{opt}^C also depends on the traffic characteristics. The p_{opt}^C value can be computed for any network configuration by numerically maximizing Equation (3). Hence, if a station has an exact knowledge of the network configuration it is possible to tune its backoff algorithm to achieve a channel utilization close to the protocol capacity. Unfortunately, in a real case a station does not have this knowledge but it can only estimate it. Using this estimate, the station can in principle compute at run time the p_{opt}^C value. However, the p_{opt}^C computation obtained by the numerical maximization of Equation (3) is too complex to be executed at run-time. Furthermore, the numerical maximization of Equation (3) does not provide a closed formula for the optimal working conditions, and hence it does not provide any insight on the optimal protocol behavior. Hence, the Equation (3) can be adopted to derive the optimal capacity state in an off-line analysis, but it would be convenient to derive a simpler relationship to provide an approximation of the p_{opt}^C value to guarantee a quasi-optimal capacity state.

4.1   Protocol Capacity: An Approximate Analysis

Equation (8) can be adopted to derive the optimal capacity state in an off-line analysis, but it is important to derive a simpler relationship to provide an approximation of the p value corresponding to optimal capacity, i.e. p_{opt}^C. In [22], the network operating point in which the time wasted on idle periods is equal to the time spent on collisions was identified as the condition to obtain the maximum protocol capacity in ALOHA and CSMA protocols where all messages require one time slot for transmission. In [12] the same network operating point was proposed to determine a quasi-optimal capacity state in the *p-persistent* IEEE 802.11 protocol where the message length was sampled from a geometric distribution. This condition can be expressed with the following relationship:

$$E[Idle\_p] = E[Coll \mid N_{tr} \geq 1] \quad , \tag{9}$$

where $E[Coll \mid N_{tr} \geq 1]$ is the average collision length given that at least a transmission occurs.

Equation (9) was proposed in previous papers using heuristic considerations. Specifically, it is straightforward to observe that $E[Idle\_p]$ is a decreasing function of the p value, whereas $E[Coll \mid N_{tr} \geq 1]$ is an increasing function of the p value. Therefore, Equation (9) suggests that a quasi-optimal capacity state is achieved when each station behaves in such a way to balance these two conflicting costs.

Hereafter, first, we give an analytical justification and a numerical validation of the above heuristic. Second, we provide closed formulas for the p_{opt}^C, and we show that the optimal capacity state, given the message length distribution, is characterized by an invariant figure: the $M \cdot p_{opt}^C$ product.

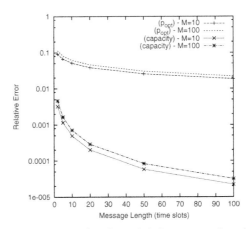

Fig. 4: Relative errors for deterministic message-length distribution

4.2 A Balancing Equation to Derive the Optimal Capacity State

Equation (9) presents a heuristic that was numerically validated. In this section we analytically investigate its validity. To make tractable the problem defined by Equation (5) in the general message-length distribution case, we assume that $E[Coll \mid Coll] = \overline{C} = \max\{l_1, l_2\}^2$. According to this assumption, substituting formulas (5) and (6) in Equation (8), after some algebraic manipulations, it follows that the p_{opt}^C value is calculated by solving:

$$\min_{p \in [0,1]} \left\{ \frac{\overline{C} - (1-p)^M (\overline{C} - 1)}{Mp(1-p)^{M-1}} \right\} = \min_{p \in [0,1]} \left\{ F\left(p, M, \overline{C}\right) \right\} \quad . \tag{10}$$

As shown by the following lemma, the solution of Equation (10) is oftem equivalent to the solution of Equation (9).

---

2 This approximation is motivated by considering that: *i)* the collision probability is low when the network is close to its optimal capacity state, and *ii)* given a collision, the probability that more than two stations collide is negligible (as shown in [11] for the *p*-persistent IEEE 802.11 protocol).

Lemma 2. For M>>1, the p value that satisfies Equation (10) can be obtained by solving the following equation:

$$E[Idle\_p] = E[Coll \mid N_{tr} \geq 1] \quad , \tag{11}$$

Proof. The proof is reported in Appendix A.

◊

Lemma 2 shows that, asymptotically (M>>1), in p-persistent CSMA protocols the optimal capacity state is characterized by the balancing between collisions' duration and idle times. To verify the existence of this relationship for small medium M values, we numerically solved both Equation (4) and Equation (9) for a wide range of M values and several message length distributions. Specifically, in Fig. 4 and 5 we show, for several the average message length (l), the relative error[3] between the optimal p (curves tagged capacity), and the p value that solve Equation (7), curves tagged capacity p_{opt}.

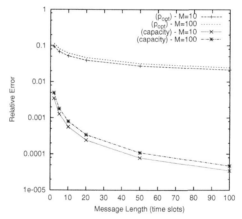

Fig. 5: Relative errors for geometric message-length distribution

4.3   Protocol Capacity: A Closed Formula

The Equation (9) allows us to evaluate a quasi-optimal p value by simply determining the p value that balance $E[Idle\_p]$ and $E[Coll \mid N_{tr} \geq 1]$ costs. By exploiting this approach it is possible to afford, at run-time, the channel-utilization maximization. Indeed, each station by exploiting the carrier sensing mechanism is able to distinguish the idle periods by collisions and by successful transmissions. Furthermore, as shown in this subsection, from Equation (10) it is easy to derive an approximated closed

---

[3]   The relative error is defined as the error between the exact value and its approximation, normalized to the exact value.

formula for the p_{opt}^C value. Note that this closed formula generalizes results already known for S-ALOHA networks [23].

Lemma 3. In an M-station network that adopts a p-persistent CSMA access scheme, in which the message lengths {Li}, normalized to t_{slot}, are a sequence of i.i.d. random variables, if the stations operate in asymptotic conditions, under the condition $Mp \ll 1$, the p_{opt}^C value is[4]

$$p_{opt}^C \cong \frac{\sqrt{1 + 2(\overline{C} - 1)\dfrac{M - 1}{M}} - 1}{(M - 1)(\overline{C} - 1)} \quad , \tag{12}$$

where $\overline{C} = E\big[\max\{L_1, L_2\}\big]$.

PROOF. The proof is reported in Appendix B.

Equation (12) is important because it allows to easily compute the p_{opt}^C value within a considered scenario (i.e. fixed the number M of stations in the network) and hence it can be used for the optimal tuning of a network if the network and traffic parameters are known, i.e. M and the message-length distribution. However, in a real networking environment, the number of active stations frequently and sharply changes. Hence, M is not a-priori known and must be estimated at run-time. Unfortunately, the M estimation could result expensive, difficult to obtain and subject to significant errors. However as shown in Proposition 1 it is possible to characterize the network optimal behavior without an explicit knowledge of M. Specifically, (given a message length distribution) the optimal state corresponds to a quasi-constant value of the $M \cdot p_{opt}^C$ product. This interesting result requires two assumption: *Mp<<1 and M>>1*. These two conditions are usually met by current WLAN traffic, i.e., long transmitted messages and several active stations. In other words, this means that for any number of active stations the optimal operating point has the same average number of stations that transmit in a slot. The following proposition provides an analytical explanation of this behavior.

Proposition 1. In an M-station network that adopts a p-persistent CSMA access scheme, in which the message lengths {Li}, normalized to t_{slot}, are a sequence of i.i.d. random variables, under the condition $Mp \ll 1$ and $M \gg 1$ the $M \cdot p_{opt}^C$ value is

$$M \cdot p_{opt}^C \cong \frac{\sqrt{1 + 2(\overline{C} - 1)} - 1}{(\overline{C} - 1)} \quad , \tag{13}$$

---

[4] This assumption is as more correct as more long is the average message length. See, for example, the numerical results reported in Figure 4 and 5.

PROOF. The proof of this proposition is straightforward. Under the condition $M \gg 1$, Equation (12) can be rewritten as (13) by noting that $(M - 1) \approx M$.

$\Diamond$

Remark. In an M-station network that adopts a p-persistent CSMA access scheme, in which the message lengths $\{Li\}$, normalized to t_{slot}, are a sequence of i.i.d. random variables, under the condition $\overline{C} \gg 1$ the p^C_{opt} value is

$$p^C_{opt} \cong \frac{1}{M \cdot \sqrt{\overline{C}/2}} \quad . \tag{14}$$

Results presented in this section indicate that the $M \cdot p^C_{opt}$ product can be easily computed by estimating only the average collision length. The average collision length estimates are easy to obtain and reliable if the average collision length does not change frequently and sharply. In addition, these results indicate that the estimation of the number of active stations is not necessary for driving the system to its optimal capacity state.

5. Energy Consumption in P-Persistent CSMA Access Schemes

As explained in the introduction, the finite battery power represents the other greatest limitation to the utility of portable computers [25], [26], [27]. The network interface is one of the main system components from the battery consumption standpoint [28]. Hence, the energy used by the network interface to successfully transmit a message is the other important figure for a mobile computer. Thus the target for our environment would be both to maximize the network capacity and to minimize the network-interface energy consumption. It may appear that these two targets cannot be achieved together. It seems that to maximize the network capacity the users must be greedy, i.e. transmitting as much as possible. On the other hand, minimization of the network-interface energy seems to indicate that the network should be lightly loaded, i.e. sporadic accesses to the network. In this paper we will show that, for *p-persistent* CSMA access schemes, the main performance figures (capacity and energy consumption) are not orthogonal, i.e. the network state that optimizes one index is not far from being optimal also for the other one. To show this result, firstly we need to study our system from an energy consumption standpoint, i.e. to identify the relationships to characterize the p value that minimizes the energy consumption.

5.1 An Analytical Model for the Energy Consumption

In this section we develop an analytical model to investigate the energy consumption From an energy consumption standpoint, the network interface alternates between two different phases: the transmitting phase, during which it consumes power to transmit the message to the physical channel, and the receiving phase, during which it consumes power to listen to the physical channel. Hereafter, we denote with *PTX* and *PRX* the power consumption (expressed in mW) of the network interface during the transmitting and receiving phase, respectively.

We assume that the message lengths are i.i.d. random variables. An analytical model for the energy consumption in *p-persistent* IEEE 802.11 MAC protocol was developed in [15].

Following the same line of reasoning of Section 4 and focusing on the successful transmission of a tagged station, we derive an analytical expression for the energy drained by a tagged-station network-interface to successfully transmit a packet. Hence, the system efficiency, from the energy standpoint, can be expressed as:

$$\rho_{energy} = \frac{PTX \cdot l \cdot t_{slot}}{E\left[Energy_{virtual\_transmission\_time}\right]} \quad , \tag{15}$$

where $E[Energy_{virtual\_transmission\_time}]$ is the energy consumed by the tagged station in a tagged_station virtual transmission time (.e., the time between two tagged station successful transmission) and l is the average message transmission time, normalized to the t_{slot}.

5.2   Energy Consumption: An Approximate Analysis

As for the throughput maximization, it is desirable to have a simpler relationship than Equation (15) to provide an approximation for the p_{opt}^{E} value. To this end, in the following we will investigate the role of the various terms of Equation (15) in determining the Energy Consumption. Specifically, in the energy consumption formula we separate the terms that are increasing function of the p value from the terms that are decreasing function of the p value.

To achieve this, it is useful to introduce the following proposition.

Proposition 2. In an *M*-station network that adopts a *p*-persistent CSMA access scheme, if the stations operate in asymptotic conditions, ρ_{energy} is equal to.

$$\rho_{energy} = PTX \cdot l \cdot t_{slot} \Big/ \Big\{ E[N_{ta}] E\left[Energy_{Idle\_p}\right] + PTX \cdot l \cdot t_{slot} + \tag{16}$$
$$+ PRX \cdot (M-1) \cdot l \cdot t_{slot} + \left(E[N_{ta}] - M\right) \cdot E\left[Energy_{Coll} \mid N_{tr} \geq 1\right] \Big\}$$

PROOF. The proof requires some algebraic manipulations of Equation (15). We first observe that the number of successful transmissions in a virtual transmission time is *M*. Furthermore, in the virtual transmission time there is exactly one successful transmission of the tagged station, and in average there are $(M-1)$ successful transmissions of the other stations. It is also straightforward to derive that the average number of collisions that we observe within a virtual transmission time is

$(E[N_{ta}] - M)$ i.e., the total number of transmission attempts in a virtual transmission time less the average number of successful transmissions, i.e.. According to these assessments, with standard probabilistic considerations Equation (16) is derived.

$\Diamond$

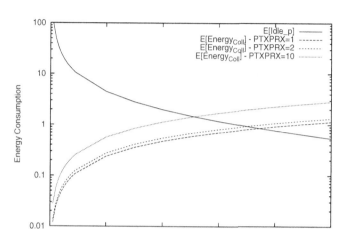

Fig. 6: p_{opt}^E approximation with $M = 10$ and $l = 2\, t_{slot}$.

From Proposition 2 it follows that p_{opt}^E corresponds to the p value that minimizes the denominator of Equation (16). It is also worth noting that the second and third terms of this denominator do not depend on the p value and hence they play no role in the minimization process. Now our problem reduces to find

$$\min_{p}\left\{ E[N_{ta}] \cdot E[Energy_{Idle\_p}] + \left(E[N_{ta}] - M\right) \cdot E[Energy_{Coll} \mid N_{tr} \geq 1]\right\} \quad . \tag{17}$$

Now let us note that the first term in Equation (17), i.e. $E[N_{ta}] \cdot E[Energy_{Idle\_p}]$, after some algebraic manipulations, reduces to $[PRX \cdot t_{slot} \cdot (1-p)]/p$, and thus this first term is a decreasing function of p. On the other hand, the second term in Equation (21) is an increasing function of p. Hence, following the same arguments that drive to propose the protocol-capacity approximation (see Equation (9)), we propose to approximate the p_{opt}^E value with the p value that balances the increasing and decreasing costs of p:

$$E[N_{ta}] \cdot E[Energy_{Idle\_p}] = \left(E[N_{ta}] - M\right) \cdot E[Energy_{Coll} \mid N_{tr} \geq 1] \quad . \tag{18}$$

Equation (22) can be re-written as:

$$E[Energy_{Idle\_p}] = E[Energy_{Coll} \mid N_{tr} \geq 1] \cdot P_{Coll\mid N_{tr} \geq 1} \quad . \tag{19}$$

To ease the computation of $E[Energy_{Coll} | N_{tr} \geq 1]$ we subdivide the collisions in two subsets depending or not they involve the tagged station. Specifically, Equation (19) can be re-written as:

$$E\left[Energy_{Idle\_p}\right] = E\left[Energy_{tag\_Coll} \mid tag\_Coll\right] \cdot P_{tag\_Coll|N_{tr} \geq 1} + \qquad (20)$$
$$E\left[Energy_{not\_tag\_Coll} \mid not\_tag\_Coll\right] \cdot P_{not\_tag\_Coll|N_{tr} \geq 1}$$

Equation (20) defines a simple but approximate relationship to characterize p_{opt}^E. Specifically, in Fig. 6 we have plotted $E[Energy_{Idle\_p}]$ and $E[Energy_{Coll} | N_{tr} \geq 1]$ versus the p value, for various PTX/PRX values. $E[Energy_{Idle\_p}]$ is equal to $E[Idle\_p]$ due to the assumption that PRX=1. The p value that corresponds to the intersection point of the $E[Energy_{Idle\_p}]$ and $E[Energy_{Coll} | N_{tr} \geq 1]$ curves is the approximation of the p_{opt}^E value, as Equation (16) indicates. As the $E[Energy_{Coll} | N_{tr} \geq 1]$ related to $PTX / PRX = 1$ is equal to the average length of a collision given a transmission attempt, i.e. $E[Coll | N_{tr} \geq 1]$, the p value that corresponds to the intersection point of the $E[Idle\_p]$ and $E[Coll | N_{tr} \geq 1]$ curves provides a good approximation of the p_{opt}^C value, as Equation (6) indicates. We note that by increasing the PTX value also $E[Energy_{Coll} | N_{tr} \geq 1]$ grows due to the rise in the energy consumption of tagged-station collisions. However, $E[Energy_{Idle\_p}]$ does not depend on the PTX value, hence, only a decrease in the p_{opt}^E value can balance the increase in $E[Energy_{Coll} | N_{tr} \geq 1]$.

5.3 Energy Consumption: A p_{opt}^E Closed Formula

Similarly to Section 4, we conclude the characterization of our system, from the Energy Consumption standpoint, by providing closed (approximate) formulas to identify the network state that minimizes the Energy Consumption.

Lemma 4. In an M-station network in which the message lengths $\{Li\}$, normalized to t_{slot}, are a sequence of i.i.d. random variables, under the condition $Mp \ll 1$ the p_{opt}^E value is

$$p_{opt}^E \cong \frac{\sqrt{1 + 2\dfrac{M-1}{M}\left[\overline{C} \cdot \dfrac{(M-2)}{M} + \dfrac{\overline{E}_{CT}}{PRX} \cdot \dfrac{1}{M} - 1\right]} - 1}{(M-1)\left[\overline{C} \cdot \dfrac{(M-2)}{M} + \dfrac{\overline{E}_{CT}}{PRX} \cdot \dfrac{1}{M} - 1\right]}, \qquad (21)$$

where $\overline{C} = E\big[\max\{L_1, L_2\}\big]$ and $\overline{E}_{CT} = E\big[Energy_{tag\_Coll}|tag\_Coll, N_{tr} = 2\big].$

PROOF. The proof of this Lemma can be found in [24]

As we have done in Proposition 1, the following proposition provides an analytical investigation of the $M \cdot p^E_{opt}$ for a large network-size population. This investigation is useful because it shows how for a large network size population the p^E_{opt} value tends to the p^C_{opt} value.

Proposition 3. In an network with a large number of active stations $(M \gg 1)$ in which the message lengths $\{Li\}$, normalized to t_{slot}, are a sequence of i.i.d. random variables, the optimal $M \cdot p^E_{opt}$ value is:

$$M \cdot p^E_{opt} \cong \frac{\sqrt{1 + 2\left(\overline{C} + \dfrac{\overline{E}_{CT}}{PRX}\dfrac{1}{M} - 1\right)} - 1}{\left(\overline{C} + \dfrac{\overline{E}_{CT}}{PRX}\dfrac{1}{M} - 1\right)} \approx \frac{\sqrt{1 + 2(\overline{C} - 1)} - 1}{(\overline{C} - 1)} \ . \tag{22}$$

PROOF. The proof of this proposition is straightforward. Under the condition $(M \gg 1)$, Equation (21) can be rewritten as (22) by noting that $(M - 1) \approx M$ and $(M - 2) \approx M$.

$\Diamond$

Equation (22) presents a tight analogy with Equation (13). For a large network-size populations it is straightforward to observe that $Mp^E_{opt} \approx Mp^C_{opt}$ (as Equation (22) and Equation (13) show). Since $\overline{E}_{CT}$ is divided by M, the energy consumption during tagged-station collisions decreases as the M value increases. Therefore, the PTX value has no significant impact on the $M \cdot p^E_{opt}$ computation for a large network-size population as it contributes only to $\overline{E}_{CT}$. Obviously $p^E_{opt} = p^C_{opt}$ when $PTX = PRX$. However, the comparison between the structure of Equation (13) and Equation (22) show also that the correspondence between the optimal p values continues to hold.

6. Effectiveness of the AOB Mechanism

In the remaining part of the paper, by means of the discrete event simulation, we extensively investigate the performance of the IEEE 802.11 protocol enhanced with the AOB mechanism. This mechanism utilize the current S_U estimate to evaluate, the opportunity to perform or to defer a transmission attempt authorized by the standard protocol (see Section 3). Specifically AOB uses the probability of transmission defined by Equation (1). As discussed before, Equation (1) requires the knowledge of the opt_S_U parameter. Below we show how results derived in Sections 4 and 5 can be used to estimate the opt_S_U value. Specifically, in the previous sections we show that the optimal capacity and energy state are characterized by invariant figures: $M \cdot p_{opt}^C$ and $M \cdot p_{opt}^E$. Hereafter we investigate the relationship between S_U and $M \cdot p_{opt}^x$ $(x \in \{C, E\})$.

We denote with N_{tr} the number of stations that make a transmission attempt in a slot. Hence, $P\{N_{tr} = i\}$ is the probability that exactly i stations transmit in a slot, and $P\{N_{tr} = 0\}$ is the probability that a slot remains empty. Let us now observe that $M \cdot p_{opt}^x$ is the average number of stations which transmits in a slot:

$$M \cdot p_{opt}^x = \sum_{i=1}^{M} i \cdot P\{N_{tr} = i\} \geq \sum_{i=1}^{M} P\{N_{tr} = i\} = 1 - P\{N_{tr} = 0\} = S\_U \quad .$$

The above formula indicates that $M \cdot p_{opt}^x \geq S\_U$. By exploiting this result we derive the opt_S_U parameter value used by AOB: $opt\_S\_U \approx M \cdot p_{opt}^x$.

6.1 Steady-State Analysis

In this section we analyze the AOB behavior when the network operates under steady-state conditions. The protocol analysis in transient conditions, and the protocol robustness are studied in the subsequent sections. The physical characteristics and parameter values of the investigated system are reported in Table 1.

The target of a MAC protocol is to share resources efficiently among several users. This efficiency can be expressed in terms of *capacity* a[25], [29]. However from the user standpoint other performance figures are needed to measure the Quality of Service (QoS) that can be relied on. The most widely used performance measure is the delay, which can be defined in several forms, depending on the time instants considered during its measurement (access delay, queueing delay, propagation delay, etc.). Hereafter, we will focus on the MAC delay. The MAC delay of a station in a LAN is the time between the instant at which a packet comes to the head of the station transmission queue and the end of the packet transmission [29].

To study the protocol performance we run a set of simulative experiments with different M of values. Active stations are assumed to operate in asymptotic conditions (i.e., with continuous transmission requirements). We use a maximum number of 200 active stations because the number of stations expected in the future for such a system could raise the order of hundreds [30]. For example, let us think to a conference room in which the participants use mobile devices with a wireless interface.

The effectiveness of the proposed AOB mechanism is shown in Fig. 7. This figure shows the channel utilization level achieved by adopting the AOB system and compares this index with the analytically defined optimal utilization levels (OPT curves in the figure). The results show that the AOB mechanism drives an IEEE 802.11 network very close to its optimal behavior at least from the channel utilization viewpoint. Only a little overhead is introduced when only few stations are active. It is worth noting that, with the AOB mechanism, the channel utilization remains close to its optimal value even in high-contention situations. In such cases, AOB almost doubles the channel utilization with respect to the standard protocol.

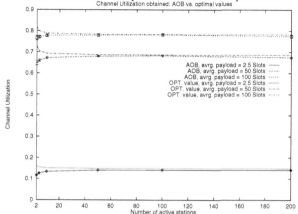

Fig. 7: Channel utilization of the IEEE 802.11 protocol with the AOB mechanism vs. optimal value

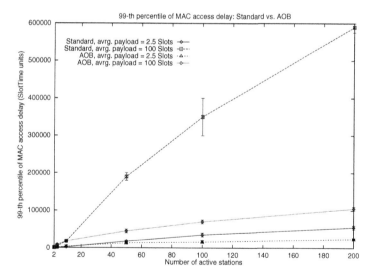

Fig. 8: 99-th percentile of MAC delay

In Fig. 8 we report the 99-th percentile of the MAC delay vs. contention level (i.e. number of active stations) for various average sizes of the transmitted frames. Simulative results show that the AOB mechanism leads to a great reduction of the tail of the MAC delay distribution with respect to the standard access scheme alone. By noting that when the network operates in asymptotic conditions the average MAC delay is the inverse of the station throughput, we can verify that AOB is really effective in reducing the tail of the MAC Delay. For example, with 100-slot average payload, the ratio between the 99-th percentile of the MAC Delay with or without the AOB mechanism is about 6 while the ratio between the average MAC Delay is only about 2.

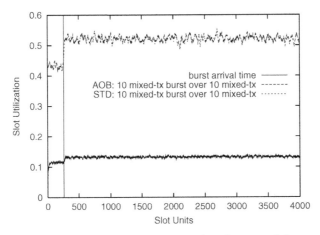

Fig. 9: A burst of 10 new stations activates when the network is operating in steady-state conditions with 10 active stations (Slot utilization)

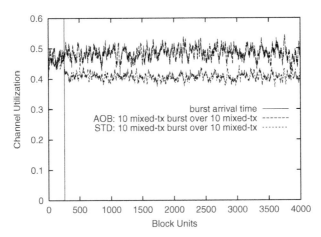

Fig. 10: A burst of 10 new stations activates when the network is operating in steady-state conditions with 10 active stations (Channel utilization)

Previous results seem to indicate that AOB, by reducing the average MAC delay, has also a positive effect on the power consumed by an IEEE 802.11 network interface. This intuition is further confirmed by the results presented in [15] showing that, by adopting AOB with current IEEE802.11 cards, the optimal capacity state closely approximates the minimum energy consumption state.

6.2 AOB Behavior in Transient Situations

In this section we analyze the protocol promptness to re-tune when the network state sharply changes. Specifically, we investigate the effectiveness the *AOB* when there is an upsurge in the number of active stations. Specifically, we analyze a network operating in steady-state conditions with 10   active stations. After 256 block units[5] (highlighted by the vertical bar "burst arrival time"), additional 10 stations become active. All stations transmit mixed traffic composed by 50% of long message (1500 bytes) and 50% of short messages (40 Bytes). Fig. 9 shows the effectiveness of the AOB mechanism. In the AOB case, the sharp increase in the number of active stations produces a negligible effect both in the slot utilization and in the channel utilization. On the other hand, the standard is negatively affected by this change: the slot utilization sharply increases (i.e., the network congestion level increases) and as a consequence the channel utilization decreases.

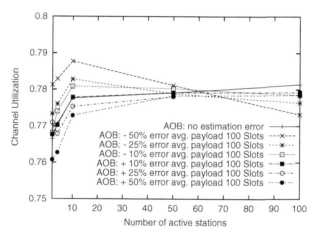

Fig. 11: Sensitiveness to errors in the estimation of the average message length (Slot utilization)

6.3 Protocol Robustness

The AOB mechanism, to tune the backoff algorithm, requires the knowledge of the network status that is identified by two parameters: the average message length (or

---

[5] A block unit corresponds to 512 slots. The block unit is introduced to smooth the trace. The smoothing was introduced to reduce the fluctuations and thus increasing the figure readability.

equivalently the q parameter) and the slot utilization. As the values of these parameters are obtained through estimations some errors may occur. Hereafter, we discuss the sensitiveness of AOB to these possible errors. To this end we compare the channel utilization in the ideal case (no estimation errors) with the channel utilization when an error is added/subtracted to the correct q and S_U estimate. Specifically, in the following figures the curve tagged with $+x\%$ ($-x\%$) error is obtained by multiplying by $1+x/100$ ($1-x/100$) the real estimate of the parameter. Results obtained are summarized in Fig. 10 (errors on q by assuming an average message length equal to 100 slots, i.e., q=0.99) and in Fig. 12 (errors on S_U). These results indicate that the AOB channel utilization is scarcely affected by estimation errors. For example, assuming constant errors of 50%, the channel utilization fluctuates in a small interval (2-3%) around the no-error value. It is worth noting that due to the way AOB is defined: i) for large M errors always have a negative impact (AOB is tuned to optimize asymptotic performance), ii) for few active stations, underestimation errors generate a channel utilization which is higher than that obtained in the no-error case. The latter behavior was expected because the ACL value is too conservative (i.e., it excessively limits the transmission rate) when there are few active stations. The parameters underestimation produces the opposite effect thus resulting in an increased channel utilization.

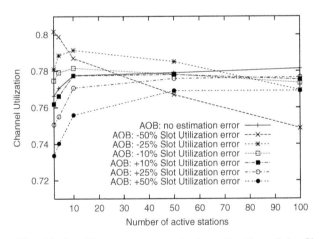

Fig. 12: Sensitiveness to errors in the estimation of the Slot Utilization

Acknoledgements

This work was partially supported by the NATO CLG.977405 project "Wireless Access to Internet exploiting the IEEE802.11 Technology" and by the the WILMA project "Wireless Internet and Location Management Architecture" funded by the Province of Trento, Italy.

References

1. ANSI/IEEE Standard 802.11, "Part 11: Wireless LAN- Medium Access Control (MAC) and Physical Layer (PHY) Specification", August 1999
2. Stallings W., Local & Metropolitan Area Networks, Fifth Edition, Prentice Hall 1996, pp. 356-383.
3. H. Woesner, J.P. Ebert, M. Schlager, A. Wolisz, "Power-saving mechanisms in emerging standards for wireless LANs: The MAC level perspective", *IEEE Personal Comm*, 1998, pp. 40-48.
4. N. Bambos, "Toward power-sensitive network architectures in wireless communications: Concepts, issues and design aspects", *IEEE Personal Comm*, 1998, pp. 50-59.
5. Weinmiller J., Woesner H., Ebert J.P., Wolisz A., "Analyzing and tuning the Distributed Coordination Function in the IEEE 802.11 DFWMAC Draft Standard", Proc. Int. Workshop on Modeling, MASCOT 96, San Jose, CA.
6. J. Weinmiller, M. Schläger, A. Festag, A. Wolisz, " Performance Study of Access control in Wireless LANs-IEEE 802.11 DFWMAC and ETSI RES 10 HIPERLAN", *Mobile Networks and Applications*, Vol. 2, 1997, pp.55-67
7. L. Bononi, M. Conti, L. Donatiello, "Design and Performance Evaluation of a Distributed Contention Control (DCC) Mechanism for IEEE 802.11 Wireless Local Area Networks", *Journal of Parallel and Distributed Computing*, Accademic Press Vol.60 N.4 di Aprile 2000.
8. M. Gerla, L. Kleinrock, "Closed loop stability control for S-Aloha satellite communications", *Proc. Fifth Data Communications Symp., Sept. 1977*, pp. 2.10-2.19.
9. B. Hajek, T. Van Loon, "Decentralized dynamic control of a multiaccess broadcast channel", *IEEE Trans Automat. Control,* Vol.27, 1982, pp. 559-569.
10. F. Kelly, "Sthocastic Models of computer communications systems", *J. Royal Statist. Soc.,* Series B, Vol. 47, 1985, pp. 379-395.
11. F. Cali' , Conti M., E. Gregori, "Dynamic Tuning of the IEEE 802.11 Protocol to Achieve a Theoretical Throughput Limit",*IEEE/ACM Transactions on Networking*, Volume 8 , No. 6 (Dec. 2000), pp. 785 - 799.
12. F. Cali' , Conti M., E. Gregori, "Dynamic IEEE 802.11: design, modeling and performance evaluation", *IEEE Journal on Selected Areas in Communications*, 18(9), September 2000. pp. 1774-1786.
13. Bianchi G., Fratta L., Olivieri M., "Performance Evaluation and Enhancement of the CSMA/CA MAC protocol for 802.11 Wireless LANs", proceedings of PIMRC 1996, 10/1996, Taipei, Taiwan, pp. 392-396.
14. J.P. Monks, V. Bharghavan, W.W. Hwu, "A Power Controlled Multiple Access Protocol for Wireless Packet Networks", in *Proc Infocom'01*, Anchorage, Alaska (Apr. 2001
15. L. Bononi, M. Conti, L. Donatiello, "A Distributed Mechanism for Power Saving in IEEE 802.11 Wireless LANs", *ACM/Kluwer Mobile Networks and Applic. Journal*, Vol. 6, N. 3 (2001), pp. 211-222.
16. http://grouper.ieee.org/groups/802/11/main.html
17. K. Bieseker, "The Promise of Broadband Wireless", IT Pro November/December 2000, pp. 31-39.
18. R. Bruno, M. Conti, E. Gregori, "WLAN technologies for mobile ad-hoc networks", Proc. HICSS-34, Maui, Hawaii, January 3-6, 2001. An extended version can be found in the Chapter 4 of *Handbook of Wireless Networks and Mobile Computing* (I. Stojmenovic Editor), John Wiley & Sons, New York, 2001.

19. Goodman J., Greenberg A.G., Madras N., March P., "Stability of Binary Exponential Backoff", app. in the Proc. of the 17-th Annual ACM Symp. on Theory of Comp., Providence, May 1985.
20. Hammond J.L., O'Reilly P.J.P., Performance Analysis of Local Computer Networks, Addison-Wesley 1988.
21. Hastad J., Leighton T., Rogoff B., "Analysis of Backoff Protocols for Multiple Access Channels", Siam J. Computing vol. 25, No. 4, 8/1996, pp. 740-774.
22. Gallagher R.G., "A perspective on multiaccess channels", IEEE Trans. Information Theory, vol. IT-31, No.2, 3/1985, pp. 124-142.
23. D. Bertsekas, R. Gallager, "Data Networks" *Prentice Hall*, 1992.
24.   R. Bruno, M. Conti, E. Gregori, " Optimization of Efficiency and Energy Consumption in p-persistent CSMA-based Wireless LANs", *IEEE Transactions on Mobile Computing*, Vol. 1 N.1, January 2002.
25. A. Chandra V. Gumalla, J.O. Limb, "Wireless Medium Access Control Protocols", IEEE Communications Surveys Second Quarter 2000.
26. G.H. Forman, J. Zahorjan, " The challenges of mobile computing", *IEEE Computer,* April 94, pp.38-47.
27. T. Imielinsky, B.R. Badrinath, "Mobile Computing: Solutions and Challenges in Data Management", *Communications of ACM* , Oct. 94.
28. R. Kravets, P. Krishnan, "Power Management Techniques for Mobile Communication", Proceedings of The Fourth Annual *ACM/IEEE International Conference on Mobile Computing and Networking* (MOBICOM'98).
29. Conti M., Gregori E., Lenzini L., "Metropolitan Area Networks", Springer Verlag, London, 1997.
30. Chen K.C., "Medium Access Control of Wireless LANs for Mobile Computing", IEEE Networks, 9-10/1994.
31. W.R.Stevens. TCP/IP Illustrated, Volume 1: The Protocols, Addison-Wesley, Reading, MA, 1994.
32. M. Stemm , R.H. Katz, "Measuring and Reducing Energy Consumption of Network Interfaces .in Hand-Held Devices", Proc. 3rd International workshop on Mobile Multimedia Communications (MoMuC-3), Princeton, NJ, September 1996.

Appendix: A

Lemma 2. For $M \gg 1$, the p value that satisfies (6) can be obtained by solving the following equation: $E[Idle\_p] = E[Coll \mid N_{tr} \geq 1]$

where $E[Coll \mid N_{tr} \geq 1]$ is the average duration of a collision given that at least a transmission occurs.

PROOF. Taking the derivative of $F(p, M, \overline{C})$ with respect p, and imposing it equal to 0, we obtain the following equation:

$$\left\{ (1-p)^M + p(1-p)^{M-1} \right\} = \tag{A.1}$$

$$= \overline{C} \left\{ p(1-p)^{M-1} - \left[1 - (1-p)^M \right] + (M-1)\frac{p}{1-p} \right\}$$

The p_{opt} value is the solution of Equation (A.1).

First we analyze the l.h.s of Equation (A.1). It is easy to observe that the l.h.s is equal to $(1-p)^{M-1}$ that $M \gg 1$ tends to $(1-p)^M$, and $E[Idle] \cdot P_{N_{tr} \geq 1} = (1-p)^M$, where $P_{N_{tr} \geq 1} = 1 - (1-p)^M$, i.e., the probability that at least a station is transmitting. Under the condition $M \cdot p < 1$, [6], the r.h.s of Equation (A.1) can be expressed as:

$$\left\{ p(1-p)^{M-1} - \left[1 - (1-p)^M\right] + (M-1)\frac{p}{1-p} \right\} = \frac{(M+2)(M-1)}{2} p^2 + O\left((Mp)^3\right) \quad \text{(A.2)}$$

By indicating with $P_{Coll|N_{tr} \geq 1}$ the collision probability conditioned to have at least a transmitting station, it also holds that:

$$P_{Coll|N_{tr} \geq 1} \cdot P_{N_{tr} \geq 1} = 1 - \left[(1-p)^M + Mp(1-p)^{M-1}\right] = \frac{M(M-1)}{2} p^2 + O\left((Mp)^3\right) \quad \text{(A.3)}$$

It is worth noting the similarity between the r.h.s of Equation (A.3) and the r.h.s of Equation (A.2). Specifically the r.h.s of Equation (A.2) can be written as:

$$\left[\frac{(M-1)}{2} p^2\right] \cdot (M+1) + O\left((Mp)^3\right) \xrightarrow[M \gg 1]{} \left[\frac{(M-1)}{2} p^2\right] \cdot M + \quad \text{(A.4)}$$

$$+ O\left((Mp)^3\right) = P_{Coll|N_{tr} \geq 1} \cdot P_{N_{tr} \geq 1}$$

Hence, Equation (A.1) can be rewritten as:

$$E[Idle] \cdot P_{N_{tr} \geq 1} = \overline{C} \cdot P_{Coll|N_{tr} \geq 1} \cdot P_{N_{tr} \geq 1}. \quad \text{(A.5)}$$

By dividing all the terms in Equation (A.5) by $P_{N_{tr} \geq 1}$, and substituting the $\overline{C}$ approximation with $E[Coll \mid Coll]$, Equation (A.5) becomes:

$$E[Idle\_p] = E[Coll \mid N_{tr} \geq 1] \quad \text{(A.6)}$$

This concludes the proof.

◊

Appendix: B

Lemma 3. In an M-station network that adopts a p-persistent CSMA access scheme, in which the message lengths $\{Li\}$, normalized to t_{slot}, are a sequence of i.i.d. random

---

[6] This assumption is always true in a stable system as the average number of transmitting stations in an empty slot must be less than one.

variables, if the stations operate in asymptotic conditions, under the condition $Mp \ll 1$· the p_{opt}^{C} value is

$$p_{opt}^{C} \cong \frac{\sqrt{1 + 2(\overline{C} - 1)\dfrac{M - 1}{M}} - 1}{(M - 1)(\overline{C} - 1)} \quad , \tag{B.1}$$

where $\overline{C} = E\big[\max\{L_1, L_2\}\big]$.

PROOF.

In [24] it is shown that if the network stations are operating close to the p_{opt}^{C} value and if the stations operate in asymptotic conditions $E[Coll \mid Collision] \approx \overline{C}$. The $E[Coll \mid Collision] \approx \overline{C}$ assumption indicates that $E[Coll \mid Collision]$ depends only on the message-length distribution and Equation (11) can be rewritten as:

$$(1 - p)^{M} - \overline{C} \cdot \left\{ 1 - \left[(1 - p)^{M} + Mp(1 - p)^{M - 1} \right] \right\} = 0 \quad . \tag{B.2}$$

Under the condition $Mp \ll 1$,

$$(1 - p)^{M} \approx 1 - Mp + \frac{M(M - 1)}{2} p^{2} - O\big((Mp)^{3}\big) \quad , \tag{B.3}$$

$$1 - \left[(1 - p)^{M} + Mp(1 - p)^{M - 1} \right] \approx \frac{M(M - 1)p^{2}}{2} - O\big((Mp)^{3}\big) \quad . \tag{B.4}$$

By substituting (B.3) and (B.4) in (B.2) the following equation is obtained:

$$\frac{M(M - 1)}{2} \cdot (\overline{C} - 1)p^{2} + Mp - 1 = 0 \quad . \tag{B.5}$$

By solving Equation (B.5) we obtain the formula (B.1) and this concludes the proof of the Lemma.

$\Diamond$

Service Centric Computing – Next Generation Internet Computing

Jerry Rolia, Rich Friedrich, and Chandrakant Patel

Hewlett Packard Labs, 1501 Page Mill Rd., Palo Alto, CA, USA, 94304
{jerry_rolia,rich_friedrich,chandrakant_patel}@hp.com
www.hpl.hp.com/research/internet

Abstract. In the not-too-distant future, billions of people, places and things could all be connected to each other and to useful services through the Internet. In this world scalable, cost-effective information technology capabilities will need to be provisioned as service, delivered as a service, metered and managed as a service, and purchased as a service. We refer to this world as service centric computing. Consequently, processing and storage will be accessible via utilities where customers pay for what they need when they need it and where they need it. This tutorial introduces concepts of service centric computing and its relationship to the Grid. It explains a programmable data center paradigm as a flexible architecture that helps to achieve service centric computing. Case study results illustrate performance and thermal issues. Finally, key open research questions pertaining to service centric computing and Internet computing are summarized.

1 Introduction

In the not-too-distant future, billions of people, places and things could all be connected to each other and to useful services through the Internet. Re-use and scale motivate the need for *service centric computing*. With service centric computing application services, for example payroll or tax calculation, may be composed of other application services and also rely on computing, networking, and storage resources as services. These services will be offered according to a *utility paradigm*. They will be provisioned, delivered, metered, managed, and purchased in a consistent manner when and where they are needed. This paper explains the components of service centric computing with examples of performance studies that pertain to resources offered as a service.

Figure 1 illustrates the components of service centric computing. Applications may be composed of application and resource services via open middleware such as Web services. Applications discover and acquire access to services via a grid service architecture. Resource utilities offer computing, network, and storage resources as services. They may also offer complex aggregates of these resources with specific qualities of service. We refer to this as *Infrastructure on Demand* (IOD).

M.C. Calzarossa and S. Tucci (Eds.): Performance 2002, LNCS 2459, pp. 463–479, 2002.
© Springer-Verlag Berlin Heidelberg 2002

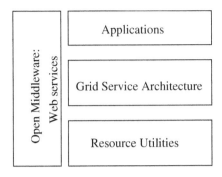

Fig. 1. Service centric computing

Section 2 describes several classes of applications and their requirements on infrastructure for service centric computing. Web service technologies are also introduced. An example of a Grid resource management system and a Grid Service Architecture are introduced in Section 3. Section 4 describes resource utilities, resources as services, and IOD. A programmable data center is introduced as an example of IOD. Next we describe a broad set of technologies that can be integrated to offer IOD with specific qualities of service. Case studies illustrate key issues with regard to IOD. A list of research challenges is offered in Section 5. Concluding remarks are given in Section 6.

2   Applications and Web Services

This section discusses the requirements of applications on service centric computing with a focus on issues that pertain to infrastructure. This is followed by a brief discussion of Web service technologies as an open middleware for service interaction.

2.1   Applications

We consider technical, commercial, and ubiquitous classes of applications and their requirements on service centric computing.

Technical applications are typically processing, data, and/or communications intensive. Examples of applications are found from life and material sciences, manufacturing CAE and CAD, national defense, high-end film and video, electronic design simulation, weather and climate modeling, geological sciences, and basic research. These applications typically present batch style jobs with a finite duration.

Commercial applications may be accessed via Intranet or Internet systems. They often rely on multi-tier architectures that include firewall, load balancer and server appliances and exploit concepts of horizontal and vertical scalability.

Examples of applications include enterprise resource management systems, E-commerce systems, and portals. These applications typically require resources continuously but may require different quantities of resources depending on factors such as time of day and day of week.

With *ubiquitous computing* there is a potential for literally billions of interconnected devices each participating in many instances of value added services. Examples of devices include personal digital assistants, tools used for manufacturing or maintenance, and fixtures. Consider the following example of a value added service for a maintenance process. Instrumentation within tools and an aircraft under service record the steps of maintenance procedures as they are completed to help verify that appropriate service schedules are being followed correctly.

Applications place many requirements on service centric computing. They include the following.

For technical computing:

- Expensive and/or specialized resources need to be easy to share
- Utilize geographically distributed resources effectively
- Share computing, storage, data, programs, and other resources
- Take advantage of underutilized resources

The above requirements have driven the development of grids for high performance computing. The following additional requirements arise for commercial and ubiquitous computing:

- Automate the deployment and evolution of complex multi-tier applications and infrastructure
- Support applications that execute continuously
- Provide access to resources with some level of assurance
- Scale: enable the deployment of many small distributed services that would not otherwise be possible
- Mobility: take computation/data closer to the client(s)

Technical computing applications express demands for numbers of resources and their capacities. For some applications these demands may constrain the topology of a supporting grid's infrastructure – for example requiring the use of high capacity low latency communication fabrics. However the actual topology of a grid's infrastructure is in general deliberately transparent to such applications. We refer to this as *infrastructure transparency*.

In contrast multi-tier commercial and ubiquitous computing applications can require explicit networking topologies that include firewalls and load balancers. Networking topology and appliance configuration may implement security and performance policies and as a result can be explicit features of such applications. As a result such applications are not necessarily infrastructure transparent. They may require changes in infrastructure in response to changes in workload, device mobility, or maintenance.

To reduce the time and skills needed to deploy infrastructure; avoid the pitfalls of over or under-provisioning; and to enable large scale and adaptive service deployment (due to changing workload demands and/or mobility), commercial and ubiquitous computing applications need automated support for the deployment and maintenance of both applications and their infrastructure. Furthermore such applications need assurances that they will be able to acquire resources when and where they need them.

2.2   Web Services

Web services [1] are a collection of middleware technologies for interactions between services in Internet environments. They are platform and application language independent. The following Web service technologies are likely to be exploited by applications to discover and bind with other application services and infrastructure services.

– XML, descriptive data
– Messaging (SOAP, etc), message formats
– Description of documents (WSDL, etc), interface/data specifications
– Registry (WSIL, UDDI), Directories/lookup

The extended markup language (XML) [2] describes data. The Simple Object Access Protocol (SOAP) [3] is a mechanism for framing data for remote procedure calls. The Web Service Description Language (WSDL) [4] defines type information for data and interfaces. The Web Service Inspection Language (WSIL) [5] and Universal Description, Discovery and Integration (UDDI) [6] offer registry and lookup services.

A business can become a service provider by encapsulating application functionality as a Web service and then offering that service over its Intranet or the Internet. Another application can reuse that functionality by binding with and then exploiting an instance of the service. In a world of Web services, applications will be an integration of locally managed and outsourced services. This is referred to as *service composition*. Grid computing has a natural relationship to the concept of Web services in that it provides resources as a service.

3   Grids and Grid Service Architectures

Today's grids largely support the needs of the technical computing community. However there are efforts underway to further develop the notion of grids to the level of Grid Service Architectures (GSA) that support both technical and commercial applications. The Global Grid Forum [7] is an organization that promotes grid technologies and architectures. As examples of Grids and GSAs, this section describes Globus [8] and the Globus Open Grid Service Architecture [9].

3.1   Globus

Globus is U.S. government sponsored organization formed to develop Grid solutions for high performance scientific computing applications. The goals are essentially those listed for technical applications in Section 2.1. The initial Grid vision for the Globus Grid development was to enable computational grids:

A computational grid is a hardware and software infrastructure that provides dependable, consistent, pervasive, and inexpensive access to high-end computing capabilities.
Ian Foster and Carl Kesselman [10]

Figure 2 illustrates the resource management architecture for the Globus grid infrastructure. The purpose of the infrastructure is to bind applications with resource schedulers. Additional Grid services provide support for large file transfer and access control.

From the figure, applications describe their resource requirements using a Resource Specification Language (RSL). They submit the RSL to Brokers. Brokers interact with Information Services to learn about resource availability. An information service receives resource availability information from resource scheduler systems. Brokers may transform RSL iteratively to find a match between the supply and demand for specific resource types. An application may then use co-allocators to reserve access to the resources managed by resource schedulers via an open Globus Resource Allocation Manager (GRAM) interface.

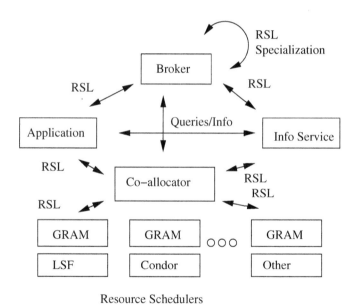

Fig. 2. Globus Resource Management Architecture

There are many examples of resource schedulers including LSF [12], Condor [13] and Legion [14]. A review of scheduling in Grid environments is given in reference [11].

Grids help to enable a utility computing paradigm by providing the mechanisms to match demands for resources with the supply of resources.

3.2   Grid Service Architectures

Recently the notion of integrating the Globus Grid with Web services has developed. The vision for the Grid has evolved to support both e-business and high performance computing applications:

> The Grid integrates services across distributed, heterogeneous, dynamic *virtual organizations* formed from the disparate resources within a single enterprise and/or from external resource sharing and service provider relationships in both e-business and e-science
> Foster, Kesselman, Nick, Tuecke [9]

The integration of Globus and Web services leads to a specification for an Open Grid Services Architecture (OGSA) [9] that treats both applications and resources uniformly as services. This uniform approach is expected to simplify the development of more advanced Grid environments.

Within an OGSA Grid, persistent services accept requests for the creation of service instances. These created instances are referred to as *transient* services. An OGSA governs the creation of and interactions between service instances. A newly defined *Grid service* interface provides a mechanism for service instance creation, registration and discovery, the management of state information, notifications, and management.

A Grid architecture based on Grid services helps to support advanced Grid environments in the following ways. For example, service instances associated with resources may exploit the Grid service interface to implement patterns for joining and departing from resource pools managed by resource schedulers and for propagating resource event information to a resource scheduler. Similarly an application may use the Grid service interface to implement a pattern for asking a resource scheduler for notification of events that pertain to a specific resource.

4   Resource Utilities

In a world of service centric computing, applications may rely on resource utilities for some or all of their resource needs. Today's grid environments offer resources in an infrastructure transparent manner. Yet some styles of applications place explicit requirements on infrastructure topology and qualities of service. In this section we describe programmable data centers as resource utilities that can offer infrastructure on demand. Technologies that contribute to infrastructure on demand are described along with several examples of research in this area.

4.1   Programmable Data Centers

A programmable data center (PDC) is composed of compute, networking, and storage resources that are physically wired once but with relationships that can be *virtually wired* programatically. Virtual wiring exploits the existing virtualization features of resources. Examples of these features are described in the next subsection.

To support automation and ease of introducing applications into the data center we introduce the notion of virtual application environments (VAE) [15]. A VAE presents an environment to an application that is consistent with the application's configuration requirements. For example, every application has certain requirements regarding server capacity, network connectivity, appliances, and storage services. It can have explicit layers of servers and many local area networks. Network and storage fabrics are configured to make a portion of the data center's resources and back end servers appear to an application as a dedicated environment. Data center management services create these VAEs by programming resource virtualization features. This is done in a manner that isolates VAEs from one another. Later, applications can request changes to their VAEs, for example to add or remove servers in response to changing workload conditions. A PDC is illustrated in Figure 3.

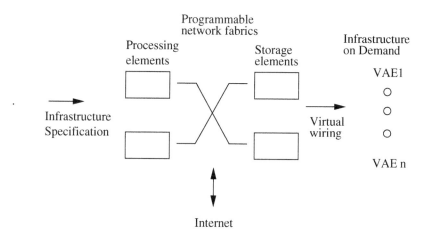

Fig. 3. Programmable Data Center

A PDC accepts a markup language description of the infrastructure required by a VAE. It must perform an admission control test to report whether it has sufficient resources to host the application with its desired qualities of service.

Applications may express requirements for many qualities of service that include: Internet bandwidth, internal communication and storage bandwidths, packet latencies and loss rates, server, storage, and network fabric reliability. They are also likely to require some assurance that it will be possible to acquire resources when they are needed.

Security and reliability are essential features of PDCs. As programmable entities strict controls must be in place to ensure that only valid changes are made to infrastructure and so that VAEs are isolated from one another. Additionally, many applications may rely on shared resources such as PDC network links so the consequences of single failures are larger than in environments without such sharing. For these reasons PDCs must have security and reliability built into their architectures.

Planetary scale computing relies on notions of PDCs and programmable networks. With planetary scale computing PDCs are joined by metro and wide area networking infrastructures providing network capacity on demand. Applications may be deployed across multiple PDCs with resources allocated near to their end-users or where capacity is least expensive. As an application's compute and storage requirements change corresponding changes must be made to network capacities between the PDCs.

4.2   Programmable Infrastructure

This section gives examples of virtualization technologies that can contribute to planetary scale computing. Subsets of these technologies can be combined to provide infrastructure as a service with specific qualities of service.

Programmable Networks. Research on programmable networks has provided a wide range of virtualization technologies. These include:

- *Virtual Private Networks* (VPN)
  - A tunneling mechanism that frames encrypted source packets for transmission to a destination appliance over an insecure network. The encrypted packets are treated as data by the appliance, decrypted, and dropped onto a secure network for delivery to the packet's true destination.
  - Properties: Security isolation
- *Virtual LANs* (VLAN)
  - Ethernet packets are augmented with a VLAN tag header. Ports on appropriate Ethernet switches can be programmed to only accept and forward frames (at line speed) with specific VLAN tags.
  - Properties: Security isolation, classes of service
- *Multiple Protocl Label Switching* (MPLS)
  - Similar to VLAN tags. However these tags can be used by switches/routers to identify specific tunnels of data. Resource reservation, class of service differentiation, and other protocols provide support for fast recovery in the event of network failures and capacity on demand for these tunnels.
  - Properties: Isolation, reliability, capacity on demand
- *Resilient Packet Rings* (RPR)

- These rings are being used to replace SONET infrastructure in metro and wide area networks. They provide a new frame specification that can carry Ethernet and other traffic, offer security isolation and have special support for fast recovery and capacity on demand.
  - Properties: Security isolation, reliability, capacity on demand
- Optical wavelength switching
  - Optical switches can support switching at the abstraction of wavelengths. In an earlier section we described virtual wiring. Wavelength switching is best described as virtual wire. With appropriate use of lasers wavelengths can each support tens of Gbps of bandwidth and fibers can support hundreds of wavelengths. Lightpaths are end-to-end circuits of wavelengths that provide true performance isolation across optical switching fabrics.
  - Properties: Security and performance isolation, reliability, capacity on demand

Programmable Servers. Since the time of early IBM mainframes server virtualization has been an important feature for resource management. With server virtualization each job or application is isolated within its own logically independent system partition. The fraction of system resources associated with each partition can be dynamically altered, permitting the vertical scaling of resources associated with an application. Server virtualization is a convenient mechanism to achieve server consolidation. Examples of systems that support server virtualization include:

- HP: Superdome and mid-range HP-UX servers [16]
- Sun: Sun Fire [17]
- IBM Mainframes [18]
- Intel [20] processor based servers with VMWare [19]

Server virtualization offers: performance isolation for partitions – when the resource consumption of each partition can bounded; capacity on demand – when the fractions of resources associated with partitions can be changed dynamically; security isolation – depending on the implementation; and can be used to support high availability solutions with redundant, but idle, application components residing in partitions on alternative servers.

Programmable Storage. Today's storage systems are utilities in and of themselves. They can contain thousands of physical disks and have sophisticated management services for backup, self-tuning, and maintenance. Storage virtualization offers the notion of virtual disks (logical units). These virtual disks are striped across a storage system's physical disks in a manner that supports the service level requirements and workload characteristics of application loads.

All major storage vendors support storage virtualization for storage systems accessed via storage area networks. Storage virtualization mechanisms support the management of performance, capacity, availability, reliability, and security.

Programmable Cooling Systems. Data centers contain thousands of single board systems deployed in racks in close proximity which results in very high heat density. Thermal management aims to extract heat dissipated by these systems while maintaining reliable operating temperatures. Air conditioning resources account for 30% of the energy costs of such installations [32].

Today's data centers rely on fixed cooling infrastructures. The PDCs of tomorrow will exploit programmable cooling controls that include:

– Variable capacity air movers
– Variable capacity compressors in air conditioners
– Variable capacity vents and air distribution systems

These features can be used to dynamically allocate cooling resources based on heat load while operating at the highest possible energy efficiency. This type of on-demand cooling is expected to reduce cooling costs by 25% over conventional designs [32].

Programmable Data centers. Programmable data centers provide infrastructure on demand for complex application infrastructures. They exploit the virtualization features of other resources to render multi-tier virtual infrastructure. This permits applications to automate the acquisition and removal of resources in proportion to their time varying workloads.

Examples of programmable data centers include:

– HP Utility Data Center with Controller Software [21], provides integrated computing, networking, and storage infrastructure as a service
– Terraspring [22], provides integrated computing, networking, and storage infrastructure as a service
– Think Dynamics [23], provides a scripting environment to enable the implementation of infrastructure on demand
– IBM Research, The Oceano Project [24], an E-business utility for the support of multi-tier E-commerce applications

These systems help to provide infrastructure on demand. For the commercial PDCs, solutions must be engineered to offer security isolation and specific internal network qualities of service that are required by their customers.

4.3   Case Studies on Infrastructure on Demand

This subsection offers several examples of research and results on infrastructure on demand. We consider *server consolidation*, presenting some otherwise unpublished results that demonstrate opportunities for resource sharing in a commercial data center environment. Next we illustrate the resource savings offered by a utility environment to two horizontally scalable Web based applications along with a mechanism to achieve those savings. We note that commercial applications are unlikely to rely on utilities unless they can receive some assurance that resources will be available when they need them. We describe some recent work on admission control for PDCs. Next, an example of a self-managing storage system is given.

Planetary scale computing relies on the co-allocation of resources, for example wide area networking as well as data center resources. Mechanisms to achieve co-allocation in Grid environments are described. The concepts of programmable data centers, programmable networks, and co-allocation help to enable wide area load balancing. Control issues regarding wide area load balancing are introduced.

Finally, we present results that pertain to the thermal management of data centers. We describe the importance of thermal management on resource reliability and on overall energy costs.

Server consolidation. Figure 4 presents the results of a server consolidation exercise for 10 identically configured 6-cpu servers from an enterprise data center. Consolidation is based on cpu utilizations as measured over 5 minute intervals for nearly 2 months. An off-line integer programming model is used to map work from the *source* servers onto as few consolidated *target* servers as possible such that the work of only one source server is allocated to a target server or the total per-interval mean cpu utilization on the target server does not exceed 50%. The following factors are considered:

- Number of CPUs per server - The number of cpus per target server: 6, 8, 16, 32
- Fast migration - whether the work of a source server may migrate between target servers at the end of each interval without penalty.
- On-line server migration - whether the pool of target servers can vary in size.

The figure shows the peak number of cpus required with and without fast migration and the mean number of servers required with fast migration and on-line server migration. In the figure, FM represents the case with fast migration while fm represents no fast migration.

We found that fast application migration enables a more effective consolidation but is sensitive to number of cpus per server. As the number of cpus per target server increases fast migration offered no benefit for the system under study. On-line server migration permits us to reclaim unused capacity for other purposes. It permits us to meaningfully characterize a system based on its average number of target servers required because we can use these resources for another purpose. Last, the figure also shows that for the system under study many small servers can be nearly as effective as fewer large servers.

Horizontal Scalability. Ranjan *et. al.*, characterize the advantages of on-line server migration for commercial E-commerce and search engine systems using a trace driven simulation environment [25]. In each case the simulation exploits an algorithm named Quality of Infrastructure on Demand (QuID) that attempts to maintain a target cpu utilization for application servers by adding and removing servers in response to changing workload conditions. The simulation takes into account the time needed to migrate servers into an application (including server

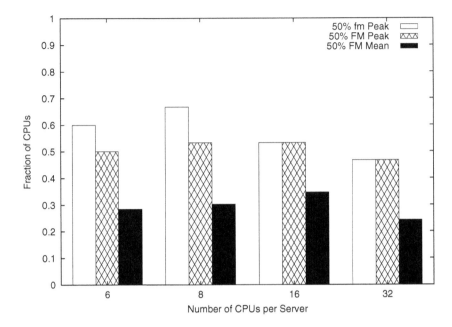

Fig. 4. Fraction of Original Number of CPUs

boot time) and time needed to drain user sessions prior to removing a server. The results show resource savings, with respect to a static allocation of resources, of approximately 29%. In both cases the peak to mean ratio for resource demand was approximately 1.6. A transformed version of the E-commerce trace with a peak to mean of 5 offered resource savings of 68% with respect to a static allocation of resources. We note that the resource savings are expected to be higher in practice since the static cases would have to be further over-provisioned.

Admission control for PDCs. Commercial applications that exploit infrastructure on demand will expect some assurance that resources will be available when they need them. An admission control approach is presented in [26]. The approach characterizes demand profiles for applications based on factors such as time of day. An aggregate of the demand profiles along with application demand correlation information are used to estimate the number of resources needed to satisfy requests for resources with a specific probability θ. Simulations suggest that the technique is relatively insensitive to correlations in application demands as long as they are taken into account when estimating the number of resources required.

Automated storage management. Reference [27] describes tools for automated storage management. Methods are used to automate an initial storage design – the layout of virtual disks over physical disks. Iterative techniques then exploit online measurements to improve the design while the system operates. Experiments showed performance results within 15% of that achieved by expert administrators.

Co-allocation. A resource co-allocation technique is described in reference [29]. The method extends the Globus resource management architecture with a component for acquiring groups of resources from multiple resource schedulers. A two phase commit protocol can be used to ensure that either all or none of the required resources are reserved.

Such a co-allocation mechanism is particularly important in the context of service centric computing as it may be necessary to acquire resources from multiple resource utilities that include network providers and programmable data centers.

Wide area load balancing. A wide area load balancing system is described in reference [30]. A goal of the work is to balance application demands over servers within and across utilities using distributed, collaborative, self-control mechanisms.

Thermal management for PDCs. Programmable cooling is a smart cooling proposition achieved through modeling, metrology and controls - by charting real-time temperature distribution through a distributed sensor network and modulating the cooling. The cooling resources are dynamically provisioned based on distributed sensing (power, air flow and temperature) in the data center and numerical modeling [31][32][33]. The capacity of compressors, condensers, and air moving devices are varied commensurate with the heat loads present in the data center. An example is an instance when high heat loads prompt an increase in the opening of "smart" cool air inlet vents and a change in speed of air movers and compressors in air conditioners to address a specific area in the data center.

In addition to this dynamic variation in cooling, distributed measurements and thermal resource allocation policies may guide the provisioning of workload within the data center. As an example we may choose to provision a resource that results in the most efficient utilization of cooling resources. In yet another example, workload allocation policies programmatically move workload and shut some systems down in response to the failure of certain air conditioning infrastructure thereby maintaining the reliability of the overall data center. Furthermore, in the context of Grid computing, workload may be provisioned in a global network of data centers based on the most cost effective energy available e.g. on diurnal basis based on the climate - e.g. Bangalore, India at night to provide a more energy efficient condensing temperature for the air conditioning vapor compression cycle. Additionally, the economics of energy production around the globe may be used to drive the choices for global load distribution.

5 Research Challenges

This section offers several performance related research challenges for service centric computing. They address issues of data center design and resource management, resource management for planetary scale computing (federations of infrastructure providers), and general control and validation for these large scale systems. We use the term resource broadly to include information technology and energy.

What is the most efficient, economical data center design?

- What high density, low power, high performance computing architectures most economically support infrastructure as a service?
- What are the simple building blocks of processing, communications and storage that support dynamic allocation at a data center level of granularity?
- What are the implications of commodity components on multi-system designs?

What are the most effective performance management techniques for utility computing?

- What measurement techniques/metrics are appropriate for large scale distributed environments?
- What automated techniques are appropriate for creating models of applications and infrastructure?
- How are models validated for this very dynamic world?

What are the most efficient dynamic resource management techniques?

- What techniques are appropriate for ensuring qualities of service within layers of shared infrastructures?
- What to do about federations of providers (co-allocation)?
- What techniques are appropriate for making good use of resources?

What control system techniques can be applied effectively to this scale and dynamism?

- What automated reasoning techniques can eliminate the complexity of controlling large scale systems?
- What control theoretic techniques are applicable to reactive and predictive events?
- What time scales are appropriate for control?
- How are control measures and decisions coordinated across federated systems?

What is the science of large scale computing that provides probabilistic assurance of large scale behavior based on small scale experiments?

- What is the equivalent to the aeronautical engineer's wind tunnel?
- What behaviors scale linearly?

6   Summary and Remarks

This paper motivates and explains the concept of service centric computing as an approach for next generation Internet computing. With service centric computing: applications, resources, and infrastructure are offered as services. This is essential for the support of commercial and ubiquitous computing applications as it enables the reuse of application functions, server consolidation, and large scale deployment.

As an architecture, service centric computing relies on middleware such as Web services and Grid service architectures as open mechanisms for service creation, interactions, discovery, and binding. Resource utilities offer access to resources and infrastructure. Today's resource utilities in Grid environments typically offer resources in an infrastructure transparent manner. Commercial applications can have explicit dependencies on networking topologies and their relationship with servers, storage, and appliances. These require resource utilities that offer infrastructure on demand.

We believe that there are many opportunities for research in this area. When realized service centric computing will enable new kinds of applications and reduce barriers to market entry for small and medium sized organizations.

7   Trademarks

Sun and Sun Fire are trademarks of the Sun Microsystems Inc., IBM is a trademark of International Business Machines Corporation, Intel is a trademark of Intel Corporation, VMware is a trademark of VMware Inc., HP Utility Data Center with Controller Software is a trademark of Hewlett Packard Company, Terraspring is a trademark of Terraspring, and Think Dynamics is a trademark of Think Dynamics.

Acknowledgements. Thanks to Xiaoyun Zhu, Sharad Singhal, Jim Pruyne, and Martin Arlitt of HP Labs for their helpful comments regarding this tutorial paper.

References

1. www.webservices.org.
2. www.w3.org/XML.
3. www.w3.org/TR/SOAP.
4. www.w3.org/TR/wsdl.
5. www-106.ibm.com/developerworks/webservices/library/ws-wsilspec.html.
6. www.uddi.org.
7. www.globalgridforum.org.
8. Czajkowski K., Foster I., Karonis N., Kesselman C., Martin S., Smith W., and Tuecke S.: A Resource Management Architecture for Metacomputing Systems. JSSPP, 1988, 62-82.

9. Foster I., Kesselman C., Nick J., and Tuecke S.: The Physiology of the Grid: An Open Grid Services Architecture for Distributed Systems Integration. www.globus.org, January, 2002.

10. The Grid: Blueprint for a New Computing Infrastructure, Edited by Ian Foster and Carl Kesselman, July 1998, ISBN 1-55860-475-8.

11. Krauter K., Buyya R., and Maheswaran M.: A taxonomy and survey of grid resource management systems for distributed computing. Software-Practice and Experience, vol. 32, no. 2, 2002, 135-164.

12. Zhou S.: LSF: Load sharing in large-scale heterogeneous distributed systems, Workshop on Cluster Computing, 1992.

13. Litzkow M., Livny M. and Mutka M.: Condor - A Hunter of Idle Workstations. Proceedings of the 8th International Conference on Distributed Computing Systems, June, 1998, 104-111.

14. Natrajan A., Humphrey M., and Grimshaw A.: Grids: Harnessing Geographically-Separated Resources in a Multi-Organisational Context. Proceedings of High Performance Computing Systems, June, 2001.

15. Rolia J., Singhal S. and Friedrich R.: Adaptive Internet Data Centers. Proceedings of the European Computer and eBusiness Conference (SSGRR), L'Aquila, Italy, July 2000, Italy, http://www.ssgrr.it/en/ssgrr2000/papers/053.pdf.

16. www.hp.com.

17. www.sun.com.

18. www.ibm.com.

19. www.vmware.com.

20. www.intel.com.

21. HP Utility Data Center Architecture, http://www.hp.com/solutions1/ infrastructure/solutions /utilitydata/architecture/index.html.

22. www.terraspring.com.

23. www.thinkdynamics.com.

24. Appleby K., Fakhouri S., Fong L., Goldszmidt G. and Kalantar M.: Oceano – SLA Based Management of a Computing Utility. Proceedings of the IFIP/IEEE International Symposium on Integrated Network Management, May 2001.

25. Ranjan S., Rolia J., Zu H., and Knightly E.: QoS-Driven Server Migration for Internet Data Centers. Proceedings of IWQoS 2002, May 2002, 3-12.

26. Rolia J., Zhu X., Arlitt M., and Andrzejak A.: Statistical Service Assurances for Applications in Utility Grid Environments. HPL Technical Report, HPL-2002-155.

27. Anderson E., Hobbs M., Keeton K., Spence S., Uysal M., and Veitch A.: Hippodrome: running circles around storage administration. Conference on File and Storage Technologies (FAST3902), 17545188 - 284530 January 2002, Monterey, CA. (USENIX, Berkeley, CA.).

28. Borowsky E., Golding R., Jacobson P., Merchant A., Schreier L., Spasojevic M., and Wilkes J.: Capacity planning with phased workloads, WOSP, 1998, 199-207.

29. Foster I., Kesselman C., Lee C., Lindell R., Nahrstedt K., and Roy A.: A Distributed Resource Management Architecture that Supports Advance Reservations and Co-Allocation. Proceedings of the International Workshop on Quality of Service, 1999.

30. Andrzejak, A., Graupner, S., Kotov, V., and Trinks, H.: Self-Organizing Control in Planetary-Scale Computing. IEEE International Symposium on Cluster Computing and the Grid (CCGrid), 2nd Workshop on Agent-based Cluster and Grid Computing (ACGC), May 21-24, 2002, Berlin.

31. Patel C., Bash C., Belady C., Stahl L., and Sullivan D.: Computational Fluid Dynamics Modeling of High Compute Density Data Centers to Assure System Inlet Air Specifications. Proceedings of IPACK'01 The Pacific Rim/ASME International Electronic Packaging Technical Conference and Exhibition July 8-13, 2001, Kauai, Hawaii, USA.
32. Patel, C.D., Sharma, R.K, Bash, C.E., Beitelmal, A: Thermal Considerations in Cooling Large Scale High Compute Density Data Centers, ITherm 2002 - Eighth Intersociety Conference on Thermal and Thermomechanical Phenomena in Electronic Systems. May 2002, San Diego, California.
33. Sharma, R.K, Bash. C.E., Patel, C.D.: Dimensionless Parameters for Evaluation of Thermal Design and Performance of Large Scale Data Centers. Proceedings of the 8th ASME/AIAA Joint Thermophysics and Heat Transfer Conf., St. Louis, MO, June 2002.

European DataGrid Project: Experiences of Deploying a Large Scale Testbed for E-science Applications

Fabrizio Gagliardi[1], Bob Jones[1], Mario Reale[2], and Stephen Burke[3]

On behalf of the EU DataGrid Project

[1] CERN, European Particle Physics Laboratory,
CH-1211 Geneve 23, Switzerland
{Fabrizio.Gagliardi, Bob.Jones}@cern.ch
http://www.cern.ch

[2] INFN CNAF, Viale Berti-Pichat 6/2,
I-40127 Bologna, Italy
mario.reale@cnaf.infn.it

[3] Rutherford Appleton Laboratory,
Chilton, Didcot, Oxon, UK
s.burke@rl.ac.uk

Abstract. The objective of the European DataGrid (EDG) project is to assist the next generation of scientific exploration, which requires intensive computation and analysis of shared large-scale datasets, from hundreds of terabytes to petabytes, across widely distributed scientific communities. We see these requirements emerging in many scientific disciplines, including physics, biology, and earth sciences. Such sharing is made complicated by the distributed nature of the resources to be used, the distributed nature of the research communities, the size of the datasets and the limited network bandwidth available. To address these problems we are building on emerging computational Grid technologies to establish a research network that is developing the technology components essential for the implementation of a world-wide data and computational Grid on a scale not previously attempted. An essential part of this project is the phased development and deployment of a large-scale Grid testbed.

The primary goals of the first phase of the EDG testbed were: 1) to demonstrate that the EDG software components could be integrated into a production-quality computational Grid; 2) to allow the middleware developers to evaluate the design and performance of their software; 3) to expose the technology to end-users to give them hands-on experience; and 4) to facilitate interaction and feedback between end-users and developers. This first testbed deployment was achieved towards the end of 2001 and assessed during the successful European Union review of the project on March 1, 2002. In this article we give an overview of the current status and plans of the EDG project and describe the distributed testbed.

M.C. Calzarossa and S. Tucci (Eds.): Performance 2002, LNCS 2459, pp. 480–499, 2002.
© Springer-Verlag Berlin Heidelberg 2002

1 Introduction

Advances in distributed computing, high quality networks and powerful and cost-effective commodity-based computing have given rise to the Grid computing paradigm [6]. In the academic world, a major driver for Grid development is collaborative science mediated by the use of computing technology, often referred to as e-science. While scientists of many disciplines have been using computing technology for decades (almost pre-dating computing science itself), e-Science projects present fresh challenges for a number of reasons, such as the difficulty of co-ordinating the use of widely distributed resources owned and controlled by many organisations. The Grid introduces the concept of the Virtual Organisation (VO) as a group of both users and computing resources from a number of real organisations which is brought together to work on a particular project.

The EU DataGrid (EDG) is a project funded by the European Union with €9.8 M through the Framework V IST R&D programme (see www.eu-datagrid.org). There are 21 partner organisations from 15 EU countries, with a total participation of over 200 people, for a period of three years starting in January 2001. The objectives of the project are to support advanced scientific research within a Grid environment, offering capabilities for intensive computation and analysis of shared large-scale datasets, from hundreds of terabytes to petabytes, across widely distributed scientific communities. Such requirements are emerging in many scientific disciplines, including particle physics, biology, and earth sciences.

The EDG project has now reached its mid-point, since the project started on January 1st 2001 and the foreseen end of the project is on December 31st 2003. At this stage, very encouraging results have already been achieved in terms of the major goals of the project, which are the demonstration of the practical use of computational and data Grids for wide and extended use by the high energy physics, bio-informatics and earth observation communities.

A production quality testbed has been set up and implemented at a number of EDG sites, while a separate development testbed addresses the need for rapid testing and prototyping of the EDG middleware. The EDG production testbed consists currently of ten sites, spread around Europe: at CERN (Geneva), INFN-CNAF (Bologna), CC-IN2P3 (Lyon), NIKHEF (Amsterdam), INFN-TO (Torino), INFN-CT (Catania), INFN-PD (Padova), ESA-ESRIN (Frascati), Imperial College (London), and RAL (Oxfordshire). The EDG development testbed currently consists of four sites : CERN, INFN-CNAF, NIKHEF, and RAL. The reference site for the EDG collaboration is at CERN, where, before any official version of the EDG middleware is released, the initial testing of the software is performed and the main functionalities are proven, before distribution to the other development testbed sites.

The EDG collaboration is currently providing free, open source software based on the Linux Red Hat 6.2 platform. A range of standard machine profiles is supported (Computing Element, Storage Element, User Interface, Resource Broker, Worker Node, Network Monitoring Node). The testbed provides a set of common shared services available to all certified users with valid X.509 PKI certificates issued by a Certificate Authority trusted by EDG. A set of tools is provided to handle the automatic update of the grid-map files on all hosts belonging to the testbed sites which allow users to be authorised to use the resources. A number of VOs have been defined for the various research groups involved in the project. Each VO has an authorisation server (using LDAP technology) to define its members, and a Replica Catalogue to store the location of its files.

In this article, besides this short introduction about the history of the project and its current status, we give an overview of the technology developed by the project so far. This is a concrete illustration of the level of maturity reached by Grid technologies to address the task of high throughput computing for distributed Virtual Organisations. The work of the project is divided into functional areas: workload management, data management, grid monitoring and information systems, fabric management, mass data storage, testbed operation, and network monitoring. In addition there are user communities drawn from high energy physics, earth observation and biomedical applications. In November-December 2001 the first testbed was set up at CERN, merging and collecting the development work performed by the various middleware developers, and the first release of the EDG software was deployed and successfully validated. The project has been congratulated "for exceeding expectations" by the European Union reviewers on March 1st, 2002, during the first official EU review .

2   The European Data Grid Middleware Architecture

The EDG architecture is based on the Grid architecture proposed by Ian Foster and Carl Kesselman [6], with a reduced number of implemented services.

Sixteen services have been implemented by the middleware developers, based on original coding for some services and on the usage of the Globus 2 toolkit (see www.globus.org) for basic Grid infrastructure services: authentication (GSI), secure file transfer (GridFTP), information systems (MDS), job submission (GRAM) and the Globus Replica Catalogue. In addition the job submission system uses software from the Condor-G project [8]. The middleware also relies on general open source software such as OpenLDAP.

The middleware development is divided into six functional areas: workload management, data management, Grid Monitoring and Information Systems, fabric management, mass data storage, and network monitoring. A sketch of the essential EDG architecture is shown in Figure 1 [1], where the relationship between the Operating System, Globus tools, the EDG middleware and the applications is shown. The EDG architecture is therefore a multi-layered architecture. At the lowest level is the operating system. Globus provides the basic services for secure and authenticated use of both operating system and network connections to safely transfer files and data and allow interoperation of distributed services. The EDG middleware uses the Globus services, and interfaces to the highest layer, the user applications running on the Grid.

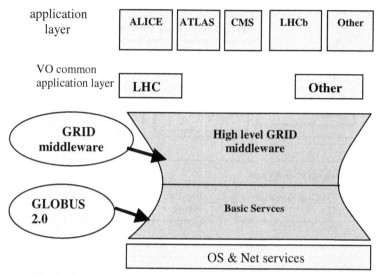

application layer

VO common application layer

GRID middleware

GLOBUS 2.0

ALICE ATLAS CMS LHCb Other

LHC Other

High level GRID middleware

Basic Servces

OS & Net services

Fig. 1. The schematic layered EDG architecture: the Globus hourglass

The multi-layered EDG Grid architecture is shown in Figure 2 and Figure 3, which show the different layers from bottom to top, namely: the Fabric layer, the underlying Grid Services, the Collective Services, the Grid Application layer and, at the top, a local application accessing a remote client machine. Figure 3 groups together and identifies the main EDG services. At the top of the whole system, the local application and the local database represent the end user machine, which executes an application requesting Grid services, either submitting a Grid job or requesting a file through the interfaces to the list of files stored on the Grid and published in a Replica Catalogue.

2.1 Workload Management System (WMS)

The goal of the Workload Management System is to implement an architecture for distributed scheduling and resource management in a Grid environment. It provides to the Grid users a set of tools to submit their jobs, have them executed on the distributed Computing Elements (a Grid resource mapped to an underlying batch system), get information about their status, retrieve their output, and allow them to access Grid resources in an optimal way (optimizing CPU usage, reducing file transfer time and cost, and balancing access to resources between users). It deals with the Job Manager of the Grid Application layer and the Grid Scheduler in the Collective Services layer. A functional view of the whole WMS system is represented in figure 4.

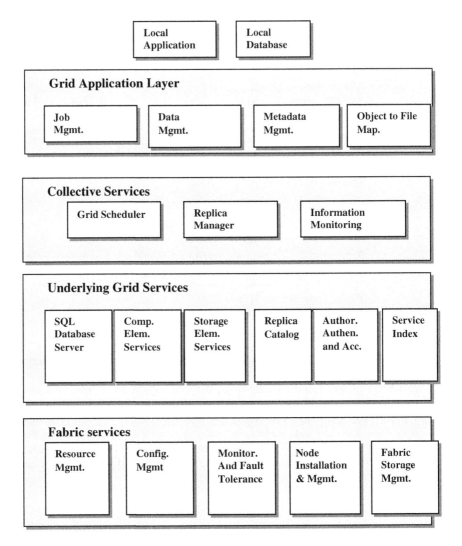

Fig. 2. The detailed multi layered EDG GRID architecture

The WMS is currently composed of the following parts:

– **User Interface** (UI): The access point for the Grid user. A job is defined using the JDL language (see below), which specifies the input data files, the code to execute, the required software environment, and lists of input and output files to be transferred with the job. The user can also control the way in which the broker chooses the best-matching resource. The job is submitted to the Resource Broker using a command line interface or a programmatic API; there are also several groups developing graphical interfaces.

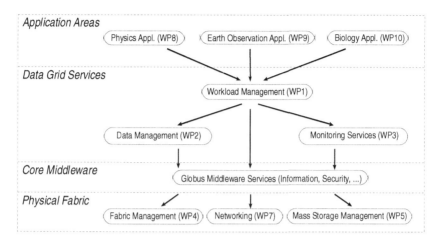

Fig. 3. The EDG service architecture

- **Resource Broker** (RB): This performs match-making between the requirements of a job and the available resources, and attempts to schedule the jobs in an optimal way, taking into account the data location and the requirements specified by the user. The information about available resources is read dynamically from the Information and Monitoring System. The scheduling and match-making algorithms used by the RB are the key to making efficient use of Grid resources. In performing the match-making the RB queries the Replica Catalogue, which is a service used to resolve logical file names (LFN, the generic name of a file) into physical file names (PFN, which gives the physical location and name of a particular file replica). The job can then be sent to the site which minimises the cost of network bandwidth to access the files.

- **Job Submission System** (JSS): This is a wrapper for Condor-G [8], interfacing the Grid to a Local Resource Management System (LRMS), usually a batch system like PBS, LSF or BQS. Condor-G is a Condor-Globus joint project, which combines the inter-domain resource management protocols of the Globus Toolkit with the intra-domain resource and job management methods of Condor to allow high throughput computing in multi-domain environments.

- **Information Index** (II): This is a Globus MDS index which collects information from the Globus GRIS information servers running on the various Grid resources, published using LDAP, and read by the RB to perform the match-making. Information items are both static (installed software, number of available CPUs etc) and dynamic (total number of running jobs, current available disk space etc). The information is cached for a short period to improve performance.

- **Logging and Bookkeeping** (LB): The Logging and Bookkeeping service stores a variety of information about the status and history of submitted jobs using a MySQL database.

Job Description Language (JDL)

The JDL allows the various components of the Grid Scheduler to communicate requirements concerning the job execution. Examples of such requirements are:

- Specification of the executable program or script to be run and arguments to be passed to it, and files to be used for the standard input, output and error streams.
- Specification of files that should be shipped with the job via Input and Output Sandboxes.
- A list of input files and the access protocols the job is prepared to use to read them.
- Specification of the Replica Catalogue to be searched for physical instances of the requested input files.
- Requirements on the computing environment (OS, memory, free disk space, software environment etc) in which the job will run.
- Expected resource consumption (CPU time, output file sizes etc).
- A ranking expression used to decide between resources which match the other requirements.

The *classified advertisements* (*ClassAds*) language defined by the Condor project has been adopted for the Job Description Language because it has all the required properties.

In order for a user to have a job correctly executed on a worker node of an available Computing Element, the user's credentials have to be transmitted by the creation of a proxy certificate. A user issues a grid-proxy-init command on a user interface machine to create an X.509 PKI proxy certificate using their locally stored private key. An authentication request containing the proxy public and private keys and the user's public key is sent to a server; the server gets the request and creates a coded message by means of the user's public key, sending it back to the user process on the User Interface machine. This message is decoded by means of the user's private key and sent back again to the server (in this case normally the Resource Broker). When the server gets the correctly decoded message it can be sure about the user's identity, so that an authenticated channel can be established and the user credentials can be delegated to the broker.

Users use Condor ClassAds-like statements inside a JDL (Job Description Language) file to describe the job they want to be executed by the Grid. This includes a list of input data residing on Storage Elements (Grid-enabled disk or tape storage), and places requirements on the features of the compute nodes on which the job will execute. These can be chosen from the set of information defined by the schema used by the information system, and includes such things as operating system version, CPU speed, available memory etc.

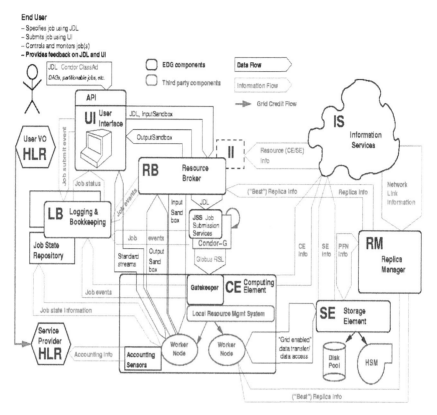

Fig. 4. The Workload Management System and its components: interaction with other EDG elements. The future component HLR (Home Location Register) is also shown.

Users can define an Input Sandbox, which is a set of files transferred to a Worker Node by means of GridFTP by the Resource Broker, so that any file required for the job to be executed (including the executable itself if necessary) can be sent to the local disk of the machine where the job will run. Similarly, the user can specify an Output Sandbox, which is a set of files to be retrieved from the Worker Node after the job finishes (other files are deleted). The files in the Output Sandbox are stored on the RB node until the user requests them to be transferred back to a UI machine.

The JDL can also specify a particular required software environment using a set of user-defined strings to identify particular features of the run-time environment (for example, locally installed application software).

A special file, called the BrokerInfo file, is created by the Resource Broker to enable a running job to be aware of the choices made in the matchmaking, in particular about the Storage Element(s) local to the chosen Computing Element, and the way to access the requested input files. The BrokerInfo file is transferred to the Worker Node along with the Input Sandbox, and can be read directly or with an API or command-line tools.

Users have at their disposal a set of commands to handle jobs by means of a command line interface installed on a User Interface machine, on which they have a normal login account and have installed their X509 certificate. They can submit a job, query its status, get logging information about the job history, cancel a job, be notified via email of the job's execution, and retrieve the job output. When a job is submitted to the system the user gets back a Grid-wide unique handle by means of which the job can be identified in other commands.

2.2 Data Management System (DMS)

The goal of the Data Management System is to specify, develop, integrate and test tools and middleware to coherently manage and share petabyte-scale information volumes in high-throughput production-quality grid environments. The emphasis is on automation, ease of use, scalability, uniformity, transparency and heterogeneity. The DMS will make it possible to securely access massive amounts of data in a universal global name space, to move and replicate data at high speed from one geographical site to another, and to manage synchronisation of distributed replicas of files or databases. Generic interfaces to heterogeneous mass storage management systems will enable seamless and efficient integration of distributed resources. The main components of the EDG Data Management System, currently provided or in development, are as follows:

– **Replica Manager**: This is still under development, but it will manage the creation of file replicas by copying from one Storage Element to another, optimising the use of network bandwidth. It will interface with the Replica Catalogue service to allow Grid users to keep track of the locations of their files.

– **Replica Catalogue**: This is a Grid service used to resolve Logical File Names into a set of corresponding Physical File Names which locate each replica of a file. This provides a Grid-wide file catalogue for the members of a given Virtual Organisation.

– **GDMP**: The GRID Data Mirroring Package is used to automatically mirror file replicas from one Storage Element to a set of other subscribed sites. It is also currently used as a prototype of the general Replica Manager service.

– **Spitfire**: This provides a Grid-enabled interface for access to relational databases. This will be used within the data managementmiddleware to implement the Replica Catalogue, but is also available for general use.

The Replica Manager
The EDG Replica Manager will allow users and running jobs to make copies of files between different Storage Elements, simultaneously updating the Replica Catalogue, and to optimise the creation of file replicas by using network performance information and cost functions, according to the file location and size. It will be a distributed system, i.e. different instances of the Replica Manager will be running on different sites, and will be synchronised to local Replica Catalogues, which will be

interconnected by the Replica Location Index. The Replica Manager functionality will be available both with APIs available to running applications and by a command line interface available to users. The Replica Manager is responsible for computing the cost estimates for replica creation. Information for cost estimates, such as network bandwidth, staging times and Storage Element load indicators, will be gathered from the Grid Information and Monitoring System.

The Replica Catalogue
The Replica Catalogue has as a primary goal the resolution of Logical File Names into Physical File Names, to allow the location of the physical file(s) which can be accessed most efficiently by a job. It is currently implemented using Globus software by means of a single LDAP server running on a dedicated machine. In future it will be implemented by a distributed system with a local catalogue on each Storage Element and a system of Replica Location Indices to aggregate the information from many sites. In order to achieve maximum flexibility the transport protocol, query mechanism, and database backend technology will be decoupled, allowing the implementation of a Replica Catalogue server using multiple database technologies (such as RDBMSs, LDAP-based databases, or flat files). APIs and protocols between client and server are required, and will be provided in future releases of the EDG middleware. The use of mechanisms specific to a particular database is excluded. Also the query technology will not be tied to a particular protocol, such as SQL or LDAP. The use of GSI-enabled HTTPS for transport and XML for input/output data representation is foreseen. Both HTTPS and XML are the most widely used industry standards for this type of system.

The Replica Manager, Grid users and Grid services like the scheduler (WMS) can access the Replica Catalogue information via APIs. The WMS makes a query to the RC in the first part of the matchmaking process, in which a target computing element for the execution of a job is chosen according to the accessibility of a Storage Element containing the required input files. To do so, the WMS has to convert logical file names into physical file names. Both logical and physical files can carry additional metadata in the form of "attributes". Logical file attributes may include items such as file size, CRC check sum, file type and file creation timestamps.

A centralised Replica Catalogue was chosen for initial deployment, this being the simplest implementation. The Globus Replica Catalogue, based on LDAP directories, has been used in the testbed so far. One dedicated LDAP server is assigned to each Virtual Organisation; four of these reside on a server machine at NIKHEF, two at CNAF, and one at CERN. Users interact with the Replica Catalogue mainly via the previously discussed Replica Catalogue and BrokerInfo APIs.

GDMP
The GDMP client-server software system is a generic file replication tool that replicates files securely and efficiently from one site to another in a Data Grid environment using several Globus Grid tools. In addition, it manages replica catalogue entries for file replicas, and thus maintains a consistent view of names and locations of replicated files. Any file format can be supported for file transfer using

plugins for pre- and post-processing, and for Objectivity database files a plugin is supplied.

GDMP allows mirroring of uncatalogued user data between Storage Elements. Registration of user data into the Replica Catalogue is also possible via the Replica Catalogue API. The basic concept is that client SEs subscribe to a source SE in which they have interest. The clients will then be notified of new files entered in the catalogue of the subscribed server, and can then make copies of required files, automatically updating the Replica Catalogue if necessary.

Spitfire
Spitfire is a secure, Grid-enabled interface to a relational database. Spitfire provides secure query access to remote databases through the Grid using Globus GSI authentication.

2.3 Grid Monitoring and Information Systems

The EDG Information Systems middleware implements a complete infrastructure to enable end-user and administrator access to status and error information in the Grid environment, and provides an environment in which application monitoring can be carried out. This permits job performance optimisation as well as allowing for problem tracing, and is crucial to facilitating high performance Grid computing. The goal is to provide easy access to current and archived information about the Grid itself (information about resources - Computing Elements, Storage Elements and the Network), for which the Globus MDS is a common solution, about job status (e.g. as implemented by the WMS Logging and Bookkeeping service) and about user applications running on the Grid, e.g. for performance monitoring. The main components are as follows:

– **MDS:** MDS is the Globus Monitoring and Discovery Service, based on soft-state registration protocols and LDAP aggregate directory services. Each resource runs a GRIS (Grid Resource Information Server) publishing local information as an LDAP directory. These servers are in turn registered to a hierarchy of GIISs (Grid Information Index Servers), which aggregate the information and again publish it as an LDAP directory.

– **Ftree**: Ftree is an EDG-developed alternative to the Globus LDAP backend with improved caching over the code in the Globus 1 toolkit.

– **R-GMA:** R-GMA is a relational GMA (Grid Monitoring Architecture) implementation which makes information from producers available to consumers as relations (tables). It also uses relations to handle the registration of producers. R-GMA is consistent with GMA principles.

– **GRM/PROVE:** GRM/Prove is an application monitoring and visualisation tool of the P-GRADE graphical parallel programming environment, modified for application monitoring in the DataGrid environment. The instrumentation library

of GRM is generalised for a flexible trace event specification. The components of GRM will be connected to R-GMA using its Producer and Consumer APIs.
A number of alternatives, MDS, Ftree and R-GMA, are being considered as the basis of the final EDG information service. These implementations are being evaluated and compared using a set of performance, scalability and reliability criteria to determine which is the most suitable for deployment.
In the current testbed all relevant Grid elements run a GRIS, which carries the information for that element to an MDS GIIS where the information is collected, to be queried by the Resource Broker and other Grid servers.

2.4 EDG Fabric Installation and Job Management Tools

The EDG collaboration has developed a complete set of tools for the management of PC farms (fabrics), in order to make the installation and configuration of the various nodes automatic and easy for the site managers managing a testbed site, and for the control of jobs on the Worker Nodes in the fabric. The main tasks are:

User Job Control and Management (Grid and local jobs) on fabric batch and/or interactive CPU services. There are two branches:

- The **Gridification** subsystem provides the interface from the Grid to the resources available inside a fabric for batch and interactive CPU services. It provides the interface for job submission/control and information publication to the Grid services. It also provides functionality for local authentication and policy-based authorisation, and mapping of Grid credentials to local credentials.

- The **Resource Management** subsystem is a layer on top of the batch and interactive services (LRMS). While the Grid Resource Broker manages workload distribution between fabrics, the Resource Management subsystem manages the workload distribution and resource sharing of all batch and interactive services inside a fabric, according to defined policies and user quota allocations.

Automated System Administration for the automatic installation and configuration of computing nodes. These three subsystems are designed for the use of system administrators and operators to perform system installation, configuration and maintenance:

- **Configuration Management** provides the components to manage and store centrally all fabric configuration information. This includes the configuration of all EDG subsystems as well as information about the fabric hardware, systems and services.

- **Installation Management** handles the initial installation of computing fabric nodes. It also handles software distribution, configuration and maintenance according to information stored in the Configuration Management subsystem.

- **Fabric Monitoring and Fault Tolerance** provides the necessary components for gathering, storing and retrieving performance, functional, setup and environmental data for all fabric elements. It also provides the means to correlate that data and execute corrective actions if problems are identified.

The fabric installation and configuration management tools are based on a remote install and configuration tool called LCFG (Local Configurator), which, by means of a server, installs and configures remote clients, starting from scratch, using a network connection to download the required RPM files for the installation, after using a disk to load a boot kernel on the client machines.

The basic architectural structure and function of LCFG are represented in Figure 5 and are as follows: abstract configuration parameters are stored in a central repository located in the LCFG server. Scripts on the host machine (LCFG client) read these configuration parameters and either generate traditional configuration files, or directly manipulate various services. A daemon in the LCFG server (mkxprof) polls for changes in the source files and converts them into XML profiles, one profile per client node. The XML profiles are then published on a web server. LCFG clients can be configured to poll at regular intervals, or to receive automatic change notifications, or they can fetch new profiles in response to an explicit command. A daemon in each LCFG client (rdxprof) then reads its associated XML profile from the web server and caches it locally (DBM file). LCFG scripts access the local cache to extract the configuration values and execute changes accordingly.

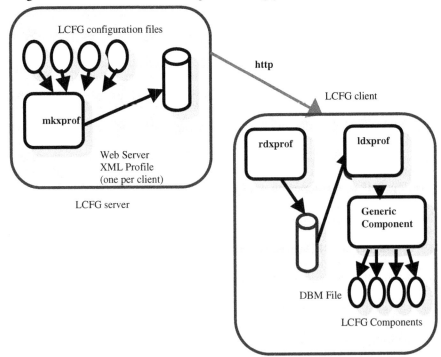

Fig. 5. LCFG internal operation

2.5 The Storage Element

The Storage Element has an important role in the storage of data and the management of files in the Grid domain, and EDG is working on its definition, design, software development, setup and testing.

A Storage Element is a complete Grid-enabled interface to a Mass Storage Management System, tape or disk based, so that mass storage of files can be almost completely transparent to Grid users. A user should not need to know anything about the particular storage system available locally to a given Grid resource, and should only be required to request that files should be read or written using a common interface. All existing mass storage systems used at testbed sites will be interfaced to the Grid, so that their use will be completely transparent and the authorisation of users to use the system will be in terms of general quantities like space used or storage duration.

The procedures for accessing files are still in the development phase. The main achievements to date have been the definition of the architecture and design for the Storage Element, collaboration with Globus on GridFTP/RFIO access, collaboration with PPDG on a control API, staging from and to the CASTOR tape system at CERN, and an interface to GDMP. Initially the supported storage interfaces will be UNIX disk systems, HPSS (High Performance Storage System), CASTOR (through RFIO), and remote access via the Globus GridFTP protocol. Local file access within a site will also be available using Unix file access, e.g. with NFS or AFS. EDG are also developing a grid-aware Unix filing system with ownership and access control based on Grid certificates rather than local Unix accounts.

3 The EDG Testbed

EDG has deployed the middleware on a distributed testbed, which also provides some shared services. A central software repository provides defined bundles of RPMs according to machine type, together with LCFG scripts to install and configure the software.

There are also automatic tools for the creation and update of grid-map files (used to map Grid certificates to local Unix accounts), needed by all testbed sites to authorise users to access the testbed resources. A new user subscribes to the EDG Acceptable Usage Policy by using their certificate, loaded into a web browser, to digitally sign their agreement. Their certificate Subject Name is then added to an LDAP server maintained for each Virtual Organisation by a VO administrator. Each site can use this information, together with local policy on which VOs are supported, to generate the local map file which authorises the user at that site. This mechanism is sketched in 6.

The testbed sites each implement a User Interface machine, a Gatekeeper and a set of Worker Nodes (i.e. a Grid Computing Element), managed by means of a Local

Resource Management System, and a Storage Element (disk only at most sites, but with tape storage at CERN, Lyon and RAL). Some sites have also set up a local Resource Broker. As a reference, Fig. 7 shows a typical site setup in terms of machine composition, for both development and production testbeds, namely the current CERN testbed, with production, development and service machines (network time server, NFS server, LCFG server, monitoring servers).

New sites are welcome to join the testbed, with a well-defined set of rules and procedures. In addition the EDG middleware is freely available, documented, and downloadable from a central repository (the exact license conditions are still under review, but will allow free use). All required RPMs are available for download to an LCFG server, which is generally the first element to be set up, by means of which all other components can be easily installed and configured following the EDG documentation. Alternatively it is possible to install and configure the software by hand. Only Red Hat Linux version 6.2 is currently supported, but more platforms will be supported in due course.

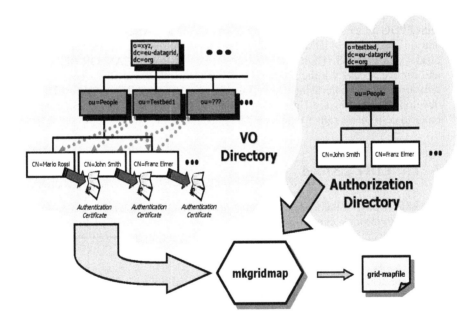

Fig. 6. The operation of the makegridmap daemon

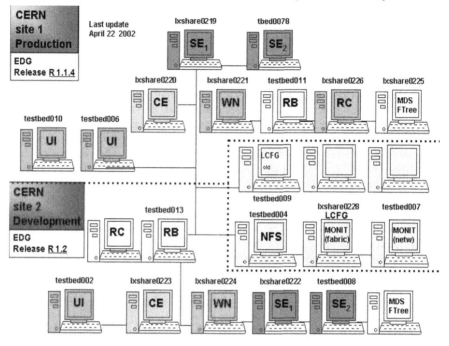

Fig. 7. The CERN testbed cluster composition

4   Future Developments

There are a number of important services still in development. The WMS will introduce an implementation for billing and accounting, advance reservation of resources, job partitioning and checkpointing. In the data management area there will be APIs for Replica Selection through a Replica Optimiser. The first full implementation of R-GMA will be used and compared with the existing information systems (MDS and Ftree). For fabric management there will be the LCAS (Local Credentials and Authorization Server) and further tools to replace the use of Grid map files to authorise users and introduce effective differentiated authorisation of users according to the Virtual Organisation they belong to (VOMS, Virtual Organisation Membership Server). Also a new high level configuration description language will be provided. Interfaces to Storage Elements will continue to be developed. Network monitoring information will be used to influence the decisions of the Resource Broker.

5   Conclusions

The European Data Grid project has already achieved many of its goals, stated at the time of the project conception two years ago. A production quality distributed computing environment has been demonstrated by the EDG testbed. It will now be enriched in functionality, further improved in reliability and extended both geographically and in terms of aggregate CPU power and storage capacity. The community of users has already successfully validated the use of a large set of applications, ranging from High Energy Physics to Bio-Informatics and Earth Observation [2, 3, 4]. At the same time development is currently ongoing to extend the range of functionality covered by the EDG middleware.

All work packages have defined an intense schedule of new research and development, which will be supported by the progressive introduction of high-speed scientific networks such as those deployed by RN GEANT. This will increase the range of possibilities available to the EDG developers. As an example, EDG has proposed the introduction of a Network Optimiser server, to establish in which cases it is preferable to access a file from a remote location or to trigger local copying, according to network conditions in the end-to-end link between the relevant sites. The development of Differentiated Services and Packet Forwarding policies is strongly encouraged, in order to make Grid applications cope better with the dynamic network performance and create different classes of services to be provided to different classes of applications, according to their requirements in terms of bandwidth, throughput, delay, jitter etc.

The impact of the new Globus features foreseen by the introduction of the OGSA paradigm suggested by the US Globus developers, where the main accent is on a Web Services oriented architecture, is being evaluated by EDG, and an evolution of the current architecture in that direction could be envisaged. This is proposed for future releases of the EDG middleware and it may be continued with initiatives in the new EU FP6 framework. An important collaboration has already been established via the GRIDSTART initiative (www.gridstart.org) with the other ten existing EU funded Grid projects. In particular, the EU CrossGrid project (www.crossgrid.org) which will exploit DataGrid technologies to support a variety of applications, all demanding guaranteed quality of service (i.e. real time environment simulation, video streaming and other applications requiring high network bandwith).

Collaboration with similar Grid projects in the US, especially PPDG (www.ppdg.net), GriPhyN (www.griphyn.org) and iVDGL (www.ivdgl.org) is being pursued in collaboration with the sister project EU DataTAG (www.datatag.org). The main goal of DataTAG is the establishment of a transatlantic testbed to deploy and test the software of the EDG project. Interest in the EDG project and its production-oriented approach has already reached beyond the borders of the European Union: after Russia and Romania, which have already installed the EDG software, some Asian sites (in Taiwan and South Korea) have applied to become members of the distributed EDG testbed, in order to participate in High Energy Physics data challenges for data production and simulation.

Reference Documents

Note: all official EDG documents are available on the web at the URL:
http://eu-datagrid.web.cern.ch/eu-datagrid/Deliverables/default.htm

[1]   DataGrid D12.4: "DataGrid Architecture"
[2]   DataGrid D8.1a: "DataGrid User Requirements and Specifications for the DataGrid Project"
[3]   DataGrid D9.1: "Requirements Specification: EO Application Requirements for Grid"
[4]   DataGrid D10.1: WP10 Requirements Document
[5]   DataGrid D8.2: "Testbed1 Assessment by HEP Applications"
[6]   "The Anatomy of the Grid", I. Foster, C. Kesselman, et al. Technical Report, Global Grid Forum, 2001, http://www.globus.org/research/papers/anatomy.pdf
[7]   DataGrid D6.1: "Testbed Software Integration Process"
[8]   Condor Project (http://www.cs.wisc.edu/condor/). Jim Basney and Miron Livny, "Deploying a High Throughput. Computing Cluster", High Performance Cluster computing,Rajkumar Buyya, Editor, Vol. 1, Chapter 5, Prentice Hall PTR,May 1999. Nicholas Coleman, "An Implementation of Matchmaking Analysis in Condor", Masters' Project report, University of Wisconsin, Madison, May 2001.
[10]   DataGrid Architecture Version 2, G. Cancio, S. Fisher, T. Folkes, F. Giacomini, W. Hoschek, D. Kelsey, B. Tierney, http://grid-atf.web.cern.ch/grid-atf/documents.html
[11]   EDG Usage Guidelines   (http://marianne.in2p3.fr/datagrid/documentation/EDG-Usage-Guidelines.html)
[12]   Software Release Plan DataGrid-12-PLN-333297; http://edms.cern.ch/document/333297
[13]   Project technical annex.
[14]   DataGrid D12.3: "Software Release Policy"

DataGrid Publications

Gagliardi, F., Baxevanidis, K., Foster, I., and Davies, H. Grids and Research Networks as Drivers and Enablers of Future Internet Architectures. *The New Internet Architecture* (to be published)

Buyya, R. Stockinger, H. Economic Models for resource management and scheduling in Grid computing. *The Journal of Concurrency and Computation: Pratice and Experience (CCPE) Special issue on Grid computing environments*. 2002

Stockinger, H. Database Replication in World-Wide Distributed Data Grids. PhD thesis, 2002.

Primet, P. High Performance Grid Networking in the DataGrid Project. Terena 2002.

Stockinger, H., Samar, A., Allcock, B., Foster, I., Holtman, K.,and Tierney, B. File and Object Replication in Data Grids. *10th IEEE Symposium on High Performance Distributed Computing (HPDC 2001)*. San Francisco, California, August 7-9, 2001.

Hoschek, W., Jaen-Martinez, J., Samar, A., Stockinger, H. and Stockinger, K. Data Management in an International Data Grid Project. *IEEE/ACM International Workshop on Grid Computing Grid'2000* – 17-20 December 2000 Bangalore, India. "Distinguished Paper" Award.

Balaton, Z., Kaczuk, P. and Podhorski, N. From Cluster Monitoring to Grid Monitoring Based on GRM and PROVE. *Report of the Laboratory of Parallel and Distributed Systems*, LPDS – 1/2000

Dullmann, D., Hoschek, W., Jean-Martinez, J., Samar, A., Stockinger, H.and Stockinger, K. Models for Replica Synchronisation and Consistency in a Data Grid. *10th IEEE Symposium on High Performance Distributed Computing (HPDC 2001)*. San Francisco, California, August 7-9, 2001.

Stockinger, H. Distributed Database Management Systems and the Data Grid. *18th IEEE Symposium on Mass Storage Systems and 9th NASA Goddard Conference on Mass Storage Systems and Technologies*, San Diego, April 17-20, 2001.

Serafini, L., Stockinger H., Stockinger, K. and Zini, F. Agent-Based Query Optimisation in a Grid Environment. *IASTED International Conference on Applied Informatics (AI2001)* , Innsbruck, Austria, February 2001.

Stockinger, H., Stockinger, K., Schikuta and Willers, I. Towards a Cost Model for Distributed and Replicated Data Stores. *9th Euromicro Workshop on Parallel and Distributed Processing PDP 2001*, Mantova, Italy, February 7-9, 2001. IEEE Computer Society Press

Hafeez, M., Samar, A. and Stockinger, H. A Data Grid Prototype for distributed Data Production in CMS. *VII International Workshop on Advanced Computing and Analysis Techniques in Physics Research (ACAT 2000)*, October 2000.

Samar, A. and Stockinger, H. Grid Data Management Pilot (GDMP): a Tool for Wilde Area Replication. . *IASTED International Conference on Applied Informatics (AI2001)* , Innsbruck, Austria, February 2001.

Ruda, M. Integrating Grid Tools to build a computing resource broker: activities of DataGrid WP1. *Conference in Computing in High Energy Physics (CHEP01)*, Beijing, September 3-7, 2001

Cerello, P. Grid Activities in ALICE. *Proceedings of the Conference in Computing in High Energy Physics (CHEP01)*, Beijing, September 3-7, 2001.

Harris, F. and Van Herwijnen, E. Moving the LHCb Monte Carlo Production system to the Grid. *Proceedings of the Conference in Computing in High Energy Physics (CHEP01)*, Beijing, September 3-7, 2001.

Fisk, I. CMS Grid Activities in the United States. *Proceedings of the Conference in Computing in High Energy Physics (CHEP01)*, Beijing, September 3-7, 2001.

Grandi, C. CMS Grid Activities in Europe. *Proceedings of the Conference in Computing in High Energy Physics (CHEP01)*, Beijing, September 3-7, 2001.

Holtman, K. CMS requirements for the Grid. *Proceedings of the Conference in Computing in High Energy Physics (CHEP01)*, Beijing, September 3-7, 2001.

Malon, D. et al, Grid-enabled Data Access in the ATLAS Athena Framework. *Proceedings of the Conference in Computing in High Energy Physics (CHEP01)*, Beijing, September 3-7, 2001.

Others Grid Publications

Foster, I., Kesselman, C., M.Nick, J. And Tuecke, S. The Physiology of the Grid: An Open Grid Services Architecture for Distributed Systems Integration.

Foster, I. The Grid: A new infrastructure for 21st Century Science. *Physics Today*, 54 (2). 2002

Foster, I. And Kesselman, C. Globus: A Toolkit-Based Grid Architecture. In Foster, I. and Kesselman, C. eds. *The Grid: Blueprint for a New Computing Infrastructure*, Morgan Kaufmann, 1999, 259-278.

Foster, I. and Kesselman, C. (eds.). *The Grid: Blueprint for a New Computing Infrastructure*, Morgan Kaufmann, 1999.

Glossary

AFS	Andrew File System
BQS	Batch Queue Service
CE	Computing Element
CVS	Concurrent Versioning System
EDG	European DataGrid
EIP	Experiment Independent Person
Ftree	LDAP-based dynamic directory service
GDMP	Grid Data Mirroring Package
II	Information Index
ITeam	Integration Team
JDL	Job Description Language
JSS	Job Submission Service
LB	Logging and Bookkeeping
LCFG	Automated software installation system
LDAP	Lightweight Directory Access Protocol
LFN	Logical File Name
LSF	Load Sharing Facility
MDS	Globus Metacomputing Directory Service
MS	Mass Storage
NFS	Network File System
PBS	Portable Batch System
RB	Resource Broker
RC	Replica Catalogue
RFIO	Remote File I/O software package
RPM	Red Hat Package Manager
SE	Storage Element
TB1	Testbed1 (project month 9 release of DataGrid)
UI	User Interface
VO	Virtual Organisation
WN	Worker Node
WP	Workpackage

Acknowledgments. The authors would like to thank the entire EU DataGrid project for contributing most of the material for this article.

Author Index

Lecture Notes in Computer Science

For information about Vols. 1–2387
please contact your bookseller or Springer-Verlag